POPULAR ACCOUNT

OF

THE ANCIENT EGYPTIANS.

A COMPLETE EGYPTIAN TEMPLE.

A

POPULAR ACCOUNT

OF

THE ANCIENT EGYPTIANS.

REVISED AND ABRIDGED FROM HIS LARGER WORK,

BY SIR J. GARDNER WILKINSON, D.C.L., F.R.S., &c.

IN TWO VOLUMES.—VOL. I.

Illustrated with Five Hundred Woodcuts.

CRESCENT BOOKS
NEW YORK

Previously published by John Murray in two volumes

This omnibus edition published 1988 by Crescent Books
distributed by Crown Publishers, Inc.,
225 Park Avenue South,
New York, New York 10003.

ISBN 0-517-67193-X

Printed in U.S.A.

hgfedcba

PREFACE.

THE present account of the " Ancient Egyptians " is chiefly an abridgment of that written by me in 1836; to which I have added other matter, in consequence of my having re-visited Egypt, and later discoveries having been made, since that time.

I have here and there introduced some remarks relating to the Greeks, thinking that a comparison of the habits and arts of other people, with those of the Egyptians, may be interesting; and the impulse now given to taste in England has induced me to add some observations on decorative art, as well as on colour, form, and proportion, so well understood in ancient times. And as many of the ideas now gaining ground in this country, regarding colour, adaptability of materials, the non-imitation of natural objects for ornamental purposes, and certain rules to be observed in decorative works, have long been advocated by me, and properly belong to the subject of Egypt, I think the opportunity well suited for expressing my opinion upon them; while I rejoice that public attention has been invited to take a proper view of the mode of improving taste.

Attention being now directed towards the question of the precious metals, some observations, on the comparative wealth of ancient and modern times, have also appeared to be not out of place.

Of the Religion and History of Egypt, I have only introduced what is necessary for explaining some points connected with them; being persuaded that a detailed account of those subjects would not be generally attractive, and might be omitted in a work not intended to treat of what is still open to conjecture. For the same reason I have abstained from all doubtful questions respecting the customs of the Egyptians; and have confined myself to as short a notice of them as possible.

References too are mostly omitted, having been given before.

Several new woodcuts have been added, and others have been introduced instead of some of the lithographic plates in the previous work; and as an Index is more useful than a mere list of contents, I have given a very copious one, which will be found to contain all the most important references.

August, 1853.

CONTENTS OF VOL. I.

(ix)

LIST OF WOODCUTS

In Vol. I.

*Those with ** prefixed are new woodcuts; with * new woodcuts copied from lithographs of the previous work.*

** Frontispiece.

A complete Egyptian Temple, surrounded by the *Temenos*, or " grove," planted with trees. A procession, with the sacred boat, or ark, advances from the hypæthral building at the extremity of the paved *dromos*.

A wooden model of the *grove* was sometimes carried in these processions, as behind the statue of Khem. It was doubtless similar to the "*grove*" which the Israelites "brought out" and "burnt."—2 Kings, xxiii. 6; Isaiah, xxvii. 9. The real grove is also mentioned, Exod. xxxiv. 13; Judges, vi. 26, &c.

CHAPTER I.

CHAPTER II.

CHAPTER IV.

CHAPTER V.

MANNERS AND CUSTOMS

OF

THE ANCIENT EGYPTIANS.

A.   Part of Cairo, showing the *Mulḳufs* on the houses of modern Egypt.

CHAPTER I.

CHARACTER OF THE EGYPTIANS — ORIGINAL POPULATIONS — SOCIAL LIFE —
HOUSES — VILLAS — FARMYARDS — GARDENS — VINEYARDS — WINEPRESS
— WINES — BEER — FURNITURE OF ROOMS — CHAIRS.

THE monumental records and various works of art, and, above all,
the writings, of the Greeks and Romans, have made us acquainted
with their customs and their very thoughts; and though the
literature of the Egyptians is unknown, their monuments, especially the paintings in the tombs, have afforded us an insight
into their mode of life scarcely to be obtained from those of any
other people. The influence that Egypt had in early times
on Greece gives to every inquiry respecting it an additional
interest; and the frequent mention of the Egyptians in the Bible

connects them with the Hebrew records, of which many satisfactory illustrations occur in the sculptures of Pharaonic times.
Their great antiquity also enables us to understand the condition
of the world long before the era of written history; all existing
monuments left by other people are comparatively modern; and
the paintings in Egypt are the earliest descriptive illustrations of
the manners and customs of any nation.

It is from these that we are enabled to form an opinion of the
character of the Egyptians. They have been pronounced a
serious, gloomy people, saddened by the habit of abstruse speculation; but how far this conclusion agrees with fact will be
seen in the sequel. They were, no doubt, less lively than the
Greeks; but if a comparatively late writer, Ammianus Marcellinus, may have remarked a "rather sad" expression, after they
had been for ages under successive foreign yokes, this can scarcely
be admitted as a testimony of their character in the early times
of their prosperity; and though a sadness of expression might be
observed in the present oppressed population, they cannot be
considered a grave or melancholy people. Much, indeed, may
be learnt from the character of the modern Egyptians; and notwithstanding the infusion of foreign blood, particularly of the
Arab invaders, every one must perceive the strong resemblance
they bear to their ancient predecessors. It is a common error to
suppose that the conquest of a country gives an entirely new
character to the inhabitants. The immigration of a whole nation
taking possession of a thinly-peopled country, will have this
effect, when the original inhabitants are nearly all driven out by
the new-comers; but immigration has not always, and conquest
never has, for its object the destruction or expulsion of the native
population; they are found useful to the victors, and as necessary
for them as the cattle, or the productions of the soil. Invaders
are always numerically inferior to the conquered nation—even to
the male population; and, when the women are added to the
number, the majority is greatly in favour of the original race,
and they must exercise immense influence on the character of
the rising generation. The customs, too, of the old inhabitants

are very readily adopted by the new-comers, especially when they are found to suit the climate and the peculiarities of the country they have been formed in ; and the habits of a small mass of settlers living in contact with them fade away more and more with each successive generation.   So it has been in Egypt ; and, as usual, the conquered people bear the stamp of the ancient inhabitants rather than that of the Arab conquerors.

Of the various institutions of the ancient Egyptians, none are more interesting than those which relate to their social life ; and when we consider the condition of other countries in the early ages when they flourished, from the 10th to the 20th century before our era, we may look with respect on the advancement they had then made in civilization, and acknowledge the benefits they conferred upon mankind during their career.   For, like other people, they have had their part in the great scheme of the world's development, and their share of usefulness in the destined progress of the human race ; for countries, like individuals, have certain qualities given them, which, differing from those of their predecessors and contemporaries, are intended in due season to perform their requisite duties.   The interest felt in the Egyptians is from their having led the way, or having been the first people we know of who made any great progress, in the arts and manners of civilization ; which, for the period when they lived, was very creditable, and far beyond that of other kingdoms of the world.   Nor can we fail to remark the difference between them and their Asiatic rivals, the Assyrians, who, even at a much later period, had the great defects of Asiatic cruelty—flaying alive, impaling, and torturing their prisoners ; as the Persians, Turks, and other Orientals have done to the present century ; the reproach of which cannot be extended to the ancient Egyptians.   Being the dominant race of that age, they necessarily had an influence on others with whom they came in contact ; and it is by these means that civilization is advanced through its various stages ; each people striving to improve on the lessons derived from a neighbour whose institutions they appreciate, or consider beneficial to themselves.   It was thus that the active

mind of the talented Greeks sought and improved on the lessons
derived from other countries, especially from Egypt ; and though
the latter, at the late period of the 7th century B. C., had lost its
greatness and the prestige of superiority among the nations of
the world, it was still the seat of learning and the resort of
studious philosophers ; and the abuses consequent on the fall of an
empire had not yet brought about the demoralization of after times.

The early part of Egyptian monumental history is coeval with
the arrivals of Abraham and of Joseph, and the Exodus of the
Israelites ; and we know from the Bible what was the state of the
world at that time.   But then, and apparently long before, the
habits of social life in Egypt were already what we find them to
have been during the most glorious period of their career ; and
as the people had already laid aside their arms, and military men
only carried them when on service, some notion may be had of
the very remote date of Egyptian civilization.   In the treatment
of women they seem to have been very far advanced beyond
other wealthy communities of the same era, having usages very
similar to those of modern Europe ; and such was the respect
shown to women that precedence was given to them over men,
and the wives and daughters of kings succeeded to the throne
like the male branches of the royal family.   Nor was this privilege rescinded, even though it had more than once entailed upon
them the troubles of a contested succession : foreign kings often
having claimed a right to the throne through marriage with an
Egyptian princess.   It was not a mere influence that they possessed, which women often acquire in the most arbitrary Eastern
communities ; nor a political importance accorded to a particular
individual, like that of the Soltána Valídeh, the Queen Mother,
at Constantinople ; it was a right acknowledged by law, both in
private and public life.   They knew that unless women were
treated with respect, and made to exercise an influence over
society, the standard of public opinion would soon be lowered,
and the manners and morals of men would suffer ; and in acknowledging this, they pointed out to women the very responsible
duties they had to perform to the community.

It has been said that the Egyptian priests were only allowed to have one wife, while the rest of the community had as many as they chose ; but, besides the improbability of such a license, the testimony of the monuments accords with Herodotus in disproving the statement, and each individual is represented in his tomb with a single consort.   Their mutual affection is also indicated by the fond manner in which they are seated together, and by the expressions of endearment they use to each other, as well as to their children.   And if further proof were wanting to show their respect for social ties, we may mention the conduct of Pharaoh, in the case of the supposed sister of Abraham, standing in remarkable contrast to the habits of most princes of those and many subsequent ages.

From their private life great insight is obtained into their character and customs ; and their household arrangements, the style of their dwellings, their amusements, and their occupations, explain their habits ; as their institutions, mode of government, arts, and military knowledge illustrate their history, and their relative position among the nations of antiquity.   In their form and arrangement, the houses were made to suit the climate, modified according to their advancement in civilization ; and we are often enabled to trace in their abodes some of the primitive habits of a people, long after they have been settled in towns, and have adopted the manners of wealthy communities ; as the tent may still be traced in the houses of the Turks, and the small original wooden chamber in the mansions and temples of ancient Greece.

As in all warm climates, the poorer classes of Egyptians lived much in the open air ; and the houses of the rich were constructed to be cool throughout the summer ; currents of refreshing air being made to circulate freely through them by the judicious arrangement of the passages and courts.   Corridors, supported on columns, gave access to the different apartments through a succession of shady avenues and areas, with one side open to the air, as in our cloisters ; and even small detached houses had an open court in the centre, planted as a garden with palms and

other trees. *Mulkufs*, or wooden wind-sails, were also fixed over
the terraces of the upper story, facing the prevalent and cool
N.W. wind, which was conducted down their sloping boards
into the interior of the house. They were exactly similar to those
in the modern houses of Cairo; and some few were double,
facing in opposite directions.

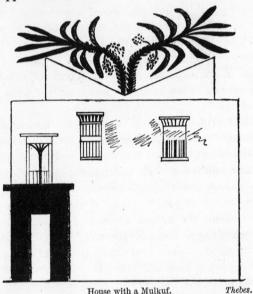

1.   House with a Mulkuf.   *Thebes.*

The houses were built of crude brick, stuccoed and painted
with all the combinations of bright colour, in which the Egyptians
delighted; and a highly decorated mansion had numerous courts,
and architectural details derived from the temples. Over the door
was sometimes a sentence, as "the good house;" or the name of
a king, under whom the owner probably held some office; many
other symbols of good omen were also put up, as at the entrances
of modern Egyptian houses; and a visit to some temple gave as
good a claim to a record, as the pilgrimage to Mekkeh at the
present day. Poor people were satisfied with very simple tene-
ments; their wants being easily supplied, both as to lodging and

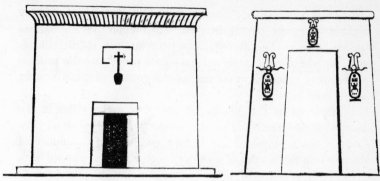

2.   Over the door is "The good house."   3. Doorway, with a king's name.

food ; and their house consisted of four walls, with a flat roof
of palm-branches laid across a split date-tree as a beam, and
covered with mats plastered over with a thick coating of mud.
It had one door, and a few small windows closed by wooden
shutters. As it scarcely ever rained, the mud roof was not
washed into the sitting room ; and this cottage rather answered
as a shelter from the sun, and as a closet for their goods, than for
the ordinary purpose of a house in other countries. Indeed at
night the owners slept on the roof, during the greater part of the
year ; and as most of their work was done out of doors, they
might easily be persuaded that a house was far less necessary for
them than a tomb. To convince the rich of this ultra-philo-
sophical sentiment was not so easy ; at least the practice differed
from the theory ; and though it was promulgated among all
the Egyptians, it did not prevent the priests and other grandees
from living in very luxurious abodes, or enjoying the good
things of this world ; and a display of wealth was found to be
useful in maintaining their power, and in securing the obedience
of a credulous people. The worldly possessions of the priests
were therefore very extensive, and if they imposed on themselves
occasional habits of abstemiousness, avoided certain kinds of
unwholesome food, and performed many mysterious observances,
they were amply repaid by the improvement of their health,

and by the influence they thereby acquired. Superior intelligence
enabled them to put their own construction on regulations
emanating from their sacred body, with the convenient persuasion that what suited them did not suit others; and the profane
vulgar were expected to do, not as the priests did, but as they
taught them to do.

In their plans the houses of towns, like the villas in the
country, varied according to the caprice of the builders. The
ground-plan, in some of the former, consisted of a number of
chambers on three sides of a court, which was often planted with
trees. Others consisted of two rows of rooms on either side of
a long passage, with an entrance-court from the street; and
others were laid out in chambers round a central area, similar to

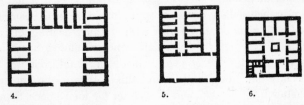

4.   5.   6.

the Roman *Impluvium*, and paved with stone, or containing a
few trees, a tank, or a fountain, in its centre. Sometimes, though
rarely, a flight of steps led to the front door from the street.

Houses of small size were often connected together, and formed
the continuous sides of streets; and a court-yard was common
to several dwellings. Others of a humbler kind consisted merely
of rooms opening on a narrow passage, or directly on the street.
These had only a basement story, or ground-floor; and few
houses exceeded two stories above it. They mostly consisted of
one upper floor; and though Diodorus speaks of the lofty houses
in Thebes four and five stories high, the paintings show that
few had three, and the largest seldom four, including as he
does the basement-story. Even the greater portion of the house
was confined to a first-floor, with an additional story in one part,
on which was a terrace covered by an awning, or a light roof
supported on columns (as in Woodcut 25). This served for the

ladies of the family to sit at work in during the day, and here
the master of the house often slept at night during the summer,
or took his *siesta* in the afternoon. Some had a tower which rose
even above the terrace.

The first-floor was what the
Italians call the "*piano nobile;*"
the ground rooms being chiefly
used for stores, or as offices, of
which one was set apart for the
porter, and another for visiters
coming on business. Sometimes
besides the parlour were receiving apartments on the base-

7.   *Thebes.*

ment-story, but guests were generally entertained on the first-
floor; and on this were the sleeping rooms also, except where the
house was of two or three stories. The houses of wealthy citizens
often covered a considerable space, and either stood directly
upon the street, or a short way back, within an open court; and
some large mansions were detached, and had several entrances
on two or three sides. Before the door was a porch supported on
two columns, decked with banners or ribands, and larger porticos
had a double row of columns, with statues between them.

Other mansions had a flight of steps leading to a raised platform, with a doorway between two towers, not unlike those before

8.   Porch. *Tel el Amarna.*   9.   Porch. *Thebes and Tel el Amarna.*

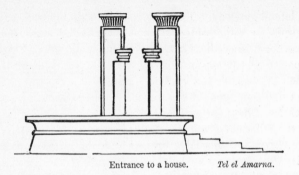

10.   Entrance to a house.   *Tel el Amarna.*

the temples. A line of trees ran parallel to the front of the
house; and to prevent injuries from cattle, or any accident, the
stems were surrounded by a low wall, pierced with square holes
to admit the air.* This custom of planting trees about town
houses was common also at Rome.

The height of the portico was about twelve or fifteen feet,
just exceeding that of the cornice of the door, which was only
raised by its threshold above the level of the ground. On either
side of the main entrance was a smaller door, which stood at an
equal distance between it and the side-wall, and was probably
intended for the servants, or those who came on business. On
entering by the porch you passed into an open court (*aula*, or
hall), containing a *mándara*, or receiving room, for visiters.
This building, supported by columns, decorated with banners,
was closed only at the lower part by inter-columnar panels, over
which a stream of cool air was admitted, and protection from the
rays of the sun was secured by an awning that covered it. On the
opposite side of the court was another door, the approach to the
mándara from the interior; and the master of the house, on the
announcement of a stranger, came in that way to receive him.
Three doors led from this court to another of larger dimensions,
which was ornamented with avenues of trees, and communicated
on the right and left with the interior of the house; and this,
like most of the large courts, had a back entrance through a central

* As in Woodcut 11, *fig.* 2, *c.*

and lateral gateway.   The arrangement of the interior was much the same on either side of the court: six or more chambers, whose doors faced those of the opposite set, opening on a corridor supported by columns on the right and left of an area, which was shaded by a double row of trees.

At the upper end of one of these areas was a sitting-room, which faced the door leading to the great court; and over this and the other chambers were the apartments of the upper-story. Here were also two small gateways towards the street.

Another plan consisted of a court, with the usual avenue of trees, on one side of which were several sets of chambers opening on corridors or passages, but without any colonnade before the doors.   The receiving room looked upon the court, and from it a row of columns led to the private sitting apartment, which stood isolated in one of the passages, near to a door communicating with the side chambers; and, in its position, with a corridor or porch in front, it bears a striking resemblance to the " summer parlour" of Eglon, king of Moab,* "which he had for himself alone," and where he received Ehud the Israelite stranger. And the flight of Ehud " through the porch," after he had shut and locked the door of the parlour, shows its situation to have been very similar to some of these isolated apartments in the houses, or villas, of the ancient Egyptians.   The side chambers were frequently arranged on either side of a corridor, others faced towards the court, and others were only separated from the outer wall by a long passage.

In the distribution of the apartments numerous and different modes were adopted, according to circumstances; in general, however, the large mansions seem to have consisted of a court and several corridors, with rooms leading from them, not unlike many of those now built in Oriental and tropical countries.† The houses in most of the Egyptian towns are quite destroyed, leaving few traces of their plans, or even of their sites; but sufficient remains of some at Thebes, at Tel el Amarna, and other

* Judges, iii. 20.			† Woodcut 11, *fig.* 1.

(Total length of fig. 1, 200 feet.)

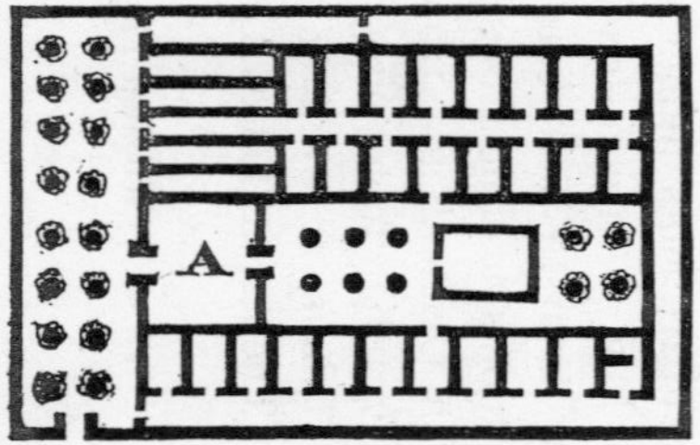

fig. 1.

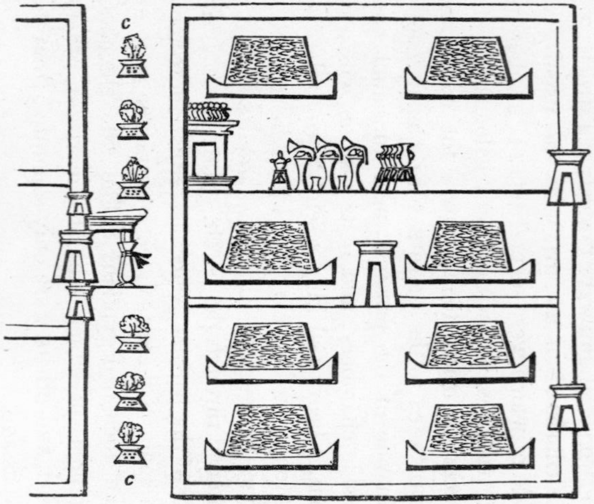

Tel el Amarna.

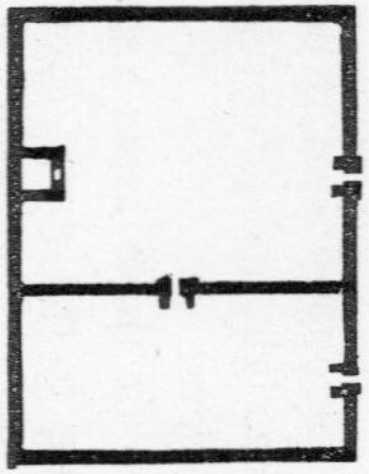

Fig. 2 shows the relative position of the house, *a*; and the granary, *b*.   *cc*, trees surrounded by low walls.

Plans of houses and a granary.

11.

places, to enable us, with the help of the sculptures, to ascertain their form and appearance.

Granaries were also laid out in a very regular manner, and varied of course in plan as much as the houses, to which there is reason to believe they were frequently attached, even in the towns; and they were sometimes only separated from the house by an avenue of trees.

Some small houses consisted merely of a court, and three or four store rooms on the ground-floor, with a single chamber above, to which a flight of steps led from the court; but they were probably only met with in the country, and resembled some still found in the *fellâh* villages of modern Egypt.* Very similar to these was the model of a house now in the British Museum,† which solely consisted of a court-yard and three small store-rooms

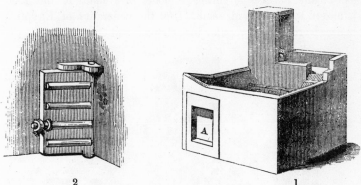

2

12.   Fig. 1. Model of a small house.   *From Thebes.*
                Fig. 2 shows how the door opened and was secured.   *British Museum.*

1

on the ground-floor, with a staircase leading to a room belonging to the storekeeper, which was furnished with a narrow window or aperture opposite the door, rather intended for the purposes of ventilation than to admit the light. In the court a woman was represented making bread, as is sometimes done at the present day in Egypt, in the open air; and the store-rooms were full of grain.

* Woodcut 11, *fig.* 4.   † Woodcuts 12, 13.

Other small houses in towns consisted of two or three stories above the ground-floor. They had no court, and stood close together, covering a small space, and high in proportion to their base, like many of those at Karnak. The lower part had merely the door of entrance and some store-rooms, over which were a first and second floor, each with three windows on the front and side, and above these an attic without windows, and a stair-case leading to a terrace on the flat roof. The floors were laid on rafters, the end of which projected slightly from the walls like dentils; and the courses of brick were in waving or concave lines, as in the walls of an enclosure at Dayr el Medeeneh in Thebes. The windows of the first-floor had a sort of mullion dividing them into two lights each, with a transom above; and the upper windows were filled with trellis-work, or cross bars of wood, as in many Turkish harems. A model of a house of this kind is also in the British Museum. But the generality of Egyptian houses were far less regular in their plan and elevation; and the

13.   Showing the interior of the court, and upper chamber in the same.

usual disregard for symmetry is generally observable in the
houses even of towns.

The doors, both of the entrances and of the inner apartments, were frequently stained to imitate foreign and rare woods.
They were either of one or two valves, turning on pins of metal,

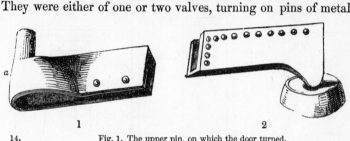

1   2

14.   Fig. 1. The upper pin, on which the door turned.
               Fig. 2. Lower pin.   *British Museum.*

and were secured within by a bar or bolts. Some of these bronze
pins have been discovered in the tombs of Thebes. They were
fastened to the wood with nails of the
same metal, whose round heads served
also as an ornament, and the upper one
had a projection at the back, in order to
prevent the door striking against the
wall. We also find in the stone lintels
and floor, behind the thresholds of the
tombs and temples, the holes in which
they turned, as well as those of the bolts
and bars, and the recess for receiving the
opened valves. The folding doors had
bolts in the centre, sometimes above as
well as below : a bar was placed across
from one wall to the other ; and in many

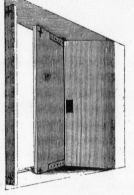

15.   A folding-door.

instances wooden locks secured them by passing over the centre,
at the junction of the two folds. For greater security they were
occasionally sealed with a mass of clay, as is proved by some
tombs found closed at Thebes, by the sculptures, and in the
account given by Herodotus of Rhampsinitus's treasury.

Keys were made of bronze or iron, and consisted of a long

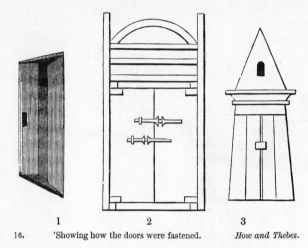

1   2   3

16. 'Showing how the doors were fastened. *How and Thebes.*

straight shank, about five inches in length, with three or more projecting teeth; others had a nearer resemblance to the wards

17.   Iron key. *From Thebes.*

of modern keys, with a short shank about an inch long; and some resembled a common ring with the wards at its back. These are probably of Roman date. The earliest mention of a key is in Judges (iii. 23-25), when Ehud having gone " through the porch, and shut the doors of the parlour upon him and locked them," Eglon's " servants took a key and opened them."

The doorways, like those in the temples, were often surmounted by the Egyptian cornice; others were variously decorated, and some, represented in the tombs, were surrounded with a variety of ornaments, as usual richly painted. These last, though sometimes found at Thebes, were more general about Memphis and the Delta; and two good instances of them are preserved at the British Museum, brought from a tomb near the Pyramids.

18.   Painted on a coffin at *Thebes*.   19.   *Thebes.*

Even at the early period when the Pyramids were built, the doors were of one or two valves; and both those of the rooms and the entrance doors opened inwards, contrary to the custom of the Greeks, who were consequently obliged to strike on the inside

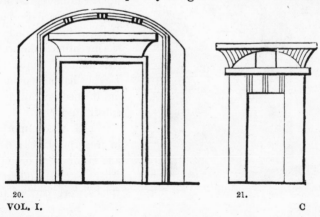

20.   21.

of the street-door before they opened it, in order to warn persons
passing by; and the Romans were forbidden to make it open
outward without a special permission.   The floors were of stone,
or a composition made of lime or other materials; but in humbler abodes they were formed of split date-tree beams, arranged
close together or at intervals, with planks or transverse layers of

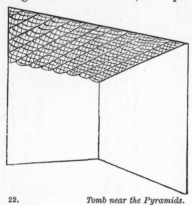

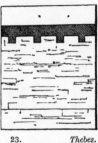

22.   *Tomb near the Pyramids.*   23.   *Thebes.*

palm branches over them, covered with mats and a coating of mud.
Many roofs were vaulted, and built like the rest of the house of
crude brick; and not only have arches been found of that material
dating in the 16th century before our era, but vaulted granaries

appear to be represented
of much earlier date.
Bricks, indeed, led to
the invention of the arch;
the want of timber in
Egypt having pointed
out the necessity of some
substitute for it.

Wood was imported
in great quantities; deal
and cedar were brought
from Syria; and rare
woods were part of the

24.   *Thebes.*

tribute imposed on foreign nations conquered by the Pharaohs. And so highly were these appreciated for ornamental purposes, that painted imitations were made for poorer persons who could not afford them ; and the panels, windows, doors, boxes, and various kinds of woodwork, were frequently of cheap deal or sycamore, stained to resemble the rarest foreign woods. And the remnants of them found at Thebes show that these imitations were clever substitutes for the reality. Even coffins were sometimes made of foreign wood ; and many are found of cedar of Lebanon. The value of foreign woods also suggested to the Egyptians the process of veneering ; and this was one of the arts of their skilful cabinet-makers.

The ceilings were of stucco, richly painted with various devices, tasteful both in their form and the arrangement of the colours ; among the oldest of which is the Guilloche, often mis-called the Tuscan or Greek border.

Both in the interior and exterior of their houses the walls were sometimes portioned out into large panels of one uniform colour, flush with the surface, or recessed, (as in Woodcuts 25 and 30,) not very unlike those at Pompeii ; and they were red, yellow, or stained to resemble stone or wood. It seems to have been the introduction of this mode of ornament into Roman houses that excited the indignation of Vitruvius ; who says that in old times they used red paint sparingly, like physic, though now whole walls are covered over with it.

Figures were also introduced on the blank walls in the sitting-rooms, or scenes from domestic life, surrounded by ornamental borders, and surmounted by deep cornices of flowers and various devices richly painted ; and no people appear to have been more fond of using flowers on every occasion. In their domestic architecture they formed the chief ornament of the mouldings ; and every visiter received a bouquet of real flowers, as a token of welcome on entering a house. It was the pipe and coffee of the modern Egyptians ; and a guest at a party was not only presented with a lotus, or some other flower, but had a chaplet placed round his head, and another round his neck ; which led the

Roman poet to remark the "many chaplets on the foreheads" of the Egyptians at their banquets. Everywhere flowers abounded; they were formed into wreaths and festoons, they decked the stands that supported the vases in the convivial chamber, and crowned the wine-bowl as well as the servants who bore the cup from it to the assembled guests.

Besides the painted panels there were other points of resemblance to Pompeian taste in the Egyptian houses; particularly the elongated columns sometimes attached to the building, sometimes painted on the walls, which were derived by the Greeks either from Egypt or from Asia. Their long slender shafts were made to reach the whole way from the ground to the very roof of

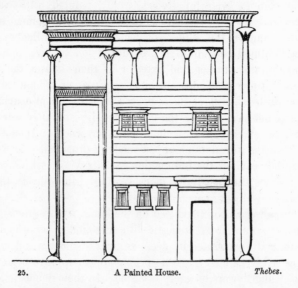

25.   A Painted House.   *Thebes.*

the house, in utter defiance of proportion or the semblance of utility; performing no more office than many of the pillars and half columns which, having nothing to support, may be said to hang up against the fronts of our modern houses, with two tiers of windows, like pictures, in the vacant space between them.

And though in their temples the horizontal line predominated,

as in Greece, the Egyptians were not averse to the contrast of
the vertical with it, which they managed by means of the long
line of their lofty pyramidal towers, and of their obelisks; and
indeed in the lengthy columns that extended up the whole front of
their houses they may claim the first introduction of the vertical
principle.   This was afterwards adopted by the Romans also;
and is very obvious in their arches of triumph, where the
column, rising from the ground on a pedestal, extends the whole
way up the front, forces the entablature to advance, and break
its uniform straight course in order to accord with the capital,
and is surmounted by a statue or a projecting attic, extending to
the summit of the edifice.

The same slender columns, or "reeds for columns," considered
so inconsistent by Vitruvius, found their way into the houses
of Rome; and we see them painted in those of Pompeii, as well
as the "buildings standing on candelabra," he equally condemns.
Incongruous they certainly were, having been merely called
in from another and proper office, in order to assist in developing
a new element of architecture; which long afterwards introduced numerous vertical lines, in the form of towers, minarets,
and other lofty edifices, that now rise above our roofs, and give
so much variety to the external aspect of modern European
and Saracenic towns.   This contrast was wanting in the low and
very uniform outline of Greek buildings, scarcely relieved by
the triangular pediment of a temple; for, however beautiful
each monument itself, a Greek city was singularly deficient in
the combination of the vertical with the horizontal line.   But
the endeavour to obtain this effect at Rome, by isolated columns
bearing a statue, which towered above the roofs, was not such
as taste could justify; for we may well condemn the inappro-
priateness of extracting from a temple one of its legitimate members, and of magnifying it to an extravagant height; and the same
Roman poverty of invention, and inapplicableness, were shown in
this as in the maimed "truncated column," called upon to support
a bust in lieu of its own head.   Nor can any justification be found
for the erection of monstrous colossi, such as Egypt, Greece, and
Rome produced; and we are now happily freed from the dilemma,

of exaggerating what ought to be limited to its proper dimensions, by the resources of modern architecture, whenever we seek
the harmonious contrast of vertical and horizontal lines.

The windows of Egyptian dwellings had merely wooden shutters of one or two valves, turning on pins; and these, like the
whole building, were painted.   The openings were small, because
where little light is admitted little heat penetrates; coolness was
the great requisite, and in the cloudless sky of Egypt there was
no want of light.   And though, as in most of our modern houses,
the windows were little more than square holes, unrelieved by
ornamental mouldings, the Egyptians did not spoil the external
appearance of the house by making them of unreasonable size,
in order to admit the light, and then inconsistently do all they
possibly could to exclude it by numerous dust-catching hangings,
such as are inflicted on innocent Englishmen by tasteless and
interested upholsterers.

The palace of a king was generally of more durable materials
than a private house, and, like the temple to which it was often
attached, was of stone, as at Medeenet Haboo in Thebes.   It
was then placed at the outer end of the avenue that led to the
sacred building; and the principal apartments stood, in two
stories, immediately over the gateway, through which all the
grand processions passed towards the temple.   The rest of the
building extended a considerable distance on the right and left
before this gateway, forming an outer approach from two lodges
at the very entrance, occupied by the guards and porters.   Some
of the chambers looked down upon this passage; others faced
in opposite directions; and the whole building was crowned
with battlements, like the walls of fortified towns.   The apartments were not large, being only 14 feet long by 12 feet 8 inches
in breadth, and 13 feet 6 inches in height; the walls being 5 to
6 feet thick were a protection against the heat, and currents of
air circulated freely through them from opposite windows.   The
walls were ornamented with subjects in low relief, or in intaglio,
representing the king and his household, with various ornamental
devices, particularly the lotus and other flowers.

Pavilions were also built in a similar style, though on a smaller scale, in various parts of the country, and in the foreign districts through which the Egyptian armies passed, for the use of the King ; and some private houses occasionally imitated these small castles, by substituting for the usual parapet wall and cornice the battlements that crowned them, and which were intended to represent Egyptian shields. The roofs of all their houses,

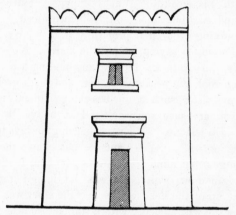

26.   *From the Sculptures at Thebes.*

whether in the town or country, were flat, like those of the modern houses of Cairo, and there (as at the present day) the women often held long conversations with their neighbours on the scandal and gossip of the day.   Many a curious subject was doubtless discussed at these animated meetings, and report affirms that some modern Cairene stories have been founded on those recorded of Pharaonic times, one of which is thus related.

A man, digging in his vineyard, having found a jar full of gold, ran home with joy to announce his good fortune to his wife ; but as he reflected on the way, that women could not always be trusted with secrets, and that he might lose a treasure which, of right, belonged to the King, he thought it better first to test her discretion.   As soon therefore as he had entered the house he called her to him, and, saying he had something of great importance to tell her, asked if she was sure she could keep a secret. "Oh, yes," was the ready answer; "when did you ever know me betray one? What is it?" "Well, then,— but you are sure you won't mention it?" "Have I not told you so? why be so tiresome? what is it?" "Now, as you promise me, I will tell you. A most singular thing happens to me; every morning I lay an egg!" at the same time producing one from beneath his cloak. "What! an egg! extraordinary!" "Yes, it is indeed: but mind you don't mention it." "Oh, no, I shall say nothing about it, I promise you." "No; I feel sure you won't;" and, so saying, he left the house. No sooner gone than his wife ran up to the terrace, and finding a neighbour on the adjoining roof, she beckoned to her, and, with great caution, said, "Oh, my sister, such a curious thing happens to my husband; but you are sure you won't tell anybody?" "No, no; what is it? Do tell me." "Every morning he lays ten eggs!" "What! ten eggs!" "Yes; and he has shown them to me; is it not strange? but mind you say nothing about it:" and away she went again down stairs. It was not long before another woman came up on the next terrace, and the story was told in the same way by the wife's friend, with a similar promise of secrecy, only with the variation of twenty instead of ten eggs; till one neighbour after another, to whom the secret was intrusted, had increased them to a hundred. It was not long before the husband heard it also, and the supposed egg-layer, learning how his story had spread, was persuaded not to risk his treasure by trusting his wife with the real secret.

The villas of the Egyptians were of great extent, and contained spacious gardens, watered by canals communicating with the Nile. They had large tanks of water in different parts of the garden, which served for ornament, as well as for irrigation when the Nile was low; and on these the master of the house occasionally amused himself and his friends by an excursion in a pleasure-boat towed by his servants. They also enjoyed the diversion of angling and spearing fish in the ponds within their grounds, and on these occasions they were generally accompanied by a friend, or one or more members of their family. Particular

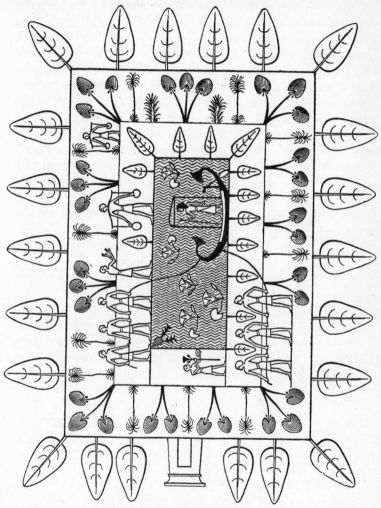

27.   Painting in a Tomb at Thebes.

care was always bestowed upon the garden, and their great fondness for flowers is shown by the number they always cultivated,
as well as by the women of the family or the attendants pre-

senting bouquets to the master of the house and his friends when
they walked there.

The house itself was sometimes ornamented with propyla
and obelisks, like the temples themselves; it is even possible
that part of the building may have been consecrated to religious purposes, as the chapels of other countries, since we find
a priest engaged in presenting offerings at the door of the
inner chambers; and, indeed, were it not for the presence of
the women, the form of the garden, and the style of the porch,
we should feel disposed to consider it a temple rather than a
place of abode. The entrances of large villas were generally
through folding-gates, standing between lofty towers, as at the
courts of temples, with a small door at each side; and others
had merely folding-gates, with the jambs surmounted by a cornice.

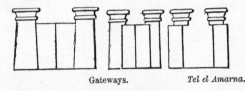

28.   Gateways.   *Tel el Amarna.*

One general wall of circuit extended round the premises, but the
courts of the house, the garden, the offices, and all the other parts
of the villa had each their separate enclosure. The walls were
usually built of crude brick, and, in damp places, or when within

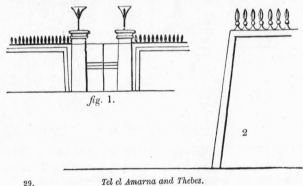

fig. 1.

2

29.   *Tel el Amarna and Thebes.*

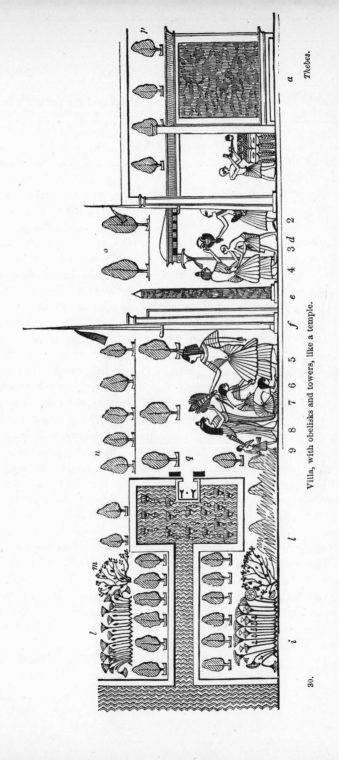

Villa, with obelisks and towers, like a temple.

Thebes.

30.

reach of the inundation, the lower part was strengthened by a basement of stone. They were sometimes ornamented with panels and grooved lines, generally stuccoed, and the summit was crowned either with Egyptian battlements, the usual cornice, a row of spikes in imitation of spear-heads, or with some fancy ornament.

The plans of the villas varied according to circumstances, but their general arrangement is sufficiently explained by the paintings. They were surrounded by a high wall, about the middle of which was the main or front entrance, with one central and two side gates, leading to an open walk shaded by rows of trees. Here were spacious tanks of water, facing the doors of the right and left wings of the house, between which an avenue led from the main entrance to what may be called the centre of the mansion. After passing the outer door of the right wing, you entered an open court with trees, extending quite round a nucleus of inner apartments, and having a back entrance communicating with the garden. On the right and left of this court were six or more store-rooms, a small receiving or waiting room at two of the corners, and at the other end the staircases which led to the upper story. Both of the inner façades were furnished with a corridor, supported on columns, with similar towers and gateways. The interior of this wing consisted of twelve rooms, two outer and one centre court, communicating by folding gates; and on either side of this last was the main entrance to the rooms on the ground-floor, and to the staircases leading to the upper story. At the back were three long rooms, and a gateway opening on the garden, which, besides flowers, contained a variety of trees, a summer-house, and a large tank of water.

The arrangement of the left wing was different. The front gate led to an open court, extending the whole breadth of the façade of the building, and backed by the wall of the inner part. Central and lateral doors thence communicated with another court, surrounded on three sides by a set of rooms, and behind it was a corridor, upon which several other chambers opened.

This wing had no back entrance, and, standing isolated, the

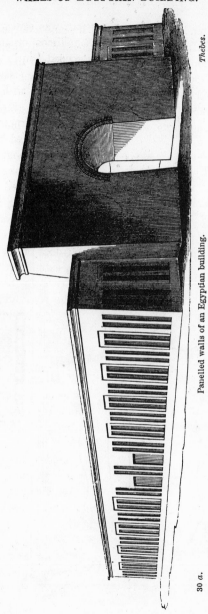

Thebes.

Panelled walls of an Egyptian building.

30 a.

outer court extended entirely round it ; and a succession of doorways communicated from the court with different sections of the
centre of the house, where the rooms, disposed like those already
described, around passages and corridors, served partly as sitting
apartments, and partly as storerooms.

The stables for the horses, and the coach-houses for the travelling chariots and carts, were in the centre, or inner part of the

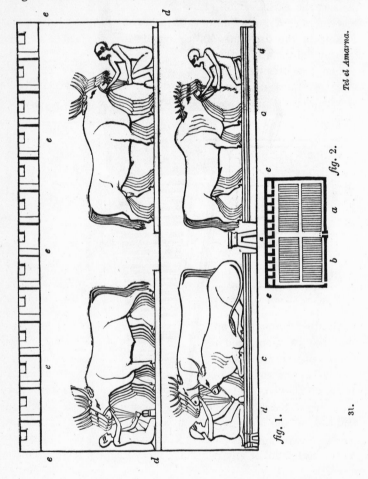

Tel el Amarna.

fig. 2.

fig. 1.

31.

building; but the farm-yard where the cattle were kept stood at some distance from the house, and corresponded to the department known by the Romans under the name of *rustica*. Though enclosed separately, it was within the general wall of circuit, which surrounded the land attached to the villa; and a canal, bringing water from the river, skirted it, and extended along the back of the grounds. It consisted of two parts: the sheds for housing the cattle, which stood at the upper end, and the yard, where rows of rings were fixed, in order to tie them while feeding in the day-time; and men always attended, and frequently fed them with the hand.

The granaries were also apart from the house, and were enclosed within a separate wall; and some of the rooms in which they housed the grain appear to have had vaulted roofs. These

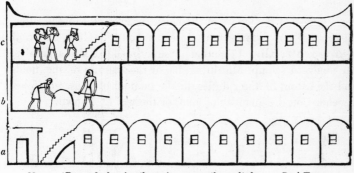

32.   Rooms for housing the grain, apparently vaulted.   *Beni Hassan.*

were filled through an aperture near the top, to which the men ascended by steps, and the grain when wanted was taken out from a door at the base.

The superintendence of the house and grounds was intrusted to stewards, who regulated the tillage of the land, received whatever was derived from the sale of the produce, overlooked the returns of the quantity of cattle or stock upon the estate, settled all the accounts, and condemned the delinquent peasants to the bastinado, or any punishment they might deserve. To one

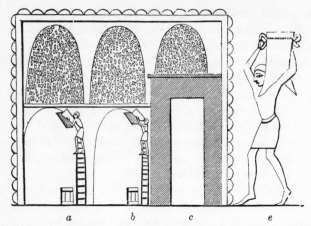

a   b   c   e

33.—Granary, showing how the grain was put in, and that the doors *a b* were intended
for taking it out.   *Thebes.*

were intrusted the affairs of the house, answering to " the ruler,"
"overseer," or "steward of Joseph's house" (Gen. xxxix. 5;
xliii. 16, 19; xliv. 1); others "superintended the granaries,"
the vineyard (comp. Matth. xx. 8), or the culture of the fields;
and the extent of their duties, or the number of those employed,
depended on the quantity of land, or the will of its owner.

2   3   4   *fig.* 1   5   6

34.   Steward (fig. 1) overlooking the tillage of the lands.   *Thebes.*

The mode of laying out their gardens was as varied as that of
the houses; but in all cases they appear to have taken particular
care to command a plentiful supply of water, by means of reservoirs and canals.   Indeed, in no country is artificial irrigation
more required than in the valley of the Nile; and, from the circumstance of the water of the inundation not being admitted into
the gardens, they depend throughout the year on the supply
obtained from wells and tanks, or a neighbouring canal.

The mode of irrigation adopted by the ancient Egyptians was exceedingly simple, being merely the *shadóof*, or pole and bucket of the present day ; and, in many instances, men were employed to carry the water in pails, suspended by a wooden yoke they bore upon their shoulders.   The same yoke was employed for

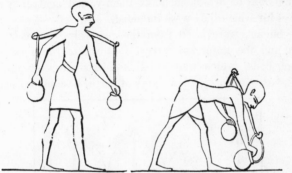

35.   Men watering the ground with pots of water.   *Beni Hassan.*

carrying other things, as boxes, baskets containing game and poultry, or whatever was taken to market ; and every trade seems to have used it for this purpose, from the potter and the brick-maker, to the carpenter and the shipwright.

The wooden bar or yoke was about three feet seven inches in length ; and the straps, which were double, and fastened together

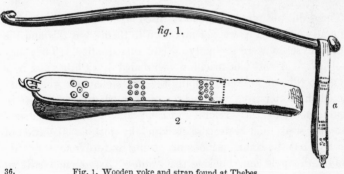

fig. 1.

2

36.   Fig. 1. Wooden yoke and strap found at Thebes.
Fig. 2 is the strap *a*, on a larger scale.

at the lower as well as at the upper extremity, were of leather, and between fifteen and sixteen inches long. The small thong at the bottom not only served to connect the ends, but was probably intended to fasten a hook, or an additional strap, if required, to attach the burden : and though most of these yokes had two, some were furnished with four or eight straps ; and the form, number, or arrangement of them varied according to the purposes for which they were intended.

The buckets were filled from the reservoirs or ponds in the garden, and the water was carried in them to the trees, or the different beds, which were small hollow squares on the level ground, surrounded by a low ledge of earth, like our saltpans.

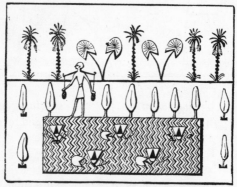

37.   Water-buckets carried by a yoke on the shoulders.   *Thebes.*

They do not appear to have used the water - wheel very generally ; though it was not unknown to them ; but this and the hydraulic screw were probably of late introduction. They may also have had the foot-machine mentioned by Philo ; and it is either to this, or to their stopping the small channels which conducted the water from one bed to another, that the sentence in Deuteronomy (xi. 40) refers—" Egypt . . . . where thou sowedst thy seed, and wateredst it with thy *foot* as a garden of herbs ;" but the common mode of raising water from the Nile was by the pole and bucket, the *shadóof*, so common still in Egypt.

Skins were much used by the Egyptians for carrying water, as

38.   Shadóof, or pole and bucket, for watering the garden.   *Thebes.*

well as for sprinkling the ground before the rooms or seats of the grandees, and they were frequently kept ready filled at the tank for that purpose.

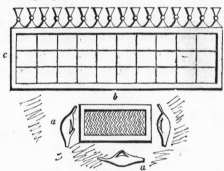

a a a Water-skins suspended close to the tank *b.*
c Beds of a garden, laid out as at the present day in Egypt, very like our saltpans.
39.   *Thebes.*

Part of the garden was laid out in walks shaded with trees, usually planted in rows, and surrounded, at the base of the stem, with a circular ridge of earth, which, being lower at the centre than at the circumference, retained the water, and directed it

D 2

more immediately towards the roots. It is difficult to say if trees were trimmed into any particular shape, or if their formal

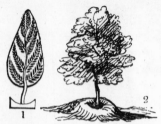

40.

1. Tree with earth raised round the roots.
2. The same according to our mode of representing it.

appearance in the sculpture is merely owing to a conventional mode of representing them; but, since the pomegranate, and some other fruit trees, are drawn with spreading and irregular branches, it is possible that sycamores, and others, which presented large masses of foliage, were really trained in that formal manner, though, from the hieroglyphic signifying " *tree*" having the same shape, we may conclude it

41. was only a general character for all trees.

Some, as the pomegranates, date-trees, and *dôm*-palms, are easily recognised in the sculptures, but the rest are doubtful, as are the flowering plants, with the exception of the lotus and a few others.

To the garden department belonged the care of the bees, which were kept in hives very like our own. In Egypt they required great attention; and so few are its plants at the present day, that the owners of hives often take the bees in boats to various spots upon the Nile, in

42. quest of flowers. They are a smaller kind than our own; and though found wild in the country, they are far less numerous than wasps, hornets, and ichneumons. The wild bees live mostly under stones, or in clefts of the rock, as in many other countries; and the expression of Moses, as of the Psalmist,

" honey out of the rock," shows that in Palestine their habits
were the same.   Honey was thought of great importance in
Egypt, both for household purposes, and for an offering to the
gods ;   that of Benha (thence surnamed *El assal*), or Athribis,
in the Delta, retained its reputation to a late time ; and a jar of
honey from that place was one of the four presents sent by John
Mekaukes, the governor of Egypt, to Mohammed.

Large gardens were usually divided into different parts ;
the principal sections being appropriated to the date and sycamore trees, and to the vineyard.   The former may be called the
orchard.   The flower and kitchen gardens also occupied a considerable space, laid out in beds ; and dwarf trees, herbs, and
flowers, were grown in red earthen pots, exactly like our own,
arranged in long rows by the walks and borders.

Besides the orchard and gardens, some of the large villas had
a park or paradise, with its fish-ponds and preserves for game,
as well as poultry-yards for keeping hens and geese, stalls for
fattening cattle, wild goats, gazelles, and other animals originally
from the desert, whose meat was reckoned among the dainties of
the table.   It was in these extensive preserves that the rich
amused themselves with the chase ; and they also enclosed a
considerable space in the desert itself with net-fences, into which
the animals were driven, and shot with arrows, or hunted with
dogs.

Gardens are frequently represented in the tombs of Thebes
and other parts of Egypt, many of which are remarkable for
their extent.   The one here introduced is shown to have been
surrounded by an embattled wall, with a canal of water passing in
front of it, connected with the river.   Between the canal and
the wall, and parallel to them both, was a shady avenue of
various trees ; and about the centre was the entrance, through a
lofty door, whose lintel and jambs were decorated with hieroglyphic inscriptions, containing the name of the owner of the
grounds, who in this instance was the king himself.   In the gateway were rooms for the porter, and other persons employed
about the garden, and, probably, the receiving room for visiters,

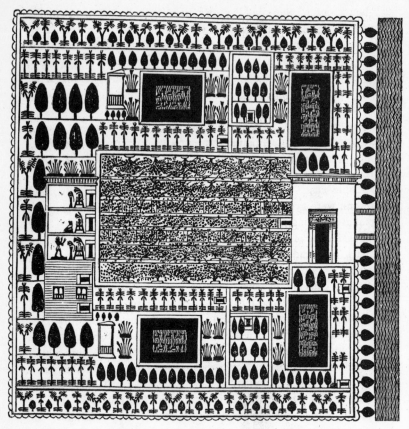

A large garden, with the vineyard and other separate enclosures, tanks of water, and a small house.   *From the Work of Prof. Rosellini.*
43.

whose abrupt admission might be unwelcome; and at the back a gate opened into the vineyard. The vines were trained on a trellis-work, supported by transverse rafters resting on pillars; and a wall, extending round it, separated this part from the rest of the garden. At the upper end were suites of rooms on three different stories, looking upon green trees, and affording a pleasant retreat in the heat of summer. On the outside of the vineyard wall were planted rows of palms, which occurred again

with the *dôm* and other trees, along the whole length of the exterior wall : four tanks of water, bordered by a grass plot, where
geese were kept, and the delicate flower of the lotus was encouraged to grow, served for the irrigation of the grounds ; and
small *kiosks* or summer-houses, shaded with trees, stood near the
water, and overlooked beds of flowers. The spaces containing
the tanks, and the adjoining portions of the garden, were each
enclosed by their respective walls, and a small subdivision on
either side, between the large and small tanks, seems to have
been reserved for the growth of particular trees, which either
required peculiar care, or bore a fruit of superior quality.

In all cases, whether the orchard stood apart from, or was
united with, the rest of the garden, it was supplied, like the other
portions of it, with abundance of water, preserved in spacious
reservoirs, on either side of which stood a row of palms, or an
avenue of shady sycamores. Sometimes the orchard and vine-

Egyptian mode of representing a tank of water with a row of palms on either side.
44.   *Thebes.*

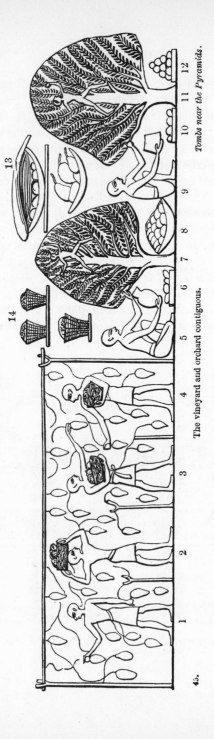

45.

The vineyard and orchard contiguous.

Tombs near the Pyramids.

yard were not separated by any wall, and figs * and other trees were planted within the same limits as the vines. But if not connected with it, the vineyard was close to the orchard, and their mode of training the vines on wooden rafters, supported by rows of columns, which divided the vineyard into numerous avenues, was both tasteful and convenient.

The columns were frequently coloured, but many were simple wooden pillars, supporting, with their forked summits, the poles that lay over them. Some vines were allowed to grow as standing bushes, and, being kept low, did not require any support; others were formed into a series of bowers; and from

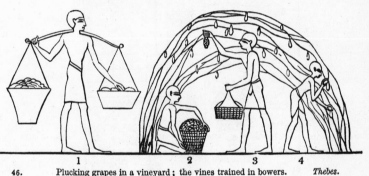

46.   Plucking grapes in a vineyard; the vines trained in bowers.   *Thebes.*

the form of the hieroglyphic, signifying vineyard, we may con-

47.   Figurative hieroglyphic signifying vineyard.

clude that the most usual method of training them was in bowers, or in avenues formed by rafters and columns. But they do not

---

* *Comp.* Luke xiii. 6, " A certain man had a fig-tree planted in his vineyard;" and 1 Kings, iv. 25, " Every man under his vine and under his fig-tree."

appear to have attached them to other trees, as the Romans often did to the elm and poplar, and as the modern Italians do to the white mulberry; nor have the Egyptians of the present day adopted this European custom.

When the vineyard was enclosed within its own wall of circuit, it frequently had a reservoir of water attached to it, as well as

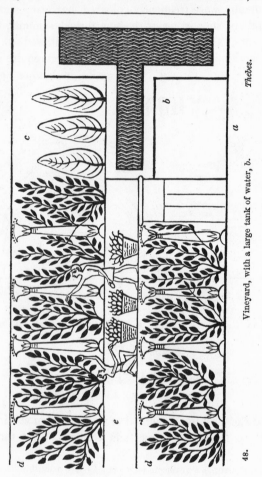

Vineyard, with a large tank of water, b.

Thebes.

48.

the building which contained the winepress;* but the various modes of arranging the vineyard, as well as the other parts of the garden, depended, of course, on the taste of each individual, or the nature of the ground.   Great care was taken to preserve the clusters from the intrusion of birds ; and boys were constantly employed, about the season of the vintage, to frighten them with a sling and the sound of the voice.

49.   Frightening away the birds with a sling.   *Thebes.*

When the grapes were gathered the bunches were carefully put into deep wicker baskets, which men carried, either on their head or shoulders, or slung upon a yoke, to the winepress ; but when intended for eating, they were put, like other fruits, into flat open baskets, and generally covered with leaves of the palm,

50.   Fig. 1. Basket containing grapes covered with leaves, from the sculptures.
             Fig. 2. Modern basket used for the same purpose.

vine, or other trees.   These flat baskets were of wicker-work, and similar to those of the present day, used at Cairo for

* *Comp.* Isaiah v. 1, 2, "And he fenced it (the vineyard), and gathered out the stones thereof, and planted it with the choicest vine, and built a tower in the midst of it, and also made a winepress therein ;" and Matthew xxi. 33, " planted a vineyard . . . . and digged a winepress in it."

the same purpose, which are made of osiers or common twigs. Monkies appear to have been trained to assist in gathering the fruit, and the Egyptians represent them in the sculptures handing

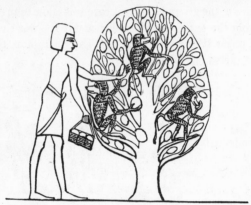

51.   Monkies assisting in gathering fruit.   *Beni-Hassan.*

down figs from the sycamore-trees to the gardeners below : but, as might be expected, these animals amply repaid themselves for the trouble imposed upon them, and the artist has not failed to show that they consulted their own wishes as well as those of their employers.

Many animals were tamed in Egypt for various purposes, as the lion, leopard, gazelle, baboon, crocodile, and others ; and in the Jimma country, which lies to the south of Abyssinia, monkies are still taught several useful accomplishments. Among them is that of officiating as torch-bearers at a supper party ; and seated in a row, on a raised bench, they hold the lights until the departure of the guests, and patiently await their own repast as a reward for their services. Sometimes the party is alarmed by an unruly monkey throwing his lighted torch into the midst of the unsuspecting guests ; but fortunately the ladies there do not wear muslin dresses ; and the stick and " no supper " remind the offender of his present and future duties.

After the vintage was over, they allowed the kids to browse upon the vines which grew as standing bushes (*comp. Hor.* ii. *Sat.*

52.   Kids allowed to browse upon the vines.   *Beni-Hassan.*

v. 43) ; and the season of the year when the grapes ripened in
Egypt was the month Epiphi, towards the end of June, or the
commencement of July.   Some have pretended to doubt that the
vine was commonly cultivated, or even grown, in Egypt ; but the
frequent notice of it, and of Egyptian wine, in the sculptures,
and the authority of ancient writers, sufficiently answer those
objections ; and the regrets of the Israelites on leaving the vines
of Egypt prove them to have been very abundant, since even
people in the condition of slaves could procure the fruit (Numb.
xx. 5, *comp.* Gen. xl. 11).

The winepress was of different kinds.   The most simple consisted merely of a bag, in which the grapes were put, and squeezed,
by means of two poles turning in contrary directions : a vase
being placed below to receive the falling juice.   Another press,

53.   Winepress.   *Beni-Hassan.*

nearly on the same principle, consisted of a bag supported in a
frame, having two upright sides, connected by beams at their
summit.   In this the bag was retained in a horizontal position,
one end fixed, the other passing through a hole in the opposite

side, and was twisted by means of a rod turned with the hand; the juice, as in the former, being received into a vase beneath; and within the frame stood the superintendent, who regulated the quantity of pressure, and gave the signal to stop.

Sometimes a liquid was heated on the fire, and, having been well stirred, was poured into the sack containing the grapes, during the process of pressure; but whether this was solely with a view of obtaining a greater quantity of juice, by moistening the husks, or was applied for any other purpose, it is difficult to determine: the fact, however, of its being stirred while on the fire suffices to show it was not simple water; and the trituration of the fruit, while it was poured upon it, may suggest its use in extracting the colouring matter for red wine.

The two Egyptian hand-presses were used in all parts of the country, but principally in Lower Egypt, the grapes in the Thebaïd being generally pressed by the feet. The footpress was also used in the lower country; and we even find the two methods of pressing the grapes represented in the same sculptures; it is not therefore impossible that, after having been subjected to the foot, they may have undergone a second pressure in

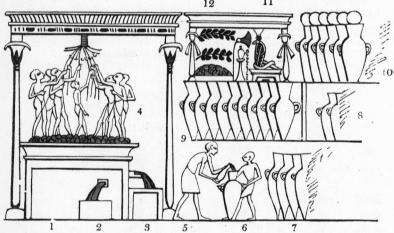

54. Large footpress; the amphoræ; and the asp, or Agathodæmon, the protecting deity of the store-room, fig. 11. *Thebes.*

the twisted bag. This does not appear to have been the case in the Thebaïd, where the *footpress* is always represented alone ; and the juice was allowed to run off by a pipe directly to an open tank (*comp.* Is. lxiii. 3, Nehem. xiii. 15, Judg. ix. 27, Virg. Georg. ii. 7).

Some of the large presses were highly ornamented, and consisted of at least two distinct parts ; the lower portion or vat, and the trough, where the men, with naked feet, trod the fruit, supporting themselves by ropes suspended from the roof ; though, from their great height, some may have had an intermediate reservoir, which received the juice in its passage to the pipe, answering to the strainer, or *colum*, of the Romans.

After the fermentation was over, the juice was taken out in small vases, with a long spout, and poured into earthenware jars, which corresponded to the *cadi* or *amphoræ* of the Romans.

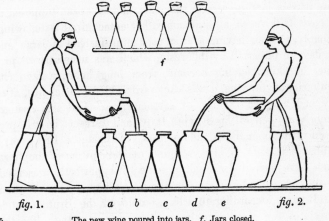

fig. 1.   *a*   *b*   *c*   *d*   *e*   *fig.* 2.

55.   The new wine poured into jars. *f.* Jars closed.

They appear also to have added something to it after or previous to the fermentation ; and an instance occurs in the sculptures of a man pouring a liquid from a small cup into the lower reservoir. When the *must* was considered in a proper state, the amphoræ were closed with a lid, resembling an inverted saucer, covered with liquid clay, pitch, gypsum, mortar, or other composition, which was stamped with a seal : they were then removed from the winehouse, and placed upright in the cellar.

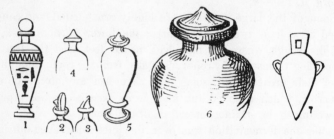

56.   Wine-jars with Covers. On *fig*. 1 is Êrp, " wine."   *Thebes.*

Previous to pouring in the wine they generally put a certain quantity of resin into the *amphoræ*, which coated the inside of those porous jars, preserved the wine, and was even supposed to improve its flavour ; a notion, or rather an acquired taste, owing, probably, to their having at first used skins·instead of jars : and the flavour imparted by the resin, which was necessary to preserve the skins, having become, from long habit, a favourite peculiarity of the wine, it was afterwards added from choice, after they had adopted the use of earthenware.   And this custom, formerly so general in Egypt, Italy, and Greece, is still preserved throughout the islands of the Archipelago.   In Egypt, a resinous substance is always found at the bottom of amphoræ which have served for holding wine ; it is perfectly preserved, brittle, and, when burnt, smells like a very fine quality of pitch. The Romans, according to Pliny, employed the Brutian pitch, or resin of the picea pine, in preference to all others, for this purpose : and if, " in Spain, they used that of the pinaster, it was little esteemed on account of its bitterness and oppressive smell." In the East, the terebinthus was considered to afford the best resin, superior even to the mastic of the lentiscus ; and the resins of Judæa and Syria only yielded in quality to that of Cyprus.

The mode of arranging amphoræ in an Egyptian cellar was

similar to that adopted by the Greeks and Romans.   They stood
upright in successive rows, the inner-
most set resting against the wall, with
their pointed ends firmly fixed in the
ground ; and each jar was secured
by means of a stone ring fitting round
its pointed base, or was raised on a
wooden stand.   Others appear occasionally to have been placed in upper
rooms, as the amphoræ in a Roman
apotheca.

57.   Vase supported by a stone ring.

The Egyptians had several different kinds of wine, some of
which have been commended by ancient authors for their excellent qualities.   That of Mareotis was the most esteemed, and in
the greatest quantity.   Its superiority over other Egyptian wines
may readily be accounted for, when we consider the nature of
the soil in that district ; being principally composed of gravel,
which, lying beyond the reach of the alluvial deposit, was free
from the rich and tenacious mud usually met with in the valley
of the Nile, so little suited for grapes of delicate quality ; and
from the extensive remains of vineyards still found on the
western borders of the Arsinoïte nome, or Fyoóm, we may conclude that the ancient Egyptians were fully aware of the advantages of land, situated beyond the limits of the inundation, for
planting the vine.   According to Athenæus, " the Mareotic
grape was remarkable for its sweetness," and the wine is thus
described by him : " Its colour is white, its quality excellent, and
it is sweet and light with a fragrant *bouquet ;* it is by no means
astringent, nor does it affect the head."   But it was not for its
flavour alone that this wine was esteemed, and Strabo ascribes to
it the additional merit of keeping to a great age.   " Still, however," says Athenæus, " it is inferior to the Teniotic, a wine which
receives its name from a place called Tenia, where it is produced.   Its colour is pale and white, and there is such a degree
of richness in it, that, when mixed with water, it seems gradually
to be diluted, much in the same way as Attic honey when a

liquid is poured into it; and besides the agreeable flavour of
the wine, its fragrance is so delightful as to render it perfectly
aromatic, and it has the property of being slightly astringent.
There are many other vineyards in the valley of the Nile, whose
wines are in great repute, and these differ both in colour and
taste : but that which is produced about Anthylla is preferred to
all the rest." Some of the wine made in the Thebaïd was particularly light, especially about Coptos, and "so wholesome,"
says the same author, " that invalids might take it without inconvenience, even during a fever." The Sebennytic was likewise one of the choice Egyptian wines ; and, as Pliny says, was
made of three different grapes ; one of which was a sort of
Thasian. The Thasian grape he afterwards describes as excelling
all others in Egypt for its sweetness, and remarkable for its
medicinal properties.

The Mendesian is also mentioned by Clemens, with rather a
sweet flavour : and another singular wine, called by Pliny
ecbolada (εκϐολας), was also the produce of Egypt ; but, from
its peculiar powers, we may suppose that men alone drank it, or
at least that it was forbidden to newly married brides. And,
considering how prevalent the custom was amongst the ancients
of altering the qualities of wines, by drugs and divers processes,
we may readily conceive the possibility of the effects ascribed to
them ; and thus it happened that opposite properties were frequently attributed to the same kind.

Wines were much used by them for medicinal purposes, and
many were held in such repute as to be considered specifics in
certain complaints ; but the medical men of the day were prudent
in their mode of prescribing them ; and as imagination has on
many occasions effected the cure, and given celebrity to a medicine,
those least known were wisely preferred, and each extolled the
virtues of some foreign wine. In the earliest times, Egypt was renowned for drugs, and foreigners had recourse to that country for
wines as well as herbs ; yet Apollodorus, the physician, in a treatise
on wines, addressed to Ptolemy, king of Egypt, recommended those
of Pontus as more beneficial than any of his own country, and

particularly praised the Peparethian, produced in an island of
the Ægean Sea ; but he was disposed to consider it less valuable
as a medicine, when its good qualities could not be discovered in
six years.

The wines of Alexandria and Coptos are also cited among the
best of Egyptian growth ; and the latter was so light as not to
affect even those in delicate health.

In offerings to the Egyptian deities wine frequently occurs,
and several different kinds are noticed in the sacred sculptures ;
but it is probable that many of the Egyptian wines are not introduced in those subjects, and that, as with the Romans, and other
people, all were not admitted at their sacrifices. According to
Herodotus, their sacrifices commenced with a libation of wine,
and some was sprinkled on the ground where the victim lay ;
yet at Heliopolis, if Plutarch may be credited, it was forbidden
to take it into the temple, and the priests of the god worshipped
in that city were required to abstain from its use. " Those of
other deities," adds the same author, " were less scrupulous,"
but still they used wine very sparingly, and the quantity
allowed them for their daily consumption was regulated by law ;
nor could they indulge in it at all times, and the use of it was
strictly prohibited during their more solemn purifications, and
in times of abstinence. The number of wines, mentioned in
the lists of offerings presented to the deities in the tombs or
temples, varies in different places. Each appears with its peculiar name attached to it ; but they seldom exceed three or four
kinds, and among them I have observed, at Thebes, that of the
" northern country," which was, perhaps, from Mareotis, Anthylla, or the nome of Sebennytus.

Private individuals were under no particular restrictions with
regard to its use, and it was not forbidden to women. In this
they differed widely from the Romans : for in early times no
female at Rome enjoyed the privilege, and it was unlawful for
women, or, indeed, for young men below the age of thirty, to
drink wine, except at sacrifices. Even at a later time the Romans considered it disgraceful for a woman to drink wine ; and

they sometimes saluted a female relation, whom they suspected, in order to discover if she had secretly indulged in its use. It was afterwards allowed them on the plea of health, and no better method could have been devised for removing the restriction.

That Egyptian women were not forbidden the use of wine, nor the enjoyment of other luxuries, is evident from the frescoes which represent their feasts ; and the painters, in illustrating this fact, have sometimes sacrificed their gallantry to a love of

58.   A servant called to support her mistress.   *Thebes.*

caricature. Some call the servants to support them as they sit, others with difficulty prevent themselves from falling on those behind them ; a basin is brought too late by a reluctant servant

59.   A party of Egyptian ladies.   *Thebes.*

and the faded flower, which is ready to drop from their heated hands, is intended to be characteristic of their own sensations.

That the consumption of wine in Egypt was very great is evident from the sculptures, and from the accounts of ancient authors, some of whom have censured the Egyptians for their excesses ; and so much did the quantity used exceed that made in the country, that, in the time of Herodotus, twice every year a large importation was received from Phœnicia and Greece.

Notwithstanding all the injunctions or exhortations of the priests in favour of temperance, the Egyptians of both sexes appear from the sculptures to have committed occasional excesses, and men were sometimes unable to walk from a feast, and were carried home by servants.   These scenes, however, do not

60.   Men carried home from a drinking p .   *Beni Hassan.*

appear to refer to members of the higher, but of the lower, classes, some of whom indulged in extravagant buffoonery, dancing in a ludicrous manner, or standing on their heads, and frequently in amusements which terminated in a fight.

At the tables of the rich, stimulants were sometimes introduced, to excite the palate before drinking, and Athenæus mentions cabbages as one of the vegetables used by the Egyptians for this purpose.

Throughout the upper and lower country, wine was the favourite beverage of the wealthy : they had also very excellent beer, called *zythus*, which Diodorus, though wholly unaccustomed to it, and a native of a wine country, affirms was scarcely inferior to the juice of the grape.   Strabo and other ancient authors have likewise mentioned it under the name of zythus; and though Herodotus pretends that it was merely used as a substitute for wine in the lowlands, where corn was principally cultivated, it is more reasonable to conclude it was drunk by the peasants in all parts of Egypt, though less in those districts where vines were abundant.   Native wines of a choice kind, whether made in the vicinity or brought from another province, were confined to the rich ; and we learn from Strabo that this was the case even at Alexandria, where wine could be obtained in greater quantity than in any other part of Egypt, owing to the proximity of the Mareotic district ; and the common people were there content with beer and the poor wine of the coast of Libya.

Egyptian beer was made from barley ; but, as hops were unknown, they were obliged to have recourse to other plants, in order to give it a grateful flavour ; and the lupin, the skirret (*Sium sisarum*), and the root of an Assyrian plant, were used by them for that purpose.

The vicinity of Pelusium was the most noted for its beer, and the Pelusiac zythus is mentioned by more than one author. The account given by Athenæus of Egyptian beer is that it was very strong, and had so exhilarating an effect that they danced, and sang, and committed the same excesses as those who were intoxicated with the strongest wines ; an observation confirmed by the authority of Aristotle, whose opinion on the subject has at least the merit of being amusing.   For we must smile at the philosopher's method of distinguishing persons suffering under the influence of wine and beer, however disposed he would have been to accuse us of ignorance in not having yet discovered how invariably the former in that state "lie upon their face, and the latter on their backs."

Besides beer, the Egyptians had what Pliny calls factitious, or artificial, wine, extracted from various fruits, as figs, *myxas*, pomegranates, as well as herbs, some of which were selected for their medicinal properties.   The Greeks and Latins comprehended every kind of beverage made by the process of fermentation under the same general name, and beer was designated as

barley-*wine;* but, by the use of the name zythos, they show that
the Egyptians distinguished it by its own peculiar appellation.
Palm-wine was also made in Egypt, and used in the process of
embalming.

The palm-wine now made in Egypt and the Oases is simply
from an incision in the heart of the tree, immediately below the
base of the upper branches, and a jar is attached to the part to
catch the juice which exudes from it. But a palm thus tapped is
rendered perfectly useless as a fruit-bearing tree, and generally
dies in consequence; and it is reasonable to suppose that so great
a sacrifice is seldom made except when date-trees are to be felled,
or when they grow in great abundance. The modern name of
this beverage in Egypt is *lowbgeh;* in flavour it resembles a
very new light wine, and may be drunk in great quantity when
taken from the tree; but, as soon as the fermentation has commenced, its intoxicating qualities have a powerful and speedy
effect.

Among the various fruit-trees cultivated by the ancient
Egyptians, palms, of course, held the first rank, as well from their
abundance as from their great utility. The fruit constituted a
principal part of their food, both in the month of August, when
it was gathered fresh from the trees, and at other seasons of the
year, when it was used in a preserved state. They had two
different modes of keeping the dates; one was by the simple
process of drying them, the other was by making them into a
conserve, like the *agweh* of the present day; and of this, which
was eaten either cooked or as a simple sweetmeat, I have found
some cakes, as well as the dried dates, in the sepulchres of
Thebes.

Pliny makes a just remark respecting the localities where the
palm prospers, and the constant irrigation it requires; and though
every one in the East knows the tree will not grow except where
water is abundant, we still read of " palm-trees of the desert," as
if it delighted in an arid district. Wherever it is found it is a
sure indication of water; and if it may be said to flourish in a
sandy soil, this is only in situations where its roots can obtain

a certain quantity of moisture. The numerous purposes for which its branches and other parts might be applied rendered the cultivation of this valuable and productive tree a matter of primary importance, for no portion of it is without its peculiar use. The trunk serves for beams, either entire, or split in half; of the *gereét*, or branches, are made wicker baskets, bedsteads, coops, and ceilings of rooms, answering every purpose for which laths or any thin woodwork are required; the leaves are converted into mats, brooms, and baskets; of the fibrous tegument at the base of the branches, strong ropes and mats are made, and even the thick ends of the *gereét* are beaten flat and formed into brooms. Besides the *lowbgeh* of the tree, brandy, wine, and vinegar are made from the fruit; and the quantity of saccharine matter in the dates might be used in default of sugar or honey.

In Upper Egypt another tree, called the *Dôm*, or Theban palm, was also much cultivated, and its wood, more solid and compact than the date-tree, is found to answer as well for rafts, and other purposes connected with water, as for beams and rafters.

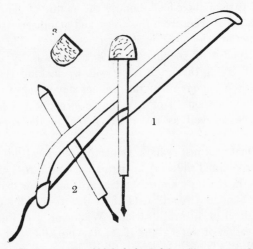

61.   Fig. 3. *Dôm* nut, which is the head of the drill.   *Found at Thebes.*

The fruit is a large rounded nut, with a fibrous exterior envelope, which has a flavour very similar to our gingerbread ; and from its extreme hardness this nut was used for the hollow socket of their drills, or centre-bits, as well as for beads and other purposes. Of the leaves of the *dôm* were made baskets, sacks, mats, fans, fly-flaps, brushes, and light sandals ; and they served as a general substitute for those of the date-tree, and for the rushes, *halfeh* or *poa* grass, the cyperus, osiers, and other materials employed for the same purposes in Egypt.

Next to the palms, the principal trees of the garden were the fig, sycamore, pomegranate, olive, peach, almond, persea, *nebk* or *sidr*, *mokhayt* or *myxa*, *kharoób* or locust-tree ; and of those that bore no fruit the most remarkable were the two tamarisks, the cassia fistula, senna, palma christi or castor-berry tree, myrtle, various kinds of " acanthus " or acacia, and some others still found in the deserts between the Nile and the Red Sea. So fond were the Egyptians of trees and flowers, and of rearing numerous and rare plants, that they even made them part of the tribute exacted from foreign countries ; and such, according to Athenæus, " was the care they bestowed on their culture, that those flowers which elsewhere were only sparingly produced, even in their proper season, grew profusely at all times in Egypt ; so that neither roses, nor violets, nor any others, were wanting there, even in the middle of winter." The tables in their sitting-rooms were always decked with bouquets, and they had even artificial flowers, which received the name of " Ægyptian." The lotus was the favourite for wreaths and chaplets ; they also employed the leaves or blossoms of other plants, as the chrysanthemum, *acinon*, acacia, *strychnus*, *persoluta*, anemone, convolvulus, olive, myrtle, *amaricus*, xeranthemum, bay-tree, and others ; and when Agesilaus visited Egypt he was so delighted with the chaplets of papyrus sent him by the Egyptian king, that he took some home with him on his return to Sparta. But it is singular that, while the lotus is so often represented, no instance occurs on the monuments of the Indian lotus, or *Nelumbium*, though the Roman-Egyptian sculptures point it out as a peculiar plant of Egypt, placing it about the figure of the god Nile; and it is stated by Latin writers to have been common in the country.

In the furniture of their houses the Egyptians displayed considerable taste; and there, as elsewhere, they studiously avoided too much regularity, justly considering that its monotonous effect fatigued the eye. They preferred variety both in the arrangement of the rooms and in the character of their furniture, and neither the windows, doors, nor wings of the house, exactly corresponded with each other. An Egyptian would therefore have been more pleased with the form of our Elizabethan, than of the box-shaped rooms of later times.

In their mode of sitting on chairs they resembled the modern Europeans rather than Asiatics, neither using, like the latter, soft *divans*, nor sitting cross-legged on carpets. Nor did they recline at meals, as the Romans, on a *triclinium*, though couches and ottomans formed part of the furniture of an Egyptian as of an English drawing-room. When Joseph entertained his brethren, he ordered them to *sit* according to their ages. And if they sometimes sat cross-legged on the ground, on mats and carpets, or knelt on one or both knees, these were rather the customs for certain occasions, and of the poorer classes. To sit on their heels was also customary as a token of respect in the presence of a

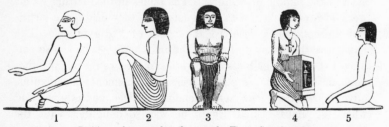

62.   Positions, when seated on the ground.   Fig. 1. Cross-legged.

superior, as in modern Egypt; and when a priest bore a shrine before the deity he assumed this position of humility; a still greater respect being shown by prostration, or by kneeling and kissing the ground. But the house of a wealthy person was always furnished with chairs and couches. Stools and low seats were also used, the seat being only from 8 to 14 inches high, and of

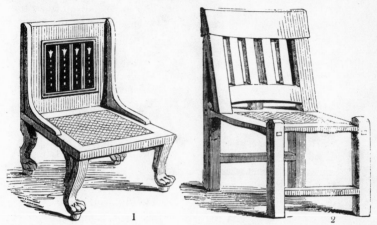

63.

64.   Chairs.   *British Museum.*

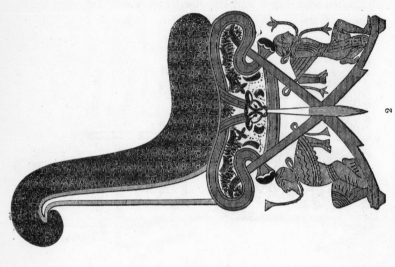

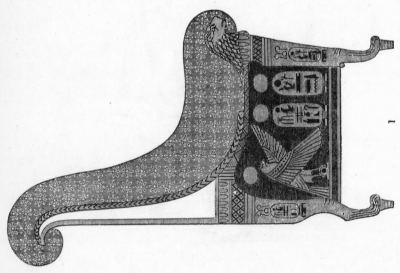

Fauteuils painted in the Tomb of Remeses III.   *Thebes.*

65.

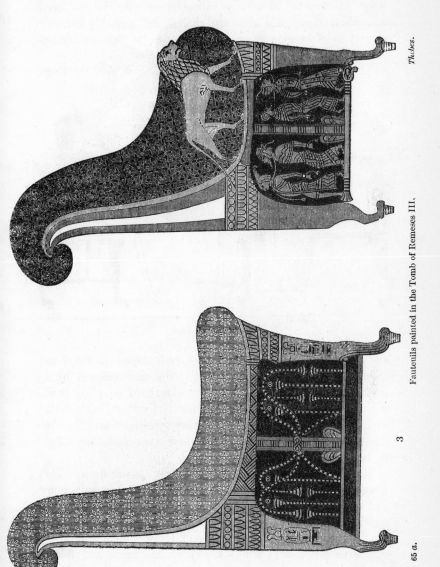

Thebes.

Fauteuils painted in the Tomb of Remeses III.

3

65 a.

wood, or interlaced with thongs; these however may be considered
equivalent to our rush-bottomed chairs, and probably belonged
to persons of humble means. They varied in their quality, and
some were inlaid with ivory and various woods.

Those most common in the houses of the rich were the single

66.   Double and Single Chairs.   *Thebes.*

and double chair (answering to the Greek *thronos* and *diphros*),
the latter sometimes kept as a family seat, and occupied by the
master and mistress of the house, or a married couple. It was
not, however, always reserved exclusively for them, nor did they
invariably occupy the same seat; they sometimes sat like their
guests on separate chairs, and a *diphros* was occasionally offered
to visiters, both men and women.

Many of the fauteuils were of the most elegant form. They
were made of ebony and other rare woods, inlaid with ivory,
and very similar to some now used in Europe. The legs were
mostly in imitation of those of an animal; and lions' heads, or
the entire body, formed the arms of large fauteuils, as in the
throne of Solomon (1 Kings x. 19). Some again had folding

legs, like our camp-stools; the seat was often slightly concave; and those in the royal palace were ornamented with the figures of captives, or emblems of his dominion over Egypt and other countries. The back was light and strong, and consisted of a single set of upright and cross bars, or of a frame receding gradually and terminating at its summit in a graceful curve, supported from without by perpendicular bars; and over this was thrown a handsome pillow of coloured cotton, painted leather, or gold and silver tissue, like the beds at the feast of Ahasuerus, mentioned in Esther; or like the feathered cushions covered with stuffs and embroidered with silk and threads of gold in the palace of Scaurus. (*Woodcuts* 65 and 65*a*.)

Seats on the principle of our camp-stools seem to have been much

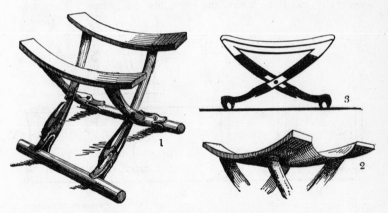

67.   Fig. 1. A stool in the British Museum, on the principle of our camp-stools.
         2. Shows the manner in which the leather seat was fastened.
         3. A similar one from the sculptures, with its cushion.

in vogue. They were furnished with a cushion, or were covered with the skin of a leopard, or some other animal, which was removed when the seat was folded up; and it was not unusual to make even head-stools, or wooden pillows, on the same principle. They were also adorned in various ways, bound with metal plates, and inlaid with ivory or foreign woods ; and the wood of common chairs was often painted to resemble that of a rarer and more valuable kind.

68.

The seats of chairs were frequently of leather, painted with flowers and fancy devices ; or of interlaced work made of string or thongs, carefully and neatly arranged, which, like our Indian cane chairs, were particularly adapted for a hot climate ; but over this they occasionally placed a leather cushion, painted in the manner already mentioned.

The forms of the chairs varied very much ; the larger ones generally had light backs, and some few had arms.   They were

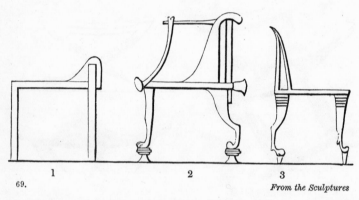

69.

1   2   3

From the Sculptures

mostly about the height of those now used in Europe, the seat nearly in a line with the bend of the knee ; but some were very low, and others offered that variety of position which we seek in the kangaroo chairs of our own drawing-room (*Woodcut* 70, *fig.* 3). The ordinary fashion of the legs was in imitation of those of some wild animal, as the lion or the goat, but more usually the former, the foot raised and supported on a short pin ; and, what is

remarkable, the skill of their cabinet-makers, even before the
time of Joseph, had already done away with the necessity of
uniting the legs with bars.   Stools, however, and more rarely

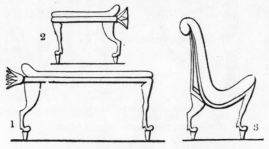

70
           Fig. 1. A δίφρος or double chair, without a back.
             2. A single chair, of similar construction.
             3. A kangaroo chair.   *Sculptures.*

chairs, were occasionally made with these strengthening members, as is still the case in our own country; but the drawing-
room fauteuil and couch were not disfigured by so unseemly and
so unskilful a support.

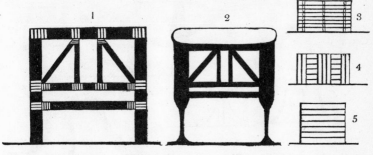

71.   Fig. 1. Stools.   2. With a cushion.   3, 4, 5. With solid sides.   *Thebes.*

The stools used in the saloon were of the same style and elegance as the chairs, frequently differing from them only in the
absence of a back; and those of more delicate workmanship
were made of ebony, and inlaid, as already stated, with ivory

VOL. I.   F

72.   Fig. 1. Stool of ebony inlaid with ivory.   *British Museum.*
        2. Shows the inlaid parts of the legs.
        3. Of ordinary construction, in the same collection.

73.   A stool with leather cushion.   *British Museum.*

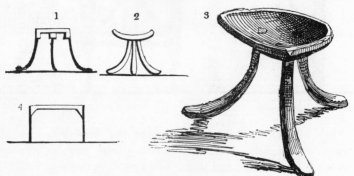

74.   Figs. 1, 2. Three-legged stools, from the Sculptures.
        3. Wooden stool, *in the British Museum.*
        4, and 1, are probably of metal.

or rare woods. Some of an ordinary kind had solid sides, and
were generally very low; and others, with three legs, not unlike
those used by the peasants of England, belonged to persons of
inferior rank.

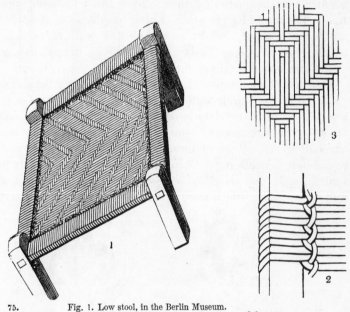

75.   Fig. 1. Low stool, in the Berlin Museum.
           2, 3. Mode of fastening, and the pattern of the seat.

The ottomans were simple square sofas, without backs, raised
from the ground nearly to the same level as the chairs. The

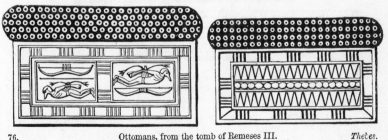

76.   Ottomans, from the tomb of Remeses III.   *Thebes.*

F 2

upper part was of leather, or a cotton stuff, richly coloured, like the cushions of the fauteuils; the base was of wood, painted with various devices; and those in the royal palace were ornamented with the figures of captives, the conquest of whose country was designated by their having this humiliating position. The same idea gave them a place on the soles of sandals, on the footstools of a royal throne, and on the walls of the palace at Medeenet Haboo, in Thebes, where their heads support some of the ornamental details of the building.

Footstools also constituted part of the furniture of the sitting-room; they were made with solid or open sides, covered at the top with leather or interlaced work, and varied in height according to circumstances, some being of the usual size now adopted by us, others of inconsiderable thickness, and rather resembling a small rug. Carpets, indeed, were a very early invention, and they are often represented sitting upon them, as well as on mats, which were commonly used in their sitting-

77.

Fig. 1. A low seat, perhaps a carpet.
2. Either similar to fig. 1, or of wood.
3. A mat.

rooms, as at the present day, and remnants of them have been found in the Theban tombs.

Their couches evinced no less taste than the fauteuils. They were of wood, with one end raised, and receding in a graceful curve; and the feet, as in many of the chairs already described, were fashioned to resemble those of some wild animal.

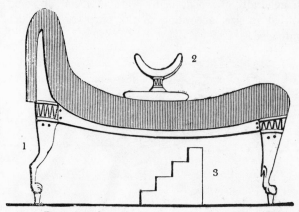

78.   Fig. 1. A couch.
        2. Pillow or head stool.
        3. Steps for ascending a lofty couch. (*Tomb of Remeses III.*) *Thebes*.

Egyptian tables were round, square, or oblong; the former were generally used during their repasts, and consisted of a circular flat summit, supported, like the *monopodium* of the Romans, on a single shaft, or leg, in the centre, or by the figure of a

79.   Fig. 1. Table, probably of stone or wood, from the sculptures.
        2. Stone table supported by the figure of a captive.
        3. Probably of metal, from the sculptures.

man, intended to represent a captive. Large tables had usually
three or four legs, but some were made with solid sides; and
though generally of wood, many were of metal or stone; and
they varied in size, according to the purposes for which they
were intended.

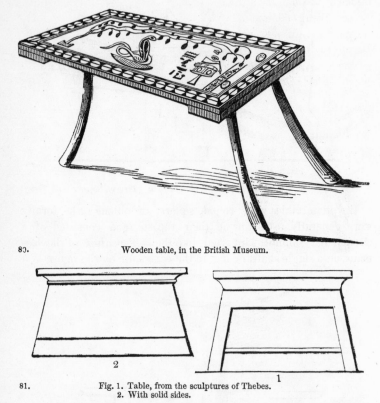

80.   Wooden table, in the British Museum.

81.   Fig. 1. Table, from the sculptures of Thebes.
                              2. With solid sides.

Of the furniture of their bed-rooms we know little or nothing :
but that they universally employed the wooden pillow above
alluded to is evident, though Porphyry would lead us to suppose its use was confined to the priests, when, in noticing their
mode of life, he mentions a half cylinder of well polished wood
" sufficing to support their head," as an instance of their simplicity

and self-denial. For the rich they were made of oriental alabaster, with an elegant grooved
or fluted shaft, ornamented with
hieroglyphics, carved in intaglio,
of sycamore, tamarisk, and other
woods of the country; the poorer
classes being contented with a
cheaper sort, of pottery or stone.
Porphyry mentions a kind of
wicker bedstead of *palm branches*,
hence called *baïs*, evidently the species of framework called

82.   Wooden pillow.

83.   Fig. 1. Wooden pillow of unusual form.
      2. Another found by me at Thebes, and now in the British Museum. The
      base was lost.

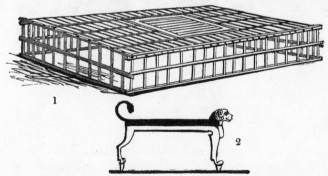

84.   Fig. 1. *Kaffass* bedstead of palm sticks used by the modern Egyptians.
      2. Ancient bier on which the bodies were placed after death.

kaffass, still employed by the modern Egyptians as a support to the *diwans* of sitting rooms, and to their beds.   Wooden, and perhaps also bronze, bedsteads (like the iron one of Og, King of Bashan), were used by the wealthier classes of the ancient Egyptians ; and it is at least probable that the couches they slept upon were as elegant as those on which their bodies reposed after death ; and the more so, as these last, in their general style, are very similar to the furniture of the sitting-room.

B. Modern *shadóof*, or pole and bucket, used for raising water, in Upper and Lower Egypt.

c.
Pavilion of Remeses III. at Medeenet Haboo. *Thebes*

CHAPTER II.

RECEPTION OF GUESTS — MUSIC — VARIOUS INSTRUMENTS — SACRED
MUSIC — DANCE.

In their entertainments they appear to have omitted nothing
which could promote festivity and the amusement of the guests.
Music,* songs, dancing,† buffoonery, feats of agility, or games of
chance, were generally introduced ; and they welcomed them with
all the luxuries which the cellar and the table could afford.

The party, when invited to dinner, met about midday,‡ and
they arrived successively in their chariots, in palanquins borne
by their servants, or on foot. Sometimes their attendants
screened them from the sun by holding up a shield, (as is still
done in Southern Africa,) or by some other contrivance ; but
the chariot of the king, § or of a princess, ‖ was often fur-

* Comp. Isaiah v. 12, " The harp and the viol, the tabret and pipe, and wine,
are at their feasts."

† Comp. the feast given on the arrival of the prodigal son : " Bring hither the
fatted calf, and kill it ; and let us eat and be merry :" and his brother, when he
drew nigh to the house, " heard music and dancing." Luke xv. 23, 25.

‡ Joseph said, " These men shall dine with me at noon." Gen. xliii. 16.

§ Woodcut 86. ‖ *See* a Chariot in Chapter vi.

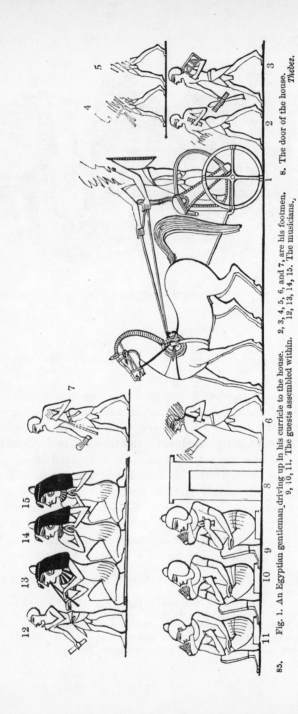

85.   Fig. 1. An Egyptian gentleman driving up in his curricle to the house.   2, 3, 4, 5, 6, and 7, are his footmen.   8. The door of the house,   *Thebes.*
9, 10, 11. The guests assembled within.   12, 13, 14, 15. The musicians.

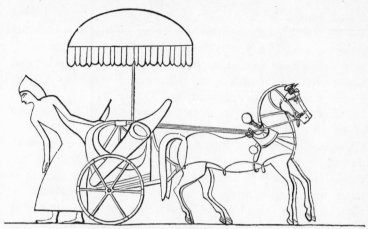

86.   Chariot with Umbrella.   *Thebes.*

Military chief carried in a sort of palanquin, an attendant bearing a parasol behind him.
87.   *Beni Hassan.*

nished with a large parasol; and the flabella borne behind
the king, which belonged exclusively to royalty, answered the
same purpose. They were composed of feathers, and were not
very unlike those carried on state occasions behind the Pope in
modern Rome. Parasols or umbrellas were also used in Assyria,
Persia, and other Eastern countries.

When a visitor came in his car, he was attended by a number
of servants, some of whom carried a stool, to enable him to
alight, and others his writing tablet, or whatever he might want
during his stay at the house. In the wood-cut (No. 85) the
guests are assembled in a sitting room within, and are entertained with music during the interval preceding the announcement of dinner; for, like the Greeks, they considered it a want
of good breeding to sit down to table immediately on arriving,
and, as Bdelycleon, in Aristophanes, recommended his father
Philocleon to do, they praised the beauty of the rooms and the
furniture, taking care to show particular interest in those objects
which were intended for admiration. As usual in all countries,
some of the party arrived earlier than others; and the consequence, or affectation of fashion, in the person who now drives
up in his curricle, is shown by his coming some time after the
rest of the company; one of his footmen runs forward to knock
at the door, others, close behind the chariot, are ready to take
the reins, and to perform their accustomed duties; and the one
holding his sandals in his hand, that he may run with greater
ease, illustrates a custom, still common in Egypt, among the
Arabs and peasants of the country, who find the power of the
foot greater when freed from the encumbrance of a shoe.

To those who arrived from a journey, or who desired it, water
was brought * for their feet, previous to entering the festive
chamber. They also washed their hands before dinner, the water
being brought in the same manner as at the present day; and

* Joseph ordered his servants to fetch water for his brethren, that they might
wash their feet before they ate. Gen. xliii. 24. *Comp.* also xviii. 4, and xxiv. 32;
1 Sam. xxv. 46. It was always a custom of the East, as with the Greeks and
Romans. *Comp.* Luke vii. 44, 46.

ewers, not unlike those used by the modern Egyptians, are represented, with the basins belonging to them, in the paintings of a
Theban tomb. In the houses of the rich they were of gold,

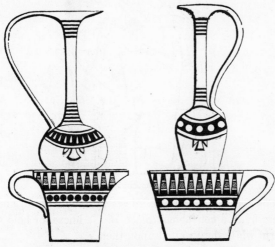

88.   Golden ewers and basins in the tomb of Remeses III.   *Thebes.*

or other costly materials. Herodotus mentions the golden
foot-pan, in which Amasis and his guests used to wash their
feet. The Greeks had the same custom of bringing water to the
guests, numerous instances of which we find in Homer ; as when
Telemachus and the son of Nestor were received at the house of
Menelaus, and when Asphalion poured it upon the hands of his
master, and the same guests, on another occasion. Virgil also
describes the servants bringing water for this purpose, when
Æneas was entertained by Dido. Nor was the ceremony thought
superfluous, or declined, even though they had previously bathed
and been anointed with oil.

It is also probable that, like the Greeks, the Egyptians
anointed themselves before they left home ; but still it was customary for a servant to attend every guest, as he seated himself,
and to anoint his head ; which was one of the principal tokens
of welcome. The ointment was sweet-scented, and was con-

tained in an alabaster, or in an elegant glass or porcelain vase, some of which have been found in the tombs of Thebes.*   Ser-

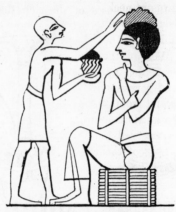

89.   A servant anointing a guest.   *Thebes.*

vants took the sandals of the guests as they arrived, and either put them by in a convenient place in the house, or held them on their arm while they waited upon them.

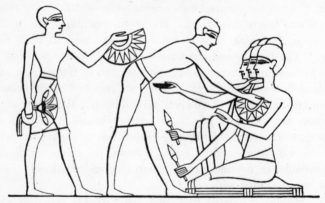

90.   Servants bringing necklaces of flowers.   *Thebes.*

After the ceremony of anointing was over, and, in some cases,

* Mary, when she washed Jesus' feet, brought an alabaster box of ointment. Luke vii. 37.   Matt. xxvi. 7.

at the time of entering the saloon, a lotus flower was presented
to each guest, who held it in his hand during the entertainment.
Servants then brought necklaces of flowers, composed chiefly of
the lotus; a garland was also put round the head, and a single
lotus bud, or a full-blown flower, was so attached as to hang over
the forehead. Many of them, made up into wreaths and other
devices, were suspended upon stands in the room ready for immediate use; and servants were constantly employed to bring
other fresh flowers from the garden, in order to supply the
guests as their bouquets faded.

The stands that served for holding the flowers and garlands
were similar to those of the amphoræ and vases, some of which
have been found in the tombs of Thebes; and the same kind of
stand was introduced into a lady's dressing-room, or the bath, for
the purpose of holding clothes and other articles of the toilet.
They varied in size according to circumstances, some being low
and broad at the top, others higher, with a small summit, merely
large enough to contain a single cup, or a small bottle. Others,

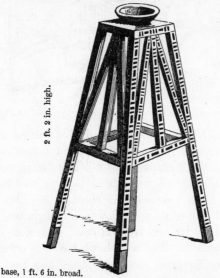

2 ft. 2 in. high.

base, 1 ft. 6 in. broad.

91.   Wooden stand, 8 in. square at the summit, holding a small cup. *British Museum.*

though much smaller than the common stands, were broader in proportion to their height, and answered as small tables, or as the supports of cases containing bottles ; and one of these last, preserved in the Berlin Museum, is supposed to have belonged to a medical man, or to the toilet of a Theban lady.

The vases are six in number, varying slightly in form and size ; five of alabaster, and the remaining one of serpentine, each standing in its own cell or compartment.

92.   A case containing bottles supported on a stand.   *Berlin Museum.*

The Greeks and Romans had the same custom of presenting guests with flowers or garlands, which were brought in at the beginning of their entertainments, or before the second course. They not only adorned their *heads*, *necks*, and *breasts*, like the Egyptians, but often bestrewed the couches on which they lay, and all parts of the room, with flowers ; though the head was chiefly regarded, as appears from Horace, Anacreon, Ovid, and other ancient authors. The wine-bowl, too, was crowned with flowers, as at an Egyptian banquet. They also perfumed the apartment with myrrh, frankincense, and other choice odours, which they obtained from Syria ; and if the sculptures do not give any direct representation of this practice among the Egyptians, we know it to have been adopted and deemed indispensable among them ; and a striking instance is recorded by Plutarch, at the reception of Agesilaus by Tachos. A sumptuous dinner was prepared for the Spartan prince, consisting, as usual, of beef, goose, and other Egyptian dishes : he was crowned with garlands of papyrus, and received with every token of welcome ; but when he refused " the sweetmeats, confections, and perfumes," the Egyptians held him in great contempt, as a person unaccustomed to, and unworthy of, the manners of civilized society.

The Greeks, and other ancient people, usually put on a particular garment at festive meetings, generally of a white colour ; but it does not appear to have been customary with the Egyptians to make any great alteration in their attire, though they evidently abstained from dresses of a gloomy hue.

The guests being seated, and having received these tokens of welcome, wine was offered them by the servants. To the ladies it was generally brought in a small vase, which, when emptied into the drinking-cup, was handed to an under servant, or slave, who followed ; but to the men it was frequently pre-

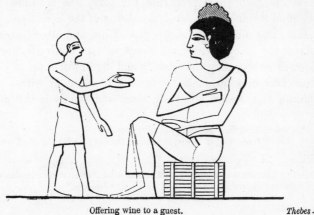

93.   Offering wine to a guest.   *Thebes.*

sented in a one-handled goblet, without being poured into any cup, and sometimes in a large or small vase of gold, silver, or other materials.

Herodotus and Hellanicus both say that they drank wine out of brass or bronze goblets; and, indeed, the former affirms that this was the only kind of drinking-cup known to the Egyptians; but Joseph* had one of silver, and the sculptures represent them of glass, and porcelain, as well as of gold, silver, and bronze. Those who could not afford the more costly kind were satisfied with a cheaper quality, and many were contented with cups of common earthenware; but the wealthy Egyptians used vases of glass, porcelain, and the precious metals, for numerous purposes, both in their houses and in the temples of the gods.

The practice of introducing wine at the commencement† of an entertainment, or before dinner had been served up, was not peculiar to this people; and the Chinese, to the present day, offer it at their parties to all the guests, as they arrive, in the same manner as the ancient Egyptians. They also drank wine during the repast,‡ perhaps to the health of one another, or of an absent friend, like the Romans; and no doubt the master of the house, or "the ruler of the feast," § recommended a choice wine, and pledged them to the cup.

While dinner was preparing, the party was enlivened by the sound of music; and a band, consisting of the harp, lyre, *guitar*, tambourine, double and single pipe, flute, and other instruments, played the favourite airs and songs of the country. Nor was it deemed unbecoming the gravity and dignity of a priest to admit musicians into his house, or to take pleasure in witnessing the dance; and, seated with their wives and family in the midst of

---

* Gen. xliv. 2, 5, "My cup, the silver cup."

† "That drink wine in bowls, and anoint themselves with the chief ointments." Amos, vi. 6.

‡ Gen. xliii. 34. "They drank wine and were merry with him." The Hebrew is יִשְׁכְּרוּ, which is to be merry from strong drink. Sikr, שֵׁכָר, implies the same in Hebrew and Arabic. *Sakrán*, in Arabic is "drunken."

§ Rex convivii, arbiter bibendi, or συμποσιαρχος, chosen by lot. John ii. 9; Hor. Od. lib. i. 4.

their friends, the highest functionaries of the sacerdotal order enjoyed the lively scene. In the same manner, at a Greek entertainment, diversions of all kinds were introduced ; and Xenophon and Plato inform us that Socrates, the wisest of men, amused his friends with music, jugglers, mimics, buffoons, and whatever could be desired for exciting cheerfulness and mirth.

Though impossible for us now to form any notion of the character or style of Egyptian music, we may be allowed to conjecture that it was studied on scientific principles ; and, whatever defects existed in the skill of ordinary performers, who gained their livelihood by playing in public, or for the entertainment of a private party, music was looked upon as an important science, and diligently studied by the priests themselves. According to Diodorus it was not customary to make music part of their education, being deemed useless and even injurious, as tending to render the minds of men effeminate ; but this remark can only apply to the custom of studying it as an amusement. Plato, who was well acquainted with the usages of the Egyptians, says that they considered music of the greatest consequence, from its beneficial effects upon the mind of youth ; and according to Strabo, the children of the Egyptians were taught letters, the songs appointed by law, and a certain kind of music, established by government.

That the Egyptians were particularly fond of music, is abundantly proved by the paintings in their tombs of the earliest times ; and we even find they introduced figures performing on the favourite instruments of the country, among the devices with which they adorned fancy boxes or trinkets. The skill of the Egyptians, in the use of musical instruments, is also noticed by Athenæus, who says that both the Greeks and barbarians were taught by refugees from Egypt, and that the Alexandrians were the most scientific and skilful players on pipes and other instruments.

In the infancy of music, as Dr. Burney observes, "no other instruments were known than those of percussion, and it was, therefore, little more than metrical." Pipes of various kinds and the flute were afterwards invented ; at first very rude, and made of reeds, which grew in the rivers and lakes, and some of these have been found in the Egyptian tombs.   To discover, we can scarcely say to invent, such simple instruments, required a very slight effort.   But it was long before music and musical instruments attained to any degree of excellence ; and the simple instruments of early times being in time succeeded by others of a more complicated kind, the many-stringed harp, lyre, and other instruments, added to the power and variety of musical sounds.

To contrive a method of obtaining perfect melody from a smaller number of strings, by shortening them on a neck during the performance, like our modern violin, was, unquestionably, a more difficult task than could be accomplished in the infancy of music, and great advances must have been already made in the science before this could be attained, or before the idea would suggest itself to the mind.   With this principle, however, the Egyptians were well acquainted ; and the sculptures unquestionably prove it, in the frequent use of the three-stringed guitar.

A harp or lyre, having a number of strings, imitating various sounds, and disposed in the order of notes, might be invented even in an early stage of the art ; but a people who had not attentively studied the nature of musical sounds would necessarily remain ignorant of the method of procuring the same tones from a limited number of strings ; nor are our means simplified till they become perfectly understood.   It is, then, evident, not only from the great fondness for music evinced by the early Egyptians, but from the nature of the very instruments they used, that the art was studied with great attention, and that they extended the same minute and serious investigation to this as to other sciences.

The fabulous account of its origin, mentioned by Diodorus, shows music to have been sanctioned, and even cultivated, by the priests themselves, who invariably pretended to have derived from the gods the knowledge of the sciences they encouraged. Hermes or Mercury was, therefore, reputed to be the first discoverer of the harmony and principle of voices or sounds, and the inventor of the lyre.

Harps, pipe, and flute, from an ancient tomb near the Pyramids.

94.

From his limiting the number of its chords to three, the historian evidently confounds the lyre with the Egyptian guitar ; yet this traditional story serves to attest the remote antiquity of stringed instruments, and proves the great respect paid to music by the Egyptian priests, who thought it not unworthy of a deity to be its patron and inventor.

It is sufficiently evident, from the sculptures of the ancient Egyptians, that their hired musicians were acquainted with the triple symphony : the harmony of instruments ; of voices ; and of voices and instruments. Their band was variously com-

95. • The harp and double pipe. *Thebes.*

posed, consisting either of two harps, with the single pipe and flute ; of the harp and double pipe, frequently with the addition of the guitar ; of a fourteen-stringed harp, a guitar, lyre, double pipe, and tambourine ; of two harps, sometimes of different sizes, one of seven, the other of four, strings ; of two harps of eight chords, and a seven-stringed lyre ; of the guitar and the square or oblong tambourine ; of the lyre, harp, guitar, double pipe, and a sort of harp with four strings, which was held upon the shoulder ; of the harp, guitar, double pipe, lyre, and square

96.   The harp, guitar, and double pipe.   *Thebes.*

97.   Harp and a smaller one of four chords.   *Thebes.*

tambourine ;* of the harp, two guitars, and the double pipe ;† of
the harp, two flutes, and a guitar ;‡ of two harps and a flute ; of a
seventeen-stringed lyre, the double-pipe, and a harp of fourteen
chords ; of the harp, and two guitars ; or of two seven-stringed

---

* Woodcut 98.   † Woodcut 101.
                    ‡ *See* Sacred Music.

Harp, guitar, double pipe, lyre, and square tambourine.

98.

Thebes.

99.   Men and women singing to the harp, lyre, and double pipe.   *Thebes.*

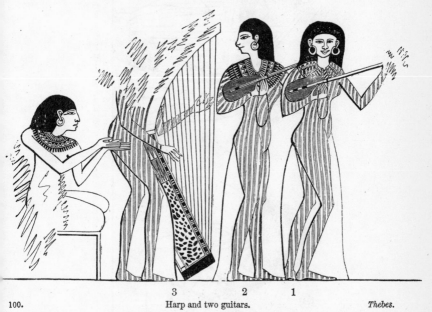

100.   Harp and two guitars.   *Thebes.*

harps and an instrument held in the hand, not unlike an eastern fan,* to which were probably attached small bells, or pieces of metal that emitted a jingling sound when shaken, like the crescent crowned *bells* of our modern bands.   There were many other combinations of these various instruments; and in the Bac-

* Woodcut 103, fig. 3.

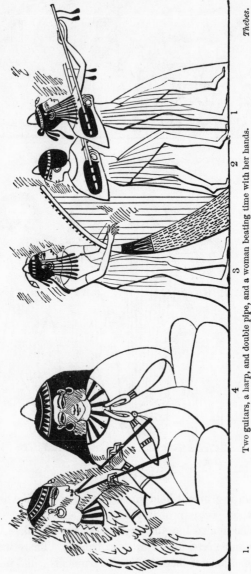

Two guitars, a harp, and double pipe, and a woman beating time with her hands.

Thebes.

1.

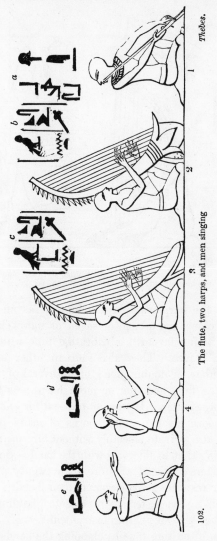

The flute, two harps, and men singing

102.

chic festival of Ptolemy Philadelphus, described by Athenæus, more than 600 musicians were employed in the chorus, among whom were 300 performers on the *cithara*.

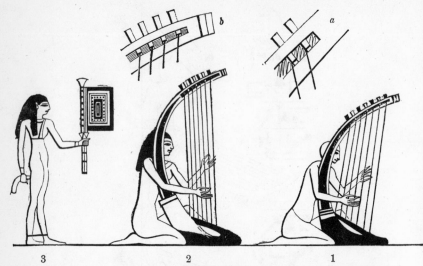

103. Two harps, and another instrument, which perhaps emitted a jingling sound. *a* and *b* show
how the strings were wound round the pegs.   *Beni Hassan.*

Sometimes the harp was played alone, or as an accompaniment to the voice ; and a band of seven or more choristers frequently sang to it a favourite air, beating time with their hands
between each stanza.   They also sang to other instruments,*
as the lyre, guitar, or double pipe ; or to several of them played
together, as the flute and one or more harps ; or to these last
with a lyre, or a guitar.   It was not unusual for one man or one
woman to perform a solo ; and a chorus of many persons occasionally sang at a private assembly without any instrument, two
or three beating time at intervals with the hand.   Sometimes the
band of choristers consisted of more than twenty persons, only
two of whom responded by clapping their hands ; and in one
instance I have seen a female represented holding what was
perhaps another kind of jingling instrument.†
The custom of beating time by clapping the hands between the
stanzas is still usual in Egypt.

* Woodcuts 99, 100, 101, and 102.   † Woodcut 104.

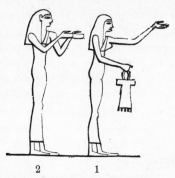

An unusual kind of instrument.   *Thebes.*

On some occasions women beat the tambourine and *darabooka* drum, without the addition of any other instrument ; dancing or singing to the sound ; and bearing palm branches or green twigs in their hands, they proceeded to the tomb of a deceased friend, accompanied by this species of music.   The same custom may still be traced in the Friday visit to the cemetery, and in some other funeral ceremonies among the Moslem peasants of modern Egypt.

If it was not customary for the higher classes of Egyptians to

7   6   5   4   3   2   1

105.   Women beating tambourines, and the *darabooka* drum (fig. 1).   *Thebes.*

learn music for the purpose of playing in society, and if few
amateur performers could be found among persons of rank, still
some general knowledge of the art must have been acquired by
a people so alive to its charms ; and the attention paid to it by
the priests regulated the taste, and prevented the introduction
of a vitiated style.   Those who played at the houses of the rich,
as well as the ambulant musicians of the streets, were of the
lower classes, and made this employment the means of obtaining
their livelihood ; and in many instances both the minstrels and
the choristers were blind.*

It was not so necessary an accomplishment for the higher
classes of Egyptians as of the Greeks, who, as Cicero says, " considered the arts of singing and playing upon musical instruments
a very principal part of learning ; whence it is related of Epaminondas, who, in my judgment, was the first of all the Greeks,
that he played very well upon the flute.   And, some time before,
Themistocles, upon refusing the harp at an entertainment, passed
for an uninstructed and ill-bred person.   Hence Greece became
celebrated for skilful musicians ; and as all persons there learned
music, those who attained to no proficiency in it were thought
uneducated and unaccomplished."   Cornelius Nepos also states
that Epaminondas "played the harp and flute, and perfectly
understood the art of dancing, with other liberal sciences," which,
" though trivial things in the opinion of the Romans, were
reckoned highly commendable in Greece."

The Israelites also delighted in music and the dance ; and
persons of rank deemed them a necessary part of their education.
Like the Egyptians with whom they had so long resided, the Jews
carefully distinguished sacred from profane music.   They introduced it at public and private rejoicings, at funerals, and in
religious services ; but the character of the airs, like the words
of their songs, varied according to the occasion ; and they had
canticles of mirth, of praise, of thanksgiving, and of lamentation.
Some were *epithalamia*, or songs composed to celebrate mar-

* As in woodcut 106.

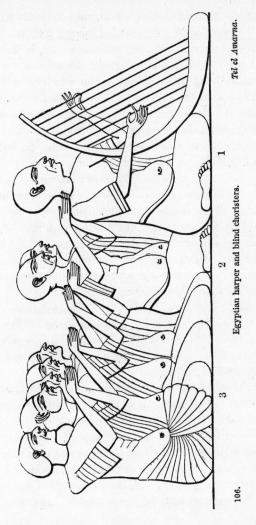

Egyptian harper and blind choristers.

Tel el Amarna.

1　2　3

106.

riages; others to commemorate a victory, or the accession of a prince; to return thanks to the Deity, or to celebrate his praises; to lament a general calamity, or a private affliction; and others, again, were peculiar to their festive meetings. On these occa-

sions they introduced the harp, lute, tabret,* and various instruments, together with songs and dancing, and the guests were
entertained nearly in the same manner as at an Egyptian feast.
In the temple, and in the religious ceremonies, the Jews had
female as well as male performers, who were generally daughters
of the Levites, as the Pallaces of Thebes were either of the royal
family, or the daughters of priests; and these musicians were
attached exclusively to the service of religion. David was not
only remarkable for his taste and skill in music, but took a delight in introducing it on every occasion. "And seeing that the
Levites were numerous, and no longer employed as formerly in
carrying the boards, veils, and vessels of the tabernacle, its abode
being fixed at Jerusalem, he appointed a great part of them to
sing and play on instruments, at the religious festivals." Solomon,
again, at the dedication of the temple, employed "120 priests,
to sound with trumpets;" and Josephus pretends that no less
than 200,000 musicians were present at that ceremony, besides
the same number of singers, who were Levites.

The method adopted by the Egyptian priests, for preserving
their melodies, has not been ascertained; but if their system of
notation resembled that of the Greeks, which was by disposing
the letters of the alphabet in different ways, it must have been
cumbrous and imperfect.

When hired to attend at a private entertainment, the musicians
either stood in the centre, or at one side, of the festive chamber,
and some sat cross-legged on the ground, like the Turks and
other Eastern people of the present day. They were usually
accompanied on these occasions by dancers, either men or women,
sometimes both; whose art consisted in assuming all the graceful or ludicrous gestures, which could obtain the applause, or
tend to the amusement, of the assembled guests. For music

---

* Comp. Luke, xv. 25, "He heard music and dancing;" and Gen. xxxi. 27,
where Laban complains that Jacob did not allow him to celebrate his departure
with a festive meeting, "with mirth and with songs, with tabret and with harp."
This last, however, in the Hebrew, is kinoor, כנור, which is rather a lyre. It
was known in the days of Seth, Gen. iv. 21, and of Job, xxi. 12.

and dancing were considered as essential at their entertainments, as among the Greeks; but it is by no means certain that these diversions counteracted the effect of wine, as Plutarch imagines; a sprightly air is more likely to have invited another glass; and sobriety at a feast was not one of the objects of the lively Egyptians.

Some of their songs, it is true, bore a plaintive character, but not so the generality of those introduced at their festive meetings. That called Maneros is said by Herodotus to be the same as the Linus of the Greeks, "which was known in Phœnicia, Cyprus, and other places;" and was peculiarly adapted to mournful occasions. Plutarch, however, asserts that it was suited to festivities and the pleasures of the table, and that, "amidst the diversions of a sociable party, the Egyptians made the room resound with the song of Maneros." We may, therefore, conclude that the Egyptians had two songs, bearing a name resembling Maneros, which have been confounded together by Greek writers; and that one of these bore a lugubrious, the other a lively, character.

The airs and words were of course made to suit the occasion, either of rejoicing and festivity, of solemnity, or of lamentation; and all their agricultural and other occupations had, as at the present day, their appropriate songs.

At the religious ceremonies and processions, certain musicians attached to the priestly order, and organised for this special purpose, were employed; who were considered to belong exclusively to the service of the temple, as each military band of their army to its respective corps.

When an individual died, it was usual for the women to issue forth from the house, and throwing dust and mud upon their heads, to utter cries of lamentation as they wandered through the streets of the town, or amidst the cottages of the village. They sang a doleful dirge in token of their grief; they, by turns, expressed their regret for the loss of their relative or friend, and their praises of his virtues; and this was frequently done to the time and measure of a plaintive, though not inharmonious, air.

Sometimes the tambourine was introduced, and the "mournful song" was accompanied by its monotonous sound.   On these occasions, the services of hired performers were uncalled for ; though during the period of seventy days, while the body was in the hands of the embalmers, mourners* were employed, who sang the same plaintive dirge to the memory of the deceased ; a custom prevalent also among the Jews, when preparing for a funeral.†

At their musical *soirées*, men or women played the harp, lyre, *guitar*, and the single or double pipe, but the flute appears to have been confined to men ; and the tambourine and *darabooka* drum were generally appropriated to the other sex.

The *darabooka* drum is rarely met with in the paintings of Thebes, being only used on certain occasions, and chiefly, as at the present day, by the peasant women, and the boatmen of the Nile.   It was evidently the same as the modern one, which is made of parchment, strained and glued over a funnel-shaped case

107.   The darabooka of modern Egypt.

of pottery, which is a hollow cylinder, with a truncated cone attached to it.   It is beaten with the hand, and when relaxed, the parchment is braced by exposing it a few moments to the sun, or the warmth of a fire.   It is generally supported by a band

* Exod. l. 3 ; Herod. ii. 86.   † Matt. ix. 23 ; Jer. xvi. 5, 7.

round the neck of the performer, who, with the fingers of the right hand, plays the air, and with the left grasps the lower edge of the head, in order to beat the bass, as in the tambourine; which we find from the sculptures was played in the same manner by the ancient Egyptians.

They had also cymbals, and cylindrical maces (*crotala*, or clappers), two of which were struck together, and probably emitted a sharp metallic sound. The cymbals were of mixed metal, apparently brass, or a compound of brass and silver, and of a form exactly resembling those of modern times, though smaller, being only seven, or five inches and a half in diameter. The handle was also of brass, bound with leather, string, or any similar substance, and being inserted in a small hole at the sum-

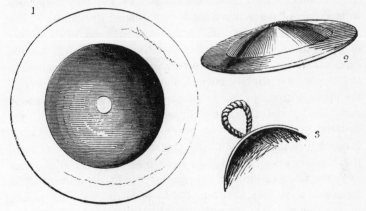

108.　　　Egyptian cymbals, 5¼ inches in diameter.　*British Museum.*

mit, was secured by bending back the two ends. The same kind of instrument is used by the modern inhabitants of the country; and from them have been borrowed the very small cymbals played with the finger and thumb, which supply the place of castanets in the *almeh* dance. These were the origin of the Spanish castanet, having been introduced into that country by the Moors, and afterwards altered in form, and made of chestnut (castaña) and other wood instead of metal.

H 2

The cymbals of modern Egypt are chiefly used by the attendants of shekhs' tombs, who travel through the country at certain periods of the year, to exact charitable donations from the credulous, or the devout, among the Moslems, by the promise of some blessing from the indulgent saint. Drums and some other noisy instruments, which are used at marriages and on other occasions, accompany the cymbals, but these last are more peculiarly appropriated to the service of the shekhs, and the external ceremonies of religion, as among the ancient Egyptians; and a female, whose coffin contained a pair of cymbals, was described in the hieroglyphics of the exterior as the minstrel of a deity.

The cylindrical maces, or clappers, were also admitted among the instruments used on solemn occasions; and they frequently formed part of the military band, or regulated the dance. They varied slightly in form; and some were of wood, or of shells; others of brass, or some sonorous metal, having a straight handle, surmounted by a head, or other ornamental device. Sometimes the handle was slightly curved, and double, with two heads at the upper extremity; but in all cases the performer held one in each hand; and the sound depended on their size, and the material of which they were made. When of wood they corresponded to the *crotala* of the Greeks, a supposed invention of the Sicilians; and reported to have been used for frightening away the fabulous birds of Stymphalus; and the paintings of the Etruscans show they were adopted by them, as by the Egyptians, in the dance. They were probably the same as the round-headed pegs, resembling large nails, seen in the hands of some dancing figures in the paintings of Herculaneum; and Herodotus describes the crotala played as an accompaniment to the flute by the votaries of the Egyptian Diana, on their way to her temple at Bubastis.

Though the Egyptians were fond of buffoonery and gesticulation, they do not seem to have had any public show which can be said to resemble a theatre. The stage is allowed to have been purely a Greek invention; and to dramatic entertainments,

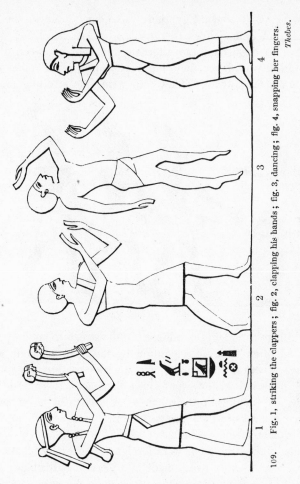

109.   Fig. 1, striking the clappers; fig. 2, clapping his hands; fig. 3, dancing; fig. 4, snapping her fingers.

Thebes.

which were originally of two kinds, comedy and tragedy, were
added the ancient Italian pantomime. The Egyptian common
people had certain jocose songs, accompanied with mimic and extravagant gestures, containing appropriate and laughable remarks
on the bystanders; extempore sallies of wit, like the Fescennine
verses of ancient Italy, which were also peculiar to the country
people. Their object was to provoke a retort from him they
addressed, or to supply one if unanswered; a custom still con-

tinued by the modern Egyptians; who have adopted the high
foolscaps of palm leaves, frequently with tassels, or foxes' tails
attached to them, and the alternate verse, or couplets, of two
performers, who dance and sing in recitative to the monotonous
sound of a hand-drum. They also went, like strolling players,

110.   Egyptian Buffoons.   *Thebes.*

from village to village, and danced in the streets to amuse passers
by; and often took up a position by the steps of some grand
mansion, where if they could only spy some children or nursery
maids at a window, they performed their parts with redoubled
energy, and holding up their hands towards them made complimentary remarks in their songs, with the same keen longing for
bakshish as their descendants.

Some of these buffoons were foreigners, generally blacks from
Africa, whose scanty dress, made of a piece of bull's hide, added
not a little to their grotesque appearance; purposely increased
by a small addition resembling a tail. (*Woodcut* 111.) They
also had tags, like beads, suspended from their elbows; which
were often put on by Egyptian performers on festive occasions; as they are still by the people of Ethiopia and Kordofan
in their dances; and they are shown by the vases to have been
adopted by the Greeks in bacchanalian and other ceremonies.
The tail was also given to Greek fauns.

111.

Men dancing in the street to the sound of the drum.

Thebes.

In their military bands some of the instruments differed from those of ordinary musicians, but the sculptures have not recorded all the various kinds used in the Egyptian army. The principal ones appear to have been the trumpet and drum: the former used to marshal the troops, summon them to the charge, and direct them in their evolutions; the latter to regulate and enliven their march.

The trumpet, like that of the Israelites, was about one foot and a half long, of very simple form, apparently of brass; and when sounded, it was held with both hands, and either used singly, or as part of the military band, with the drum and other instruments.

112.   1   2   A military band.   3   4   5   *Thebes.*

The trumpet was particularly, though not exclusively, appropriated to martial purposes. It was straight, like the Roman tuba, or our common trumpet, and was used in Egypt at the earliest times. In Greece it was also known before the Trojan war; it was reputed to have been the invention of Minerva, or of Tyrrhenus, a son of Hercules; and in later times it was generally adopted, both as a martial instrument, and by the ambulant musicians of the streets. In some parts of Egypt a prejudice existed against the trumpet; and the people of Busiris and Lycopolis would never use it, because the sound resembled the braying of an ass, which, being the emblem of Typhon, gave them very unpleasant sensations, by reminding them of the Evil Being.   The same kind of notion prevents the Moslems using bells, which, if they do not actually bring bad spirits into the house, keep away good ones ; and many seem to think that dogs are also in league with the powers of darkness.

113.   The trumpet.   *Thebes.*

The Israelites had trumpets for warlike, as well as sacred purposes, for festivals and rejoicings ; and the office of sounding them was not only honourable, but was committed solely to the priests.   Some were of silver, which were suited to all occasions ; others were animals' horns (like the original *cornu* of the Romans), and these are stated to have been employed at the siege of Jericho.   The Greeks had six kinds of trumpets ; the Romans four,—the tuba, cornu, buccina, and lituus, and, in ancient times, the *concha*, so called from having been originally a shell—which were the only instruments employed by them for military purposes, and in this they differed from the Greeks and Egyptians.

The only drum represented in the sculptures is a long drum, very similar to one of the *tomtoms* of India.   It was about two feet or two feet and a half in length, and was beaten with the hand, like the Roman tympanum.   The case was of wood or copper, covered at either end with parchment or leather, braced by cords extending diagonally over the exterior of the cylinder, and when played, it was slung by a band round the neck of the drummer, who during the march

114.   The drum.   *Thebes.*

carried it in a vertical position at his back. Like the trumpet,
it was chiefly employed in the army;
and the evidence of the sculptures
is confirmed by Clement of Alexandria, who says the drum was
used by the Egyptians in going to
war.* It was also common at the
earliest period of which we have
any account from the sculptures of
Thebes, or about the sixteenth century before our era.

When a body of troops marched
to the beat of drum, the drummer
was often stationed in the centre or
the rear, and sometimes immediately

115. Mode of slinging the drum behind
them, when on a march.

behind the standard bearers; the trumpeter's post being generally at the head of the regiment, except when summoning them
to form or advance to the charge; but the drummers were not
always alone, or confined to the rear and centre; and when
forming part of the band, they marched in the van, or, with the
other musicians, were drawn up on one side while the troops
defiled.

Besides the long drum, the Egyptians had another, not very
unlike our own, both in form and size, which was much broader
in proportion to its length than the *tomtom* just mentioned, being
two feet and a half high, and two feet broad. It was beaten with
two wooden sticks; but as there is no representation of the mode
of using it, we are unable to decide whether it was suspended
horizontally and struck at both ends, as the drum of the same
kind still used at Cairo, or at one end only, like our own;
though, from the curve of the sticks, I am inclined to think it
was slung and beaten as the *tamboor* of modern Egypt. Sometimes the sticks were straight, and consisted of two parts, the
handle and a thin round rod, at whose end a small knob pro-

* Clemens Alex. Stromat. ii. 164.

jected, for the purpose of fastening the leather pad with which
the drum was struck; they were about a foot in length, and,

116.   Drum-stick.   *Berlin Museum.*

judging from the form of the handle of one in the Berlin Museum, we may conclude they belonged, like those above mentioned, to a drum beaten at both ends. Each extremity of the
drum was covered with red leather, braced with catgut strings
passing through small holes in its broad margin, and extending
in direct lines over the copper body, which, from its convexity,
was similar in shape to a cask.

In order to tighten the strings, and thereby to brace the drum,
a piece of catgut extended round each end, near the edge of the
leather; and crossing the strings at right angles, and being
twisted round each separately, braced them all in proportion as
it was drawn tight: but this was only done when the leather and
the strings had become relaxed by constant use; and as this
piece of catgut was applied to either end, they had the means of
doubling the power of tension on every string.

3   1   2
117.   Fig. 1. The drum.   2. shows how the strings were braced.   3. The sticks.
                                                   Found at Thebes.

Besides the ordinary forms of Egyptian instruments, several
were constructed according to a particular taste or accidental
caprice. Some were of the most simple kind, others of very

118.   Harpers painted in the tomb of Remeses III.,

costly materials, and many were richly ornamented with brilliant colours and fancy figures ; particularly the harps and lyres.
The harps varied greatly in form, size, and the number of their

known as Bruce's, or the Harper's tomb.   *Thebes.*

strings ; they are represented in the ancient paintings with four,
six, seven, eight, nine, ten, eleven, twelve, fourteen, seventeen,
twenty, twenty-one, and twenty-two chords : that in the Paris

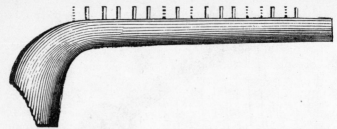

119.   Head of a harp brought by me from Thebes, and now in the British Museum.

collection appears also to have had twenty-one; and the head of
another I found at Thebes was made for seventeen strings. They
were frequently very large, even exceeding the height of a man,
tastefully painted with the lotus and other flowers, or with fancy
devices; and those of the royal minstrels were fitted up in the
most splendid manner, adorned with the head or bust of the
monarch himself: like those in Bruce's tomb at Thebes.

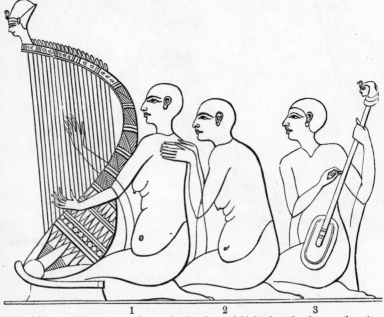

1   2   3
120. A richly painted harp on a stand, a man beating time with his hands, and a player on the guitar.

The oldest harps found in the sculptures are in a tomb, near the pyramids of Geezeh, upwards of four thousand years old. They are more rude in shape than those usually represented ; and though it is impossible to ascertain the precise number of their chords,* they do not appear to have exceeded seven or eight, and are fastened in a different manner from ordinary Egyptian harps. These date long before the Shepherd invasion, and the fact of the Egyptians being already sufficiently advanced to combine the harmony of various instruments with the voice shows they were not indebted for music to that Asiatic race.   The combination of harps and lyres of great compass with the flute, single and double pipes, guitars, and tambourines, prove the proficiency to which they had arrived ; and even in the reign of Amosis, the first king of the 18th dynasty, about 1570 B.C., nine hundred years before Terpander's time, the ordinary musicians of Egypt used harps of fourteen, and lyres of seventeen strings.

The Greeks were indebted to Asia for their stringed instruments, and even for the cithara ($\kappa\iota\theta\acute{a}\rho a$), which was originally styled " Asiatic," and was introduced from Lesbos.   It had only seven chords, till Timotheus of Miletus added four others, about 400 B.C.; and Terpander, who lived 200 years after Homer, was the first to lay down any laws for this instrument, some time before they were devised for the flute or pipe. The harp, indeed, seems always to have been unknown to the Greeks.

The strings of Egyptian harps were of catgut, as of the lyres still used in Nubia.   Some harps stood on the ground while played, having an even, broad, base ; others were placed on a stool, or raised upon a stand, or limb, attached to the lower part.† Men and women often used harps of the same compass, and even the smallest, of four strings, were played by men ; ‡ but the largest were mostly appropriated to the latter, who stood during the performance.   These large harps had a flat base, so as to stand without support, like those in Bruce's tomb ; § and a lighter kind was also squared for the same purpose, || but, when played, was frequently inclined towards the performer, who supported

* Woodcut 94.   † Woodcuts 96, 97, 121, 122.   ‡ Woodcuts 96, 97, 103.
§ Woodcuts 118, 118 a, and 99. || Woodcut 101.

121.   Minstrel standing, while playing the harp.   *Dendera.*

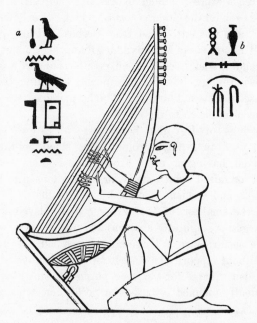

122.   Harp raised on a stand, or support.   *Thebes.*

the instrument in the most convenient position.* Many harps were of wood, covered with bull's hide,† or with leather, sometimes of a green or red colour, and painted with various devices, vestiges of which may be traced in that of the Paris collection; ‡ and small ones were sometimes made, like many Greek lyres, of tortoise shell. (*Woodcuts* 96, 97.)

The Egyptians had no means of shortening the harp strings during the performance, by any contrivance resembling our modern pedals, so as to introduce occasional sharps and flats; they could, therefore, only play in one key, until they tuned the instrument afresh, by turning the pegs. Indeed it was not more necessary in their harp than in the lyre, since the former was always combined with other instruments, except when used as a mere accompaniment to the voice. But they seem occasionally to have supplied this deficiency by a double set of pegs; and their great skill in music during so many centuries would necessarily suggest some means of obtaining half notes.

The Egyptian harps have another imperfection, for which it is not easy to account,—the absence of a pole, and consequently of a support to the bar, or upper limb, in which the pegs were fixed; and it is difficult to conceive how, without it, the chords could have been properly tightened, or the bar sufficiently strong to resist the effect of their tension; particularly in those of triangular form. The pole is not only wanting in those of the paintings, but in all that have been found in the tombs; and even in that of the Paris Collection, which, having twenty-one strings, was one of the highest power they had, since they are seldom represented on the monuments with more than two octaves. This last, however, may hold an intermediate place between a harp and the many triangular stringed instruments of the Egyptians.

The harp was thought to be especially suited for the service of religion; and it was used on many occasions to celebrate the praises of the gods. It was even represented in the hands of the deities themselves, as well as the tambourine and the sacred sistrum.

* Woodcuts 95, 98, 100.   † Woodcuts 97, fig. 2, 98, 100, 101.
‡ Woodcut 123.

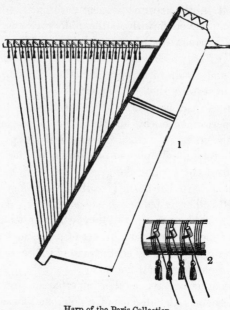

Harp of the Paris Collection.

The Egyptian lyre was not less varied in form, and the number
of its chords, than the harp, and they ornamented it in many
ways, as their taste suggested ; some with the head of an animal
carved in wood, as the horse, ibex, or gazelle ; while others were
of more simple shape.

Mercury has always obtained the credit of its invention, both
among the Egyptians and the Greeks ; and Apollodorus gravely
explains how it came into his head : " The Nile," he says, " after
having overflowed the whole land of Egypt, returned once more
within its banks, leaving on the shore a great number of dead
animals of various kinds, and among the rest a tortoise. Its flesh
was quite dried up by the hot Egyptian sun, so that nothing
remained within the shell but nerves and cartilages ; and these,
being braced and contracted by the heat, had become sonorous.
Mercury, walking by the river side, happened to strike his foot
against this shell, and was so pleased with the sound produced,

that the idea of a lyre presented itself to his imagination. He therefore constructed the instrument in the form of a tortoise, and strung it with the sinews of dead animals."

124.   Lyre ornamented with the head of an animal.   *Thebes .*

Many Egyptian lyres were of considerable power, having 5, 7, 10, and 18 strings. They were usually supported between the elbow and the side ; and the mode of playing them was with the hand, or sometimes with the plectrum, which was made of bone, ivory, or wood, and was often attached to one limb of the lyre by a string.

The Greeks also adopted both methods, but more generally used the plectrum ; and in the frescoes of Herculaneum are lyres of 3, 6, 9, and 11 strings played with it ; of 4, 5, 6, 7, and 10 with the hands ; and of 9 and 11 strings played with the plectrum and fingers at the same time.

The strings were fastened at the upper end to a cross bar connecting the two limbs or sides, and at the lower end they were attached to a raised ledge or hollow sounding board, about the

125.   Lyres played with and without the plectrum.   *Thebes.*

centre of the body of the instrument, which was entirely of wood.
In the Berlin and Leyden museums are lyres of this kind, which,
with the exception of the strings, are perfectly preserved.   That

126.   Lyre in the Berlin Museum.

in the former collection has the two limbs terminating in horses' heads ; and in form and principle, and in the alternate long and short chords, resembles some of those represented in the paintings ;* though the board to which the strings are fastened is nearer the bottom of the instrument, and the number of chords is 13 instead of 10.

We have thus an opportunity of comparing real Egyptian lyres with those represented at Thebes in the reign of Amunoph, and other kings, who reigned more than three thousand years ago.

The body of the Berlin lyre is about ten inches high, and fourteen and a half broad, and the total height of the instrument is two feet. That of Leyden is smaller, and less ornamented ; but it is equally well preserved, and highly interesting from a hieratic inscription written in ink upon the front. It had no extra sounding board ; its hollow body sufficiently answered this purpose ; and the strings passed over a moveable bridge, and were secured at the bottom by a small metal ring or staple. Both these lyres were entirely of wood ; and one of the limbs, like many represented in the paintings, was longer than the opposite one, so that the instrument might be tuned by sliding the strings upwards along the bar, as well as round it, which was the usual method, and is continued to the present day in the *Kisírka* of modern Nubia.

127.   Lyre of the Leyden Collection.
Fig. 2 shows the lower end.

In Greece the lyre had at first only four chords, till the addi-

---

* Woodcuts 98, 125.

tional three were introduced by Amphion, who seems to have
borrowed his knowledge of music from Lydia ; and was, as
usual, reputed to have been taught by Mercury.   Terpander
(670 B.C.) added several more notes ; and the lyres represented
at Herculaneum have 3, 4, 5, 6, 7, 8, 9, 10, and 11 chords.

Numerous other instruments, resembling harps or lyres in
principle, were common in Egypt, which varied so much in
form, compass, and sound, that they were considered quite distinct from them, and had each its own name.   They have been
found in the tombs, or are represented in the paintings of Thebes
and other places.   Those of a triangular shape were held under
the arm while played, and, like the rest, were used as an accom-

128. Triangular instrument. *Thebes.*   129. Another, held under the arm. *Dakkeh.*

paniment to the voice ; they were mostly light, but when of any
weight were suspended by a band over the shoulder of the performer.

The strings were of catgut, as in the harps ; and those of *woodcut*
130, *fig.* 1, were so well preserved that, when found at Thebes,
in 1823, they sounded on being touched, though buried two or three
thousand years.   It was an instrument of great compass, having
twenty strings wound round a rod at the lower end, which was

probably turned in order to tighten them ; and the frame was of
wood, covered with leather, on which could be traced a few

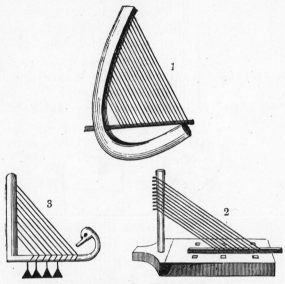

130.   *Fig.* 1 found at Thebes in 1823.

hieroglyphics.   That in fig. 2, given by Professor Rosellini, has
the peculiarity of being tuned by pegs ; but its ten strings are
fastened to a rod in the centre of its sounding-board, as in other
instruments.

Another, which may be called a standing-lyre, was of great
height. It consisted of a round body, probably of wood and
metal, in the form of a vase, from which two upright limbs rose,
supporting the transverse bar to which the upper ends of its
eight strings were fastened ; and the minstrel sang to it, as he
touched the chords with his two hands.

A still more jingling instrument was used as an accompaniment to the lyre.   It consisted of several bars, probably of wire,
attached to a frame, or some sounding body ; which were struck
by a rod held in both hands by the performer.   (*Woodcut* 132.)

More common was a light instrument of four strings, which

131.   A standing lyre.   *Tel el Amarna.*

132.   An instrument played as an accompaniment to the lyre.   *Tel el Amarna.*

was carried on the shoulder while played, and was mostly used
by women, who chanted to it as the Jews did " to the sound

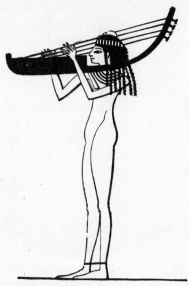

133.   A light kind of instrument borne on the shoulder.   *Thebes.*

of the (*nabl*) viol" (Amos, vi. 5).   Some of these have been
found in the tombs of Thebes, and the most perfect one is that
in the British Museum, which is 41 inches long, the neck 22,
and the breadth of the body 4 inches.   Its exact form, the pegs,
the rod to which the chords were fastened, and even the parchment covering its wooden body and serving as a sounding-board,

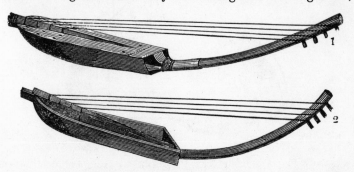

134.   Instrument differing from the harp, lyre, and guitar.   *British Museum.*

still remain, and all it wants are the four strings. The mode of fastening the strings to the rod is not quite evident, and they seem to have passed through the parchment to the rod lying beneath it, which has notches at intervals to receive them. It is of hard wood, apparently acacia; and sufficient remains of one of the strings to show they were of catgut.

Similar in principle to this was a small instrument of five chords, having a hollow wooden body, over which was stretched a covering of parchment, or of thin wood; and the strings extended in the same manner from a rod in the centre, to the pegs at the end of the neck.

135.   The instrument restored.

Three have been found in the tombs; one of which is in the Berlin, and two in the British Museum; the former with the five pegs entire, and the body composed of three pieces of sycamore

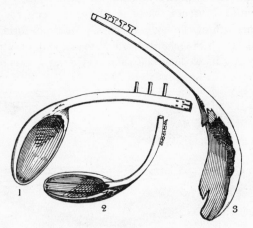

136.   Figs. 1. 3. Instruments *in the British Museum.*
               Fig. 2. *In the Berlin Museum.*

wood.   Their whole length is 2 feet, the neck about 1 foot 3 inches, in the under side of which are the five pegs, placed in a direct line, one after the other.   At the opposite end of the body are two holes for fastening the rod that secured the strings.

Besides harps and lyres, the Egyptians had a sort of guitar with three chords, which have been strangely supposed to correspond to the three seasons of the Egyptian year: and here again Thoth or Mercury has received the credit of the invention ; for the instrument having only three strings, and yet equalling the power of those of great compass, was considered by the Egyptians worthy of the God ; whose intervention on this and similar occasions is, in fact, only an allegorical mode of expressing the intellectual gifts communicated from the Divinity to man.

The guitar consisted of two parts : a long flat neck, or handle, and a hollow oval body, either wholly of wood, or covered with parchment, having the upper surface perforated with holes to allow the sound to escape.   Over this body, and the whole length of the handle, were stretched three strings of catgut, secured at the upper extremity either by the same number of pegs, or by passing through an aperture in the handle ; they were then bound round it, and tied in a knot.   It does not appear to have had any bridge, but the chords were fastened at the lower end to a triangular piece of wood or ivory, which raised them to a sufficient height ; and they were sometimes elevated at the upper extremity of the handle by means of a small crossbar, immediately below each

137.   Female playing the guitar.   *Thebes.*

of the apertures where the strings were passed through and tightened.*   This answered the same purpose as the depressed

* Woodcuts 96, 98, 101, 138, 139.

end of our modern guitar; and, indeed, since the neck was in a
straight line with the body of the instrument, some contrivance
of the kind was absolutely required.

The length of the handle was from twice, to thrice, that
of the body; and the whole instrument measured about 4
feet, the breadth of the body being equal to half its length.
It was struck with the plectrum, which was attached by a
string to the neck, and the performers usually stood as they
played. It was considered equally suited to men or women;
and some danced while they touched its strings, supporting it on
the right arm. It was sometimes slung by a band round the
neck, like the modern Spanish guitar, to which it also corresponded in being an accompaniment to the voice, though this did
not prevent its being part of a band with other instruments.*

138. Dancing while playing the guitar. *Thebes.*   139. Supported by a strap. *Thebes.*

It is from an ancient instrument of this kind, sometimes called
kithára (κιθάρα), that the modern name guitar (*chitarra*) has
been derived; though the cithara of the Greeks and Romans, in
early times, at least, was a lyre. The Egyptian guitar may be

* Woodcuts 96, 98, 100, 101.

called a lute, but it does not appear to correspond to the three-stringed lyre of Greece.

An instrument of an oval form, with a circular or cylindrical handle, was found at Thebes, not altogether unlike the guitar; but, owing to the imperfect state of its preservation, nothing could be ascertained respecting the pegs, or the mode of tightening the chords. The wooden body was faced with leather, the handle extending down it to the lower end, and part of the string remained which attached the plectrum. Three small holes indicated the place where the chords were secured, and two others, a short distance above, appear to have been intended for fastening some kind of bridge.

140.   An instrument like the guitar found at Thebes.

Wire strings were not used by the Egyptians in any of their instruments, catgut being alone employed, and the twang of this in the warlike bow doubtless led to its adoption in the peaceful lyre, owing to the accidental discovery of its musical sound; for men hunted animals, and killed each other, with the bow and arrow, long before they recited verses, or indulged in music. It is, therefore, not surprising that the Arabs, a nation of hunters, were the inventors of the *monochordium*, an instrument of the most imperfect kind (except when the skill of a Paganini is employed to command its tones); for, with all the accumulated practice of ages, the modern Cairenes have not succeeded in making their one-stringed *rahab* a tolerable accompaniment to the voice. No doubt the instrument was very ancient; for, being used by the reciters of poems, it evidently belonged to the early bards, the first musicians of every country; and the wild Montenegrins still sing their primitive war and love songs to the sound of the one-stringed *gûsla*, handed down to them from the "wizards" of the ancient Slavonians.

If we are surprised at the number of stringed instruments of the Egyptians (and many more are of course unknown to us), and if we wonder what sort of tones, and what variety of sounds, could be obtained from them, what shall we think of those mentioned by the Greeks, who seem to have adopted every one they could obtain from other countries? Some, as the phorminx, barbiton, and other lyres, are known; the first of which, according to Clemens, was not very different from the cithara; but the bare recital of the names of the rest is bewildering.

There were the *nablum, sambuca*,* pandurum, magadis, trigon (one of the three-cornered instruments) Phœnicica, pêctis, scindapsus, enneachordon ("of nine strings"), the square shaped psithyra or ascarum, heptagona (septangles) psaltery, spadix, pariambus, clepsiambus, jambyce, epigoneum, and many more; and even most Jewish instruments are uncertain, as the *kitharus* or harp, "the ten stringed" ashûr, the triangular *sambukê*, or *sabka*, the *nabl* or viol, the *kinnóor* or lyre of six or nine strings, and the *psanterin* or psaltery. And though the last is said to have had twelve notes, and to have been played with the fingers, and the *ashur*, or ten stringed viol, to have been played with the bow (or rather plectrum), we have no definite idea of their appearance; so that the Egyptian paintings give by far the best insight into the instruments used in those early times.

The flute was of great antiquity; for in a tomb near the Great Pyramid, built more than four thousand years ago, is a concert of vocal and instrumental music, where two harps, a pipe, a flute, and several voices are introduced.†

In Greece it was at first very simple, "with few holes," which were limited to four, until Diodorus of Thebes, in Bœotia, added others, and made a lateral opening for the mouth. It was originally of reed; afterwards of bone or ivory, and covered with bronze. But even this improved instrument was very small; and I have seen part of one, measuring 5½ inches in length and

---

* Described by Athenæus as a " ship with a ladder placed over it ;" by Suidas, as a triangular instrument.

† Woodcut 94.

½ an inch in diameter, broken off at the fifth hole ; the first of
the five holes being distant only 1¼ inch from that of the mouth.

The Egyptian flute was of great length ; for, reaching the
ground when the performer was seated, it
could not be less than 2 feet 3 inches ; and
some were so long that, when playing, he
was obliged to extend his arms below his
waist, to touch the holes.* Those who played
it generally sat on the ground ; and in every
instance I have met with they are men.

It was made of reed, of wood, of bone, or of
ivory ; and from the word *sêbi*, written over
the instrument in the hieroglyphics, which is
the same as its Coptic name, we may suppose it was originally the leg-bone of some
animal.　The Latin *tibia* has the same
meaning ; and flutes are said to have been made in Bœotia of those
hollow bones.　The Egyptians probably had several kinds of flutes,
some suited to mournful, others to festive, occasions, like the
Greeks ; and it is evident they used them both at banquets and
religious ceremonies.　But no Egyptian deity is represented
playing the flute ; and the gods and goddesses may have felt the
same aversion to it as Minerva, when she perceived " the deformed appearance of her mouth,"— an allegory signifying,
according to Aristotle, that it " interfered with mental reflection,"
and had most immoral effects, which in these ignorant days we
are unable to perceive.

Flute-player.　The flute is
of great length.

141.　　　　*Thebes.*

The pipe was of equal antiquity with the flute,† and belonged also to male performers ; but, as it is seldom represented
at concerts, and all those discovered are of common reed,
it appears not to have been in great repute.　In most countries
it has been the instrument of the peasantry ; but if the pipe
" made of the straw of barley " was the invention of Osiris, it does
not speak well for the musical talents of that deity.　It was a

* Woodcuts 94, 141.　　　　　† Woodcut 94

straight tube, without any increase at the mouthpiece, and when played was held with both hands. Its length did not exceed a foot and a half: two in the British Museum are 9 and 15 inches long, and those in the Collection at Leyden vary from 7 to 15 inches. Some have three, others four, holes, as is the case with fourteen of those at Leyden; and one at the British Museum had a small mouthpiece of reed or thick straw, inserted into the hollow of the pipe, the upper end so compressed as to leave a very small aperture for the admission of the breath.

(9 inches long)

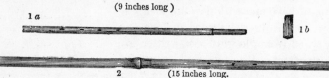

1 a   1 b

2   (15 inches long.

142.   Reed pipes, of Mr. Salt's Collection, now in the British Museum.

The double pipe was quite as common in Egypt, as in Greece. It consisted of two tubes, one played by the right, the other by the left hand, the latter giving a deep sound for the base, the right a sharp tone for the tenor. The double *zummára* of the modern Egyptians is a rude imitation of it, but its piping harshness and monotonous drone exclude it even from their imperfect bands; and it is only used by the boatmen of the Nile, and by the peasants, who seem to think it a suitable accompaniment to the tedious camel's pace. Fortunately this national instrument delights

1   2   3

143.   Woman dancing, while playing the double pipe.   *Thebes.*

its admirers out of doors, like the bagpipes of the Abbruzzi and other countries, which, at a little distance, it so much resembles.

The double, like the single pipe, was at first of reed, and afterwards of wood and other materials; and it was introduced both on solemn and festive occasions among the Egyptians, as among the Greeks. Men, but more frequently women, performed upon it, occasionally dancing as they played; and, from its repeated occurrence in the sculptures of Thebes, it was evidently preferred to the single pipe.

The tambourine was a favourite instrument in religious ceremonies and at private banquets. It was played by men and women, but more usually by the latter, who often danced and sang to its sound; and it was used as an accompaniment to other instruments.* It was of three kinds; one circular, like our own; another square or oblong; and the third consisted of two squares, separated by a bar; all of which were beaten by the hand;† but there is no appearance of balls, or moveable pieces of metal attached to the frame, as in the Greek and modern tambourine. The *taph*, "timbrel," or "tabret" of the Jews was the same instrument,‡ and was of very early use among them, as well as the harp, even before they "went down into Egypt;" and the Jewish, like the Egyptian, women, danced to its sound.

Nearly all their instruments were admitted by the Egyptians into their *sacred music*, as the harp, lyre, flute, double pipe, tambourine, cymbals, and guitar; and neither the trumpet, drum, nor clappers, were excluded from the religious processions in which the military were engaged. The harp, lyre, and tambourine performed a part in the services of the temple; and two goddesses in the frieze at Dendera are represented playing the harp and tambourine, in honour of Athor, the Egyptian Venus. The priests, bearing sacred emblems, often walked in procession to the sound of the flute; and, excepting those of Osiris at Abydus, the sacred rites of an Egyptian deity did not forbid the introduction of the harp and flute, or the voice of singers.

* Woodcuts 98, 121.   † Woodcuts 105, 151.
‡ Gen. xxi. 27; Exod. xv. 20; Job xxi. 12; Judges xi. 34; 1 Sam. xviii. 6.

The harp, indeed, was considered particularly suited to religious purposes; the title "minstrels of Amun" applied to some harpers, and the two performers before the god in the tomb of Remeses III., show the honour in which it was held; and it was played either alone, or in combination with other instruments. The minstrel often chanted as he touched its strings; and the harp, guitar, and two flutes joined in a sacred air, while the high priest offered incense to the deity. The *crotala*, or clappers, were also used with the flute during pilgrimages and processions to the shrine of a god, accompanied by choristers who chanted hymns in his honour.

144.   Sacred musicians, and a priest offering incense.   *Leyden Museum.*

The Jews, in like manner, regarded music as indispensable for religious rites; their favourite instruments were the harp, lute or psaltery, and ten-stringed *ashur*, the tabret, trumpet, cornet, cymbals, and others;* and many "singing men and

* Psalm xxxiii. 2; lxxxi. 2. 1 Chron. xvi. 5; and xxv. 1. 2 Sam. vi. 5. Exod. xv. 20, &c.

singing women" attended in the processions to the Jewish sanctuary.*

The sistrum was the sacred instrument *par excellence*, and belonged as peculiarly to the service of the temple, as the small tinkling bell to that of a Roman Catholic chapel. Some pretend it was used to frighten away Typhon, and the rattling noise of its moveable bars was sometimes increased by the addition of several loose rings. It had generally three, rarely four, bars; and the whole instrument was from 8 to 16 or 18 inches in length, entirely of brass or bronze. It was sometimes inlaid with silver, or gilt, or otherwise ornamented; and, being held upright, was shaken, the rings moving to and fro upon the bars. These last were frequently made to imitate the sacred asp, or were simply bent at each end to secure them. Plutarch mentions a cat with a human face on the top of the instrument, and at the upper part of the handle, beneath the bars, the face of Isis on one side, and of Nepthys on the other.

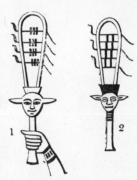

145.   146.

Fig. 1. The sistrum of four bars.
    2. Of unusual form.

Thebes.

The British Museum possesses an excellent specimen of the sistrum, well preserved, and of the best period of Egyptian art. It is 1 foot 4 inches high, and had three moveable bars, which have been unfortunately lost. On the upper part are represented the goddess Pasht, or Bubastis, the sacred vulture, and other emblems; and on the side below is the figure of a female, holding in each hand one of these instruments.

The handle is cylindrical, and surmounted by the double face of Athor, wearing an "asp-formed crown," on whose summit appears to have been the cat, now scarcely traced in the remains of its feet. It is entirely of bronze; the handle, which is hollow, and closed by a moveable cover of the same metal, is

* Psalm lxviii. 25; 2 Sam. xix. 35.

supposed to have held something appertaining to the sistrum; and the lead, still remaining within the head, is a portion of that used in soldering it.

Two others, in the same collection, are highly preserved, but of a late time, and another is of still more recent date; they have four bars, and are of very small size.

 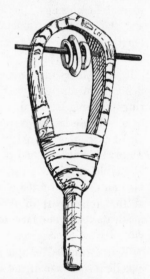

1   2
147.   Sistra in the British Museum.

Rude model of a sistrum in the
148.   Berlin Museum.

One of the Berlin sistra is 8, the other 9 inches in height: the former has four bars, and on the upper or circular part lies a cat, crowned with the disc or sun. The other has three bars: the handle is composed of a figure, supposed to be of Typhon, surmounted by the heads of Athor; and on the summit are the horns, globe, and feathers of the same goddess. They are both destitute of rings; but the rude Egyptian model of another, in the same collection, has three rings upon its single bar, agreeing in this respect, if not in the number of the bars, with those represented in the sculptures. They are not of early date.

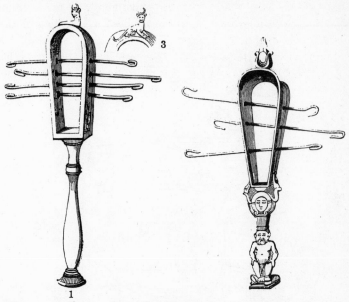

149.　　　　　Sistra in the Berlin Museum.　　　　150.

It was so great a privilege to hold the sacred sistrum in the temple, that it was given to queens, and to those noble ladies who had the distinguished title of "women of Amun," and were devoted to the service of the deity; and the Jews seem, in like manner, to have intrusted the principal sacred offices held by women to the daughters of priests, and of persons of rank.

The χνουη, an instrument said by Eustathius to have been used by the Greeks, at sacrifices, to assemble the congregation, was reputed to have been of Egyptian origin; but it has not been met with in the sculptures. It was a species of trumpet, of a round shape, and was said to have been the invention of Osiris.

The dance consisted mostly of a succession of figures, in which the performers endeavoured to exhibit a great variety of gesture: men and women danced at the same time, or in separate parties, but the latter were generally preferred, from their superior grace and elegance. Some danced to slow airs, adapted

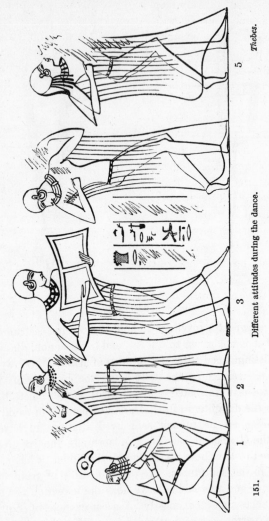

151.

to the style of their movement : the attitudes they assumed frequently partook of a grace not unworthy of the Greeks ;* and

* Woodcut 151.

others preferred a lively step, regulated by an appropriate tune. Men sometimes danced with great spirit, bounding from the ground more in the manner of Europeans than of an Eastern people : on which occasions the music was not always composed of many instruments, but consisted only of *crotala* or maces, a man clapping his hands, and a woman snapping her fingers to the time.*

Graceful attitudes and gesticulation were the general style of their dance ; but, as in other countries, the taste of the performance varied according to the rank of the person by whom they were employed, or their own skill ; and the dance at the house of a priest differed from that among the uncouth peasantry, or the lower classes of townsmen.

It was not customary for the upper orders of Egyptians to indulge in this amusement, either in public or private assemblies, and none appear to have practised it but the lower ranks of society, and those who gained their livelihood by attending festive meetings.   The Greeks, however, though they employed women who professed music and dancing, to entertain the guests, looked upon the dance as a recreation in which all classes might indulge, and an accomplishment becoming a gentleman ; and it was also a Jewish custom for young ladies to dance at private entertainments,† as it still is at Damascus and other Eastern towns.

The Romans, on the contrary, were far from considering it worthy of a man of rank, or of a sensible person ; and Cicero says, " No man who is sober dances, unless he is out of his mind, either *when alone*, or in any decent society ; for dancing is the companion of wanton conviviality, dissoluteness, and luxury." Nor did the Greeks indulge in it to excess; and effeminate dances, or extraordinary gesticulation, were deemed indecent in men of character and wisdom.   Indeed, Herodotus tells a story of Hippoclides, the Athenian, who had been preferred before all the nobles of Greece, as a husband for the daughter of Clisthenes, king of Argos, having been rejected on account of his extravagant gestures in the dance.

* Woodcut 109.   † Matth. xiv. 6.

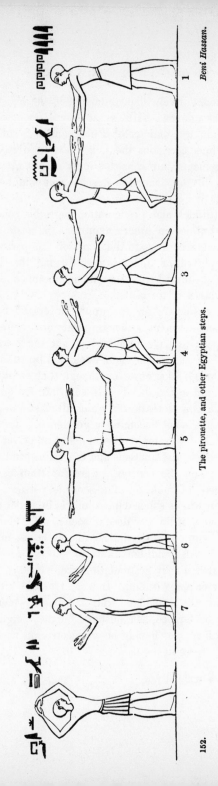

Beni Hassan.

The pirouette, and other Egyptian steps.

152.

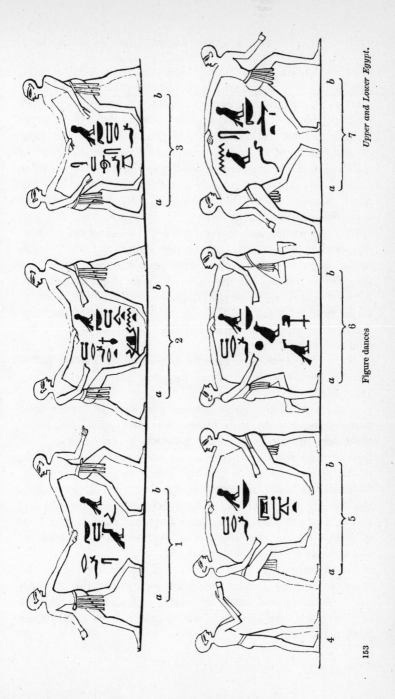

Figure dances

Upper and Lower Egypt.

153

Of all the Greeks, the Ionians were most noted for their fondness of this art; and, from the wanton and indecent tendency of their songs and gestures, dances of a voluptuous character (like those of the modern Alméhs of the East) were styled by the Romans "Ionic movements." Moderate dancing was even deemed worthy of the gods themselves. Jupiter, "the father of gods and men," is represented dancing in the midst of the other deities; and Apollo is not only introduced by Homer thus engaged, but received the title of ορχηστης, "the dancer," from his supposed excellence in the art.

Grace in posture and movement was the chief object of those employed at the assemblies of the rich Egyptians; and the ridiculous gestures of the buffoon were permitted there, so long as they did not transgress the rules of decency and moderation. Music was always indispensable, whether at the festive meetings of the rich or poor; and they danced to the sound of the harp, lyre, guitar, pipe, tambourine, and other instruments, and, in the streets, even to the drum.

Many of their postures resembled those of the modern ballet, and the *pirouette* delighted an Egyptian party four thousand years ago.*

The dresses of the female dancers were light, and of the finest texture, showing, by their transparent quality, the forms and movement of the limbs: they generally consisted of a loose flowing robe, reaching to the ankles, occasionally fastened tight at the waist; and round the hips was a small narrow girdle, adorned with beads, or ornaments of various colours. Sometimes the dancing figures appear to have been perfectly naked; but this is from the outline of the transparent robe having been effaced; and, like the Greeks, they represented the contour of the figure as if seen through the dress.

Slaves were taught dancing as well as music; and in the houses of the rich, besides their other occupations, that of dancing to entertain the family, or a party of friends, was required of them; and free Egyptians also gained a livelihood by their performances.

* Woodcut 152.

Some danced by pairs, holding each other's hands; others went through a succession of steps alone;* and sometimes a man performed a *solo* to the sound of music, or the clapping of hands.†

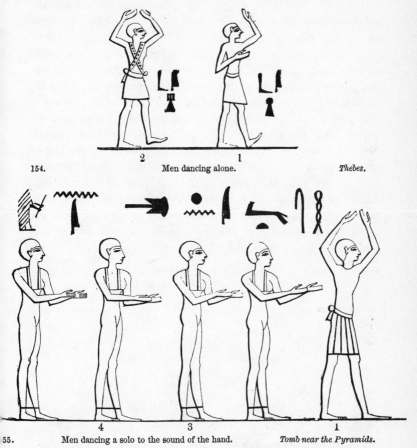

154.   Men dancing alone.   *Thebes.*

55.   Men dancing a solo to the sound of the hand.   *Tomb near the Pyramids.*

The dances of the lower orders generally had a tendency towards a species of pantomime; and the rude peasantry were more delighted with ludicrous and extravagant dexterity, than with gestures which displayed elegance and grace.

Besides the pirouette and the steps above mentioned, a

* Woodcut 154.   † Woodcut 155.

favourite figure dance was universally adopted throughout the country, in which the two partners, who were usually men, advanced towards each other, or stood face to face upon one leg, and, having performed a series of movements, retired again in opposite directions, continuing to hold by one hand, and concluding by turning each other round.*

In another they struck the ground with the heel, standing on one foot, changing, perhaps, alternately from the right to the left; which is not very unlike a step of the present day.†

The Egyptians also danced at the temples in honour of the gods, and in some processions, as they approached the precincts of the sacred courts; and though this custom may at first sight appear inconsistent with the gravity of religion, we may recollect with what feelings David himself danced ‡ before the ark, and that the Jews considered it part of their religious duties to approach the Deity with the dance, § with tabret, and with harp. Their mode of worshipping the golden calf also consisted of songs and dancing; and this was immediately derived from the ceremonies of the Egyptians.

* Woodcut 153.   † Woodcut 154.   ‡ 1 Chron. xv. 29.   2 Sam. vi. 14.
§ Psalm cxlix. 3, " Let them praise his name in the dance." Exod. xv. 20.

D. The palace-temple of Remeses the Great, generally called the Memnonium, at Thebes, during the inundation.

E.   The two Colossi of Thebes before the temple built by Amunoph III., with the ruins of
Luxor in the distance, during the inundation.

CHAPTER III.

AMUSEMENT OF THE GUESTS — VASES — ORNAMENTS OF THE HOUSE — PRE-
PARATION FOR DINNER — THE KITCHEN — MODE OF EATING — SPOONS —
WASHING BEFORE MEALS — FIGURE OF A DEAD MAN BROUGHT IN — GAMES
WITHIN, AND OUT OF, DOORS — WRESTLING — BOAT-FIGHTS — BULL-FIGHTS.

WHILE the party was amused with music and dancing, and the
late arrivals were successively announced, refreshments continued to be handed round, and every attention was shown to the
assembled guests. Wine was offered to each new comer, and
chaplets of flowers were brought by men servants to the gentlemen, and by women or white slaves to the ladies, as they took
their seats.* An upper servant, or slave, had the office of handing the wine, and a black woman sometimes followed, in an inferior
capacity, to receive an empty cup when the wine had been poured
into the goblet. The same black slave also carried the fruits
and other refreshments; and the peculiar mode of holding a
plate with the hand reversed, so generally adopted by women
from Africa, is characteristically shown in the Theban paintings.†

* Woodcut 157; *figs.* 4, 5, 8, 9, 12, 21.   † Woodcut 158.

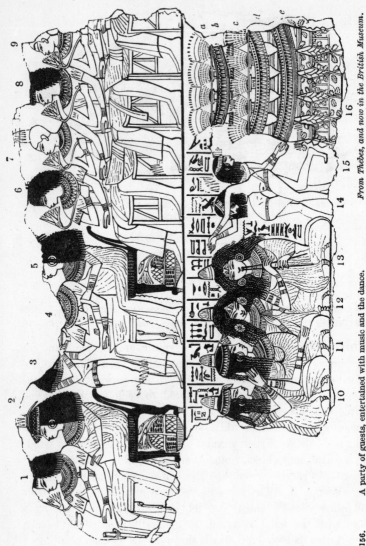

156.

A party of guests, entertained with music and the dance.

From Thebes, and now in the British Museum.

Figs. 1, 2, 4, 5, 6, 7, 8, 9. Men and Women seated together at the feast.   3. A servant offering a cup of wine.
10, 11, 12. Women singing and clapping their hands to the sound of the double pipe, 13.   14, 15. Dancing women.
16. Vases on stands, stopped with heads of wheat, and decked with garlands.

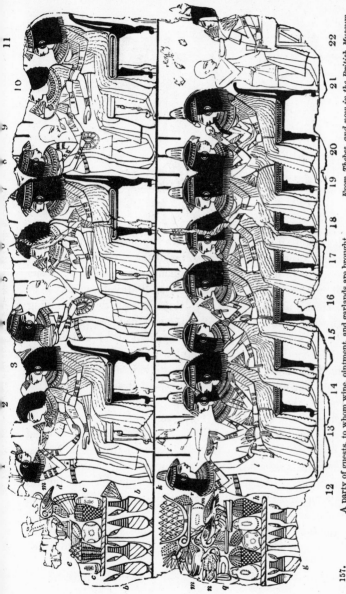

157.

A party of guests, to whom wine, ointment, and garlands are brought.   *From Thebes, and now in the British Museum.*

Fig. 1. A maid-servant presenting a cup of wine to a gentleman and lady, seated on chairs with cushions, probably of leather.

4. Another holding a vase of ointment and a garland.

5. presents a lotus flower; and 9, a necklace or garland, which he is going to tie round the neck of the guest, 10.

12. A female attendant offering wine to a guest; in her left hand is a napkin, *l,* for wiping the mouth after drinking.

The tables, *a, f,* have cakes of bread, *c r*; meat, *d, q*; geese, *e*; and other birds, *m*; figs, *e, k*; grapes in baskets, *h*; flowers *p*; and other things prepared for the feast: and beneath them are glass bottles of wine, *b, g.*

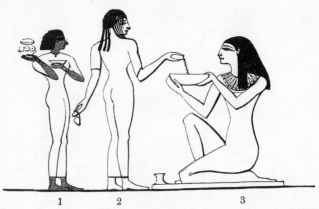

1   2   3

A black and white slave waiting upon a lady at a party   *Thebes.*

To each person after drinking a napkin was presented for wiping the mouth,* answering to the *máhrama* of the modern Egyptians; and the bearer of it uttered a complimentary sentiment, when she offered it and received back the goblet: as, " May it benefit you!" and no oriental at the present day drinks water without receiving a similar wish.   But it was not considered rude to refuse wine when offered, even though it had been poured out;† and a teeto-taller might continue smelling a lotus without any affront.   Men and women either sat together, or separately, in a different part of the room; but no rigid mistrust prevented strangers, as well as members of the family, being received into the same society; which shows how greatly the Egyptians were advanced in the habits of social life.   In this they, like the Romans, differed widely from the Greeks, and might say with Cornelius Nepos, " Which of us is ashamed to bring his wife to an entertainment? and what mistress of a family can be shown who does not inhabit the chief and most frequented part of the house?   Whereas in Greece she never appears at any entertainments, except those to which relations alone are invited, and constantly lives in the women's apartments at the upper part of the house, into which

* Woodcut 157; *figs.* 12, 21.   † Woodcut 157; *fig.* 13.

no man has admission, unless he be a near relation." Nor were married people afraid of sitting together, and no idea of their having had too much of each other's company made it necessary to divide them. In short, they were the most Darby and Joan people possible, and they shared the same chair at home, at a party, and even in their tomb, where sculpture grouped them together.

The master and mistress of the house accordingly sat side by side on a large fauteuil, and each guest as he arrived walked up to receive their welcome. The musicians and dancers hired for the occasion also did obeisance to them, before they began their part. To the leg of the fauteuil was tied a favourite monkey, a dog, a gazelle, or some other pet; and a young child was permitted to sit on the ground at the side of its mother, or on its father's knee.

In the mean time the conversation became animated, especially in those parts of the room where the ladies sat together, and the numerous subjects that occurred to them were fluently discussed. Among these the question of dress was not forgotten, and the patterns, or the value of trinkets, were examined with propor-

159.   Ladies at a party talking about their earrings.   *Thebes.*

tionate interest. The maker of an earring, and the shop where it was purchased, were anxiously inquired; each compared the workmanship, the style, and the materials of those she wore, coveted her neighbour's, or preferred her own ; and women of every class vied with each other in the display of " jewels of silver and jewels of gold," in the texture of their " raiment," the neatness of their sandals, and the arrangement or beauty of their plaited hair.

It was considered a pretty compliment to offer each other a flower from their own bouquet, and all the vivacity of the Egyptians was called forth as they sat together. The hosts omitted nothing that could make their party pass off pleasantly, and keep up agreeable conversation, which was with them the great charm of accomplished society, as with the Greeks, who thought it " more requisite and becoming to gratify the company by cheerful conversation, than with variety of dishes." The guests, too, neglected no opportunity of showing how much they enjoyed themselves ; and as they drew each other's attention to the many knick-knacks that adorned the rooms, paid a well-turned compliment to the taste of the owner of the house. They admired the vases, the carved boxes of wood or ivory, and the light tables on which many a curious trinket was displayed ; and commended the elegance and comfort of the luxurious fauteuils, the rich cushions and coverings of the couches and ottomans, the carpets and the other furniture. Some, who were invited to see the sleeping apartments, found in the ornaments on the toilet-tables, and in the general arrangements, fresh subjects for admiration ; and their return to the guest-chamber gave an opportunity of declaring that good taste prevailed throughout the whole house. On one occasion, while some of the delighted guests were in these raptures of admiration, and others were busied with the chitchat, perhaps the politics, or the scandal, of the day, an awkward youth, either from inadvertence, or a little too much wine, reclined against a wooden column placed in the centre of the room to support some temporary ornament, and threw it down upon those who sat beneath it.*

* I regret having lost the copy of this amusing subject. It was in a tomb at Thebes.

The confusion was great : the women screamed ; and some, with uplifted hands, endeavoured to protect their heads and escape from its fall.   No one, however, seems to have been hurt ; and the harmony of the party being restored, the incident afforded fresh matter for conversation ; to be related in full detail to their friends, when they returned home.

The vases were very numerous, and varied in shape, size, and materials ; being of hard stone, alabaster, glass, ivory, bone, porcelain, bronze, brass, silver, or gold ; and those of the poorer classes were of glazed pottery, or common earthenware.   Many of their ornamental vases, as well as those in ordinary use, were of the most elegant shape, which would do honour to the Greeks, the Egyptians frequently displaying in these objects of private *luxe* the taste of a highly refined people ; and so strong a resemblance did they bear to the productions of the best epochs of ancient Greece, both in their shape and in the fancy devices upon them, that some might even suppose them borrowed from Greek patterns.   But they were purely Egyptian, and had been universally adopted in the valley of the Nile, long before the graceful forms we admire were known in Greece ; a fact invariably acknowledged by those who are acquainted with the remote age of Egyptian monuments, and of the paintings that represent them.

160.   Gold vases of the time of Thothmes III.   *Thebes.*

For some of the most elegant date in the early age of the third Thothmes, who lived between fourteen and fifteen hundred years before our era ; and we not only admire their forms, but the richness of the materials of which they were made, their colour, as well as the hieroglyphics, showing them to have been of gold and silver, or of this last, inlaid with the more precious metal.

Those of bronze, alabaster, glass, porcelain, and even of ordinary pottery, were also deserving of admiration, from the beauty of their shapes, the designs which ornamented them, and the superior quality of the material; and gold and silver cups were often beautifully engraved, and studded with precious stones. Among these we readily distinguish the green emerald, the purple amethyst, and other gems; and when an animal's head adorned their handles, the eyes were frequently composed of them, except when enamel, or some coloured composition, was employed as a substitute.

That the Egyptians made great use of precious stones for their vases, and for women's necklaces, rings, bracelets, and other ornamental purposes, is evident from the paintings at Thebes,

and from the numerous articles of jewellery discovered in the tombs; and they appear sometimes to have been sent to Egypt in bags, similar to those containing the gold dust brought by the conquered nations tributary to the Egyptians, which

161. Bags, generally containing gold dust, tied up and sealed. *Thebes.*

were tied up and secured with a seal.

Many bronze vases found at Thebes, and in other parts of Egypt, are of very excellent quality, and prove the skill possessed by the Egyptians in the art of working and compounding metals. We are surprised at the rich sonorous tones they emit on being struck, the fine polish of which some are still susceptible, and the high finish given them by the workmen: nor are the knives and daggers, made of the same materials, less deserving of notice; the elastic spring they possessed, and even retain to the present day, being such as could only be looked for in a blade of steel. The exact proportions of the copper and alloys, in all the different specimens preserved in the museums of Europe, have not yet been ascertained; but it would be curious to know

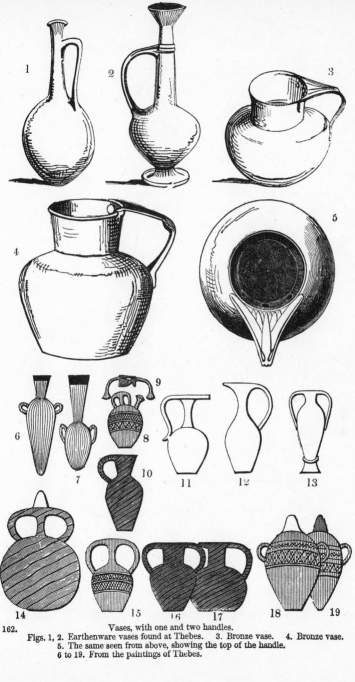

162.   Vases, with one and two handles.

Figs. 1, 2. Earthenware vases found at Thebes.   3. Bronze vase.   4. Bronze vase.
5. The same seen from above, showing the top of the handle.
6 to 19. From the paintings of Thebes.

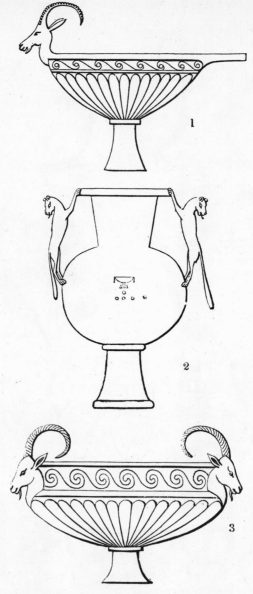

163.   Vases ornamented with one and two heads, or the whole animal.   *Thebes.*
Fig. 2 has the word "gold" upon it.

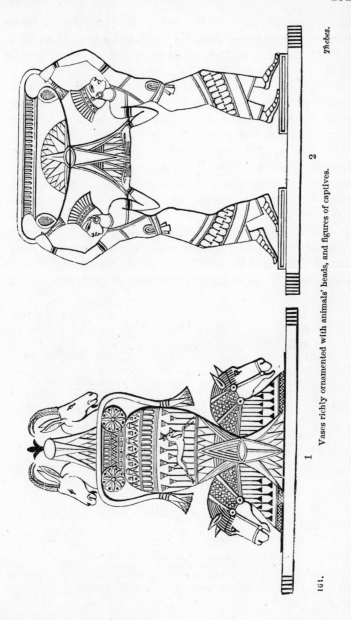

1   Vases richly ornamented with animals' heads, and figures of captives.   2   *Thebes.*

164.

their composition, particularly the interesting dagger of the Berlin collection, which is as remarkable for the elasticity of its blade, as for the neatness and perfection of its finish.   Many contain 10 or 20 parts tin, to 90 and 80 copper.

Some vases had one, others two handles; some were ornamented with the heads of wild animals, as the ibex, oryx, or gazelle; others had a head on either side, a fox, a cat, or something similar; and many were ornamented with horses' heads, a whole quadruped, a goose's head, figures of captives, or fancy devices.   They were occasionally grotesque, and monstrous; especially when introduced among the offerings brought by the conquered people of the north, which may be Asiatic rather than Egyptian; and one of them (fig. 1) appears to have for its cover the head of the Assyrian god represented in the Nimroud sculptures, supposed to be a vulture, a bird whose name, *nisr*, recalls that of " Nisroch, the god " of Nebuchadnezzar.   They were either made of porcelain, or an enamel on gold, and were re-

165.

Fig. 1. Vase, with the head of a bird as a cover.
2. With head of a Typhonian monster.
3. A golden vase, without handles.   *Thebes.*

They are of the time of the 18th and 19th dynasties.

markable for the brilliancy of their colours. The head of a
Typhonian monster also served for the cover of some of these
vases, as it often did for the support of a mirror (contrasted
daily with the beauty of an Egyptian lady) ; but both this, and
the head of the bird, are of early time, being found on vases
brought as part of the tribute from Asia to the kings of the
18th and 19th dynasties. The Typhonian head bears some
analogy to that of Medusa. It is thought to be of the Syrian god
Baal ; whose name was sometimes associated with that of Seth,
or Typhon, the Evil Being.

There was also a *rhyton*, or drinking-cup, in the form of a
cock's head, represented among the tribute of the people of Kûfa
brought to Thothmes III.

These very highly ornamented vases, with a confused mixture of
flower and scroll patterns, appear to have been mostly brought
from Asia ; and it is remarkable that the Nineveh ornaments have
much the same kind of character. They are occasionally as
devoid of taste as the wine bottles and flower-pots of an English
cellar and conservatory ; but many of those brought by the
people of Rotūn have all the beauty of form found in those of
Greece.

Some had a single handle fixed to one side, and were in shape
not unlike our cream jugs,* ornamented with the heads of oxen,
or fancy devices ; others were of bronze, bound with gold, having
handles of the same metal. Several vases had simple handles or
rings on either side ; others were destitute of these, and of every
exterior ornament ; some again were furnished with a single ring
attached to a neat bar,† or with a small knob, projecting from the
side ;‡ and many of those used in the service of the temple, highly
ornamented with figures of deities in relief,§ had a moveable
curved handle, on the principle of, though more elegant in form
than that of their common culinary utensils. ‖ They were of
bronze, ornamented with figures, in relief, or engraved upon

* Woodcut 166, *figs*. 1, 2.   † Woodcut 167, *figs*. 1, 2.
‡ Woodcut 167, *figs*. 3, 4, 5.   § Woodcut 168, *fig*. 1.
‖ Woodcut 168 *fig*. 3.

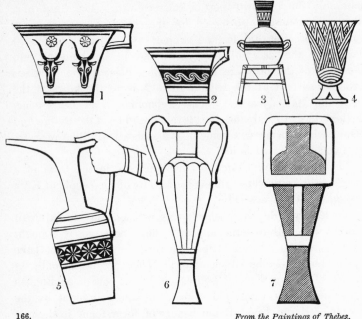

166.   *From the Paintings of Thebes.*
Figs. 1 and 2. Vases of an early period.   3. Vase on a stand.
4. Drinking-cup of porcelain.   7. Bronze vase, bound with gold.

them; and one of those found by Mr. Salt showed, by the
elastic spring of its cover, and the nicety with which this fitted
the mouth of the vase, the great skill of the Egyptian workmen.*

Another, of much larger dimensions, and of a different form,
brought by me from Thebes, and presented to the British
Museum, is also of bronze, with two large handles fastened on
with pins; and, though it resembles some of the caldrons represented by the paintings in an Egyptian kitchen, its lightness
seems to show that it was rather intended as a basin, or for a
similar purpose.†

Vases, surmounted with a human head forming the cover,

* Woodcut 172.   † Woodcut 169.

167.   Fig. 1. Bronze vase brought by me from Thebes, now in the British Museum.
        2. Showing how the handle is fixed.
        3. Alabaster vase from Thebes, of the time of Neco.
        4. Vase at Berlin of cut glass.   5. Stone vase.
        6 to 9. From the sculptures of Thebes.

appear to have been frequently used for keeping gold and other
precious objects, as in certain small side chambers of Medeenet
Haboo, which were the treasury of King Remeses III. And if
this Remeses was really the same as the wealthy Rhampsinitus
of Herodotus, these chambers may have been the very treasury
he mentions, where the thieves displayed so much dexterity.

Bottles, small vases, and pots used for holding ointment, or

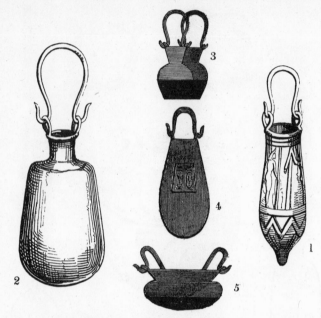

168.   Fig. 1. Bronze vase used in the temple.
            2. A larger one in the Berlin Museum.
            3, 4, 5. Culinary utensils in the sculptures at Thebes.

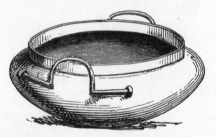

169.   Large bronze vase brought by me from Thebes.

other purposes connected with the toilet, were of alabaster, glass,
porcelain, and hard stone, as granite, basalt, porphyry, serpentine,
or breccia; some were of ivory, bone, and other materials,
according to the choice or means of individuals; and the porous

170.   Fig. 1. Alabaster vase in my possession, from Thebes.
          2. Porcelain vase in Mr. Salt's Collection.

Fig. 1. Alabaster vase, containing sweet scented ointment, in the Museum of Alnwick Castle.
   2. Hieroglyphics on a vase, presenting the name of a queen, the sister of Thothmes III.
   3. The stopper.   4 and 9. Porcelain vases, from the paintings of Thebes.
   5. Porcelain cup, in my possession, from Thebes.
   6. Small ivory vase, in my possession, containing a dark-coloured ointment, from Thebes.
   7. Alabaster vase, with its lid (8), in the Museum of Alnwick Castle.
171.

172. Bronze vase of Mr. Salt's Collection.   173. Glass bottle.   *Thebes.*

earthenware jars and water-bottles of Coptos, like the modern
ones of Ballas and Kéneh in the same neighbourhood, were
highly prized, even by foreigners.

Small boxes, made of wood or ivory, were also numerous ; and,
like the vases, of many different forms ; and some, which contained cosmetics of divers kinds, served to deck the dressing
table, or a lady's boudoir. They were carved in various ways,
and loaded with ornamental devices in relief ; sometimes representing the favourite lotus flower, with its buds and stalks, a
goose, gazelle, fox, or other animal. Many were of considerable
length, terminating in a hollow shell, not unlike a spoon in
shape and depth, covered with a lid turning on a pin ; and to
this, which may properly be styled the box, the remaining part
was merely an accessory, intended for ornament, or serving as a
handle.

They were generally of sycamore wood, sometimes of tamarisk,* or of acacia ; and occasionally ivory, and inlaid work, were

* Woodcuts 174, 175.

substituted for wood. To many, a handle of less disproportionate
length was attached, representing the usual lotus flower, a figure,
a Typhonian monster, an animal, a bird, a fish, or a reptile ; and

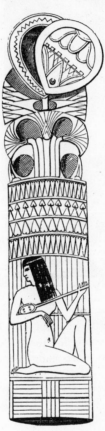

174. Box with a long handle.
      Mr. Salt's Collection.

175. Box in the Berlin Museum,
      showing the lid open.

the box itself, whether covered with a lid or open, was in character with the remaining part. Some shallow ones were probably intended to contain small portions of ointment, taken from
a large vase at the time it was wanted, or for other purposes

176.   Wooden boxes, or saucers without covers.   *Mr. Salt's Collection.*

connected with the toilet, where greater depth was not required;
and in many instances they rather resembled spoons than boxes.

Many were made in the form of a royal oval, with and without

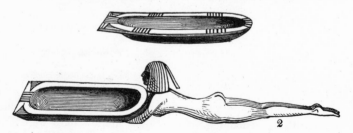

177.   Other open boxes, whose form is taken from the oval of a king's name.
Alnwick Castle, and Leyden Museum.

a handle ;* and the body of a wooden fish was scooped out, and
closed with a cover imitating the scales, to deceive the eye by the

178.   Box in the form of a fish, with turning lid.   *Mr. Salt's Collection.*

appearance of a solid mass.   Sometimes a goose was represented,
ready for table,† or swimming on the water,‡ and pluming itself ;
the head being the handle of a box formed of its hollow body ;

179   Box with and without its cover.   *Museum of Alnwick Castle.*

180.   Boxes in form of geese.   *Mr. Salt's Collection and Leyden Museum.*

some consisted of an open part or cup, attached to a covered box ;§
others of different shapes offered the usual variety of fancy devices,
and some were without covers, which may come under the de-

* Woodcut 177.   † Woodcut 179.   ‡ Woodcut 180, *fig.* 2.
                § Woodcut 181.

nomination of saucers. Others bore the precise form and character of a box, being deeper and more capacious; and these
were probably used for holding trinkets, or occasionally as repositories for the small pots of ointment, or scented oils, and bottles
containing the collyrium, which women applied to their eyes.

181.   One part open, and one covered.   *Mr. Salt's Collection.*

182.   Box with the lid turning, as usual, on a pin.   *Mr. Salt's Collection.*

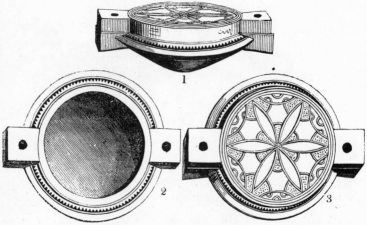

183.   A box with and without its lid.   *Mr. Salt's Collection.*

Some were divided into separate compartments, covered by a common lid, either sliding in a groove,* or turning on a pin at one end; and many of still larger dimensions sufficed to contain a mirror, combs, and perhaps even some articles of dress.

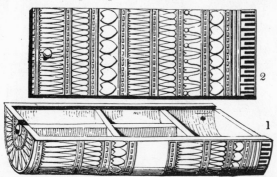

184.　Fig. 1. A box, with devices carved in relief, divided into cells.
　　　2. The lid, which slides into a groove.　　*Mr. Salt's Collection.*

These boxes were frequently of costly materials, veneered with rare woods, or made of ebony, inlaid with ivory, painted with various devices, or stained to imitate materials of a valuable nature; and the mode of fastening the lid, and the curious substitute for a hinge given to some of them, show the former was entirely removed, and that the box remained open, while used. The principle of this will be better understood by reference to woodcut 185, where fig. 1 represents a side section of the box, and fig. 2 the inside of the lid. At the upper part of the back c, fig. 3, a small hole E is cut, which, when the box is closed, receives the nut D, projecting from the cross-bar B, on the inside of the lid; and the two knobs F and G, one on the lid, the other on the front of the box itself, serve not only for ornament but for fastening it, a band being wound round them, and secured with a seal.

Knobs of ebony, or other hard wood, were very common. They were turned with great care, and inlaid with ivory and silver; an instance of which is given in fig. 5.

* Woodcut 184.

M 2

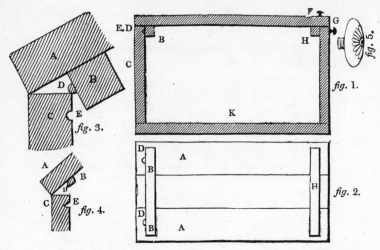

185.   Fig. 1. Section of the box. A, the lid. K, the bottom. C, D, the two sides.
       2. The inside of the lid. B, H, cross-bars nailed inside the lid. *Found at Thebes.*

Some boxes were made with a pointed summit, divided into two parts, one of which alone opened, turning on small pivots at the base, and the two ends of the box resembled in form the gable ends, as the top, the shelving roof, of a house.* The sides were, as usual, secured by glue and nails, generally of wood, and dovetailed, a method of joining adopted in Egypt at the most remote period ; but the description of these belongs more properly to cabinet work, as those employed for holding the combs, and similar objects, to the toilet.

Some vases have been found in boxes, made of wicker-work, closed with stoppers of wood, reed, or other materials, supposed to belong either to a lady's toilet or to a medical man ; one of which, now in the Berlin Museum, has been already noticed.†

Bottles of terra cotta are also met with, in very great abundance, of the most varied forms and dimensions, made for every kind of purpose of which they were susceptible ; and I have seen one which appears to have belonged to a painter, and

---

* See the boxes in Chap. vii. in the department of the Carpenters.
† Page 80, Woodcut 92.

to have been intended for holding water to moisten the colours ; the form and position of the handle suggesting that it was held on the thumb of the left hand, while the person wrote or painted with his right.

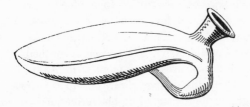

186. Terra-cotta bottle, perhaps used by painters for holding water, and carried on the thumb.   *Mr. Salt's Collection.*

Besides vases and bottles of stone, and of the materials above mentioned, the Egyptians made them of leather or prepared skin ; and some of these were imported into Egypt from foreign countries. As with the Greeks and Romans, skins were often used for carrying wine ; but leathern bottles are never seen at an Egyptian party, either for drawing wine from the amphora, or for handing it to table.

Bottles and narrow-mouthed vases, placed in the sitting-room, and holding water, were frequently closed with some light substance, through which the warm air could pass, as it rose, during the cooling process, being submitted to a current of air, to increase the evaporation : leaves were often employed for this purpose, as at the present day, those of a fragrant kind being probably selected ; and the same prejudice against leaving a vase uncovered evidently existed among the ancient, as among the modern, inhabitants of Egypt.*

While the guests were entertained with music and the dance, dinner was prepared ; but as it consisted of a considerable number of dishes, and the meat was killed for the occasion, as at the present day in Eastern and tropical climates, some time elapsed before it was put upon table. An ox, kid, wild goat, gazelle, or an oryx, and a quantity of geese, ducks, teal, quails, and other

* Woodcut 156, *figs. a, b, c, d, e.*

birds, were generally selected ; but mutton was excluded from a Theban table.   Plutarch even states that " no Egyptians would eat the flesh of sheep, except the Lycopolites," who did so out of compliment to the wolves they venerated ; and Strabo confines the sacrifice of them to the Nome of Nitriotis.   But, though sheep were not killed for the altar or the table, they abounded in Egypt, and even at Thebes ; and large flocks were kept for their wool, particularly in the neighbourhood of Memphis. Sometimes a flock consisted of more than 2000 ; and in a tomb below the Pyramids, dating upwards of 4000 years ago, 974 rams are brought to be registered by his scribes, as part of the stock of the deceased ; implying an equal number of ewes, independent of lambs.*

Beef and goose constituted the principal part of the animal food throughout Egypt ; and by a prudent foresight, in a country possessing neither extensive pasture lands, nor great abundance of cattle, the cow was held sacred, and consequently forbidden to be eaten.   Thus the risk of exhausting the stock was prevented, and a constant supply of oxen was kept up for the table and for agricultural purposes.   A similar fear of diminishing the number of sheep, so valuable for their wool, led to a preference for such meats as beef and goose ; though they were much less light and wholesome than mutton.   In Abyssinia it is a sin to eat geese or ducks ; and modern experience teaches that in Egypt, and similar climates, beef and goose are not eligible food, except in the winter months.

A considerable quantity of meat was served up at those repasts, to which strangers were invited, as among people of the East at the present day ; whose *azooma*, or feast, prides itself in the quantity and variety of dishes, in the unsparing profusion of viands, and, whenever wine is permitted, in the freedom of the bowl.   An endless succession of vegetables was also required on all occasions ; and, when dining in private, dishes composed chiefly of them, were in greater request than joints, even at the tables of

* See the seventh woodcut in Chapter viii.

the rich ; and consequently the Israelites, who, by their long residence there, had acquired similar habits, regretted them equally
with the meat and fish * of Egypt.

Their mode of dining was very similar to that now adopted in
Cairo, and throughout the East ; each person sitting round a
table, and dipping his bread into a dish placed in the centre,
removed on a sign made by the host, and succeeded by others,
whose rotation depends on established rule, and whose number
is predetermined according to the size of the party, or the quality
of the guests.

Among the lower orders, vegetables constituted a very great
part of their ordinary food, and they gladly availed themselves
of the variety and abundance of esculent roots growing spontaneously, in the lands irrigated by the rising Nile, as soon as its
waters had subsided ; some of which were eaten in a crude state, and
others roasted in the ashes, boiled, or stewed : their chief aliment,
and that of their children, consisting of milk and cheese, roots,
leguminous, cucurbitaceous, and other plants, and the ordinary
fruits of the country.   Herodotus describes the food of the workmen, who built the Pyramids, to have been the "*raphanus*,
onions, and garlic ;" the first of which, now called *figl*, is like a
turnip-radish in flavour ; but he has omitted one more vegetable,
lentils, which were always, as at the present day, the chief article
of their diet ; and which Strabo very properly adds to the number.

The nummulite rock, in the vicinity of those monuments, frequently presents a conglomerate of testacea imbedded in it,
which, in some positions, resemble small seeds ; and Strabo
imagines they were the petrified residue of the lentils brought
there by the workmen, from their having been the ordinary food
of the labouring classes, and of all the lower orders of Egyptians.

Much attention was bestowed on the culture of this useful
pulse, and certain varieties became remarkable for their excellence,
the lentils of Pelusium being esteemed both in Egypt and in
foreign countries.

* Numbers xi. 4, 5.

In few countries were vegetables more numerous than in Egypt; as is proved by ancient writers, the sculptures, and the number of persons who sold them; and at the time of the Arab invasion, when Alexandria was taken by Amer, the lieutenant of the caliph Omer, no less than 4000 persons were engaged in selling vegetables in that city.

The lotus, the papyrus, and other similar productions of the land, during and after the inundation, were, for the poor, one of the greatest blessings nature ever provided for any people; and, like the acorn in northern climates, constituted perhaps the sole aliment of the peasantry, at the early period when Egypt was first colonised. The fertility of the soil, however, soon afforded a more valuable produce to the inhabitants; and long before they had made any great advances in civilisation, corn and leguminous plants were grown to a great extent throughout the country. The palm was another important gift bestowed upon them: it flourished spontaneously in the valley of the Nile, and, if it was unable to grow in the sands of the arid desert, yet wherever water sufficed for its nourishment, this useful tree produced an abundance of dates, a wholesome and nutritious fruit, which might be regarded as an universal benefit, being within the reach of all classes of people, and neither requiring expense in the cultivation, nor interfering with the time demanded for other agricultural occupations.

Among the vegetables above mentioned, is one which requires some observations. Juvenal says that they were forbidden to eat the onion, and it is reported to have been excluded from an Egyptian table. But even if, as Plutarch supposes, onions were prohibited to the priests, who "abstained from most kinds of pulse; they were not excluded from the altars of the gods, either in the tombs or temples; and a priest is frequently seen holding them in his hand, or covering an altar with a bundle of their leaves and roots. They were introduced at private as well as public festivals; and brought to table with gourds, cucumbers, and other vegetables; and the Israelites, when they left the country, regretted "the onions" as well as the cucumbers, the water-melons,* the leeks, the garlic, and the meat they " did eat " in Egypt.†

The onions of Egypt were mild, and of an excellent flavour. They were eaten crude as well as cooked, by persons both of the higher and the lower classes; but it is difficult to say if they introduced them to table like the cabbage, as a *hors-d'œuvre*, to stimulate the appetite, which Socrates recommends in the Banquet of Xenophon. On this occasion, some curious reasons for their use are brought forward, by different members of the party. Nicerates observes that onions relish well with wine, and cites Homer in support of his remark; Callias affirms that they inspire courage in the hour of battle; and Charmidas suggests their utility " in deceiving a jealous wife, who, finding her husband return with his breath smelling of onions, would be induced to believe he had not saluted any one while from home."

In slaughtering for the table, it was customary to take the ox, or whatever animal had been chosen for the occasion, into a court-yard near the house; to tie its four legs together, and then

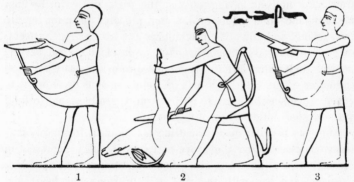

187. A butcher killing and cutting up an ibex or wild goat: the other two sharpening their knives on a *steel*.   *Thebes.*

to throw it upon the ground; in which position it was held by one or more persons, while the butcher, sharpening his broad

* *Abtikhim, comp.* Arabic *batikh,* " water-melon."
† Exod. xvi. 3; Numb. xi. 5.

knife upon a *steel* attached to his apron, proceeded to cut the throat, as near as possible from one ear to the other; sometimes continuing the opening downwards.* The blood was frequently received into a vase or basin for the purposes of cookery,† which was repeatedly forbidden to the Israelites by the Mosaic law ;‡ and the reason of the explicit manner of the prohibition is readily explained, from the necessity of preventing their adopting a custom they had so recently witnessed in Egypt. Nor is it less strictly denounced by the Mohammedan religion; and all Moslems look upon this ancient Egyptian, and modern European, custom with unqualified horror and disgust. But black-puddings were popular in Egypt.

The head was then taken off, and they proceeded to skin the animal, beginning with the leg and neck. The first joint removed was the right foreleg or shoulder; the other parts following in succession, according to custom or convenience; and the same rotation was observed, in cutting up the victims offered in sacrifice to the gods. Servants carried the joints to the kitchen on wooden trays, and the cook having selected the parts suited for boiling, roasting, and other modes of dressing, prepared them for the fire by washing, and any other preliminary process he thought necessary. In large kitchens, the *chef*, or head cook, had several persons under him; who were required to make ready and boil the water of the caldron, to put the joints on spits or skewers, to cut up or mince the meat, to prepare the vegetables, and to fulfil various other duties assigned to them.

The very peculiar mode of cutting up the meat frequently prevents our ascertaining the exact part they intend to represent in the sculptures; the chief joints, however, appear to be the head, shoulder, and leg, with the ribs, tail, or rump, the heart, and kidneys; and they occur in the same manner on the altars of the temple, and the tables of a private house. One is remarkable,

* The Israelites sometimes cut off the head at once. Deut. xxi. v. 4, 6.
† Woodcut 191, *fig.* 2.
‡ Deut. xv. 23. "Only thou shalt not eat the blood thereof: thou shalt pour it upon the ground as water." And c. xii. 16, 23; "be sure that thou eat not the blood, for the blood is the life." Gen. ix. 4, and Levit. xvii. 10, 11, 14, &c.

not only from being totally unlike any of our European joints,
but from its exact resemblance to that commonly seen at table in
modern Egypt: it is part of the leg, consisting of the flesh
covering the bone, whose two extremities project slightly beyond
it ; and the accompanying drawing from the sculptures, and a
sketch of the same joint from a modern table in Upper Egypt,
show how the mode of cutting it has been preserved by traditional custom to the present day.

188.   Peculiar joint of meat at an ancient and modern Egyptian table.

The head was left with the skin and horns ; and was sometimes
given away to a poor person, as a reward for holding the walking
sticks of those guests who came on foot ; but it was frequently

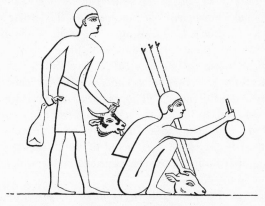

189.   One head given to a poor man.   *Thebes.*

taken to the kitchen with the other joints ; and, notwithstanding the positive assertion of Herodotus, we find that even in the temples themselves it was admitted at a sacrifice, and placed with other offerings on the altars of the gods.

The historian would lead us to suppose that a strict religious scruple prevented the Egyptians of all classes from eating this part, as he affirms, " that no Egyptian will taste the head of any species of animal," in consequence of certain imprecations having been uttered upon it at the time it was sacrificed ; but as he is speaking of heifers slaughtered for the service of the gods, we may conclude that the prohibition did not extend to those killed for table, nor even to all those offered for sacrifice in the temple ; and as with the scapegoat of the Jews, that important ceremony was perhaps confined to certain occasions, and to chosen animals, without extending to every victim which was slain.

The formula of the imprecation was probably very similar with the Jews and Egyptians. Herodotus says the latter pray the gods " that if any misfortune was about to happen to those who offered, or to the other inhabitants of Egypt, it might fall upon that head :" and with the former it was customary for the priest to take two goats and cast lots upon them, " one lot for the Lord, and the other lot for the scapegoat," which was presented alive " to make atonement " for the people. The priest was then required to " lay both his hands upon the head of the live goat, and confess over him all the iniquities of the children of Israel, and all their transgressions in all their sins, putting them upon the head of the goat, and send him away by the hand of a fit man into the wilderness." The remark of Herodotus should then be confined to the head, on which their imprecation was pronounced ; and being looked upon by every Egyptian as an abomination, it may have been taken to the market and sold to foreigners, or if no foreigners happened to be there, it may have been given to the crocodiles.

The same mode of slaughtering, and of preparing the joints, extended to all the large animals ; but geese, and other wild and

tame fowl, were served up entire, or, at least, only deprived
of their feet and pinion joints.
Fish were also brought to table
whole, whether boiled or fried,
the tails and fins being removed.
For the service of religion, they
were generally prepared in the
same manner as for private feasts;
sometimes, however, an ox was
brought entire to the altar, and
birds were often placed among

190.   An ox and a bird placed entire on
the altar.

the offerings, without even having the feathers taken off.

In Lower Egypt, or, as Herodotus styles it, "the corn country,"
they were in the habit of drying and salting birds of various
kinds, as quails, ducks, and others;* and fish were prepared by
them in the same manner both in Upper and Lower Egypt.†

Some joints were boiled, others roasted : two modes of dressing
their food to which Herodotus appears to confine the Egyptians,
at least in the lower country ; but the various modes of artificial
cookery which Menes introduced, and which offended the simple
habits of King Tnephachthus, had long since taught them to make
" savoury meats," such as prevented Isaac's distinguishing the
flesh of kids from venison.

For though the early Greeks were contented with roast meats,
and, as Athenæus observes, the heroes of Homer seldom " boil
their meat, or dress it with sauces," the Egyptians were far more
advanced in the habits of civilisation in those remote times.

The Egyptians never committed the same excesses as the
Romans under the Empire ; but they gave way to habits of in-
temperance and luxury after the Persian conquest, and the
accession of the Ptolemies ; so that writers who mention them
at that period, describe the Egyptians as a profligate and luxurious
people, addicted to an immoderate love of the table, and to every

* *See* Fowlers, in chap. viii.   † *See* Fishermen, chap. viii.

excess in drinking. They even used excitants for this purpose, and *hors d'œuvres* were provided to stimulate the appetite ; crude cabbage, provoking the desire for wine, and promoting the continuation of excess.

As is the custom in Egypt, and other hot climates, at the present day, they cooked the meat as soon as killed ; with the same view of having it tender, which makes northern people keep it until decomposition is beginning ; and this explains the order of Joseph to "slay and make ready" for his brethren to dine with him the same day at noon. As soon, therefore, as this had been done, and the joints were all ready, the kitchen presented an animated scene, and the cooks were busy in their different departments. One regulated the heat of the fire, raising it with a poker, or blowing it with bellows, worked by the feet ;* another superintended the cooking of the meat, skimming the water with a spoon, or stirring it with a large fork ;† while a third pounded salt, pepper, or other ingredients, in a large mortar, which were added from time to time during this process. Liquids of various kinds also stood ready for use, which were sometimes drawn off by means of siphons ;‡ and those things they wished to raise beyond the reach of rats, or other intruders, were placed upon trays, and pulled up by ropes running through rings in the ceiling, answering the purposes of a safe.§

Other servants took charge of the pastry, which the bakers or confectioners had made for the dinner table ; and this department, which may be considered as attached to the kitchen, appears even more varied than that of the cook. Some sifted and mixed the flour,‖ others kneaded the paste with their hands,¶ and formed it into rolls, which were then prepared for baking, and, being placed on a long tray or board, were carried on a man's

---

* *See* chap. ix.   † Woodcut 191, *figs.* 4 and 5.
   ‡ This part of the picture is very much damaged, but sufficient remains to show them using the siphons ; which occur again, perfectly preserved, in a tomb at Thebes. *See* chap. ix.
   § At *h* and *f* in woodcut 191.
   ‖ Woodcut 191*a*, *figs.* 13 and 14.   ¶ *Fig.* 15.

An Egyptian kitchen, from the tomb of Remeses III., at Thebes.

Fig. 1. Killing and preparing the joints, which are placed at *a*, *b*, *c*.
2. Catching the blood for the purposes of cookery, which is removed in a bowl by fig. 3.
4 and 5. Employed in boiling meat, and stirring the fire.
7. Preparing the meat for the caldron, which fig. 6 is taking to the fire
8. Pounding some ingredients for the cook.
f, *h*. Apparently siphons.
i, *j*. Ropes passing through rings, and supporting different things, as a sort of safe.
s. Probably plates.
u, *v*. Tables.

191.

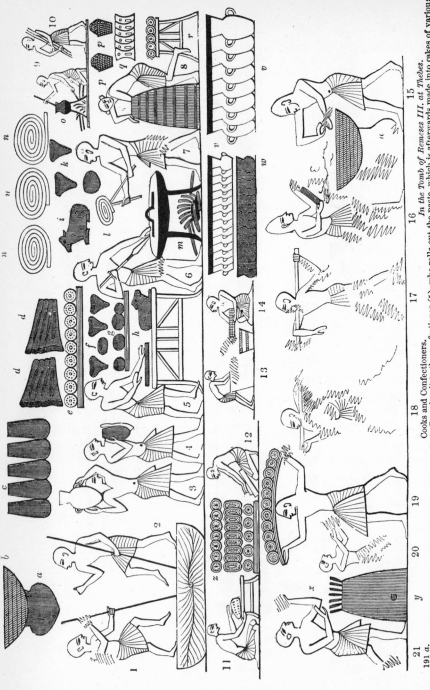

In the *Tomb of Rameses III. at Thebes.*

Cooks and Confectioners.

Fig. 1, 2. Kneading the dough with their feet.
3, 4. Carrying it to the confectioner (5), who rolls out the paste, which is afterwards made into cakes of various
forms. 1, 2, 3, 4, 5. 6, 7. Making a sort of macaroni (1, *w*, *v*) on a pan over the fire, *m*. 9. Cooking lentils, which are in the baskets, *p*, *p*.

191 *a*.

head * to the oven.† Certain seeds were previously sprinkled upon the upper surface of each roll,‡ and, judging from those still used in Egypt for the same purpose, they were chiefly the *nigella sativa*, or *kamóon aswed*, the *simsim*,§ and the caraway. Pliny also mentions this custom, and says that seeds of cummin were put upon cakes of bread in Egypt, and that condiments were mixed with them.

Sometimes they kneaded the paste with their feet,|| having placed it in a large wooden bowl upon the ground; it was then in a more liquid state than when mixed by the hand, and was carried in vases to the pastrycook, who formed it into a sort of maccaroni, upon a shallow metal pan over the fire. Two persons were engaged in this process; one stirring it with a wooden spatula, and the other taking it off when cooked, with two pointed sticks,¶ who arranged it in a proper place, where the rest of the pastry was kept. This last was of various kinds, apparently made up with fruit, or other ingredients, with which the dough, spread out with the hand, was sometimes mixed; and it assumed the shape of a three-cornered cake, a recumbent ox, a leaf, a crocodile's head, a heart, or other form,** according to the fancy of the confectioner. That his department was connected with the kitchen†† is again shown, by the presence of a man in the corner of the picture, engaged in cooking lentils for a soup or porridge; ‡‡ his companion §§ brings a bundle of faggots for the fire, and the lentils themselves are seen standing near him in wicker baskets.||||

---

* As at the present day. *Comp.* Pharaoh's chief baker, with "three white baskets on his *head*." Gen. xl. 16, and Herod. ii. 35. "Men carry loads on their *heads*, women on their shoulders." But it was not the general custom.

† Woodcut 191*a*, *figs.* 19 and *x*.

‡ *Figs.* 11 and *z*. Called *oŧk* by the Egyptians.   § Sesamum Orientale, Linn.

|| Herod. ii. 36, and *figs.* 1 and 2.   ¶ *Figs.* 6 and 7, and *l*.

** *Figs. d, f, g, h, i, k. f* and *g* appear to have the fruit apart from the pastry. Cakes of the form of *f* have been found in a tomb at Thebes, but without any fruit or other addition.

†† The chief baker (שר האפים) of Pharaoh carried in the uppermost basket "all manner of bake-meats," not only "bread," but "all kind of food." כל מאכל. Gen. xl. 17. Anciently, the cook and baker were the same with the Romans.

‡‡ *Fig.* 9.   §§ *Fig.* 10. |||| At *p*.

The large caldrons containing the meat for boiling, having been taken from the dresser,* where they were placed for the convenience of putting in the joints, stood over a wood fire upon the hearth, supported on stones, or on a metal frame or tripod.† Some of smaller dimensions, probably containing the stewed meat, stood over a pan ‡ containing charcoal, precisely similar

192.   Cooking geese and different joints of meat.   *Tomb near the Pyramids.*
   Figs. *a a.* Joints in caldrons, on the dresser *b.*   *c.* A table.
         1. Preparing a goose for the cook (2), who puts them into the boiler *d.*
         3. Roasting a goose over a fire (*e*) of peculiar construction.
         4. Cutting up the meat.   *l.* Joints on a table.
         g. Stewed meat over a pan of fire, or *magoor.*

to the *magoor,* used in modern Egypt ;§ and geese, or joints of meat, were roasted over a fire of a peculiar construction, intended solely for this purpose ;‖ the cook passing over them a fan,¶ which served for bellows. In heating water, or boiling meat, faggots of wood were principally employed; but for the roast meat charcoal, as in the modern kitchens of Cairo; and the sculptures represent servants bringing this last in mats, of the same form as those of the present day. They sometimes used round

* At *b.*   † Woodcut 192, at *d.*   ‡ At *c.*   § At *g.*
          ‖ At *e.*   ¶ At *f.*

balls for cooking, probably a composition of charcoal, and other ingredients, which a servant is represented taking out of a basket, and putting on the stove, while another blows the fire with a fan.

That dinner was served up at midday, may be inferred from the invitation given by Joseph to his brethren; but it is probable that, like the Romans, they also ate supper in the evening, as is still the custom in the East. The table was much the same as that of the present day in Egypt: a small stool, supporting a round tray, on which the dishes are placed; but it differed from this in having its circular summit fixed on a pillar, or leg, which was often in the form of a man, generally a captive, who supported the slab upon his head; the whole being of stone, or some hard wood. On this the dishes were placed, together with loaves of bread, some of which were not unlike those of the present day in Egypt, flat and round as our crumpets. Others had the form of rolls or cakes, sprinkled with seeds.

It was not generally covered with any linen, but, like the Greek table, was washed with a sponge, or napkin, after the dishes were removed, and polished by the servants, when the company had retired; though an instance sometimes occurs of a napkin spread on it, at least on those which bore offerings in honour of the dead. One or two guests generally sat at a table, though from the mention of persons seated in rows according to rank, it has been supposed the tables were occasionally of a long shape, as may have been the case when the brethren of Joseph " sat before him, the first born according to his birth-right, and the youngest according to his youth," Joseph eating alone at another table where " they set on for him by himself." But even if round, they might still sit according to rank; one place being always the post of honour, even at the present day, at the round table of Egypt.

In the houses of the rich, bread was made of wheat; the poorer classes being contented with cakes of barley, or of *doora* (holcus sorghum), which last is still so commonly used by them; for Herodotus is as wrong in saying that they thought it " the greatest disgrace to live on wheat and barley," as that " no one drank out of any but bronze (or brazen) cups." The drinking cups of the Egyptians not only varied in their materials, but also in their forms. Some were plain and unornamented ; others, though of small dimensions, were made after the models of larger vases ; many were like our own cups without handles ; and others may come under the denomination of beakers, and saucers. Of these the former were frequently made of alabaster, with a round base, so that they could not stand when filled, and were held in the hand, or, when empty, were turned downwards upon their rim : and the saucers, which were of glazed pottery, had some-times lotus blossoms, or fish, represented on their concave surface.

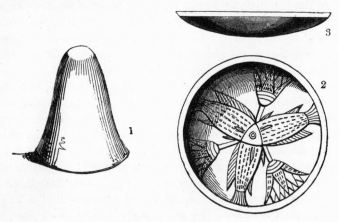

193.   Drinking cups.
Fig. 1. An alabaster beaker, in the Museum of Alnwick Castle.
2. A saucer or cup of blue glazed pottery, in the Berlin Collection.
3. Side view of the same.

The tables, as at a Roman repast, were occasionally brought in, and removed, with the dishes on them ; sometimes each joint was served up separately, and the fruit, deposited in a plate or trencher, succeeded the meat at the close of dinner ; but in less fashionable circles, particularly of the olden time, fruit was brought in baskets, which stood beside the table. The dishes consisted of fish ; meat boiled, roasted, and dressed in various ways ; game,

poultry, and a profusion of vegetables and fruit, particularly figs
and grapes, during the season; and a soup, or "pottage of

194.   The table brought in with the dishes upon it.   *Tomb near the Pyramids.*

lentils," as with the modern Egyptians, was not an unusual dish.
Of figs and grapes they were particularly fond, which is shown
by their constant introduction, even among the choice offerings
presented to the gods; and figs of the sycamore must have been
highly esteemed, since they were
selected as the heavenly fruit, given
by the goddess Netpe to those who
were judged worthy of admission to
the regions of eternal happiness.
Fresh dates during the season, and
in a dried state at other periods of
the year, were also brought to table,
as well as a preserve of the fruit,
made into a cake of the same form
as the tamarinds now brought from
the interior of Africa, and sold in
the Cairo market.

195.   A cake of preserved dates, found
by me at Thebes.   At *a* is a date stone.

The guests sat on the ground, or on stools and chairs, and, having neither knives and forks, nor any substitute for them answering to the chopsticks of the Chinese, they ate with their fingers,
like the modern Asiatics, and invariably with the right hand;

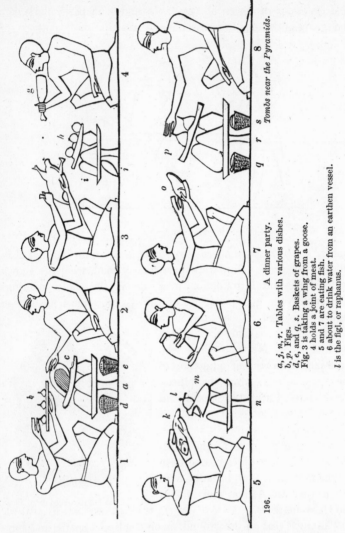

196.   A dinner party.

a, j, n, r. Tables with various dishes.
b, p. Figs.
d, e, and *q, s.* Baskets of grapes.
Fig. 3 is taking a wing from a goose.
4 holds a joint of meat.
5 and 7 are eating fish.
6 about to drink water from an earthen vessel.
l is the figl, or raphanus.

Tombs near the Pyramids.

nor did the Jews * and Etruscans, though they had forks for
other purposes, use any at table.

* 1 Sam. ii. 14.

Spoons were introduced when required for soup, or other liquids; and, perhaps, even a knife was employed on some occasions, to facilitate the carving of a large joint, which is sometimes done in the East at the present day.

197.　Fig. 1. Ivory spoon, about 4 inches long, in the Berlin　　198.　Of wood, in Mr.
　　　　　　Museum, found with the vases of wood-cut 181.　　　　　　Salt's Collection.
　　　　2. Bronze spoon, in my possession, 8 inches in length.
　　　　3, 4. Bronze spoons, found by Mr. Burton, at Thebes.

The Egyptian spoons were of various forms and sizes. They were principally of ivory, bone, wood, or bronze, and other metals; and in some the handle terminated in a hook, by which, if required, they were suspended to a nail.* Many were ornamented with the lotus flower; the handles of others were made to repre-

* Woodcut 197, *fig.* 2.

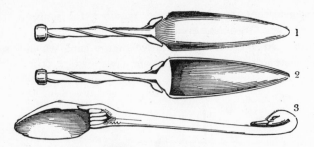

199.   Figs. 1, 2. Front and back of a wooden spoon.
                        3. Ivory spoon.   *Mr. Salt's Collection.*

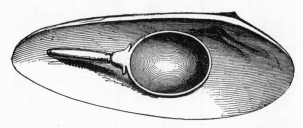

200.   Alabaster shell and spoon.   *Museum of Alnwick Castle.*

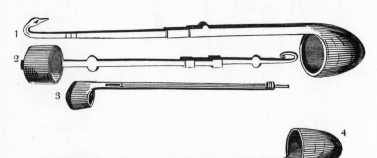

201.   Figs. 1, 2. Bronze simpula in the Berlin Museum.
             3. Of hard wood, in the same Museum.
             4. Bronze simpulum, in my possession, 1 foot 6 inches long.   It has been gilt.

sent an animal, or a human figure; some were of very arbitrary
shape; and a smaller kind, of round form, probably intended for

taking ointment out of a vase, and transferring it to a shell or cup for immediate use, are occasionally discovered in the tombs of Thebes.   One in the Museum of Alnwick Castle is a perfect specimen of these spoons, and is rendered more interesting from having been found with the shell, its companion at the toilet-table.*

Simpula, or ladles, were also common, and many have been found at Thebes.   They were of bronze, frequently gilt, and the curved summit of the handle, terminating in a goose's head, a favourite Egyptian ornament, served to suspend them at the side of a vessel, after having been used for taking a liquid from it; and, judging from a painting on a vase in the Naples Museum, where a priest is represented pouring a libation from a vase with the simpulum, we may conclude this to have been the principal purpose to which they were applied.   The length of some was eighteen inches, and the lower part or ladle nearly three inches deep, and two and a half inches in diameter; but many were much smaller.

Some simpula were made with a joint, or hinge, in the centre of the handle, so that the upper half either folded over the other, or slided down behind it; the extremity of each being furnished with a bar which held them together, at the same time that it allowed the upper one to pass freely up and down (*figs*. 1, 2).   Two of these are preserved in the Berlin Museum.   There is also a ladle of hard wood, found with a case of bottles.   It is very small; the lower part, which may properly be called the handle, being barely more than five inches long, of very delicate workmanship; and the sliding rod, which fits into a groove in the centre of the handle, is about the thickness of a needle (*fig*. 3).

Small strainers, or cullenders, of bronze have also been found at Thebes, about five inches in diameter; and several other utensils.

The Egyptians washed after, as well as before, dinner; an invariable custom throughout the East, as among the Greeks,

* Woodcut 200.

Romans, Hebrews,* and others; and Herodotus speaks of a golden basin, belonging to Amasis, which was used by the King, and "the guests who were in the habit of eating at his table."

An absorbent seems also to have been adopted for scouring the hands; and a powder of ground lupins, the *doqáq* of modern Egypt, is no doubt an old invention, handed down to the present inhabitants.

Soap was not unknown to the ancients, and a small quantity has been found at Pompeii. Pliny, who mentions it as an invention of the Gauls, says it was made of fat and ashes; and Aretæus, the physician of Cappadocia, tells us, that the Greeks borrowed their knowledge of its medicinal properties from the Romans. But there is no evidence of soap having been used by the Egyptians; and if by accident they discovered something of the kind, while engaged with mixtures of natron or potash, and other ingredients, it is probable that it was only an absorbent, without oil or grease, and on a par with steatite, or the argillaceous earths, with which, no doubt, they were long acquainted.

The Egyptians, a scrupulously religious people, were never remiss in expressing their gratitude for the blessings they enjoyed, and in returning thanks to the gods for that peculiar protection they were thought to extend to them and to their country, above all the nations of the earth. They therefore never sat down to meals without saying grace; and Josephus says that when the seventy-two elders were invited by Ptolemy Philadelphus to sup at the palace, Nicanor requested Eleazer to say grace for his countrymen, instead of those Egyptians, to whom that duty was committed on other occasions.

It was also a custom of the Egyptians, during or after their repasts, to introduce a wooden image of Osiris, from one foot and a half to three feet in height, in the form of a human mummy, standing erect, or lying on a bier, and to show it to each of the guests, warning him of his mortality, and the transitory nature of human pleasures. He was reminded that some day he would

* The Pharisees "marvelled that he had not first washed before dinner." Luke xi. 38.

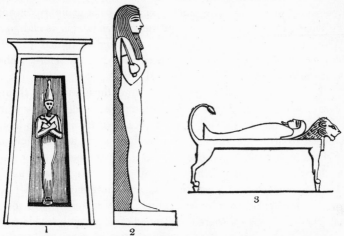

202.   Figure of a mummy in the form of Osiris, brought to an Egyptian table,
and shown to the guests.

be like that figure ; that men ought " to love one another, and
avoid those evils which tend to make them consider life too long,
when in reality it is too short ;" and while enjoying the blessings
of this world, to bear in mind that their existence was precarious,
and that death, which all ought to be prepared to meet, must
eventually close their earthly career.   Thus, while the guests
were permitted, and even encouraged, to indulge in conviviality,
the pleasures of the table, and the mirth so congenial to their
lively disposition, they were exhorted to put a certain degree of
restraint upon their conduct ; and though this sentiment was
perverted by other people, and used as an incentive to present
excesses, it was perfectly consistent with the ideas of the Egyptians to be reminded that this life was only a lodging, or " inn "
on their way, and that their existence here was the preparation
for a future state.

Widely different was the exhortation of Trimalchio, thus given
by Petronius : " To us, who were drinking, and admiring the splendour of the entertainment, a silver model of a man was brought
by a servant, so contrived that its joints and moveable vertebræ
could be bent in any direction.   After it had been produced

upon the table two or three times, and had been made, by means of springs, to assume different attitudes, Trimalchio exclaimed, ' Alas, unhappy lot, how truly man is nought! similar to this shall we all be, when death has carried us away : therefore, while we are allowed to live let us live well.' "

" The ungodly," too, of Solomon's time, thus expressed themselves : " Our life is short and tedious, and in the death of a man there is no remedy ; neither was there any man known to have returned from the grave. For we are born at all adventure, and we shall be hereafter as though we had never been, ... come on, therefore, let us enjoy the good things that are present, ... let us fill ourselves with costly wine and ointments ; and let no flower of the spring pass by us ; let us crown ourselves with rose-buds, before they be withered ; let none of us go without his part of our voluptuousness ; let us leave tokens of our joyfulness in every place." *

But even if the Egyptians, like other men, neglected a good warning, the original object of it was praiseworthy ; and Plutarch expressly states that it was intended to convey a moral lesson. The idea of death had nothing revolting to them ; and so little did the Egyptians object to have it brought before them, that they even introduced the mummy of a deceased relative at their parties, and placed it at table, as one of the guests ; a fact which is recorded by Lucian, in his " Essay on Grief," and of which he declares himself to have been an eyewitness.

After dinner, music and singing were resumed ; hired men and women displayed feats of agility ; swinging each other round by the hand ; throwing up and catching the ball ; or flinging themselves round backwards head-over-heels, in imitation of a wheel ; which was usually a performance of women. They also stood on each other's backs, and made a somerset from that position ; and a necklace, or other reward, was given to the most successful tumbler.

The most usual games within doors were odd and even, *mora*,

* Book of Wisdom, ii. 1, et seq. *Comp*. Is. xxii. 13, and lvi. 12. Eccles. ii. 24. Luke xii. 19, and 1 Cor. xv. 32.

203.   Tumblers. *Fig.* 1, one of four holding the rewards.   *Beni Hassan.*

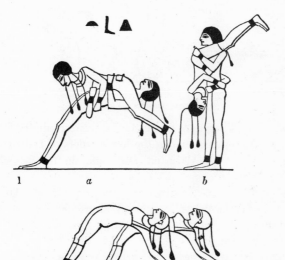

204.   Women tumbling, and performing feats of agility.   *Beni Hassan.*

and draughts ; for the first of which (called by the Romans " ludere
par et impar ") they used bones, nuts, beans, almonds, or shells ;
and any indefinite number was held between the two hands.

   The game of mora was common in ancient as well as modern
Italy, and was played by two persons, who each simultaneously
threw out the fingers of one hand, while one party guessed the

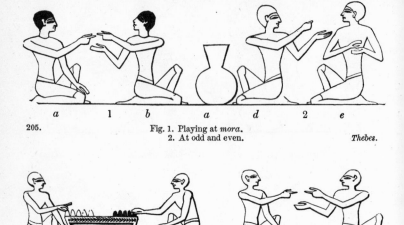

205.

Fig. 1. Playing at *mora*.
2. At odd and even.

Thebes.

206.   Games of draughts and *mora*.   *Beni Hassan.*

sum of both. They were said in Latin, "micare digitis," and this game, still so common among the lower orders of Italians, existed in Egypt, about four thousand years ago, in the reigns of the Osirtasens.

The same, or even a greater, antiquity may be claimed for the game of draughts, or, as it has been erroneously called, chess. As in the two former, the players sat on the ground, or on chairs, and the pieces, or men, being ranged in line at either end of the tables, moved on a chequered board, as in our own chess and draughts.

The pieces were all of the same size and form, though they varied on different boards, some being small, others large with round summits: some were surmounted by human heads; and many were of a lighter and neater shape, like small nine-pins, probably the most fashionable kind, since they were used in the palace of king Remeses. These last seem to have been about one inch and a half high, standing on a circular base of half an inch in diameter; but some are only one inch and a quarter in

207.   Draughtsmen.
        Fig. 1. From the sculptures of Remeses III.
            2. Of wood, and 4, 5, of ivory, in my possession.
            3. Of glazed pottery, from Thebes.

height, and little more than half an inch broad at the lower end. Others have been found, of ivory, one inch and six-eighths high, and one and an eighth in diameter, with a small knob at the top, exactly like those represented at Beni Hassan, and the tombs near the Pyramids (*fig.* 4).

They were about equal in size upon the same board, one set black, the other white or red; or one with round, the other with flat heads, standing on opposite sides;* and each player, raising it with the finger and thumb, advanced his piece towards those of

        * Woodcuts 206, *fig.* 1, and 208, *fig.* 1.

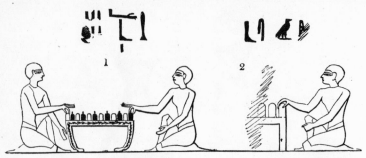

208.   Game of draughts.   *Beni Hassan and Thebes.*

his opponent; but though we are unable to say if this was done in a direct or a diagonal line, there is reason to believe they could not take backwards as in the Polish game of draughts, the men being mixed together on the board.*

It was an amusement common in the houses of the lower classes, as in the mansions of the rich; and king Remeses is himself portrayed on the walls of his palace at Thebes, engaged in the game of draughts with the ladies of his household.

The modern Egyptians have a game of draughts, very similar, in the appearance of the men, to that of their ancestors, which they call *dámeh,* and play much in the same manner as our own.

209.   A game perhaps similar to the Greek *kollabismos.*   *Beni Hassan.*

* As in woodcut 208, *fig.* 1.

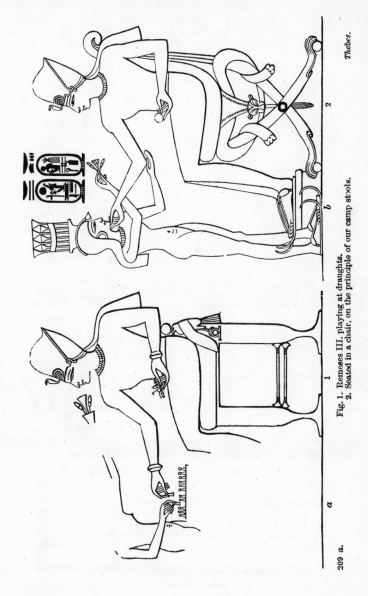

Fig. 1. Remeses III. playing at draughts.
2. Seated in a chair, on the principle of our camp stools.

Thebes.

209 a.

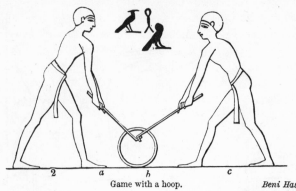

210.   Game with a hoop.   *Beni Hassan.*

211.   Other games.   *Beni Hassan.*

212.   Wooden boards.   *In the Collection of Dr. Abbott.*

Analogous to the game of odd and even was one, in which two of the players held a number of shells, or dice, in their closed hands, over a third person who knelt between them, with his face towards the ground, and who was obliged to guess the combined number ere he could be released from this position.

Another game consisted in endeavouring to snatch from each other a small hoop, by means of hooked rods, probably of metal; and the success of a player seems to have depended on extricating his own from an adversary's rod, and then snatching up the hoop, before he had time to stop it.

There were also two games, of which the boards, with the men, are in the possession of Dr. Abbott. One is eleven inches long by three and a half, and has ten spaces or squares in three rows; the other twelve squares at the upper end (or four squares in three rows) and a long line of eight squares below, forming an approach to the upper part, like the arrangement of German tactics. The men in the drawer of the board are of two shapes, one set ten, the other nine in number.

Other games are represented in the paintings, but not in a manner to render them intelligible; and many, which were doubtless common in Egypt, are omitted both in the tombs, and in the writings of ancient authors.

The dice discovered at Thebes, and other places, may not be of a Pharaonic period, but, from the simplicity of their form, we may suppose them similar to those of the earliest age, in which too the conventional number of six sides had probably always been adopted. They were marked with small circles, representing units, generally with a dot in the centre; and were of bone or ivory, varying slightly in size.

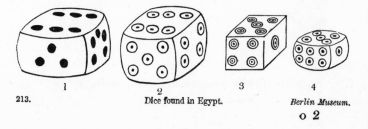

213.

1   2   3   4

Dice found in Egypt.   Berlin Museum.

Plutarch shows that dice were a very early invention in Egypt, and acknowledged to be so by the Egyptians themselves, since they were introduced into one of their oldest mythological fables; Mercury being represented playing at dice with the Moon, previous to the birth of Osiris, and winning from her the five days of the epact, which were added to complete the 365 days of the year.

It is probable that several games of chance were known to the Egyptians, besides dice and *mora*, and, as with the Romans, that many a doubtful mind sought relief in the promise of success, by having recourse to fortuitous combinations of various kinds; and the custom of drawing, or casting lots, was common, at least as early as the period of the Hebrew Exodus.

The games and amusements of children were such as tended to promote health by the exercise of the body, and to divert the mind by laughable entertainments. Throwing and catching the ball, running, leaping, and similar feats, were encouraged, as soon as their age enabled them to indulge in them; and a young

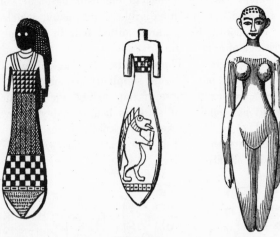

214.   Wooden dolls.

child was amused with painted dolls, whose hands and legs, moving on pins, were made to assume various positions by means of strings. Some of these were of rude form, without legs, or with an imperfect representation of a single arm on one side. Some had numerous beads, in imitation of hair, hanging from the doubtful place of the head; others exhibited a nearer approach to the form of a man; and some, made with considerable attention to proportion, were small models of the human figure. They were coloured according to fancy; and the most shapeless had usually the most gaudy appearance, being intended to catch the eye of an infant. Sometimes a man was figured washing, or kneading dough, who was made to work by pulling a string; and a typhonian monster, or a crocodile, amused a child by its grimaces, or the motion of its opening mouth. In the toy of the crocodile, we have sufficient evidence that the notion of this

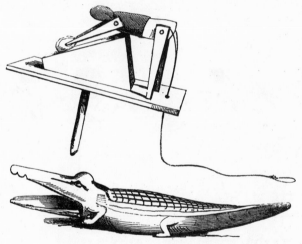

215.   Children's toys.   *Leyden Museum.*

animal " not moving its lower jaw, and being the only creature which brings the upper one down to the lower," is erroneous. Like other animals, it moves the lower jaw *only ;* but when seizing its prey, it throws up its head, which gives an appearance of motion in the upper jaw, and has led to the mistake.

216.   Playing the game of ball mounted on each other's backs.   *Beni Hassan.*

217.   Throwing up and catching one, two, and three balls.   *Beni Hassan.*

The game of ball was of course generally played out of doors. It was not confined to children, nor to one sex, though the mere amusement of throwing and catching it appears to have been considered more particularly adapted to women. They had different modes of playing. Sometimes a person unsuccessful in catching the ball was obliged to suffer another to ride on her

Different positions in the game of ball.

Beni Hassan

1   2   3   4   5   6

218.

back, who continued to enjoy this post until she also missed it:
the ball being thrown by an opposite player, mounted in the
same manner, and placed at a certain distance, according to the

space previously agreed upon; and, from the beast-of-burden office of the person who had failed, the same name was probably applied to her as to those in the Greek game, " who were called ονοι (asses), and were obliged to submit to the commands of the victor."

Sometimes they caught three or more balls in succession, the hands occasionally crossed over the breast; they also threw it up to a height and caught it, like the Greek ουρανια, our " sky ball ;" and the game described by Homer to have been played by Halius and Laodamus, in the presence of Alcinöus, was known to them ; in. which one party threw the ball as high as he could, and the other, leaping up, caught it on its fall, before his feet again touched the ground.

When mounted on the backs of the losing party, the Egyptian women sat sidewise.   Their dress consisted merely of a short petticoat, without a body, the loose upper robe being laid aside on these occasions : it was bound at the waist with a girdle, supported by a strap over the shoulder, and was nearly the same as the undress garb of mourners, worn during the funeral lamentation on the death of a friend.

The balls were made of leather or skin, sewed with string, crosswise, in the same manner as our own, and stuffed with bran, or husks of corn ; and those which have been found at Thebes are about three inches in diameter.   Others were made of string, or of the stalks of rushes, platted together so as to form a circular mass, and covered, like the former, with leather.   They appear also

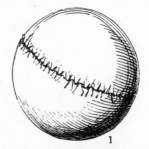

2

1

219.   Fig. 1. Leather ball, three inches in diameter.
                            2. Of painted earthenware.   *From Mr. Salt's Collection.*

to have had a smaller kind of ball, probably of the same materials,
and covered, like many of our own, with slips of leather of a
rhomboidal shape, sewed together longitudinally, and meeting in
a common point at both ends, each alternate slip being of a different colour; but these have only been met with in pottery.

In one of their performances of strength and dexterity, two
men stood together side by side, and, placing one arm for-

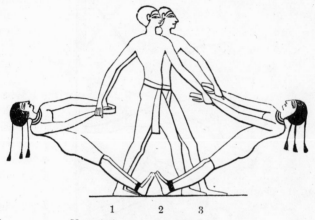

1   2   3

220.   Men swinging women round by the arms.   *Beni Hassan.*

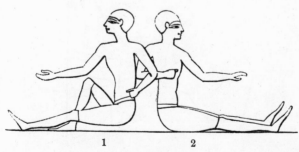

1   2

221.   Rising from the ground.   *Beni Hassan.*

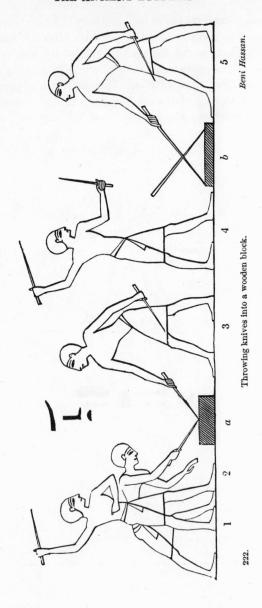

222.   Throwing knives into a wooden block.   Beni Hassan.

ward and the other behind them, held the hands of two women, who reclined backwards, in opposite directions, with their whole weight pressed against each other's feet, and in this position were whirled round ; the hands of the men who held them being occasionally crossed, in order more effectually to guarantee the steadiness of the centre, on which they turned.

Sometimes two men, seated back to back on the ground, at a given signal tried who should rise first from that position, without touching the ground with the hand. And in this, too, there was probably the trial who should first make good his seat upon the ground, from a standing position.

Another game consisted in throwing a knife, or pointed weapon, into a block of wood, in which each player was required to strike his adversary's, or more probably to fix his own in the centre, or at the circumference, of a ring painted on the wood ; and his success depended on being able to ring his weapon most frequently, or approach most closely to the line.

Conjuring appears also to have been known to them, at least thimble-rig, or the game of cups, under which a ball was put,

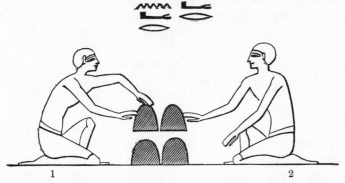

223.   Conjurors, or thimble-rig.   *From the work of Professor Rosellini.*

while the opposite party guessed under which of four it was concealed.

The Egyptian grandees frequently admitted dwarfs, and deformed persons, into their household ; originally, perhaps, from a

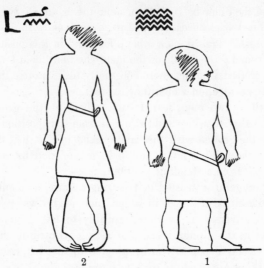

224.   Dwarfs and deformed persons in the service of the Egyptian grandees.

Beni Hassan.

The stone is broken in that part where the hands should be.

humane motive, or from some superstitious regard for men who bore the external character of one of their principal gods, Pthah-Sokari-Osiris, the misshapen Deity of Memphis; but, whatever may have given rise to the custom, it is a singular fact, that already as early as the age of Osirtasen, or about 4000 years ago, the same fancy of attaching these persons to their suite existed among the Egyptians, as at Rome, and even in modern Europe, till a late period.

The games of the lower orders, and of those who sought to invigorate the body by active exercises, consisted of feats of agility and strength. Wrestling was a favourite amusement; and the paintings at Beni Hassan present all the varied attitudes and modes of attack and defence of which it is susceptible. And, in order to enable the spectator more readily to perceive the position of the limbs of each combatant, the artist has availed himself of a dark and light colour, and even ventured to introduce alternately a black and red figure. The subject covers a whole wall;

205

Beni Hassan.

Some of the positions of wrestlers.

Fig. 1. A man holding his girdle.
2. The other binding on his girdle.
Fig. 3, 4. Advancing to the attack.
13, 14. Continuing the attack on the ground.

225.

but the selection of a few groups will suffice to convey an idea of the principal positions of the combatants. (*Woodcut* 225.)

It is probable that, like the Greeks, they anointed the body with oil, when preparing for these exercises, and they were entirely naked, with the exception of a girdle, apparently of leathern thongs.

The two combatants generally approached each other, holding their arms in an inclined position before the body; and each endeavoured to seize his adversary in the manner best suited to his mode of attack. It was allowable to take hold of any part of the body, the head, neck, or legs; and the struggle was frequently continued on the ground, after one or both had fallen; a mode of wrestling common also to the Greeks.

They also fought with the single stick, the hand being apparently protected by a basket, or guard projecting over the knuckles; and on the left arm they wore a straight piece of wood, bound on with straps, serving as a shield to ward off their adversary's blow. They do not, however, appear to have used the *cestus*, nor to have known the art of boxing; though in one group, at Beni Hassan, the combatants appear to strike each other. Nor is there an instance, in any of these contests, of the

226.   Singlestick.   *From the work of Professor Rosellini.*

Greek sign of acknowledging defeat, which was by holding up a finger in token of submission; and it was probably done by the

Egyptians with a word. It is also doubtful if throwing the discus, or quoit, was an Egyptian game; but there appears to be one instance of it, in a king's tomb of the 19th dynasty.

One of their feats of strength, or dexterity, was lifting weights; and bags full of sand were raised with one hand from the ground

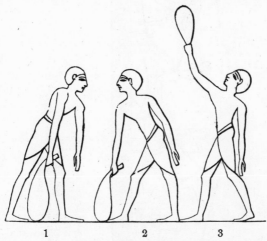

227.   Raising weights.   *From the work of Professor Rosellini.*

and carried with a straight arm over the head, and held in that position.

Mock fights were also an amusement, particularly among those of the military class, who were trained to the fatigues of war, by these manly recreations. One party attacked a temporary fort, and brought up the battering ram, under cover of the testudo; another defended the walls and endeavoured to repel the enemy; others, in two parties of equal numbers, engaged in single stick, or the more usual *nebóot*, a pole wielded with both hands; and the pugnacious spirit of the people is frequently alluded to in the scenes portrayed by their artists.

The use of the *nebóot* seems to have been as common among the ancient, as among the modern, Egyptians; and the quarrels of villages were often decided or increased, as at present, by this

208

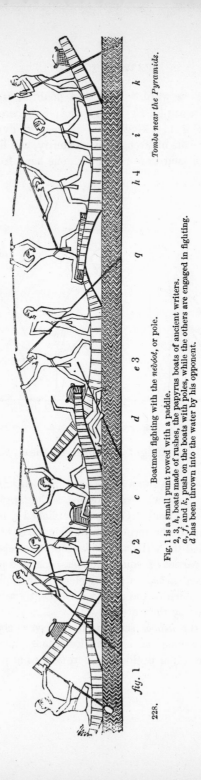

fig. 1   b 2   c   d   e 3   q   h 4   i   k

Tombs near the Pyramids.

Boatmen fighting with the *neboot*, or pole.

Fig. 1 is a small punt rowed with a paddle.
2, 3, *h*, boats made of rushes, the papyrus boats of ancient writers.
a, *f*, and *k*, push on the boats with poles, while the others are engaged in fighting.
d has been thrown into the water by his opponent.

228.

efficient weapon. Crews of boats are also represented attacking each other with the earnestness of real strife. Some are desperately wounded, and, being felled by their more skilful opponents, are thrown headlong into the water; and the truth of Herodotus's assertion, that the heads of the Egyptians were harder than those of other people, seems fully justified by the scenes described by their own draughtsmen. It is fortunate that their successors have inherited this peculiarity, in order to bear the violence of the Turks, and their own combats.

Many singular encounters with sticks are mentioned by ancient authors; among which may be noticed one at Papremis, the city of Mars, described by Herodotus. When the votaries of the deity presented themselves at the gates of the temple, their entrance was obstructed by an opposing party; and all being armed with sticks, they commenced a rude combat, which ended, not merely in the infliction of a few severe wounds, but even, as the historian affirms, in the death of many persons on either side.

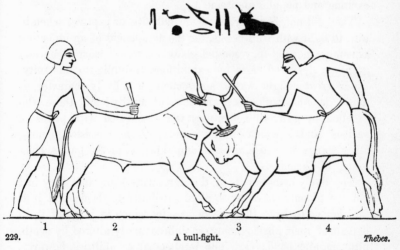

229.   A bull-fight.   *Thebes.*
1   2   3   4

Bull-fights were also among their sports; which were sometimes exhibited in the *dromos*, or avenue, leading to the temples, as at Memphis before the temple of Vulcan; and prizes were

awarded to the owner of the victorious combatant.   Great care
was taken in training them for this purpose ; Strabo says as
much as is usually bestowed on horses ; and herdsmen were not

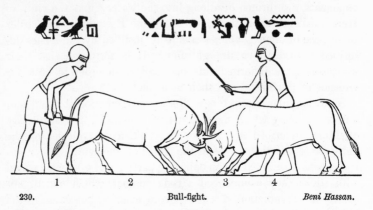

230.   Bull-fight.   *Beni Hassan.*

loth to allow, or encourage, an occasional fight for the love of the
exciting and popular amusement.

They did not, however, condemn culprits, or captives taken in
war, to fight with wild beasts, for the amusement of an unfeeling
assembly ; nor did they compel gladiators to kill each other, and
gratify a depraved taste by exhibitions revolting to humanity.
Their great delight was in amusements of a lively character, as
music, dancing, buffoonery, and feats of agility ; and those who
excelled in gymnastic exercises were rewarded with prizes of
various kinds ; which in the country towns consisted, among
other things, of cattle, dresses, and skins, as in the games celebrated in Chemmis.

The lively amusements of the Egyptians show that they had
not the gloomy character so often attributed to them ; and it is
satisfactory to have these evidences by which to judge of it, in
default of their physiognomy, so unbecomingly altered by death,
bitumen, and bandages.   The intellectual capabilities, however,
of individuals may yet be subject to the decision of the phreno-
logist ; and if they have escaped the ordeal of the *supposed*
spontaneous rotation of a pendulum under a glass bell, their

handwriting is still open to the
criticisms of the wise, who discover by it the most minute secrets
of character ; and some of the old
scribes may even now be amenable
to this kind of scrutiny. But they
are fortunately out of reach of the
surprise, that some in modern days
exhibit, at the exact likeness of
themselves, believed to be presented to them from their own
handwriting by a few clever gene-
ralities; forgetting that the sick
man, in each malady he reads of
in a book of medicine, discovers
his own symptoms, and fancies
they correspond with his own particular case. For though a certain
neatness, or precision, carelessness,
or other habit, may be discovered
by handwriting, to describe from
it all the minutiæ of character is
only feeding the love of the marvellous, so much on the increase
in these days, when a reaction of
credulity bids fair to make nothing
too extravagant for our modern
gobe-mouches.

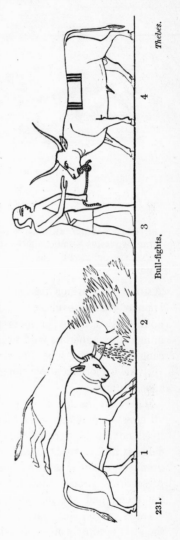

231.   Bull-fights.   Thebes.

View of the Ruins and Vicinity of Philæ.

CHAPTER IV.

THE CHASE — WILD ANIMALS — DOGS — BIRDS — FISHING — CHASE OF THE
HIPPOPOTAMUS — CROCODILE — ITS EGGS — THE TROCHILUS — LIST OF THE
ANIMALS OF EGYPT — BIRDS — PLANTS — EMBLEMS — OFFERINGS — CERE-
MONIES.

AMONG the various pastimes of the Egyptians, none was more
popular than the chase; and the wealthy aristocracy omitted
nothing that could promote their favourite amusement. They
hunted the numerous wild animals in the desert; they had them
caught with nets, to be turned out on some future day; and some
very keen sportsmen took long journeys to spots noted for abundance of game.

The taste, as far as it could be indulged, was general with
all classes; and the peasants hunted down the wild beasts that
lived on the borders of the desert, and invaded the flocks and
fields at night, with the same alacrity as the priestly and military
grandees, or other wealthy land owners, chased the game in their
preserves.   Some shot them with arrows, others laid traps
for them, and various methods were devised for securing the
enemies of the farm-yard.   Watchers and dogs were always on
the alert against wolves and jackals, the poachers of their flocks
and poultry; and when the peasants heard the melancholy howls
and yelping bark of the large packs of jackals, collecting every
evening in anticipation of a foray among the geese, they waited

for their well-known passage through a ravine, on the desert's edge, or longed that some, in spite of Anubis, might fall into their traps.

The hyæna, an enemy of flocks and herds, a gourmand in the flesh of the peasant's very useful donkey, and, when none of these could be had, a very destructive devourer of the crops, was especially hateful; and the agricultural heart rejoiced when a hyæna, caught in a trap, was brought home muzzled, as a harmless spectacle to the children of the village, and a triumph among the neighbours.

232.   Hyæna caught in a trap.   *Thebes.*

When a grand chase took place in the domain of some grandee, or in the extensive tracts of the desert, a retinue of huntsmen, beaters, and others in his service attended, to manage the hounds, to carry the game-baskets and hunting poles, to set the nets, and to make other preparations for a good day's sport. Some took a fresh supply of arrows, a spare bow, and various requisites for remedying accidents; some were merely beaters, others were to assist in securing the large animals caught by the *lasso*, others had to mark or turn the game, and some carried a stock of provisions for the chasseur and his friends. These last were borne upon the usual wooden yoke, across the shoulders, and consisted of a skin of water, and jars of good wine placed in wicker baskets, with bread, meats, and other eatables. The skin used for holding water was precisely the same as that of the present day, being of a goat, or a gazelle, stripped from the body by a longitudinal opening at the throat; the legs serving as handles, to which ropes for slinging them were attached; and a soft pendent tube of leather, sewed to the throat, in the place of the head, formed the mouth of the water skin, which was secured by a thong fastened round it.

Sometimes a portion of the desert, of considerable extent, was enclosed by nets, into which the animals were driven by beaters; and the place chosen for fixing them was, if possible, across narrow valleys, or torrent beds, lying between some rocky hills. Here a sportsman on horseback, or in a chariot, could waylay them, or get within reach with a bow; for many animals, particularly gazelles, when closely pressed by dogs, fear to take a steep ascent, and are easily overtaken, or shot as they double back.

The spots thus enclosed were usually in the vicinity of the water brooks, to which they were in the habit of repairing in the morning and evening : and having awaited the time when they went to drink, and ascertained it by their recent tracks on the accustomed path, the hunters disposed the nets, occupied proper positions for observing them unseen, and gradually closed in upon them. Such are the scenes partially portrayed in the Egyptian paintings, where long nets are represented surrounding the space they hunted in; and the hyænas, jackals, and various wild beasts unconnected with the sport, are intended to show that they have been accidentally enclosed, within the same line of nets with the antelopes and other animals.

In the same way Æneas and Dido repaired to a wood at break of day, after the attendants had surrounded it with a temporary fence, to enclose the game.

The long net was furnished with several ropes, and was supported on forked poles, varying in length, to correspond with the inequalities of the ground, and was so contrived as to enclose any space, by crossing hills, valleys, or streams, and encircling woods, or whatever might present itself; smaller nets for stopping gaps were also used; and a circular snare, set round with wooden or metal nails, and attached by a rope to a log of wood, which was used for catching deer, resembled one still made by the Arabs.

The dresses of the attendants and huntsmen were generally of a suppressed colour, " lest they should be seen at a distance by the animals," tight fitting, and reaching only a short way down the thigh; and the horses of the chariots were divested of the feathers, and showy ornaments, used on other occasions.

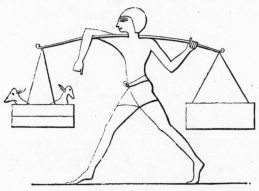

233.   Carrying young animals.   *Tomb near the Pyramids.*

Besides the portions of the open desert and the valleys, which were enclosed for hunting, the parks and covers on their own domains in the valley of the Nile, though of comparatively limited dimensions, offered ample space and opportunity for indulging in the chase; and a quantity of game was kept there; principally the wild goat, oryx, and gazelle.

They had also fishponds, and spacious poultry-yards set apart for keeping geese, and other wild fowl, which they fattened for the table.

It was the duty of the huntsmen, or the gamekeepers, to superintend the preserves; and at proper periods of the year wild fawns were obtained, to increase the herds of gazelles and other animals, which always formed part of the stock of a wealthy Egyptian.

Being fed within pastures enclosed with fences, they were not

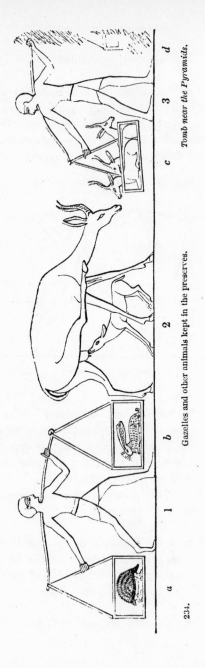

231.

a   1   b   2   c   3   d

Gazelles and other animals kept in the preserves.   *Tomb near the Pyramids.*

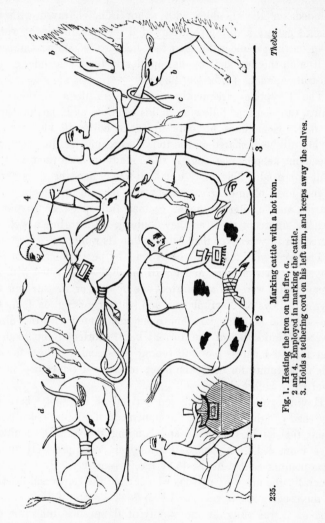

Fig. 1. Heating the iron on the fire, *a*.
2 and 4. Employed in marking the cattle.
3. Holds a tethering cord on his left arm, and keeps away the calves.

Marking cattle with a hot iron.

Thebes.

235.

marked in any particular way like the cattle, which, being let loose, in open meadows, and frequently allowed to mix with the herds of the neighbours, required some distinguishing sign by which they might be recognised. These last were, therefore, branded on the shoulder with a hot iron, engraved with the owner's name; and the paintings of Thebes represent the cattle lying on the ground with their feet tied, while one person heats an iron on the fire, and another applies it to the shoulder of the prostrate animal. (*Woodcut* 235.)

The Egyptians frequently coursed with dogs in the open plains, the chasseur following in his chariot, and the huntsmen on foot. Sometimes he only drove to cover in his car, and having alighted, shared in the toil of searching for the game, his attendants keeping the dogs in slips, ready to start them as soon as it appeared. The more usual custom, when the dogs threw off in a level plain of great extent, was for him to remain in his chariot, and, urging his horses to their full speed, endeavour to turn or intercept them as they doubled, discharging a well directed arrow whenever they came within its range.

The dogs were taken to the ground by persons expressly employed for that purpose, and for all the duties connected with the kennel; and were either started one by one, or in pairs, in the narrow valleys or open plains: and when coursing on foot, the chasseur and his attendant huntsmen, acquainted with the direction and sinuosities of the torrent beds, shortened the road, as they followed across the intervening hills, and sought a favourable opportunity for using the bow; or enjoyed the course in the level space before them.

Having pursued on foot, and arrived at the spot where the dogs had caught their prey, the huntsman, if alone, took up the game, tied its legs together, and hanging it over his shoulders, once more led by his hand the coupled dogs, precisely in the same manner as the Arabs do at the present day. But this was generally the office of persons who carried the cages and baskets on the usual wooden yoke, and who took charge of the game as soon as it was caught; the supply of these substitutes for our game cart being in proportion to the proposed range of the chase, and the number of head they expected to kill. Sometimes an ibex, oryx, or wild ox, being closely pressed by the hounds, faced round and kept them at bay, with its formidable horns, and

236.   A huntsman carrying home the game, with his coupled dogs.   *Thebes.*

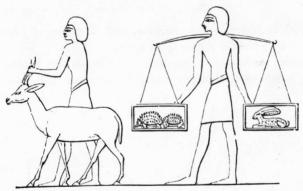

237.   Bringing home the game: a gazelle, porcupines, and hare.   *Beni Hassan.*

the spear of the huntsman, as he came up, was required to decide the success of the chase.

It frequently happened, when the chasseur had many attendants, and the district to be hunted was extensive, that they divided into parties, each taking one or more dogs, and starting them on whatever animal broke cover; sometimes they went without hounds, merely having a small dog for searching the bushes, or laid in wait for the larger and more formidable animals, and attacked them with the lance.

The noose, or *lasso*, was also employed to catch the wild ox, the antelope, and other animals; but this could only be thrown

238.   Catching a gazelle with the noose.   *Beni Hassan.*

by lying in ambush for the purpose, and was principally adopted when they wished to secure them alive.

Besides the bow, the hounds, and the noose, they hunted with lions, which were trained expressly for the chase, like the *cheeta*,

239.   Catching a wild ox with the noose or *lasso*.   *Beni Hassan.*

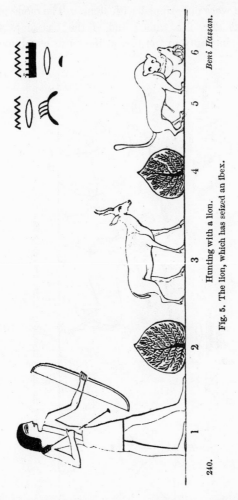

Fig. 5. The lion, which has seized an ibex.

Hunting with a lion.

Beni Hassan.

240.

or hunting leopard of India, being brought up from cubs in a
tame state; and many Egyptian monarchs were accompanied in
battle by a favourite lion. But there is no instance of hawking.

The bow used for the chase was very similar to that employed
in war; the arrows were generally the same, with metal heads,

though some were only tipped with stone. . The mode of drawing
the bow was also the same; and if the chasseurs sometimes
pulled the string only to the breast, the more usual method was

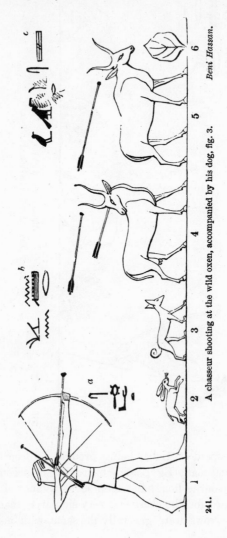

241. A chasseur shooting at the wild oxen, accompanied by his dog, fig. 3. *Beni Hassan.*

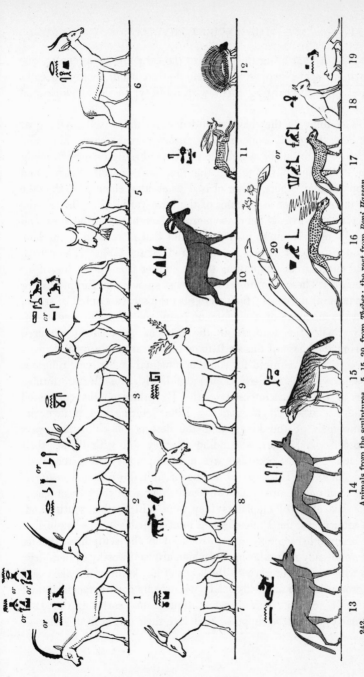

242.

Animals from the sculptures. 5, 15, 20, from *Thebes*; the rest from *Beni Hassan.*

1. The ibex. 2. The oryx. 3, 4. Wild oxen. 5. Humped or Indian ox. 6. Gazelle. 7. Probably the antilope addax. 8. Goat. 9. Stag. 10. The kebsh. 11. Hare. 12. Porcupine. 13. Wolf. 14. Fox. 15. Hyæna. 16, 17. Species of leopard. 18. Cat. 19. Rat. 20. Ichneumon. 10 is coloured red in the paintings: it is the *kebsh*, which is of a sandy colour.

to raise it, and bring the arrow to the ear; and occasionally, one or more spare arrows were held in the hand, to give greater facility in discharging them with rapidity, on the antelopes and wild oxen.

The animals they chiefly hunted were the gazelle, wild goat or *ibex*, the oryx, wild ox, stag, *kebsh* or wild sheep, hare, and porcupine; of all of which the meat was highly esteemed among the delicacies of the table; the fox, jackal, wolf, hyæna, and leopard, and others, being chased as an amusement, for the sake of their skins, or as enemies of the farm-yard. For though the fact of the hyæna being sometimes bought with the ibex and· gazelle might seem to justify the belief that it was also eaten, there is no instance of its being slaughtered for the table. The ostrich held out a great temptation to the hunter from the value of its plumes. These were in great request among the Egyptians for ornamental purposes; they were also the sacred symbol of truth; and the members of the court on grand occasions decked themselves with the feathers of the ostrich. The labour endured during the chase of this swift-footed bird was amply repaid; even its eggs were required for some ornamental or for some religious use (as with the modern Copts); and, with the plumes, formed part of the tribute imposed by the Egyptians on the conquered countries where it abounded. Lion hunting was a favourite amusement of the kings, and the deserts of Ethiopia always afforded good sport, abounding as they did with lions; their success on those occasions was a triumph they often recorded; and Amunoph III. boasted having brought down in one *battue* no less than one hundred and two head, either with the bow or spear. For the chase of elephants they went still further south; and, in after times, the Ptolemies had hunting palaces in Abyssinia.

Many other animals are introduced in the sculptures, besides those already noticed, some of which are well worthy of heraldry; as winged quadrupeds with the heads of hawks, or of a snake; and a crocodile with a hawk's head; with others equally fanciful; and were it not for their great antiquity (as early as the 12th dynasty), might be supposed to derive their origin from Asia.

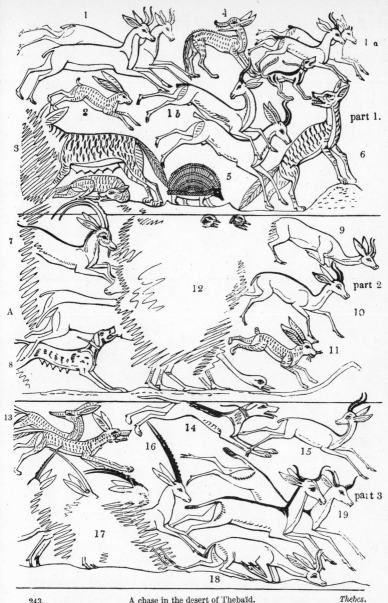

243.   A chase in the desert of Thebaïd.   *Thebes.*

To the left of A was the chasseur in his chariot shooting with the bow, *now defaced.*
Figs. 1, 9, 15, 18. Gazelles. 2, 11. Hares. 3. Female hyæna, with its young. 4, 13. Foxes.
5. Porcupine. 6. Hyæna arrived at the top of a hill, and looking towards the chasseur.
7. The ibex. 8, 14. Hounds. 12. Ostriches (*defaced*). 16. The oryx. 19. Wild oxen.

The Egyptian sphinx was usually an emblematic figure, representative of the king, and may be considered, when with the head of a man and the body of a lion, as the union of intellect and physical force; it is therefore scarcely necessary to observe that it is not female, as that of the Greeks. Besides the ordinary sphinx, compounded of a lion and a man, was one with

244.   Monsters, in the paintings of Beni Hassan and Thebes.

the head of a ram, another with the hawk's head and lion's body, and the asp-headed and the hawk-headed sphinx with wings.

The wild animals now most noted in Egypt, either in the Valley of the Nile, or in the desert, are the gazelle, ibex, *kebsh*, hare, fox, jackal, wolf, hyæna, *jerbóa*, hedgehog, and ichneumon.

The *oryx** is a native of Ethiopia, as is the spotted hyæna or *marafeén;* which last is once represented in the Egyptian sculptures. The oryx has long annulated horns, tapering to a sharp point, and nearly straight, with a slight curve or inclination backwards. It frequently occurs in the sculptures, being among the animals tamed by the Egyptians, and kept in great numbers in their preserves.

The *beïsa* is very like the oryx, except in the black marks upon its face, and a few other points; and the *addax*, another antelope, inhabiting Upper Ethiopia, differs principally from the oryx in its horns, which have a waving or spiral form. It appears to be represented in the sculptures of Beni Hassan.†

The wild ox, which is also of the genus *antilope*, the *defassa* of modern zoologists, though not a native of Egypt, is found in the African desert, and I believe in Eastern Ethiopia; it is of a reddish sandy and grey colour, with a black tuft terminating its tail, and stands about four feet high at the shoulder. At Beni Hassan‡ it is made too much to resemble a common ox, but it is more correctly represented in the Theban sculptures.§

The stag with branching horns,‖ figured at Beni Hassan, is also unknown in the Valley of the Nile; but it is still seen in the vicinity of the Natron Lakes, as about Tunis, though not in the desert between the river and the Red Sea.

The *ibex*,¶ which is common in the Eastern desert, is very similar to the bouquetin of the Alps, and is called in Arabic *Beddan*, or *Táytal*. The former appellation is exclusively applied to the male, which is readily distinguished by a beard and large knotted horns, curving backwards over its body; the female having short erect horns, scarcely larger than those of the gazelle, and being of a much smaller and lighter structure.

The *kebsh*, or wild sheep, is found in the Eastern desert,

* Woodcut 242, *fig.* 2.   † Woodcut 242, *fig.* 7.
  ‡ Woodcut 241, *figs.* 4 and 5.   § Woodcut 243, *fig.* 19.
‖ Woodcut 242, *fig.* 9.   ¶ Woodcut 242, *fig.* 1; 243, *fig.* 7.

Q 2

principally in the ranges of primitive mountains, which, commencing about latitude 28° 40′, at the back of the limestone hills of the Valley of the Nile, extend thence into Ethiopia and Abyssinia. The female kebsh is between two and three feet high at the shoulder, and its total length from the tail to the end of the nose is a little more than four feet: but the male is larger, and is provided with stronger horns, which are about five inches in diameter at the roots, and are curved backwards on each side of the neck. The whole body is covered with hair, like many of the Ethiopian sheep, and the throat and thighs of the fore legs are furnished with a long pendent mane; a peculiarity not omitted in the sculptures, and which suffices to prove the identity of the kebsh, wherever its figure is represented. (*Woodcut* 242, *fig*. 10.)

The porcupine is no longer a native of Egypt; nor is the leopard met with on this side of Upper Ethiopia. Bears are altogether unknown, and, if they occur twice in the paintings of the Theban tombs, they are only brought by foreigners, together with the productions of their country, which were deemed rare and curious to the Egyptians.

The wolf is common, and, as Herodotus says, "scarcely larger than a fox;" and the tombs in the mountain above Lycopolis, the modern O'Sioot, contain the mummies of wolves, which were the sacred animals of the place.

The Egyptian hare is a native of the Valley of the Nile, as well as of the two deserts; and is remarkable for the length of its ears, which the Egyptians have not failed to indicate in their sculptures. It is a smaller species than those of Europe; which accords with Denon's remark on the comparative size of animals common to Egypt and Europe, that the former are always smaller than our own.

The *wabber* or *hyrax*, though a native of the eastern desert of Egypt, is not represented in the sculptures; but this is probably owing to its habits, and to their hunting principally in the valleys of the secondary mountains; the wabber only venturing a short distance from its burrow in the evening, and living in the primitive ranges where the *sealeh* or acacia grows. It was probably the *saphan* of the Bible, as Bruce has remarked, and that enterprising traveller is perfectly correct in placing it among ruminating animals. The hedgehog was always common, as at present, in the Valley of the Nile.

The lion is now unknown to the north of Upper Ethiopia: there, however, it is common, as well as the leopard, and other carnivorous beasts; and the abundance of sheep in those districts amply supplies them with food, and has the happy tendency of rendering them less dangerous to man. In ancient times, however, the lion inhabited the deserts of Egypt, and Athenæus mentions one killed by the Emperor Adrian, while hunting near Alexandria. They are even said, in former times, to have been found in Syria, and in Greece.

Among the animals confined to the Valley of the Nile, and its immediate vicinity, may be mentioned the ichneumon, which lives principally in Lower Egypt and the Fyoom, and which, from its enmity to serpents, was looked upon by the Egyptians with great respect. Its dexterity in attacking the snake is truly surprising. It seizes the enemy at the back of the neck, as soon as it perceives it rising to the attack, one firm bite sufficing to destroy it; and when wounded by the venomous fangs of its opponent, it is said by the Arabs to have recourse to some herb, which checks the effect of the deadly poison.

The ichneumon is easily tamed, and is sometimes seen in the houses of Cairo, where, in its hostility to rats, it performs all the duties of a cat; but, from its indiscriminate fondness for eggs, poultry, and many other requisites for the kitchen, it is generally reckoned troublesome, and I have often found reason to complain of those I kept.

Eggs are its favourite food, and it is said to have been greatly venerated by those who held the crocodile in abhorrence, in consequence of its destroying the eggs of that hateful animal: but it is now rarely met with in places where the crocodile abounds; and at all periods its principal recommendation was its hostility to serpents. It is frequently seen in the paintings, where its habits are distinctly alluded to by the Egyptian artists, who represent it in search of eggs, among the bushes, and the usual resorts of the feathered tribe.

The wild cat, the *felis chaus* of Linnæus, is common in the vicinity of the Pyramids and Heliopolis, but it does not occur among the pictured animals of ancient Egypt. Nor is the *jerbóa*, so frequently met with both in the upper and lower country, represented in the sculptures.

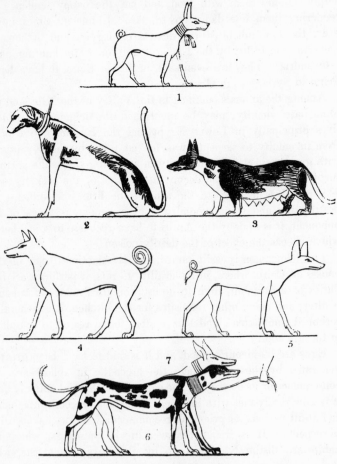

245.   Various kinds of dogs, from the sculptures.

The giraffe was not a native of Egypt, but of Ethiopia, and is only introduced in subjects which relate to that country, where it is brought with apes, rare woods, and other native productions, as part of the tribute annually paid to the Pharaohs.

The Egyptians had several breeds of dogs, some solely used for the chase, others admitted into the parlour, or as companions of their walks; and some, as at the present day, were chosen for their peculiar ugliness. The most common kinds were a sort of fox-dog, and a hound ; they had also a short-legged dog, not unlike our turnspit, which was a great favourite, especially in the reigns of the Osirtasens ; and, as in later days, the choice of a king, or some noted personage, brought a particular breed into fashion.

Mummies of the fox-dog are common in Upper Egypt; and this was doubtless the parent stock of the modern red wild dog of Egypt, so common in Cairo, and other parts of the lower country.

Pigs, though an abomination to the Egyptians, formed part of a farmer's stock; but, attentive to the habits of animals, they allowed them to range and feed out of doors, under the care of a herdsman; knowing that cleanliness is as beneficial for, as the confinement in a sty is contrary to, the nature of a pig.

Their cattle were of different kinds; the most common being the short and long horned varieties, and the Indian or humped ox ; and the two last, though no longer natives of Egypt, are common in Abyssinia and Upper Ethiopia. The buffalo, which abounds in Abyssinia and in modern Egypt, is never represented on the monuments.

Horses and asses were abundant, and the latter were employed as beasts of burden, for treading out corn (particularly in Lower Egypt) and for many other purposes. Like those of the present day, they were small, active, and capable of bearing great fatigue ; and, as these hardy animals were maintained at a very trifling expense, their numbers in the agricultural districts were very great, and one individual had as many as seven hundred and sixty employed on different parts of his estate.

246.   Some of the birds of Egypt.   *Beni Hassan and the Tombs near the Pyramids.*
            Figs. 18, 19, 20. Bats. 21. The locust.   *From Thebes.*

Some of the birds of Egypt. *Beni Hassan.*

Egyptian horses were greatly esteemed; they were even exported to the neighbouring countries, and Solomon bought them at a hundred and fifty shekels of silver, from the merchants who traded with Egypt by the Syrian Desert.

It is remarkable that the camel, though known in Egypt as early at least as the time of Abraham (being among the presents given by Pharaoh to the Patriarch), has never been met with, even in the latest paintings or hieroglyphics. Yet this does not prove it was even rare in the country; since the same would apply to fowls and pigeons, of which no instance occurs on the monuments among the stock of the farmyard. Cocks and hens, however, as well as horses, appear to have come originally from Asia.

The birds of Egypt were very numerous, especially wild fowl, which abounded on the lakes and marsh-land of the Delta; they also frequented the large pieces of water on the estates of the rich landed proprietors, in all parts of the country.

Large flights of quails afforded excellent sport at certain seasons, and the bustard and other birds, found on the edge of the desert, were highly prized for the table.

Many are represented by the Egyptian sculptors; some sacred, others that served for food; and in the tombs of Thebes and Beni Hassan, the Egyptians have not omitted to notice bats, and even some of the insects that abound in the Valley of the Nile; and the well-known locust, the butterfly, and the beetle are introduced in the fowling and fishing scenes, and in sacred subjects. (*Woodcuts* 246, 249, 250, 251.)

Fowling was one of the great amusements of all classes. Those who followed this sport for their livelihood used nets and traps; but the amateur sportsman pursued his game in the thickets, and felled them with the throw-stick, priding himself on his dexterity in its use. The bow was not employed for this purpose, nor was the sling adopted, except by gardeners and peasants, to frighten the birds from the vineyards and fields. The throw-stick was made of heavy wood, and flat, so as to offer little resistance to the air in its flight; and the distance to which

248.   A sportsman using the throw-stick.   *Thebes.*
Figs. 2 and 3. His sister and daughter.   4. A decoy bird.   5, 5. Birds struck with the stick.

Williams de'.

an expert arm could throw it was considerable; though they always endeavoured to approach the birds as near as possible, under cover of the bushes and reeds. It was from one foot and a quarter to two feet in length, and about one and a half inch in breadth, slightly curved at the upper end; but in no instance had it the round shape and flight of the Australian *boomerang*.

On their fowling excursions, they usually proceeded with a party of friends and attendants, sometimes accompanied by the members of their family, and even by their young children, to the jungles and thickets of the marsh-lands, or to the lakes of their own grounds, which, especially during the inundation, abounded with wild fowl; and seated in punts made of the papyrus, they glided, without disturbing the birds, amidst the lofty reeds that grew in the water, and masked their approach. This sort of boat was either towed, pushed by a pole, or propelled by paddles, and the Egyptians fancied that persons who used it were secure from the attacks of crocodiles.

The attendants collected the game as it fell, and one of them was always ready to hand a fresh stick to the chasseur, as soon as he had thrown. They frequently took with them a decoy-bird; and in order to keep it to its post, a female was selected, whose nest, containing eggs, was deposited in the boat.

249.   Sportsman using the throw-stick.   *British Museum.*
Fig. 2 keeps the boat steady by holding the stalks of a lotus.   4. A cat se izing the game in
the thicket.   5. A decoy-bird.

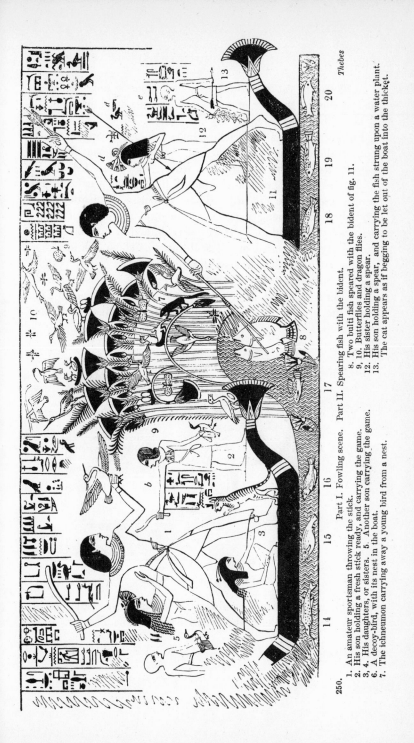

250.   Part I. Fowling scene.   Part II. Spearing fish with the bident.

1.   An amateur sportsman throwing the stick.
2.   His son holding a fresh stick ready, and carrying the game.
3, 4.   His daughters, or sisters.   5.   Another son carrying the game.
6.   A decoy-bird, with its nest in the boat.
7.   The ichneumon carrying away a young bird from a nest.
8.   Two bulti fish speared with the bident of fig. 11.
9, 10.   Butterflies and dragon flies.
12.   His sister holding a spear.
13.   His son holding a spear, and carrying the fish strung upon a water plant.
      The cat appears as if begging to be let out of the boat into the thicket.

Thebes

A favourite cat sometimes attended them on these occasions, and performed the part of a retriever, amidst the thickets on the bank. (*Woodcut* 249, *fig.* 4.)

Fishing was also a favourite pastime of the Egyptian gentleman; both in the Nile and in the spacious "sluices, or ponds for fish,"* constructed within his grounds, where they were fed for the table, and where he amused himself by angling,† and the dexterous use of the *bident*.‡ These favourite occupations were not confined to young persons, nor thought unworthy of men of serious habits; and an Egyptian of rank, and of a certain age, is frequently represented in the sculptures catching fish in a canal or lake, with the line, or spearing them as they glided past the bank. Sometimes the angler posted himself in a shady spot by the water's edge, and, having ordered his servants to spread a mat upon the ground, sat upon it as he threw his line; and some,

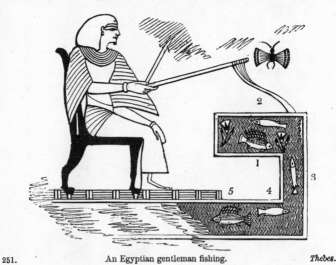

251.   An Egyptian gentleman fishing.   *Thebes.*

with higher notions of comfort, used a chair; as "stout gentlemen" now do in punts, upon retired parts of the Thames.

* Isaiah xix. 10.   † Isaiah xix. 8.   ‡ Woodcut 250, *fig.* 11.

The rod was short, and apparently of one piece; the line usually single, though instances occur of a double line, each with its own hook, which was of bronze. In all cases they adopted a ground bait, as is still the custom in Egypt, without any float; and though several winged insects are represented in the paintings hovering over the water, it does not appear that they ever put them to the hook; and still less that they had devised any method similar to our artificial-fly fishing; which is still as unknown to the unsophisticated modern Egyptians as to their fish.

To spear them with the bident was thought the most sportsmanlike way of killing fish. In throwing it they sometimes stood on the bank, but generally used the papyrus punt, gliding smoothly over the water of a lake in their grounds, without disturbing the fish as they lay beneath the broad leaves of the lotus. Those who were very keen sportsmen even made parties to the lowlands of the Delta; as they did at other times, for shooting, to the highlands of the desert.

The bident was a spear with two barbed points, which was either thrust at the fish with one or both hands as they passed by, or was darted to a short distance; a long line fastened to it preventing its being lost, and serving to recover it with the fish when struck. It was occasionally furnished with feathers like an arrow, and sometimes a common spear was used for the purpose; but in most cases it was provided with a line, the end of which was held by the left hand, or wound upon a reel. This mode of fishing is still adopted in many countries; and the fish-spears of the South Sea islanders have two, three, and four points, and are thrown nearly in the same manner as the bident of the ancient Egyptians. Their attendants, or their children, assisted in securing the fish, which, when taken off the barbed point of the spear, were tied together by the stalk of a rush passed through the gills. (*Woodcut* 250, *fig.* 13.)

The chase of the hippopotamus was a favourite amusement of the sportsman; for it then frequented Lower Egypt, though now confined to Upper Ethiopia. Like the crocodile, it was looked upon as an enemy, from the ravages it committed at night in the fields; and was also killed for its hide, of which they made shields, whips, javelins, and helmets.

252.   *Thebes.*
Attendant carrying a whip, or *corbág.*

The whips, known by the name of *corbág* (*corbaj*), are still very generally used in Egypt and Ethiopia, in riding the dromedary, or for chastising a delinquent peasant; for which purposes it was applied by the ancient Egyptians; and an attendant sometimes followed the steward of an estate, with this implement of punishment in his hand.

The mode of attacking and securing the hippopotamus appears, from the sculptures of Thebes, to have been very similar to that now adopted about Sennar; where, like the ancient Egyptians, they prefer chasing it in the river, to an open attack on shore: and the modern Ethiopians are contented to frighten it from the corn-fields by the sound of drums and other noisy instruments.

It was entangled by a running noose, at the extremity of a long rope wound upon a reel, at the same time that it was struck by a spear. This weapon consisted of a broad flat blade, furnished with a deep tooth, or barb, at the side; having a strong line of considerable length attached to its upper end, and running over the notched summit of a wooden shaft, which was inserted into the head, or blade, like a common javelin. It was thrown in the same manner; but, on striking, the shaft fell, and the iron head alone remained in the body of the animal; which, on receiving a wound, plunged into deep water, the line having been immediately let out. When fatigued by exertion, the hippopotamus was dragged to the boat, from which it again plunged, and the same was repeated till it became perfectly exhausted; frequently receiving additional wounds, and being entangled by

other nooses, which the attendants held in readiness, as it was
brought within their reach.

253.   Spear used in the chase of the hippopotamus.   *Thebes.*

The line attached to the blade was also wound upon a reel,
generally carried by some of the attendants, which was of very
simple construction, consisting of a half ring
of metal, as a handle, and the bar turning
in it, on which the line was wound.

Neither the hippopotamus nor the crocodile were used as food by the ancient Egyptians; but the people of Apollinopolis ate
the crocodile, upon a certain occasion, in
order to show their abhorrence of Typho,
the evil genius, of whom it was an emblem.
" They had also a solemn hunt of this animal
upon a particular day, set apart for the purpose, at which time they killed as many of them
as they could, and afterwards threw their dead
bodies before the temple of their god, assigning this reason for

254. A reel held by an
attendant. *Beni Hassan.*

their practice, that it was in the shape of a crocodile Typho eluded the pursuit of Orus."

In some parts of Egypt it was sacred, "while in other places they made war upon it; and those who lived about Thebes and the Lake Mœris (in the Arsinoïte nome) held it in great veneration."

It was there treated with the most marked respect, and kept at a considerable expense; it was fed and attended with the most scrupulous care; geese, fish, and various meats were dressed purposely for it; they ornamented its head with ear-rings, its feet with bracelets, and its neck with necklaces of gold and artificial stones; it was rendered perfectly tame by kind treatment; and after death its body was embalmed in a most sumptuous manner. This was particularly the case in the Theban, Ombite, and Arsinoïte nomes; and at a place now called Maabdeh, opposite the modern town of Manfaloot, are extensive grottoes, cut far into the limestone mountain, where numerous crocodile mummies have been found, perfectly preserved, and evidently embalmed with great care.

The people of Apollinopolis, Tentyris, Heracleopolis, and other places, on the contrary, held the crocodile in abhorrence, and lost no opportunity of destroying it; and the Tentyrites were so expert, from long habit, in catching, and even in overcoming this powerful animal in the water, that they were known to follow it into the Nile, and bring it by force to the shore. Pliny and others mention the wonderful feats performed by them, not only in their own country, but in the presence of the Roman people: and Strabo says that on the occasion of some crocodiles being exhibited at Rome, the Tentyrites, who were present, fully confirmed the truth of the report of their power over those animals; for, having put them into a spacious tank of water, with a shelving bank artificially constructed at one side, the men boldly entered the water, and, entangling them in a net, dragged them to the bank, and back again into the water; which was witnessed by numerous spectators.

The crocodile is in fact a timid animal, flying on the approach of man; and little danger need be apprehended from it, except by any one incautiously standing on a sloping bank of sand near the river, when it can approach unseen. Egypt produces two varieties, distinguished by the number and position of the scales on the neck, and by one being black, the other of a greener colour. They do not exceed eighteen or twenty feet, though travellers have mentioned some of awful size. The story of the " *trochilus* " entering its mouth as it sleeps on the sandbanks, and relieving it of the leeches in its throat, would be " remarkable, if true " that any leeches existed in the Nile; but the friendly offices of this winged toothpick may have originated in the habits of the small " *running bird*," a species of *charadrius*, or dottrel, so common there; which, by its shrill cry on the approach of man, warns the crocodile (quite unintentionally) of its danger. And its proximity to the crocodile is readily explained by its seeking the flies and other insects, that are attracted to the sleeping beast.

255.   The Trochilus, or Charadrius melanocephalus, Linn.

The eggs of the crocodile are remarkably small; only three inches long, by two in breadth (or diameter); being less than those of a goose. They are equally thick at each end. They are laid in the sand, till hatched by the warmth of the sun; and the small crocodile, curled up with its tail to its nose, awaits the time for breaking the shell. But the ichneumon is far more dangerous to the eggs, than the trochilus is useful to their parents; and its destruction of the unhatched young obtained for it great veneration in those places where the crocodile was not held sacred.

There were various modes of catching it. One was " to fasten a piece of pork to a hook, and throw it into the middle of the stream, as a bait; then, standing near the water's edge, they beat a young pig, and the crocodile, being enticed to the spot by its cries, found the bait on its way, and, swallowing it, was caught by the hook. It was then pulled ashore, and its eyes being quickly covered up with mud, it was easily overcome."

It is singular that the wild boar is never represented among the animals of Egypt, though a native of the country, and still frequenting the Fyoom and the Delta. It is even eaten at the present day, in spite of the religious prejudices of the Moslems, by some of the people about Damietta. Even if it never inhabited Upper Egypt, it ought to be figured in some of the fowling and hunting scenes, which relate to the marsh lands of the Delta; and the fabled chase of it by Typho shows it was known in Egypt at the earliest times. Nor is the wild ass met with in the paintings either of Upper or Lower Egypt, though it is common in the deserts of the Thebaïd; and other animals have already been shown to be wanting in the sculptures. We are, therefore, more reconciled, by these omissions, to the absence of several from the monuments, which appear in all probability to have existed in the country.

And here it may not be out of place to give a list of the different animals, birds, reptiles, fish, and plants; noticing at the same time those that were sacred, and adding an account of the emblems connected with the religion.

256.   257.   a.   b.   c.   d.

The name of "Egypt."

Div. I.—VERTEBRATA.

Class I.—MAMMALIA.

Name.	If sacred.	To what Deity.	In what Place (particularly).	Where mentioned.	Where found embalmed.
Orders 1 and 2.					
BIMANA AND QUADRUMANA.					
Cynocephalus Ape	Sacred	Thoth	Hermopolis	The sculptures. Strabo, xvii. Horapollo, i. 15, 16.	Thebes and Hermopolis.
Green Monkey of Ethiopia, or *Cercopithecus*?	Sacred	Thoth?	At Thebes?	Juvenal, Sat. xv. 4. Sculptures	Thebes.
Order 3.					
CARNARIA.					
Bat	Not sacred				
Hedgehog	Not sacred			Sculptures.	
Shrew-mouse, or *Mygale*	Sacred	Buto or Latona	Athribis, Butos	Represented in ornaments. Strabo, xv. Herodot. ii. 59.	Thebes.
Bear	Not sacred		Not found in Egypt.	Herodot. ii. 67; and sculptures.	
Weasel	Not sacred			Plutarch de Is. s. 74.	
Otter	Not sacred		Not found in Egypt.	Herodotus, ii. 72.	
Dog	Sacred	Anubis?	Cynopolis	Plut., Plato, &c.	Thebes, El Harcib, &c.
Wolf	Sacred	Anubis?	Lycopolis	Strabo, xvii. Plut. s. 72; and sculptures	Lycopolis.
Fox	Sacred?	Anubis?	Lycopolis?		

Name.	If sacred.	To what Deity.	In what Place (particularly).	Where mentioned.	Where found embalmed.
CARNARIA—*continued.*					
Jackal	Sacred	Anubis	Lycopolis ?	Sculptures.	Lycopolis.
Ichneumon	Sacred		Heracleopolis	Clem. Alex. Orat. Adhort. p. 17. Strabo, xvii.; and sculptures.	
Hyaena vulgaris	Not sacred			In sculptures.	
Spotted Hyaena, or *Crocuta*	Not sacred.				
Cat	Sacred	Pasht or Bubastis	Bubastis	Cicero, Diodor., &c.; and sculptures.	} Thebes, &c.
Lion	Sacred	Gom or Hercules	Leontopolis	Strabo, xvii. Diodor. i. 84. Porphyr. de Abst. iv. 9.	
Panther	Not sacred			Sculptures.	
Leopard	Not sacred				
Felis Chaus	Not sacred.				
Order 5.					
RODENTIA.					
Mouse	Not sacred			Sculptures. Plin. x. 65.	Thebes.
Rat	Not sacred				Thebes.
Dipus, or *Jerboa*	Not sacred.				
Porcupine	Not sacred			Sculptures.	
Hare	Not sacred. An emblem			Sculptures. Horapollo.	
Order 7.					
PACHYDERMATA.					
Elephant	Not sacred			Sculptures.	
Hippopotamus	Sacred Emblem of Typho	Mars of Typho	Papremis	Herodot. ii. 71. Diodor., &c.	Thebes ?

Pig . . .	Emblem	of Typho		Plut., Ælian, Herodot., &c. Plut. de Is. s. 8.	
Wild Boar . .	Not sacred				
Hyrax (Arab. *Wabber*) .	Not sacred.			Sculptures, &c.	
Horse . . .	Not sacred.			Plutarch.	
Ass . . .	Sacred to, or emblem of	} Typho			
Order 8. **RUMINANTIA.**					
Camel . . .	Not sacred				
Stag, or *Cervus Elaphus* .	Not sacred			*Vide suprà,* p. 234. *Vide suprà,* p. 227.	
Camelopardalis, or Giraffe	Not sacred? perhaps an emblem .	}		Sculptures at Hermonthis, &c.	At Thebes?
Gazelle . . .	Not sacred?				
Antilope Addax ? .	Not sacred				
— *Defassa* .					
Oryx Beisa . .				Sculptures.	
Oryx and *Leucoryx* .	An emblem	{ of Pthah-Sokari-Osiris.	} Thebes, &c.	Plin. ii. 40. Sculptures.	
Goat . . .	Sacred	Mendes ? .	{ Mendesian nome ?	Clem. Orat. Adhort. p. 17; and Strabo, xvii. Diodor. i. 84.	
Ibex . . .	Not sacred			Sculptures.	
Sheep, Ram . .	Sacred		{ Thebes and Saïs	Clem. Alex. Oratio Adhort., p. 17. Strabo, xvii. p. 559 and 552 . .	} Thebes, &c.
Kebsh, or *Ovis Tragelaphus* . .	Not sacred			Sculptures.	

Name.	If sacred.	To what Deity.	In what Place (particularly).	Where mentioned.	Where found embalmed.
RUMINANTIA—continued.					
Cow	Sacred	Athor		Sculptures	Thebes, &c.
The Sacred Bulls.					
Apis	Sacred	A God, and the type of Osiris	Memphis	Plut. Herodot. Diodor. i. 84 and 21.	
Mnevis	Sacred	The Sun, or Apollo	Heliopolis	Diodor. i. 84 and 21. Plut. s. 33.	
Basis, Bacchis	Sacred		Hermonthis	Macrob. Sat. i. 26. Strabo, xvii. Ælian, xii. 11.	
Onuphis	Sacred			Not represented.	
Buffalo	Not sacred			Sculptures.	
Indian or humped Ethiopian Ox	Not sacred ?				
Order 9.					
CETACEA.					
Dolphin	Not sacred			Strabo, xvii. Plin. & Seneca.	
FABULOUS ANIMALS.					
Sphinx {with Man's head, Hawk's head, Ram's head.				Sculptures. Clemens, &c.	
Other monsters				Sculptures.	

The principal Birds are—

Class II.—AVES.

Name.	Sacred to what Deity.	In what Place.	Where mentioned.	Where found embalmed.
Order 1.				
ACCIPITRES, or RAPTORES.				
Vultur Nubicus, or *Barbarus* (*Arab.* the *Nisser*)	Sacred to Eileithyia	At Eileithyias	Sculptures	Thebes.
V. percnopterus, Pharaoh's Hen (*Arab. Rákham*)	?	.	Sculptures.	
Eagle (*Arab. Okáb* or *Ogáb*)	Sacred?	In Thebes?	Strabo, xvii. Diodor. i. 87.	
Falco Aroeris? the sacred Hawk of Re	Sacred to Re, and other Deities	Heliopolis, and other towns	Diodor., Strabo, and others; and the sculptures	Thebes, &c.
F. tenunculoides, or small brown Hawk	?	.	Sculptures	Thebes.
Falco miluus (*F. cinereo-ferugineus*, Forsk., *F. arda* of Savigny), the Kite	Not sacred?	.	Sculptures.	
Horned Owl, or *Bubo maximus*	Not sacred?	.	Sculptures	Thebes.
White Owl, or *Strix flammea*	?	.	Sculptures	Thebes.
Small Owl, or *Strix passerina*, Minerva's Owl	?	.	Sculptures.	

Name.	Sacred to what Deity.	In what Place.	Where mentioned.	Where found embalmed.
Order 2.				
INSESSORES, or PASSERINÆ.				
Lanius excubitor, Butcher Bird.	Not sacred		Sculptures ?	
Motacilla, alba and *flava*, Wag-tail	Not sacred		Sculptures	
Swallow	Not sacred	•	Sculptures	
Sparrow	Not sacred		Horapollo, ii. 115.	Thebes.
Raven, or *Corvus corax*	Not sacred		Sculptures.	
C. cornix, the Royston Crow	Not sacred		Sculptures.	Horapollo.
Upupa epops	Not sacred		Sculptures ?	Horapollo.
Turdus viscivorus, Thrush	Not sacred		Sculptures ?	
Alauda cristata, Crested Lark	Not sacred		Sculptures ?	
Alauda arenaria, Sand Lark	Not sacred	•	Sculptures ?	
Hirundo rustica, Swallow	Not sacred		Sculptures ?	
Alcedo Ispida, Kingfisher	Not sacred		Sculptures ?	
Alcedo Rutteis, id. of the Nile	Not sacred		Sculptures ?	
Fringilla, several species	Not sacred		Sculptures ?	
Order 3.				
RASORES, or GALLINACEÆ.				
Fowls, Cocks	White and saffron-coloured cocks sacrificed to Anubis	•	Plut. de Is. s. 61.	
Columba turtur, Turtle-dove	Not sacred	•	Sculptures.	
Columba domestica, Pigeon	Not sacred		Sculptures.	
Pterocles melanogaster (*Arab.* *Gutta*), Sand-grouse	Not sacred	•	Sculptures ?	
Quail, *Perdix Coturnix*	Not sacred		Sculptures.	
Ostrich, or *Struthio Camelus*	Not sacred		Sculptures.	
Otis Hebara, Ruffed Bustard	Not sacred	•	Sculptures ?	

Order 4.				
GRALLATORIÆ.				
Charadrius Œdicnemus .	Not sacred .	•	Sculptures ?	
—— (*Trochilus?*), or *Melanocephalus* .	Not sacred ?	•	Herodot. ii. 68.	
—— *armatus,* Spurwinged Plover . —— *cristatus,* Peewit	Not sacred .	•	Sculptures ?	
Ardea cinerea, Grey Heron .	Not sacred ?	•	Sculptures.	
Ardea garzetta, Little Egret, perhaps the Benno, which was	sacred to Osiris		Sculptures.	
Ardea minuta, small Bittern . *Ciconia alba,* White Stork . *Grus cinerea,* Common Crane, and some other species .	Not sacred .	•	Sculptures.	
Tantulus, or *Numenius Ibis,* or *Ibis religiosa,* Cuv. .	Sacred to Thoth	Hermopolis •	{ Herodot., Plato, &c.; and sculptures . . . . }	{ Thebes, Memphis, Hermopolis, Abydus, &c. }
Ibis falcinellus, small Ibis . *Plataleu leucorodia,* Spoonbill . *Scolopax gallinago,* Snipe .	Not sacred .	•	Sculptures ?	
Fulica atra, Common Coot . *Phœnicopterus ruber,* Flamingo .	Not sacred.	•	Sculptures.	
Order 5.				
NATATORES, or PALMIPEDES.				
Goose, or *Anser Ægyptius,* the *Chenalopex,* or *Vulpanser* .	Emblem of Seb.	•	Herodot. ii. 72. Sculptures	Thebes.
Anas, various species of Ducks .	Not sacred .	•	Sculptures.	
Anas creca, Teal .	Not sacred ?	•	Horapollo. Sculptures.	
Pelicanus Onocratulus .	Not sacred .	•	Sculptures.	
Recurvirostra avosetta, Avoset .				

Name.	Sacred to what Deity.	In what Place.	Where mentioned.	Where found embalmed.
FABULOUS AND UNKNOWN BIRDS.				
Phenix (perhaps the *Benno*?	sacred to Osiris)	·	Sculptures.	
The "Pure Soul" of the King (a bird with man's head and arms)	·	·	Sculptures.	
Emblem of the Soul	·	·	Sculptures.	
Vulture with a Snake's head	·	·	Sculptures.	
Hawk with Man's and Ram's head	·	·	Sculptures.	
Class III.—REPTILES.				
CHELONIA. Order 1.				
Tortoise	{ A tortoise head-ed God · }	·	Sculptures.	
SAURIA. Order 2.				
Crocodile	Sacred to Savak	{ The Arsinoïte nome and its capital, Crocodilopolis. Lake Mœris, Thebes, &c. }	Herodot. Strabo, xvii. Diodor. i. 48. Sculptures, &c.	Thebes, Maabdeh, &c.

Waran el bahr, *Monitor* of the Nile, *Lacerta Nilotica*	Not sacred?			
Waran el ard, Land *Monitor*, *Lac. scincus*	Not sacred?			
The *Dthobb*, or *Lac. Caudiverbera*	Not sacred?			
Lac. Gecko, or *Boorse*, and many other of the Lizard tribe	Not sacred?	.	.	Thebes.
ORDER 3. OPHIDIA.				
Asp, *Coluber Haje*, or *Naja Haje*	Sacred to Neph and Ranno	.	Sculptures. Plut. s. 74, &c.	Thebes.
The common Snake of Egypt	Not sacred?	.	Sculptures.	
The *Coluber*, or *Vipera Cerastes*, the horned Snake	Not sacred to Amun?	Thebes	{ Herodot., and sculptures, &c.	Thebes.
The small spotted Viper of Egypt, *Echis pavo*?	Not sacred.	.		
Order 4. BATRACHIANS.				
Frog	Emblem of Pthah?	.	Sculptures. Horapollo.	Thebes.
Toad	Not sacred?			
FABULOUS REPTILES.				
Snakes { with Human head, Hawk's head, Lion's head.		.	Sculptures.	

The Fish are noticed elsewhere ; I shall therefore content myself with the names of those which were held sacred.

Class IV.—Fishes.

Name.	Sacred to what Deity.	In what Place.	Where mentioned.	Where found embalmed.
Oxyrhinchus	Sacred . . .	At Oxyrhinchus, &c.	Plut., Strabo. Sculptures	Several fish found embalmed at Thebes.
Phagrus, the Eel . .	Sacred . . .	Among the Syenite, and at Phagrorio-polis	Clemens, Orat. Adhort. p. 17. Athenaeus, Deipn. vii. Sculptures.	
Lepidotus	Sacred . . .	In most parts of Egypt	Plut., &c. Sculptures.	
Latus	Sacred . . .	At Latopolis . .	Strabo, xvii. Sculptures ?	
Mæotes	Sacred . . .	At Elephantine . .	Clemens Alex. Orat. Ad-hort. p. 17. Sculptures ?	

Of the second division of the animal kingdom, the Mollusca, containing shellfish, nothing is known which connects any of them with the religion of Egypt : and of the third, or Articulata, the only one which appears to have been sacred to, or emblematic of, any Deity, is the Scorpion, in the third class, or ARACHNIDES.

Div. III.—ARTICULATA.

Class III.—ARACHNIDES.

Scorpion	Emblem of the Goddess Selk . .		Sculptures.	

Class IV.—Insects.

Name.	Sacred to what Deity.	In what Place.	Where mentioned.	Where found embalmed.
COLEOPTERA. Scarabæus, and probably different genera and species of Beetles . . .	Sacred to the Sun and to Pthah, and adopted as an emblem of the world, and sometimes also of Hor-Hat.	.	Horapollo. Sculptures, &c. (The modern Nubians, confounding those who venerated it with the scarabæus itself, have called it a *Käfer,* "infidel.")	Thebes.
HYMENOPTERA. Bees . . . Wasps . . . Ichneumons . . .	Not sacred? . .	.	Sculptures.	
DIPTERA. Flies . . .	Not sacred	.	Sculptures, and in pottery.	Thebes.

Locusts, butterflies, moths, and other insects, are represented in the sculptures; but none appear to claim the honour of being sacred.

Some fabulous insects may also be cited, as well as fabulous quadrupeds, which were chiefly emblems appropriated to particular gods, or representative of certain ideas connected with religion, the most remarkable of which were scarabæi with the heads of hawks, rams, and cows. Of these, many are found made of pottery, stone, and other materials, and the sculptures represent the beetle with a human head. Such changes did not render them less fit emblems of the gods: the Scarabæus of the Sun appears with the head of a ram as well as a hawk; and the god Pthah was sometimes figured with the body of a scarabæus, and the head and legs of his usual human form.

Among the Vegetables of Egypt, the following were sacred, or connected with religion :—

Name.	Sacred to what Deity.	In what Place.	Where mentioned.	Where found embalmed.
The Persea	Sacred to Athor	•	Sculptures.	
Peach?	Supposed to be sacred to Harpocrates	•	Plut. de Is. s. 68.	
Pomegranate, Vine, and Acanthus	Used for sacred purposes	•	Athen. xv. 680. Sculp.	
Sycomore Fig	Sacred to Netpe	•	Sculptures.	
Tamarisk	Sacred to Osiris	•	Plut. s. 15, 21. Sculp.	
Lotus. Perhaps the modern name *Nufar* may be related to Nofr, the epithet "good" attached to the god	Emblem of the God Nofr Atmoo?, and connected with Harpocrates.	•	Sculptures and Ancient Authors.	
Garlick				
Onion	Not sacred	•	Plin. xix. 6; Juvenal, Sat. xv.	
Leek				
Palm-branch	Symbol of Astrology, and type of a year	•	Clem. Strom. 6; Horapollo, &c. Plut. s. 38.	
Melilotus?		•	Sculptures & Anc. Auth.	
Papyrus		•	Plut. s. 37. Diodor. i. 17.	
Ivy?	Sacred? to Osiris	•	Sculptures?	
Periploca Secamone?				

Many of these were conspicuous among the offerings made to the gods.

The most remarkable emblems, independent of the types of the deities, were the signs of, 1, Life; 2, 3, of Goodness; 4, of Power (or of Purity); 5, of Majesty and Dominion (the flail and crook of Osiris); 6, of Authority; 7, 8, 9, 10, of Royalty; 11, of Stability; which were principally connected with the gods and kings.

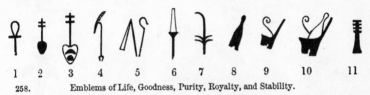

1 2   3 4   5   6 7   8   9 10   11

258.   Emblems of Life, Goodness, Purity, Royalty, and Stability.

Many others belonged to religious ceremonies; a long list of which may be seen in the chamber of Osiris at Philæ, and in the coronation ceremony at Medeenet Haboo.

The sign of Life (*tau*, or *crux ansata*) is held by the gods in one hand, and the sceptre of Power (or Purity) generally in the other. The lotus was always a favourite symbol; the palm branch was the sign of " the year;" and a frog with the young palm leaf, as it springs from the date stone, rising from its back, was the type of man in embryo. The eye of Osiris was sometimes a representation of " Egypt," (*see page* 244;) and was placed at the head of their boats; and numerous other emblems occur 259. in the sacred subjects represented on the monuments. Among flowers, two frequently occur, the papyrus head and another water plant, which were the emblems of Lower and Upper Egypt.

Flowers were presented in different ways; either loosely, tied together by the stalks,* or in carefully formed bouquets, without any other gifts. Sometimes those of a particular kind were offered alone; the most esteemed being the lotus, papyrus, convolvulus, and other favourite productions of the garden: and a bouquet of peculiar form was occasionally presented,† or two smaller ones, carried in each of the donor's hands.‡

---

* Woodcut 260. † Woodcut 260, *fig.* 12. ‡ Woodcut 260, *fig.* 13.

260.   Various flowers from the sculptures.   *Thebes.*

In fig. 8 is an attempt at perspective. The upper part (*a*) appears to be the papyrus; *b* is a lotus; and *c* probably the melilotus. From fig. 1 *a*, it would seem that one bell-formed flower is a convolvulus; though 1 *b*, 4, 6, 7, and 9 *a*, may be the papyrus; and the shafts of columns with that kind of capital have an indication of the triangular form of its stalk. 3. The lotus. 2, 11, 12, 13. Different bouquets. 10. A flower from an ornamental cornice. 5. Perhaps the same as 4. *See* Flowers in Chapter VI.

Chaplets and wreaths of flowers were also laid upon the altars, and offered to the deities, whose statues were frequently crowned with them.   In the selection of them, as of herbs and roots, those most grateful, or useful, to man, were chosen as most acceptable to the gods; and it was probably the utility, rather than the flavour, that induced them to show a marked preference for the onion, the *Raphanus*, and cucurbitaceous plants, which so generally found a place amongst the offerings.

Of fruits, the sycamore, fig, and grapes were the most esteemed for the service of the altar. They were presented on baskets or trays, frequently covered with leaves to keep them fresh; and sometimes the former were represented placed in such a manner, on an open basket, as to resemble the hieroglyphic signifying "*wife*."*

Ointment often formed part of a large donation, and always entered into the list of those things which constituted a complete set of offerings. It was placed before the deity in vases of alabaster or other materials; the name of the god to whom it was vowed being frequently engraved upon the vase that contained it. Sometimes the king, or priest, took out a certain portion to anoint the statue of the deity, which was done with the little finger of the right hand.

261.

Ointment was presented in different ways, according to the ceremony performed in honour of the gods; and the various kinds of sweet-scented ointments used by the Egyptians were liberally offered at every shrine. According to Clemens, the *psagdæ* of Egypt were among the most noted; and Pliny and Athenæus both bear testimony to the variety of Egyptian ointments, as well as the importance attached to them; which is confirmed by the sculptures, and even by the vases discovered in the tombs.

* Woodcut 284, *figs.* 1, 2, 3, 4.

Rich vestments, necklaces, bracelets, jewellery of various kinds, and other ornaments, vases of gold, silver, and porcelain, bags of gold, and numerous gifts of the most costly description, were also presented to the gods. They constituted the riches of the treasury of the temples; and the spoils taken from conquered nations were deposited there by a victorious monarch, as a votive gift for the success of his arms, or as a token of gratitude for favours already received. Tables of the precious metals, and rare woods, were among the offerings; and an accurate catalogue of his votive presents was engraved on the walls of the temple, to commemorate the piety of the donor, and the wealth of the sanctuary. They do not, however, properly come under the denomination of offerings to the gods, but are rather dedications to their temples; and it was in presenting them that some of the grand processions took place.

But it was not only customary to deposit the necklaces and other " precious gifts " collectively in the temple; the kings frequently offered each singly to the gods, decorating their statues with them, and placing them on their altars.

They also presented numerous emblems, connected with the vows they had made, the favours they desired, or the thanksgivings they returned to the gods : among which the most usual were a small figure of Truth ; the symbol of the assemblies

262.   " He gives (fig. 1) ; the cow of Athor (2); the hawk-headed
Truth (or Justice)
to his father."   necklace of Sokari (3) ; a cynocephalus (4) ; parts of dress? (5) ; ointment (6) ; gold and silver in bags, or in rings (7 a and b); three feathers, or heads of reeds, the emblem of a field (8) ; a scribe's tablet and ink-stand (9 a and b); a garland or wreath (10); and an emblem of pyramidal form, perhaps a particular kind of " white " cake (11).

Thanksgivings for the birth of a child, escape from danger, or other marks of divine favour, were offered by individuals through the medium of the priests. The same was also done in private; and secret as well as public vows were made in the hope of future

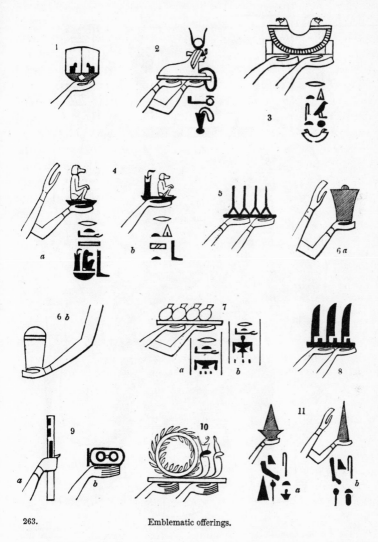

263.   Emblematic offerings.

favours. The quality of these oblations depended on the god
to whom presented, or the occupation of the donor; a shepherd

264.   Offerings on the Altar.   *British Museum.*

1, 2, 3. Vases of ointment, &c., on stands crowned with lotus flowers.
4. Bouquets of lotus and other flowers presented by the son of the deceased.
5. Table of offerings; the most remarkable of which are cakes, grapes, figs, fore leg
   and head of a victim, two hearts, a goose, lotus flowers, and cucumbers or gourds.
6. Four vases on stands, with their mouths closed with ears of corn; over them is a
   wreath of leaves.
7. The person of the tomb seated.

bringing from his flocks, a husbandman from his fields, and others according to their means; provided the offering was not forbidden by the rites of the deity.

Though the Egyptians considered certain oblations suited to particular gods, others inadmissible to their temples, and some more peculiarly adapted to prescribed periods of the year, the greater part of the deities were invoked with the same offerings; the most usual of which were fruit, flowers, vegetables, ointment, incense, grain, wine, milk, beer, oil, cakes, and the sacrifice of animals and birds. These last were either offered whole, with the feathers, or plucked and trussed; and when presented alone, they were sometimes placed upon a portable stand, furnished with spikes, over which the bird was laid.

265.   Stands for bearing offerings.

The bronze instruments with long curved spikes, found in the Etruscan tombs, were probably intended for a similar purpose; though they were once thought to be for torturing Christian martyrs.

Even oxen and other animals were sometimes offered entire, though generally after the head had been taken off; and it does not appear that this depended on any particular ceremony.

In slaying a victim, the Egyptians suffered the blood to flow upon the ground, or over the altar, if placed upon it; and the mode of cutting it up appears to have been the same as when killed for the table. The head was first taken off; and, after the skin had been removed, they generally cut off the right leg and shoulder, and the other legs and parts in succession; which, if required for the table, were placed on trays, and carried to the kitchen, or if intended for sacrifice, were deposited on the altar, with fruit, cakes, and other offerings.

The joints, and parts, most readily distinguished in the sculptures, are the head, the fore leg (fig. 1), with the shoulder (which was styled *sapt*, " the chosen part ;") the upper joint of the hind

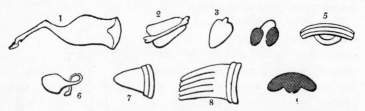

266.   Different joints placed on the altars or the tables.   *Thebes*

leg (2), the kidneys (4), the ribs (5 and 8), the heart (3), and the rump (6) ; and those most commonly seen on the altars are the head, the leg, and the ribs. When the Egyptians offered a holocaust, they commenced with a libation of wine, a preliminary ceremony common, according to Herodotus, to all their sacrifices; and, after it had been poured upon the altar, the victim was slain. They first removed the head and skin (a statement, as I have already shown, fully confirmed by the sculptures) ; they then took out the stomach, leaving only the entrails and the fat; after which the thighs, the upper part of the haunches, the shoulders, and the neck, were cut off in succession. Then, filling the body with cakes of pure flour, honey, dried raisins, figs, incense, myrrh, and other odoriferous substances, they burnt it on the fire, pouring over it a considerable quantity of oil. The portions which were not consumed were afterwards given to the votaries, who were present on the occasion, no part of the offering being left; and it was during the ceremony of burning the sacrifice at the fête of Isis, that they beat themselves in honour of Osiris.

The ordinary subjects, in the interior of the temples, represent the king presenting offerings to the deities worshipped there; the most remarkable of which are the sacrifices already mentioned, incense, libation, and several emblematic figures or devices connected with religion. He sometimes made an appropriate offering to the presiding deity of the sanctuary, and to

each of the contemplar gods, as Diodorus says Osymandyas was
represented to have done; the memorial of which act of piety
was preserved in the sculptures of his tomb.

Incense was presented to all the gods, and introduced on every
grand occasion when a *complete* oblation was made. For they
sometimes merely offered a libation of wine, oil, and other liquids,
or a single gift, a necklace, a bouquet of flowers, or whatever
they had vowed. Incense was also presented alone, though more
usually accompanied by a libation of wine. It consisted of
various ingredients, according to circumstances; and in offerings
to the sun, Plutarch says that resin, myrrh, and a mixture of
sixteen ingredients, called *kuphi*, were adapted to different times
of the day.

In offering incense, the king held in one hand the censer, and
with the other threw balls or pastiles of incense into the flame.

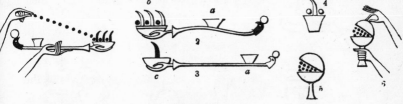

267.   Offering of incense.

Then, addressing the God, before whose statue he stood, with a
suitable prayer, to invoke his aid and favour, he begged him to
accept the incense he presented: in return for which the deity
granted him " a long, pure, and happy life," with other favours
accorded by the gods to men.

A libation of wine was frequently offered, together with incense; or two censers of incense, with several
oxen, birds, and other consecrated gifts. And
that it was customary to present several of
the same kind is shown by the ordinary
formula of presentation, which says, " I give
you a thousand (*i.e.* many) cakes, a thousand
vases of wine, a thousand head of oxen, a
thousand geese, a thousand vestments, a thousand censers of

268. Offering of incense
and a libation.

incense, a thousand libations, a thousand boxes of ointment."
The cakes were of various kinds. Many were round, oval, or
triangular; and others had the edges folded over, like the
fateereh of the present day. They also assumed the shape of
leaves, or the form of an animal, a crocodile's head, or some
capricious figure; and it was frequently customary to sprinkle
them (particularly the round and oval cakes) with seeds.

Wine was presented in two cups. It was not then a libation,
but merely an offering of wine; and since the pouring out of wine
upon the altar was a preliminary ceremony, as Herodotus observes, common to all their sacrifices, we find that the king is
often represented making a libation upon an altar covered with
offerings of cakes, flowers, and the joints of a victim killed for the
occasion.

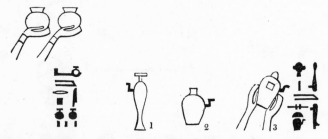

269. Wine HPII offered in two cups.   270. Vases used for libations.

Two kinds of vases were principally used for libations; but
that used on grand occasions, and carried in procession by the
Prophet, or by the king, was of long shape, with the usual spout
(fig. 1).

The various kinds of wine were indicated by the names affixed to them. White and red wines, those of the Upper and
Lower Country, grape juice or wine of the vineyard (one of the

271.   Offering
       of milk, ⲉⲡⲱϯ.

most delicious beverages of a hot climate,
and one which is commonly used in Spain
and other countries at the present day),
were the most noted.

Beer and milk, as well as oils of various

kinds, for which Egypt was famous, were also common among the offerings.

No people had greater delight in ceremonies and religious pomp than the Egyptians; and grand processions constantly took place, to commemorate some legendary tale connected with superstition. Nor was this tendency of the Egyptian mind neglected by the priesthood; whose influence was greatly increased by the importance of the post they held on those occasions: there was no ceremony in which they did not participate; and even military regulations were subject to their influence.

One of the most important ceremonies was " the procession of

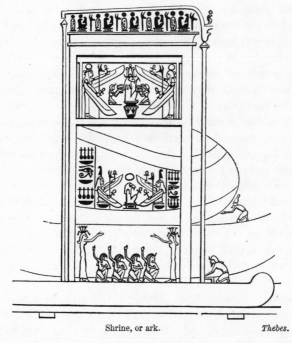

271a.   Shrine, or ark.   *Thebes.*

shrines," which is mentioned in the Rosetta Stone, and is frequently represented on the walls of the temples. The shrines were of two kinds : the one a sort of canopy ; the other an ark or sacred boat, which may be termed the great shrine.   This was carried with grand pomp by the priests, a certain number being selected for that duty, who, supporting it on their shoulders by means of long staves, passing through metal rings at the side of the sledge on which it stood, brought it into the temple, where it was placed upon a stand or table, in order that the prescribed ceremonies might be performed before it.

The stand was also carried in the procession by another set of priests, following the shrine, by means of similar staves; a method usually adopted for transporting large statues, and sacred emblems, too heavy or too important to be borne by one person. The same is stated to have been the custom of the Jews in some of their religious processions, as in carrying the ark " to its place, into the oracle of the house, to the most holy place," when the temple was built by Solomon.

The number of shrines in these processions, and the splendour of the ceremony performed on the occasion, depended on the particular festival they intended to commemorate.   In many instances the shrine of the deity of the temple was carried alone, sometimes that of other deities accompanied it, and sometimes that of the king was added ; a privilege granted as a peculiar mark of esteem, for some great benefit conferred by him upon his country, or for his piety in having beautified the temples of the gods.   Such is the motive mentioned in the description of the Rosetta Stone ; which, after enumerating the benefits conferred upon the country by Ptolemy, decrees, as a return for them, " that a statue of the king shall be erected in every temple, in the most conspicuous place ; that it shall be called the statue of Ptolemy, the defender of Egypt ; and that near it shall be placed the presiding deity, presenting to him the shield of victory.   Moreover, that the priests shall minister three times every day to the statues, and prepare for them the sacred dress, and perform the accustomed ceremonies, as in honour of other gods at feasts and festivals. That there shall be erected an image, and *golden shrine*, of King Ptolemy, in the most honourable of the temples, to be set up in the sanctuary among the other shrines; and that on the great festivals, when the *procession of shrines* takes place, that of the god Epiphanes shall accompany them; ten royal golden crowns being deposited upon the shrine, with an asp attached to each; and the (double) crown *Pshent*, which he wore at his coronation, placed in the midst." (*See the Pshent, in Woodcut* 258, *fig.* 10.)

It was also usual to carry this statue of the principal Deity, in whose honour the procession took place, together with that of the king, and the figures of his ancestors, borne in the same manner on men's shoulders; like the Gods of Babylon mentioned by Jeremiah.

Diodorus speaks of an Ethiopian festival of Jupiter, when his statue was carried in procession, probably to commemorate the supposed refuge of the gods in that country; which may have been a memorial of the flight of the Egyptians with their gods, at the time of the Shepherd invasion, mentioned by Josephus on the authority of Manetho. Diodorus also says, " Homer derived from Egypt his story of the embraces of Jupiter and Juno, and their travelling into Ethiopia, because the Egyptians every year carry Jupiter's shrine over the river into Africa, and a few days after bring it back again, as if the gods had returned out of Ethiopia. The fiction of their nuptials was taken from the solemnization of these festivals; at which time both their shrines, adorned with all sorts of flowers, are carried by the priests to the top of a mountain."

The usual number of priests, who performed the duty of bearers, was generally twelve or sixteen, to each shrine. They were accompanied by another of a superior grade, distinguished by a lock of hair pendent on one side of his head, and clad in a leopard skin, the peculiar badge of his rank, who, walking near them, gave directions respecting the procession, its position in the temple, and whatever else was required during the ceremony; which agrees well with the remark of Herodotus, that " each deity had many priests, and one high priest." Sometimes two priests of the same peculiar grade attended, both during the

procession, and after the shrine had been deposited in the temple.
These were the Pontiffs, or highest order of priests : they had
the title of " Sem," and enjoyed the privilege of offering sacrifices on all grand occasions.

When the shrine reached the temple, it was received with
every demonstration of respect by the officiating priest, who was
appointed to do duty upon the day of the festival; and if the
king happened to be there, it was his privilege to perform the
appointed ceremonies.   These consisted of sacrifices and prayers;
and the shrine was decked with fresh-gathered flowers and rich
garlands.   An endless profusion of offerings was placed before
it, on several separate altars; and the king, frequently accompanied by his queen, who held a sistrum in one hand, and in the
other a bouquet of flowers made up into the particular form required for these religious ceremonies, presented incense and
libation.   This part of the ceremony being finished, the king
proceeded to the presence of the god (represented by his statue),
from whom he was supposed to receive a blessing, typified by the
sacred *tau*, the sign of Life.   Sometimes the principal contemplar deity was also present, usually the second member of the
triad of the place; and it is probable that the position of the

272. One of the sacred boats or arks, with two figures resembling Cherubim. *a* and
      b represent the king; the former under the shape of a sphinx.

statue was near to the shrine, alluded to in the inscription of the Rosetta Stone.

Some of the sacred boats, or arks, contained the emblems of life and stability, which, when the veil was drawn aside, were partially seen; others, the figure of the Divine Spirit, Nef, or Nou; and some presented the sacred beetle of the sun, overshadowed by the wings of two figures of the goddess Thmei or Truth, which call to mind the cherubim of the Jews.   (*Woodcut* 272.)

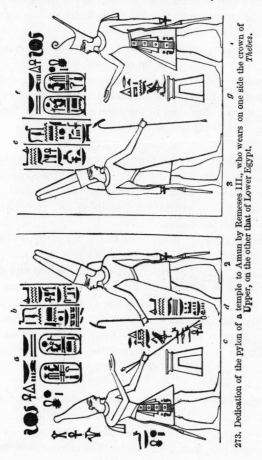

273. Dedication of the pylon of a temple to Amun by Remeses III., who wears on one side the crown of Upper, on the other that of Lower Egypt.

The dedication of the whole or part of a temple was, as may be reasonably supposed, one of the most remarkable solemnities, at which the king presided. And if the actual celebration of the rites practised on the occasion, the laying of the foundation stone, or other ceremonies connected with it, are not represented on the monuments, the importance attached to it is shown by the conspicuous manner in which it is recorded in the sculptures, the ostentation with which it is announced in the dedicatory inscriptions of the monuments themselves, and the answer returned by the god in whose honour it was erected.

Another striking ceremony was the transport of the dedicatory offerings made by the king to the gods, which were carried in great pomp to their respective temples. The king and all the priests attended the procession, clad in their robes of ceremony : and the flag-staffs attached to the great towers of the façade were decked, as on other grand festivals, with banners.

The coronation of the king was a peculiarly imposing ceremony. It was one of the principal subjects represented in the court of the temples ; and some idea may be formed of the pomp displayed on the occasion, even from the limited scale on which the monuments are capable of describing it. It is thus represented at Medeenet Haboo.

First comes the king, borne in his shrine or canopy, and seated on a throne, ornamented with the figures of a lion and a sphinx, which is preceded by a hawk.   Behind him stand two figures of Truth and Justice, with outspread wings. Twelve Egyptian princes, his sons, bear the shrine ; officers wave flabella around the monarch ; and others, of the sacerdotal order, attend on either side, carrying his arms and insignia. Four others follow ; then six of the king's sons, behind whom are two scribes and eight attendants of the military class, bearing stools and the steps of the throne.

In another line are members of the sacerdotal order, four others of the king's sons, fan-bearers, and military scribes ; a guard of soldiers bringing up the rear of the procession. Before the shrine, in one line, march six officers bearing sceptres and other insignia; in another a scribe reads aloud the contents of a scroll he holds unfolded in his hand, preceded by two of the king's sons, and two distinguished persons of the military and priestly orders. The rear of both these lines is closed by a pontiff, who, turning round towards the shrine, burns incense before the monarch; and a band of music, composed of the trumpet, drum, double-pipe, and other instruments, with choristers, forms the van of the procession.

The king, alighted from his throne, officiates as priest before the statue of Amun-Khem, or Amun-Re *generator;* and, still wearing his helmet, he presents libations and incense before the altar, which is loaded with flowers, and other suitable offerings. The statue of the god, attended by officers bearing flabella, is carried on a palanquin, covered with rich drapery, by twenty-two priests; behind it follow others, bringing the table and the altar of the deity. Before the statue is the sacred bull, followed by the king on foot, wearing the cap of the "Lower country." Apart from the procession itself stands the queen, as a spectator of the ceremony; and before her, a scribe reads a scroll he has unfolded. A priest turns round to offer incense to the white bull; and another, clapping his hands, brings up the rear of a long procession of *hieraphori*, carrying standards, images, and other sacred emblems; and the foremost bear the statue of the king's ancestors.

This part of the picture refers to the *coronation* of the king, who, in the hieroglyphics, is said to have "put on the crown of the Upper and Lower countries;" which the birds, flying to the four sides of the world, are to announce to the gods of the south, north, east, and west.

In the next compartment, the president of the assembly reads a long invocation, the contents of which are contained in the hieroglyphic inscription above; and the six ears of corn which the king, once more wearing his helmet, has cut with a golden sickle, are held out by a priest towards the deity. The white bull and images of the king's ancestors are deposited in his temple, in the presence of Amun-Khem, the queen still witnessing the ceremony, which is concluded by an offering of incense and libation, made by Remeses to the statue of the god.

Clemens gives an account of an Egyptian procession; which, as it throws some light on similar ceremonies, and is of interest from having some points of resemblance with the one before us, I here transcribe.

" In the solemn pomps of Egypt the singer generally goes first, bearing one of the symbols of music. They say it is his duty to carry two of the books of Hermes; one of which contains hymns of the gods, the other precepts relating to the life of the king. The singer is followed by the Horoscopus, bearing in his hand the measure of time (hour-glass) and the palm (branch), the symbols of astrology (astronomy), whose duty it is to be versed in (or recite) the four books of Hermes, which treat of that science. Of these, one describes the position of the fixed stars, another the conjunctions (eclipses) and illuminations of the sun and moon, and the others their risings. Next comes the Hierogrammat (or sacred scribe), having feathers on his head, and in his hands a book (papyrus), with a ruler (palette) in which is ink, and a reed for writing. It is his duty to understand what are called hieroglyphics, the description of the world, geography, the course of the sun, moon, and planets, the condition of the land of Egypt and the Nile, the nature of the instruments or sacred ornaments, and the places appointed for them, as well as weights and measures, and the things used in holy rites. Then follows the *Stolistes*, or ' dresser,' bearing the cubit of justice and the cup of libation. He knows all subjects relating to education, and the choice of calves for victims, which are comprehended in ten books. These treat of the honours paid to the gods, and of the Egyptian religion, including sacrifice, first fruits, hymns, prayers, processions, holydays, and the like. Last of all comes the prophet, who carries in his bosom a water jar, followed by persons bearing loaves of bread. He presides over all sacred things, and is obliged to know the contents of the ten books called sacerdotal, relating to the gods, the laws, and all the discipline of the priests."

One of the principal solemnities connected with the coronation was the anointing of the king, and his receiving the emblems of majesty from the gods.   The sculptures represent the deities themselves officiating on this as on other similar occasions, in order to convey to the Egyptian people, who beheld these records, a more exalted notion of the special favours bestowed on their monarch.

We, however, who at this distant period are less interested in the direct intercourse between the Pharaohs and the gods, may be satisfied with a more simple interpretation of such subjects, and conclude that it was the priests who performed the ceremony, and bestowed upon the prince the title of " the anointed of the gods."

With the Egyptians, as with the Jews, the investiture to any sacred office, as that of king or priest, was confirmed by this external sign; and as the Jewish lawgiver mentions the ceremony of pouring oil upon the head of the high priest *after* he had put on his entire dress, with the mitre and crown, the Egyptians represent the anointing of their priests and kings *after* they were attired in their full robes, with the cap and crown upon their head.   Some of the sculptures introduce a priest pouring oil over the monarch, in the presence of Thoth, Hor-Hat, Seth, and Nilus; which may be considered a representation of the ceremony, before the statues of those gods.   The functionary who officiated was the high priest, or prophet, clad in a leopard skin; the same who attended on all occasions which required him to assist, or assume the duties of, the monarch in the temple.

There was also the ceremony of anointing the statues of the gods, which was done with the little finger of the right hand; and another, of pouring from two vases, alternate emblems of life and purity, over the king, in token of purification, previous to his admittance into the presence of the god of the temple. This was performed by Thoth on one side, and the hawk-headed Hor-Hat on the other; sometimes by Hor-Hat and Seth, or by two hawk-headed deities, or by one of these last and the god Nilus.   The deities Seth and Horus are also represented placing

the crown of the two countries upon the head of the king, saying
" Put this cap upon your head like your father Amun-Re :" and
the palm branches they hold in their hands allude to the long
series of years they grant him to rule over his country. The
emblems of Dominion and Majesty, the crook and flagellum of
Osiris, have been already given him, and the asp-formed fillet is
bound upon his head.

Another mode of investing the sovereign with the diadem is
figured on the apex of some obelisks, and on other monuments,
where the god, in whose honour they were raised, puts the crown

upon his head as he kneels before him, with
the announcement that he " grants him dominion over the whole world." Goddesses,
in like manner, placed upon the heads of
queens the peculiar insignia they wore ; which
were two long feathers, with the globe and
horns of Athor ; and they presented them
their peculiar sceptre.

274.   Sceptre of a Queen.

The custom of anointing was not confined to the appointment
of kings and priests to the sacred offices they held : it was the
ordinary token of welcome to guests in every party at the house
of a friend ; and in Egypt, no less than in Judæa, the metapho-
rical expression, " anointed with the oil of gladness," was fully
understood, and applied to the ordinary occurrences of life. It
was not confined to the living ; the dead were made to participate
in it, as if sensible of the token of esteem thus bestowed upon
them ; and a grateful survivor, in giving an affectionate token of
gratitude to a regretted friend, neglected not this last unction of
his mortal remains. Even the head of the bandaged mummy,
and the case which contained it, were anointed with oils and the
most precious ointments.

Another ceremony, represented in the temples, was the blessing
bestowed by the gods on the king, at the moment of his assuming
the reins of government. They laid their hands upon him ;
and, presenting him with the symbol of life, they promised that
his reign should be long and glorious, and that he should enjoy

tranquillity, with certain victory over his enemies. If about to undertake an expedition against foreign nations, they gave him the falchion of victory, to secure the defeat of the people whose country he was about to invade, saying, "Take this weapon, and smite with it the heads of the impure Gentiles."

To show the special favour he enjoyed from heaven, the gods were even represented admitting him into their company and communing with him; and sometimes Thoth, with other deities, taking him by the hand, led him into the presence of the great Triad, or of the presiding divinity, of the temple. He was welcomed with suitable expressions of approbation; and on this, as on other occasions, the sacred *tau*, or sign of life, was presented to him,—a symbol which, with the sceptre of purity, was usually placed in the hands of the gods. These two were deemed the greatest gifts bestowed by the deity on man.

The origin of the *tau* I cannot precisely determine; but this curious fact is connected with it in later times,—that the early Christians of Egypt adopted it in lieu of the cross, which was afterwards substituted for it, prefixing it to inscriptions in the same manner as the cross in later times; and numerous inscriptions headed by the *tau* are preserved to the present day in early Christian sepulchres at the Great Oasis.

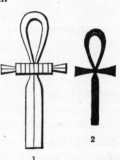

275.   Tau, or Sign of Life.

The triumph of the king was a grand solemnity. Flattering to the national pride of the Egyptians, it awakened those feelings of enthusiasm which the celebration of victory naturally inspires, and led them to commemorate it with the greatest pomp. When the victorious monarch, returning to Egypt after a glorious campaign, approached the cities which lay on his way, from the confines of the country to the capital, the inhabitants flocked to meet him, and with welcome acclamations greeted his arrival and the success of his arms. The priests and chief people of each place advanced with garlands and bouquets of flowers; the principal person present addressed him in an appropriate speech; and as the troops defiled through the streets, or passed without the walls, the people followed with acclamations, uttering earnest thanksgivings to the gods, the protectors of Egypt, and praying them for ever to continue the same marks of favour to their monarch and their nation.

Arrived at the capital, they went immediately to the temple, where they returned thanks to the gods, and performed the customary sacrifices on this important occasion. The whole army attended, and the order of march continued the same as on entering the city. A corps of Egyptians, consisting of chariots and infantry, led the van in close column, followed by the allies of the different nations, who had shared the dangers of the field and the honour of victory. In the centre marched the body guards, the king's sons, the military scribes, the royal arm-bearers, and the staff corps, in the midst of whom was the monarch himself, mounted in a splendid car, attended by his fan-bearers on foot, bearing over him the state flabella. Next followed other regiments of infantry, with their respective banners; and the rear was closed by a body of chariots. The prisoners, tied together with ropes, were conducted by some of the king's sons, or by the chief officers of the staff, at the side of the royal car. The king himself frequently held the cord which bound them, as he drove slowly in the procession; and two or more chiefs were sometimes suspended beneath the axle of his chariot, contrary to the usual humane principles of the Egyptians, who seem to have refrained from unnecessary cruelty to their captives, extending this feeling so far as to rescue, even in the heat of battle, a defenceless enemy from a watery grave.

Having reached the precincts of the temple, the guards and royal attendants selected to be the representatives of the whole army entered the courts, the rest of the troops, too numerous for admission, being drawn up before the entrance; and the king, alighting from his car, prepared to lead his captives to the shrine of the god. Military bands played the favourite airs of the country; and the numerous standards of the different regiments, the banners floating in the wind, the bright lustre of arms, the immense concourse of people, and the grandeur of the lofty towers of the temple, decked with their bright-coloured flags streaming above the cornice, presented an imposing scene. But the most striking feature of this pompous ceremony was the brilliant cortége of the monarch, who was either borne in his chair of state by the principal officers of state under a rich canopy, or walked on foot, overshadowed with rich flabella and fans of waving plumes. As he approached the inner gateway, a long procession of priests advanced to meet him, dressed in their robes of office; censers full of incense were burnt before him; and a sacred scribe read from a papyrus roll the glorious deeds of the victorious monarch, and the tokens he had received of the divine favour. They then accompanied him into the presence of the presiding deity of the place; and having performed sacrifice, and offered suitable thanksgivings, he dedicated the spoil of the conquered enemy, and expressed his gratitude for the privilege of laying before the feet of the god, the giver of victory, those prisoners he had brought to the vestibule of the divine abode.

In the mean time, the troops without the sacred precincts were summoned by sound of trumpet, to attend the sacrifice prepared by the priests, in the name of the whole army, for the benefits they had received from the gods, the success of their arms, and their own preservation in the hour of danger. Each regiment marched up by turn to the altar, temporarily raised for the occasion, to the sound of the drum, the soldiers carrying in their hand a twig of olive, with the arms of their respective corps; but the heavy-armed soldier laid aside his shield on this occasion, as if to show the security he enjoyed in the presence of the deity. An ox was then killed; and wine, incense, and the customary offerings of cakes, fruit, vegetables, joints of meat, and birds, were presented to the god. Every soldier deposited the twig of olive he carried at the altar; and as the trumpet summoned them, so also it gave the signal for each regiment to withdraw, and cede its place to another. The ceremony being over, the king went in state to his palace, accompanied by the troops; and having distributed rewards to them, and eulogised their conduct in the field, he gave his orders to the commanders of the different corps, and they withdrew to their cantonments, or to the duties to which they were appointed.

Of the fixed festivals, one of the most remarkable was the celebration of the grand assemblies, or panegyries, held in the great halls of the principal temples, at which the king presided in person. That they were of the greatest importance is abundantly proved by the frequent mention of them in the sculptures; and that the post of president of the assemblies was the highest possible honour may be inferred, as well from its being enjoyed by the sovereign alone of all men, as from its being assigned to the

1

2

276.

deity himself in these legends: "Phrah (Pharaoh), lord of the panegyries, like Re," or "like his father Pthah;" which so frequently occur on the monuments of Thebes and Memphis.

Their celebration was fixed to certain periods of the year; as were the festivals of the new moons, and those recorded in the great calendar, sculptured on the exterior of the S.W. wall of Medeenet Haboo, which took place during several successive days of each month, and were even repeated in honour of different deities every day during some months, and attended by the king in person.

Another important religious ceremony is often alluded to in the sculptures, which appears to be connected with the assemblies just mentioned. In this the king is represented running, with a vase or some emblem in one hand, and the flagellum of Osiris, a type of majesty, in the other, as if hastening to enter the hall where the panegyries were held; and two figures of him are frequently introduced, one crowned with the cap of the Upper, the other with that of the Lower country, as they stand beneath a canopy indicative of the hall of assembly. The same deities, who usually preside on the anointing of the king, present him with the sign of life, and bear before him the palm branch, on which the years of the assemblies are noted. Before him stands the goddess Milt, bearing on her head the water-plants, her emblem; and around are numerous emblems appropriated to this subject. The monarch sometimes runs into the presence of the god bearing two vases, which appears to be the commencement of, or connected with, this ceremony; and the whole may be the anniversary of the foundation of the temple, or of the sovereign's reign. An ox (or cow) is in some instances represented running with the king, on the same occasion.

The birthdays of the kings were celebrated with great pomp. They were looked upon as holy; no business was done upon them; and all classes indulged in the festivities suitable to the occasion. Every Egyptian attached much importance to the day, and even to the hour of his birth; and it is probable that, as in Persia, each individual kept his birthday with great rejoicings, welcoming his friends with all the amusements of society, and a more than usual profusion of the delicacies of the table.

They had many other public holydays, when the court of the king and all public offices were closed. This was sometimes owing to a superstitious belief of their being unlucky; and such was the prejudice against the "third day of the Epact, the birthday of Typho, that the sovereign neither transacted any business upon it, nor even suffered himself to take any refreshment till the evening." Other fasts were also observed by the king and the priesthood, out of respect to certain solemn purifications they deemed it their duty to undergo for the service of religion.

Among the ordinary rites the most noted, because the most frequent, were the daily sacrifices offered in the temple by the sovereign pontiff. It was customary for him to attend there early every morning, after he had examined and settled his epistolary correspondence relative to the affairs of state; and the service began by the high priest reading a prayer for the welfare of the monarch, in the presence of the people.

Of the anniversary festivals one of the most remarkable was

the Niloa, or invocation of the blessings of the inundation, offered to the tutelary deity of the Nile. According to Heliodorus, it was one of the principal festivals of the Egyptians. It took place about the summer solstice, when the river began to rise; and the anxiety with which they looked forward to a plentiful inundation induced them to celebrate it with more than usual honour. Libanius asserts that these rites were deemed of so much importance by the Egyptians, that unless· they were performed at the proper season, and in a becoming manner, by the persons appointed to this duty, they felt persuaded that the Nile would refuse to rise and inundate the land. Their full belief in the efficacy of the ceremony, secured its annual performance on a grand scale. Men and women assembled from all parts of the country in the towns of their respective nomes, grand festivities were proclaimed, and all the enjoyments of the table were united with the solemnity of a holy festival. Music, the dance, and appropriate hymns, marked the respect they felt for the deity; and a wooden statue of the river god was carried by the priests through the villages in solemn procession, that all might appear to be honoured by his presence, while invoking the blessings he was about to confer.

Another festival, particularly welcomed by the Egyptian peasants, and looked upon as a day of great rejoicing, was (if it may be so called) the harvest home, or the close of the labours of the year, and the preparation of the land for its future crops by the inundation; when, as Diodorus tells us, the husbandmen indulged in recreations of every kind, and showed their gratitude for the benefits the deity had conferred upon them by the blessings of the inundation. This, and other festivals of the peasantry, I shall notice in treating of the agriculture of Egypt.*

Games were also celebrated in honour of certain gods, in which wrestling and other gymnastic exercises were practised.

The investiture of a chief was a ceremony of considerable importance, when the post conferred was connected with any high dignity

* In chap. vi.

about the person of the monarch, in the army, or the priesthood. It took place in the presence of the sovereign seated on his throne ; and two priests, having arrayed the candidate in a long loose vesture, placed necklaces round his neck. One of these ceremonies frequently occurs in the monuments, which was some-times performed immediately after a victory ; in which case we may conclude that the honour was granted in return for distin-guished services in the field : and as the individual, on all occa-sions, holds the flabella, crook, and other insignia of the office of fan-bearer, it appears to have been either the appointment to that post, or to some high command in the army.

A similar mode of investiture appears to have been adopted in all appointments to the high offices of state, both of a civil and military kind. In this, as in many customs detailed in the sculptures, we find an interesting illustration of a ceremony mentioned in the Bible, which describes Pharaoh taking a ring from his hand and putting it on Joseph's hand, arraying him in vestures of fine linen, and putting a gold chain about his neck.

In a tomb, opened at Thebes by Mr. Hoskins, another instance occurs of this investiture to the post of fan-bearer ; in which the two attendants, or inferior priests, are engaged in clothing him with the robes of his new office. One puts on the necklace, the other arranges his dress, a fillet being already bound round his head ; and he appears to wear *gloves* upon his uplifted hands. In the next part of the same picture (for, as is often the case, it presents two actions and two periods of time) the individual holding the insignia of fan-bearer, and followed by the two priests, presents himself before the king, who holds forth his hand to him to touch, or perhaps to kiss.

The office of fan-bearer to the king was a highly honourable post, which none but the royal princes, or the sons of the first nobility, were permitted to hold. These constituted a principal part of his staff; and in the field they either attended on the monarch to receive his orders, or were despatched to take the command of a division ; some having the rank of generals of cavalry, others of heavy infantry or archers, according to the service to which they belonged. They had the privilege of presenting the prisoners to the king, after the victory had been gained, announcing at the same time the amount of the enemy's slain, and the booty that had been taken; and those, whose turn it was to attend upon the king's person, as soon as the enemy had been vanquished, resigned their command to the next in rank, and returned to their post of fan-bearers. The office was divided into two grades,—the one serving on the right, the other on the left, hand of the king; the most honourable post being given to those of the highest rank, or to those most esteemed for their services. A certain number were always on duty; and they were required to attend during the grand solemnities of the temple, and on every occasion when the monarch went out in state, or transacted public business at home.

At Medeenet Haboo is a remarkable instance of the ceremony of carrying the sacred boat of Pthah-Sokari-Osiris, which may represent the funeral of Osiris. It is frequently introduced in the sculptures; and in one of the tombs of Thebes this solemnity occurs, which, though on a smaller scale than on the walls of Medeenet Haboo, offers some interesting peculiarities. First comes the boat, carried as usual by several priests, superintended by the pontiff, clad in a leopard skin; after which two *hieraphori*, each bearing a long staff, surmounted by a hawk; then a man beating the tambourine, behind whom is a flower with the stalk bound round with ivy (or the periploca, which so much resembles it). These are followed by two *hieraphori* (or bearers of holy emblems), carrying each a staff with a jackal on the top, and another carrying a flower; behind whom is a priest turning round to offer incense to the emblem of Nofre-Atmoo. The latter is placed horizontally upon six columns, between each of which stands a human figure, with uplifted arms, either in the act of adoration, or aiding to support the sacred emblem; and behind it is an image of the king kneeling; the whole borne on the usual staves by several priests, attended by a pontiff in his leopard-skin dress. In this ceremony, as in some of the tales related of Osiris, we may trace those analogies which led the

Greeks to suggest the resemblance between that deity and their Bacchus; as the tambourine, the ivy-bound flower or thyrsus, and the leopard skin, which last recalls the leopards that drew his car. The spotted skin of the nebris, or fawn, may also be traced in that suspended near Osiris in the region of Amenti.

At Medeenet Haboo the procession is on a more splendid scale: the ark of Sokari is borne by sixteen priests, accompanied by two pontiffs, one clad in the usual leopard skin; and Remeses himself officiates on the occasion. The king also performs the singular ceremony of holding a rope at its centre, the two ends being supported by four priests, eight of his sons, and four other chiefs; before whom two priests turn round to offer incense, while a sacred scribe reads the contents of a papyrus he holds in his hands. These are preceded by one of the *hieraphori* bearing the hawk on a staff decked with banners (the standard of the king, or of Horus), and by the emblem of Nofre-Atmoo, borne by eighteen priests, the figures standing between the columns, over which it is laid, being of kings, and the columns themselves being surmounted by the heads of hawks.

In the same ceremony at Medeenet Haboo, it appears that the king, when holding the rope, has the cubit in his hand, and, when following the ark, the cup of libation; which calls to mind the office of the Stolistes mentioned by Clemens, " having in his hand the cubit of justice, and the cup of libation;" and he, in like manner, is preceded by the sacred scribe.

The mode of carrying the sacred arks on poles borne by priests, or by the nobles of the land, was extended to the statues of the gods, and other sacred objects belonging to the temples. The former, as Macrobius states, were frequently placed in a case or canopy; and the same writer is correct in stating that the chief people of the nome assisted in this service, even the sons of the king being proud of so honourable an employment. What he afterwards says of their " being carried forward according to divine inspiration, whithersoever the deity urges them, and not by their own will," cannot fail to call to mind the supposed dictation of a secret influence, by which the bearers of the dead, in the funeral processions of modern Egypt, pretend to be actuated. To such an extent do they carry this superstitious belief of their ancestors, that I have seen them in their solemn march suddenly stop, and then run violently through the streets, at the risk of throwing the body off the bier, pretending that they were obliged, by the irresistible will of the deceased, to visit a certain mosk, or seek the blessing of a particular saint.

Few other processions of any great importance are represented in the sculptures; nor can it be expected that the monuments would give more than a small proportion of the numerous festivals, or ceremonies, which took place in the country.

Many of the religious festivals were indicative of some peculiar attribute or supposed property of the deity in whose honour they were celebrated. One, mentioned by Herodotus, was emblematic of the generative principle, and the same that appears to be alluded to by Plutarch under the name of Paamylia, which he says bore a resemblance to one of the Greek ceremonies. The assertion, however, of these writers, that such figures belonged to Osiris, is contradicted by the sculptures, which show them to have been emblematic of the god Khem, or Pan; and this is confirmed by another observation of the latter writer, that the leaf of the fig-tree represented the deity of that festival, as well as the land of Egypt. The tree does indeed represent Egypt, and always occurs on the altar of Khem; but it is not in any way connected with Osiris, and the statues mentioned by Plutarch evidently refer to the Egyptian Pan.

According to Herodotus, the only two festivals, in which it was lawful to sacrifice pigs, were those of the Moon and Bacchus (or Osiris): the reason of which restriction he attributes to a sacred reason, which he does not think it right to mention. " In sacrificing a pig to the Moon, they killed it; and when they had put together the end of the tail, the spleen, and the caul, and covered them with all the fat from the inside of the animal, they burnt them; the rest of the victim being eaten on the day of the full Moon, which was the same on which the sacrifice was offered, for on no other day were they allowed to eat the flesh of the pig.   Poor people who had barely the means of subsistence made a paste figure of a pig, which being baked, they offered as a sacrifice."   The same kind of substitute was, doubtless, made for other victims, by those who could not afford to purchase them : and some of the small glass and clay figures of animals found in the tombs, have probably served for this purpose.   " On the fête of Bacchus, every one immolated a pig before the door of his house, at the hour of dinner ; he then gave it back to the person of whom it had been bought."   " The Egyptians," adds the historian, " celebrate the rest of this fête nearly in the same manner as the Greeks, with the exception of the sacrifice of pigs."

The procession on this occasion was headed, as usual, by music, a flute-player, according to Herodotus, leading the van ; and the first sacred emblem they carried was a *hydria*, or water-pitcher.   A festival was also held on the 17th of Athyr, and three succeeding days, in honour of Osiris, during which they exposed to view a gilded ox, the emblem of that deity ; and commemorated what they called the " *loss of Osiris.*"   Another followed in honour of the same deity, after an interval of six months, or 179 days, " upon the 19th of Pachon ; when they marched in procession towards the sea-side, whither, likewise, the priest and other proper officers carried the sacred chest, inclosing a small boat or vessel of gold, into which they first poured some fresh water, and then all present cried out with a loud voice, ' Osiris is found.'   This ceremony being ended, they threw a little fresh mould, together with rich odours and spices, into the water, mixing the whole mass together, and working it up into a little image in the shape of a crescent.   The image was afterwards dressed and adorned with a proper habit ; and the whole was intended to intimate that they looked upon these gods as the essence and power of Earth and Water."

Another festival in honour of Osiris was held " on the new Moon of the month Phamenoth, which fell in the beginning of spring, called the entrance of Osiris into the Moon ;" and on the 11th of Tybi (or the beginning of January) was celebrated the fête of Isis's return from Phœnicia, when cakes, having a hippopotamus bound stamped upon them, were offered in her honour, to commemorate the victory over Typho. A certain rite was also performed in connection with the fabulous history of Osiris, in which it was customary to throw a cord in the midst of the assembly and then chop it to pieces; the supposed purport of which was to record the desertion of Thueris, the concubine of Typho, and her delivery from a serpent, which the soldiers killed with their swords as it pursued her in her flight to join the army of Horus.

Among the ceremonies connected with Osiris, the fête of Apis holds a conspicuous place.

For Osiris was also worshipped under the form of Apis, the Sacred Bull of Memphis, or as a human figure with a bull's head, accompanied by the name " Apis-Osiris." According to Plutarch, " Apis was a fair and beautiful image of the Soul of Osiris ;" and the same author tells us that " Mnevis, the Sacred Ox of Heliopolis, was also dedicated to Osiris, and honoured by the Egyptians with a reverence next to that paid to Apis, whose sire some pretend him to be." This agrees with the statement of Diodorus, who says, Apis and Mnevis were both sacred to Osiris, and worshipped as gods throughout the whole of Egypt; and Plutarch suggests that, from these well-known representations of Osiris, the people of Elis and Argos derived the idea of Bacchus with an ox's head; Bacchus being reputed to be the same as Osiris. Herodotus, in describing him, says, " Apis, also called Epaphus, is a young bull, whose mother can have no other offspring, and who is reported by the Egyptians to conceive from lightning sent rom heaven, and thus to produce the god Apis. He is known by certain marks : his hair is black ; on his forehead is a white triangular spot, on his back an eagle, and a beetle under his tongue, and the hair of his tail is double." Ovid represents him of various colours. Strabo says his forehead and some parts of his body are of a white colour, the rest being black ; " by which signs they fix upon a new one to succeed the other, when he

dies;" and Plutarch thinks that, "on account of the great
resemblance they imagine between Osiris and the Moon, his
more bright and shining parts being shadowed and obscured by
those that are of a darker hue, they call the Apis the living image
of Osiris, and suppose him begotten by a ray of generative light,
flowing from the moon, and fixing upon his mother, at a time
when she was strongly disposed for it."

Pliny speaks of Apis "having a white spot in the form of a
crescent upon his right side, and a lump under his tongue in the
form of a beetle." Ammianus Marcellinus says the white crescent on his right side was the principal sign, and Ælian mentions twenty-nine marks, by which he was recognized, each
referable to some mystic signification. But he pretends that the
Egyptians did not allow those given by Herodotus and Arista-
goras. Some suppose him entirely black; and others contend
that certain marks, as the predominating black colour, and the
beetle on his tongue, show him to be consecrated to the sun, as
the crescent to the moon. Ammianus and others say that
"Apis was sacred to the Moon, Mnevis to the Sun;" and most
authors describe the latter of a black colour.

It is difficult to decide if Herodotus is correct respecting the
peculiar marks of Apis. There is, however, evidence from the
bronzes, found in Egypt, that the vulture (not eagle) on his

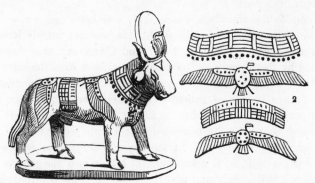

277.
    1. Bronze figure of Apis.

In the possession of Miss Rogers.
2. The marks on his back.

back was one of his characteristics, supplied, no doubt, like many others, by the priests themselves; who probably put him to much inconvenience, and pain too, to make the marks and hairs conform to his description.

To Apis belonged all the clean oxen, chosen for sacrifice; the necessary requisite for which, according to Herodotus, was, that they should be entirely free from black spots, or even a single black hair; though, as I shall have occasion to remark in treating of the sacrifices, this statement of the historian is far from accurate. It may also be doubted if the name Epaphus, by which he says Apis was called by the Greeks in their language, was of Greek origin.

He is called in the hieroglyphic legends Hapi; and the bull, the demonstrative and figurative sign following his name, is accompanied by the *crux ansata*, or emblem of life. It has

278.   Hieroglyphical name of Apis.

seldom any ornament on its head; but the figure of Apis-(or Hapi-)Osiris generally wears the globe of the sun, and the Asp, the symbol of divine majesty; which are also given to the bronze figures of this bull.

Memphis was the place where Apis was kept, and where his worship was particularly observed. He was not merely looked upon as an emblem, but, as Pliny and Cicero say, was deemed "a god by the Egyptians:" and Strabo calls "Apis the same as Osiris." Psammaticus there erected a grand court (ornamented with figures in lieu of columns 12 cubits in height, forming an inner peristyle), in which he was kept when exhibited in public. Attached to it were the two stables ("delubra," or "thalami"), mentioned by Pliny: and Strabo says, "Before the enclosure where Apis is kept, is a vestibule, in which also the mother of the sacred bull is fed; and into this vestibule Apis is introduced, in order to be shown to strangers. After being brought out for a little while, he is again taken back; at other times he is only seen through a window." "The temple of Apis is close to that of Vulcan; which last is remarkable for its architectural beauty, its extent, and the richness of its decoration."

The festival in honour of Apis lasted seven days; on which occasion a large concourse of people assembled at Memphis. The priests then led the sacred bull in solemn procession, all people coming forward from their houses to welcome him as he passed; and Pliny and Solinus affirm, that children who smelt his breath were thought to be thereby gifted with the power of predicting future events.

Diodorus derives the worship of Apis from the belief of "the soul of Osiris having migrated into this animal, who was thus supposed to manifest himself to man through successive ages; though some report that the members of Osiris, when killed by Typho, having been deposited in a wooden ox, enveloped in byssine cloths, gave the name to the city of Busiris, and established its worship there."

When the Apis died, certain priests, chosen for this duty, went in quest of another, who was known from the signs mentioned in the sacred books. As soon as he was found, they took him to the city of the Nile, preparatory to his removal to Memphis, where he was kept 40 days; during which period women alone were permitted to see him. These 40 days being completed, he was placed in a boat, with a golden cabin prepared to receive him, and he was conducted in state upon the Nile to Memphis.

Pliny and Ammianus, however, declare that they led the bull Apis to the fountain of the priests, and drowned him with much ceremony, as soon as the time prescribed in the sacred books was fulfilled. This Plutarch limits to 25 years ("the square of five, and the same number as the letters of the Egyptian alphabet"), beyond which it was forbidden that he should live; and having put him to death, they sought another to succeed him. His body was embalmed, and a grand funeral procession took place at Memphis, when his coffin, "placed on a sledge, was followed by the priests," "dressed in the spotted skins of fawns (leopards), bearing the thyrsus in their hands, uttering the same cries, and making the same gesticulations as the votaries of Bacchus during the ceremonies in honour of that god."

When the Apis died a natural death, his obsequies were celebrated on the most magnificent scale; and to such extravagance was this carried, that those who had the office of taking charge of him were often ruined by the heavy expenses entailed upon them. On one occasion, during the reign of the first Ptolemy, upwards of 50 talents were borrowed to defray the necessary cost of his funeral; "and in our time," says Diodorus, "the curators of other sacred animals have expended 100 talents in their burial."

As soon as he was buried, permission was given to the priests to enter the temple of Sarapis, though previously forbidden during the whole festival.

The burial-place of the Apis bulls has lately been discovered by M. Mariette, near Memphis. It consists of an arched gallery hewn in the rock, about 20 feet in height and breadth, and 2000 feet in length (besides a lateral gallery). On each side is a series of chambers, or recesses, which might be called sepulchral *stalls;* every one containing a large sarcophagus of granite, 15 feet by 8, in which the body of a sacred bull was deposited; and when visited by Mr. Harris (in March, 1852) 30 sarcophagi had been already found. One only had an inscription, with the blank oval of a king; but on the walls were several tablets, and fragments of others lay on the ground, containing dedications to Apis, in behalf of some person deceased; one with the name of Amasis, and another of Ptolemaïc time. Mention was also made of the birth, death, and burial of the bulls. They mostly lived 17 to 20 years (25 being the prescribed limit of their life), so that the 30 would only go back to about the beginning of the 26th dynasty. Many more have, therefore, to be discovered.

Before this is a paved road, with lions ranged on each side, about 8 feet high, which forms the approach; and before this again is a temple, supposed to be the Sarapeum, with a sort of vestibule; and at the door-way, between these two, are, on either side, a crouched lion and a tablet, on one of which king Nectanebo, followed by a priest of Apis-Osiris (Sarapis?), is represented making an offering; and in the upper line are eight deities, with an altar before them—Amunra, Maut, Khons, Horus, Athor, Mandoo (Month), Khem, and Osiris.   In the vestibule are statues of 11 divinities, of Greek form (one of whom is Jupiter), seated in a half circle.   These are of Greek or Roman time; but near the spot have been found the names of Amyrtæus, and of some late unknown Egyptian kings; and that of the second Remeses on the surface of the ground above.

From whatever cause the death of Apis took place, the people performed a public lamentation, as if Osiris himself had died: and this mourning lasted until the other Apis, his successor, had been found.   They then commenced the rejoicings, which were cele-brated with an enthusiasm equal to the grief exhibited during the previous mourning.

Of the discovery of a new Apis, Ælian gives the following account :—" As soon as a report is circulated that the Egyptian god has manifested himself, certain of the sacred scribes, well versed in the mystical marks, known to them by tradition, ap-proach the spot where the divine cow has deposited her calf, and then (following the ancient ordonnance of Hermes) feed him with milk during four months, in a house facing the rising sun.   When this period has passed, the sacred scribes and prophets resort to the dwelling of Apis, at the time of the new moon, and placing him in a boat prepared for the purpose, convey him to Memphis, where he has a convenient and agreeable abode, with pleasure grounds, and ample space for wholesome exercise.   Female com-panions of his own species are provided for him, the most beauti-ful that can be found, kept in apartments, to which he has access when he wishes.   He drinks out of a well or fountain of clear water; for it is not thought right to give him the water of the Nile, which is considered too fattening.

" It would be tedious to relate what pompous processions and sacred ceremonies the Egyptians perform, on the celebration of the rising of the Nile, at the fête of the Theophania, in honour of this god, or what dances, festivities, and joyful assemblies are appointed on the occasion, in the towns and in the country." He then says, " the man from whose herd the divine beast has sprung, is the happiest of mortals, and is looked upon with admiration by all people ; " which refutes his previous statement respecting the divine cow : and the assertions of other writers, as well as probability, show that it was not the mother which was *chosen to produce* a calf with particular marks, but that the Apis was selected from its having them. The honour conferred on the cow which bore it was retrospective, being given her *after* the Apis with its proper marks " had been found " by the priests ; and this is consistent with the respect paid to the possessor of the favoured herd, in which the sacred bull had been discovered. " Apis," continues the naturalist, " is an excellent interpretation of futurity. He does not employ virgins, or old women, sitting on a tripod, like some other gods, nor require that they should be intoxicated with the sacred potion ; but inspires boys, who play around his stable, with a divine impulse, enabling them to pour out predictions in perfect rhythm."

The Egyptians not only paid divine honours to the bull Apis, but, considering him the living image and representative of Osiris, they consulted him as an oracle, and drew from his actions good or bad omens. They were in the habit of offering him any kind of food with the hand : if he took it, the answer was considered favourable ; if he refused, it was thought to be a sinister omen. Pliny and Ammianus observe, that he refused what the unfortunate Germanicus presented to him ; and the death of that prince, which happened shortly after, was thought to confirm most unequivocally the truth of those presages. The Egyptians also drew omens respecting the welfare of their country, according to the stable in which he happened to be. To these two stables he had free access ; and when he spontaneously entered one, it foreboded benefits to Egypt, as the other the reverse ; and many other tokens were derived from accidental circumstances connected with this sacred animal.

Pausanias says, that those who wished to consult Apis first

burnt incense on an altar, filling the lamps with oil which were lighted there, and depositing a piece of money on the altar to the right of the statue of the god. Then placing their mouth near his ear, in order to consult him, they asked whatever question they wished. This done, they withdrew, covering their two ears until they were outside the sacred precincts of the temple ; and there listening to the first expression any one uttered, they drew from it the desired omen.

Children, also, according to Pliny and Solinus, who attended in great numbers during the processions in honour of the divine bull, received the gift of foretelling future events ; and the same authors mention a superstitious belief at Memphis, of the influence of Apis upon the Crocodile, during the seven days when his birth was celebrated. On this occasion, a gold and silver patera was annually thrown into the Nile, at a spot called from its form the "Bottle ;" and while this festival was held, no one was in danger of being attacked by crocodiles, though bathing carelessly in the river. But it could no longer be done with impunity after the sixth hour of the eighth day. The hostility of that animal to man was then observed invariably to return, as if permitted by the deity to resume its habits.

Apis was usually kept in one or other of the two stables—seldom going out, except into the court attached to them, where strangers came to visit him. But on certain occasions he was conducted through the town with great pomp. He was then escorted by numerous guards, who made a way amidst the crowd, and prevented the approach of the profane ; and a chorus of children singing hymns in his honour headed the procession.

The greatest attention was paid to the health of Apis ; they took care to obtain for him the most wholesome food; and they rejoiced if they could preserve his life to the full extent prescribed by law. Plutarch also notices his being forbidden to drink the water of the Nile, in consequence of its having a peculiarly fattening property. "For," he adds, " they endeavour to prevent fatness, as well in Apis, as in themselves ; always studious that their bodies may sit as light about their souls as possible, in order that their mortal part may not oppress and weigh down the more divine and immortal."

Many fêtes were held at different seasons of the year ; for, as Herodotus observes, far from being contented with one festival, the Egyptians celebrate annually a very great number : of which that of Diana (Pasht), kept at the city of Bubastis, holds the first rank, and is performed with the greatest pomp. Next to it is that of Isis, at Busiris, a city situated in the middle of the Delta, with a very large temple, consecrated to that Goddess, the Ceres of the Greeks. The third in importance is the fête of Minerva (Neith), held at Saïs ; the fourth, of the Sun, at Heliopolis ; the fifth, of Latona in the city of Buto ; and the sixth is that performed at Papremis, in honour of Mars.

In going to celebrate the festival of Diana at Bubastis, it was customary to repair thither by water ; and parties of men and women were crowded together on that occasion in numerous boats, without distinction of age or sex. During the whole of the journey, several women played on *crotala* (clappers) and some men on the flute ; others accompanying them with the voice and the clapping of hands, as was usual at musical parties in Egypt. Whenever they approached a town, the boats were brought near to it ; and while the singing continued, some of the women, in the most abusive manner, scoffed at those on the shore as they passed by.

Arrived at Bubastis, they performed the rites of the festival, by the sacrifice of a great number of victims ; and the quantity of wine consumed on the occasion was said to be more than during all the rest of the year. The number of persons present was reckoned by the inhabitants of the place to be 700,000, without including children ; and it is probable that the appearance presented by this concourse of people, the scenes which occurred, and the picturesque groups they presented, were not altogether unlike those witnessed at the modern fêtes of Tanta and Dessook in the Delta, in honour of the Sayd el Beddawee, and Shekh Ibrahim e' Dessookee.

The number stated by the historian is beyond all probability, notwithstanding the population of ancient Egypt ; and cannot fail to call to mind the 70,000 pilgrims, reported by the Moslems to be annually present at Mekkeh ; whose explanation of the mode adopted, for keeping up that exact number, is very ingenious ; every deficiency being supplied by a mysterious complement of angels, obligingly presenting themselves for the purpose ; and some contrivance of the kind may have suggested itself to the ancient Egyptians, at the festival of Bubastis.

The fête of Isis was performed with great magnificence. The votaries of the Goddess prepared themselves beforehand by fastings .and prayers, after which they proceeded to sacrifice an ox. When slain, the thighs and upper part of the haunches, the shoulders, and neck were cut off ; and the body was filled with unleavened cakes of pure flour, with honey, dried raisins, figs, incense, myrrh, and other odorific substances. It was then burnt, and a quantity of oil was poured on the fire during the process. In the mean time those present scourged themselves in honour of Osiris, uttering lamentations around the burnt offering ; and this part of the ceremony being concluded, they partook of the remains of the sacrifice.

This festival was celebrated at Busiris, to commemorate the death of Osiris, who was reported to have been buried there, as well as in other places, and whose tomb gave the name to the city. It was probably on this occasion that the branch of absinthium, mentioned by Pliny, was carried by the priests of Isis ; and dogs were made to head the procession, to commemorate the recovery of his body.

Another festival of Isis was held at harvest time, when the Egyptians throughout the country offered the first-fruits of the earth, and with doleful lamentations presented them at her altar. On this occasion she seems to answer to the Ceres of the Greeks, (as has been observed by Herodotus) ; and the multiplicity of names she bore may account for the different capacities in which she was worshipped, and remove the difficulty any change appears to present in the wife and sister of Osiris. One similarity is observable between this last and the fête celebrated at Busiris

—that the votaries presented their offerings in the guise of mourners ; and the first-fruits had probably a direct reference to Osiris, in connection with one of those allegories which represented him as the beneficent property of the Nile.

The festival of Minerva at Saïs was performed on a particular night, when every one, who intended to be present at the sacrifice, was required to light a number of lamps in the open air around his house. They were small vases filled with salt and oil, on which a wick floated, and being lighted continued to burn all night. They called it the Festival of Burning Lamps. It was not observed at Saïs alone : every Egyptian who could not attend in person was required to observe the ceremony of lighting lamps, in whatever part of the country he happened to be ; and it was considered of the greatest consequence to do honour to the deity, by the proper performance of this rite.

On the sacred lake of Saïs they represented, probably on the same occasion, the allegorical history of Osiris, which the Egyptians deemed the most solemn mystery of their religion, and which Herodotus always mentions with great caution.

The lake of Saïs still exists, near the modern town of Sa-el-Hagar ; and the walls and ruins of the town stand high above the level of the plain.

Those who went to Heliopolis, and to Buto, merely offered sacrifices. At Papremis the rites were much the same as in other places ; but when the Sun went down, a body of priests made certain gestures about the statue of Mars, while others, in greater numbers, armed with sticks, took up a position at the entrance of the temple. A numerous crowd of persons, amounting to upwards of 1000 men, armed with sticks, then presented themselves with a view of performing their vows ; but no sooner did the priests proceed to draw forward the statue, which had been placed in a small wooden gilded shrine, upon a four-wheeled car, than they were opposed by those in the vestibule, who endeavoured to prevent their entrance into the temple. Each party attacked its opponents with sticks ; when an affray ensued, which, as Herodotus observes, must, in spite of all the assertions of the Egyptians to the contrary, have been frequently attended with serious consequences, and even with loss of life.

Another festival, mentioned by Herodotus, is said to have been founded on a mysterious story of King Rhampsinitus, of which he witnessed the celebration.

On that occasion the priests chose one of their number, whom they dressed in a peculiar robe, made for the purpose on the very day of the ceremony, and then conducted, with his eyes bound, to a road leading to the temple of Ceres. Having left him there, they all retired; and two wolves were said to direct his steps to the temple, a distance of twenty stades (2 to 2½ miles), and afterwards to reconduct him to the same spot.

On the 19th of the first month was celebrated the fête of Thoth, from whom that month took its name. It was usual for those who attended "to eat honey and eggs, saying to each other, '*How sweet a thing is truth!*'" And a similar allegorical custom was observed in Mesoré, the last month of the Egyptian year, when, on "offering the first-fruits of their lentils, they exclaimed 'The tongue is fortune, the tongue is God!'"

Most of their fêtes appear to have been celebrated at the new or the full moon, the former being also chosen by the Israelites for the same purpose; and this, as well as a month being represented in hieroglyphics by a moon, may serve to show that the months of the Egyptians were originally lunar; as in many countries, to the present day.

The historian of Halicarnassus speaks of an annual ceremony, which the Egyptians informed him was performed at Saïs, in memory of the daughter of Mycerinus.

But this was evidently connected with the rites of Osiris; and if Herodotus is correct in stating that it was a heifer (and not an ox), it may have been the emblem of Athor, in the capacity she held in the regions of the dead. The honours paid to it on such an occasion could not have referred solely to a princess, whose body was deposited within it: they were evidently intended for the Deity of whom it was the emblem; and the introduction of Athor, with the mysterious rites of Osiris, may be explained by the fact of her frequently assuming the character of Isis.

Plutarch, who seems to have in view the same ceremony, states the animal exposed to public view on this occasion was an ox, in commemoration of the misfortunes reported to have happened to Osiris. "About this time (the month of Athyr, when the Etesian winds have ceased to blow, and the Nile, returning to its own channel, has left the country everywhere bare and naked), in consequence of the increasing length of the nights, the power of darkness appears to prevail, whilst that of light is diminished and overcome. The priests, therefore, practise certain doleful rites ; one of which is to expose to public view, as a proper representation of the present grief of the goddess (Isis), an ox covered with a pall of the finest black linen, that animal being looked upon as the living image of Osiris. The ceremony is performed four days successively, beginning on the 17th of the above-mentioned month. They represent thereby four things which they mourn :—1. The falling of the Nile and its retiring within its own channel : 2. The ceasing of the northern winds, which are now quite suppressed by the prevailing strength of those from the south : 3. The length of the nights and the decrease of the days : 4. The destitute condition in which the land now appears, naked and desolate, its trees despoiled of their leaves. Thus they commemorate what they call the '*loss of Osiris ;*' and on the 19th of the month (Pachons?) another festival represents the '*finding of Osiris.*' "

Small tablets in the tombs sometimes represent a black bull, bearing the corpse of a man to its final abode in the regions of the dead. The name of this bull is shown by the sculptures in the Oasis to be Apis, the type of Osiris; it is therefore not unreasonable to suppose it, in some way, related to this fable.

There were several festivals in honour of Re, or the Sun. Plutarch states that a sacrifice was performed to him, on the fourth day of every month, as related in the books of the genealogy of Horus, by whom that custom was said to have been instituted ; and so great was the veneration paid to the Sun, that they burnt incense to him three times a day—resin at his " first rising, myrrh when in the meridian, and a mixture called kuphi " at the time of setting.   The principal worship of Re was at Helio-polis, of which he was the presiding deity ; and every city had certain holy days peculiarly consecrated to its patron, besides those common to the whole country.

Another festival in honour of the Sun was held on the 30th day of Epiphi, called the birth-day of Horus's eyes, when the Sun and Moon were in the same right line with the earth ; and " on the 22d day of Phaophi, after the autumnal equinox, was a similar one, to which, according to Plutarch, they gave the name of ' the nativity of the staves of the Sun :' intimating that the Sun was then removing from the earth ; and as its light became weaker and weaker, that it stood in need of a staff to support it.   In reference to which notion," he adds, " about the winter solstice, they lead the sacred Cow seven times in pro-cession around her temple ; calling this the searching after Osiris, that season of the year standing most in need of the Sun's warmth."

Clemens mentions the custom of carrying four golden figures in the festivals of the gods.   They were, two dogs, a hawk, and an ibis, which, like the number four, had a mysterious meaning. The dogs represented the Hemispheres, the hawk the Sun, and the ibis the Moon ; but he does not state if this was usual at all festivals, or confined to those in honour of particular deities.

In their religious solemnities music was permitted, and even required, as acceptable to the gods ; except, if we may be-lieve Strabo, in the temple of Osiris, at Abydus.   It probably differed much from that used on ordinary festive occasions, and was, according to Apuleius, of a lugubrious character.   But this I have already mentioned in treating of the music of the Egyptians.*

* Chapter ii. p. 129.

The Pyramids, during the Inundation, from near the Fork of the Delta.

CHAPTER V.

ORIGIN OF THE EGYPTIANS — POPULATION OF EGYPT AND OF THE WORLD OF
OLD — HISTORY — THE KING — PRINCES — PRIESTS — THEIR SYSTEM —
RELIGION — GODS — TRIADS — DRESSES AND MODE OF LIFE OF THE PRIESTS
— SOLDIERS — ARMS — CHARIOTS — SHIPS AND NAVY — ENEMIES OF EGYPT
— CONQUESTS.

HAVING mentioned those customs particularly connected with the
private life of the Egyptians, I proceed to notice their early
history, government, and institutions; as well as the occupations
of the different classes of the community.

The origin of the Egyptians is enveloped in the same obscurity
as that of most people; but they were undoubtedly from Asia;
as is proved by the form of the skull, which is that of a Caucasian race, by their features, hair, and other evidences; and the
whole valley of the Nile throughout Ethiopia, all Abyssinia, and
the coast to the south, were peopled by Asiatic immigrations.
Nor are the Kafirs a Negro race. Pliny is therefore right in
saying that the people on the banks of the Nile, south of Syene,
were Arabs (or a Semitic race) "who also founded Heliopolis."

At the period of the colonization of Egypt, the aboriginal
population was doubtless small, and the change in the peculiarities of the new comers was proportionably slight; little variation being observable in the form of the skull from the Caucasian
original. Still there was a change: and a modification in
character as well as conformation must occur, in a greater or
less degree, whenever a mixture of races has taken place.

I may even venture to suggest that while the present races in

Europe are all traceable to an Asiatic origin, they must there have found at the period of their immigration an indigenous population, which, though small, had its influence upon them. And this conclusion is confirmed by the fact, that while in N. America the people who have become its new inhabitants are (as they always will continue to be) essentially European, the Europeans are decidedly not Asiatics, and differ entirely from them in character, habits, and appearance. The difference between all Europeans and the Asiatics is as palpable, as the identity of the new American race and their European ancestors; and this is readily explained by the Asiatic tribes who peopled Europe having mixed with the indigenous races of our continent, while the Europeans who colonised America have kept themselves distinct from the aborigines. It is not necessary that the primitive Europeans should, as some have thought, be traceable in the Basques, or any other people, and the absorption of all of them is rather to be expected after so many ages.

The Egyptians probably came to the Valley of the Nile as conquerors. Their advance was through Lower Egypt southwards; and the extraordinary notion that they descended, and derived their civilisation, from Ethiopia has long since been exploded. Equally obsolete is the idea that the Delta occupies a tract once covered by the sea, even after Egypt was inhabited; and the argument derived from Homer's "Isle of Pharos" having been a day's sail "from Ægyptus" has failed before the fact of his "Ægyptus" being the name he applies to the Nile, not to the coast of Egypt; which being rock in that part, is exactly the same distance from the Pharos now as at any previous period, though the intermediate channel has been filled up by a causeway that unites it to the shore. The oldest towns, too, on the coast of the Delta occupy the same site, close to the sea, as of old; and whatever may be the accumulation of soil, it is counterbalanced by a sinking of the land, from subterraneous agency, along the whole of the northern coast of Egypt.

Though a country which played a distinguished part in the early history of the world, its extent was very limited; Egypt itself consisting merely of the narrow strip of land between the Mediterranean and the first cataract, about seven degrees and a half of latitude. For, with the exception of the northern part about the Delta, the average width of the valley of the Nile, between the eastern and western hills, is only about seven miles, and that of the cultivable land scarcely more than five and a half, being in the widest part ten and three-quarters, and in the narrowest two miles, including the river. And that portion between Edfoo and Asouan, at the first cataract, is still narrower, barely leaving room for any soil, so that those sixty miles do not enter into the general average.

The extent in square miles of the northernmost district, between the Pyramids and the sea, is considerable; and that of the Delta alone, which forms a portion of it, may be estimated at 1976 square miles; for though it is very narrow about its apex, at the junction of the modern Rosetta and Damietta branches, it gradually widens on approaching the coast, where the base of this somewhat irregular triangle is eighty-one miles. And as much irrigated land stretches on either side E. and W. of the two branches, the northern district, with the intermediate Delta included, will be found to contain about 4500 square miles, or double the whole arable land of Egypt, which may be computed at 2255 square miles, exclusive of the Fyoom, a small province consisting of about 340.

The number of towns and villages reported to have stood on this tract, and in the upper parts of the valley of the Nile, appears incredible; and Herodotus affirms that 20,000 populous *cities* existed in Egypt during the reign of Amasis. Diodorus calculates 18,000 large villages and towns; and states that, under Ptolemy Lagus, they amounted to upwards of 30,000, a number which remained even at the period when he wrote, or about forty-four years before our era. But the population was already greatly reduced, and of the seven millions who once inhabited Egypt, about three only remained in the time of the historian; so that Josephus must overstate it when, in the reign of Vespasian, he still reckons seven millions and a half in the valley of the Nile, besides the population of Alexandria, which amounted to more than 300,000 souls. To such an extent has the population of Egypt diminished, that it now scarcely amounts to two millions; but this decrease is not peculiar to Egypt; and other countries, once more remarkable for their populousness, have undergone a similar change; while others, then scantily peopled, now teem with inhabitants. Indeed, the question suggests itself, whether the world, within historic times at least, has not always had the same amount of population as at the present day? Whatever increase has taken place in some parts of the globe, the total will not surpass that of olden times; and when we compare the populous condition of Assyria, and the neighbouring countries, Persia, India, Asia Minor, Syria, and Scythia, which, till Tartar times, spread its hordes over distant countries, we are led to the conviction that the inhabitants of the small continent of Europe, and the rising population of America, do not exceed the numbers that crowded the ancient world. This, however, is only a question I offer (with great deference) to those who are competent to decide it.

Besides the inhabitants of the country between the first cataract and the sea, Egypt included those of the neighbouring districts under her sway, who greatly increased her power; and in her flourishing days, the Ethiopians, Libyans, and others, united with her, and formed part of her permanent dominions.

The produce of the land was doubtless much greater in the earlier periods of its history than at the present day, owing as well to the superior industry of the people as to a better system of government, and sufficed for the support of a very dense population; yet Egypt, if well cultivated, could now maintain many more inhabitants than at any former period, owing to the increased extent of the irrigated land : and if the ancient Egyptians enclosed those portions of the uninundated edge of the desert which were capable of cultivation, the same expedient might still be resorted to; and a larger proportion of soil now overflowed by the rising Nile offers additional advantages. That the irrigated part of the valley was much less extensive than at

present, at least wherever the plain stretches to any distance E.
and W., or to the right and left of the river, is evident from the
fact of the alluvial deposit constantly encroaching in a horizontal direction upon the gradual slope of the desert; and, as a
very perceptible elevation of the river's bed, as well as of the
land of Egypt, has always been going on, it requires no argument to prove that a perpendicular rise of the water must cause
it to flow to a greater distance over an open space to the E.
and W.

Thus the plain of Thebes, in the time of Amunoph III., or
about 1400 years before our era, was not more than two thirds of
its present breadth; and the statues of that monarch, around which
the alluvial mud has accumulated to the height of nearly seven
feet, are based on the sand that once extended some distance before them. This at once explains why the ancient Egyptians were
constantly obliged to raise mounds round the old towns, to prevent
their being overwhelmed by the inundation of the Nile; the increased height of its rise, which took place after a certain number
of years, keeping pace with the gradual elevation of the bed of the
river. How erroneous, then, is it to suppose that the drifting sands
of the encroaching desert threaten the welfare of this country, or
have in any way tended to its downfall! and how much more
reasonable is it to ascribe the degraded condition, to which
Egypt is reduced, to causes of a far more baneful nature,—
foreign despotism, the insecurity of property, and the effects of
that old age which is the fate of every country, as well as of every
individual, to undergo! For though the sand has encroached in a
few places on the west side, from the Libyan desert, the general en-
croachment is vastly in favour of the alluvial deposit of the Nile.

Besides the numerous towns and villages in the plain, many
were prudently placed by the ancient Egyptians on the slope of
the desert, at a short distance from the irrigated land, in order
not to occupy more than was necessary of the soil so valuable for
its productions; and frequently with a view of encouraging some
degree of cultivation in the desert plain; which, though above
the reach of the inundation, might be irrigated by artificial ducts,

or by water raised from inland wells.   Mounds and ruined walls still mark the sites of those villages, in different parts of Egypt; and in a few instances the remains of magnificent temples, or the authority of ancient authors, attest the existence of large cities in similar situations.   Thus Abydus, Athribis, Tentyris, parts of Memphis, and Oxyrhinchus, stood on the edge of the desert; and the town that once occupied the vicinity of Kasr Kharóon, at the western extremity of the Fyoom, was far removed from the fertilising influence of the inundation.   This province, formerly the Nome of Crocodilopolis, or Arsinoë, was indebted entirely for its fertility to artificial irrigation; and a supply of water was conducted to it by a canal from the Nile, and kept up all the year in the immense reservoir made there by King Mœris.

The Egyptians seem at first to have had a hierarchical form of government, which lasted a long time, until Menes was chosen king, probably between 2000 and 3000 years before our era. Menes was of This, in Upper Egypt; and at his death, or that of his son, the country was divided into the southern and northern kingdoms, a Thinite and Memphite dynasty ruling at the same time.   Other independent kingdoms, or principalities, also started up, and reigned contemporaneously in different parts of Egypt. The Memphite kings of the 3rd and 4th, who built the Pyramids, and Osirtasen I., the leader of the 12th, or 2nd Theban dynasty, were the most noted among them.   The latter was the original Sesostris; but his exploits having been, many generations afterwards, eclipsed by those of Remeses the Great, they were transferred together with the name of Sesostris to the later and more glorious conqueror ; and Remeses II. became the traditional Sesostris of Egyptian history.   Osirtasen, who seems to have ruled all Egypt as lord paramount, ascended the throne about 2080 B.C.; but the contemporaneous kingdoms continued, till a new one arose which led to the subjugation of the country, and to the expulsion of the native princes from Lower, and apparently for a time from Upper Egypt also; when they were obliged to take refuge in Ethiopia.   This dominion of the Shepherd kings lasted upwards of half a century.   At length about 1530 B.C. Amosis, the leader of the 18th dynasty, having united in his own hands the previously divided power of the kingdom, drove the Shepherds out of the country, and Egypt was thenceforth governed by one king, bearing the title of " Lord of the Upper and Lower Country." Towards the latter end of this dynasty, some " Stranger kings " obtained the sceptre, probably by right of marriage with the royal family of Egypt ; (a plea on which the Ethiopian princes and others obtained the crown at different times,) and Egypt again groaned under a hateful tyranny.   They even introduced very heretical changes into the religion, they expelled the favourite God Amun from the Pantheon, and introduced a Sun worship unknown in Egypt.   Their rule was not of very long duration ; and having been expelled, their monuments, as well as every record of them, were purposely defaced.

The kings of the 18th dynasty had extended the dominion of Egypt far into Asia, and the interior of Africa, as the sculptures of the Thothmes, the Amunophs, and others show ; but Sethos and his son Remeses II., of the 19th, who reigned from about 1370 to 1270 B.C., advanced them still farther.   The conquests of the Egyptians had been pushed into Mesopotamia as early as the reign of Thothmes III., about 1445 B.C. ; the strong fortress of Carchemish remained in their hands nearly all the time till the reign of Necho ; and whenever the Egyptians boasted, in after ages, of the power of their country, they referred to the glorious era of the 18th and 19th dynasties. Remeses III., of the 20th dynasty, also carried his victorious arms into Asia and Africa, about a century after his namesake ; enforcing the tributes, previously levied by Thothmes III. and his successors, from many countries that formed part of the Assyrian empire.   But little was done by the kings who followed him, until the time of Sheshonk (Shishak), who pillaged the temple of Jerusalem, and laid Judæa under tribute B.C. 971.   The power of the Pharaohs was on the decline; and Assyria, becoming the dominant kingdom, threatened to wrest from Egypt all the possessions she had obtained during a long career of conquest.   Tirhaka (Tehrak), who with the Sabacos composed the 25th Ethiopian dynasty, checked the advance of the Assyrians, and forcing Sennacherib to retire from Judæa, restored the influence of Egypt in Syria. The Saïte kings of the 26th dynasty continued to maintain it, though with doubtful success, until the reign of Necho; when it was entirely lost; for soon after Necho had defeated and killed Josiah, king of Judah, the " king of Babylon" " smote " his army " in Carchemish,"* and took from the Egyptians " all that pertained to the king of Egypt," from the boundary torrent† on the Syrian confines " unto the river Euphrates."

No permanent conquests of any extent were henceforth made, "out of his land," by the Egyptian king; and though Apries sent an expedition against Cyprus, defeated the Syrians by sea, besieged and took Gaza and Sidon, and recovered much of the influence in Syria which had been taken from Egypt by Nebuchadnezzar, these were only temporary successes; the prestige of Egyptian power had vanished; it had been found necessary to employ Greek mercenaries in the army; and in the reign of Amasis, another still greater power than Assyria, or Babylon, arose to threaten and complete the downfall of Egypt. In the reign of his son Psammenitus, B.C. 525, Cambyses invaded the country, and Egypt submitted to the arms of Persia.

Several attempts were made by the Egyptians to recover their lost liberty; and at length, the Persian garrison having been over-powered, and the troops sent to reconquer the country having been defeated, the native kings were once more established (B.C. 414). These formed the 28th, 29th, and 30th dynasties; but the last of the Pharaohs, Nectanebo II., was defeated by Ochus, or Arta-xerxes III., B.C. 340, and Egypt again fell beneath the yoke of Persia. Eight years after this, Alexander the Great liberated it from the Persians, and Ptolemy and his successors once more erected it into an independent kingdom, though governed by a foreign dynasty, which lasted until it became a province of the Roman Empire.

Though far better pleased with the rule of the Macedonian

---

* Jerem. xlvi. 2; 2 Chron. xxxv. 20.   † *Nahal*, "rivulet."   2 Kings xxiv. 7.

kings than of the Persians, the Egyptians were never thoroughly satisfied to be subject to foreigners, whose manners and customs were so different from their own; and, however much the Ptolemies courted their goodwill, consulted their prejudices, and flattered the priesthood, they never ceased to be discontented; and occasionally showed their impatience by sudden and ill-judged outbreaks. To the Romans they were equally troublesome; but they had then ceased to be the Egyptians of bygone days; and oppression under the Persians, and loss of independence, had changed their character, and introduced the bad qualities of cunning, deceit, perverseness, and insubordination; which a shrewd and vain people often have recourse to, as their offensive and defensive weapons against an unwelcome master.

Proud of the former greatness of their nation, they could never get over the disgrace of their fallen condition; and so strong was their bias towards their own institutions and ancient form of government, that no foreign king, whose habits differed from their own, could reconcile them to his rule. For no people were more attached to their own country, to their own peculiar institutions, and to their own reputation as a nation; and the sentiments of attachment that their ancestors had always felt for their kings never lost an opportunity of displaying themselves, as was shown by the repeated and almost hopeless efforts they made to expel the Persians, as well as by the delight they manifested in once more re-establishing a native dynasty.

The king was to them the representative of the deity; his name, Phrah (Pharaoh), signifying "the sun," pronounced him the emblem of the god of light, and his royal authority was directly derived from the gods. He was the head of the religion and of the state; he was the judge and lawgiver; and he commanded the army and led it to war. It was his right and his office to preside over the sacrifices, and pour out libations to the gods; and, whenever he was present, he had the privilege of being the officiating high priest.

The sceptre was hereditary; but, in the event of a direct heir failing, the claims for succession were determined by proximity of parentage, or by right of marriage. The king was always either of the military or priestly class, and the princes also belonged to one of them. The army or the priesthood were the two professions followed by all men of rank, the navy not being an exclusive service; and the "long ships of Sesostris" and other kings were commanded by generals and officers taken from the army, as was the custom of the Turks, and some others in modern Europe to a very recent time. The law too was in the hands of the priests; so that there were only two professions. Most of the kings, as might be expected, were of the military class, and during the glorious days of Egyptian history, the younger princes generally adopted the same profession. Many held offices also in the royal household, some of the most honourable of which were fanbearers on the right of their father, royal scribes, superintendents of the granaries, or of the land, and treasurers of the king; and they were generals of the cavalry, archers, and other corps, or admirals of the fleet.

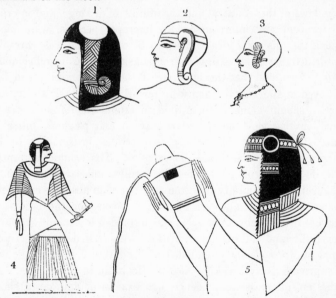

279.   Princes and Children.   *Thebes.*
1. Head-dress of a prince. 2 and 3. Lock of hair worn by children. 4. Dress of a son of
Remeses III. 5. Head-dress of a prince, Remeses.

Princes were distinguished by a badge hanging from the side
of the head, which enclosed, or represented, the lock of hair emblematic of a " son;" in imitation of the youthful god " Horus,
the son of Isis and Osiris," who was held forth as the model for
all princes, and the type of royal virtue.   For though the
Egyptians shaved the head, and wore wigs or other coverings to
the head, children were permitted to leave certain locks of hair;
and if the sons of kings, long before they arrived at the age of
manhood, had abandoned this youthful custom, the badge was
attached to their head-dress as a mark of their rank as princes;
or to show that they had not, during the lifetime of their father,
arrived at *kinghood;* on the same principle that a Spanish prince,
of whatever age, continues to be styled an " infant."

When the sovereign was a military man, it was his duty, as
well as his privilege, on ascending the throne, to be instructed in
the mysteries of the religion, and the various offices of a pontiff.
He learnt all that related to the gods, the service of the temple,
the laws of the country, and the duties of a king; and in order
to prevent any intercourse with improper persons, who might
instil into his mind ideas unworthy of a prince, it was carefully
provided that no slave or hired servant should hold any office about
his person, and that the children of the first families, who had
arrived at man's estate, and were remarkable for their ability and
piety, should alone be permitted to attend him; from the persuasion that no monarch gives way to evil passions, unless he
finds those about him ready to serve as instruments to his
caprices, and to encourage his excesses.   His conduct and mode
of life were regulated by prescribed rules, and care was taken to
protect the community from the caprices of an absolute monarch;
laws being laid down in the sacred books, for the order and
nature of his occupations.   He was forbidden to commit excesses;
even the kind and quality of his food were settled with precision;
and he was constantly reminded of his duties, both in public and
in private.   At break of day public business commenced; all
the epistolary correspondence was examined, and despatched;
the ablutions for prayer were then performed, and the monarch,
having put on his robes of ceremony, and attended by proper

officers with the insignia of royalty, repaired to the temple to superintend the customary sacrifices to the gods of the sanctuary. The victims being brought to the altar, it was usual for the high priest to place himself close to the king, while the whole congregation present on the occasion stood round at a short distance from them, and to offer up prayers for the monarch, beseeching the gods to bestow on him " health, victory, power, and all other blessings," and to " establish the kingdom unto him and his children for ever." His qualities were then separately enumerated; and the high priest particularly noticed his piety towards the gods, and his conduct towards men. He lauded his self-command, his justice, his magnanimity, his love of truth, his munificence and generosity, and, above all, his entire freedom from envy and covetousness. He exalted his moderation in awarding the most lenient punishment to those who had transgressed, and his benevolence in requiting with unbounded liberality those who had merited his favours. These and other similar encomiums having been passed on the character of the monarch, the priest proceeded to review the general conduct of kings, and to point out those faults which were the result of ignorance and misplaced confidence. And it is a curious fact, that this ancient people had already adopted the principle, that the king " could do no wrong:" and while he was exonerated from blame, every curse and evil were denounced against his ministers, and those advisers who had given him injurious counsel. The idea, too, of the king " never dying" was contained in their common formula of " life having been given him for ever."

The object of this oration, says Diodorus, was to exhort the sovereign to live in fear of the deity, and to cherish that upright line of conduct and demeanour, which was deemed pleasing to the gods; and they hoped that, by avoiding the bitterness of reproach, and by celebrating the praises of virtue, they might stimulate him to the exercise of those duties which he was expected to fulfil. The king then proceeded to examine the entrails of the victim, and to perform the usual ceremonies of sacrifice: and the hierogrammat, or sacred scribe, read those extracts from the holy writings which recorded the deeds and sayings of the most celebrated men.

These regulations were instituted by a cautious people, when the change took place which introduced the kingly form of government. The law could, if required, be repealed, to protect the country from the arbitrary conduct of a king; and even if he had the means of defying its power, there still remained a mode of avenging its dignity, for the voice of the people could punish the refractory tyrant at his death, by the disgrace of excluding his body from interment in his own tomb. It was, however, rather as a precaution that these laws were set forth: they were seldom enforced, and the indulgence of the Egyptians to their king gave him no excuse for tyranny or injustice. Nor were the rigid regulations respecting his private life vexatiously enforced; and though the quantity of wine he was allowed to drink, and numerous punctilious observances, were laid down in some old statute, he was not expected to regard them to the very letter, provided he benefited society by his general conduct. It was no difficult task for a king to be popular; the Egyptians were prone to look upon him with affection and respect; and if he had done nothing to obtain their approbation as prince, the moment he ascended the throne he was sure to be regarded with favour.

Nor did it require any great effort on his part to conform to the general rules laid down for his conduct: and by consulting the welfare of the country, he easily secured for himself that good will which was due from children to a parent; the whole nation being as anxious for the welfare of the king as for that of their own wives and children, or whatever was most dear to them. To this Diodorus ascribes the duration of the Egyptian state; which not only lasted long, but enjoyed the greatest prosperity, both at home, and in its wars with distant nations, and was enabled by its immense riches, resulting from trade and foreign conquest, to display a magnificence, in its provinces and cities, unequalled by that of any other country.

Love and respect were not merely shown to the sovereign during his lifetime, but were continued to his memory after his

death ; and the manner in which his funeral obsequies were celebrated tended to show, that, though their benefactor was no more,
they retained a grateful sense of his goodness, and admiration for
his virtues.   And what, says the historian, can convey a greater
testimony of sincerity, free from all colour of dissimulation,
than the cordial acknowledgment of a benefit, when the person
who conferred it no longer lives to witness the honour done to
his memory?

On the death of every Egyptian king, a general mourning was
instituted throughout the country for seventy days,* hymns com-
memorating his virtues were sung, the temples were closed,
sacrifices were no longer offered, and no feasts or festivals were
celebrated during the whole of that period.   The people tore
their garments, and, covering their heads with dust and mud,

280.   People throwing dust on their heads, in token of grief.   *Thebes*.

formed a procession of 200 or 300 persons of both sexes, who
met twice a day in public to sing the funeral dirge.   A general
fast was also observed, and they neither allowed themselves to
taste meat nor wheat bread, and abstained, moreover, from wine
and every kind of luxury.

* Gen. l. 3, " The Egyptians mourned for Jacob threescore and ten days," for
" so are fulfilled the days of those which are embalmed."

In the mean time the funeral was prepared, and on the last day the body was placed in state within the vestibule of the tomb, and an account was then given of the life and conduct of the deceased.

The Egyptians are said to have been divided into castes, similar to those of India; but though a marked line of distinction was maintained between the different ranks of society, they appear rather to have been classes than castes, and a man did not necessarily follow the precise occupation of his father. Sons, it is true, usually adopted the same profession or trade as their parent, and the rank of each depended on his occupation; but the children of a priest frequently chose the army for their profession, and those of a military man could belong to the priesthood.

The priests and military men held the highest position in the country after the family of the king, and from them were chosen his ministers and confidential advisers, "the wise counsellors of Pharaoh," * and all the principal officers of state.

The priests consisted of various grades—as the chief priests, or pontiffs; the prophets; judges; sacred scribes; the sphragistæ, who examined the victims for sacrifice; the stolistæ, dressers, or keepers of the sacred robes; the bearers of the shrines, banners, and other holy emblems; the sacred sculptors, draughtsmen, and masons; the embalmers; the keepers of sacred animals; and various officers employed in the processions and other religious ceremonies; under whom were the beadles, and inferior functionaries of the temple. There was also the king's own priest; and the royal scribes were chosen either from the sacerdotal or the military class.

Women were not excluded from certain offices in the temple; there were priestesses of the gods, of the kings and queens, and they had many employments connected with religion. They even attended in some religious processions; as well as at the funeral of a deceased relation; and an inferior class of women

* Isa. xix. 11; Diodor. i. 73.

acted as hired mourners on this occasion. The queens, indeed,
and other women of high rank, held a very important post in the
service of the gods; and an instance occurs of the title "pourer
out of libations" being applied to a queen, which was only given
to the priests of the altar. They usually accompanied their husbands as they made offerings in the temple, holding two sistra, or

281.   King offering, and the Queen holding two emblems.   *Thebes.*

other emblems, before the statue of the deity. This was the
office of those "holy women," whose duties in the temple of the
Theban Jupiter led to the strange mistake respecting the "Pel-
lices Jovis," or Pallacides of Amun; but its dignity and importance is sufficiently shown by its having been filled by women
of the first families in the country, and by the wives and daughters
of the kings. They were of various grades—the highest of them
were the queens, princesses, and the wives and daughters of the
high priests, who held the sistra; others praised the deity with
various instruments; and from being often called "minstrels"
of the god, their office seems to have been particularly connected
with the sacred music of the temple. The institution may have

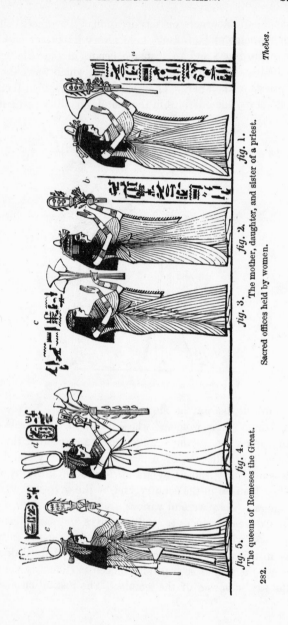

Thebes.

fig. 1.
fig. 2.   The mother, daughter, and sister of a priest.
fig. 3.   Sacred offices held by women.
fig. 4.   The queens of Remeses the Great.
fig. 5.
282.

been a sort of college, or convent; but as married women and
even young children might belong to it, they were evidently not
immured within the precincts of any place resembling a modern
nunnery; and if they were obliged to take certain vows, and
attend to the duties attached to their honourable office, nothing
prevented their performing all others of a public and social kind.
It was not forbidden to strangers naturalized in Egypt to belong
to it; and one instance occurs on a papyrus of a "foreign"
woman having the same holy office in the service of Amun.

The priests enjoyed great privileges. They were exempt from
taxes; they consumed no part of their own income in any of
their necessary expenses; and they had one of the three portions
into which the land of Egypt was divided, free from all duties.
They were provided for from the public stores, out of which they
received a stated allowance of corn, and all the other necessaries
of life; and we find that when Pharaoh, by the advice of Joseph,
took all the land of the Egyptians in lieu of corn, the priests
were not obliged to make the same sacrifice of their landed property, nor was the tax of the fifth part of the produce entailed
upon it, as on that of the other people.

In the sacerdotal as among the other classes, a great distinction
existed between the different grades; and the various orders of
priests ranked according to their peculiar office. The chief or
high priests held the first and most honourable station; but the
one who offered sacrifice and libation in the temple had the
highest post. He appears to have been called "the prophet,"
and his title in the hieroglyphic legends is "*Sem*." He superintended the sacrifice of the victims, the processions of the sacred
boats or arks, the presentation of the offerings at the altar, and
at funerals, and the anointing of the king; and the same office
was held by the sovereign, when he presented incense and libations to the gods. He was marked by a peculiar dress; a leopard
skin fitting over his linen robes; and the same was worn by the
king on similar occasions.

The duty of the prophet was to be fully versed in all matters
relating to religion, the laws, the worship of the gods, and the

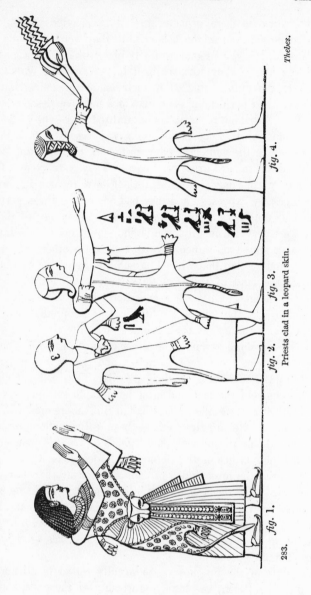

283.

fig. 1.   fig. 2.   fig. 3.   fig. 4.

Priests clad in a leopard skin.

Thebes.

discipline of the whole order of the priesthood; he presided over the temple and the sacred rites, and directed the management of the priestly revenues. In the processions he bore the holy *hydria*, or vase, which the king also carried on similar occasions; and when any new regulations were introduced in matters of religion, the prophets with the chief priests headed the conclave.

It was the great privilege of the priests to be initiated into the mysteries; though they were not all admitted indiscriminately to that honour; and " the Egyptians neither entrusted them to every one, nor degraded the secrets of divine matters by disclosing them to the profane; reserving them for the heir-apparent of the throne, and for *such priests* as excelled in virtue and wisdom." The mysteries were also distinguished into the greater and the less;—the latter preparatory to a fuller revelation of their secrets. This, and the superior knowledge they possessed, gave the priests a great ascendency over the rest of the people; and though all might enjoy the advantages of education, some branches of learning were reserved for particular persons.

Diodorus says, " The children of the priests are taught two different kinds of writing,—what is called the sacred, and the more general; and they pay great attention to geometry and arithmetic. For the river, changing the appearance of the country very materially every year, causes many and various discussions among neighbouring proprietors, about the extent of their property; and it would be difficult for any person to decide upon their claims without geometrical proof, founded on actual observation.

" Of arithmetic they have also frequent need, both in their domestic economy, and in the application of geometrical theorems, besides its utility in the cultivation of astronomical studies; for the orders and motions of the stars are observed at least as industriously by the Egyptians as by any people whatever; and they keep a record of the motions of each for an incredible number of years, the study of this science having been, from the remotest times, an object of national ambition with them. They have also most punctually observed the motions, periods, and stations of the planets, as well as the powers which they possess with respect to the nativities of animals, and what good or evil influences they exert; and they frequently foretel what is to happen to a man throughout his life, and not uncommonly predict the failure of crops, or an abundance, and the occurrence of epidemic diseases among men and beasts: foreseeing also earthquakes and floods, the appearance of comets, and a variety of other things which appear impossible to the multitude.

" But the generality of the common people learn only from their parents, or relations, that which is required for the exercise of their peculiar occupations; a few only being taught anything of literature, and those principally the better classes of artificers."

If the priests were anxious to establish a character for learning and piety, they were not less so in their endeavours to excel in the propriety of outward demeanour, and to set forth a proper example of humility and self-denial; and if not in their houses, at least in their mode of living, they were remarkable for simplicity and abstinence. They committed no excesses either in eating or drinking; their food was plain, and in a stated quantity, and wine was used with the strictest regard to moderation. And so fearful were they lest the body should not " sit light upon the soul," and excess should cause a tendency to increase " the corporeal man," that they paid a scrupulous attention to the most trifling particulars of diet; and similar precautions were extended even to the deified animals: Apis not being allowed to drink the water of the Nile, since it was thought to possess a fattening property.

They were not only scrupulous about the quantity, but the quality of their food ; and certain viands were alone allowed to appear at their table. Above all meats, that of swine was particularly obnoxious ; and fish both of the sea and the Nile was forbidden them, though so generally eaten by the rest of the Egyptians. And indeed, on the 9th of the month Thoth, when a religious ceremony obliged all the people to eat a fried fish before the door of their houses, the priests were not even then expected to conform to the general custom, and they were contented to substitute the ceremony of burning theirs at the appointed time. Beans they held in utter abhorrence ; and Herodotus affirms that " beans were never sown in the country, and if they grew spontaneously, they neither formed an article of food, nor even if cooked were ever eaten by the Egyptians." But this aversion, which originated in a supposed sanitary regulation, and which was afterwards so scrupulously adopted by Pythagoras, did not prevent their cultivation ; nor were the people obliged to abstain from them ; and they were allowed to eat them in common with other pulse and vegetables, which abounded in Egypt. Not only beans, but lentils, peas, garlick, leeks, and onions were forbidden to the priests ; who were not permitted to eat them under any pretence. The prohibition, however, regarding them, as well as certain meats, was confined to the sacerdotal order ; and even swine, if we may believe Plutarch, were not forbidden to the other Egyptians at all times : " for those who sacrificed a sow to Typho once a year, at the full moon, afterwards ate its flesh."

It is a remarkable fact that onions, as well as the first fruits of their lentils, were admitted among the offerings placed upon the altars of the gods, together with gourds, figs, garlic, *raphanus* (or *figl*), cakes, beef, goose, or wild fowl, grapes, wine, and the

284.   Fig. 1. A basket of sycamore figs.
    2, 3, 4. Hieroglyphic signifying " wife," apparently taken from it.
    5, 6. Cucurbita Lagenaria, γ, or Karra-toweel.   7. Garlic (?)
    8. Raphanus sativus *var*. edulis, or *figl*.   9. Onions.

head of the victim. Onions were generally bound in a single bundle, seldom presented singly ; and they were sometimes arranged in a hollow circular bunch, which, descending upon the table or altar, enveloped and served as a cover to whatever was placed upon it. And the privilege of presenting them in this

orm appears to have been generally enjoyed by that class of
priests who wore the leopard-skin dress.

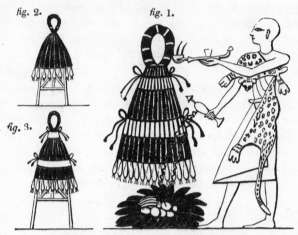

fig. 2.   fig. 1.

fig. 3.

285.   Mode of tying up the onions for some offerings.   *Thebes.*

In general, "the priests abstained from most sorts of pulse,
from mutton, and swine's flesh; and in their more solemn purifications even excluded salt from their meals;" but some vegetables
were considered lawful food, being remarkable for their wholesome nature; and many of the leguminous productions and fruits
of Egypt represented on the tables placed before priests, as part
of the *inferiæ*, or offerings to the dead, must have been acceptable
to them while living.

In their ablutions, as in their diet, they were equally severe,
and they maintained the strictest observance of numerous religious
customs. They bathed twice a day, and twice during the night;
and some who pretended to a more rigid observance of religious
duties, washed themselves with water which had been tasted by
the ibis, supposed in consequence to bear an unquestionable
evidence of purity; and shaving the head and the whole body
every third day, they spared no pains to promote the cleanliness
of their persons, without indulging in the bath, as a luxury. A
grand ceremony of purification took place, previous and pre-

paratory to their fasts, many of which lasted from seven to forty-two days, and sometimes even a longer period : during which time they abstained entirely from animal food, from herbs and vegetables, and from all extraordinary indulgences.

These " numerous religious observances," as well as the dependence of all classes upon them for instruction, and the possession of secrets known only to themselves, gave them that influence they so long possessed ; but they had obtained a power, which, while it raised their own class, could not fail to degrade the rest of the people ; who, allowed to substitute superstition for religion, and credulity for belief, were taught to worship the figures of imaginary beings, while they were excluded from a real knowledge of the Deity, and of those truths which constituted " the wisdom of the Egyptians." It was to liberate mankind from the dark superstition, in which the selfish views of the priesthood of those days had kept the world, that Moses received his grand and important mission. Men were by him taught to offer their prayers directly to the Deity, without the necessity of depending on a frail mortal, like themselves, for his pretended intercession with One equally accessible to all ; and they learnt that heaven was not to be purchased by money paid to the cupidity of a privileged class, whose assumed right of pronouncing against a man his exclusion from future happiness was an unwarrantable assumption of divine authority, and an attempt to fabricate a judgment in this world, which alone belonged to the Deity.

Privilege and power the priests certainly did enjoy, when they could reach a man after his death, by refusing him a passport to eternal happiness, and could still force his family to pay them for pretended prayers for their deceased relative ; and nothing could be better devised to enforce obedience to their will. It must, however, be allowed that they deserved credit for setting a good example by their abstinence and moral conduct ; their wisdom was shown by their tact and good policy in giving no occasion for scandal and discontent ; and they did not affect to be superior to the world by disregarding all social ties. Thus while performing the affectionate duties of fathers and husbands, they still kept up their influence over society, and ruled a flourishing country, without prostrating its resources, or checking the industry of the inhabitants; and, though we may censure an artful piece of priestcraft, we must remember that it was established long before mankind enjoyed the advantages of a thorough revelation.

The long duration of their system, and the feeling with which it was regarded by the people, may also plead some excuse for it; and while the function of judges and the administration of the laws gave them unusual power, they had an apparent claim to those offices, from having been the framers of the codes of morality, and of the laws they superintended. Instead of setting themselves above the king, and making him succumb to their power, like the unprincipled Ethiopian pontiffs, they acknowledged him as the head of the religion and the state; nor were they above the law; no one of them, nor even the king himself, could govern according to his own arbitrary will; his conduct was amenable to an ordeal of his subjects at his death, the people being allowed to accuse him of misgovernment, and to prevent his being buried in his tomb on the day of his funeral.

But though the regulations of the priesthood may have suited .the Egyptians in early times, certain institutions being adapted to men in particular states of society, they erred in encouraging a belief in legends they knew to be untrue, instead of purifying and elevating the religious views of the people, and committed the fault of considering their unbending system perfect, and suited to all times. Abuses therefore crept in; credulity, already shamefully encouraged, increased to such an extent that it enslaved the mind, and paralyzed men's reasoning powers; and the result was that the Egyptians gave way to the grossest superstitions, which at length excited universal ridicule and contempt.

The religion of the Egyptians is a subject of too great extent to be treated fully in a work of limited dimensions: little more can therefore be given of it than a general outline.

The fundamental doctrine was the unity of the Deity; but this unity was not represented, and He was known by a sentence, or an idea, being, as Jamblichus says, " worshipped in silence." But the attributes of this Being were represented under positive forms; and hence arose a multiplicity of gods, that engendered idolatry, and caused a total misconception of the real nature of the Deity, in the minds of all who were not admitted to a knowledge of the truth through the mysteries. The division of God into his attributes was in this manner. As soon as he was thought to have any reference to his works, or to man, he ceased to be quiescent; he became an agent; and he was no longer the One, but distinguishable and divisible, according to his supposed character, his actions, and his influence on the world. He was then the Creator, the Divine Goodness, (or the abstract idea of Good,) Wisdom, Power, and the like; and as we speak of Him as the Almighty, the Merciful, the Everlasting, so the Egyptians gave to each of his various attributes a particular name. But they did more: they separated them; and to the uninitiated they became distinct gods. As one of these, the Deity was Amun; probably, the divine mind in operation, the bringer to light of the secrets of its *hidden* will; and he had a complete human form, because man was the intellectual animal, and the principal design of the divine will in the creation. As the " Spirit of God " that moved on the face of the *waters*, the Deity was Nef, Nû, or Nûm; over whom the asp, the emblem of royalty and of the good genius, spread itself as a canopy, while he stood in his *boat*. As the Creator he was Pthah; and in this character he was accompanied by the figure of Truth,—a combination of it with the creative power which recalls this sentence in the Epistle of St. James, " Of his own will begat he us with the word of truth." As the principle of generation he was Khem, called " the father of his own father " —the abstract idea of father; as the goddess Maut was that of mother,—who consequently " proceeded from herself;" and other attributes, characters, and offices of the Deity held a rank according to their closer, or more distant, relation to his essence and operations.

In order to specify and convey an impression of these abstract notions to the eyes of men, it was thought necessary to distinguish them by some fixed representation; and the figures of Pthah, Osiris, Amun, Maut, Neith, and other gods or goddesses, were invented as the signs of the various attributes of the Deity. But it did not stop there; and as the subtlety of philosophical speculation entered into the originally simple theory, numerous subdivisions of the divine nature were made; and at length anything which appeared to partake of, or bear analogy to it, was admitted to a share of worship. Hence arose the various grades of deities: and they were known as the gods of the first, second, and third orders. But Herodotus is quite right in saying that the Egyptians gave no divine honours to heroes.

The Egyptian figures of gods were only vicarious forms, not intended to be looked upon as real personages; and no one was expected to believe that a being could exist with the head of an animal joined to a human body; but credulity will always do its work; the uneducated failed to take the same view of them, as the initiated portion of the community; and mere emblems soon assumed the importance of the divine personages to which they belonged. These abuses were the natural consequences of such representations; and experience has often shown how readily the mind may be drawn away from the most spiritual worship to a superstitious veneration for images, whether at first intended merely to fix the attention, or to represent some legendary tale or abstract idea. The religion of the Egyptians was a pantheism rather than a polytheism; and their admitting the sun and moon to divine worship may rather be ascribed to this than to any admixture of Sabæism. The sun was thought to possess much of the divine influence in its vivifying power, and its various other effects; and it was not only one of the grandest works, but was one of the direct *agents*, of the deity. The moon was in another similar capacity; and, as the regulator of *time* and the messenger of heaven, was figured as the Ibis-headed Thoth, the god of letters, and the deity who registered man's actions and the events of his life.

They not only attributed to the sun and moon, and to other

supposed agents, a participation in the divine essence, but even stones and plants were thought to have some portion of it; and certain peculiarities were often discovered in the habits or appearance of animals, which were supposed to bear a resemblance to the divine character. Even a king was sometimes represented making offerings to another figure of himself in the temples, signifying that his human did homage to his divine nature.

They also represented the same deity under different names and characters; Isis, from the number of her titles, was called "Myriônymus," or "with ten thousand names." A god or goddess was also worshipped as residing in some particular place, or as gifted with some peculiar quality; like the Minerva Polias, and various Minervas, the several Venuses, the Jupiters, and others; and modern custom has made a variety of Madonnas from the one Virgin.

Among other remarkable theories of the Egyptians, was the union of certain attributes into triads; the third number of which proceeded from the other two; and in every city one of these combinations was the triad of the place. The first members were not always of the first order of gods, nor was it necessary they should be; and an attribute of the deity might be combined with some abstract idea to form a result.

This notion had been held by them at the earliest periods of the Egyptian monarchy; it is, therefore, an anachronism to derive this, and other Egyptian doctrines, from the peninsula of India, in which part of the country the Hindoos did not settle till long after the age of the 18th dynasty, when they gradually dispossessed, and confined to certain districts, those original populations, who are supposed to be of Scythian origin; and if there is any connexion between the two religions of Egypt and India, this must be ascribed to the period before the two races left Central Asia.

Certain innovations were introduced in early days into the religion of Egypt, but they were partial, and such as might be expected from the progress of superstition; and if instances occur of sudden and positive changes, there is reason to believe they were brought about by the influence of strangers; as the banishment of Amun from the Pantheon for a short time, through the usurpation of the Stranger kings, towards the end of the 18th dynasty.

The expulsion of Seth, or Evil, seems also to have been the result of foreign influence. The children of Seb and Netpe (Saturn and Rhea) were Osiris, Seth, Aroeris, Isis, and Nepthys. Osiris and Seth (or Typho) were brothers; the former represented "good," the latter "evil." In early times they were both adored as gods throughout Upper and Lower Egypt, and were considered part of the same divine system. For Evil had not yet been confounded with sin or wickedness; and this last was figured as Apôp (Apophis) "the giant," who, in the form of the "great serpent," the enemy of gods and of mankind, was pierced by the spear of Horus, Atmoo, and other deities. Osiris and Seth were even placed synonymously in the names of some kings at the same period, and on the same monument; the latter was figured instructing the monarch in the use of the bow, being a cause of evil; and Seth's pouring from a vase, in conjunction with Horus, the emblems of life and power over the newly-crowned king, was intended to show that good and evil affected the world equally, as a necessary condition of human existence.

As soon as the change was resolved upon, the name and figure of the square-eared Seth were everywhere hammered out; he was branded as the enemy of Osiris; not merely opposed as a necessary consequence, but as if it were from his own agency, as Ariman to Ormusd, or the Manichæan Satan to God. The exact period when he was "expelled from Egypt" is uncertain. It may have been at the time of the 22nd dynasty; and if Seshonk (Shishak), and the other kings of that dynasty, were Assyrians, as Mr. Birch supposes, the reason of it may be readily explained.

The conflict of *wickedness* and *goodness* was not, however, a novel theory with the Egyptians, as is shown by the most ancient representations of the snake-giant Apôp, the symbol of sin; nor was the peculiar office of Osiris a late introduction, after Seth (or Typho) had been banished from the Pantheon. The unphilo-

sophical innovation was, in Seth being converted from *evil* into
sin, and made the *enemy*, instead of the *necessary antagonistic
companion*, of good.

The peculiar character of Osiris, his coming upon earth for
the benefit of mankind, with the titles of "manifester of good
and truth," his being put to death by the malice of the evil one ;
his burial and resurrection, and his becoming the judge of the
dead, are the most interesting features of the Egyptian religion.
This was the great mystery ; and this myth and his worship were
of the earliest times, and universal in Egypt. He was to every
Egyptian the great judge of the dead ; and it is evident that
Moses abstained from making any very pointed allusion to the
future state of man, because it would have recalled the well-
known Judge of the dead, and all the funeral ceremonies of Egypt,
and have brought back the thoughts of the "mixed multitude,"
and of all whose minds were not entirely uncontaminated by
Egyptian habits, to the very superstitions from which it was his
object to purify them. Osiris was to every Egyptian the great
deity of a future state ; and though different gods enjoyed particular honours in their respective cities, the importance of
Osiris was admitted throughout the country.

Certain cities and districts were appropriated to certain gods,
who were the chief deities of the place ; and while Amun had his
principal temple at Thebes, Memphis was the great city of
Pthah, as Heliopolis of Re or the Sun, and other cities of other
divinities ; no two neighbouring districts, or chief cities, being
given to the same god. But although Amun was the great god
of Thebes, as Pthah was of Memphis, it is not to be supposed that
their separate worship originated in two parts of Egypt, or that
the religions of the Upper and Lower country were once distinct,
and afterwards united into one. They were members of the
same Pantheon.

"A balance of power," as of honour, was thus established for
the principal gods ; minor deities being satisfied with towns of
minor importance. Other divinities shared the honours of the
sanctuary ; and different triads, or single gods, were admitted to a

post in the various temples of Egypt: thus Pthah had a suitable
position in a Theban adytum; Amun, and Nef, or the triads of
Thebes and of the Cataracts, of which they were respectively the
first persons, were figured on the temples at Memphis; and none
were necessarily excluded, provided room could be found for
them, except purely local deities.   Those of a neighbouring
town were more readily admitted to a place among the contemplar gods; it was at least a neighbourly compliment; and it
suited the convenience of the priests, quite as much as the gods
themselves.   Many minor divine beings, whose worship was
ordained for some particular object, and certain emblems, or
sacred animals, were admitted in one and excluded from another
place.   Thus the reverence for the crocodile, encouraged in some
inland town, in order that the canals might be properly kept up,
was found unnecessary in places by the river side, where he was
probably held in abhorrence; and the same animal, which was
highly regarded in one district, was a symbol of evil in another.

Still all was part of the same system; and however changed and
perverted it afterwards became, the original composition of the
Pantheon dates from the most remote periods of Egyptian history;
and the few innovations introduced in early times occasioned no
real alteration in the principle of the religion itself.   Changes
certainly took place in the speculations of the Egyptians, as in
their mode of representing them; and some foreign deities were
occasionally admitted into their Pantheon; yet the original progress of their ideas may readily be traced, from the one God, to
the Deity in action under various characters, as well as numerous
abstract ideas made into separate gods.   Of these last, two are
particularly worthy of notice, from being common to many other
religions; which have treated them according to their peculiar
views.   They are the Nature gods; sometimes represented as the
sun and earth, by people who were inclined to a physical rather
than an ideal treatment of the subject; but which the speculative
Egyptians considered as the vivifying or generative principle, the
abstract idea of "father," and the producing principle of nature,
or "mother;" both consequent upon the creative action.   Of

these, the latter was originally (as one of the great deities) only the abstract idea of " mother," *Maut*, whose emblem was a vulture ; and if another—Isis (sometimes identified with Athor, the Egyptian Venus), holding the child Horus, her offspring—was a direct representation of the maternal office, she may be considered an offset of the myth.   Two other goddesses also belonged to it, the one of parturition (Lucina), and the other of gestation ; the former connected with the maternal idea by having the vulture as her emblem, the latter related to Isis as the " mother of the child ;" and thus the analogies and relationships of various deities were kept up on one side, while on the other the subdivisions and minute shades of difference increased the number and complication of these ideal beings.   Thus too the relationship of deities in many mythologies may be recognised ; representing as they do the same original idea ; and the Alitta, or Mylitta (*i. e.*, " the child-bearing " goddess) of the Arabs and Assyrians, the Anaitis of Persia, the Syrian Astarte, and Venus-Urania, Cybele, and " the Queen of heaven," the " Mother of the child " found in Western Asia, Egypt, India, ancient Italy, and even in Mexico, the prolific Diana of Ephesus, and others, are various characters of the Nature goddess.

The dress of the priests was simple ; but the robes of ceremony were grand and imposing ; and besides the leopard-skin dress of the prophet were other peculiarities of costume, that marked their respective grades.   Necklaces, bracelets, garlands, and other ornaments were also put on, during the religious ceremonies in the temple.   The material of their robes was linen ; but they sometimes wore cotton garments ; and it was lawful to have an upper one of wool as a cloak ; though they were not permitted to enter a temple with this last, nor to wear woollen garments next the skin. Nor could any body be buried in bandages of that material.

The dresses of the priests consisted of an under garment, like the usual apron worn by the Egyptians, and a loose upper robe with full sleeves, secured by a girdle round the loins ; or of the apron, and a shirt with short, tight sleeves, over which was thrown a loose robe, leaving the right arm exposed.   Sometimes a priest,

when officiating in the temple, laid aside the upper vestment,
and was satisfied to wear an ample robe bound round the waist,
and descending over the apron to his ankles (which answers to

286.
1   2   3   4   5   6   7   8   9

Dresses for Priests.   *Thebes.*

8, 9. Hierogrammat, or sacred scribe.

the dress of the Stolistes mentioned by Clemens, "covering only
the lower part of the body"); and occasionally he put on a long
full garment, reaching from below the arms to the feet, and supported over the neck with straps.* Others again, in the sacred
processions, were entirely covered with a dress of this kind, reaching to the throat, and concealing even the hands and arms.†

The costume of the hierogrammat, or sacred scribe,‡ consisted

* *Fig.* 4.   † *Fig.* 5.   ‡ *Fig.* 8.

of a large kelt or apron, either tied in front, or wound round the
lower part of the body ; and the loose upper robe with full sleeves,
which, in all cases, was of the finest linen.   He had sometimes
one or two feathers on his head, as described by Clemens and
Diodorus.*   Those who bore the sacred emblems wore a long,
full apron reaching to the ankles, tied in front with long bands ;
and a strap, also of linen, passed over the shoulder to support it.†
Sometimes a priest, who offered incense, was clad in this long
apron, and the full robe with sleeves, or only in the former ;
and the dress of the same priest varied on different occasions.
Their sandals were made of the papyrus and palm-leaves, and the
simplicity of their habits extended to the bed they slept upon,
which was sometimes a skin stretched on the ground, or a sort of
wicker bedstead of palm branches,‡ covered with a mat or a skin ;
and their head was supported by a wooden concave pillow.

The same mode of resting the head was common to all the

287.   Alabaster pillow for the head.   *Alnwick Museum.*

Egyptians, and a considerable number of these stools § have been
found in the tombs of Thebes : generally of sycamore, acacia, or

* Woodcut 286, *fig.* 9.   † *Fig.* 6.   ‡ Woodcut 84, *fig.* 1, p. 71.
        § Woodcuts 287, and 82, 83, p. 71.

tamarisk wood; or of alabaster, not inelegantly formed, and frequently ornamented with coloured hieroglyphics.   In Abyssinia, and in parts of Upper Ethiopia, they still adopt the same support for the head; and the materials of which they are made are either wood, stone, or common earthenware.   Nor are they peculiar to Abyssinia and the valley of the Nile: the same custom prevails in far distant countries; and we find them used in Japan, China, and Ashantee, and even in the island of Otaheite (Tahiti), where they are also of wood, but longer and less concave than those of Africa.

Next in rank to the priests were the military.   To them was assigned one of the three portions into which the land of Egypt was divided by an edict of Sesostris, in order, says Diodorus, " that those who exposed themselves to danger in the field might be more ready to undergo the hazards of war, from the interest they felt in the country as occupiers of the soil; for it would be absurd to commit the safety of the community to those who possessed nothing which they were interested in preserving."   Each soldier, whether on duty or no, was allowed 12 arouræ of land (a little more than eight English acres) free from all charge; and another important privilege was, that no soldier could be cast into prison for debt; Bocchoris, the framer of this law, considering that it would be dangerous to allow the civil power the right of arresting those who were the chief defence of the state.   They were instructed from their youth in the duties and requirements of soldiers, and trained in all the exercises that fitted them for an active career; and a sort of military school appears to have been established for the purpose.

Each man was obliged to provide himself with the necessary arms, offensive and defensive, and everything requisite for a campaign; and he was expected to hold himself in readiness for taking the field when required, or for garrison duty.   The principal garrisons were posted in the fortified towns of Pelusium, Marea, Eileithyias, Hieraconpolis, Syene, Elephantine, and other intermediate places; and a large portion of the army was frequently called upon, by their warlike monarchs, to invade a foreign country, or to suppress those rebellions which occasionally broke out in the conquered provinces.

The whole military force, consisting of 410,000, was divided into two corps, the Calasiries and Hermotybies. They furnished a body of men to do the duty of royal guards, 1000 of each being annually selected for that purpose; and each soldier had an additional allowance of " five *minæ* of bread, with two of beef, and four *arusters* of wine," as daily rations, during the period of his service.

The Calasiries (*Klashr*) were the most numerous, and amounted to 250,000 men, at the time that Egypt was most populous. They inhabited the nomes of Thebes, Bubastis, Aphthis, Tanis, Mendes, Sebennytus, Athribis, Pharbæthus, Thmuis, Onuphis, Anysis, and the Isle of Myecphoris, which was opposite Bubastis; and the Hermotybies, who lived in those of Busiris, Saïs, Chemmis, Papremis, the Isle of Prosopitis, and the half of Natho, made up the remaining 160,000. It was here that they abode while retired from military service, and in these nomes their farms or portions of land were situated, which tended to encourage habits of industry, and keep up a taste for active employment.

Besides the native corps they had mercenary troops, who were enrolled either from the nations in alliance with the Egyptians, or from those who had been conquered by them. They were divided into regiments, sometimes disciplined in the same manner as the Egyptians, though allowed to retain their arms and costume; but they were not on the same footing as the native troops; they had no land, and merely received pay, like other hired soldiers. Strabo speaks of them as mercenaries; and the million of men he mentions must have included these foreign auxiliaries. When formally enrolled in the army they were considered a part of it, and accompanied the victorious legions on their return from foreign conquest; and they sometimes assisted in performing garrison duty in Egypt, in the place of those Egyptian troops which were left to guard the conquered provinces.

The strength of the army consisted in archers, whose skill con-

          fig. 1.   *fig.* 2.   *fig.* 3.   *fig.* 4.

288.   Allies of the Egyptians.   *Thebes.*

tributed mainly to the successes of the Egyptians; as of our
own ancestors; and their importance is shown by the Egyptian
" soldier" being represented as an archer kneeling, often preceded by the word " *Klashr*," converted by Herodotus into
" *Calasiris*." They fought either on foot or in chariots, and
may therefore be classed under the separate heads of a mounted
and unmounted corps; and they constituted a great part of both
wings. Several bodies of heavy infantry, divided into regiments,
each distinguished by its peculiar arms, formed the centre; and
the cavalry (which, according to the Scriptural accounts, was
numerous) covered and supported the foot.

    Though Egyptian horsemen are rarely found on any monu-
ments, they are too frequently and positively noticed in sacred
and profane history to allow us to question their employment;
and an ancient battle-axe represents a mounted soldier on its
blade.*

* Woodcut 355.

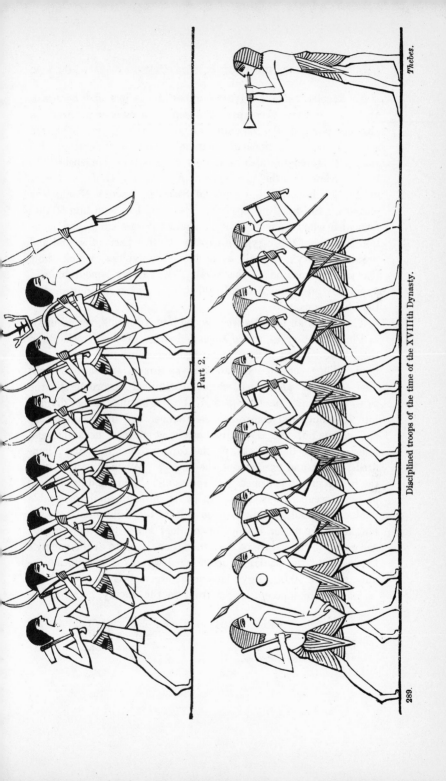

Part 2.

Disciplined troops of the time of the XVIIIth Dynasty.

Thebes.

At Jacob's funeral a great number of chariots and *horsemen* are said to have accompanied Joseph;* *horsemen* as well as chariots pursued the Israelites on their leaving Egypt;† the song of Moses mentions in Pharaoh's army the " horse an his rider;"‡ Herodotus also represents Amasis " on horseback " in his interview with the messenger of Apries; and Diodorus speaks of 24,000 horse in the army of Sesostris, besides 27,000 war chariots. Shishak, the Egyptian Sheshonk, had with him 60,000 horsemen when he went to fight against Jerusalem;§ and mention is made of the Egyptian cavalry in other parts of sacred and profane history; as well as in the hieroglyphics, which show that the " command of the cavalry " was a very honourable and important post, and generally held by the most distinguished of the king's sons.

The Egyptian infantry was divided into regiments, very similar, as Plutarch observes, to the λοχοι and ταξεις of the Greeks; and these were formed and distinguished according to the arms they bore. They consisted of bowmen, spearmen, swordsmen, clubmen, slingers, and other corps, disciplined according to the rules of regular tactics; || and the regiments being divided into battalions and companies, each officer had his peculiar rank and command, like the chiliarchs, hecatontarchs, decarchs, and others among the Greeks, or the captains over thousands, hundreds, fifties, and tens, among the Jews.¶ When in battle array, the heavy infantry, armed with spears and shields, and a falchion, or other weapon, was drawn up in the form of an impregnable phalanx;** and the bowmen as well as the light infantry were taught either to act in line, or to adopt more open movements, according to the nature of the ground, or the state of the enemy's battle. But the phalanx once formed was fixed and unchangeable, and the 10,000 Egyptians in the army of Crœsus could not be induced to oppose a larger front to the enemy, being accus-

* Gen. l. 9.   † Exod. xiv. 28: *comp.* 2 Kings, xviii. 24; Isa. xxxvi. 9.
‡ Exod. xv. 21.   § 2 Chron. xii. 3.
|| See woodcuts 289, 290.   ¶ Deut. i. 15.
** See woodcut next page.

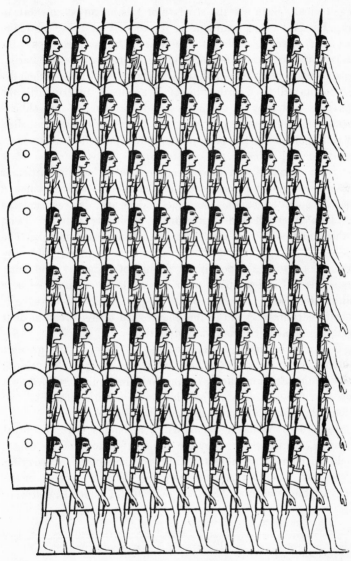

290.   Phalanx of heavy infantry.   *Thebes.*

tomed always to form in a compact body, having 100 men in
each face.   Such was the strength of this mass that no efforts of
the Persians could avail against it; and Cyrus being unable to
break it, after he had defeated the rest of Crœsus's army, gave the
Egyptians honourable terms, assigning them the cities of Larissa
and Cyllene, near Cumæ and the sea, for an abode; where their descendants still lived in the time of Xenophon.   In that battle the
phalanx had adopted the huge shields, reaching to the soldiers'
feet, and completely covering them from the enemy's missiles,
which some of the Egyptian infantry are represented to have used
at the period of the VIth Dynasty.*

Each battalion, and indeed each company, had its particular
standard, which represented a sacred subject,—a king's name, a
sacred boat, an animal, or some emblematic device; and the
soldiers either followed or preceded it, according to the service on
which they were employed, or as circumstances required.   The
objects chosen for their standards were such as were regarded by
the troops with a superstitious feeling of respect;† and being
raised, says Diodorus, on a spear (or staff), which an officer bore
aloft,‡ they served to point out to the men their respective regiments, encouraged them to the charge, and offered a conspicuous
rallying point in the confusion of battle.

The post of standard-bearer was at all times of the greatest
importance.   He was an officer, and a man of approved valour;
and in the Egyptian army he was sometimes distinguished by a
peculiar badge suspended from his neck, which consisted of two
lions, the emblems of courage, and other devices.

Besides the ordinary standards of regiments were the royal
banners, and those borne by the principal persons of the household near the king himself.   The peculiar office of carrying
these, and the *flabella*, was reserved for the royal princes, or the
sons of the nobility.   They had the rank of generals, and were

---

* See woodcut 300.
† Solomon, in his Song, says, "Terrible as an army with banners," vi. 4.
They were used by the Jews, Ps. xx. 5; lx. 4; Isa. xiii. 2.   Woodcut 291.
‡ Woodcut 289.

291.   Egyptian standards.   *Thebes.*

either despatched to take command of a wing, or a division, and
remained in attendance upon the monarch; and their post during
the royal triumph, the coronation, or other grand ceremonies, was
close to his person. Some bore the fans of state behind the
throne, or supported the seat on which he was carried to the

292.   Officers of the household.   *Thebes.*

temple; others held the sceptre, and waved flabella before him; and the privilege of serving on his right, or left, hand depended on the grade they enjoyed. A wing was called "*horn*," as by the Greeks and Romans.

The troops were summoned by sound of trumpet*—an instrument, as well as the long drum, used by the Egyptians at the earliest period;† and the trumpeters are represented in the battle-scenes of Thebes either standing still, and summoning the troops to form, or in the act of leading them to the charge.

The offensive weapons of the Egyptians were the bow, spear, two species of javelin, sling, a short and straight sword, dagger, knife, falchion or *ensis falcatus*, axe or hatchet, battle-axe, pole-axe, mace or club, and the *lissán*,—a curved stick similar to that still in use among the modern Ethiopians. Their defensive arms consisted of a helmet of metal, or a quilted headpiece; a cuirass, or coat of armour, made of metal plates, or quilted with metal

* Woodcut 289.   † See above, woodcuts, pp. 104, 105.

bands, and an ample shield. But they had no greaves; and the only coverings to the arms were a part of the cuirass, forming a short sleeve, and extending about half way to the elbow.

The soldier's chief defence was his shield, which, in length, was equal to about half his height, and generally double its own breadth. It was most commonly covered with bull's hide, having the hair outwards, sometimes strengthened by one or more

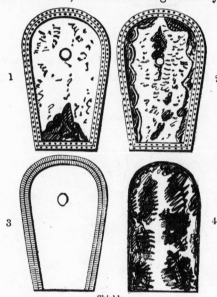

293.   Shields.   *Thebes.*

rims of metal, and studded with nails or metal pins, the inner part being a wooden frame. It was on this account that the shields of the Egyptians, who had fallen in the battle between Artaxerxes and the younger Cyrus, were collected by the Greeks for firewood, together with arrows, baggage-waggons, and other things made of wood.

In shape, the Egyptian shield resembled the ordinary funereal tablets found in the tombs, circular at the summit and squared at the base, frequently with a slight increase or swell towards the top; and near the upper part of the outer surface was a circular

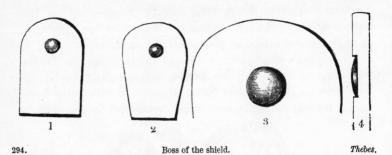

294. Boss of the shield. *Thebes.*

cavity in lieu of a boss, the use of which is not easily explained. To the inside of the shield was attached a thong, by which they

295. Thong inside the shield. *Thebes.*

suspended it upon their shoulders, as described by Xenophon; and an instance occurs of a shield so supported, which is shown

to be concave within; like that used in Assyria.*   It appears that
the handle was so made that they might pass their arm through

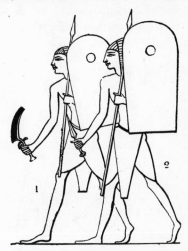

296. Concave shield.   *Thebes.*   297. Mode of carrying the shield. *Thebes.*

it and grasp a spear: but this may only be another mode of representing the shield slung at their back. The handle was sometimes

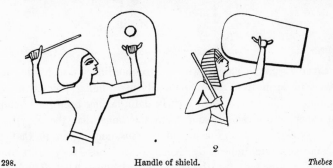

298.   Handle of shield.   *Thebes*

placed horizontally, across the shield, sometimes vertically; but
the latter was its more usual position.†

* Woodcut 296. Layard, N. and Bab., p. 457.   † Woodcuts 295 and 298.

Some lighter bucklers, furnished with a wooden bar, placed across the upper part, which was held with the hand, are represented at Beni-Hassan; but these appear to have belonged rather to foreigners than to Egyptian soldiers.

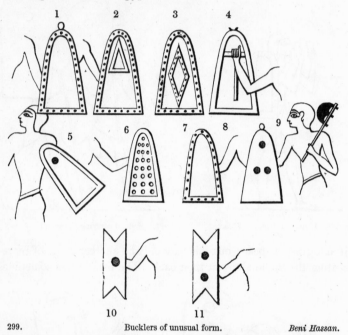

299.   Bucklers of unusual form.   *Beni Hassan.*

Some Egyptian shields were of extraordinary dimensions, and varied in form from those generally used, being pointed at the summit. They were of very early date, having been used before the Shepherd invasion; and were the same that the Egyptian phalanx carried in the army of Crœsus, and again in that of Artaxerxes, mentioned by Xenophon. But they were not generally adopted by the Egyptian troops, who found the common shield sufficiently large, and more convenient.

The Egyptian bow was not unlike that used in later times by European archers. The string was either fixed upon a projecting piece of horn, or inserted into a groove or notch in the wood,

300.   Large shield of early time.   *O'Sioot.*

at either extremity, differing in this respect from that of the Koofa, and some other Asiatic people, who secured the string by passing it over a small nut which projected from the circular ends of the bow.

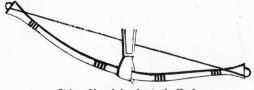

301.   String of bow belonging to the Koofa.   *Thebes.*

The Ethiopians and Libyans, who were famed for their skill in archery, adopted the same method of fastening the string as the Egyptians, and their bow was similar in form and size to that of their neighbours.

The Egyptian bow was a round piece of wood, from five to five feet and a half in length, either almost straight, and tapering to a point at both ends; some of which are represented in the sculptures, and have even been found at Thebes; or curving

fig. 1.

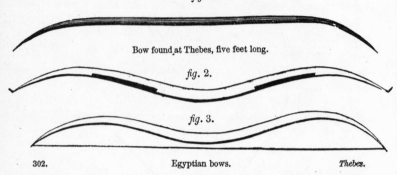

Bow found at Thebes, five feet long.

fig. 2.

fig. 3.

302.   Egyptian bows.   *Thebes.*

inwards in the middle, when unstrung, as in the paintings of the
tombs of the kings; and in some instances a piece of leather
or wood was attached to or let into it, above and below the
centre.

In stringing it, the Egyptians fixed the lower point in the
ground, and, standing or seated, the knee pressed against the

303. Usual mode of stringing the bow. *Thebes and Beni Hassan.*   304. Stringing a bow. *Beni Hassan.*

inner side of the bow, they bent it with one hand, and then
passed the string with the other into the notch at the upper extremity; and one instance occurs of a man resting the bow on

his shoulder, and bracing it in that position. While shooting, they frequently wore a guard on the left arm, to prevent its being hurt by the string; and this was fastened round the wrist, and secured by a thong tied above the elbow. Sometimes a groove of metal was fixed upon the fore knuckle, in which the arrow rested and ran when discharged; and the chasseur, whose bow appears to have been less powerful than those used in war, occasionally held spare arrows in his right hand, while he pulled the string. (*Woodcut* 306.)

305.   A guard worn on the wrist.   *Thebes.*

Their mode of drawing it was either with the forefinger and thumb, or the two forefingers; and though in the chase they often brought the arrow merely to the breast, (—a sort of snap-shooting adopted in the buffalo hunts of America—), their custom in war, as with the old English archers, was to carry it to the ear, the shaft of the arrow passing very nearly in a line with the eye.

The Egyptian bow-string was generally of catgut; and so great was their confidence in the strength of it and of the bow, that an archer from his car sometimes used them to entangle his opponent, whilst he smote him with a sword.

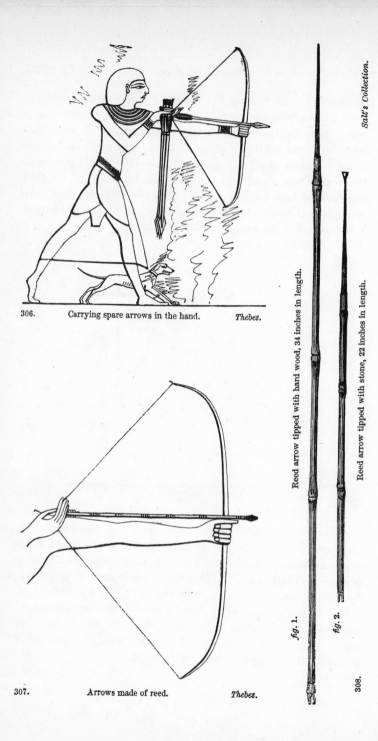

306.   Carrying spare arrows in the hand.   *Thebes.*

307.   Arrows made of reed.   *Thebes.*

Salt's Collection.

Reed arrow tipped with hard wood, 34 inches in length.

Reed arrow tipped with stone, 22 inches in length.

fig. 1.

fig. 2.

308.

Their arrows varied from twenty-two to thirty-four inches in length; some were of wood, others of reed;* frequently tipped with a metal head; and winged with three feathers,† glued longitudinally, and at equal distances, upon the other end of the shaft, as on our own arrows. Sometimes, instead of the metal head, a piece of hard wood was inserted into the reed, which terminated in a long tapering point;‡ but these were of too light and powerless a nature to be employed in war, and could only have been intended for the chase; in others, the place of the metal was supplied by a small piece of flint, or other sharp stone, secured by a firm black paste;§ and though used occasionally in battle, they appear from the sculptures to have belonged more particularly to the huntsman; and the arrows of archers are generally represented with bronze heads,‖ some barbed, others

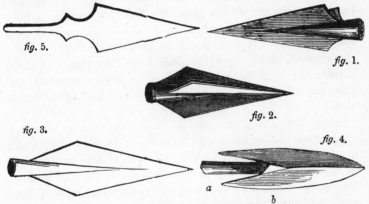

fig. 5.			fig. 1.

fig. 3.			fig. 2.

fig. 4.

a

b

309.			Metal heads of arrows.			*Alnwick Museum and Thebes.*
Fig. 4 had its shank (a) let into the hollow end of the shaft, and the projection above b acted as a stop.

triangular, and many with three or four projecting blades, placed at right angles, and meeting in a common point. Stone-tipped arrows were not confined to an ancient era, nor were they peculiar to the Egyptians; the Persians and other eastern people frequently used them, even in war; and recent discoveries have

* Woodcuts 307 and 308.		† Woodcut 306.		‡ Woodcut 308, *fig.* 1.
§ Woodcut 308, *fig.* 2.			‖ Woodcuts 309 and 348.

ascertained that they were adopted by the Greeks themselves, several having been found in places unvisited by the troops of Persia, as well as on the plain of Marathon, and other fields of battle where they fought.

Each bowman was furnished with a capacious quiver, about four inches in diameter, and consequently containing a plentiful supply of arrows, which was supported by a belt, passing over the shoulder, and across the breast, to the opposite side. Their mode of carrying it differed from that of the Greeks, who bore it upon their shoulder, and from that of some Asiatic people, who suspended it vertically at their back, almost on a level with the elbow; or at their thigh; the usual custom of the Egyptian soldier being to fix it nearly in a horizontal position, and to draw out the arrows from beneath his arm.* Instances also occur in the sculptures of the quiver placed at the back, and projecting above the top of the shoulder; but this appears to have been only during the march, or at a time when the arrows were not required.† It was closed by a lid or cover, like the quiver itself, highly decorated; and, when belonging to a chief, surmounted with the head of a lion, or other ornament; and this, on being thrown open, remained attached by a leather thong.

They had also a case for the bow, intended to protect it against the sun or damp, and to preserve its elasticity; which was opened by drawing off a moveable cap of soft leather sewed to the upper end. It was always attached to the war-chariots; and across it, inclined in an opposite direction, another large case, containing two spears and an extra supply of arrows;‡ and, besides the quiver he wore, the warrior had frequently three others attached to his car.

Archers of the infantry were furnished with a smaller sheath for the bow,§ of which it covered the centre, leaving the two ends exposed; and, being of a pliable substance, probably leather, it was put round the bow, as they held it in their hand

* Woodcut 348.
‡ Woodcuts 326, 327, 331.
† Woodcut 325, *fig.* 2.
§ Woodcut 289, part 1.

during a march. Besides the bow, their principal weapon of offence, they, like the mounted archers who fought in cars, were provided with a falchion, dagger, curved stick, mace, or battle-axe, for close combat when their arrows were exhausted; and their defensive arms were the helmet, or quilted headpiece, and a coat of the same materials; but they had no shield, that being an impediment to the free use of the bow.

The spear, or pike, was of wood,* between five and six feet in length, with a metal head, into which the shaft was inserted and fixed with nails. The head was of bronze or iron, often very large, and with a double edge; but the spear does not appear to have been furnished with a metal point at the other extremity, called σαυρωτηρ by Homer,† which is still adopted in Turkish, modern Egyptian, and other spears, in order to plant them upright in the ground; as the spear of Saul was fixed near his head, while he "lay sleeping within the trench." ‡ Spears of this kind may sometimes come under the denomination of javelins, the metal being intended as well for a counterpoise in their flight as for the purpose above mentioned; but such an addition to those of the heavy-armed infantry was neither requisite nor convenient.

The javelin, lighter and shorter than the spear, was also of wood, and similarly armed with a strong two-edged metal head, of an elongated diamond, or leaf shape, either flat, or increasing in thickness at the centre, and sometimes tapering to a very long point;§ and the upper extremity of its shaft terminated in a bronze knob, surmounted by a ball with two thongs or tassels, intended both as an ornament and a counterpoise to the weight of its point. It was used like a spear, for thrusting, being held with one or with two hands; and occasionally, when the adversary was within reach, it was darted, and still retained in the warrior's grasp; the shaft being allowed to pass through his hand till stopped by the blow, or by the fingers suddenly closing

* Woodcuts 289, 290, 297, 310 a.　　　　† Hom. Il. x, 151.
‡ 1 Sam. xxvi. 7.　Comp. Virg. Æn. xii. 130.
§ Woodcut 355, fig. 9.

2 A 2

on the band of metal at the end; a custom still common among the modern Nubians and Ababdeh. They had another javelin,

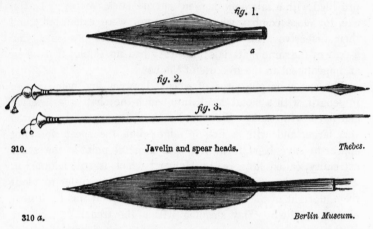

310.   Javelin and spear heads.   *Thebes.*

310 *a.*   *Berlin Museum.*

apparently of wood, tapering to a sharp point, without the usual metal head;* and a still lighter kind, armed with a small bronze

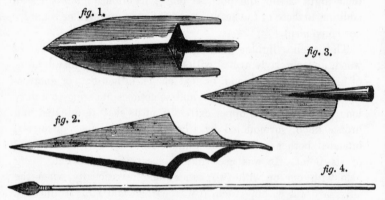

311.   Heads of small javelins.   *Alnwick Museum and Thebes.*

point,† which was frequently four-sided, three-bladed,‡ or broad and nearly flat;§ and, from the upper end of the shaft being desti-

* Woodcut 310, *fig.* 3.   † Woodcut 310, *fig.* 1; and woodcut 355, *fig.* 8.
‡ Woodcut 311, *fig.* 2.   § *Fig.* 3.

tute of any metal counterpoise,* it resembled a dart now used by
the people of Dar-Foor, and other African tribes, who, without
any scientific knowledge of projectiles, and of the curve of a para-
bola, dexterously strike their enemy with its falling point.

Another inferior kind of javelin was made of reed, with a metal
head; but this can scarcely be considered a military weapon, nor
would it hold a high rank among those employed by the Egyptian
chasseur, most of which were of excellent workmanship.

The sling was a thong of leather, or string plaited;† broad in
the middle, and having a loop at one end, by which it was fixed
upon and firmly held with the hand; the other extremity terminating in a lash, which escaped from the finger as the stone was
thrown: and when used, the slinger.whirled it two or three times
over his head, to steady it and increase the impetus.‡

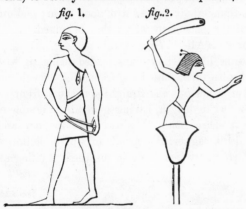

fig. 1.   *fig.* 2.

312.   Slingers.   *Beni Hassan and Thebes.*

It was an arm looked upon by many of the Greeks with great
contempt; but, when exposed to the missiles of the Persians, the
" Ten thousand " found the necessity of adopting it; and the leaden
bullet of the Rhodian slingers proved, by its greater range, its superiority over the large stones thrown by the enemy.   Other Greeks

* Woodcut 311, *fig.* 4.
† As that still used in Egypt to drive away birds from the corn-fields.
‡ Woodcuts 49 and 355, *figs.* 4 and 5.

were also skilful with the sling, as the Achæans and Acarnanians ; but the people most renowned for it were the natives of the Balearic Islands, who considered the sling of so much importance that the principal care of a parent was to instruct a boy in its use ; and he was not permitted to have his breakfast, until he had dislodged it from a beam with the sling.   This unpleasant alternative does not appear to have been imposed on the more fortunate sons of an Egyptian family, nor was the same consequence attached to the sling as to the bow and many other weapons.

Most Greeks, who used the sling, threw leaden plummets of an elongated spherical shape, or, rather, like an olive pointed at each end ;—proving that the principle of " *the pointed ball*" was not unknown to them ; and, indeed, all boys have long since found that an oval-shaped stone goes farther than a round one. Some had a thunderbolt represented upon them ; and others bore the name of the person to whom they belonged, or a word, as ΑΓΩΝΙΣ, or ΔΕΞΑΙ—" *Take that.*"

The Achæans, like the Egyptians, loaded their sling with a round pebble ; and a bagful of these hung from a belt over the shoulder.*

The Egyptian sword was straight and short, from two and a half to three feet in length, having generally a double edge, and tapering to a sharp point.   It was used for cut and thrust. They had also a dagger, the handle of which, hollowed in the centre, and gradually increasing in thickness at either extremity,

fig. 1.

fig. 2.

313.   Daggers in their sheaths, with inlaid handles.   *Thebes.*

was inlaid with costly stones, precious woods, or metals ; and the pommel of that worn by the king in his girdle was frequently surmounted by one or two heads of a hawk, the symbol

* Woodcut 312, *fig.* 1.

314.   Stabbing an enemy.   *Thebes.*

of Phrah, or the Sun, the title given to the monarchs of the Nile.
It was much smaller than the sword: its blade was about ten or
seven inches in length, tapering gradually in breadth, from one

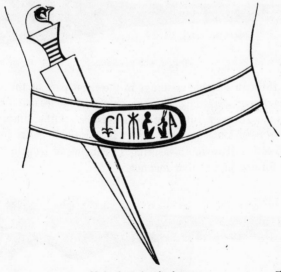

315.   Mode of wearing the dagger.   *Thebes.*

inch and a half to two-thirds of an inch, towards the point; and the total length, with the handle, only completed a foot or sixteen inches. The blade was bronze, thicker in the middle than at the edges, and slightly grooved in that part; and so exquisitely was the metal worked, that some retain their pliability and spring after a period of several thousand years, and almost resemble steel in elasticity. Such is the dagger of the Berlin collection, which was discovered in a Theban tomb, together with its leathern sheath. The handle is partly covered with metal, and adorned with numerous small pins and studs of gold, which are purposely

fig. 1.

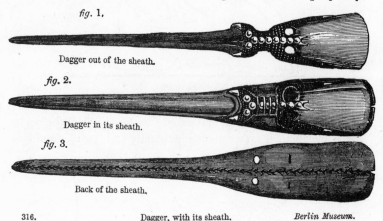

Dagger out of the sheath.

fig. 2.

Dagger in its sheath.

fig. 3.

Back of the sheath.

316.　　　　　　　Dagger, with its sheath.　　　　*Berlin Museum.*

shown through suitable openings in the front part of the sheath; but the upper extremity consists solely of bone, neither ornamented nor covered with any metal casing. Other instances of this have been found; and a dagger in Mr. Salt's collection, now in the British Museum, measuring 11½ inches in length, had the handle formed in a similar manner.

317.　　　　　　　Egyptian dagger, 11½ inches.　　　　*British Museum.*

I have the blade of a smaller dagger, also of bronze, bearing the Amunoph II., 5¼ inches long, found at Thebes; and a knife, apparently of steel, is represented in the paintings, which had a single edge.

There was also a falchion called Shopsh, or Khopsh; resembling in form and name the κοπις of the Argives, reputed to be an Egyptian colony. It was more generally used than the sword, being borne by light as well as heavy armed troops; and that it was a most efficient weapon is evident, as well from the size and form of the blade as from its weight; the back of this bronze or iron blade being sometimes cased with brass.*

Officers as well as privates carried the falchion; and the king himself is frequently represented in close combat with the enemy, armed with it, or with the hatchet, battle-axe, pole-axe, or mace. A simple stick is more usually seen in the hand of officers commanding corps of infantry; but they had also other weapons; and, in leading their troops to the charge, they were armed in the same manner as the king when he fought on foot.

The axe, or hatchet, was small and simple, seldom exceeding two, or two feet and a half, in length: it had a single blade, and no instance is met with of a double axe resembling the *bipennis* of the Romans. It was of the same form as that used by the Egyptian carpenters; and served for close combat as well as for breaking down the gates of a town, and felling trees to construct engines for an assault. Independent of the bronze pins which secured the blade, the

318.   Axes and hatchets.
Thebes, and Salt's Collection.

* Woodcut 297, *fig.* 1.

handle was bound in that part with thongs of hide, in order
to prevent the wood, grooved to admit the metal, from splitting,
when a blow was struck.

The axe was less ornamented than other weapons: some bore
the figure of an animal, a boat, or fancy device, engraved upon
the blade; and the handle, frequently terminating in the shape
of a gazelle's foot, was marked with circular and diagonal lines,
representing bands, as on the projecting torus of an Egyptian
temple, or like the ligature of the Roman fasces.* The soldier,
on his march, either held it in his hand, or suspended it at his
back with the blade downwards; but it does not appear from
the sculptures to have been covered by a sheath, nor is any
mode of wearing a sword indicated by them, except as a dagger
in the girdle, the point sloping to the left.†

The blade of the battle-axe was, in form, not unlike the

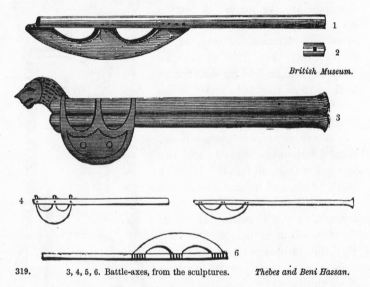

British Museum.

319.   3, 4, 5, 6. Battle-axes, from the sculptures.   *Thebes and Beni Hassan.*

Parthian shield; a segment of a circle, divided at the back into
two smaller segments, whose three points were fastened to the

---

* Woodcuts 318, and 355, *fig.* 3.   † As in woodcut 315.

handle with metal pins.   It was of bronze, and sometimes (as the colour of those in the paintings shows) of steel; and the length of the handle was equal to, or more than double that of, the blade.   In the British Museum is a portion of one of these weapons.*   Its bronze blade is thirteen inches and a half long, and two and a half broad, inserted into a silver tube, secured with nails of the same metal.   The wooden handle once fixed into this tube is wanting; but, judging from those represented at Thebes, it was considerably longer than the tube, and even protruded a little beyond the extremity of the blade, where it was sometimes ornamented with the head of a lion or other device, receding slightly,† so as not to interfere with the blow.   The total length of these battle-axes may have been from three to four feet, and sometimes much less;‡ and their blades varied slightly in shape.§

The pole-axe was about three feet in length, but apparently more difficult to wield than the preceding, owing to the great weight of a metal ball to which the blade was fixed; and required, like the mace, a powerful as well as a skilful arm.   The handle was generally about two feet in length, sometimes much longer; the

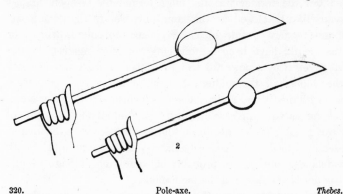

320.   Pole-axe.   *Thebes.*

ball four inches in its greatest diameter, and the blade varied from ten to fourteen inches, by two and three in breadth.

The mace was very similar to the pole-axe, without a blade.

---

* Woodcut 319, *fig.* 1.   † As *fig.* 3.
‡ As *fig.* 6, which is from the sculptures.   § *Figs.* 3 and 6.

It was of wood, bound with bronze, about two feet and a half in length, and furnished with an angular piece of metal, projecting from the handle, which may have been intended as a guard, though in many instances they represent the hand placed above it, while the blow was given.*

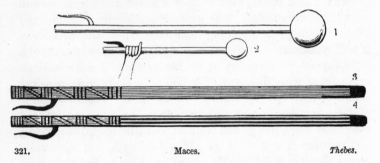

321.   Maces.   *Thebes.*

They had another mace,† similar in many respects to this, without the ball, and, to judge from its frequent occurrence in the sculptures, more generally used, and evidently far more manageable; but the former was the most formidable weapon against armour (like that used for the same purpose by the Memlooks, and the modern people of Cutch); and no shield, helmet, or cuirass, could have been a sufficient protection against the impetus given it by a powerful arm. Neither of these was peculiar to the chiefs: all the soldiers in some infantry regiments were armed with them; and a charioteer was furnished with one or more, which he carried in a case attached with the quiver to the side of his car. ‡ A club has also been found, and is now in the British Museum, armed with wooden teeth, similar to those in the South Sea Islands; but it was probably of some rude, foreign people, and is not represented on the monuments.

In ancient times, when the fate of a battle was frequently decided by personal valour, the dexterous management of such arms was of great importance; and a band of resolute veterans, headed by a gallant chief, spread dismay among the ranks of an enemy.

---

* Woodcut 321, *fig.* 2.   † Woodcut 321, *figs.* 3 and 4.
‡ Egyptian chariot, in woodcut 331, p. 376.

They had another kind of mace, sometimes of uniform thickness through its whole length, sometimes broader at the upper
end,* without either the ball or guard; and many of their allies
carried a rude, heavy club; † but no body of native troops was
armed with this last, and it cannot be considered an Egyptian
weapon.

The curved stick, or club (now called *lissán* "tongue"), was
used by heavy and light-armed troops as well as by archers; and if
it does not appear a formidable arm, yet the experience of modern

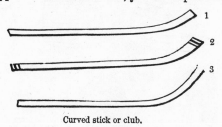

322.   Curved stick or club.   *Thebes.*

times bears ample testimony to its efficacy in close combat. To the
Bisharieen it supplies the place of a sword; and the Ababdeh,
content with this, their spear, and shield, fear not to encounter other
tribes armed with the matchlock and the *yatagán*. In length it
is about two feet and a half, and is made of a hard acacia wood.

The helmet was usually quilted; and though bronze helmets
are said to have been worn by the Egyptians, they generally
adopted the former, which being thick, and well padded, served
as an excellent protection to the head, without the inconvenience
of metal in so hot a climate. Some of them descended to the
shoulder,‡ others only a short distance below the level of the
ear; § and the summit, terminating in an obtuse point, was ornamented with two tassels. ‖ They were of a green, red, or black
colour; and a longer one, which fitted less closely to the back of
the head, was fringed at the lower edge with a broad border,¶ and
in some instances consisted of two parts, or an upper and under
fold. ** Another, worn by the spearmen, and many corps of in-

* Woodcut 322, *figs.* 1 and 2.   † Woodcut 288, *fig.* 3.
‡ Woodcut 323, *figs.* 1, 2, 3, 4.   § *Figs.* 5, 6, 7.
‖ *Figs.* 3, 4, 5, 6, 7.   ¶ *Fig.* 3.   ** *Fig.* 4.

fantry and charioteers, was also quilted, and descended to the shoulder with a fringe ; but it had no tassels, and, fitting close to the top of the head, it widened towards the base, the front, which covered the forehead, being made of a separate piece, attached to the other part. *

There is no representation of an Egyptian helmet with a crest,

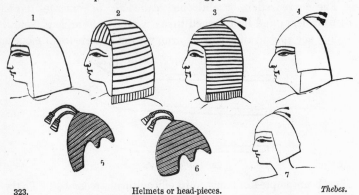

323.   Helmets or head-pieces.   *Thebes.*

but that of the Shairetana, once enemies and afterwards allies of the Pharaohs, shows they were used long before the Trojan war.

The outer surface of the corslet of mail, or coat of scale-armour, consisted of about eleven horizontal rows of metal plates, well secured by bronze pins ; and at the hollow of the throat a narrower range of plates was introduced, above which were two more, completing the collar or covering of the neck. The breadth of each plate or scale was little more than an inch, eleven or twelve of them sufficing to cover the front of the body ; and the sleeves, which were sometimes so short as to extend less than half way to the elbow, consisted of two rows of similar plates. Many, indeed most, of the corslets were without collars ; in some the sleeves were rather longer, reaching nearly to the elbow, and they were worn both by heavy infantry and bowmen. The ordinary corslet may have been little less than two feet and a half in length ; it sometimes covered the thighs nearly to the knee ; and in order to prevent its pressing heavily upon the shoulder, they bound their girdle

* *Fig. 2.*

over it, and tightened it at the waist.   But the thighs, and that
part of the body below the girdle, were usually covered by a
kelt, or other robe, detached from the corslet; and many of the
light and heavy infantry were clad in a quilted vest of the same
form as the coat of armour, for which it was a substitute; and

fig. 2.

fig. 1.

Fig. 2. Corslet, with metal scales.
        Tomb of Remeses III.   Thebes.

324.   *Fig. 1.* Corslet, worked in colours.

some wore corslets, reaching only from the waist to the upper

324 *a.* Plates of scale-armour.
Fig. 1. With the name of Sheshonk.

part of the breast, and supported by straps over the shoulder, which were faced with bronze plates.* A portion of one is in Dr. Abbott's collection. It is made of bronze plates (in the form of Egyptian shields), overlapping each other, and sewed upon a leathern doublet; two of which have the name of Sheshonk (Shishak), showing it either belonged to that king, or to some great officer of his court.

Among the arms painted in the tomb of Remeses III., at Thebes, is a corslet made of rich stuff, with the figures of lions and other animals worked upon it, and edged with a neat border, terminating below in a fringe; evidently the same kind of corslet, " ornamented with animals embroidered upon it," which was sent by Amasis as a present to Minerva in Lindus. (*Woodcut* 324, *fig.* 1.)

Heavy-armed troops were furnished with a shield and spear; some with a shield and mace; and others, though rarely, with a battle-axe, or a pole-axe, and shield. They also carried a sword, falchion, curved stick or *lissan,* simple mace, or hatchet; which may be looked upon as their side-arms.†

The light troops had nearly the same weapons, but their defensive armour was lighter; and the slingers and some others fought, like the archers, without shields.

The chariot corps constituted a very large and effective portion of the Egyptian army. Each car contained two persons, like the *diphros* (διφρος) of the Greeks. On some occasions it carried three, the charioteer or driver and two chiefs; but this was rarely the case, except in triumphal processions, when two of the princes accompanied the king in their chariot, bearing the regal sceptre, or the *flabella,* and required a third person to manage the reins.‡

* Woodcut 325, *figs.* 10, 11, 12.　　　　† Woodcut 325.
‡ Woodcut 326, *fig.* 1.

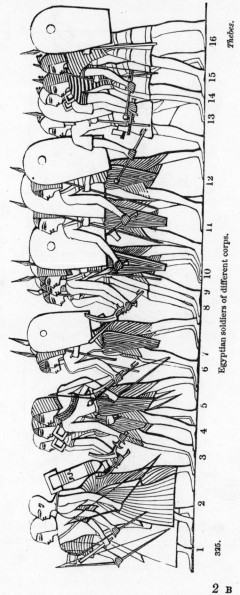

Egyptian soldiers of different corps.   *Thebes.*

325.

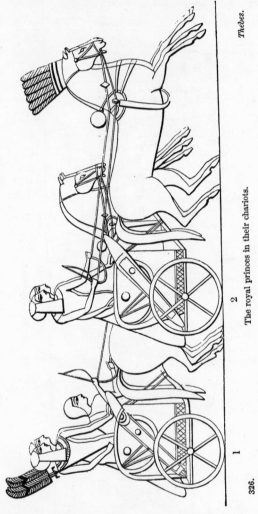

Thebes.

The royal princes in their chariots.

2

1

326.

In the field each had his own car, with a charioteer; and the
insignia of his office being attached behind him by a broad belt,*

* Woodcut 327.

his hands were free for the use of the bow and other arms. The driver generally stood on the off-side, in order to have the whip-hand free; and this interfered less with the use of the bow, than the Greek custom of driving on the near-side; which last was adopted in Greece as being more convenient for throwing the spear. When on an excursion for pleasure, or on a visit to a friend, an Egyptian gentleman mounted alone, and drove himself, footmen and other attendants running before and behind the car;* and sometimes an archer used his bow and acted as his own charioteer.†

In the battle scenes of the Egyptian temples, the king is represented alone in his car, unattended by any charioteer;‡ with the reins fastened round his body, while engaged in bending his bow against the enemy; though it is possible that the driver was omitted, in order not to interfere with the principal figure. The king had always a " second chariot," in order to provide against accidents; as Josiah is stated to have had when defeated by Necho;§ and the same was in attendance on state occasions.‖

327.   The son of King Remeses with his charioteer.   *Thebes.*

The cars of the whole chariot corps contained each two war-

* Woodcut 85.   † Woodcut 329.
‡ Like Homer's gods and heroes; Iliad, θ, 116; κ, 513; O, 352, &c.
§ 2 Chron. xxxv. 24.   ‖ Gen. xli. 43, " the second chariot."

riors, comrades of equal rank; and the charioteer who accompanied a chief was a person of confidence, as we see from the
familiar manner in which one of them is represented conversing
with a son of the great Remeses.* (*Woodcut* 327.)

In driving, the Egyptians used a whip, like the heroes and
charioteers of Homer; and this, or a short stick, was generally
employed even for beasts of burden, and for oxen at the plough,
in preference to the goad. The whip consisted of a smooth round
wooden handle, and a single or double thong: it sometimes had

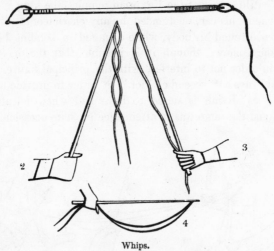

328.   Whips.   *Thebes.*

a lash of leather, or string, about two feet in length, either
twisted or plaited; and a loop being attached to the lower end,
the archer was enabled to use the bow, while it hung suspended
from his wrist.†

When a hero encountered a hostile chief, he sometimes dis-
mounted from his car, and substituting for his bow and quiver
the spear, battle-axe, or falchion, he closed with him hand to
hand, like the Greeks and Trojans described by Homer: and the
lifeless body of the foe being left upon the field, was stripped of its

---

* *Comp.* Hom. Il., θ, 120; and λ, 518.   † Woodcut 329.

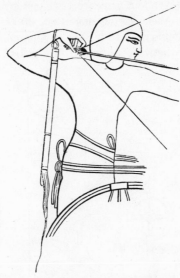

329.   Whip suspended from the wrist of the archer.   *Thebes.*

arms by his companions.   Sometimes a wounded adversary, incapable of further resistance, having claimed and obtained the
mercy of the victor, was carried from the field in his chariot;
and the ordinary captives, who laid down their arms and yielded
to the Egyptians, were treated as prisoners of war, and were sent
bound to the rear under an escort, to be presented to the monarch,
and to grace his triumph, after the termination of the conflict.
The hands of the slain were then counted before him; and this
return of the enemy's killed was duly registered, to commemorate
his success, and the glories of his reign.

The Egyptian chariots had no seat; but the bottom part consisted of a frame interlaced with thongs or rope, forming a species
of network, in order, by its elasticity, to render the motion of a
carriage without springs more easy: and this was also provided
for by placing the wheels as far back as possible, and resting
much of the weight on the horses, which supported the pole.

That the chariot was of wood is sufficiently proved by the

sculptures, wherever workmen are seen employed in making it;
and the fact of their having more than 3000 years ago already
invented and commonly used a form of pole, only introduced into
our own country between forty and fifty years,* is an instance of

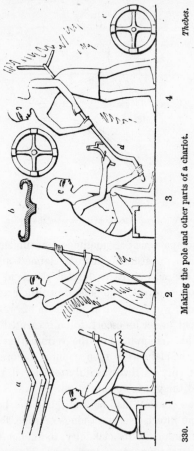

Making the pole and other parts of a chariot.

330.

Thebes.

the truth of Solomon's assertion, " there is no new thing under
the sun," and shows the skill of their workmen at that remote
time.

* Woodcut 330, *fig.* 3 *d.*

The body of the car was exceedingly light, consisting of a painted wooden framework, strengthened and ornamented with metal and leather binding, like many of those mentioned by Homer: the bottom part rested on the axle-tree and lower extremity of the pole, which was itself inserted into the axle, or a socket attached to it; and some chariots are shown by the monuments to have been " inlaid with silver and gold, others painted;" —the latter, as might be expected, the most numerous, 61 of them being mentioned to 9 of the former. The upper rim of its front was fastened to the pole by a couple of thongs or straps, to steady it, like the straps at the back of our modern chariots and coaches; and when the horses were taken out, the pole was supported on a crutch, or the wooden figure of a man, representing a captive, or enemy, who was considered fitted for this degrading office.

The greater portion of the sides, and the whole of the back, were open; the latter indeed entirely so, without any rim or framework above; and the hinder part of the lateral framework commenced nearly in a line with the centre of the wheel, and rising perpendicularly, or slightly inclined backwards, from the base of the car, extended with a curve, at the height of about two feet and a half, to the front, serving as well for a safeguard to the driver, as a support for his quivers and bow-case. To strengthen it, three thongs of leather were attached at either side, and an upright of wood connected it with the base of the front part immediately above the pole, where the straps before mentioned were fastened.

The bow-case, frequently richly ornamented, with the figure of a lion or other devices, was placed in an inclined position, pointing forwards; its upper edge, immediately below the flexible leather cover, being generally on a level with the summit of the framework of the chariot; so that when the bow was drawn out, the leather cover fell downwards, and left the upper part on an uninterrupted level. In battle this was of course a matter of no importance; but in the city, where the bow-case was considered an elegant part of the ornamental hangings of a car, and conti-

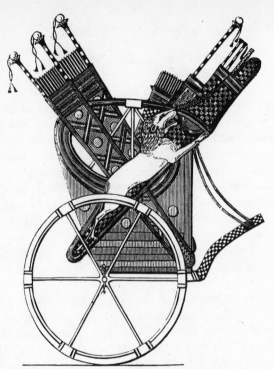

331.   A war chariot, with bow-cases and complete furniture.   *Thebes.*

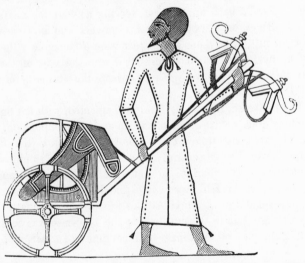

332.   Chariot of the Rot-ṅ-n.   *Thebes*

nued to be attached to it, they paid some attention to the position and fall of the pendent cover, deprived, as it there was, of its bow ; for, as I have observed, the civilised state of Egyptian society required the absence of all arms, except on service.   The quivers and spear-cases were suspended in a contrary direction, pointing backwards ; sometimes an additional quiver was attached close to the bow-case, with a mace and other arms, and every war chariot containing two men was furnished with the same number of bows.

The processes of making the pole, wheels, and other parts of the chariot are often represented, and even the mode of bending the wood for the purpose.*   In the ornamental trappings, hangings, and binding of the framework and cases, leather was principally used, dyed of various hues, and afterwards adorned with metal edges and studs ; and the wheels, strengthened at the joints of the felly with bronze or brass bands, were bound with a hoop of metal.†   The Egyptians themselves have not failed to point out what parts were the peculiar province of the carpenter, and of the currier.   The body and framework of the car, the pole, yoke, and

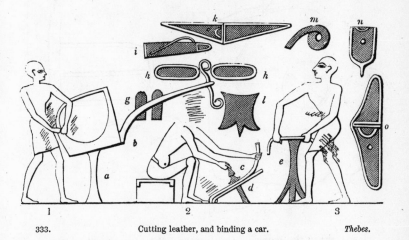

333.   Cutting leather, and binding a car.   *Thebes.*

* Woodcut 334, next page.   † *Comp.* Hom. Il., ε, 724.

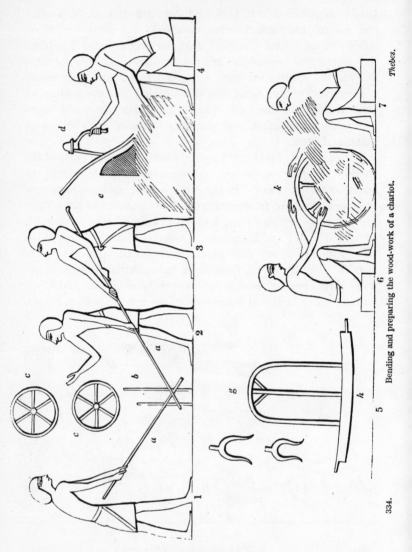

Bending and preparing the wood-work of a chariot. *Thebes.*

334.

wheels, were the work of the former; the cases for the bows and
other arms, the saddle and harness, the binding of the framework,

and the coverings of the body, were finished by the currier; and lest it should not be sufficiently evident that they are engaged in cutting and bending the leather for this purpose, the artist has distinctly pointed out the nature of the substance they employed, by figuring an entire skin, and the soles of a pair of shoes,* or sandals, suspended in the shop; and we find a semicircular knife† used by the Egyptians to cut leather precisely similar to our own, even in the remote age of king Amunoph II., who lived 14 centuries before our era.

In war chariots, the wheels had six spokes, generally round; in many curricles, or private cars, employed in towns, only four; and the wheel was fixed to the axle by a small linch-pin, sometimes surmounted with a fanciful head, and secured by a thong which passed through the lower end.

The harness of curricles and war chariots was nearly similar; and the pole in either case was supported on a curved yoke fixed to its extremity by a strong pin, and bound with straps or thongs of leather. The yoke, resting upon a small well-padded saddle, was firmly fitted into a groove of metal; and the saddle, placed upon the horses' withers, and furnished with girths and a breast-band, was surmounted by an ornamental knob; and in front of it a small hook secured the bearing-rein. The other reins passed through a thong or ring at the side of the saddle, and thence over the projecting extremity of the yoke; and the same thong secured the girths, and even appears in some instances to have been attached to them. In the war chariots, a large ball, placed upon a shaft, projected above the saddle, which was either intended to give a greater power to the driver, by enabling him to draw the reins over a groove in its centre; or was added solely for an ornamental purpose, like the fancy head-dresses of the horses, and fixed to the yoke immediately above the centre of the saddle,‡ or rather to the head of a pin which connected the yoke to the pole.§

---

* Woodcut 333, *l* and *g*.
† It occurs frequently.   See woodcut 333, *c*.
‡ Woodcut 335, *fig.* 2.   § Woodcut 335, *fig.* 1.

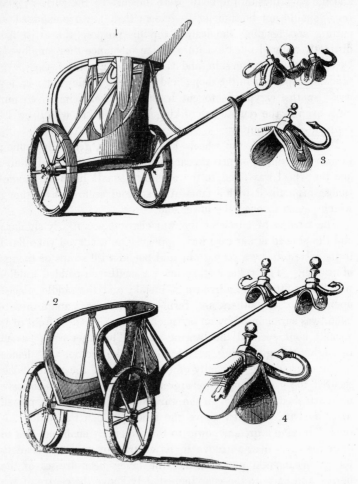

335.   Chariots in perspective, from a comparison of different sculptures.

The traces were single, one only on the inner side of each horse, fastened to the lower part of the pole, and thence extending to the saddle; but no exterior trace was thought necessary:

and no provision was made for attaching it to the car. Indeed the yoke sufficed for all the purposes of draught as well as for backing the chariot; and being fixed to the saddle, it kept the horses at the same distance and in the same relative position, and prevented their breaking outwards from the line of draught. In order to render this more intelligible, I shall introduce a pair of horses yoked to a chariot according to the rules of European drawing, derived from a comparison of the numerous representations in the sculptures, omitting only their housings and head-dress, which may be readily understood in an Egyptian picture. I have also followed the Egyptian fashion of putting a chesnut and a grey together, which was thought quite as correct in ancient Egypt, as it now is in England.

On grand occasions the Egyptian horses were decked with fancy ornaments: a rich striped or checkered housing, trimmed with a broad border and large pendent tassels, covered the whole body; and two or more feathers inserted in lions' heads, or some other device of gold, formed a crest upon the summit of the head-stall. But this display was confined to the chariots of the monarch, or the military chiefs; and it was thought sufficient, in the harness of other cars, and in the town curricle, to adorn the bridles with rosettes, which resemble those used in England at the present day.*

They had no blinkers; but the head and upper part of the neck were frequently enveloped in a rich covering similar to the housing, trimmed with a leather fringe; and the bridle consisted of two check pieces, a throat-lash, head-stall, and the forehead and nose straps.

No instance occurs of Egyptian chariots with more than two horses; nor is there any representation of a carriage with shafts drawn by one horse; but a pair of shafts have been found, with a wheel of curious construction, having a wooden tire to the felly, and an inner circle, probably of metal, which passed through, and connected, its six spokes a short distance from the

* Woodcuts 85 and 326.

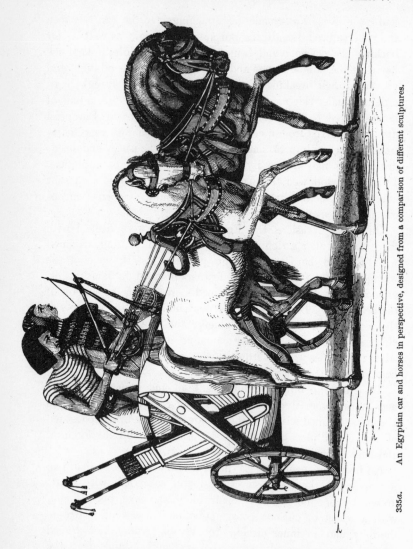

An Egyptian car and horses in perspective, designed from a comparison of different sculptures.

335a.

nave (A A). The diameter of the wheel was about 3 ft. 1 in. The felly was in six pieces, the end of one overlapping the other; and the tire was fastened to it by bands of raw hide passing

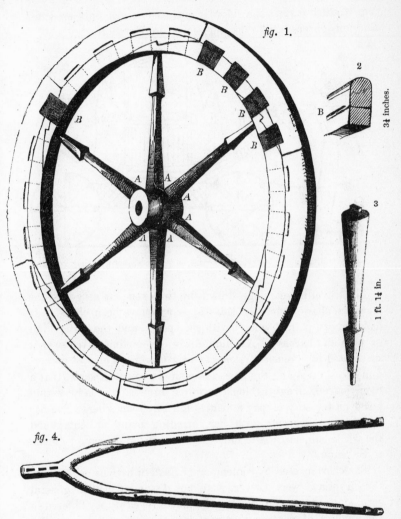

fig. 1.

2

3¼ inches.

3

1 ft. 1¼ in.

fig. 4.

336.   *Fig.* 1. Wheel; 3 ft. 1 in. diameter.   *In the Collection of Dr. Abbott.*
                Fig. 4. Shafts; 11 feet in total length.

through long narrow holes made to receive them (B B). It is
uncertain whether the carriage they belonged to had two or
four wheels; for though an instance does occur of an Egyptian

four-wheeled car, it is a singular one, and it was only used for religious purposes, like that mentioned by Herodotus.*

337.   Singular instance of a four-wheeled carriage, on the bandages of a mummy, belonging
to S. d'Athanasi.

The travelling carriage drawn by two oxen was very like the common chariot; but the sides appear to have been closed. It had also one pair of wheels with six spokes, and the same kind of pole and harness. An umbrella was sometimes fixed over it when used for women of rank, as over the king's chariot on certain occasions;† and the bow-case with the bow in it shows that a long journey from Ethiopia required arms; the lady within being on her way to pay a visit to the Egyptian king. She has a very large retinue with her, bringing many presents: and the whole subject calls to mind the visit of the Queen of Sheba to Solomon.

The chariots used by contemporary Eastern nations, with whom the Egyptians were at war, were not dissimilar in their general form, or in the mode of yoking the horses (even if they differed in the number of persons they contained, having usually three instead of the two in Egyptian and Greek cars); as may be seen from that which is brought, with its two unyoked horses, as a

* Herod. ii. 63.   † Woodcut 86, in p. 75.

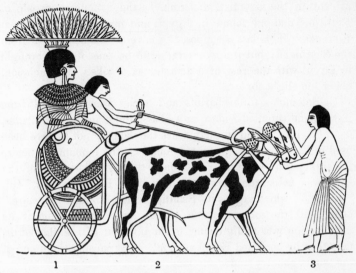

338.   An Ethiopian princess travelling in a *plaustrum*, or car drawn by oxen.   Over her is a
       sort of umbrella.   3. An attendant.   4. The charioteer or driver.   *Thebes*.

339.   Car and bow, in the collection at Florence (from the great work of Professor
                                Rosellini).

present to the Egyptian monarch, by the conquered people of Rot-ñ-n,* and one found in Egypt, and now in the museum at Florence. This last is supposed to have been taken in war from the Scythians; but it appears rather to be one of those brought to Egypt with the rest of a tribute, as a token of submission, being too slight for use.

In Solomon's time chariots and horses were exported from Egypt, and supplied Judæa, as well as "the kings of the Hittites, and of Syria;" † but in early times they appear not to have been used in Egypt, and they are not found on the monuments before the eighteenth dynasty. For though the Egyptian name of the horse was *hthor*, the *mare* was called, as in Hebrew, "*sûs*," (pl. "*susim;*") which argues its Semitic origin; *fáras*, "the mare," being still the generic name of the Arab horse; and if its introduction was really owing to the invasion of the Shepherds, they thereby benefited Egypt as much, as by causing the union of the whole country under one king.

The Egyptians sometimes drove a pair of mules, instead of horses, in the chariots used in towns, or in the country; an instance of which occurs in a painting now in the British Museum.

The Egyptian chariot corps, like the infantry, were divided into light and heavy troops, both armed with bows: the former chiefly employed in harassing the enemy with missiles, and in evolutions requiring rapidity of movement; the latter called upon to break through opposing masses of infantry, after having galled them during their advance with a heavy shower of arrows; and, in order to enable them to charge with greater security, they were furnished with a shield, which was not required for the other mounted archers, and a long spear was substituted on these occasions for the missiles they had previously employed. The light-armed chariot corps were also supplied with weapons adapted to close combat, as the sword, club, and javelin; but they had neither spear nor shield. The heavy infantry, and light

Woodcut 339.   † 1 Kings, x. 29.   2 Chron. i. 16, 17.

troops employed in the assault of fortified towns, were all provided with shields, under cover of which they made approaches
to the place; and so closely was the idea of a siege connected
with this arm,* that a figure of the king, who is sometimes introduced in the sculptures, as the representative of the whole army,
advancing with the shield before him, is intended to show that
the place was taken by assault.

In attacking a fortified town, they advanced under cover of
the arrows of the bowmen; and either instantly applied the
scaling-ladder to the ramparts, or undertook the routine of a
regular siege: in which case, having advanced to the walls, they
posted themselves under cover of *testudos*, and shook and dislodged the stones of the parapet with a species of battering-ram,†
directed and impelled by a body of men expressly chosen for this
service: but when the place held out against these attacks, and
neither a *coup de main*, the ladder, nor the ram, were found to
succeed, they used the testudo for concealing and protecting the
sappers, while they mined the place; and certainly, of all people,
the Egyptians were the most likely to have recourse to this
stratagem of war, from the great practice they had in under-
ground excavations, and in directing shafts through the solid
rock.

The testudo was of frame-work, sometimes supported by poles
having a forked summit, and covered, in all probability, with
hides; it was sufficiently large to contain several men, and so
placed that the light troops might mount upon the outside, and
thus obtain a footing on more elevated ground, apply the ladders
with greater precision, or obtain some other important advantage; and each party was commanded by an officer of skill, and
frequently by those of the first rank.‡

They also endeavoured to force open the gates of the town, or

---

* Conf. 2 Kings xix. 32. " Nor come before it (the city) with *shield*, nor
cast a bank against it." Isaiah xxxvii. 33.

† See woodcut 340.

‡ Woodcut 341. Four of the king's sons command the four testudos, *a,
b, c, d.*

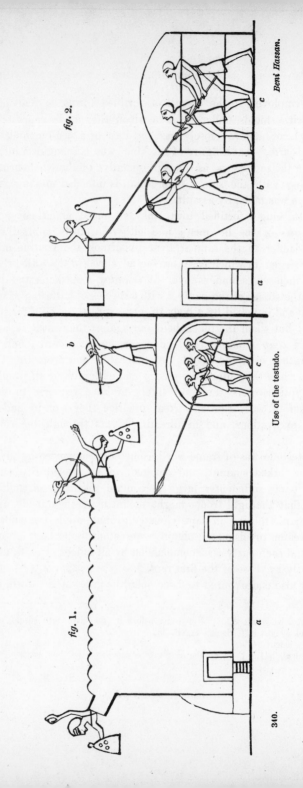

fig. 2.

Beni Hassan.

fig. 1.

Use of the testudo.

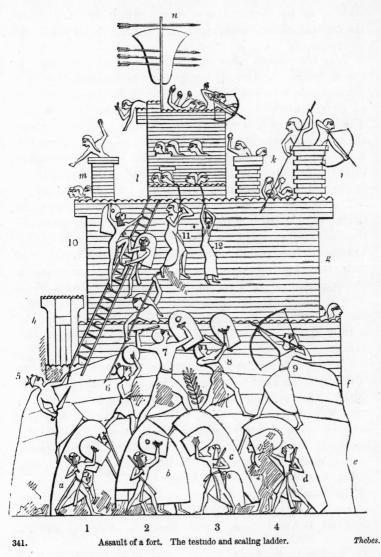

341.   Assault of a fort. The testudo and scaling ladder.   *Thebes.*

hew them down with axes; and when the fort was built upon
a rock, they escaladed the precipitous part by means of the

testudo, or by short spikes of metal, which they forced into the crevices of the stone,* and then applied the ladder to the ramparts.

They had several other engines for sieges not represented in the sculptures ; and the bulwarks used by the Jews,† on their march to the promised land, were doubtless borrowed from those of Egypt, where they had lived until they became a nation. The bulwarks, or moveable towers, were of wood, and made on the spot during the siege, the trees of the neighbouring country being cut down for the purpose : but the Jews were forbidden to fell a fruit-tree for the construction of warlike engines, or any except those which grew wild, or in an uncultivated spot.‡

The northern and eastern tribes, against whom the Egyptians fought, were armed in many instances with the same weapons as the disciplined troops of the Pharaohs, as bows and spears ; they had besides long swords, rude massive clubs, and knives ; and their coats of mail, helmets, and shields varied in form according to the custom of each nation. They also used stones, which were thrown with the hand, while defending the walls of a besieged town ; but it does not appear that either the Egyptians, or their enemies, threw them on any other occasions, except with a sling.

The most distinguished peculiarities of some of the nations at war with the Egyptians were the forms of the head-dress and shield. One of these, the Shairetana, a people inhabiting a country of Asia, near a river, a lake, or a sea, wore a helmet ornamented with horns, projecting from its circular summit, and frequently surmounted by a crest, consisting of a ball raised upon a small shaft ; which is the earliest instance of a crest, and shows that it really had an Asiatic origin.

The Shairetana were also distinguished by a round shield, and the use of long spears and javelins, with a pointed sword ; they were clad in a short dress, and frequently had a coat of mail, or

---

* *See* woodcut 341, *fig.* 5.   † Deut. xx. 20.
‡ " For the tree of the field is man's life."   Deut. xx. 19.

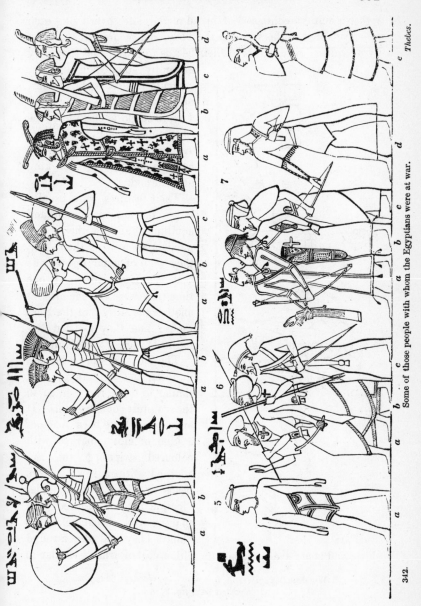

342.

Some of those people with whom the Egyptians were at war.

Thebes.

rather a cuirass, composed of broad metal plates overlaying each other, adapted to the form of the body, and secured at the waist by a girdle.   Some allowed their beards to grow ; and they very

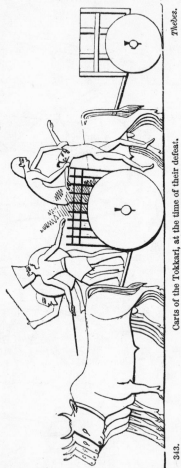

generally adopted a custom, common to most early nations, of wearing large ear-rings.* Layard supposes them to be the Sharutinians (near the modern Antioch) mentioned among the conquests of the Assyrian king at Nimroud.

Their features were usually large, the nose prominent and aquiline ; and in their complexion, as well as their hair, they were of a far lighter hue than the Egyptians.   At one time they were the enemies, at another the allies,† of the Pharaohs : and they assisted Remeses II. against the Khita.

The Tokkari wore a helmet, in form and appearance very similar to those represented in the sculptures of Persepolis.   It appears to have been made of a kind of cloth, marked with coloured stripes ; ‡ the rim adorned with a row of large beads or other ornamental devices, and it was secured by a thong or riband tied below the chin.   They had also a round shield and short dress, frequently with a coat of armour similar to

Thebes.

Carts of the Tokkari, at the time of their defeat.

343.

shield and short dress, frequently with a coat of armour similar to

* Woodcut 342, *fig.* 1, *a, b.*   † Woodcut 341, *figs* 5, 6.
‡ Woodcut 342, *fig.* 2, *a, b.*

that of the Shairetana; and their offensive weapons consisted principally of a spear, and a large pointed knife, or straight sword.   They sometimes, though rarely, had a beard, which was still more unusual with the chiefs: their features were regular, the nose slightly aquiline: and whenever the Egyptian artists have represented them on a large scale, their face presents a more pleasing outline than the generality of these Asiatic people. They fought, like the Egyptians, in chariots; and had carts or waggons, with two solid wheels, drawn by a pair of oxen; which appear to have been placed in the rear, as in the Scythian and Tartar armies, and were used for carrying off the old men, women, and children, in defeat.   They were also at one time allies of the Pharaohs, and assisted them in their long wars against the Rebo.

Another people, whose name is lost,* were distinguished by a costume of a very Oriental character, consisting of a high fur-cap, not unlike one worn by the ancient Persians and that of the modern Tartars; a tight dress, with the usual girdle; and a short kelt, common to many Asiatic nations, which, apparently divided and folding over in front, was tied at the bottom with strings.   Round their neck, and falling upon the breast, was a large round amulet,† very similar to those of agate worn by the dervishes of the East, in which they resembled the Assyrian captives of Tirhakah, represented on the walls of Medeenet Haboo.‡ Their features were remarkable; and though in the sculptures they occasionally vary in appearance, from the presence or the absence of a beard, the strongly defined contour of the face and the high bridge of their prominent nose sufficiently distinguish them from other people, and show that the artist has intended to convey a notion of these peculiar characteristics.

Their arms consisted of two javelins, a club, and falchion, and a shield like that of the Egyptians, with a round summit.   They were on terms of friendship with the third Remeses, and assisted

* It begins with the letters Sha . . . . Woodcuts 288, *fig.* 2, and 342, *fig.* 3.
† Woodcut 342, *fig.* 3 a.   ‡ Woodcut 344, *fig.* 1.

him in his wars against the Rebo ; and though they occur among the foreigners who had been conquered by the arms of Egypt, the same feeling of inveterate enmity, arising from a repeated succession of conflicts, did not exist towards them as towards many other Asiatic tribes.   The same remark applies to another people, represented at Medeenet Haboo,* as allies of the Egyptians, whose name has been unfortunately lost : they were clad in a short tight dress, and carried a shield, like the former, with a bow and a heavy club ; but of their features we have little or no knowledge, owing to the imperfect state of the sculptures.

Among the most formidable Asiatic enemies encountered by the Egyptians were the Rebo,† with whom they had frequent and severe contests.

One of the principal military events in the glorious reign of the great Remeses was his success against them ; and three victories gained over the Rebo by Remeses III., about a century later, were great triumphs for the Egyptians.

From the style of their costume, and the lightness of their complexion, it is evident they inhabited a northern as well as an Asiatic country, very distant from Egypt, and of a far more temperate climate.   Their dress consisted of an under garment, with the usual short kelt, and a long outer robe, highly coloured, and frequently ornamented with fancy devices, or a broad rich border, which descended to the ankles, and was fastened at the neck with a large bow, or by a strap over the shoulder, the lower part being open in front.   Beneath this they wore a highly ornamented girdle, the end of which, falling down in front, terminated in a large tassel ; and so fond were they of decorating their persons, that besides earrings, necklaces, and trinkets, common to Asiatic and other tribes, the chiefs decked their heads with feathers, and some painted or tattooed their arms and legs.

They were evidently a people of consequence, being selected as the type of Asia, or of the nations of the East, in the tombs of the kings at Thebes.

---

* See the allies, in woodcut 288, *fig.* 3.   † Woodcut 342, *fig.* 4.

Their hair was not less singular than their dress: it was divided into separate parts, one of which fell in ringlets over the forehead, and the other over the back of the head; and a plaited lock of great length, passing nearly over the ear, descended to the breast, and terminated in a curled point. In features they were as remarkable as in costume; and the Egyptians have not failed to indicate their most striking peculiarities, as blue eyes, aquiline nose, and small red beards. Their arms consisted principally of the bow, and a long straight sword, with an exceedingly sharp point; and it is probable that, to their skill in the use of the former, we may attribute their effectual resistance to the repeated invasions of the Egyptians.

Another Eastern nation, with whom the Egyptians were already at war in the remote age of Amun-m-he II., nearly 2000 years before our era, was the Pount;* who were tributary to Egypt in the reign of the third Thothmes.

Their features were less marked than those of many Oriental people represented in the sculptures: they shaved their beards, and wore their hair enveloped in a large cap, bound with a fillet, like many of the tribes of the interior, and the Syrians who bordered upon Egypt. Their dress consisted chiefly of a short kelt, secured with the usual girdle: and they appear to have inhabited a region lying more to the south than the Rot-ñ-n, or the Koofa, who were also tributary at the same period to Thothmes III. They probably lived on the borders of Arabia; and some suppose there was one tribe of this name in Africa, and another in Asia. Among the presents brought by them to the Egyptian monarch were some gold, with a little silver, the ibex, leopard, baboon, ape, ostrich eggs and feathers, dried fruits and skins, baskets full of a brown substance called *ana* (?), with two obelisks made of it, and a red mineral (?), called " *min* " (apparently *minium*, " red lead," or vermilion) ; and exotic shrubs, with ebony and ivory, seem to prove that they lived in a cultivated country as well as a warm climate.

The Shari were another Asiatic people, against whom the

* Or Pouônt.   Woodcut 342, *fig.* 5.

Egyptians waged a successful war, principally in the reigns of
Osirei (or Sethos) and his son, the great Remeses. I am inclined
to think them a tribe of Northern Arabia, or *Shur;* and their name
seems to agree with that of the Arabian Gulf, called by the Egyptians "the Sea of Shari." Their features were marked by a prominent aquiline nose and high cheek bones : they had a large beard ;
and their head-dress consisted either of a cap bound, like that of
the Pount, with a fillet, or a skull-cap fitting loosely to the head,
secured by a band, and terminating at the end, which fell down
behind, in a ball or tassel.* Their dress consisted of a long loose
robe reaching to the ankles, and fastened at the waist by a girdle,
the upper part furnished with ample sleeves. The girdle was
sometimes highly ornamented : men as well as women wore earrings ; and they frequently had a small cross suspended to a
necklace, or to the collar of their dress. The adoption of this
last was not peculiar to them ; it was also appended to, or
figured upon, the robes of the Rot-n̄-n ; and traces of it may be

344.   Prisoners of Tirhaka.   *Thebes.*

* Woodcut 342, *fig.* 6 *c.*

seen in the fancy ornaments of the Rebo, showing that this very simple device was already in use as early as the 15th century before the Christian era.

Some wore a sort of double belt, crossing the body, and passing over each shoulder, which, together with the pointed cap, resembles the dress of Tirhaka's captives.*   Their principal arms were the bow, spear, two javelins, and a sword or club; and their country was defended by several strongly fortified towns.

The Rot-n̄-no,† or Rot-n̄-n, were a nation with whom the Egyptians waged a long war, commencing at least as early as, and perhaps prior to, the reign of the third Thothmes.   Their white complexion, tight dresses, and long gloves,‡ decide them to have been natives of a much colder climate than Egypt or Southern Syria; and the productions of their country, which they bring as a tribute to the victorious Pharaoh, pronounce them to have lived in the East. These consist of horses, and even chariots, with four spoked wheels,§ (very similar to the Egyptian curricle,) rare woods, ivory, elephants and bears, a profusion of elegant gold and silver vases, with rings of the same precious metals, porcelain, and jars filled with choice gums and resins used for making incense, as well as bitumen, called "zift," the common name for "pitch" in Arabic and Hebrew.   And it is a curious fact that one of the same kind of jars is now in the British Museum, having on it the word "tribute." Their country was in the vicinity, or part, of Mesopotamia, and consisted of an "Upper and Lower" province; and in the record of the tributes paid to Thothmes III. at Karnak, the Rot-n̄-n are mentioned with Nahrayn (Mesopotamia), Neniee (Nineveh), Shinar (Singar), Babel, and other places.

Their features were regular, without the very prominent nose that characterises some Eastern people represented in the sculptures; and they were of a very light colour, with brown or red hair, and blue eyes.   Their long dress, usually furnished with

---

* Woodcut 344.   † Woodcut 342, fig. 7.
‡ There are other instances of gloves in Egyptian sculptures; but they are very rare.   The expression shoe, in Ruth iv. 7, is in the Targum "right-hand glove."   § Woodcut 332.

tight sleeves, and fastened by strings round the neck, was either closed or folded over in front, and was sometimes secured by a girdle.   Beneath the outer robe they wore a kelt ; and an ample cloak, probably woollen, like the modern *herám*, or blanket, of the coast of Barbary, was thrown over the whole dress ;* the head being generally covered with a close cap, or a fuller one, bound by a fillet.

The women wore a long garment secured by a girdle, and trimmed in the lower part with three rows of flounces ; the sleeves sometimes large and open, sometimes fastened tight round the wrist ; and the hair was either covered with a cap, to which a long tassel was appended, or descending in ringlets was encircled by a simple band.†

The Toersha,‡ a people who lived near a river or the sea, are also mentioned among the enemies of Egypt, and their close cap, from whose pointed summit a crest of hair falls to the back of the neck, readily distinguishes them from other Eastern tribes.   Their features offer no peculiarity; and we know them only by being introduced among the tribes conquered by the third Remeses.   The same applies to the Mashoash,§ another Asiatic nation ; who resemble the former in their general features, and the shape of their beards ; but their head-dress is low, and

345.   Other enemies of the Egyptians.   *Thebes.*

rather more like that of some of Tirhaka's prisoners,‖ descending in two points at the side and back of the head, and bound with a fillet.

* Woodcuts 353, and 342, *fig.* 7, *d.*   † Woodcuts 353, and 342, *fig.* 7, *e.*
‡ Woodcut 345, *fig.* 1.   § Woodcut 345, *fig.* 2.   ‖ Woodcut 344.

The people of Kufa (Koofa) were also an Asiatic race; and their long hair, rich dresses, and sandals of the most varied form and colour, render them remarkable among the nations represented in Egyptian sculpture. In complexion they were much darker than the Rot-ñ-n, but far more fair than the Egyptians; and to judge from the tribute they brought to the Pharaohs, they were a rich people, and, like the Rot-ñ-n, far advanced in the arts and customs of civilised life. This tribute, which is shown to have been paid to the Egyptians as early as the reign of Thothmes III., consisted almost entirely of gold and silver, in rings and bars, and vases of the same metals. Many of the latter were silver, inlaid with gold, tastefully ornamented, of elegant form, and similar to those already in use among the Egyptians; and from the almost exclusive introduction of the precious metals, and the absence of animals, woods, and such productions as were brought to Egypt by other people, we may suppose the artist intended to convey a notion of the great mineral riches of their country; where silver seems to have been even more abundant than gold. They are occasionally represented carrying knives or daggers, beads, a small quantity of ivory, leathern bottles, and a few bronze and porcelain cups. Their dress was a simple kelt, richly worked and of varied colour, folding over in front, and fastened with a girdle; and their sandals, which, being closed like boots, differed entirely from those of the Egyptians, appear to have been of cloth or leather, highly ornamented, and reaching considerably above the ankle. Their long hair hung loosely in tresses, reaching more than half way down the back; and from the top of the head projected three or four curls, either of real or artificial hair. (*Woodcut* 347, *fig.* 1.)

The Khita, or Sheta, were a warlike people of Asia, who had made considerable progress in military tactics, both with regard to manœuvres in the field, and the art of fortifying towns; some of which they surrounded with a double fosse, crossed by *bridges*. But whether these were supported on arches, or simply of wooden rafters resting on piers of the same materials, we are unable to decide, since the view is given as seen from above, and

is therefore confined to the level upper surface.*   Their troops
were disciplined; and the close array of their phalanxes of

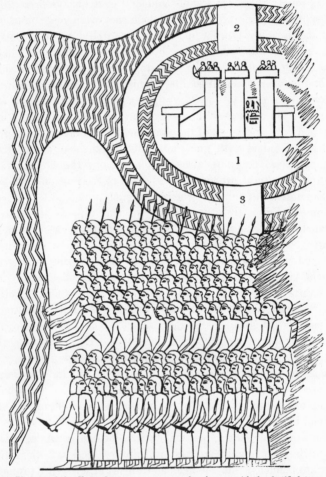

346.   Phalanx of the Sheta, drawn up as a corps de réserve, with the fortified town, surrounded by double ditches, over which are *bridges* (figs. 2 and 3).   *Thebes.*

infantry, the style of their chariots, and the arms they used, indicate a great superiority in military tactics, compared with other

* Woodcut 346, *figs.* 2 and 3.

Eastern nations of that early period. The wars waged against the Khita by the Egyptians, and the victories obtained over them by the great Remeses, are pictured on the walls of his palace at Thebes,* and are again alluded to in the sculptures of Remeses III., at Medeenet Haboo, where this people occurs in the list of nations conquered by the Pharaohs. Their arms were the bow, sword, and spear; and their principal defence was a wicker shield, either rectangular, or concave at the sides and convex at each end, approaching in form the Theban buckler.

Their dress consisted of a long robe, reaching to the ankles, with short sleeves, open or folding over in front, and secured by a girdle round the waist; but though frequently made of a very thick stuff, and perhaps even quilted, it was by no means an effectual substitute for armour, nor could it resist the spear or the metal-pointed arrow. They either wore a close or a full cap; and their arms were occasionally decked with bracelets, as their dresses with brilliant colours. Their cars were drawn by two horses, like those of Egypt, but they each contained three men, and some had wheels with four instead of six spokes; in both which respects they differed from those of their opponents. They had some cavalry: but large masses of infantry, with a formidable body of chariots, constituted the principal force of their numerous and well-appointed army; and if, from the manner in which they posted their *corps de réserve*, we may infer them to have been a people skilled in war, some idea may also be formed of the strength of their army from the numbers composing that division, which amounted to 24,000 men,† drawn up in three close phalanxes, consisting each of 8000.

The nation of Khita seems to have been composed of two distinct tribes,‡ both comprehended under the same name. They differed in their costume and general appearance; one having a large cap, and the long loose robe, with open sleeves or capes covering the shoulders, worn by many Asiatic people already mentioned, a square or oblong shield, and sometimes a large

* Usually called the Memnonium.   † At the Memnonium.
‡ Woodcut 347, *figs.* 2, 3, 4, and 5.

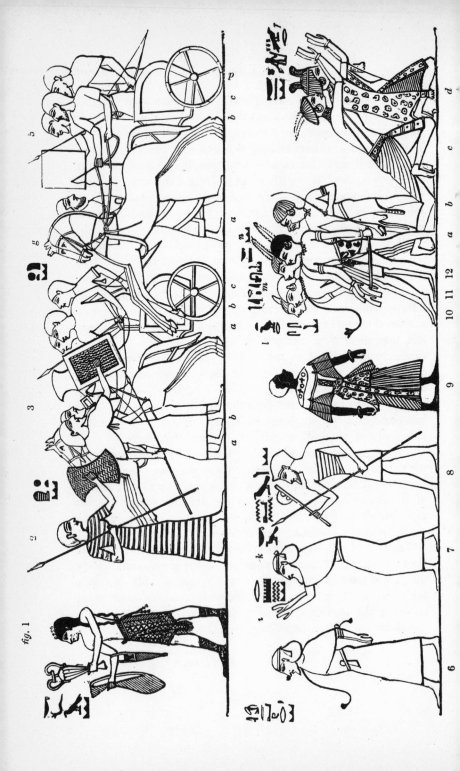

fig. 1

beard; the other the dress and shield before described, and no beard. They both fought in cars, and used the same weapons; and we find they lived together, or garrisoned the same towns.

They were evidently in the vicinity of Mesopotamia, or " Nahrayn ;" and the strong fort of Atesh, or Kadesh,* belonged to them. It is supposed that they were the Hittites.

Several other nations and tribes, who inhabited parts of Asia, are shown by the monuments to have been invaded and reduced to subjection by the arms of the Pharaohs; and in the names of some we recognise towns or districts of Syria, as in Asmaori (Samaria?), Lemanon, Kanana, or Kanaan, and Ascalon. The inhabitants of the two first are figured with a round full head-dress, bound with a fillet : and those of Kanaan are distinguished by a coat of mail and helmet, and the use of spears, javelins, and a battle-axe similar to that of Egypt.† (*Woodcut* 347, figs. 6, 7, 8.)

The country of Lemanon is shown by the artist to have been mountainous, inaccessible to chariots, and abounding in lofty trees, which the affrighted mountaineers are engaged in felling, in order to impede the advance of the invading army. Having taken by assault the fortified towns on the frontier, the Egyptian monarch advances with his light infantry in pursuit of the fugitives, who had escaped, and taken refuge in the woods; and sending a herald to offer terms on condition of their surrender, the chiefs are induced to trust to his clemency, and return to their allegiance; as are those of Kanaan, whose strongholds yield in like manner to the arms of the conqueror.

These two names seem to point out the inhabitants of Mount Lebanon and Canaan, since the campaign is said to have taken place in the first year, or soon after the accession, of Osirei, or Sethi, the father of the great Remeses; and the events which previously occurred in Egypt, during the rule of the Stranger kings, may have given an opportunity to these people, though so near Egypt, to rebel, and assert their independence.

Many black nations were also conquered by the early mon-

* Woodcut 346, *fig.* 1.　　　　　† Woodcut 347, *fig.* 8.

archs of the 18th and 19th dynasties, as the Toreses, the Tareáo, the Cush,* or Ethiopians, and others.

The Blacks, like the Ethiopians, wore short aprons of bulls' hides, or the skins of wild beasts, frequently drawn by the Egyptian artists with the tail projecting from the girdle, for the purpose of adding to their grotesque appearance: the chiefs, decked with ostrich and other feathers, had large circular gold earrings, collars, and bracelets; and many of the Ethiopian grandees were clad in garments of fine linen, with leathern girdles highly ornamented, a leopard skin being occasionally thrown over their shoulder.† The chief arms of the Ethiopians and Blacks were the bow, the spear, and club: they fought mostly on foot, and the tactics of a disciplined army appear to have been unknown to them.

The Ethiopian tribute consisted of gold, mostly in dust, a little silver, *shishm* perhaps "antimony," ostrich feathers, skins, ebony, ivory, apes, oxen of the long-horned breed still found in Abyssinia, lions, oryxes, leopards, giraffes, and hounds; and they were obliged to supply the victors with slaves, which the Egyptians sometimes exacted even from the conquered countries of Asia.

When an expedition was resolved upon against a foreign nation, each province furnished its quotum of men. The troops were generally commanded by the king in person; but in some instances a general was appointed to that post, and intrusted with the sole conduct of the war. A place of rendezvous was fixed, in early times generally at Thebes, Memphis, or Pelusium; and the troops having assembled in the vicinity, remained encamped there, awaiting the leader of the expedition. As soon as he arrived, the necessary preparations were made; a sacrifice was performed to the gods whose assistance was invoked in the approaching conflict; and orders having been issued for their march, a signal was given by sound of trumpet; the troops fell in, and with a profound bow each soldier in the ranks saluted the

* It is the Scriptural as well as the hieroglyphical name. Woodcut 347, *fig.* 13, *a*, *b*, *c*, and *d*.

† Woodcut 347, *fig.* 13, *c*, *d*.

royal general, and prepared to follow him to the field. The march then commenced, as Clemens and the sculptures inform us, to the sound of the drum; the chariots led the van; and the king, mounted in his car of war, and attended by his chief officers carrying flabella, took his post in the centre, preceded and followed by bodies of infantry armed with bows, spears, or other weapons, according to their respective corps.

On commencing the attack in the open field, a signal was again made by sound of trumpet. The archers drawn up in line first discharged a shower of arrows on the enemy's front, and a considerable mass of chariots advanced to the charge; the heavy infantry, armed with spears or clubs, and covered with their shields, moved forwards at the same time in close array, flanked by chariots and cavalry, and pressed upon the centre and wings of the enemy, the archers still galling the hostile columns with their arrows, and endeavouring to create disorder in their ranks.

348.　　　　　　　　A body of archers.　　　　　　　*Thebes.*

Their mode of warfare was not like that of nations in their infancy, or in a state of barbarism; and it is evident, from the number of prisoners they took, that they spared the prostrate who asked for quarter: and the representations of persons slaughtered by the Egyptians, who have overtaken them, are intended to allude to what happened in the heat of action, and not to any wanton cruelty on the part of the victors. Indeed in the naval fight of Remeses III., the Egyptians, both in the ships and on the shore, are seen rescuing the enemy, whose galley has been sunk, from a watery grave; and the humanity of that people is strongly argued, whose artists deem it a virtue, worthy of being recorded among the glorious actions of their countrymen.

Those who sued for mercy and laid down their arms, were spared and sent bound from the field; and the hands of the slain being cut off, and placed in heaps before the king, immediately after the action, were counted by the military secretaries in his presence, who thus ascertained and reported to him the amount of the enemy's slain. Sometimes their tongues, and occasionally other members, were laid before him in the same manner; in all instances being intended as authentic returns of the loss of the foe: for which the soldiers received a proportionate reward, divided among the whole army: the capture of prisoners probably claiming a higher premium, exclusively enjoyed by the captor.

The arms, horses, chariots, and booty, taken in the field or in the camp, were also collected, and the same officers wrote an account of them, and presented it to the monarch. The booty was sometimes collected in an open space, surrounded by a temporary wall, indicated in the sculptures by the representation of shields placed erect, with a wicker gate, on the inner and outer face of which a strong guard was posted, the sentries walking to and fro with drawn swords. It was forbidden to the Spartan soldier, when on guard, to have his shield, in order that, being deprived of this defence, he might be more cautious not to fall asleep; and the same appears to have been a custom of the Egyptians, as the watch here on duty at the camp-gates are only armed with swords and maces, though belonging to the heavy-armed corps, who, on other occasions, were in the habit of carrying a shield.

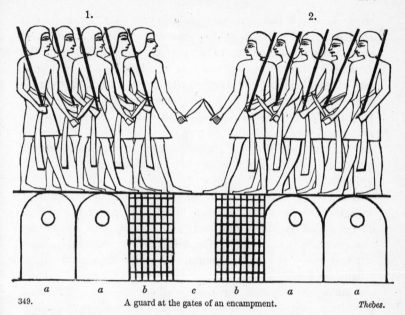

1.   2.

a   a   b   c   b   a   a

349.   A guard at the gates of an encampment.   *Thebes.*

The sculptures at the Memnonium in Thebes show their mode
of encamping on the field, when they had been victorious and no
longer feared an attack ; but the permanent station, or regular
encampment, was constructed with greater attention to the principles of defence, and furnished with ditches and a strong efficient
rampart.

A system of regular fortification was adopted in the earliest
times. The form of the fortresses was quadrangular; the walls
of crude brick 15 feet thick, and often 50 feet high, with square
towers at intervals along each face. These were generally the
same height as the walls, and when they only reached part of the
way up they were rather buttresses ; and sometimes the whole wall
was doubled by an outer casing, leaving a space between the two,
filled in here and there by a solid buttress, which strengthened
and united them, and prevented any one passing freely round the
inner wall when the outer one was broken through. The
towers, like the rest of the walls, consisted of a rampart and

parapet, which last was crowned by the usual round-headed battlements, in imitation of Egyptian shields, like those on their stone walls. But a singular arrangement was followed in the position of the towers at the corners, two being placed not upon, but at each side of the very angle, which remained recessed between them, and was slightly rounded off. Whenever it was possible, the fortress was square, with one or occasionally two entrances; but generally with one, and a sally-port, or a water-gate, if near the river: and, when built on an irregularly-shaped height, the form of the works was regulated by that of the ground.

One great principle in the large fortresses was to have a long wall, on the side most exposed to attack, projecting from 70 to 100 feet, at right angles from, and at the same height as, the main wall, upon which the besieged were enabled to run out and sweep the faces, or curtains, by what we should call a "flanking fire." But the great object was, of course, to keep the enemy as far from the main wall as possible. This was done by raising it on a broad terrace or basement, or by having an outer circuit, or low wall of circumvallation, parallel to the main wall, and distant from it, on every side, from 13 to 20 feet; and a tower stood at each side of the entrance, which was towards one corner of the least exposed face. This low wall answered the purpose of a second rampart and ditch; it served to keep the besiegers' moveable towers and battering rams at a distance from the main wall, who had to carry the outer circuit before they could attempt a breach in, or an assault on, the body of the fortress; while, from the lowness of the outer circuit, they were exposed to the missiles of the besieged.

Another more effectual defence, adopted in larger fortifications, was a ditch with a counterscarp, and in the centre of the ditch a continuous stone wall, parallel to the face of the curtain and the counterscarp (—a sort of ravelin, or a tenaille), and then came the scarp of the platform on which the fortress stood. Over the ditch was a wooden bridge, which was removed during a siege.

Occasionally, as at Semneh, there was a glacis of stone, sloping down from the counterscarp of the ditch towards the level country ; so that they had in those early days some of the peculiarities of our modern works, the glacis, scarps, and counterscarps, and a sort of ravelin (or a tenaille) in the ditch.   But though some were kept up after the accession of the 18th dynasty, the practice of fortifying towns seems to have been discontinued, and fortresses or walled towns were not then used, except on the edge of the desert, and on the frontiers where large garrisons were required.   To supply their place, the temples were provided with lofty pyramidal stone towers, which, projecting beyond the walls, enabled the besieged to command and rake them, while the parapet-wall over the gateway shielded the soldiers who defended the entrance ; and the whole plan of an outer wall of circumvallation was carried out by the large crude brick enclosure of the *temenos*, within which the temple stood.   Each temple was thus a detached fort, and was thought as sufficient a protection for itself and for the town as a continuous wall, which required a large garrison to defend it ; and neither Thebes nor Memphis, the two capitals, were walled cities.

The field encampment was either a square, or a parallelogram, with a principal entrance in one of the faces ; and near the centre were the general's tent, and those of the principal officers.   The general's tent was sometimes surrounded by a double rampart or fosse, enclosing two distinct areas, the outer one containing three tents, probably of the next in command, or of the officers on the staff ; and the guards slept or watched in the open air.   Other tents were pitched outside these enclosures ; and near the external circuit, a space was set apart for feeding horses and beasts of burthen, and another for ranging the chariots and baggage. It was near the general's tent, and within the same area, that the altars of the gods, or whatever related to religious matters, the standards, and the military chest, were kept ; and the sacred emblems were deposited beneath a canopy, within an enclosure similar to that of the general's tent.

To judge from the mode of binding their prisoners, we might suppose they treated them with unnecessary harshness and even cruelty, at the moment of their capture, and during their march with the army. They tied their hands behind their backs, or

A captive secured by a handcuff.
350.   *Thebes.*

over their heads, in the most strained positions, and a rope passing round their neck fastened them to each other ; and some had their hands enclosed in an elongated fetter of wood, made of two opposite segments, nailed together at each end ; such as are used for securing prisoners in Egypt, at the present day. In the capture of a town some were beaten with sticks, in order to force from them the secret of the booty that had been concealed ; many were compelled to labour for the benefit of the victors ; and others were insulted by the wanton soldiery, who pulled their beards and derided their appearance. But when we remember how frequently instances of harsh treatment have occurred, even among civilized Europeans, at an epoch which deemed itself much more enlightened than the fourteenth century before our era, we are disposed to excuse the occasional insolence of an Egyptian soldier ; and the unfavourable impressions conveyed by such scenes are more than counterbalanced by the proofs of Egyptian humanity, as in the sea-fight above mentioned. Allowance is also to be made for a licence of the sculptors, who, as Gibbon observes, " in every age have felt the truth of a system, which derives the sublime from the principle of terror."

Indeed, when compared with the Assyrians, and other Asiatic conquerors, the Egyptians hold a high position among the nations of antiquity from their conduct to their prisoners ; and the cruel custom of flaying them alive, and the tortures represented in the sculptures of Nineveh, show the Assyrians were guilty of barbarities, at a period long after the Egyptians had been accustomed to the refinements of civilized communities.

The captives, too, represented on the façades of their temples, bound at the feet of the king, who holds them by the hair of the head, and with an uplifted arm appears about to immolate them in the presence of the deity, are merely an emblematical record of his successes over the enemies of Egypt;* as is shown by the same subject being represented on monuments erected by the Ptolemies and Cæsars.†

The sailors of the "king's ships," or royal navy, were part of the military class, a certain number of whom were specially trained for the sea; though all the soldiers were capable of handling galleys, from their constant practice at the oar on the Nile. The Egyptian troops were therefore employed on board ship by Xerxes, in his war against Greece, "being," as Herodotus says, "all sailors." And as ships of war then depended on the skill of their crews in the use of the oar, the employment of the Egyptian soldiers in a sea fight is not so extraordinary. Many, too, of the Nile boats were built purposely for war, and were used in the expeditions of the Pharaohs into Ethiopia; officers who commanded them are often mentioned on the monuments; and chief, or captain, of the king's ships is not an uncommon title.

Herodotus and Diodorus both mention the fleet of long vessels, or ships of war, fitted out by Sesostris on the Arabian Gulf. They were four hundred in number; and there is every reason to believe that the trade, and the means of protecting it by ships of war, existed there at least as early as the 12th dynasty, about two thousand years before our era.

The galleys, or ships of war, used in their wars out of Egypt differed from those of the Nile. They were less raised at the head and stern; and on each side, throughout the whole length of the vessel, a wooden bulwark, rising considerably above the gunwale, sheltered the rowers, who sat behind it, from the missiles of the enemy; the handles of the oars passing through an aperture at the lower part.

* Herodotus justly blames the Greeks for their ignorance of the Egyptian character, in taking literally their allegorical tales of human sacrifices, ii. 45.
† At E'Dayr, near E'sné, at Dendera, and other places.

The ships in the sea fight represented at Thebes fully confirm the statement of Herodotus that the Egyptian soldiers were employed on board them; as their arms and dress are exactly the same as those of the heavy infantry and archers of the army; and the quilted helmet of the rowers shows they also were part of the same corps. Besides the archers in the raised poop and forecastle, a body of slingers was stationed in the tops, where they could with more facility manage that weapon, and employ it with effect on the enemy.

351.   War galley; the sail being pulled up during the action.   *Thebes.*
a. Raised forecastle, in which the archers were posted.   *c.* Another post for the archers,
   and the pilot *d.*   *e.* A bulwark, to protect the rowers.   *f.* Slingers, in the top.

On advancing to engage a hostile fleet, the sail was used till they came within a certain distance, when the signal or order having been given to clear for action, it was reefed by means of ropes running in pulleys, or loops, upon the yard. The ends of these ropes, which were usually four in number, dividing the sail as it rose into five folds, descended and were attached to the lower part of the mast, so as to be readily worked, when the sail required to be pulled up at a moment's notice, either in a squall of wind or on any other occasion; and in this respect, and in the absence of a lower yard, the sail of the war galley greatly differed from that of the boats on the Nile. Having prepared for the attack, the rowers, whose strength had been hitherto reserved, plied their oars ; the head was directed towards an enemy's vessel, and showers of missiles were thrown from the forecastle and tops as they advanced. It was of great importance to strike their opponent on the side ; and when the steersman, by a skilful manoeuvre, could succeed in this, the shock was so great that they sank it, or obtained a considerable advantage by crippling the oars.

The small Egyptian galleys do not appear to have been furnished with a beak, like those of the Romans, which being of bronze sharply pointed, and sometimes below the water's surface, often sank a vessel at once ; but a lion's head fixed to the prow supplied its place, and being probably covered with metal, was capable of doing great execution, when the galley was impelled by the force of sixteen or twenty oars. This head occasionally varied in form, and perhaps served to indicate the rank of the commander, the name of the vessel, or the deity under whose protection they sailed ; unless indeed the lion was always chosen for their war galleys, and the ram, oryx, and others, confined to the boats connected with the service of religion.

Some of the war galleys on the Nile were furnished with forty-four oars, twenty-two being represented on one side ; which, allowing for the steerage and prow, would require their total length to be about 120 feet. They were furnished, like all the others, with one large square sail ; but the mast, instead of being single, was made of two limbs of equal length, sufficiently open at the top to admit the yard between them, and secured by several strong stays, one of which extended to the prow, and others to the steerage of the boat. Over the top of the mast a light rope was passed, probably intended for furling the sail, which last, from the horizontal lines represented upon it, appears to have been like those of the Chinese, and is a curious instance of a sail, apparently made of the papyrus.

This double mast was common of old, during the 4th and other early dynasties ; but it afterwards gave place entirely to the single one, with bars, or rollers, at the upper part, serving

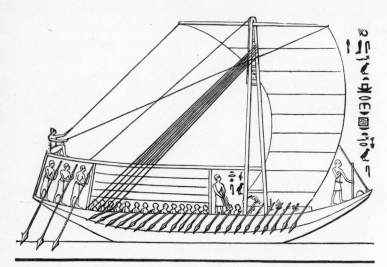

352.   Large boat with sail, apparently made of the papyrus, a double mast, and many
       rowers.   *In a tomb at Kom Ahmar, above Minieh.*

for pulleys, over which the ropes passed; and sometimes rings
were fixed to it, in which the halliards worked.

In this, as in other Egyptian boats, the braces were fixed to the
end of the yard; which being held by a man seated in the steerage,
or upon the cabin, served to turn the sail to the right and left;
they were common to all boats; and at the lower end of the sail
(which in these boats had no yard) were the sheets, which were
secured within the gunwale.   The mode of steering is different
from that usually described in the Egyptian paintings; and
instead of a rudder in the centre of the stern, or at either side,
it is furnished with three on the same side: a peculiarity which,
like the double mast and the folding sail, was afterwards abandoned as cumbrous and imperfect.   This boat shows satisfactorily
their mode of arranging the oars, while not required during a
favourable wind: they were drawn up, through the ring or band
in which they turned, and they were probably held in that position
by a thong or loop passing over the handle.   The ordinary boats

of the Nile were of a different construction; which will be mentioned in describing the boat-builders, one of the members of the fourth class of the Egyptian community.

On returning from war, the troops marched according to the post assigned to each regiment, observing the same order and regularity as during their advance through the enemy's country : and the allies who came with them occupied a position towards the rear of the army, and were followed by a strong corps of Egyptians. Rewards were afterwards distributed to the soldiers, and the triumphant procession of the conqueror was graced by the presence of the captives, who were conducted in bonds beside his chariot.

On traversing countries tributary to, or in alliance with, Egypt, the monarch received the homage of the friendly inhabitants, who, greeting his arrival with joyful acclamations and rich presents, complimented him on the victory he had obtained; and the army, as it passed through Egypt, was met at each of the principal cities by a concourse of people, who, headed by the priests, and chief men of the place, bearing bouquets of flowers, green boughs, and palm branches, received them with loud acclamations, and welcomed their return. Then addressing themselves to the king, the priests celebrated his praises; and, enumerating the many benefits he had conferred on Egypt by the conquest of foreign nations, the enemies of his country, they affirmed that his power was exalted in the world "like the sun" in the heavens, and his beneficence only equalled by that of the deities themselves.

Having reached the capital, preparations commenced for a general thanksgiving in the principal temple : and suitable offerings were made to the presiding deity, the guardian of the city, by whose special favour and intercession the victory was supposed to have been obtained. The prisoners were presented to him, as well as the spoils taken from the enemy, and the monarch acknowledged the manifest power of his all-protecting hand, and his own gratitude for so distinguished a proof of heavenly favour to him and to the nation. And these subjects, represented on the walls of the temples, not only served as a record of the victory, but tended to impress the people with a religious veneration for the deity, towards whom their sovereign set them so marked an example of respect. The troops were also required to attend during the performance of the prescribed ceremonies, and to return thanks for the victories they had obtained, as well as for their personal preservation; and a priest offered incense, meat offerings, and libations, in their presence.*

The captives, being brought to Egypt, were employed in the service of the monarch, in building temples, cutting canals, raising dykes and embankments, and other public works: and some, who were purchased by the grandees, were employed in the same capacity as the Memlooks of the present day. Women slaves were also engaged in the service of families, like the Greeks and Circassians in modern Egypt, and other parts of the Turkish empire; and from finding them represented in the sculptures of Thebes, accompanying men of their own nation,

1   2   3 4 5 6 7 8   9

353.   Women of the Rot-n-n sent to Egypt.   *Thebes.*

* *See* above, p. 278.

Black slaves, with their women and children.   *Thebes.*

who bear tribute to the Egyptian monarch, we may conclude
that a certain number were annually sent to Egypt from the
conquered provinces of the North and East, as well as from
Ethiopia.   It is evident that both white and black slaves were
employed as servants : they attended on the guests when invited
to the house of their master ; and from their being in the families
of priests, as well as of the military chiefs, we may infer that
they were purchased with money, and that the right of possessing
slaves was not confined to those who had taken them in war.
The traffic in slaves was tolerated by the Egyptians ; and doubtless many persons were engaged, as at present, in bringing them
to Egypt for public sale, independent of those who were sent as
part of the tribute; and the Ishmaelites,* who bought Joseph from
his brethren, sold him to Potiphar on arriving in Egypt.   It was
the common custom in those days : the Jews had their bondsmen
bought with money ; † the Phœnicians, who traded in slaves,
sold "the children of Judah and Jerusalem" to the Greeks ; ‡
and the people of the Caucasus sent their boys and girls to

* Gen. xxxvii. 28.   *See* also Gen. xliv. 9.   † Levit. xxv. 44, &c.
‡ Amos iii. 6.

Persia*, as the modern Circassians do to that country and to Turkey.

Diodorus, in mentioning the military punishments of the Egyptians, says that they were not actuated by any spirit of vengeance; but solely by the hope of reclaiming an offender, and of preventing for the future the commission of a similar crime. They were, therefore, averse to making desertion and insubordination capital offences: the soldier was degraded, and condemned publicly to wear some conspicuous mark of ignominy, which rendered him an object of reproach to his comrades; and, without fixing any time for his release, he was doomed to bear it, till his subsequent good conduct had retrieved his character, and obtained for him the forgiveness of his superiors. "For," says the historian, "by rendering the stigma a more odious disgrace than death itself, the legislator hoped to make it the most severe of punishments, at the same time that it had a great advantage in not depriving the state of the services of the offender; and deeming it natural to every one, who had been degraded from his post, to desire to regain the station and character he had lost, they cherished the hope that he might eventually reform, and become a worthy member of the society to which he belonged." For minor offences they inflicted the bastinado, which was commonly employed for punishing peasants and other people; but the soldier who treacherously held communication with the enemy was sentenced to the excision of his tongue; in accordance with the ancient practice of punishing the offending member.

This brief outline of the military customs of Egypt suffices to show that the monuments contain abundant records of those early days; and though many others have long since perished, some belonging to the most glorious periods have fortunately been preserved; and the sculptures of Thothmes III., of the Amunophs, of Sethos, of the Second and Third Remeses, and other kings, confirm the testimony of historians respecting the power of ancient Egypt.

* Herod. iii. 97.

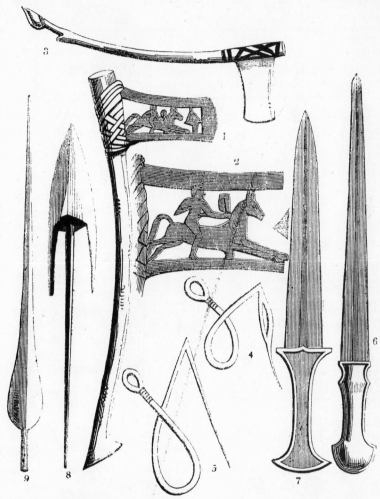

355.　　　Egyptian arms.　　*Collections of S. D'Athanasi and Mr. Salt, and from Thebes.*

Fig. 1. Hatchet, 1 foot 5 inches in length.
　　4 and 5. Slings, from the sculptures.
　　6. Dagger, 15¼ inches in length.

Fig. 7. Dagger, 10½ inches long.
　　8. Head of dart, 3 inches.
　　9. Javelin head, 14 inches long.

END OF VOL. I.

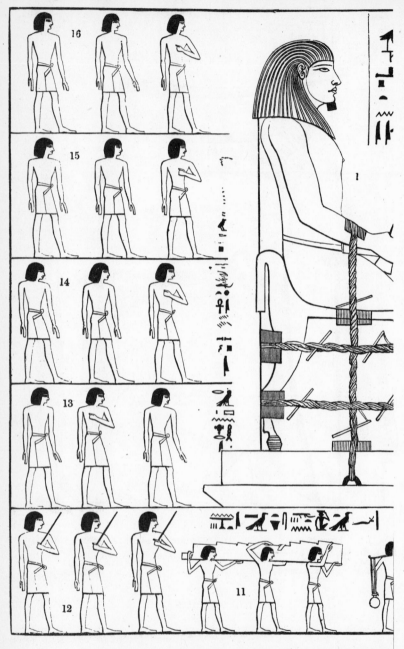

1. The statue bound upon a sledge with ropes. It is of a private individual,
2. Man, probably beating time with his hands, and giving out the verse of a

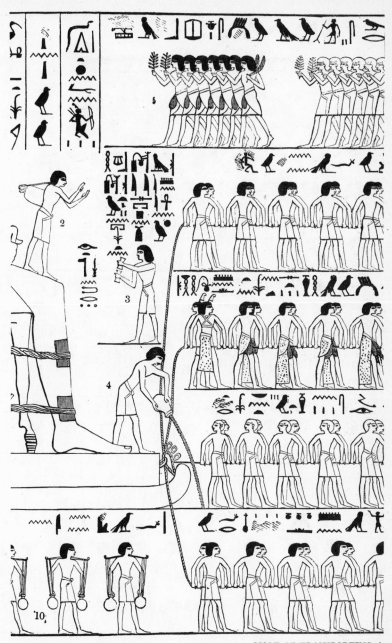

MODE OF TRANSPORTING A

not of a king.
song, to which the men responded.

3. Seems from the hieroglyphics to be offering incense.
4. Pouring grease from a vase.

COLOSSUS FROM THE QUARRIES.

| 5. Egyptian soldiers. | 10. Men carrying water |
| 6, 7, 8, 9. Four rows, of forty-three men each, dragging the statue. | 11. Some implements. |

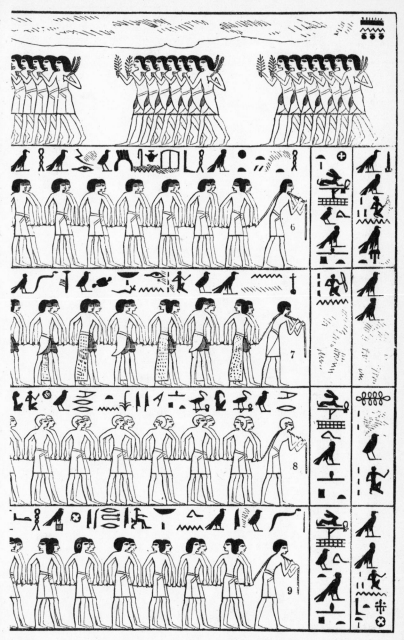

In a grotto at El Bersheh.

or grease. | 12. Taskmasters, or "Superintendents."
13, 14 ,15 16. " Superintendents," and perhaps reliefs of men.

A

POPULAR ACCOUNT

OF

THE ANCIENT EGYPTIANS.

REVISED AND ABRIDGED FROM HIS LARGER WORK,

BY SIR J. GARDNER WILKINSON, D.C.L., F.R.S., &c.

IN TWO VOLUMES.—Vol. II.

Illustrated with Five Hundred Woodcuts.

CONTENTS OF VOL. II.

CHAPTER VI.

CHAPTER VII.

CHAPTER VIII.

CHAPTER IX.

CHAPTER X.

LIST OF WOODCUTS

In Vol. II.

*Those with ** prefixed are new woodcuts; with * new woodcuts copied from lithographs of the previous work.*

** Frontispiece

Mode of transporting a large colossus from the quarries. The statue is bound upon a sledge with ropes; on the knee stands a man beating time with his hands, and giving out a verse of a song; another stands on the base, and pours a green liquid, evidently grease, from a vase, before the sledge. In the upper line are companies of soldiers carrying green twigs; then four rows of men, forty-three in each, dragging the statue with ropes; and in the lowest line are others bearing implements, and vases of grease, or other liquids, followed by " superintendents," or task-masters; and behind the statue are other " superintendents," and perhaps reliefs of men.

CHAPTER VI.

CHAPTER VII.

CHAPTER VIII.

CHAPTER X.

MANNERS AND CUSTOMS

OF

THE ANCIENT EGYPTIANS.

H. *Khonfud,* or clod-crushing machine used after the land is ploughed. *Heliopolis—Cairo in the distance.*

CHAPTER VI.

THE DIFFERENT CLASSES OF EGYPTIANS — THE THIRD CLASS —. THE HUSBANDMEN — AGRICULTURE — PRODUCTIONS OF EGYPT — HARVEST — FESTIVALS OF THE PEASANTS — GARDENERS, HUNTSMEN, BOATMEN OF THE NILE.

THE high estimation in which the priestly and military professions were held in Egypt placed them far above the rest of the community; but the other classes had also their degrees of consequence, and individuals enjoyed a position and importance in proportion to their respectability, their talents, or their wealth.

According to Herodotus, the whole Egyptian community was divided into seven tribes, one of which was the sacerdotal, another of the soldiers, and the remaining five of the herdsmen, swineherds, shopkeepers, interpreters, and boatmen. Diodorus states that, like the Athenians, they were distributed into three classes—the priests ; the peasants or husbandmen, from whom the soldiers were levied ; and the artizans, who were employed in handicraft and other similar occupations, and in common offices among the people—but in another place he extends the number to five, and reckons the pastors, husbandmen, and artificers independent of the soldiers and priests.   Strabo limits them to three, the military, husbandmen, and priests ; and Plato divides them into six bodies, the priests, artificers, shepherds, huntsmen, husbandmen, and soldiers ; each peculiar art or occupation, he observes, being confined to a certain subdivision of the caste, and every one being engaged in his own branch without inter-fering with the occupation of another.   Hence it appears that the first class consisted of the priests ; the second of the soldiers ; the third of the husbandmen, gardeners, huntsmen, boatmen of the Nile, and others ; the fourth of artificers, tradesmen and shopkeepers, carpenters, boatbuilders, masons, and probably potters, public weighers, and notaries ; and in the fifth may be reckoned pastors, poulterers, fowlers, fishermen, labourers, and, generally speaking, the common people.   Many of these were again subdivided, as the artificers and tradesmen, according to their peculiar trade or occupation ; and as the pastors, into ox-herds, shepherds, goatherds, and swineherds ; which last were, according to Herodotus, the lowest grade, not only of the class, but of the whole community, since no one would either marry their daughters or establish any family connexion with them. So degrading was the occupation of tending swine, that they were looked upon as impure, and were even forbidden to enter a temple without previously undergoing a purification ; and the prejudices of the Indians against this class of persons almost justify our belief in the statement of the historian.

Without stopping to inquire into the relative rank of the different subdivisions of the third class, the importance of agriculture in a country like Egypt, where the richness and pro-ductiveness of the soil have always been proverbial, suffices to claim the first place for the husbandmen.

The abundant supply of grain and other produce gave to Egypt advantages which no other country possessed. Not only was her dense population supplied with a profusion of the necessaries of life, but the sale of the surplus conferred considerable benefits on the peasant, in addition to the profits which thence accrued to the state ; for Egypt was a granary where, from the earliest times, all people felt sure of finding a plenteous store of corn ;* and some idea may be formed of the immense quantity produced there, from the circumstance of " seven plenteous years" affording, from the superabundance of the crops, a sufficiency of corn to supply the whole population during seven years of dearth, as well as " all countries" which sent to Egypt " to buy " it, when Pharaoh by the advice of Joseph† laid up the annual surplus for that purpose.

The right of exportation, and the sale of superfluous produce to foreigners, belonged exclusively to the government, as is distinctly shown by the sale of corn to the Israelites from the royal stores, and the collection having been made by Pharaoh only ; and it is probable that even the rich landowners were in the habit of selling to government whatever quantity remained on hand at the approach of each successive harvest ; while the agricultural labourers, from their frugal mode of living, required very little wheat and barley, and were generally contented, as at the present day, with bread made of the *Doora*‡ flour ; children, and even grown persons, according to Diodorus, often living on roots and esculent herbs, as the papyrus, lotus, and others, either raw, toasted, or boiled.

The Government did not interfere directly with the peasants respecting the nature of the produce they intended to cultivate ; and the vexations of later times were unknown under the Pharaohs. They were thought to have the best opportunities of obtaining, from actual observation, an accurate knowledge on all subjects connected with husbandry ; and, as Diodorus observes, " being from their infancy brought up to agricultural

* Gen. xii. 2, and xlii. 2.   † Gen. xli. 29.
‡ The Holcus Sorghum.

pursuits, they far excelled the husbandmen of other countries, and had become acquainted with the capabilities of the land, the mode of irrigation, the exact season for sowing and reaping, as well as all the most useful secrets connected with the harvest, which they had derived from their ancestors, and had improved by their own experience." "They rented," says the same historian, "the arable lands belonging to the kings, the priests, and the military class, for a small sum, and employed their whole time in the tillage of their farms;" and the labourers who cultivated land for the rich peasant, or other landed proprietors, were superintended by the steward or owner of the estate, who had authority over them, and the power of condemning delinquents to the bastinado. This is shown by the paintings of the tombs; which frequently represent a person of consequence inspecting the tillage of the field, either seated in a chariot, walking, or leaning on his staff, accompanied by a favourite dog.*

Their mode of irrigation was the same in the field of the peasant as in the garden of the villa;† and the principal differ-

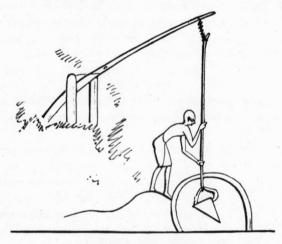

356.   *Shadóof* for watering the lands.   *Thebes.*

* *See* woodcut 368, *fig.* 1, and vol. i. p. 32.   † Vol. i. pp. 33, 34, 35.

ence in the mode of tilling the former consisted in the use of the plough.

The usual contrivance for raising water from the Nile for watering the crops was the *shadóof*, or pole and bucket, so common still in Egypt ; and even the water-wheel appears to have been employed in more recent times.

The sculptures of the tombs frequently represent canals conveying the water of the inundation into the fields ; and the proprietor of the estate is seen, as described by Virgil, plying in a light painted skiff or papyrus punt, and superintending the maintenance of the dykes, or other important matters connected with the land. Boats carry the grain to the granary, or remove the flocks from the lowlands ; as the water subsides, the husbandman ploughs the soft earth with a pair of oxen ; and the same subjects introduce the offering of first-fruits to the gods, in acknowledgment of the benefits conferred by " a favourable Nile." The main canal was usually carried to the upper or southern side of the land, and small branches, leading from it at intervals, traversed the fields in straight or curving lines, according to the nature or elevation of the soil.

The inundation began about the end of May, sometimes rather later : but about the middle of June the gradual rise of the river was generally perceived ; and the comparatively clear stream assumed a red and turbid appearance, caused by the floods of the rainy season in Abyssinia : the annual cause of the inundation. It next assumed a green appearance, and being unwholesome during that short period, care was taken to lay up in jars a sufficient supply of the previous turbid but wholesome water, which was used until it reassumed its red colour. This explains the remark of Aristides, " that the Egyptians are the only people who preserve water in jars, and calculate its age as others do that of wine ;" and may also be the reason of water-jars being an emblem of the inundation ; though the calculation of the " age " of the water is an exaggeration. Perhaps, too, the god Nilus being represented of a blue and a red colour may allude to the two different appearances of the low and high Nile.

In the beginning of August, the canals were opened, and the
waters overflowed the plain.   That part nearest the desert, being

357.   Cattle rescued from the inundation.

Part 1.   Figs. 1 and 3. Men calling to others to drive the cattle towards the boat.   2. Rower.   4. Pulling a cow by a noose to the boat.
Part 2.   Fig. 5. Driving the cattle towards the boat.   6. Throwing a noose, in order to drag them after the boat (the end of it is effaced).
           7. The rowers.   8. A man on the bank fishing.   (See the Vignette at the head of Chap. VIII.)

the lowest level, was first inundated; as the bank itself, being the highest, was the last part submerged, except in the Delta, where the levels were more uniform, and where, during the high inundations, the whole land, with the exception of its isolated villages, was under water. As the Nile rose, the peasants were careful to remove the flocks and herds from the lowlands; and when a sudden irruption of the water, owing to the bursting of a dyke, or an unexpected and unusual increase of the river, overflowed the fields and pastures, they were seen hurrying to the spot, on foot, or in boats, to rescue the animals, and to re-move them to the high grounds above the reach of the inunda-tion. Some, tying their clothes upon their heads, dragged the sheep and goats from the water, and put them into boats; others swam the oxen to the nearest high ground; and if any corn or other produce could be cut or torn up by the roots, in time to save it from the flood, it was conveyed on rafts or boats to the next village. And though some suppose the inundation does not now attain the same height as of old, those who have lived in the country have frequently seen the villages of the Delta standing, as Herodotus describes them, like islands in the Ægean Sea, with the same scenes of rescuing the cattle from the water.

Guards were placed to watch the dykes, which protected the lowlands, and the utmost care was taken to prevent any sudden influx of water, which might endanger the produce still growing there, the cattle, or the villages. And of such importance was the preservation of the dykes, that a strong guard of cavalry and infantry was always in attendance for their protection; certain officers of responsibility were appointed to superintend them, being furnished with large sums of money for their mainten-ance and repairs; and in the time of the Romans, any person found destroying a dyke was condemned to hard labour in the public works or in the mines, or was branded and transported to the Oasis. According to Strabo, the system was so admirably managed, "that art contrived sometimes to supply what nature denied, and, by means of canals and embankments, there was little difference in the quantity of land irrigated, whether the inundation was deficient or abundant." "If," continues the geographer, " it rose only to the height of eight cubits, the usual idea was that a famine would ensue ; fourteen being required for a plentiful harvest : but when Petronius was præfect of Egypt, twelve cubits gave the same abundance, nor did they suffer from want even at eight :" and it may be supposed that long experience had taught the ancient Egyptians to obtain similar results from the same means, which, neglected at a subsequent period, were revived, rather than, as Strabo thinks, first introduced, by the Romans.

In some parts of Egypt, the villages were liable to be overflowed, when the Nile rose to a more than ordinary height ; by which the lives and property of the inhabitants were endangered ; and when their crude brick houses had been long exposed to the damp, the foundations gave way, and the fallen walls, saturated with water, were once more mixed with the mud from which they had been extracted. On these occasions, the blessings of the Nile entailed heavy losses on the inhabitants ; for, according to Pliny, " if the rise of the water exceeded sixteen cubits, a famine was the result, as when it only reached the height of twelve." In another place he says, " a proper inundation is of sixteen cubits . . . . in twelve cubits, the country suffers from famine, and feels a deficiency even in thirteen ; fourteen cause joy, fifteen security, sixteen delight ; the greatest rise of the river to this period being of eighteen cubits, in the reign of Claudius ; the least during the Pharsalic war."

From all that can be learnt respecting the rise of the Nile, it is evident that the actual height of the inundation is the same now as in former times, and maintains the same proportion with the land it irrigates ; and that, in order to arrive at great accuracy in its measurement, the scales of the Nilometers ought, after certain periods, to be raised in an equal ratio ; as may be seen by any one who visits those of Cairo and Elephantine. For the bed of the river gradually rises from time to time ; and the level of the land, which always keeps pace with that of the river, increases in a ratio of six inches in a hundred years in some places (as about Elephantine), and in others less—varying according to the distance down the stream. The consequence, and indeed the proof, of which is, that the highest scale in the Nilometer at the island of Elephantine, which served to measure the inundation in the reigns of the early Roman emperors, is now far below the level of the ordinary high Nile; and the obelisk of Matareeh or Heliopolis, the Colossi of the Theban plain, and other similarly situated monuments, are flooded to a certain height by the waters of the inundation, and imbedded in a stratum of alluvial soil deposited around their base.

The continual increase in the elevation of the bed of the river naturally produced those effects mentioned by Herodotus and other writers, who state that the Egyptians were obliged from time to time to raise their towns and villages, in order to secure them from the effects of the inundation; and that the same change in the levels of the Nile and the land took place in former ages, as at the present day, is shown by the fact of Sabaco having found it necessary to elevate the towns throughout the country, which had been previously protected by similar means in the reign of Sesostris. This was done by the inhabitants of each place, who had been condemned for great crimes to the public works. Bubastis was raised more than any other city; and the lofty mounds of Tel Basta, which mark its site, fully confirm the observation of Herodotus, and show, from the height of those mounds above the present plain, after a lapse of 770 years, that " the Ethiopian monarch elevated the sites of the towns much more than his predecessor Sesostris had done," when that conqueror employed his captives in making the canals of Egypt. And if its height was in proportion to the number of its criminals, Bubastis could not boast of the morality of its inhabitants.

On a rough calculation, it may be said that the land about Elephantine has been raised about nine feet in 1700 years; at Thebes, about seven; and in a less degree towards the Delta and the sea, where the extensive surface of the land (compared to the narrow valley above Memphis) alters the proportions in

its elevation, until at the mouths of the Nile there is no perceptible rise of the soil from alluvial deposit.

There is another singular fact connected with the inundation in
different places : that throughout the valley lying to the S. of the
Delta, the actual banks of the Nile are much more elevated than
the land of the interior at a distance from the river, and are
seldom quite covered with water even during the highest
inundations ; though the bank then projects very little above the
level of the stream ; and, in some places, the peasant is obliged
to keep out the water by temporary embankments. This difference
of level may be accounted for partly by the continued cultivation
of the soil by the river side, which, being more conveniently
situated for artificial irrigation, has a constant succession of
crops ; for it is known that tillage has the effect of raising land,
from the accumulation of decayed vegetable substances, the
addition of dressing, and other causes ; and the greater depression of the plain in the interior is owing, in some degree, to the
numerous channels in that direction, and to the effect of the
currents which pass over it as the water covers the land : though
they are not sufficient to account for the great difference between
the height of the bank and the land near the edge of the desert,
which is often 12 or 15 feet, as may be seen from the comparative
height of the same horizontal dyke at those two points.

These elevated roads, the sole mode of communication by
land from one village to another during the inundation, commence on a level with the bank of the river, and, as they extend
to the interior, are there so much higher than the fields, that room
is afforded for the construction of arches to enable the water to
pass through them ; though the larger bridges are only built on
those parts, where ancient or modern canals . have caused a still
greater depression of the land.

The canals, like the dykes, were the constant care of the
magistrates in old times ; and they were furnished with sluices
and other appliances to regulate the supply of water, and to turn
the fisheries to good account.

The water of the inundation was differently managed in

various districts.   This depended either on the relative levels of
the adjacent lands, or on the crops they happened to be cultivating at the time.   When a field lay fallow, or the last crop had
been gathered, the water was permitted to overflow it as soon as
its turn came to receive it from the nearest sluices ; or, in those
parts where the levels were low and open to the ingress of the
rising stream, as soon as the Nile had arrived at a sufficient height ;
but when the last autumn crop was in the ground, every precaution was taken to keep the field from being inundated ; and
" as the water rose gradually, they kept it out by small dams,
which could be opened if required, and closed again without
much trouble."*

As the Nile subsided, the water was retained in the fields by
proper embankments ; and the mouths of the canals being again
closed, it was prevented from returning into the falling stream.
By this means the irrigation of the land was prolonged considerably, and the fertilising effects of the inundation continued until
the water was absorbed.   And so rapidly does the hot sun of
Egypt, even at this late period of the season,—in the months of
November and December,—dry the mud when once deprived of
its covering of water, that no fevers are generated, and no illness visits those villages which have been entirely surrounded by
the inundation.

The land being cleared of the water, and presenting in some
places a surface of liquid mud, in others nearly dried by the sun
and the strong N.W. winds (that continue at intervals to the
end of autumn and the commencement of winter), the husbandman prepared the ground to receive the seed ; which was either
done by the plough and hoe, or by more simple means, according
to the nature of the soil, the quality of the produce they intended
to cultivate, or the time the land had remained under water.

When the levels were low, and the water had continued long
upon the land, they often dispensed with the plough, and, like
their successors, broke up the ground with hoes, or simply
dragged the moist mud with bushes after the seed had been
thrown upon the surface ; and then merely drove a number of

* Diodor. i. 36.

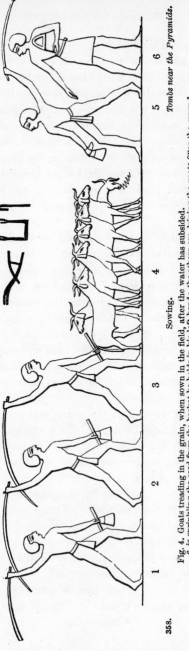

CHAP. VI.

Tombs near the Pyramids.

Sowing.

Fig. 4. Goats treading in the grain, when sown in the field, after the water has subsided. 6 is sprinkling the seed from the basket he holds in his left hand; the others are driving the goats over the ground. The hieroglyphic word above, Sk, or Skai, signifies "tillage," and is followed by the demonstrative sign, a plough.

358.

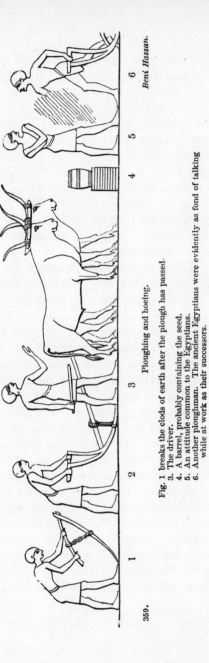

359.

Ploughing and hoeing.

Fig. 1 breaks the clods of earth after the plough has passed.
3. The driver.
4. A barrel, probably containing the seed.
5. An attitude common to the Egyptians.
6. Another ploughman. The ancient Egyptians were evidently as fond of talking while at work as their successors.

Beni Hassan.

cattle, asses, pigs, sheep, or goats into the field to tread in the grain. "In no country," says Herodotus, "do they gather their seed with so little labour. They are not obliged to trace deep furrows with the plough, and break the clods, nor to partition out their fields into numerous forms, as other people do ; but when the river of itself overflows the land, and the water retires again, they sow their fields, driving the pigs over them to tread in the seed ; and this being done, every one patiently awaits the harvest." On other occasions they used the plough, but were contented, as we are told by Diodorus and Columella, with " tracing slight furrows with light ploughs on the surface of the land ;" and others followed with wooden hoes* to break the clods of the rich and tenacious soil.

The modern Egyptians sometimes substitute for the hoe a machine,† called *khonfud*, "hedgehog," which consists of a cylinder studded with projecting iron pins, to break the clods after the land has been ploughed ; but this is only used when great care is required in the tillage of the land ; and they frequently dispense with the hoe ; contenting themselves, also, with the same slight furrows as their predecessors, which do not exceed the depth of a few inches, measuring from the lowest part to the summit of the ridge. It is difficult to say if the modern Egyptians derived the hint of the " *hedgehog* " from their predecessors ; but it is a curious fact that a clod-crushing machine, not very unlike that of Egypt, has only lately been invented in England, which was shown at the Great Exhibition of 1851.

The ancient plough was entirely of wood, and of as simple a form as that of modern Egypt. It consisted of a share, two *handles*, and the pole or beam ; which last was inserted into the lower end of the stilt, or the base of the handles, and was strengthened by a rope connecting it with the heel. It had no coulter, nor were wheels applied to any Egyptian plough : but it is probable that the point was shod with a metal sock, either of bronze or iron. It was drawn by two oxen ; and the plough-

* Woodcuts 359, *fig.* 1, 361 and 362.
† See the Vignette at the beginning of this Chapter.

man guided and drove them with a long goad, without the assistance of reins, which are used by the modern Egyptians. He was sometimes accompanied by another man, who drove the animals,* while he managed the two handles of the plough; and sometimes the whip was substituted for the more usual goad.

Cows were occasionally put to the plough; and it may not have been unknown to them that the cow ploughs quicker than the ox.

The mode of yoking the beasts was exceedingly simple. Across the extremity of the pole, a wooden yoke or cross-bar, about fifty-five inches or five feet in length, was fastened by a strap lashed backwards and forwards over a prominence projecting from the centre of the yoke, which corresponded to a similar peg, or knob, at the end of the pole; and occasionally,

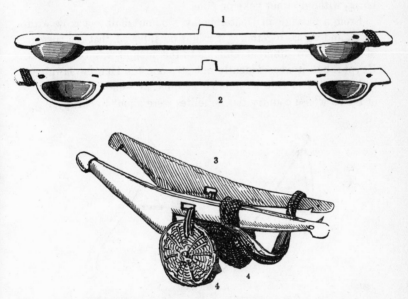

360.　　　　Yoke of an ancient plough found in a tomb.　　*Collection of S. D'Anastasy.*

Figs. 1, 2. The back and front of the yoke.
3. Collar or shoulder pieces attached to the yoke.
4, 4. The pieces of matting for protecting the two shoulders from friction.

* *See* instances of both in woodcut 34, vol. i. p. 32.

in addition to these, was a ring passing over them as in some
Greek chariots.   At either end of the yoke was a flat or slightly
concave projection, of semi-circular form, which rested on a pad
placed upon the withers of the animal ; and through a hole on
either side of it passed a thong for suspending the shoulder-
pieces which formed the collar.   These were two wooden bars,
forked at about half their length, padded so as to protect the
shoulder from friction, and connected at the lower end by a
strong broad band passing under the throat.

Sometimes the draught, instead of being from the withers,
was from the head, the yoke being tied to the base of the horns ;*
and in religious ceremonies oxen frequently drew the bier, or
the sacred shrine, by a rope fastened to the upper part of the
horns, without either yoke or pole.

From a passage in Deuteronomy, " Thou shalt not plow with
an ox and an ass together," it might be inferred that the custom
of yoking two different animals to the plough was common in
Egypt : but it was evidently not so ; and the Hebrew lawgiver
had probably in view a practice adopted by some of the people
of Syria, whose country the Israelites were about to occupy.

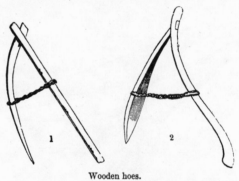

361.   Wooden hoes.
        Fig. 1. From the sculptures.   Fig. 2. Found in a tomb.

The hoe was of wood, like the fork, and many other implements of husbandry, and in form was not unlike our letter A,

* As in woodcut 359, p. 13.

with one limb shorter than the other, and curving inwards. The longer limb, or handle, was of uniform thickness, round and smooth, sometimes with a knob at the end; and the lower extremity of the blade was of increased breadth, and either terminated in a sharp point, or was rounded at the end. The blade was frequently inserted into the handle,* and they were bound together, about the centre, with a twisted rope. Being the most common tool, answering for hoe, spade, and pick, it is frequently represented in the sculptures; and several, which have been found in the tombs of Thebes, are preserved in the museums of Europe.

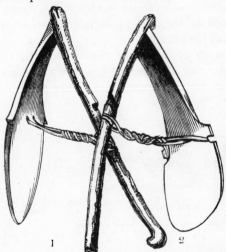

362.   Wooden hoes.   *Berlin Museum.*

The hoe in hieroglyphics stands for the letter M, though the name of this instrument was in Egyptian, as in Arabic, *Tóré*. It forms the commencement of the word *Mai*, " *beloved*," and enters into numerous other combinations.

There are no instances of hoes with metal blades, except of very late time, nor is there any proof of the ploughshare having been sheathed with metal.

* Woodcut 361, *fig.* 2.

363.   Hoeing and sowing the land, and felling trees.   *Thebes.*

The axe had a metal blade, either bronze or iron; and the peasants are sometimes represented felling trees with this implement; while others are employed in hoeing the field preparatory to its being sown,—confirming what I before observed, that the ancient, as well as the modern, Egyptians frequently dispensed with the use of the plough.

The admission of swine into the fields, mentioned by Herodotus, should rather have been before than after they had sowed the land, since their habits would do little good to the farmer,

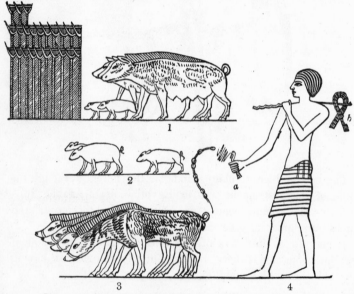

364.   Pigs; rarely seen in the sculptures; and never before the 18th dynasty.   *Thebes.*
1. Sows with young pigs.   2. Young pigs.   3. Boars.
a is a whip, knotted like some of our own.   *b* a *gayd*, or noose, often used as the emblem of a shepherd.

and other animals would answer as well for " treading in the grain ;" but they may have been used before for clearing the fields of the roots and weeds encouraged by the inundation ; and this seems to be confirmed by the herd of pigs with water plants represented in the tombs.

They sometimes used a top dressing of nitrous soil, which was spread over the surface ; a custom continued to the present day : but this was confined to certain crops, and principally to those reared late in the year ; the fertilising properties of the alluvial deposit answering all the purposes of the richest manure. Its peculiar quality is not merely indicated by its effects, but by the appearance it presents ; and when left upon rock, and dried by the sun, it resembles pottery, from its brittleness and consistence. Its component parts, according to the analysis given by Regnault in the " Mémoires sur l'Egypte," are—

                11 water.
                 9 carbon.
                 6 oxide of iron.
                 4 silica.
                 4 carbonate of magnesia.
                18 carbonate of lime.
                48 alumen.
                ———
               100

the quantity of silica and alumen varying according to the places whence the mud is taken, which frequently contains a great admixture of sand near the banks, and a larger proportion of argillaceous matter at a distance from the river.

The same quality of soil and alluvial deposit seems to accompany the Nile in its course from Abyssinia to the Mediterranean ; and though the *White* River is the principal stream, being much broader, bringing a larger supply of water, and coming from a greater distance than the Blue (*Black*) River, or Abyssinian branch, which rises a little beyond the lake Dembea, still this last claims the merit of possessing the real peculiarities of the Nile, and of supplying those fertilising properties which mark its course

to the sea.   The White River, or western branch, likewise overflows its banks, but no rich mud accompanies its inundation ;
and though, from the force of its stream (which brings down
numbers of large fish and shells at the commencement of its rise,
probably from passing through some large lakes), there is evidence of its being supplied by an abundance of heavy rain, we
may conclude that the nature of the soil, along the whole of its
course, differs considerably from that of the Abyssinian branch.

And here I may mention that the name Bahr el Azrek, opposed
to Bahr el Abiad, or " *White* River," should be translated *Black*
(not *Blue*) River; azrek, though signifying " blue," being also
used in the sense of our " jet black ;" and hossán *azrek* is a
" *black* (not a blue) horse."

Besides the admixture of nitrous earth, the Egyptians made
use of other kinds of dressing ; and sought for different productions, the soils best suited to them.   They even took advantage
of the edge of the desert, for growing the vine and some other
plants, which, being composed of clay and sand, was peculiarly
adapted to such as required a light soil ; and the cultivation of
this additional tract, which only stood in need of proper irrigation to become highly productive, had the advantage of increasing
considerably the extent of the arable land of Egypt.   In many
places we still find evidence of its having been tilled by the
ancient inhabitants, even to the late time of the Roman empire ;
and in some parts of the Fyoom, the vestiges of beds and channels for irrigation, as well as the roots of vines, are found in
sites lying far above the level of the rest of the country.

The occupation of the husbandman depended much on the
produce he had determined on rearing.   Those who solely cultivated corn had little more to do than to await the time of harvest ; but many crops required constant attention, and some
stood in need of frequent artificial irrigation.

In order to give a general notion of the quality of the crops,
and other peculiarities relating to their agriculture, I shall introduce the principal productions of Egypt in the two following
tables ; of which the first presents those raised after the retire-
ment of the inundation :—

English Name.	Botanical Name.	Remarks.
Wheat	Triticum sativum. (Arab. *Kumh.*)	Sown in November; reaped in beginning of April, a month later than barley. *Comp.* Exod. ix. 32.
Barley	Hordeum vulgare. (Arab. *Shayéer.*)	Sown at the same time; reaped, some in 90 days, some in the 4th month.*
Beans	Vicia faba. (Arab. *Fool.*)	Sown in October or November; cut in about 4 months.
Peas ?	Pisum arvense. (Arab. *Bisilleh.*)	Sown in the middle of November; ripen in 90 or 100 days.
Lentils	Ervum lens. (Arab. *Ads.*)	Sown in the middle or end of November; ripen in 100 or 110 days.
Vetches	(Hommos) Cicer arietinum. (Arab. *Hommos.*)	
Lupins	Lupinus Termis. (Arab. *Termus.*)	*Id.* Called *Θαρμος* in Coptic, which is still retained in the modern Arabic name Termus.
Clover	Trifolium Alexandrinum. (Arab. *Bersim.*)	Sown in beginning of October; first crop after 60 days, second after 50 more days, third left for seed; if a fourth crop is raised by irrigation, it produces no seed.
	Trigonella fœnum-græcum. (Arab. *Helbeh.*)	The Helbeh, or Trigonella fœnum-græcum, sown in November; cut in about 2 months.
	Lathyrus sativus. (Arab. *Gilbán.*)	Lathyrus sativus, a substitute for clover, gathered in 60 days; seed ripens in 110.
A sort of French Bean	Dolichos lubia. (Arab. *Loobieh.*)	Sown at same time as wheat in November, ripens in 4 months. A crop raised by the *Shadoof* in August, gathered in about 3 months; its beans for cooking in 60 days.

* Pliny says in the sixth, and wheat in the seventh, month after sowing, xviii. 7.

English Name.	Botanical Name.	Remarks.
Safflower	Carthamus tinctorius. (Arab. *Kortum.*)	The flowers used for dyeing : the seeds giving an oil. Sown middle of November ; seeds ripen in 5 months.
Lettuce	Lactuca sativa. (Arab. *Khus.*)	Cultivated for oil. Sown in middle of November ; seeds ripen in 5 months.
Flax	Linum usitatissimum. (Arab. *Kettán.*)	Sown middle of November ; plucked in 110 days.
Coleseed	Brassica oleifera. (Arab. *Selgam.*)	Yields an oil. Sown middle of November ; cut in 110 days.
Hemp ?	Cannabis sativa. (Arab. *Hasheésh.*)	
Cummin	Cuminum Cyminum. (Arab. *Kammoon.*)	
Coriander	Coriandrum sativum. (Arab. *Koosbera.*)	Sown middle of December ; cut in 4 months.
Poppy	Papaver somniferum. (Arab. *Aboonóm.*)	Sown end of November ; seeds ripen in April. The Arabic name signifies father (of) sleep.
Water Melon, and several other Cucurbitæ	Cucurbita citrullus. (Arab. *Bateékh.*)	Sown middle of December ; cut in 90 days.
Cucumber, and other Cucumis	Cucumis sativus. (*Kheár*) &c.	Cut in 60 days.
Doora	Holcus Sorghum. (Arab. *Doora Sayfee.*)	Independent of the crop raised by the *Shadoof*, and that *during* the inundation ; sown middle of November ; ripens in 5½ months.

All these, the ordinary productions of modern Egypt, appear
to have been known and cultivated in old times: and according
to Dioscorides, from the *Helbeh*, or Trigonella, was made the
ointment, called by Athenæus ' Telinon.'   The Carthamus tinctorius and the pea are now proved, by the discovery of their
seeds in a tomb at Thebes, to have been ancient Egyptian plants ;
the coleseed appears also to have been an indigenous production ;
and hemp is supposed to have been used of old for its intoxicating
qualities.

The Carthamus was not only cultivated for the dye its flower
produced, but for the oil extracted from its seeds.   The ancient,
as well as the modern Egyptians, also obtained oil from other
plants, as the olive, *simsim* or sesamum, the *cici* or castor-berry
tree, lettuce, flax, and *selgam* or coleseed.   This last, the Bras-
sica oleifera of Linnæus, appears to be the Egyptian *raphanus*
mentioned by Pliny, as " celebrated for the abundance of its
oil," unless he alludes to the *seemga*, or Raphanus oleifer of
Linnæus, which is now only grown in Nubia and the vicinity of
the first cataract.   The seeds of the *simsim* also afforded an excellent oil, and they were probably used, as at the present day,
in making a peculiar kind of cake, called by the Arabs *Koosbeh*,
which is the name it bears when the oil has been previously extracted.   When only *bruised* in the mill, and still containing the
oil, it is called *Taheéneh;* and the unbruised seeds are strewed
upon cakes, or give their name and flavour to a coarse conserve
called *Haloweh simsemeéh*.   The oil of *simsim* (called *seerig*) is
considered the best lamp oil of the country ; it is also used for
cooking, but is reckoned inferior in flavour to that of the lettuce.

The castor-berry tree is called by Herodotus Sillicyprion, and
the oil kiki (*cici*), which he says is not inferior to that of the
olive for lamps, though it has the disadvantage of a strong unpleasant smell.   Pliny calls the tree *cici*, which, he adds, " grows
abundantly in Egypt, and has also the names of croton, trixis,
tree sesamum, and ricinus ;" and he records his very natural dislike of castor-oil.   The mode he mentions of extracting the oil
by putting the seeds into water over a fire, and skimming the

surface, is the manner now adopted in Egypt; though he says
the ancient Egyptians merely pressed them after sprinkling them
with salt.   The press, indeed, is employed for this purpose at the
present day, when the oil is only wanted for lamps; but by the
other method it is more pure, and the coarser qualities not being
extracted, it is better suited for medicinal purposes.   Strabo
says, " Almost all the natives of Egypt used its oil for lamps,
and workmen, as well as all the poorer classes, both men and
women, anointed themselves with it," giving it the same name,
kiki, as Pliny, which he does not confine, like Herodotus, to the
oil: and of all those by which it was formerly known in Egypt
or Greece, no one is retained by the modern Egyptians.   It
grows in every part of Upper and Lower Egypt; but the oil is
now little used, in consequence of the extensive culture of the
lettuce, the coleseed, the olive, the carthamus, and the *simsim*,
which afford a better quality for burning : it is, therefore, seldom
employed except for the purpose of adulterating the lettuce and
other oils; and the Ricinus, though a common plant, is rarely
cultivated in any part of the country.

" The *cnicon*, a plant unknown in Italy, according to Pliny,
was sown in Egypt for the sake of the oil its seeds afforded;"
the chorticon, urtica, and amaracus were cultivated for the same
purpose, and the cypros, " a tree resembling the ziziphus in its
foliage, with seeds like the coriander, was noted in Egypt, particularly on the Canopic branch of the Nile, for the excellence
of its oil."   Egypt was also famed for its " oil of bitter almonds ;"
and many other vegetable productions were encouraged for the
sake of their oil, for making ointments, or for medicinal purposes.

In the length of time each crop took to come to maturity, and
the exact period when the seed was put into the ground, much
depended on the duration of the inundation, the state of the soil,
and other circumstances ; and in the two accompanying tables
I have been guided by observations made on the crops of modern
Egypt, which, as may be supposed, differ in few or no particulars
from those of former days ; the causes that influence them being
permanent and unvarying.

English Name.	Botanical Name.	Remarks.
Rice	Oryza sativa. (Arab. *Rooz* or *Aroos.*)	Cut in 7 months: in October. Grown in the Delta.
Doora	Holcus Sorghum. (Arab. *Doora Kaydee.*)	Sown in beginning or end of April; cut at rise of Nile in 100 days. Its seed sown as Byoód.
Byoód or autumn *Doora*	Holcus Sorghum. (Arab. *D. Byoód,* or *Di-méeree.*)	Sown middle of August; cut in 4 months; but its seed, no longer prolific, is all used for bread.
Yellow Doora	Id. (Arab. *D. Saffra.*)	Sown when the Nile is at its height, in middle of August, and banked up from the inundation: ripens in 120 days.
Millet	Holcus saccharatus. (Arab. *Dokhn.*)	Only in Nubia and the Oases: sown at same time as the Doora.
Cotton	Gossypium herbaceum. (Arab. *Koton.*)	Planted in March and summer. In good soil some is gathered the 5th month.
Simsim, Sesame	Sesamum orientale. (Arab. *Simsim.*)	Gives an oil. Ripens in about 100 days. Sown 10 days after the Doora Byoód. *See above,* p. 23.
Indigo	Indigofera argentea. (Arab. *Néeleh.*)	Sown in April: the first crop in 70 days; second in 40; third in 30; fourth in 25, in the first year: it is then left without water all the winter, and watered again in March. Then the first crop is cut after 40 days; second in 30; third in 30; and the same in the third year. After three years it is renewed from seed. The first year's crop is the best.
Henneh	Lawsonia spinosa et inermis.	Used for the dye of its leaves.
Water Melon	and other Cucurbitæ. (Arab. *Bateekh,* &c.)	During the rise of the Nile, and in March, on the sand-banks of the river.
Onion (Leek, and Garlic)	Allium Cepa, &c. (Arab. *Bussal.*)	Sown in August.
Bámia	Hibiscus esculentus. (Arab. *Bámia.*)	Mostly in gardens. Gathered in 50 or 60 days, in September and October. Many other vegetables raised at different seasons, by artificial irrigation.

In the foregoing table are enumerated the chief productions sown the half year before, or during the inundation. They may be called the plants of the summer season; which succeeding the other crops, either immediately or after a short interval, are produced solely by artificial irrigation. But the use of the *shadoof* is not confined to the productions of summer; it is required for some in spring, and frequently throughout the winter, as well as in autumn, if the inundation be deficient; and the same system was, of course, adopted by the ancient Egyptians.

Having, in the preceding tables, shown the seasons when the principal productions of Egypt were raised, I proceed to mention those which appear from good authority to have been grown by the ancient Egyptians. Wheat, barley, *doora*, peas, beans, lentils, *hommos*, *gilbán?* (Lathyrus sativus), carthamus, lupins, *bamia* (Hibiscus esculentus), *figl* (Raphanus sativus, *var.* edulis), *simsim*, indigo, sinapis or mustard, origanum, succory,* flax, cotton, cassia senna, colocinth, cummin, coriander, several Cucurbitæ, " cucumbers, melons, leeks, onions, garlic," lotus, nelumbium, cyperus esculentus, papyrus, and other Cyperi, are proved to have been cultivated by them: and the learned Kircher mentions many productions of the country, principally on the authority of Apuleius, and early Arab writers. But the greater part of these last are wild plants: and, indeed, if all the indigenous productions of Egypt (which unquestionably grew there in ancient as well as modern times) were enumerated, a large catalogue might be collected, those of the desert alone amounting to nearly 250 species. For though the Egyptian Herbarium is limited to about 1300, the indigenous plants constitute a large proportion of that number, and few countries have a smaller quantity introduced from abroad than Egypt, which, except in a few instances, has remained contented with the herbs and trees of its own soil; and the plants of the desert may be considered altogether indigenous, without, I believe, one single exception.

The following is a brief enumeration of those mentioned by Pliny, together with the most striking characteristics or properties he ascribes to them. I have arranged them in the order in which they are given by the naturalist, not according to their botanical classification, some being unknown.

Name from Pliny.	lib.	c.	Botanical Name.	Remarks.
A plant producing ladanum	12	17	Cistus ladaniferus.	"The plant which produces ladanum, introduced into Egypt by the Ptolemies." *Plin.*
Tree producing Myrobalanum, Myrobalanus	12 23	21 5	Moringa aptera? (Arab. *Yessur*; fruit, *Hab-ghálee*.)	"Producing a fruit from which an oil or ointment was extracted. Growing in the Thebaïd." *Plin.*
Palma called Adipsos	12	22	?	"Gathered before ripe: that which is left is called Phœnicobalanus, and is intoxicating." *Plin.*
Sphagnos, Bryon, or Sphacos	12 24	23 28 6	Parmelia parietina? (Arab. *Shegeret e'neddeh*.)	"Said to grow in Egypt," *Plin.* A sort of lichen growing on trees. Oil extracted from it. *Plin.* 13, 1.
Cypros	12 13 23	24 1 4	Lawsonia spinosa et inermis. (Arab. *Henneh*.)	"Bearing leaves like the Zizyphus. Cooked in oil to make the ointment called Cyprus. The best grown about Canopus. Leaves dye the hair." *Plin.*
Maron	12	24	Teucrium Iva? (Arab. *Miskeh?*)	There are four or five other species of Teucrium in Egypt.
(——————)	12	25	Amyris Opobalsamum. (Arab. *Belisán*.)	Balsam in Egypt, according to Dioscorides and Strabo, till lately cultivated at Heliopolis.
Elate (Abies?), Palma, or Spathe	12 23	28 5	?	"Of use for ointments." *Plin.* It is supposed to be the sheath of the palm flowers. *Vide Dioscor.* 1. 150. (Arab. *Sabát*, comp. *Spathe*.)
Amygdalus, Almond	13	1	Amygdalus communis. (Arab. *Lóz*.)	"Oil of bitter almonds made in Egypt." *Plin.*
Palma, Palm	13	4	Phœnix dactylifera. (Arab. *Nakhl*.)	See Vol. I., p. 55. "Thebaïc palms." *Plin.* 23. 4.
Myxa	13	5	Cordia Myxa, Sebestena. domestica, *Alpin.* (Arab. *Mokháyt*.)	"Wine made from the fruit in Egypt." *Plin.* They now make birdlime from it.
Ficus Ægyptia	13 23	7 7	Ficus Sycamorus. (Arab. *Gimmayz*.)	"Fruit growing on the stem itself." *Plin.* and *Athen. Deipn.* ii. p. 51.
(*Ceraunia siliqua*)	13	8	Ceratonia Siliqua. (Arab. *Kharoob*.)	(Locust tree, or *Kharoób*, said by Pliny *not* to grow in Egypt. It is now an Egyptian tree.)

Name from Pliny.	lib.	c.	Botanical Name.	Remarks.
Persica or Peach	13 15	9 13	Amygdalus Persica. (Arab. *Khokh.*)	"Pliny rejects the idle tale of the peach being a poisonous fruit introduced by the Persians into Egypt." *See* lib. xv. 13.
Cuci	13	9	Cucifera Thebaïca. (Arab. *Dôm.*)	"Like to a palm, but with spreading branches. Fruit fills a man's hand; of a brown yellow colour. That within large and hard; turned and made into pulleys or sail rings. The nucleus within it eaten when young; exceedingly hard when dry (and ripe)." *See above,* Vol. I. p. 56.
Spina Ægyptia, the Acanthus of Herodotus and Strabo.	13 24	9 11 11 12	Mimosa Nilotica. (Arab. *Sont.*)	"Seed pods used for tanning." "Produces gum." *Plin. See Athen.* xv. p. 680. Groves of it at Thebes, Memphis, and Abydus: the two last still remain. Many other Mimosas in Egypt. Pliny (xiii. 10) mentions a sensitive acacia about Memphis. One is now common on the banks of the Nile above Dongola (the *Acacia Asperata?*). The mimosa Lebbek also grew of old in Egypt, and the Copt Christians have a silly legend of its worshipping the Saviour.
Quercus, Oak	13	9	Quercus ——	"About Thebes, where the Persica, olive (and spina) grow." *Plin.* The oak is unknown in Egypt.
(Perséa)	13	9	Balanites Ægyptiaca. (Arab. *Egléeg;* fruit, *Lalob.*)	Grows in the Eastern desert of the Thebaïd. *See Descr. de l'Egypte. Bot.,* pl. 28, fig. 1.
Oliva, Olive	13 15	9 3	Olea Europæa. (Arab. *Zaytoon.*)	"The olives of Egypt very fleshy, but with little oil." *Plin.* xv. 13. This is very true. Strabo says, "the Arsinoïte nome alone (excepting the gardens of Alexandria) produces the olive. The oil is very good if carefully extracted; if not, the quantity is great, but with a strong odour," xvii. p. 556.

Prunus Ægyptia	13	10	Rhamnus Spina Christi or R. Nabeca, Forsk. (Arab. *Nebk.*)	"Near Thebes."
Papyrus or Biblus	13 24	11 12 11	Cyperus papyrus. (Arab. *Berdi?*)	*See* below in Chap. vii. Strabo, xvii. p. 550.
Lotus	13 24	17 2	Nymphaea Lotus. (Arab. *Beshnín.*)	*See* Vol. I. pp. 57, 79, 256, 257.
Punicum malum or Granatum, Pomegranate	13	19	Punica Granatum. (Arab. *Roomán.*)	"The flower called Balaustium." *Plin.* It is the ancient *rhodon* or rose, which was used for its dye, and gave its name to the Island of Rhodes. It is therefore on the reverse of the coins of that island.
Tamarix, Myrice, Tamarisk	13 24	21 9	Tamarix Gallica. (Arab. *Turfa.*)	"Called also Myrice, or wild brya, very abundant in Egypt and Syria." "Brya, or bryonia, commonly called Arbor infelix," *Plin.*
Ferula	13 20	22 23	Ferula communis? or Bubon tortuosum? (The Crythmum Pyrenaicum of Forskal.) (Arab. *Shebet e' Gebel.*)	"Knotted and hollow stem, very light, good for matches. Some call the seed *Thapsia.*" *Plin.* Two kinds, like the anethum. A large umbelliferous plant, supposed to be a sort of wild fennel.
Capparis	13	23	Capparis spinosa. (Arab. *Lussuf.*)	The Caper. The fruit of the Egyptian caper, or *Lussuf,* is very large, like a small cucumber, about 2½ inches long, which is eaten by the Arabs.
Sari	13	23	Cyperus dives? or C. fastigiatus? (Arab. *Dees.*)	*See Theophr.* iv. 9. "It grows on the banks of the Nile, with a head (*coma*) like the papyrus, and is eaten in the same manner." *Plin.*
Vitis, Vine	14 16	3 7 18	Vitis vinifera. (Arab. *Enéb.*)	*See* above, Vol. I. pp. 39 to 45. Pliny says that no trees, not even vines, lose their leaves about Memphis and Elephantine. Lib. xvi. 21.
Cici, Croton, Trixis, or wild Sesamum	15	3	Ricinus communis. (Arab. *Kharwah.*)	Castorberry tree, or Palma Christi. "Oil extracted from it abounds in Egypt." *Plin.*

Name from Pliny.	lib.	c.	Botanical Name.	Remarks.
Raphanus . . .	15 19	7 5	Raphanus oleïfer, or the Brassica oleïfer. (*Seemga* of Nubia; or the *Selgam* of Egypt?)	"Oil made from its seeds in Egypt." *Plin.* It is probably the *Seemga* or Raphanus oleïfer, and not the sativus, that he alludes to. He may perhaps have had in view the *Selgam* (Brassica oleïfer), or coleseed, so common throughout Egypt. The seemga is now confined to Nubia and the southern extremity of the Thebaïd.
Chorticon, a Grass . .	15	7		"Oil extracted from it." *Plin.*
Sesama	15	7	Sesamum orientale. (Arab. *Simsim.*)	"Cultivated for its oil." *See above*, p. 23.
Urtica, called Cneci-mum, or Cnidium	15 22	7 13	Urtica pilullifera. (Arab. *Fiss el Kelab.*)	"Giving an oil." "The Alexandrian the best quality," "Used also medicinally." *Plin.* Supposed to be a nettle.
Pyrus Alexandria, Pear of Alexandria	15	15	Pyrus communis ? (Arab. *Koomitree.*)	Perhaps of Greek introduction.
Ficus, Fig . . .	15	18	Ficus Carica. (Arab. *Tin.*)	It is a singular fact, that the small fruit of the wild fig of the Egyptian desert, and of Syria, is called by the Arabs *Kottayn*, since Pliny says, "the small Syrian figs are called *Cottana.*" Lib. xiii. c. 5. The tree is called *Hamát.*
Myrtus. Myrtle . .	15 21	29 11	Myrtus communis. (Arab. *As*, or *Mersia.*)	"The myrtle of Egypt is the most odoriferous." *Plin.* and *Athen.* 15. It is only now grown in gardens. Pliny in another place says, "the flowers of Egypt have very little odour," xxi. 7, probably on the authority of Theophrastus. *Hist. Plant.* vi. 6.; *De Caus. Plant.* vi. 27.
Calamus, Reed . .	16	36	Arundo Donax, and Arundo Isiaca. (Arab. *Kussub* and *Boos.*)	"Used by many nations for arrows, so that half the world has been conquered by reeds." *Plin.* (*See* Vol. I. pp. 352, 353.)
Hordeum, Barley .	18	7	Hordeum vulgare. (Arab. *Shayîr.*)	

Triticum, Wheat .	18	8	Triticum sativum (Arab. *Kumh.*)	"The Egyptians make a medicinal decoction of olyra for children, which they call Athara." *Plin.* xxii. 25.
Zea .	18	8	Triticum Zea?	
Olyra		10	Holcus Sorghum? (Arab. *Dóora.*)	
Tiphe .	18	11	Triticum Spelta?	"With a prickly stalk." *Plin.*
Faba, Beans .		12	Vicia Faba. (Arab. *Fool.*)	
Lens, Lentils	18	12	Ervums Lens, (Arab. *Atz, Adz,* or *Adduz.*)	"Two kinds of lentils in Egypt." *Plin.*
Linum, Flax .	19	1	Linum usitatissimum. (Arab. *Kettán.*)	"Four kinds, the Tanitic, Pelusiac, Butic, and Tentyritic." *Plin.*
Gossipion, Cotton .	19	1	Gossypium herbaceum. (Arab. *Kóton.*)	"Called Gossipion, or Xylon: the cloths made from it hence named Xylina." *Plin.*
Aron .	19 / 24	5 / 16	Arum Colocasia? (Arab. *Kolkás.*)	"About the size of a squill", "with a bulbous root." *Plin.*
Aris .	24	16	Arum Arisarum?	"Like the Aron, but smaller; the root being the size of an olive." *Plin.*
Allium, Garlic .	19	6	Allium sativum. (Arab. *Tóm.*)	"Both ranked by the Egyptians among gods, in taking an oath." *Plin.*
Cepa, Onion .	19	6	Allium Cepa. (Arab. *Bussal.*)	
Porrum, Leek .	19	6	Allium Porrum. (Arab. *Korrát.*)	"The best kind is in Egypt." *Plin.*
Cuminum, Cummin .	19 / 20	8 / 15	Cuminum Cyminum, and Nigella sativa. (Arab. *Kammoon-abiad* and *Kammoon-aswed.*)	Pliny speaks of two, one whiter than the other, used for the same purpose, and put upon cakes of bread at Alexandria. The white and black Cuminum are called by the Arabs *Kammoon abiad* and *Kammoon aswed*: the latter is the Nigella sativa. *See* above, Vol. I, pp. 177, 266.
Origanum .	19 / 20 / 25	8 / 17 / 4	Origanum Egyptiacum. (Arab. *Burdakoosh.*)	

Name from Pliny.	lib.	c.	Botanical Name.	Remarks.
Sinapis, Mustard	19	8	Sinapis juncea. (Arab. *Khardel*, or *Kubbr*.)	"The best seed is the Egyptian. Called also Napy, Thaspi, and Saurion." *Plin.*
Cichorium, or Intubus erraticus Seris	20 21 20	8 15 8	Cichorium Intybus. (Arab. *Shikôrieh*.) Cichorium Endivia? (Arab. *Hendebeh*.)	"In Egypt, the wild endive is called Cichorium; the garden endive, Seris." *Plin.*
Anisum, Aniseed	20	17	Pimpinella Anisum. (Arab. *Yensoôn*.)	"The Egyptian is the best quality after the Cretan." *Plin.*
Coriandrum	20	20	Coriandrum sativum. (Arab. *Kuzber* or *Koozbareh*.)	"The best is from Egypt." *Plin.*
Buceros, or Fœnum Græcum	21 24	7 19	Trigonella Fœnum Græcum. (Arab. *Helbeh*.)	"Without any scent." *Plin.*
(*Helenium*)	21 21	10 21	Teucrium Creticum ?	(Helenium (according to Dioscorides), a native of Egypt. This and four other species of Teucrium now grow there.)
Amaracus	21 21	11 22	Origanum Majorana.	"What is called by Diocles, and the Sicilians, Amaracus, is known in Egypt and Syria as the Sampsuchum." "An oil made from it." *Plin.* Athenæus (xv. p. 676) says, "the Amaracus abounds in Egypt;" and in lib. v, he mentions "Amaracine ointment."
Melilotus.	21	11	Trifolium Melilotus Indica. (Arab. *Rekrak* or *Nafâl?*)	"Grows every where." *Plin.*
Rosa, Rose		11	Rosa centifolia. (Arab. *Werd*.)	If by "In Ægypto sine odore hæc omnia," Pliny means that *all* the flowers mentioned in this chapter are Egyptian, many others might be here introduced.
Viola, Violet	21	11	Viola odorata. (Arab. *Benefsig*.)	

Plant	Ref.			Botanical identification	Remarks
Colocasia or Cyamus, or Faba Ægyptia.	21	15		Nymphaea. Nelumbo, or Nelumbium.	"Growing in the Nile;" "one of the wild plants, which abound so plentifully in Egypt." *Plin.* *Athen.* iii. p. 72. *Strabo*, xvii. p. 550.
Anthalium	21	15		Supposed to be the Cyperus esculentus?? (which is in Arab. *Hab el āzeez.*)	"Grows some distance from the Nile," "Fruit like a medlar, without husk or kernel. Leaf of the Cyperus. No other use but for food." *Plin.* Some suppose it the Cyperus esculentus, which is very doubtful.
	21	29			
Œtum	21	15		Supposed to be the Arachis hypogæa?	"Also eaten in Egypt. Few leaves; large root." *Plin.* Theophrastus says, it has a long root, gathered at the time of the inundation, and used for crowning the altars. Lib. i. c. 1. 11.
Arachidna	21	15		?	"These two have spreading and numerous roots; but no leaf, nor anything above the ground." *Plin.*
Aracos	21	15		?	
Condrylla	21	15		Lactuca sativa? (Arab. *Khuss.*)	Lettuce?
Hypocheris	21	15		Hyoseris lucida.	
Caucalis	21	15		Caucalis daucoïdes? Caucalis anthriscus. (Arab. *Gezzer e'shaytán.*)	
Anthriscum	21	15			
Scandix, or Tragopogon.	21	15		Tragopogon picroïdes? (Arab. *Edthbáh?*)	"Leaves like a crocus." *Plin.* The *Edthbáh* is of the order *Syngenesia*, and the flower is of a purplish colour. Dioscorides describes its flower with a white circuit and yellow within.
Parthenium	21	15	30	Matricaria Parthenium, or M. Chamomilla.	
	22	17			
	25	5			
Strychnum, or Strychnus, or Trychos, or Solanum.	21	15		Solanum Dulcamara, or Solanum nigrum. (Arab. *Eneb e' deeb.*)	"Used in Egypt for chaplets: the leaves like ivy: of two kinds; one has red berries (in a sort of bladder) full of grains, and is called Halicacabus, or Callion, and, in Italy, Vesicaria: the third kind is very poisonous." Nightshade.
	21	31			
	27	13			

All esculent plants.

Name from Pliny	lib.	c.	Botanical Name	Remarks.
Corchorus	21	15	Corchorus olitorius. (Arab. *Melokheïh.*)	"Eaten at Alexandria." *Plin.*
Aphace	21 / 21	32 / 15	Leontodon Taraxacum.	"Flowers all the winter and spring, till the summer." *Plin.* Dandelion.
Acinos	21 / 21	15 / 27	Thymus Acinos, or Ocymum Zátarhendi. (Arab. *Zátar.*)	"The Egyptians grow the Acinos for making chaplets and for food. It appears the same as the Ocimum, but its leaves and stalks are more hirsute." *Plin.*
Epipetron	21	15	Sedum confertum. (Arab. *Heïalem.*)	"Never flowers." *Plin.* Some editions of Pliny make this and the Acinos the same; but they are generally believed to be different.
Cnicus, or Atractylis	21 / 21	15 / 32	Carthamus tinctorius? (Arab. *Koortum.*) The other is perhaps the Carthamus Creticus?	Supposed to be the Carthamus. "Unknown in Italy. Oil extracted from the seeds, and of great value. Two kinds; the wild and the cultivated; and two species of the former. Remedy against the poison of scorpions and other reptiles." *Plin.* It is supposed that the Cnicus and Atractylis are not the same plant.
Tribulus	21	16	Trapa natans?	"Grows about the Nile in marshes, and is eaten. Leaf like the elm." *Plin.*
Pirdicium	22 / 21 / 22	10 / 17 / 17	?	"Eaten by other people, as by the Egyptians." "Grows on walls and tiles of houses." *Plin.*
Ornithogale	21	17	Ornithogalum Arabicum? (Arab. *Sumár.*)	"Sieves made of it in Egypt." *Plin.*
Juncus	21	18	Juncus acutus?	
Cypirus	21	18	Gladiolus communis.	"With a bulbous root." *Plin.*
Cyperus	21	18	Cyperus Niloticus, and many other species.	"A triangular rush." *Plin.*

Heliochrysum, or Chrysanthemum.	21	25	Gnaphalium Stœchas.	"Gods crowned with it; a custom particularly observed by Ptolemy, King of Egypt." *Plin.*
Persoluta	21	33	——?	"Grown in gardens in Egypt, for making chaplets." *Plin.*
Lotometra	22	21	A large kind of cultivated lotus, or Nymphœa Lotus.	"Coming from the garden lotos, from whose seed, like millet, the Egyptian bakers make bread." *Plin.*
(*Rhus*)	24	11	Rhus oxyacanthoides. (Arab. *Errin.*)	("Rhus: leaves like myrtle, used for dressing skins." Though Pliny does not mention it as an Egyptian plant, it is indigenous in the desert, and the leaves and wood are used by the Arabs for tanning.)
Egyptian Clematis, or Daphnoides, or Polygonoides.	24	15	Vinca major et minor?	"Mostly produced in Egypt." *Plin.*
Ophiusa	24	17	——?	"About Elephantina." *Plin.*
Stratiotis	24	18	Pistia Stratiotes. (Arab. *Heialem el ma.*)	"Only in Egypt during the inundation of the Nile." *Plin.*
Nepenthes	25 / 21	2 / 21	Perhaps the *Bust* or *Hasheesh*, a preparation of the Cannabis sativa.	"Homer attributes the glory of herbs to Egypt. He mentions many given to Helen by the wife of the Egyptian King, particularly the Nepenthes, which caused oblivion of sorrow." *Plin.*
Absinthium marinum, or Seriphium.	27 / 21	7 / 21	Artemisia Judaica? (Arab. *Bytherân.*)	"The best at Taposiris in Egypt: a bunch of it carried at the fête of Isis." *Plin.*
Myosotis	27	12	Myosotis arvensis.	"The Egyptians believe that if, on the 27th day of Thiatis (Thoth), which answers nearly to our August, any one anoints himself with its juice before he speaks in the morning, he will be free from weakness of the eyes all that year." *Plin.*

The trees of ancient Egypt represented on the monuments are the date, *dôm*, sycamore, pomegranate, persea, tamarisk, and Periploca Secamone : and the fruit, seeds, or leaves of the *nebk*, vine, fig, olive, *Mokhayt* (Cordia Myxa), *Kharoob* or locust-tree, palma Christi or *cici*, *Sont* or acanthus, bay, and *Egleeg* or balanites, have been found in the tombs of Thebes ; as well as of the Areca, Tamarind, Myrobalanus, and others, which are the produce either of India, or the interior of Africa.   And though these last are not the actual productions of Egypt, they are interesting, as they show the constant intercourse maintained with those distant countries.   One instance has been met with of the pine apple, in glazed pottery.   The sculptures also represent various flowers, some of which may be recognised ; while others are less clearly defined, and might puzzle the most expert botanist.

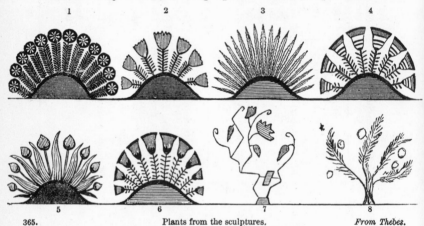

365.   Plants from the sculptures.   *From Thebes.*

Figs. 1 to 6, inclusive, from the tomb of Remeses III.
Figs. 1 and 5 perhaps the same as the two flowers in *fig.* 10, woodcut 260.

Little attention is paid by the inhabitants of modern Egypt to the cultivation of plants, beyond those used for the purpose of food, or to the growth of trees, excepting the palm, large groves of which are met with in every part of the country ; and if the statement of Strabo be true, that, "in all (Lower) Egypt the palm was sterile, or bore an uneatable fruit, though of excellent quality in the Thebaïd," this tree is now cultivated with more success in Lower Egypt than in former times, some of the best quality of dates being produced there, particularly at Korayn, to the E. of the Delta, where the kind called A'maree is superior to any produced to the N. of Nubia.

Few timber trees are reared in these days either in Upper or Lower Egypt. Some sycamores, whose wood is required for water wheels and other purposes ; a few groups of *Athuls*, or Oriental tamarisks, used for tools and other implements requiring a compact wood ; and two or three groves of *Sont*, or Mimosa Nilotica, valuable for its hard wood, and for its pods used in tanning, are nearly all that the modern inhabitants retain of the many trees grown by their predecessors. But their thriving condition, as that of the mulberry-trees (planted for the silkworms), which form, with the Mimosa Lebbek, some shady avenues in the vicinity of Cairo, and of the Cassia fistula (bearing its dense mass of blossoms in the gardens of the metropolis), shows that it is not the soil, but the industry of the people, which is wanting to encourage the growth of trees.

The *Egleeg*, or balanites, (the supposed Persea,) no longer thrives in the valley of the Nile ; many other trees are rare, or altogether unknown ; and the extensive groves of Acanthus, or *Sont*, are rather tolerated than encouraged, as the descendants of the trees planted in olden times near the edge of the cultivated land.

The thickets of Acanthus, alluded to by Strabo, still grow above Memphis, at the base of the low Libyan hills : in going from the Nile to Abydus, you ride through the grove of Acacia, once sacred to Apollo, and see the rising Nile traversing it by a canal, as when the geographer visited that city, even then reduced to the condition of a small village : and groves of the same tree may here and there be traced in other parts of the Thebaïd, from which it obtained the name of the Thebaïc thorn.

Above the cataracts, the *Sont* grew in profusion a few years ago upon the banks of the Nile, enabling the poor Nubians to

send abundance of charcoal for sale to Cairo ; and its place is
supplied in the desert by the *Séáleh* and other of the Mimosa
tribe, which are indigenous to the soil.

The principal woods used by the Egyptians were the date,
Dôm, sycamore, several acacias, the two tamarisks, the *Egleeg* or
balanites, ebony, fir, and cedar.   The various purposes, to which
every part of the palm or date-tree was applied, have been
already noticed, as well as of the *Dôm*, or Theban palm.   Sycamore wood was employed for coffins, boxes, small idols, doors,
window shutters, stools, chairs, and cramps for building ; for
handles of tools, wooden pegs or nails, cramps, idols, small
boxes, and those parts of cabinet work requiring hard compact
wood, the *Sont* (Acacia Nilotica) was usually preferred ; and
spears were frequently made of other acacias, which grew in the
interior, or on the confines of the desert.

For cramps in walls, and tools of various kinds, the wood of the
Tamarix orientalis was much used, and even occasionally for pieces
of furniture, for which purpose the Egleeg was also employed ; but
the principal woods adopted by the cabinet-maker for fine
work were ebony, fir, and cedar.   Of these three the first came
from Africa, and formed, with ivory, gold, ostrich feathers,
dried fruits, and skins, the principal object of the annual tribute
brought to Egypt by the conquered tribes of Ethiopia and the
Soodán ; but fir and cedar were imported from Syria ; the two
last being in great demand for common furniture, small boxes,
coffins, and various objects connected with the dead.

Other woods of a rare and valuable kind were brought to
Egypt by the people of Asia tributary to the Pharaohs ; and the
importance attached to them may be estimated by their being
frequently imitated, for the satisfaction of those who could not
afford to purchase furniture or trinkets of so expensive a material.

Egypt also produced some fungi useful for dyeing ; the pods
of the Acacia Nilotica, the bark of the *séáleh* acacia, and the wood
and bark of the *Errin*, or Rhus oxyacanthoïdes, for tanning ;
and the Periploca Secamone for curing skins.

White crops were of course the principal cultivated productions in the valley of the Nile, and wheat and barley were grown in every part of Egypt.

Like the Romans, they usually brought the seed in a basket, which the sower held in his left hand, or suspended on his arm (sometimes with a strap round his neck), while he scattered the seed with his right; and he sometimes followed the plough, in those fields which required no further preparation with the hoe, or were free from the roots of noxious weeds. The mode of sowing was what we term broadcast; the seed was scattered loosely over the surface, whether ploughed, or allowed to remain in its unbroken muddy state; and in no agricultural scene is there any evidence of drilling or dibbling.

Corn, and those productions which did not require constant irrigation, were sown in the open field, as in other countries; but for indigo, esculent vegetables, and herbs, the fields were portioned out into the usual square beds,* surrounded by a raised border of earth to keep in the water, which was conducted into them by channels from the *shadóof*, or poured in with buckets.†

Wheat was cut in about five, barley in four months; the best quality, according to Pliny, being grown in the Thebaïd. The wheat, as at the present day, was all bearded, and the same varieties, doubtless, existed in ancient as in modern times; among which may be mentioned the seven-eared quality described in Pharaoh's dream.‡ This is the kind which has been lately grown in England, and which is *said* to have been raised from grains found in the tombs of Thebes. It is no longer cultivated in Upper Egypt, being only grown in small quantities in the Delta; and this is the more remarkable as it renders the substitution of modern for ancient wheat at Thebes very improbable.

The wheat was cropped a little below the ear § with a toothed sickle, and carried to the threshing-floor in wicker paniers upon asses,‖ or in rope ¶ nets, the gleaners following to collect the

---

* *See* these square beds in woodcut 39, *fig.* c., vol. i. p. 35.
† *See* p. 4, and vol. i. p. 33.   ‡ Gen. xli. 22.
§ *Comp.* Job xxiv. 24, "Cut off as the tops of the ears of corn."
‖ Woodcut 368, *figs.* 4 and 5.   ¶ Woodcut 367, *figs.* 5 and 7.

Part 1.

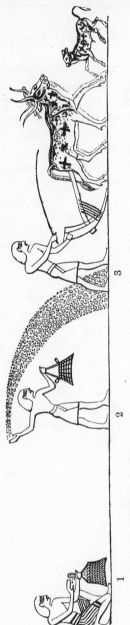

3   2   1

Fig. 1 puts the seed into the basket.
   2 sowing the land after the plough has passed. The handle of the plough has a peg at the side like the modern Egyptian plough,
      which may be seen in the Vignette.

Part 2.

2   1

Ploughing, sowing, and reaping.
Fig. 1. Plucking up the doora by the roots.
   2. Reaping wheat.

Tombs of the Kings—Thebes.

366.

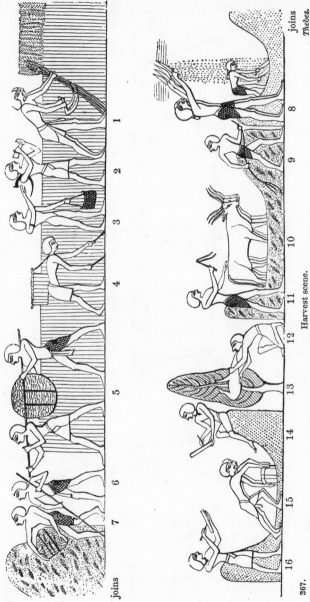

joins

joins
Thebes.

Harvest scene.

Fig. 1. The reapers.   2. A reaper drinking from a cup.   3, 4. Gleaners: the first of these asks the reaper to allow him to drink.   8. Winnowing.
5. Carrying the ears in a rope basket: the length of the stubble showing the ears alone are cut off.   12 drinks from a water-skin suspended in a tree.   14. Scribe who notes down
10. The *tritura*, answering to our threshing.   16 Checks the account by noting those taken away to the granary.
the number of bushels measured from the heap.

367.

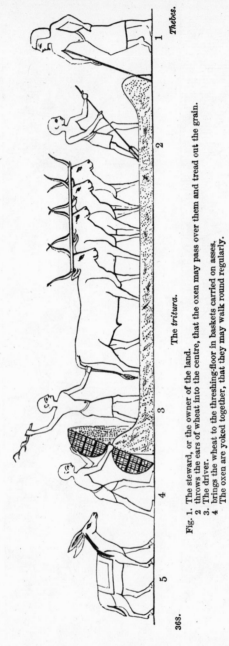

368.

The *tritura*.

Fig. 1. The steward, or the owner of the land.
2 throws the ears of wheat into the centre, that the oxen may pass over them and tread out the grain.
3. The driver.
4 brings the wheat to the threshing-floor in baskets carried on asses.
4 The oxen are yoked together, that they may walk round regularly.

Thebes.

fallen ears in hand baskets. The rope net, answering to the
Shenfeh of modern Egypt, was borne on a pole by two men;
and the threshing-floor was a level circular area near the field, or
in the vicinity of the granary, where, when it had been well
swept, the ears were deposited, and cattle were driven over it to
tread out the grain. While superintending the animals so employed, the Egyptian peasants, like their modern successors, relieved their labours by singing; and in a tomb at Eileithyias
this song of the threshers is written in hieroglyphics over oxen

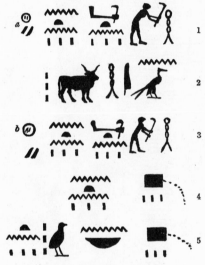

369.   Song of the threshers *to* the oxen.   *Eileithyias.*

treading out the grain :—" (1) Thresh for yourselves (*twice, a*),
(2) O oxen, (3) thresh for yourselves (*twice, b*), (4) measures for
yourselves, (5) measures for your masters." The discovery and
translation of this are due to Champollion, to whom all who
study hieroglyphics are under such infinite obligations, and whose
talents were beyond all praise.

A certain quantity was first strewed in the centre of the area,
and when this had been well triturated by the animals' feet,
more was added by means of large wooden forks, from the main

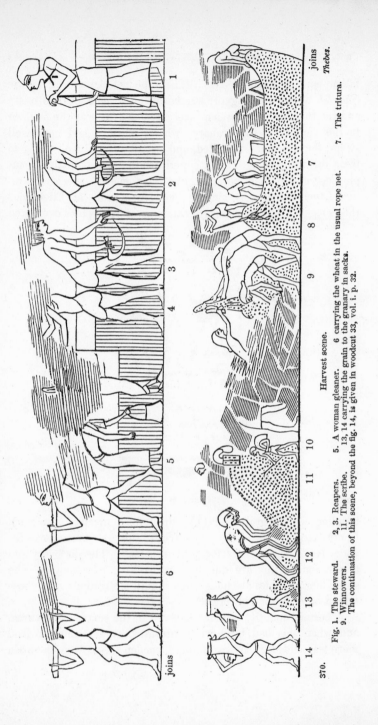

joins

370.

Harvest scene.

Fig. 1. The steward.   2, 3. Reapers.   5. A woman gleaner.   6 carrying the wheat in the usual rope net.   7. The tritura.
9. Winnowers.   11. The scribe.   13, 14 carrying the grain to the granary in sacks.
The continuation of this scene, beyond the fig. 14, is given in woodcut 33, vol. i. p. 32.

Thebes.

joins

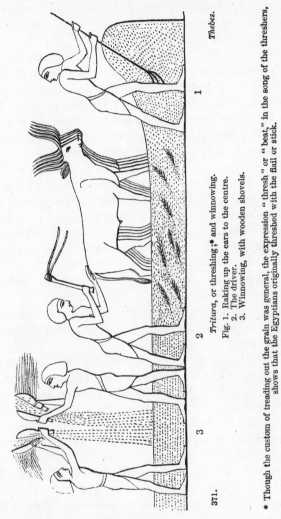

Tritura, or threshing;* and winnowing.

Fig. 1. Raking up the ears to the centre.
    2. The driver.
    3. Winnowing, with wooden shovels.

Thebes.

371.

* Though the custom of treading out the grain was general, the expression "thresh" or "beat," in the song of the threshers, shows that the Egyptians originally threshed with the flail or stick.

heap, raised around, and forming the edge of, the threshing-floor ; and so on till all the grain was trodden out. This process, called *trituration*, was generally adopted by ancient, as by some modern people. Sometimes the cattle were bound together by a piece of wood or a rope fastened to their horns or necks, in order to force them to go round the heap, and tread it regularly, the driver following behind them with a stick.*

After the grain had been trodden out, they winnowed it with wooden shovels; it was then carried to the granary in sacks, each containing a fixed quantity, which was determined by wooden measures; a scribe noting down the number, as called by the teller who superintended its removal. Sweepers with small hand-brooms were employed to collect the scattered grain that fell from the measure; and the "immense heaps of corn" mentioned by Diodorus, collected from "the field which was round every city," † accord well with the representation of the paintings in the tombs,‡ and with those seen at the present day in the villages of the Nile. Sometimes two scribes § were present; one to write down the number of measures taken from the heap of corn, and the other to check them by entering the quantity removed to the granary,|| as well as the number of sacks actually housed :—a precaution quite in character with the circumspect habits of the Egyptians.

Oxen, as Herodotus says, were generally used for treading out the grain; and sometimes, though rarely, asses were employed for that purpose.

The Jews had the same custom, and, like the Egyptians, they suffered the ox to tread out the corn unmuzzled, according to the express order of their lawgiver.¶ In later times, however, it appears that the Jews used "threshing instruments;" though, from the offer made to David by Ornan, of "the oxen also," and the use of the word *dus*, "treading," in the sentence, "Ornan was *threshing* wheat," ** it is possible that the *trituration* is here alluded to, and that the threshing instruments only refer to the winnowing-shovels, or other implements used on those occasions : though the "new sharp threshing instrument having teeth,"

---

* Woodcuts 368, 373.   † Gen. xli. 48.   Diodor. i. 36.
‡ Woodcuts 367, 370.   § Woodcut 367.
|| Of the granary, see vol. i., woodcuts 11, 32, 33.   ¶ Deut. xxv. 4.
     ** 1 Chron. xxi. 20, and 23.

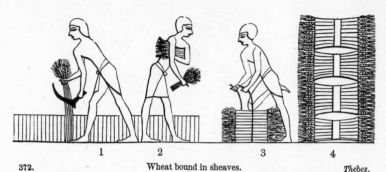

372.   Wheat bound in sheaves.   *Thebes.*

Fig. 1. Reaping.   2. Carrying the ears.   3. Binding them in sheaves put up at fig. 4.

mentioned in Isaiah,* seems to be the *nóreg*, or corn-drag, still employed in Egypt, which the Hebrew name "*moreg*" so closely resembles; and this same word is applied to the "threshing instruments" of Ornan. The Jews, like the Greeks, bound up the wheat, when cut, into sheaves;† which was sometimes done by the Egyptians, though their usual custom was to put it into baskets or rope nets, and to carry it loose to the threshing-floor.

The modern Egyptians cut the wheat close to the ground,—barley and doora being plucked up by the roots,—and having bound it in sheaves, carry it to a level and cleanly swept area near the field, in the centre of which they collect it in a heap, and then taking a sufficient quantity, spread it upon the open area, and pass over it the *nóreg* drawn by two oxen: the difference in the modern and ancient method being that in the former the *nóreg* is used, and the oxen go round the heap, which is in the centre, and not at the circumference, of the threshing floor. Some instances, however, occur of the heap being in the centre, as at the present day.

The *nóreg* is a machine consisting of a wooden frame, with three cross-bars or axles, on which are fixed circular iron plates, for the purpose of bruising the ears of corn and extracting the grain, at the same time that the straw is chopped up: the first and last axles having each four plates, and the central one three:

* Isaiah xli. 15.   † Gen. xxxvii. 7.   Levit. xxiii. 10.   Deut. xxiv. 19, &c.

373.   The oxen driven round the heap; contrary to the usual custom.   *Thebes.*

and at the upper part is a seat on which the driver sits, his weight giving additional effect to the machine.* Indeed, the Roman *tribulum*, described by Varro, appears not to have been very unlike the *nóreg*. It was " a frame made rough by stones or pieces of iron, on which the driver, or a great weight, was placed; and this being drawn by beasts yoked to it, pressed out the grain from the ear."

While some were employed in collecting the grain and depositing it in the granary, others gathered the long stubble from the field, and prepared it as provender to feed the horses and cattle; for which purpose it was used by them, as by the Romans, and the modern Egyptians. They probably preferred reaping the corn close to the ear, in order to facilitate the trituration; and afterwards cutting the straw close to the ground, or plucking it by the roots, they chopped it up for the cattle; and this, with dried clover (the *drees* of modern Egypt), was laid by for autumn, when the pastures being overflowed by the Nile, the flocks and herds were kept in sheds or pens on the higher grounds, or in the precincts of the villages.

This custom of feeding some of their herds in sheds accords with the Scriptural account of the preservation of the cattle,

---

* See Vignette at the end of this Chapter.

which had been " brought home" from the field ; and explains
the apparent contradiction of the destruction of " *all* the cattle
of Egypt " by the murrain, and the *subsequent* destruction of the
cattle by the hail ;* those which " were in the field " alone having suffered from the previous plague, and those in the stalls or
" houses " having been preserved.

An instance of stall-fed oxen from the sculptures has been
given in the account of the farmyard† and villas of the Egyptians.

The first crop of wheat having been gathered, they prepared
the land for whatever produce they next intended to rear ; the
field was ploughed and sowed, and, if necessary, the whole was
inundated by artificial means, as often as the quality of the crop
or other circumstances required. The same was repeated after
the second and third harvest, for which the peasant was indebted
to his own labours in raising water from the Nile,—an arduous
task, and one from which no showers relieved him throughout
the whole season. For in Upper Egypt rain may be said to be
unknown : five or six slight showers, that annually fall there,
scarcely deserving that name ; and in no country is artificial
irrigation so indispensable, as in the valley of the Nile.

In many instances, instead of corn they reared clover, or
leguminous herbs, which were sown as soon as the water began
to subside, generally about the commencement of October ; and
at the same time that corn, or other produce, was raised on the
land just left by the water, another crop was procured by artificial irrigation. This, of course, depended on the choice of
each individual, who consulted the advantages obtained from
certain kinds of produce, the time required for their succession,
or the benefit of the land : for though no soil recovers more
readily from the bad effects arising from a repetition of similar
crops, through the equalising influence of the alluvial deposit, it
is at length found to impoverish the land ; and the Egyptian
peasant is careful not to neglect the universal principle in husbandry, of varying the produce on the same ground.

* Exod. ix. 6 and 19, &c.　　　† Woodcut 31, vol. i. p. 27.

Besides wheat, other crops are represented in the paintings of the tombs; one of which, a tall grain, is introduced as a production both of Upper and Lower Egypt. From the colour, the height to which it grows, compared with the wheat, and the appearance of a round yellow head it bears on the top of its bright green stalk, it is evidently intended to represent the *doora*, or Holcus Sorghum. It was not reaped by a sickle, like the wheat and barley, but men, and sometimes women, were employed to pluck it up;* which being done, they struck off the earth that adhered to the roots with their hands, and having bound it in sheaves, they carried it to what may be termed the threshing floor, where, being forcibly drawn through an instrument armed

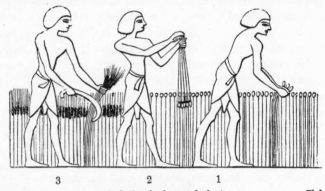

3   2   1

374.   Gathering the doora and wheat.   *Thebes.*

Fig. 1. Plucking up the plant by the roots.
2. Striking off the earth from the roots.
3. Reaping wheat.

at the summit with metal spikes, the grain was stripped off, and fell upon the well-swept area below. This ancient contrivance is the more remarkable as something of the kind has lately been proposed in England, for a similar purpose.†

Much flax was cultivated in Egypt, and the various processes of watering it, beating the stalks when gathered, making it into twine, and lastly into a piece of cloth, are represented in the

* Woodcuts 374 and 375.   † Woodcut 375, *fig.* 3.

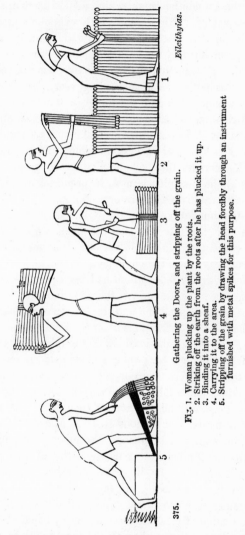

Gathering the Doora, and stripping off the grain.

Fig. 1. Woman plucking up the plant by the roots.
   2. Striking off the earth from the roots after he has plucked it up.
   3. Binding it into a sheaf.
   4. Carrying it to the area.
   5. Stripping off the grain by drawing the head forcibly through an instrument furnished with metal spikes for this purpose.

Eileithyias.

375.

paintings. These will be mentioned in the account of the arts and manufactures of Ancient Egypt.

At the end of summer, the peasant looked anxiously for the

E 2

return of the inundation, upon which all his hopes for the ensuing year depended. He watched with scrupulous attention the
first rise of the river ; the state of its daily increase was noted
down and proclaimed by the curators of the Nilometers at Memphis and other places ; and the same anxiety for the approaching
inundation was felt on each succeeding year. But during this
interval he was not idle, and the quantity of water required for
artificial irrigation entailed on the peasant incessant labour,
except when the Nile was at its highest ; and even while watch-
ing his water-melons, and various cucurbitaceous plants (like the
modern *felláh*, under the shade of a rude " lodge in a garden of
cucumbers "), he occupied himself in preparing something that
might be serviceable on a future occasion.

During the inundation, when the Nile had been admitted by
the canals into the interior, and the fields were covered with
water, the peasantry indulged in various amusements which this
leisure period gave them time to enjoy. Their cattle were housed,
and supplied with dry food, which had been previously prepared
for the purpose; the tillage of the land and all agricultural
occupations were suspended ; and this season was celebrated as
a harvest home, with recreations of every kind. They indulged
in feasting, and in all the luxuries of the table that they could
afford ; they attended the public games held in some of the
principal towns, where the competitors contended for prizes
of cattle, skins, and other things well suited to the taste or
wants of the peasant ; and they amused themselves with wrestling-
matches, bull-fights, and various sports. Many a leisure hour
was passed in singing and dancing ; and among the songs of the
Egyptian peasant, Julius Pollux mentions that of Maneros ; who
was even celebrated as the inventor of husbandry,—an honour
generally given to the still more mysterious Osiris. But some
songs and games were exclusively appropriated to certain festivals ;
and this adaptation of peculiar ceremonies to particular occasions,
is quite consistent with the character of the Egyptians.

They had many festivals connected with agriculture and the
produce of the soil, which happened at different periods of the

year. In the month Mesoré, they offered the firstfruits of their lentils to the God Harpocrates, "calling out at the same time, The tongue is Fortune, the tongue is God;" and the allegorical festival of "the delivery of Isis was celebrated immediately after the Vernal Equinox," to commemorate the beginning of harvest. " Some," says Plutarch, " assimilate the history of those Gods to the various changes which happen in the air, during the several seasons of the year, or to those accidents which are observed in the production of corn, in its sowing and ripening; 'for,' they observe, 'what can the burial of Osiris more aptly signify, than the first covering the seed in the ground after it is sown? or his reviving and reappearing, than its first beginning to shoot up? and why is Isis said, upon perceiving herself to be with child, to have hung an amulet about her neck on the 6th of the month Phaophi, soon after sowing time, but in allusion to this allegory? and who is that Harpocrates, whom they tell us she brought forth about the time of the winter *tropic*, but those weak and slender shootings of the corn, which are yet feeble and imperfect?'—for which reason it is, that the firstfruits of their lentils are dedicated to this God, and they celebrate the feast of his mother's delivery just after the vernal equinox."   From this it may be inferred that the festival of the lentils was instituted when the month Mesoré coincided with the end of March; for since they were sown at the end of November, and ripened in about 100 or 110 days, the firstfruits might be gathered in three months and a half, or, " just after the vernal equinox," or the last week in March: which would carry back the original institution of the festival to about 2650 years before our era, or some time after the reign of Menes.

" On the 19th day of the first month (Thoth), which was the feast of Hermes, they eat honey and figs, saying to each other, 'how sweet a thing is truth!' "—a satisfactory proof that the month itself, and not the first day alone, was called after and dedicated to Thoth, the Egyptian Hermes; and another festival, answering to the " Thesmophoria of the Athenians," was established to commemorate the period when " the husbandmen began to sow their corn, in the Egyptian month Athyr.

Many of the sacred festivals of the Egyptians were connected with agriculture; but these I have already introduced among their religious ceremonies. The gardeners have also been noticed, in mentioning the villas of the Egyptians.*

The huntsmen formed another subdivision of this class.

They were employed in great numbers to attend and assist the amateur sportsmen, during their excursions in pursuit of the wild animals of the country; the scenes of which were chiefly in the deserts of Upper Egypt.† They conducted the dogs to the field; they had the management of them in loosing them for the chase, and they secured and brought home the game, after having contributed by their own skill to increase the sport of the chasseur. They also followed the occupation on their own account; making a considerable profit by catching the animals most prized for the table; by the reward they received for destroying the hyæna, and other animals hostile to the husbandman or the shepherd; and by the lucrative chase of the ostrich, which was highly valued for its plumes and eggs, and was sold to the wealthier Egyptians.

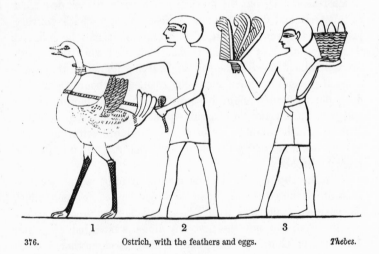

1   2   3

376.   Ostrich, with the feathers and eggs.   *Thebes.*

* Vol. i. pp. 296 to 301, and 33 to 45, and 55, 56, 57.
† *See* beginning of chap. iv.

The boatmen of the Nile belonged to the same third class.

They were of different grades ; some belonging to the private sailing or pleasure boats of the grandees ; others to those of burden. They also differed from the sailors of the " long ships " employed at sea, and even from those of the war galleys on the Nile, which acted as guard-boats, and were also used in the expeditions undertaken by the Pharaohs into Ethiopia.* These government boatmen were sometimes employed by the Kings in transporting large blocks of stone to ornament the temples ; and the immense monolith of granite, brought by Amasis from the first cataract to Saïs, was dragged overland by 2000 boatmen ; but those who carried stones in lighters from the quarries were an inferior order, and ranked among the common boatmen of the Nile. Even among them the office of steersman seems always to have been very important ; and as the pilots of the ships of war had a high rank above the " able seamen " of the fleet, so the helmsman in the ordinary boats of the Nile was looked upon as little inferior to the captain ; standing in the same relative position as the *Mestámel* to the *Ryïs* of the modern *Cangia*.

* See above, vol. i. p. 411, on their sailors and ships of war.

i.   The *Nóreg*, a machine used by the modern Egyptians for threshing corn.

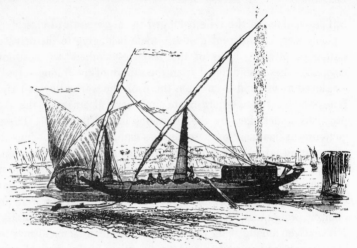

K.   Modern boats of the Nile.   On the opposite bank is a whirlwind of sand.

CHAPTER VII.

FOURTH CLASS:— ARTIFICERS, TRADESMEN OR SHOPKEEPERS, MUSICIANS,
    BUILDERS, CARPENTERS, BOATBUILDERS, MASONS, POTTERS, PUBLIC
    WEIGHERS AND NOTARIES, POUNDERS — GLASS — FALSE STONES — LAMPS
    — FINE LINEN — LOOMS — FLAX — LEATHER — PAPYRUS — POTTERS —
    CARPENTERS — BOXES — BOATS — METALS — TIN — GOLD MINES — IRON —
    BRONZE — CASTING — STONE KNIVES — POUNDING IN MORTARS.

In the fourth class were included the workers in glass, metals,
wood, and leather; the manufacturers of linen and various stuffs;
dyers, tanners, carpenters, cabinet-makers, masons; and all who
followed handicraft employments, or any kind of trade. The musicians, who gained their livelihood by singing and playing, the
leather-cutters and the carvers in stone, and ordinary painters (distinct of course from sculptors and artists) were included in the
same class, which was mostly composed of people living in towns.
Each craft (as is generally the case in Modern Egypt also) had
its own quarter of the town, called after it; as the quarter of the
goldsmiths, of the leather-cutters, and others; and no one pre-
sumed to interfere with the occupation of a different trade from
his own.   It is even said that every one was obliged by law to

follow the very same trade as his father ; at all events, whether allowed in the beginning of his career to choose for himself or no, he was forced to continue in the one he first belonged to ; and each vied with his neighbour in improving his own branch.

According to Diodorus, " no tradesman was permitted to meddle in political affairs, or to hold any civil office in the state, lest his thoughts should be distracted by the inconsistency of his pursuits, or by the jealousy and displeasure of the master in whose business he was employed. They feared that, without such a law, constant interruptions would take place, in consequence of the necessity, or the desire, of becoming conspicuous in a public station ; that their proper occupations would be neglected ; and that many would be led, by vanity and self-sufficiency, to interfere in matters out of their sphere. They also considered that to follow more than one occupation would be detrimental to their own interests, and to those of the community ; and that when men, from a motive of avarice, are induced to engage in numerous branches of art, the result generally is that they are unable to excel in any. Such," he adds, " is the case in some countries, where artizans engage in agricultural pursuits, or in commercial speculations, and frequently in two or three different arts at once. Many, again, in those communities which are governed on democratic principles, are in the habit of frequenting popular assemblies, and dreaming only of their own interests, receive bribes from the leaders of parties, and do incredible mischief to the state. But with the Egyptians, if any artizan meddled with political affairs, or engaged in any other employment than the one to which he had been brought up, a severe punishment was instantly inflicted upon him ; and it was with this view that the regulations respecting their public and private occupations were instituted by the early legislators of Egypt."

Many arts and inventions were in common use in Egypt for centuries before they are generally supposed to have been known ; and we are now and then as much surprised to find that certain things were old 3000 years ago, as the Egyptians would be if they could hear us talk of them as late discoveries. One of them is the use of glass, with which they were acquainted, at least, as early as the reign of the first Osirtasen, more than 3800 years ago; and the process of glass-blowing is represented, during his reign, in the paintings of Beni Hassan, in the same manner as it is on later monuments, in different parts of Egypt, to the time of the Persian conquest.

Part 1.

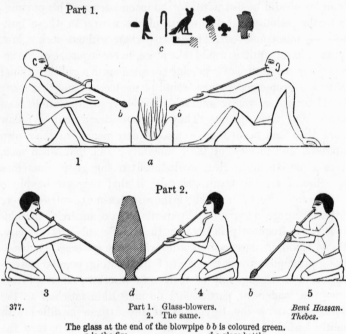

377. Part 1. Glass-blowers.
      2. The same.   *Beni Hassan.*
                                                Thebes.
The glass at the end of the blowpipe *b b* is coloured green.
a is the fire.   *d* a glass bottle.

The form of the bottle and the use of the blow-pipe are unequivocally indicated in those subjects; and the green hue of the fused material, taken from the fire at the point of the pipe, sufficiently proves the intention of the artist. But, even if we had not this evidence of the use of glass, it would be shown by those well-known images of glazed pottery, which were common at the same period; the vitrified substance that covers them being of the same quality as glass, and containing the same in-

gredients fused in the same manner. And besides the many
glass ornaments known to be of an earlier period is a bead, found
at Thebes, bearing the name of a Pharaoh who lived about
1450 B.C., the specific gravity of which, 25° 23', is precisely
the same as of crown glass, now manufactured in England.

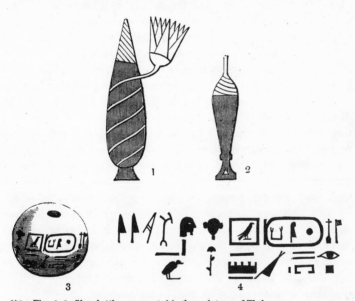

378. Figs. 1, 2. Glass bottles represented in the sculptures of Thebes.
         3. Captain Henvey's glass bead.   About the real size.
         4. The hieroglyphics on the bead, containing the name of Amun-m̄-het,
             who lived about B.C. 1450.

Glass bottles, similar to those in the above woodcut (*figs.* 1, 2),
are even met with on monuments of the 4th dynasty, dating
long before the Osirtasens, or more than 4000 years ago ; the
transparent substance shows the red wine they contained ; and this
kind of bottle is represented in the same manner among the
offerings to the gods, and at the fêtes of individuals, wherever
wine was introduced, from the earliest to the latest times.
Bottles, and other objects of glass, are commonly found in the
tombs ; and though they have no kings' names or dates in-

scribed upon them (glass being seldom used for such a purpose), no doubt exists of their great antiquity; and we may
consider it a fortunate chance that has preserved *one* bead with
the name of a sovereign of the 18th dynasty.   Nor is it necessary to point out how illogical is the inference that, because other
kinds of glass have not been found bearing a king's name, they
were not made in Egypt, at, or even before, the same early period.

Pliny ascribes the discovery of glass to some Phœnician
sailors accidentally lighting a fire on the sea-shore ; but if an
effect of chance, the secret is more likely to have been arrived at
in Egypt, where natron (or subcarbonate of soda) abounded, than
by the sea side ; and if the Phœnicians really were the first to
discover it on the *Syrian* coast, this would prove their migration from the Persian Gulf to have happened at a very remote
period.   Glass was certainly one of the great exports of the
Phœnicians ; who traded in beads, bottles, and other objects of
that material, as well as various manufactures, made either in
their own or in other countries ; but Egypt was always famed for
its manufacture ; a peculiar kind of earth was found near
Alexandria, without which, Strabo says, " it was impossible to
make certain kinds of glass of many colours, and of a brilliant
quality ;" and some vases, presented by an Egyptian priest to
the Emperor Hadrian, were considered so curious and valuable
that they were only used on grand occasions.

Glass bottles, of various colours, were eagerly bought from
Egypt, and exported into other countries ; and the manufacture,
as well as the patterns of many of those found in Greece, Etruria,
and Rome, show that they were of Egyptian work ; and though
imitated in Italy and Greece, the original art was borrowed from
the workmen of the Nile.

Such, too, was their skill in making glass, and in the mode of
staining it of various hues, that they counterfeited with success
the emerald, the amethyst, and other precious stones ; and even
arrived at an excellence in the art of introducing numerous
colours into the same vase, to which our European workmen, in
spite of their improvements in many branches of this manufac-

ture, are still unable to attain. A few years ago the glass-makers of Venice made several attempts to imitate the variety of colours found in antique cups; but as the component parts were of different densities, they did not all cool, or set, at the same rapidity, and the vase was unsound. And it is only by making an inner foundation of one colour, to which those of the outer surface are afterwards added, that they have been able to produce their many-coloured vases; some of which were sent to the Great Exhibition of 1851.

Not so the Egyptians; who combined all the colours they required in the same cup, without the interior lining: those which had it being of inferior and cheaper quality. They had even the secret of introducing gold between two surfaces of glass; and in their bottles, a gold band alternates within a set of blue, green, and other colours. Another curious process was also common in Egypt in early times, more than 3000 years ago, which has only just been attempted at Venice; whereby the pattern on the surface was made to pass in right lines directly through the substance; so that if any number of horizontal sections were made through it, each one would have the same device on its upper and under surface. It is in fact a Mosaic in glass; made by fusing together as many delicate rods of an opaque glass, of the colour required for the picture; in the same manner as the woods in Tunbridge-ware are glued together, to form a larger and coarser pattern. The skill required in this exquisite work is not only shown by the art itself, but the fineness of the design; for some of the feathers of birds, and other details, are only to be made out with a lens; which means of magnifying was evidently used in Egypt, when this Mosaic glass was manufactured. Indeed the discovery of a lens of crystal by Mr. Layard, at Nimroud, satisfactorily proves its use at an early period in Assyria; and we may conclude that it was neither a recent discovery there, nor confined to that country.

Winckelmann is of opinion that " the ancients carried the art of glassmaking to a higher degree of perfection than ourselves, though it may appear a paradox to those who have not seen

their works in this material ;" and we may even add that they
used it for more purposes; excepting of course windows, the
inconvenience of which in the hot sun of Egypt would have
been unbearable; or even in Italy; and only one pane of glass
has been found at Pompeii, in a place not exposed to the outer
light.

Winckelmann also mentions two pieces of glass mosaic,
" one of which, though not quite an inch in length, and a
third of an inch in breadth, exhibits on a dark and variegated
ground, a bird resembling a duck, in very bright and varied
colours, rather in the manner of a Chinese painting than a
copy of nature. The outlines are bold and decided, the colours
beautiful and pure, and the effect very pleasing ; in consequence
of the artist having alternately introduced an opaque and a
transparent glass. The most delicate pencil of a miniature
painter could not have traced with greater sharpness the circle
of the eyeball, or the plumage of the neck and wings; at which
part this specimen has been broken. But the most surprising
thing is, that the reverse exhibits the same bird, in which it is
impossible to discover any difference in the smallest details ;
whence it may be concluded that the figure of the bird continues
through its entire thickness. The picture has a granular appearance on both sides, and seems to have been formed of single
pieces, like mosaic work, united with so much skill, that the
most powerful magnifying glass is unable to discover their junction. From the condition of this fragment, it was at first difficult
to form any idea of the process employed in its manufacture :
and we should have remained entirely ignorant of it, had not the
fracture shown that filaments of the same colours, as on the
surface of the glass, and throughout its whole diameter, passed
from one side to the other ; whence it has been concluded that
the picture was composed of different cylinders of coloured glass,
which, being subjected to a proper degree of heat, united by
(partial) fusion. I cannot suppose they would have taken so
much trouble, and have been contented to make a picture only
the sixth of an inch thick, while, by employing longer filaments,

they might have produced one many inches in thickness, without occupying any additional time in the process; it is therefore probable this was cut from a larger or thicker piece, and the number of the pictures taken from the same depended on the length of the filaments, and the consequent thickness of the original mass. The other specimen, also broken, and about the size of the preceding one, is made in the same manner. It exhibits ornaments of a green, yellow, and white colour, on a blue ground, which consist in volutes, strings of beads, and flowers, ending in pyramidical points. All the details are perfectly distinct and unconfused, and yet so very minute, that the keenest eye is unable to follow the delicate lines in which the volutes terminate; the ornaments, however, are all continued, without interruption, through the entire thickness of the piece."

Winckelmann is quite right respecting the mode of forming these glass mosaics; which was made more intelligible by a specimen found in Egypt. It consisted of separate squares, whose original division was readily discovered in a bright light, as well as the manner of adjusting the different parts, and of uniting them in one mass; and here and there the heat applied to cement the squares had caused the colours to run between them, in consequence of partial fusion from too strong a fire.

Not only were these various parts made at different times, and afterwards united by heat, rendered effective on their surfaces by means of a flux applied to them, but each coloured line was at first separate, and, when adjusted in its proper place, was connected with those around it by the same process.

The immense emeralds mentioned by ancient authors were doubtless glass imitations of those precious stones. Such were the colossal statue of Serapis, in the Egyptian labyrinth, nine cubits, or thirteen feet and a half, in height; an emerald presented by the king of Babylon to an Egyptian Pharaoh, which was four cubits, or six feet, long, and three cubits broad; and an obelisk in the temple of Jupiter, which was forty cubits, or sixty feet, in height, and four cubits broad, composed of four emeralds; and to have formed statues of glass of such dimensions, even

allowing them to have been of different pieces, was a greater
triumph of skill than imitating the stones.

That the Egyptians, more than 3000 years ago, were well
acquainted not only with the manufacture of common glass, for
beads and bottles of ordinary quality, but with the art of staining
it of divers colours, is sufficiently proved by the fragments found
in the tombs of Thebes; and so skilful were they in this complicated process, that they imitated the most fanciful devices, and
succeeded in counterfeiting the rich hues, and brilliancy, of
precious stones. The green emerald, the purple amethyst, and
other expensive gems, were successfully imitated; a necklace of
false stones could be purchased at an Egyptian jeweller's, to
please the wearer, or deceive a stranger, by the appearance of
reality; and some mock pearls (found by me at Thebes) have
been so well counterfeited, that even now it is difficult with a
strong lens to detect the imposition.

Pliny says the emerald was more easily counterfeited than any
other gem, and considers the art of imitating precious stones a
far more lucrative piece of deceit than any devised by the ingenuity of man; Egypt was, as usual, the country most noted for
this manufacture; and we can readily believe that in Pliny's time
they succeeded so completely in the imitation as to render it
" difficult to distinguish false from real stones."*

Many, in the form of beads, have been met with in different
parts of Egypt, particularly at Thebes; and so far did the
Egyptians carry this spirit of imitation, that even small figures,
scarabæi, and objects made of ordinary porcelain, were counterfeited; being composed of still cheaper materials. A figure,
which was entirely of earthenware, with a glazed exterior, underwent a somewhat more complicated process than when cut out of
stone, and simply covered with a vitrified coating; this last
could therefore be sold at a low price : it offered all the brilliancy
of the former, and its weight alone betrayed its inferiority; by
which means, whatever was novel, or pleasing from its external

* Plin. xxxvii. 12.

appearance, was placed within reach of all classes; or at least the possessor had the satisfaction of seeming to partake in each fashionable novelty.

Such inventions, and successful endeavours to imitate costly ornaments by humbler materials, not only show the progress of art among the Egyptians, but strongly argue the great advancement they had made in the customs of civilised life; since it is certain, that until society has arrived at a high degree of luxury and refinement, artificial wants of this nature are not created, and the poorer classes do not yet feel the desire of imitating the rich, in the adoption of objects dependent on taste or accidental caprice.

Glass bugles and beads were much used by the Egyptians for necklaces, and for a sort of network, with which they covered the wrappers and cartonage of mummies. They were arranged so as to form, by their varied hues, numerous devices or figures, in the manner of our bead purses; and women sometimes amused themselves by stringing them for ornamental purposes, as at the present day.

The principal use to which glass was applied by the Egyptians, (besides the beads and fancy work already noticed,) was for the manufacture of bottles, vases, and other utensils; wine was frequently brought to table in a bottle, or handed to a guest in a cup of this material; and a body was sometimes buried in a glass coffin. Occasionally a granite sarcophagus was covered with a coating of vitrified matter, usually of a deep green colour, which displayed, by its transparency, the sculptures or hieroglyphic legends engraved upon the stone; a process well understood by the Egyptians, and the same they employed in many of the blue figures of pottery and stone, commonly found in their tombs.

In their glass mosaics, the colours have a wonderful brilliancy; the blues which are given by copper are vivid and beautifully clear; and one of the reds has all the intenseness of rosso antico, with the brightness of the glassy material in which it is found; thus combining the qualities of a rich enamel.

Many of the porcelain cups discovered at Thebes present a tasteful arrangement of varied hues, and show the skill of the

Egyptians, and the great experience they possessed in this branch of art. The manner in which the colours are blended and arranged; the minuteness of the lines, frequently tapering off to an almost imperceptible fineness; and the varied directions of twisted curves, traversing the substance, but strictly conforming to the pattern designed by the artist, display no ordinary skill, and show that they were perfect masters of the means they employed.

The Egyptian porcelain should perhaps be denominated glass-porcelain, as partaking of the quality of the two, and not being altogether unlike the porcelain-glass invented by the celebrated Réaumur; who discovered, during his curious experiments on different qualities of porcelain, the method of converting glass into a substance very similar to chinaware.

The ground of Egyptian porcelain is generally of one homogeneous quality and hue, either blue or green, traversed in every direction by lines or devices of other colours—red, white, yellow, black, light or dark blue, and green, or whatever the artist chose to introduce; and these are not always confined to the surface, but frequently penetrate into the ground, sometimes having passed half, or entirely, through the fused substance; in which respect they differ from the porcelain of China, where the flowers or patterns are applied to the surface, and justify the use of the term glass-porcelain. In some instances, the yellows were put on after the other colours, upon the surface of the vase, which was then again subjected to a proper degree of heat; and after this, the handles, the rim, and the base, were added, and fixed by a repetition of the same process. It was not without considerable risk that these additions were made to their porcelain and glass vases, and many were broken during the operation; to which Martial alludes, in an epigram on these fragile cups of the Egyptians.

That the Egyptians possessed considerable knowledge of chemistry and the use of metallic oxides, is evident from the nature of the colours applied to their glass and porcelain; and they were even acquainted with the influence of acids upon colour, being able, in the process of dyeing or staining cloth, to bring about certain changes in the hues, by the same means adopted in our own cotton works, as I shall show in describing the manufactures of the Egyptians.

The art of cutting glass was known to them at the most remote periods; hieroglyphics and various devices being frequently engraved upon vases and beads; they also ground glass; and some, particularly that which bears figures or ornaments in relief, was cast in a mould. Some have supposed that the method of cutting glass was unknown to the ancients, and have limited the period of its invention to the commencement of the 17th century of our era, when Gaspar Lehmann, at Prague, first succeeded in it, and obtained a patent from the Emperor Rodolph II.; but the specimens of ancient glass, cut, engraved, and ground, discovered in Egypt, suffice to prove the art was practised there of old.

We find that in Rome the diamond was used for cutting hard stones; for Pliny tells us that diamonds were eagerly sought by lapidaries, who set them in iron handles, having been found to penetrate anything, however hard. He also states that emeralds and other hard stones were engraved, though in early times it was "considered wrong to violate gems with any figures or devices;" and " all gems could be engraved by the diamond." And though we do not know the precise method adopted by the Egyptians for cutting glass and hard stones, we may reasonably conclude they were acquainted with the diamond, and adopted it for engraving them. Emery powder and the lapidary's wheel were also used in Egypt; and there is little doubt that the Israelites learnt the art of cutting and engraving stones in that country.*

Some glass bottles were enclosed in wicker-work very nearly resembling what is now called by the Egyptians a *damagán*: which holds from one to two gallons of fluid; and some of a smaller size, from six to nine inches in height, were protected by a covering made of the stalks of the papyrus or *cyperus* rush, like the modern bottles containing Florence oil: others again appear

---

* The stones engraved by the Israelites were the " sardius, topaz, and carbuncle; the emerald, sapphire, and *diamond;* the ligure, agate, and amethyst; the beryl, onyx, and jasper." Exod. xxviii. 17, 18, 19, 20, 21, and xxxix. 6.

379.   Fig. 1 has apparently leather sewed over the glass.
          2 glass *damagán* enclosed in wickerwork.
          3 small glass bottle covered with papyrus rush, like the Florence oil flasks.
          4 a piece of cloth with a border of a blue colour.

to have been partly cased in leather, sewed over them, much in
the same manner as some now made for carrying liquids on a
journey. (*Figs.* 1, 3, *and* 2.)

Among the many bottles found in the tombs of Thebes, and
other places, none have excited greater curiosity and surprise
than those of Chinese manufacture, presenting inscriptions in
that language.   Their number is considerable, and I have seen
more than twenty from Thebes and other places.   But though
found in ancient tombs, there is no evidence of their having really
been deposited there in early Pharaonic or even Ptolemaic times ;
and so many of the tombs have been occupied till a recent period by
the Moslem population, that they may have been left there by
these their more recent inmates.   Professor Rosellini, however,
mentions one he met with " in a previously unopened tomb, of
uncertain date, which " he refers, " from the style of the sculptures, to a Pharaonic period, not much later than the 18th
dynasty ; " and, were it not for this, we might suppose them
brought from India by Arab traders.   They are about two

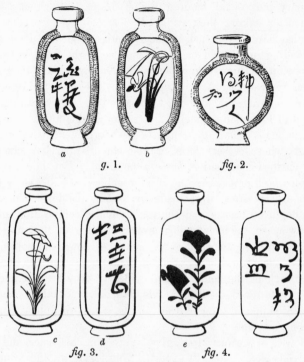

a   g. 1.   b   fig. 2.

c   fig. 3.   d   e   fig. 4.

380.   Chinese bottles found in the Egyptian tombs.
        Fig. 1, in the Museum of Alnwick Castle.
           2, one of two presented by me to the British Museum.
           3, belonging to Mr. W. Hamilton.
           4, in my possession.   From Thebes.

inches in height: one side presents a flower, and the other an
inscription, containing, according to Sir J. Davis (in three out of
eight he examined), the following legend:—"The flower opens,
and lo! another year;" and another has been translated by Mr.
Thoms:—"During the shining of the moon the fir-tree sends
forth its sap," (which in a thousand years becomes amber.)

The quality of these bottles is very inferior, and of a time,
as Sir J. Davis thought, "when the Chinese had not yet arrived
at the same perfection in making porcelain as at present."
They appear to have been only prized for their contents; and
after they were exhausted, the valueless bottle was applied to the

ordinary purpose of holding the *Kohl*, or Collyrium, used by women for staining their eyelids.*

It has been questioned, if the Egyptians understood the art of enamelling upon gold or silver, but we might infer it from an expression of Pliny, who says : " The Egyptians paint their silver vases, representing Anubis upon them, the silver being painted and not engraved ;" and M. Dubois had in his possession a specimen of Egyptian enamel. The reason of the doubt is our finding so many small gold figures with ornamented wings, and bodies, whose feathers, faces, or other coloured parts are composed of a vitrified composition, *let into* the metal. But they may have adopted both processes ; and it is probable that many early specimens of *encaustum* were made by tooling the devices to a certain depth on bronze, and pouring a vitrified composition into the hollow space, the metal being properly heated, at the same time ; and, when fixed, the surface was smoothed down and polished.

Both the encaustic painting in wax, and that which consisted in burning in the colours, were evidently known to the ancients, being mentioned by Pliny, Ovid, Martial, and others ; and the latter is supposed to have been on the same principle as our enamelling on gold.

Bottles of various kinds, glass, porcelain, alabaster, and other materials were frequently exported from Egypt to other countries. The Greeks, the Etruscans, and the Romans received them as articles of luxury, which being remarkable for their beauty were prized as ornaments of the table; and when Egypt became a Roman province, part of the tribute annually paid to the conquerors consisted of glass vases, from the manufactories of Memphis and Alexandria.

The intercourse between Egypt and Greece had been constantly kept up after the accession of Psammitichus and Amasis ;

---

* Since the above was written, a paper has been presented by Mr. Medhurst to the Royal Asiatic Society, which would establish the fact of their having been brought by the Arab traders, if, as there stated, the style of the characters did not come into use till the 3rd century of our era; and the poems, from which the sentences were taken, were not written till the 8th and 11th centuries. The earliest mention of porcelain in China is also limited to the 2nd century B.C. A similar bottle was found by Mr. Layard at Arban, on the Khaboor.

and the former country, the parent of the arts at that period, supplied the Greeks and some of the Syrian tribes with numerous manufactures. The Etruscans, too, a commercial people, appear to have had an extensive trade with Egypt, and we repeatedly find small alabaster, as well as coloured glass, bottles in their tombs, which have all the character of the Egyptian ; and not only does the stone of the former proclaim by its quality the quarries from which it was taken, but the form and style of the workmanship leave no doubt of the bottles themselves being the productions of Egyptian artists. The same remark applies to many objects found at Nineveh.

It is uncertain of what stone the famous murrhine vases, mentioned by Pliny, Martial, and other writers, were made; it was of various colours, beautifully blended, and even iridescent, and was obtained in greater quantity in Carmania than in any country. It was also found in Parthia and other districts of Asia, but unknown in Egypt; a fact quite consistent with the notion of its being fluor-spar, which is not met with in the valley of the Nile; and explaining the reason why the Egyptians imitated it with the composition known under the name of false murrhine, said to have been made at Thebes and Memphis. The description given by Pliny certainly bears a stronger resemblance to the fluor-spar than to any other stone, and the only objection to this having been murrhine, is our not finding any vases, or fragments, of it ; and some may still doubt if the substance is known to which the naturalist alludes. But the fluor-spar appears to have the strongest claim ; and the glass-porcelain of Egypt, whose various colours are disposed in waving lines, as if to imitate the natural undulations of that crystallised substance, may be the false murrhine of the ancients. (*Woodcuts* 170, *fig.* 2 ; 171, *fig.* 5.)

It is difficult to say whether the Egyptians employed glass for the purpose of making lamps or lanterns : ancient authors give us no direct information on the subject; and the paintings offer few representations of lamps, torches, or any other kind of light.*

Herodotus mentions a " fête of burning lamps," which took

* In the funeral processions one person carries what seems to be a candle or torch.

place at Saïs, and indeed throughout the country, at a certain period of the year, and describes the lamps used on this occasion

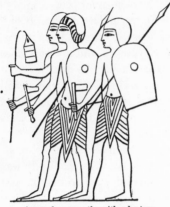

as "small vases filled with salt and olive oil, on which the wick floated, and burnt during the whole night;" but he does not say of what materials those vases were made, and they may either have been of glass, or of earthenware.

The sculptures of Tel-el-Amarna, again, represent a guard of soldiers, one of whom holds before him what appears to be a lamp, and resembles the cloth or paper lanterns so common in Egypt at the present day.

A guard apparently with a lantern.
381.   *Tel-el-Amarna.*

The Egyptians were always celebrated for their manufacture of linen and other cloths, and the produce of their looms was exported to, and eagerly purchased by, foreign nations. The fine linen and embroidered work, the yarn and woollen stuffs, of the upper and lower country are frequently mentioned, and were highly esteemed. Solomon purchased many of those commodities, as well as chariots and horses, from Egypt; and Chemmis, the city of Pan, retained the credit it had acquired in making linen stuffs, till about the period of the Roman conquest.

Woollen garments were chiefly used by the lower orders : sometimes also by the rich, and even by the priests, who were permitted to wear an upper robe in the form of a cloak of this material : but under garments of wool were strictly forbidden them, upon a principle of cleanliness ; and as they took so much pains to cleanse and shave the body, they considered it inconsistent to adopt clothes made of the hair of animals. No one was allowed to be buried in a woollen garment, in consequence of its engendering worms, which would injure the body ; nor could any priest enter a temple without taking off this part of his dress.*

* *See* Vol. i. p. 333. Herodot. ii. 81.

The quantity of linen manufactured and used in Egypt was very great; and, independent of that made up into articles of dress, the numerous wrappers required for enveloping the mummies, both of men and animals, show how large a supply must have been kept ready for the constant demand at home, as well as for that of the foreign market.

That the bandages employed in wrapping the dead are of linen, and not, as some have imagined, of cotton, has been already ascertained by the most satisfactory tests; and though no one among the unscientific inhabitants of modern Egypt ever thought of questioning the fact, received opinion in Europe had till lately decided that they were cotton; and it was forbidden to doubt that "the bands of *byssine* linen," said by Herodotus to have been used for enveloping the mummies, were cotton.

The accurate experiments made, with the aid of powerful microscopes, by Mr. Bauer, Mr. Thomson, Dr. Ure, and others, on the nature of the fibres of linen and cotton threads, have shown that the former invariably present a cylindrical form, transparent, and articulated, or jointed like a cane, while the latter offer the appearance of a flat riband, with a hem or border at each edge; so that there is no possibility of mistaking the fibres of either, except, perhaps, when the cotton is in an unripe state, and the flattened shape of the centre is less apparent. The results having been found similar in every instance, and the structure of the fibres thus unquestionably determined, the threads of mummy cloths were submitted to the same test, and no exception was found to their being linen; nor were they even a mixture of linen and cotton thread.

The fact of the mummy cloths being linen is therefore decided. The name *byssus*, it is true, presents a difficulty; owing to the Hebrew *shash* being translated "*byssus*" in the Septuagint version, and, in our own, "fine linen;" and to shash being the name applied at this day by the Arabs to fine muslin, which is of cotton and not of linen; but as the mummy cloths said by Herodotus to be "of *byssine sindon*," are known to be invariably linen, the byssus cannot be cotton. Herodotus, indeed, uses the expression "tree wool" to denote cotton; and Julius Pollux adopts the same name, distinguishing it also from byssus, which he calls a species of Indian flax. The use of the two words *byssus* and *linon* presents no difficulty, since they might be employed, like our flax and linen, to signify the plant, and the substance made from it.

Cotton cloth, however, was among the manufactures of Egypt, and dresses of this material were worn by all classes. Pliny states that the Egyptian priests, though they used linen, were particularly partial to cotton robes; and "cotton garments," supplied by the government for the use of the temples, are distinctly mentioned in the Rosetta Stone. Herodotus and Plutarch affirm that linen was preferred, owing as well to its freshness in a hot climate, as to its great tendency to keep the body clean, and that a religious prejudice forbade the priests to wear vestments of any other quality; this, however, refers to the inner portion of the dress; and the prohibition of entering a temple with cotton or woollen garments led to the notion that none but linen were worn by them at any time. The same custom was adopted by the votaries of Isis, when her rites were introduced by the Greeks and Romans; and linen dresses were appropriated to those who had been initiated in the sacred mysteries.

Whatever restrictions may have been in force respecting the use of cotton among the priesthood, other individuals were permitted to consult their own choice on this point; and it was immaterial whether they preferred, during life, the coolness of flax, or the softness of cotton raiment, provided the body, after death, was enveloped in bandages of linen; and this regulation accounts for the mummy cloths of the poorest individuals being also found of that material.

It was not only for articles of dress that cotton was manufactured by the Egyptians: a great quantity was used for the furniture of their houses, the coverings of chairs and couches, and various other purposes; and a sort of cloth was made of the united filaments of flax and cotton. This is mentioned by Julius Pollux, who, after describing the cotton-plant as an Egyptian production, and stating that cloth was manufactured of the " wool of its nut," says they sometimes " make the woof of it, and the warp of linen;" a quality of cloth still manufactured by the modern Egyptians.

From the few representations which occur in the tombs of Thebes, it has been supposed that the Egyptian looms were of rude construction, and totally incapable of producing the fine linen so much admired by the ancients; and as the paintings in which they occur were executed at a very early period, it has been conjectured that, in after times, great improvements took place in their construction. But when we consider with what simple means oriental nations are in the habit of executing the most delicate and complicated work, we cease to feel surprised at the apparent imperfection of the mechanism, or instruments, used by the Egyptians; and it is probable that their far-famed " fine linen," mentioned in Scripture, and by ancient writers, was produced from looms of the same construction as those represented in the paintings of Thebes and Eileithyias. Nor was the praise bestowed upon that manufacture unmerited; and the quality of one piece of linen found near Memphis fully justifies it, and excites equal admiration at the present day, being to the touch comparable to silk, and not inferior in texture to our finest cambric.

The mummy cloths are generally of a very coarse quality; and little attention was bestowed on the disposition of the threads, in the cloths of ordinary manufacture. Mr. Thomson, who examined many specimens of them, is of opinion that the number of threads in the warp invariably exceeded those of the woof, occasionally even by four times the quantity; and as his observations are highly interesting, I shall introduce an extract from his pamphlet on the subject.

" Of the products of the Egyptian loom, we know scarcely more than the mummy pits have disclosed to us; and it would be as unreasonable to look through modern sepulchres for specimens and proofs of the state of manufacturing art amongst ourselves, as to deduce an opinion of the skill of the Egyptians, from those fragments of cloth which envelope their dead, and have come down, almost unchanged, to our own time. The curious or costly fabrics which adorned the living, and were the pride of the industry and skill of Thebes, have perished ages ago. There

are, however, amongst these remains, some which are not unworthy of notice, which carry us back into the workshops of
former times, and exhibit to us the actual labours of weavers and
dyers of Egypt, more than 2000 years ago.

" The great mass of the mummy cloth, employed in bandages
and coverings, whether of birds, animals, or the human species,
is of coarse texture, especially that more immediately in contact
with the body, which is generally impregnated with resinous or
bituminous matter. The upper bandages, nearer the surface, are
finer. Sometimes the whole is enveloped in a covering coarse
and thick, and very like the sacking of the present day : sometimes in cloth coarse and open, like that used in our cheese-
presses, for which it might easily be mistaken. In the College
of Surgeons are various specimens of these cloths, some of which
are very curious.

" The beauty of the texture and peculiarity in the structure of
a mummy cloth given to me by Mr. Belzoni were very striking.
It was free from gum, or resin, or impregnation of any kind, and
had evidently been originally white. It was close and firm, yet
very elastic. The yarn of both warp and woof was remarkably
even and well spun. The thread of the warp was *double*, consisting of two fine threads twisted together. The woof was single.
The warp contained 90 threads in an inch ; the woof, or weft,
only 44. The fineness of these materials, estimated after the
manner of cotton yarn, was about 30 hanks in the pound.

" The subsequent examination of a great variety of mummy
cloths showed, that the disparity between the warp and woof
belonged to the system of manufacture, and that the warp generally had twice or thrice, and not seldom four times, the number
of threads in an inch that the woof had : thus, a cloth containing
80 threads of warp in the inch, of a fineness of about 24 hanks in
the pound, had 40 threads in the woof : another with 120 threads
of warp, of 30 hanks, had 40 ; and a third specimen only 30
threads in the woof. These have each respectively double, treble,
and quadruple the number of threads in the warp that they have
in the woof. This structure, so different from modern cloth,
which has the proportions nearly equal, originated, probably, in

the difficulty and tediousness of getting in the woof, when the shuttle was thrown by hand, which is the practice in India at the present day, and which there are weavers still living old enough to remember the universal practice in this country."

Mr. Thomson then mentions some fragments of mummy cloths, sent to England by the late Mr. Salt, which he saw in the British Museum. They were " of different degrees of fineness ; some fringed at the ends, and some striped at the edges." " My first impression," he continues, " on seeing these cloths, was, that the finest kinds were *muslin*, and of Indian manufacture, since we learn from the ' Periplus of the Erythrean Sea,' ascribed to Arrian, but more probably the work of some Greek merchant himself engaged in the trade, that muslins from the Ganges were an article of export from India to the Arabian Gulf : but this suspicion of their being cotton was soon removed by the microscope of Mr. Bauer, which showed that they were all, without exception, linen. Some were thin and transparent, and of very delicate texture. The finest appeared to be made of yarns of near 100 hanks in the pound, with 140 threads in the inch in the warp, and about 64 in the woof. A specimen of muslin in the museum of the East India House, the finest production of the Dacca loom, has only 100 threads in an inch in the warp, and 84 in the woof; but the surprising fineness of the yarns, which, though spun by hand, is not less than 250 hanks in the pound, gives to this fabric its unrivalled tenuity and lightness.

" Some of the cloths were fringed at the ends, and one, a sort of scarf, about four feet long, and twenty inches wide, was fringed at both ends. Three or four threads twisted together with the fingers to form a strong one, and two of these again twisted together, and knotted at the middle and at the end to prevent unravelling, formed the fringe, precisely like the silk shawls of the present day.

" The selvages of the Egyptian cloths are generally formed with the greatest care, and are well calculated by their strength to protect the cloth from accident. Fillets of strong cloth or tape also secure the ends of the pieces from injury, showing a knowledge of all the little resources of modern manufacture.

Several of the specimens, both of fine and coarse cloth, were bordered with blue stripes of various patterns, and in some alternating with narrow lines of another colour. The width of the patterns varied from half an inch to an inch and a quarter. In the latter were seven blue stripes, the broadest about half an inch wide nearest the selvage, followed by five very narrow ones, and terminated by one an eighth of an inch broad. Had this pattern, instead of being confined to the edge of the cloth, been repeated across its whole breadth, it would have formed a modern gingham, which we can scarcely doubt was one of the articles of Egyptian industry.

" A small pattern about half an inch broad formed the edging of one of the finest of these cloths, and was composed of a stripe of blue, alternating with three lines of a fawn colour, forming a simple and elegant border. These stripes were produced in the loom by coloured threads previously dyed in the yarn. The nature of the fawn colour I was unable to determine. It was too much degraded by age, and the quantity too small, to enable me to arrive at a satisfactory conclusion. Though I had no doubt the colouring matter of the blue stripes was indigo, I subjected the cloth to the following examination. Boiled in water for some time, the colour did not yield in the least ; nor was it at all affected by soap, nor by strong alkalies : sulphuric acid, diluted only so far as not to destroy the cloth, had no action on the colour. Chloride of lime gradually reduced, and at last destroyed it. Strong nitric acid, dropped upon the blue, turned it orange, and in the same instant destroyed it. These tests prove the colouring matter of the stripes to be indigo.

" This dye was unknown to Herodotus, for he makes no mention of it. It was known to Pliny, who, though ignorant of its true nature, and the history of its production, has correctly described the most characteristic of its properties, the emission of a beautiful purple vapour when exposed to heat. Had his commentators been acquainted with the sublimation of indigo, it would have saved many learned doubts. We learn from the Periplus, that it was an article of export from Barbarike on the Indus, to Egypt, where its employment by the manufacturers of that country, probably from a remote period, is clearly established by the specimens here described."

In *woodcut* 379, *fig.* 4, is a piece of cloth, brought from Thebes, which offers a very good instance of the coloured border mentioned by Mr. Thomson. It is of ordinary quality; the number of threads in the inch is ninety-six in the warp, and thirty-four in the woof; and the border consists of one broad band and six narrow stripes, of a blue colour, evidently dyed with indigo; the band which is nearest the selvage is one inch and two tenths in breadth, the others consist each of two threads, in the direction of the warp, with the exception of the innermost one, which is of five threads; and the dividing line between the fourth and fifth is varied by the introduction of a blue thread down the centre. The rest of the cloth has the usual yellowish tinge, " supposed to arise from some astringent preparation employed for its preservation," which, according to Mr. Thomson, imparts to water a similar colour, but offers no trace of tannin. " In none of the specimens I have examined," he adds, " did either gelatine or albumen, or solution of iron, afford any precipitate; but the subacetate of lead produced a cloud, indicating the presence of extractive matter."

It is evident that the colour was imparted to the threads previous to the cloth being made,* as the blue remains unaltered; and the cloths with broad coloured borders are the more curious, as they illustrate the representations in the paintings, and show that they were similar to those made by the looms in the age of the Pharaohs of the 12th and 18th dynasties; and the Nubians wear shawls with the same blue borders, manufactured in the valley of the Nile, at the present day. The Egyptians also dyed old dresses, as in these days.

Another piece of linen, from Thebes, has 152 threads in the warp, and 71 in the woof, to each inch; it is of a much darker hue than the cloth just mentioned, and was perhaps dyed with the *carthamus tinctorius*, or saff flower. But the most remarkable piece of fine linen is that found near Memphis, before mentioned;

* As with the threads used by the Israelites, Exod. xxxv. 25. " And all the women that were wise-hearted did spin with their hands, and brought that which they had spun, both of blue, and of purple, and of scarlet, and of fine linen."

and some idea may be given of its texture, from the number of threads in the inch, which is 540 (or 270 double threads) in the warp; and the limited proportion of 110 in the woof, shows the justness of Mr. Thomson's observation, that this disparity belonged to their "system of manufacture," since it is observable even in the finest quality of cloth. It is also of a light brown colour. Another very remarkable circumstance in this specimen is, that it is covered with small figures and hieroglyphics, so finely drawn, that here and there the lines are with difficulty followed by the eye; and as there is no appearance of the ink having run in any part of the cloth, it is evident they had previously prepared it for this purpose. The perfection of its threads is equally surprising; the knots and breaks, seen in our best cambric, are not found in holding it to the light—an ancient mode of proving fine cloth which led to that beautiful Greek expression εἰλικρινής, "sincere," borrowed from this test of light; which is far superior to the Latin *sincerus*, derived from honey, *sine cerâ*.

Pliny cites four qualities of linen, particularly noted in Egypt: the Tanitic and Pelusiac, the Butine and the Tentyritic; and mentions in the same place the cotton tree of Egypt, which he confines to the Upper country. He also states that the quantity of flax, cultivated in Egypt, was accounted for, by their exporting linen to Arabia and India; and the quality of that produced by the Egyptian looms was far superior to any other.

The threads used for nets were remarkable for their fineness; and Pliny says "some of them were so delicate that they would pass through a man's ring, and a single person could carry a sufficient number of them to surround a whole wood. Julius Lupus, who died while governor of Egypt, had some of these nets, each string of which consisted of 150 threads; a fact perfectly surprising to those who are not aware, that the Rhodians preserve to this day, in the Temple of Minerva, the remains of a linen corslet presented to them by Amasis, king of Egypt, whose threads are composed each of 365 fibres; and in proof of the truth of this, Mutianus, who was thrice consul, lately affirmed at Rome, that he had examined it; and the reason of so few fragments remaining was attributable to the curiosity of those who had frequently subjected it to the same scrutiny."

Herodotus mentions this corslet, and another, presented by Amasis to the Lacedæmonians, which had been carried off by the Samians; " it was of linen, ornamented with numerous figures of animals, worked in gold and cotton. Each thread of the corslet was worthy of admiration. For, though very fine, every one was composed of 360 other threads, all distinct; the quality being similar to that dedicated to Minerva, at Lindus, by the same monarch."

Many of the Egyptian stuffs presented various patterns worked in colours by the loom, independent of those produced by the dyeing or printing process, and so richly composed, that Martial says they vied with the Babylonian cloths embroidered with the needle.

The art of embroidery * was commonly practised in Egypt; and the Hebrews, on leaving the country, took advantage of the knowledge they had there acquired to make a rich " hanging for the door of the tent, of blue, and purple, and scarlet, and fine twined linen, wrought with needlework ;" † a coat of fine linen was embroidered for Aaron ; and his girdle was " of fine twined linen, and blue, and purple, and scarlet, of needlework." ‡

The gold thread used for these purposes is supposed to have been beaten out with the hammer,§ and afterwards rounded ; and even the delicate net made by Vulcan, which was so fine that the gods themselves were unable to see it, is represented to have been forged on his anvil with the hammer.|| Pliny mentions cloth woven with gold threads, sometimes entirely of those materials, without any woollen or linen ground, as were the garment of Agrippina, the tunic of Heliogabalus, and that worn by Tarquinius Priscus, mentioned by Verrius.

Pliny says, " Coloured dresses were known in the time of Homer, from which the robes of triumph were borrowed : and from the Phrygians having been the first to devise the method of

* Ezekiel, xxvii. 7, " Fine linen, with broidered work from Egypt."
† Exod. xxvi. 36, xxvii. 16, xxxvi. 37, and xxxviii. 18.
‡ Exod. xxviii. 39, and xxxix. 29.
§ Exod. xxxix. 3, " And they did beat the gold into thin plates, and cut it into wires, to work it in the blue, and in the purple, and in the scarlet, and in the fine linen." || Hom. Od. viii. 274.

giving the same effect with the needle, they have been called *Phrygiones*. But to weave cloth with gold thread was the invention of an Asiatic king, Attalus, from whom the name Attalic was derived ; and the Babylonians were most noted for their skill in weaving cloths of various colours."

The question still remains undecided respecting the time when silver thread came into use ; and as no mention of silver stuffs occurs in the writings of ancient authors, it has been supposed that its introduction was of late date. Silver wire, however, was already known in Egypt about 3300 years ago, being found at Thebes of the third Thothmes : nor is there any reason to suppose it was then a novel invention ; and it was probably known and used nearly as soon as gold wire, which we find attached to rings bearing the name of Osirtasen the First, who lived more than 600 years earlier.

This wire is supposed not to have been drawn, like our own, through holes in metal plates, but to have been beaten out, and rounded with the file : but the appearance of some found at Thebes justifies the conclusion that a mode of drawing it was not unknown to them ; and the omission of every representation of the process in the paintings is no argument against it, since they have also failed to introduce the casting of metals, and various other arts, with which we see they were acquainted.

Wire-drawing was first attempted with the most ductile metals, gold and silver being used before brass and iron, because the wire was originally employed for ornamental purposes. Gold thread and wire were always made entirely of metal, even to the time of the latter Roman Emperors ; and there is no instance of flattened wire wound round silk or linen threads, or of silver or other wire gilt ; though gilding was so common on vases and other articles of bronze. That the Egyptians had arrived at great perfection in the art of making the thread is evident, from its being sufficiently fine for weaving into cloth, and for embroidery ; and the exceeding delicacy of the linen corslet of Amasis, on which numerous figures of animals were worked in gold, required a proportionate degree of fineness in the gold thread used for the purpose.

The coloured dresses represented in the Egyptian paintings, worn by women of rank, and by the deities, much resemble our modern chintzes, in the style of their patterns, though it is probable that they were generally of linen instead of calico : some appear to have been worked with the needle, and others woven with gold threads.

Another very remarkable discovery of the Egyptians was the use of mordants. They were acquainted with the effect of acids on colour, and submitted the cloth they dyed to one of the same processes adopted in our modern manufactories ; and while, from his account, we perceive how little Pliny understood the process he was describing, he at the same time gives us the strongest evidence of its truth. " In Egypt," he says, " they stain cloths in a wonderful manner. They take them in their original state, quite white, and imbue them, not with a dye, but with certain drugs which have the power of absorbing and taking colour. When this is done, there is still no appearance of change in the cloths; but so soon as they are dipped into a bath of the pigment, which has been prepared for the purpose, they are taken out properly coloured. The singular thing is, that though the bath contains only one colour, several hues are imparted to the piece, these changes depending on the nature of the drug employed : nor can the colour be afterwards washed off; and surely if the bath had many colours in it, they must have presented a confused appearance on the cloth."

From this it is evident that the cloth was prepared before steeping ; the *momentary* effect he mentions could only be produced by the powerful agency of mordants ; and they not only used them to make the cloth take the colour equally, but also to change the hues.

Whether the Egyptians really understood the principle, on which the salts and acids of the mordants acted, or calculated their effects solely from the experience they had acquired, it is difficult to decide. They had long been used in Europe, before their chemical agency was properly explained ; and when the term mordant was first applied by the French dyers, they imagined " that the intention of passing the substances, which were to be dyed, through certain saline liquors, was to corrode something that opposed the entering of the colouring principle, and to enlarge the pores of the substances " (the effect of acids in changing the hues being a later discovery) ; we cannot therefore positively prove that the Egyptians had a knowledge of chemistry, though from their long experience, and from their skill in the employment of the metallic oxides, we may find strong reasons to infer it. For if at first ignorant of the reason of such changes, it is probable that in process of time, they were led to investigate the causes, by which they were effected.

Many discoveries, and even inventions, are more the effect of chance than of studious reflection, and the principle is often the last to be understood. In discoveries this is generally the case, in inventions frequently. But when men have observed, from long practice, a fixed and undeviating result, their curiosity naturally becomes excited, the thirst for knowledge, and above all the desire of benefiting by the discovery, prompt them to scrutinise the causes to which they have been so much indebted ; and few people, who have made any advance in the arts of civilised life, long remain ignorant of the means of improving their knowledge.

We may, therefore, suppose some general notions of chemistry, or at least of chemical agency, were known to the Egyptians ; and the beautiful colours they obtained from copper, the composition of various metals, and the knowledge of the effects produced on different substances by the salts of the earth, tend to confirm this opinion.

The Egyptian yarn seems all to have been spun with the hand, and the spindle is seen in all the pictures representing the manufacture of cloth. Spinning was principally the occupation of women ; and our word "wife" is nearly related to "woof," "weaving," and " web." But men were also employed at the spindle and the loom ; though not, as Herodotus would lead us to suppose, to the exclusion of women, who he pretends undertook the duties of men in other countries, " by going to market, and engaging in business, while the men, shut up in the house, worked at the loom." Men, to this day, are employed in making cloth in

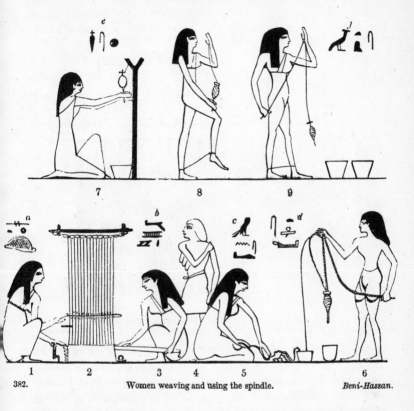

382.   Women weaving and using the spindle.   *Beni-Hassan.*

Egypt and in other countries, but it cannot be said that they
have relinquished their habits for those of women; and we
find from the paintings executed by the Egyptians themselves,
that both men and women were employed in manufacturing
cloth.

"Other nations," continues the historian, "make cloth by
pushing the woof upwards, the Egyptians, on the contrary, press
it down;" and this is confirmed by the paintings * which
represent the process of manufacturing cloth; but at Thebes,† a
man who is engaged in making a piece of cloth, with a co-

* In woodcut 382, *fig.* 2.   † Woodcut 384, *fig.* 2.

Part 1.

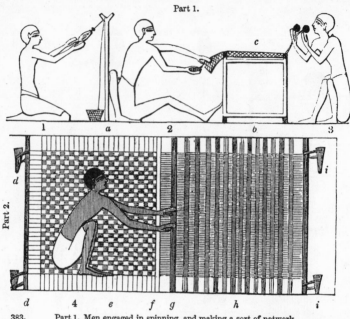

383.   Part 1. Men engaged in spinning, and making a sort of network.
                2. The horizontal loom, or perhaps mat-making.   *Beni Hassan.*

loured border or selvage, appears to push the woof upwards,
the cloth being fixed above him to the upper part of the frame.
They had also the horizontal loom, which occurs at Beni Hassan
and other places; and, at El Bersheh we see the mode of taking
up the increasing length of the cloth by pegs in the ground (as
still done in Ethiopia), and how the women wound off numerous
threads from balls placed within a slight framework, the fineness
of which is indicated by the number taken to form one twist.

    In the hieroglyphics over persons employed with the spindle,
it is remarkable that the word *saht*, which in Coptic signifies to
"twist," constantly occurs.   The spindles were generally small,
being about one foot three inches in length, and several, found at
Thebes, are now in the museums of Europe.*   They were generally of wood, and in order to increase their impetus in turning,

    * One of those in the British Museum, which I found at Thebes, had some of
the linen thread with it.   Woodcut 385, *fig.* 2.

384.   Fig. 1. A piece of cloth on a frame.   *Eileithyias.*
                        2. A loom.   *Thebes.*

k is a shuttle, not thrown, but put in with the hand. It had a hook at each end. *See* woodcut 382, fig. 2.

the circular head was occasionally of gypsum, or composition; some, however, were of a light plaited work, made of rushes, or palm leaves, stained of various colours, and furnished with a loop of the same materials, for securing the twine after it was wound.*

Besides the use of the spindle, and form of the loom, we find the two principal purposes, to which flax was applied, represented in the paintings of the tombs: and at Beni Hassan the mode of

* Woodcut 385, *fig.* 5.   Another of wood, *fig.* 6.

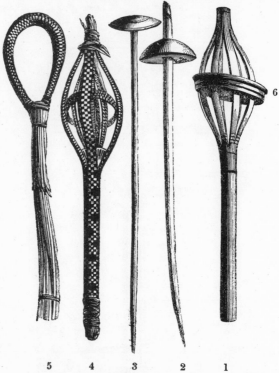

385.

5 4 3 2 1

Spindles. *British and Berlin Museums.*

Fig. 1 is a sort of cane split at the top to give it a globular shape.
2 has the head of gypsum.
3 entirely of wood.
4 of plaited or basket work.
5 the loop to put over the twine.
6 a ring of wood for securing the twine.

cultivating the plant, in the same square beds now met with throughout Egypt (much resembling our salt pans), the process of beating the stalks, and making them into ropes, and the manufacture of a piece of cloth, are distinctly pointed out.

It is, however, possible that the part of the picture, where men are represented pouring water from earthen pots, may refer to the process of steeping the stalks of the plant, after they were cut; the square spaces would then indicate the different pits in which they were immersed, containing some less, some more,

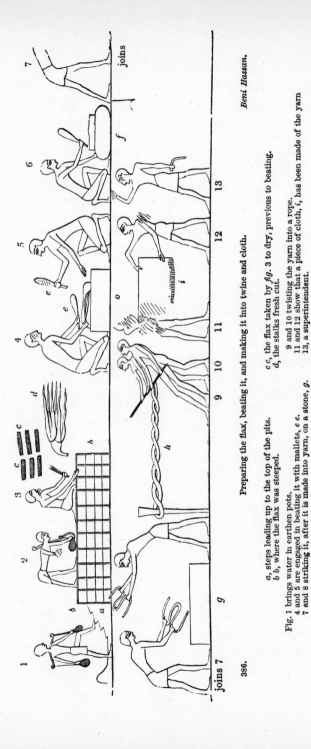

386.

Preparing the flax, beating it, and making it into twine and cloth.

a, steps leading up to the top of the pits.
b b, where the flax was steeped.

c c, the flax taken by *fig.* 3 to dry, previous to beating.
d, the stalks fresh cut.

Fig. 1 brings water in earthen pots.
4 and 5 are engaged in beating it with mallets, *e e.*
7 and 8 striking it, after it is made into yarn, on a stone, *g.*

9 and 10 twisting the yarn into a rope.
11 and 12 show that a piece of cloth, *i,* has been made of the yarn
13, a superintendent.

Beni Hassan.

water, according to the state in which they were required; and this is rendered more probable by the flight of steps, for ascending to the top of the raised sides of the pits; which would not have been introduced if the level ground were intended.

The steeping, and the subsequent process of beating the stalks with mallets, illustrate the following passage of Pliny upon the same subject :—" The stalks themselves are immersed in water, warmed by the heat of the sun, and are kept down by weights placed upon them ; for nothing is lighter than flax.   The membrane, or rind, becoming loose is a sign of their being sufficiently macerated.   They are then taken out, and repeatedly turned over in the sun, until perfectly dried; and afterwards beaten by mallets on stone slabs.   That which is nearest the rind is called *tow*, inferior to the inner fibres, and fit only for the wicks of lamps. It is combed out with iron hooks, until all the rind is removed. The inner part is of a whiter and finer quality.   Men are not ashamed to prepare it. . . . . After it is made into yarn, it is polished by striking it frequently on a hard stone, moistened with water; and when woven into cloth it is again beaten with clubs, being always improved in proportion as it is beaten."

They also parted and cleansed the fibres of the flax with a sort of comb, probably answering to the iron hooks mentioned by Pliny; two of which, found with some tow at Thebes, are preserved in the Berlin Museum ; one having twenty-nine, the other forty-six, teeth.   (*Woodcut* 387.)

The border of some of their cloths consists of long fringes, formed by the projecting threads of the warp, twisted together, and tied at the end in one or more knots, to prevent their unravelling, " precisely," as Mr. Thomson observes, " like the silk shawls of the present day ;" and specimens of the same borders, in pieces of cloth found in the tombs, may be seen in the British Museum, and other collections.

The sculptures, as well as the cloths which have been discovered, perfectly bear out Herodotus in his statement that they had the custom of leaving a fringe to their pieces of linen, which, when the dresses were made up, formed a border round the legs ; but they do not appear to have been universally worn.   This

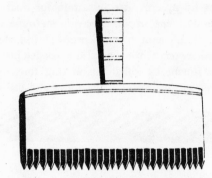

387.   Wooden comb found with some tow.   *Berlin Museum*

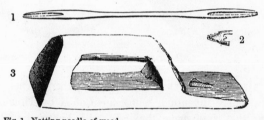

388.   Fig. 1. Netting needle of wood.
        2. Part of another of bronze, of later date, found by me at Berenice.
        3. Wooden plane for smoothing or pressing cloth.   *From Thebes.*

kind of dress he says was called *calasiris*. When the fringe
was wanting, the border was hemmed, which had the same effect
of preventing the unravelling of the cloth; and a fringe was
sometimes sewed on, as in many of our imitation shawls. The
Jews wore a similar kind of fringed dress, and Moses commanded
the children of Israel to "make them fringes in the borders of
their garments . . . and . . . put upon the fringe of the borders a riband of blue." (*Numbers* xv. 38.)

Besides the process of making cloth, that of smoothing, or
calendering, is represented in the paintings; which seems to
have been done by means of wooden rods, passed to and fro over
the surface; but from the appearance of some of the fine linen
found in the tombs, we may conjecture that much greater pressure
was sometimes used for this purpose, such as could only be
applied by a press, or cylinders of metal.

For smoothing linen, a wooden substitute for what we call an *iron* was also used; some of which have been found at Thebes, six inches in length, made of tamarisk wood;* but this belonged chiefly to the washerwomen, who had also a wooden instrument for goeffreying fine linen; by which the waving lines were made, so commonly seen in the dresses of the kings and priests.

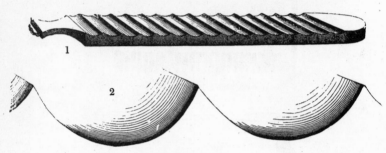

389.   Goeffreying Machine.   *Florence Museum.*

I have already stated that the Egyptians had carpets, which were a very early invention, being mentioned by Homer, who gives them the same name they are still known by, *Tapeta*, whence *tapis* and *tapestry*. They were used in houses, and were even spread for the sacred animals in Egypt. They were of wool, but of their quality we are unable to form any opinion, the fragments discovered in the tombs being very imperfectly preserved; though there is no doubt of their being portions of carpets. A small rug was also brought to England, and is now in the possession of Mr. Hay.

It is eleven inches long by nine broad; and is made like many carpets of the present day, with woollen threads on linen string. In the centre is the figure of a boy in white, with a goose above it, the hieroglyphic of " child," upon a green ground; around which is a border composed of red and blue lines; the remainder is a ground of yellow, with four white figures above and below, and one at each side, with blue outlines and red ornaments; and the outer border is made up of red, white, and blue lines, with a fancy

* Woodcut 388, *fig.* 3.

device projecting from it, with a triangular summit, which extends entirely round the edge of the carpet. Its date is uncertain; but from the child, the combination of the colours, and the ornament of the border, I am inclined to think it really Egyptian.

I have noticed the use of flax for making ropes, string, and various kinds of twine; for large ropes, however, of ordinary quality, and for common purposes, the *leef* or fibres of the date tree, were employed, as at the present day; and many specimens of these durable materials have been found in the excavations of Upper and Lower Egypt.

In a tomb at Thebes, of the time of Thothmes III., is represented the process of twisting thongs of leather, which, as it is probably the same as that adopted in rope-making, may be properly introduced here.

The ends of four thongs were inserted and fastened into a hollow tube, from the side of which a bar projected, surmounted by a heavy metal ball; and the man, who twisted them, held the tube in his right hand, whirling it round, as he walked backwards, by means of the impetus given from the ball. A band, attached to a ring at the other end of the tube, went round his body, in order to support it and give it a free action, and the ring turned upon a nut, to prevent the band itself from twisting.

At the other extremity of the walk, his companion, seated on the ground, or on a low three-legged stool, let out the separate thongs, and kept them from becoming entangled. Behind him sat another, who, with the usual semicircular knife, cut the skin into strips, as he turned it round; showing that what we term "the circular cut" was known to the ancient Egyptians 3300 years ago, and that they had already adopted this mode of obtaining the longest thongs from a single piece of leather. Such, too, was Dido's method, when she persuaded the unsophisticated natives to give up a piece of land as large as she could cover with a bull's hide, upon which she built Byrsa, the citadel of Carthage.

But the name Byrsa, said to be derived from the " hide," seems rather to be related to the fortress itself; being found in the names of Birs-Nimroud, Borsippa, the mounds of Boursa, and other places in the East, where towers, or citadels, once stood.

Part 1. Cutting and twisting thongs of leather.

a, a skin hanging up in the shop, indicating the trade of leather cutter.   *b*, cutting thongs out of a circular piece of skin.
d arranges the separate thongs, which are twisted by *i*, and when finished are bound together and hung up in the shop, *g h*.
k, a weight, which gives a greater impetus to the tube, *l*, when thrown round.
m, cobbler, perforating the sole of a sandal to receive the thong.
o, pieces of leather, ready for cutting into soles.

n n, thongs ready for fixing to the sole.
p, an awl.   *q*, a stand.

Part 1.

Part 2.

Part 2.   Carpenters.

r, drills a hole in the seat of a chair, *s*.   *t t*, legs of chairs.   *u u*, hatchets.
v, a right angle.   *w*, man planing or polishing the leg of a chair.

390.

When finished, the twisted thongs were wound round a hollow centre, through which the end was passed, and repeatedly bound over the concentric coils in the same manner as we tie up ropes.

Some, indeed, have supposed the present subject to represent rope-making; but the presence of the skin on the left, and the shoemakers on the right, forming a continuation of the picture, sufficiently prove that they are engaged in preparing leathern thongs for sandals, and other similar purposes.

Their nets were made of flax-string,* both for fishing and fowling; and portions of them have been discovered at Thebes. The netting-needles † were of wood, very like our own, split at each end, and between ten and eleven inches in length, and others were of bronze, with the point closed.

Sieves were often made of string, but some of an inferior quality, and for coarse work, were constructed of small thin rushes or reeds (very similar to those used by the Egyptians for writing, and frequently found in the tablets of the scribes); a specimen of which kind of sieve is in the Paris Museum. The paintings also represent them made of the same materials; and the first they used were evidently of this humble quality, since the hieroglyphic indicating a sieve is borrowed from them. Horse-hair sieves are ascribed by Pliny to the Gauls; the Spaniards, he says, made them of string; and the Egyptians of papyrus-stalks and rushes.

The Egyptians were not less famed for their manufacture of paper, than for the delicate texture of their linen. The plant from which it was made, the *Cyperus papyrus* of modern botanists, mostly grew in Lower Egypt, in marshy land, or in shallow brooks and ponds formed by the inundation of the Nile, where they bestowed much pains on its cultivation.

The right of growing and selling it belonged to the government, who made a great profit by its monopoly; and though we frequently read of the *byblus* or *papyrus* being used for constructing canoes or rude punts, for making baskets, parts of

---

* *Comp.* Isaiah xvii. 9, "They that work in fine flax, and they that weave networks." Plin. 19, 1, and above, p. 80.

† Woodcut 388, *figs.* 1, 2.

sandals, sails, and for numerous other common purposes, it is evident, that we are to understand, in these instances, some other species of the numerous family of Cyperus; which is also shown by Strabo's distinguishing the *common* from " the *hieratic* byblus."

The real *papyrus*, or hieratic *byblus*, was particularly cultivated in the Sebennytic nome : other parts of the Delta also produced it, and probably even some districts in Upper Egypt. The paper made from it differed in quality, being dependent upon the growth of the plant, and the part of the stalk whence it was taken; and we find many of the papyri which have been preserved vary greatly in their texture and appearance. They are generally fragile, and difficult to unrol, until rendered pliant by gradual exposure to steam, or the damp of our climates; and some are as brittle as if they had been purposely dried.

We are however less surprised at the effect of the parched climate of Upper Egypt, when we consider the length of time they have been kept beyond the reach of moisture; and our drawing paper, after a very few years, becomes so dry in that country, that it is too brittle to fold without breaking. Indeed, those papyri which have not been exposed to the same heat, being preserved in the less arid climate of Lower Egypt, still keep their pliability; and I have a fragment of one from Memphis, which may be bent, and even twisted in any way, without breaking, or without being more injured than a piece of common paper. The hieroglyphics from their style show it to be of an ancient Pharaonic age, and they contain the name of the city where the papyrus was found, " Menofr (or Memphis), the land of the Pyramid."

The mode of making papyri was this :—The interior of the stalks of the plant, after the rind had been removed, was cut into thin slices in the direction of their length, and these being laid on a flat board, in succession, similar slices were placed over them at right angles ; and their surfaces being cemented together by a sort of glue, and subjected to a proper degree of pressure, and well dried, the papyrus was completed. The length of the slices depended of course on the breadth of the intended sheet, as that of the sheet on the number of slices placed in succession beside each other, so that though the breadth was limited, the papyrus might be extended to an indefinite length.

The papyrus is now no longer used, paper from linen rags and other materials having superseded it; but some few individuals continue to make it in Sicily as a curiosity; and sheets from the plant, which still grows in the Anapus, near Syracuse, are offered to travellers, as curious specimens of an obsolete manufacture. I have seen many of these small sheets of papyrus; the manner of placing the pieces is the same as that practised in former times; but the quality of the paper is very inferior to that of ancient Egypt, owing either to the preparation of the slices of the stalk, before they are glued together, or to the coarser texture of the plant itself, certain spots occurring here and there throughout the surface, which are never seen on those discovered in the Egyptian tombs. The plant is now unknown in Egypt; and the only streams that produce it are the Anapus in Sicily, and a small one two miles north of Jaffa, where it was found by the Rev. S. Malan.

Pliny thus describes the plant and the mode of making paper: —" The papyrus grows in the marsh lands of Egypt, or in the stagnant pools left inland by the Nile, after it has returned to its bed, which have not more than two cubits in depth. The root of the plant is the thickness of a man's arm; it has a triangular stalk, growing not higher than ten cubits (fifteen feet), and decreasing in breadth towards the summit, which is crowned as with a thyrsus, containing no seeds, and of no use except to deck the statues of the gods. They employ the roots as fire-wood, and for making various utensils. They even construct small boats of the plant; and out of the rind, sails, mats, clothes, bedding, and ropes; they eat it either crude or cooked, swallowing only the juice; and when they manufacture paper from it, they divide the stem, by means of a kind of needle, into thin plates, or laminæ, each of which is as large as the plant will admit. . . . ."

" All the paper is woven upon a table, and is continually moistened with Nile water, which being thick and slimy, furnishes an effectual species of glue. In the first place, they form, upon a table perfectly horizontal, a layer the whole length of the papyrus;

which is crossed by another placed transversely, and afterwards inclosed within a press. The different sheets are then hung in a situation exposed to the sun, in order to dry, and the process is finally completed by joining them together, beginning with the best. There are seldom more than twenty slips or stripes, produced from one stem of the plant.

" Different kinds of broad paper vary in breadth. The largest, in old times, was the Hieratic, for holy purposes. . . . . The best is now thirteen digits broad; the hieratic two less. . . . The Saitic is under nine, being only the breadth of the mallet; and the paper used for business is only six digits broad. Besides the breadth, the fineness, compactness, whiteness, and smoothness are particularly regarded; . . . . when it is coarse it is polished with a (boar's) tooth, or a shell; but then the writing is more readily effaced, as it does not take the ink so well." Some sheets of papyrus, of ancient date, were much broader than any he mentions, thirteen digits or fingers being only about nine inches and two-thirds; and the Turin Papyrus of Kings was at least fourteen inches and a half in breadth.

Pliny makes a strange mistake when he supposes that the papyrus was not used for making paper before the time of Alexander the Great, as papyri are of the most remote Pharaonic periods; and the same mode of writing on them is shown from the sculptures to have been common in the age of Suphis, or Cheops, the builder of the Great Pyramid, 2000 years before Alexander's conquest of Egypt.

It is uncertain until what period paper made of the papyrus continued in general use : there are some deeds and other documents in the Vatican of the fifth and sixth centuries, and in the Munich Library of the seventh, in *minuscules;* and there is evidence of its having been occasionally employed, to the end of the seventh century, when it was superseded by parchment. All public documents, under Charlemagne and his dynasty, were written on this last, and the papyrus was then entirely given up.

Parchment, indeed, had been invented long before, and is supposed to have been first used for writing in the year 250 before our era, by Eumenes, king of Pergamus ; who being desirous of collecting a library which should vie with that of Alexandria, and being prevented by the jealousy of the Ptolemies from obtaining a sufficient quantity of papyrus, had recourse to this substitute ; and this adoption of it at Pergamus obtained for it the lasting name of Pergamena (*parchment*). It was made of the skins of sheep and of calves ; but to the former the name of parchment is more correctly applied, as to the latter that of vellum. The use of parchment, or of prepared skins, for writing upon, was not however first suggested at Pergamus ; it had been known ages before in Egypt ; and "records kept in the temple" are mentioned in the time of the eighteenth Dynasty, 1200 years before Eumenes, written upon skins called *Thr*, or *Takar*—a name which, as Mr. Birch thinks, resembles the Chaldee *Tzar*. Rolls of leather are also found in the tombs, buried with the deceased in lieu of papyri, which are of a very early period, and were adopted in consequence of the high price of the papyrus paper.

The monopoly of the papyrus in Egypt so increased the price of the commodity, that persons in humble life could not afford to purchase it for ordinary purposes ; few documents, therefore, are met with written on papyrus, except funereal rituals, the sales of estates, and official papers, which were absolutely required : and so valuable was it, that they frequently obliterated the old writing, and inscribed another document on the same sheet. The same happened afterwards with those on parchment ; Cicero mentions *palimpsests* in his time ; and one of his own treatises (de Republicâ) was subjected to this treatment.

For common purposes, pieces of broken pottery, stone, board, and leather were used ; an order to visit some monument, a soldier's leave of absence, accounts, and various memoranda, were often written on the fragments of an earthenware vase ; an artist sketched a picture, which he was about to introduce in a temple or a sepulchre, on a large flat slab of limestone, or on a wooden panel prepared with a thin coating of stucco : and even parts of funereal rituals were inscribed on square pieces of stone, on stuccoed cloth, or on leather. But though a rigid monopoly secured the value of the paper, it did not ensure the employment of the plant in its manufacture; other and better materials were at length discovered for making paper; and the remarkable prophecy of Isaiah (xix. 7) has come to pass, which foretold the papyrus should " be no more" in Egypt : " The paper reeds by the brooks, by the mouth of the brooks, ... shall wither, be driven away, and be no more:" and this Egyptian plant no longer grows in Egypt. Yet its name is destined to survive: the " Bible," or book, is so called from the *byblus*, and its other name, *papyrus*, will be perpetuated in " paper."

It was perhaps the desire to increase its value that caused its disappearance from Egypt, having been rooted out from every spot except where its cultivation was permitted by the Government; and Pliny either says " it *only* grew in the nome of Sebennytus ;" or that " nothing was grown in that district but the papyrus."

In the infancy of society various materials were employed for writing, as stones, bricks, tiles, plates of bronze, lead and other metals, wooden tablets, the inner bark (hence *liber*) and leaves of trees, and the shoulder bones of animals. Wooden tablets, covered with wax, were long in use among the Romans, as well as the papyrus; and the inner bark of trees and pieces of linen had been previously adopted by them about B.C. 440.

Many Eastern people still write on the leaves of trees, or on wooden tablets, and *wáraka* continues to signify, in Arabic, both " paper" and " a *leaf*."

The early Arabs committed their poetry and compositions to the shoulder-bones of sheep : they afterwards obtained the papyrus paper from Egypt, on which the poems called *Moallaqât* were written, in gold letters; and after their conquests in Asia and Africa, these people so speedily profited by the inventions of the nations they subdued, that parchment was manufactured in Syria, Arabia, and Egypt, which in colour and delicacy might vie with our modern paper. It speedily superseded the use of the papyrus, and continued to be employed until the discovery of the method of making paper from cotton, and silk, called *Carta bombycina*, which is proved by Montfaucon to have been known at least as early as A.D. 1100; and is supposed to have been invented about the beginning of the ninth century. Being introduced into Spain from Syria, it was denominated *Carta Damascena*; and manuscripts on cotton paper are said to exist in the Escurial, written in the eleventh century. There are also some on cotton paper in the Munich library, of the eleventh century; and of linen at the beginning of the fourteenth.

It is a matter of doubt to what nation, and period, the invention of paper manufactured from linen ought to be ascribed. The Chinese were acquainted with the secret of making it from various vegetable substances long before it was known in Europe; the perfection to which they have carried this branch of art continues to excite our admiration; and " the librarian Casiri relates," according to Gibbon, " from credible testimony, that paper was first imported from China to Samarcand A.H. 30 (A.D. 652), and *invented*, or rather introduced, at Mecca A.H. 88 (A.D. 710)."

It may, however, be questioned whether it was made from linen at that early period, and we have no positive proof of linen paper being known even by the Saracens, prior to the eleventh century. The Moors, as might be expected, soon introduced it into Spain, and the Escurial library is said to contain manuscripts written on this kind of paper, as old as the twelfth century.

But paper of mixed cotton and linen, which was made at the same time, appears to have been in more general use; and linen paper continued to be rare in most European countries till the fifteenth century. That it was known in Germany as early as the year 1312 has been satisfactorily ascertained by existing documents, and a letter on linen paper, written from Germany to Hugh Despencer, about the year 1315, is preserved in the Chapter-house at Westminster; which, even to the water-mark, resembles that made at the present day.

It was not till the close of the sixteenth century that paper was manufactured in England. The first was merely of a coarse brown quality, very similar to that of the modern Arabs, whose skill in this, as in many arts and sciences, has been transferred to people once scarcely known to them, and then greatly their inferiors; and writing or printing paper was not made in London before 1690; France and Holland having, till that time, supplied us with an annual importation, to the amount of nearly 100,000 pounds.

The tanning and preparation of leather was also a branch of art, in which the Egyptians evinced considerable skill; the leather cutters constituted one of the principal subdivisions of the fourth-class; and a district of the city was exclusively appropriated to them, in the Libyan part of Thebes; where they were known as " the leather-cutters of the Memnonia."

Leather is little capable of resisting the action of damp, and other causes of destruction, so that we cannot reasonably expect to find much of it in a good state of preservation; but the fine quality of the straps, placed across the bodies of mummies, discovered at Thebes, and the beauty of the figures stamped upon them, satisfactorily prove the skill of " the leather cutters," as well as the antiquity of embossing; and those bearing the names of Sheshonk (Shishak), the contemporary of Solomon, and the other kings of that dynasty, are perfectly preserved.

Many of the occupations of their trade are portrayed on the painted walls of the tombs at Thebes. They made shoes, sandals, the coverings and seats of chairs or sofas, bow-cases, and most of the ornamental furniture of the chariot; harps were also adorned with coloured leather, and shields and numerous other things were covered with skin prepared in various ways. They also made skins for carrying water, wine, and other liquids; coated within with a resinous substance, as is still the custom in Egypt.

Part of the process of curing the skins is introduced in the sculptures; and that of dyeing them is mentioned in the Bible,* being doubtless borrowed by the Jews from Egypt. In one instance, a man is represented dipping the hide into a vase, probably containing water, in which it was suffered to soak, preparatory to the lime being applied to remove the hair; a process very similar to that adopted at the present day in the East.

The Arabs prefer the acrid juice of a plant growing in the desert, for the purpose; as its effect is still more rapid, and as it has the advantage of making the skin better and more durable.

* Exod. xxv. 5, " And rams' skins dyed red."

This plant is the Periploca Secamone; its stalks contain a white milky juice, which exudes from it when bruised, and which is so acrid as to be highly injurious to the eye, or to the wounded skin. It supports itself by winding around every neighbouring shrub, and its not ungraceful stalks appear to have been occasionally used by the ancient Egyptians, for the same ornamental purpose as the ivy, the nightshade, and the convolvulus, in forming festoons. But though there is no proof of its having been employed by them in curing skins, it is very probable, as they were so well acquainted with the properties of the plants of the desert and the valley of the Nile; and curriers are represented in the sculptures of Thebes, pounding something in a mortar, which is either the *periploca*, lime, or some other substance required for the purpose.

According to the Arabs, the method of preparing skins with the periploca (their *Ghulga*) is as follows:—" The skins are first put into flour and salt for three days, and are cleansed of all the fat and impurities of the inside. The stalks of the plant, being pounded between large stones, are then put into water, which is applied to the inner side of the skin for one day, and the hair having fallen off, the skin is left to dry for two or three days, and the process is completed."

The mode of stretching or bending leather over a form is frequently represented at Thebes; and the semicircular knife, similar to that of our modern curriers, is commonly used by them. The curriers and shoemakers had also a sort of chisel, the common awl (specimens of which have been found at Thebes, similar to our own), a stone for polishing the leather, the cutting table, the bending form, the horn, and a few other utensils; and a prepared skin, the emblem of their trade, was suspended, together with ready-made shoes and other articles, to indicate their skill, and to invite a customer. (*Woodcuts* 333, 390, *and* 392, *part* 1.)

The shops of an Egyptian town were probably similar to those of Cairo and other Eastern cities, which consist of a square room, open in front, with falling or sliding shutters to close it at night; and the goods, ranged on shelves or suspended against the walls, are exposed to the view of those who pass. In front is generally a raised seat, where the owner of the shop and his customers sit

during the long process of concluding a bargain previous to the
sale and purchase of the smallest article ; and here an idle lounger
frequently passes whole hours, less intent on benefiting the shop-
keeper than in amusing himself with the busy scene of the passing
crowd.

Among the many curious customs introduced in the paintings,
and still retained in the East, is that of holding a strap of leather,
or other substance, with the toes, which, if always free and unin-

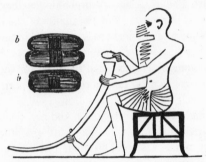

391.   Currier holding a strap of leather with his toes, while cutting it.   *Thebes.*
                b b are straps tied up, and deposited in the shop.

cumbered with tight shoes, retain their full power and pliability ;
and the singular, I may say primitive, mode of tightening a thong
with the teeth, while sewing a shoe, is also portrayed in the paintings of the same time.

It is probable that, as at the present day, they ate in the open
front of their shops, exposed to the view of every one who passed ;
and to this custom Herodotus may allude, when he says, " the
Egyptians eat in the street."

There is no direct evidence that the ancient Egyptians affixed
the name and trade of the owner of the shop, though the presence
of hieroglyphics, denoting this last, together with the emblem
which indicated it, may seem to argue in favour of the custom ;
and the absence of many individuals' names in the sculptures is
readily accounted for by the fact, that these scenes refer to the
occupation of the whole trade, and not to any particular person.

Of all people, we may suppose Egyptian shopkeepers most
likely to display the patronage received from royalty, the name

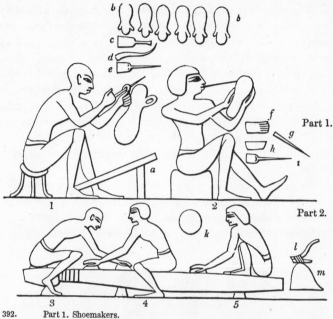

392.   Part 1. Shoemakers.
            Part 2. Men employed in polishing a column, probably of wood.   *Thebes.*
            Fig. 1. Making a hole with an awl.   2. Tightening a thong with his teeth.
            b b. Sandals hanging up in the shop.   *c* to *i.* Various tools; *l* an adze.

of a monarch being so often introduced in the most conspicuous
manner on the coffins of private individuals, and in the paintings
of the tombs; many of the scarabæi they wore presenting the
name of a king; and the most ordinary devices being formed to
resemble a royal oval.   But whether or not they had this custom,
or that of affixing the name and occupation of the tradesman, it is
difficult to determine; and indeed in those cities where certain
districts were set apart for particular trades, the latter distinction
was evidently uncalled for and superfluous.

The great consumption of leather in Egypt, and the various
purposes to which skins, both in the tanned and raw state, were
applied, created a demand far greater than could be satisfied by
the produce of the country; they, therefore, imported skins from
foreign countries, and part of the tribute levied on the conquered
tribes of Asia and Africa consisted of hides, and the skins of wild

animals, as the leopard, fox, and others; which are frequently represented in the paintings of Thebes, laid before the throne of a
Pharaoh, together with gold, silver, ivory, rare woods, and the
various productions of each vanquished country.

For tanning they used the pods of the *Sont*, or Acacia (Acacia,
or Mimosa, Nilotica), the *acanthus* of Strabo and other writers,
which was cultivated in many parts of Egypt, being also prized
for its timber, charcoal, and gum; and it is probable that the bark
and wood of the Rhus oxyacanthoïdes, and the bark of the Acacia
Séál, both natives of the desert, were employed for the same
purpose.

Many persons, both men and women, were engaged in cleaning
cloths and stuffs of various kinds; and the occupations of the
fuller form some of the numerous subjects of the sculptures. It
is probable that they were only a subdivision of the dyers. In

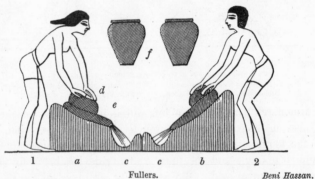

393.   Fullers.   *Beni Hassan.*
   a b. Inclined tables.   *c c.* The water running off into the trough below.

early times, before, and even after, the invention of soap, potash,
nitre, and several earths, were employed for cleansing cloths,
as well as various herbs, many of which are still in use among the
Arabs, one of which was doubtless the alkaline plant *boréeth*,
mentioned by Jeremiah (ii., 22) and Malachi (iii., 2). Many of
the Suædas and Salsolas, and other alkaline plants, are found in
the Egyptian deserts, as well as the *gilloo*, also called "the soap
plant;" and the people of Cairo and the Barbary coast use certain woods for cleansing manufactured stuffs.

A far more numerous class were the potters ; and all the processes of mixing the clay, and of turning, baking, and polishing
the vases, are represented in the tombs of Thebes and Beni
Hassan.

They frequently kneaded the clay with their feet, and after it
had been properly worked up, they formed it into a mass of convenient size with the hand, and placed it on the wheel, which was
of very simple construction, and generally turned with the hand.
The various forms of the vases were made out by the finger
during their revolution ; the handles, if they had any, were
afterwards affixed to them ; and the devices and other ornamental
parts were traced with a wooden or metal instrument, previous to
their being baked. They were then suffered to dry, and for this
purpose were placed on planks of wood ; they were afterwards
arranged with great care in trays, and carried, by means of the
usual yoke, borne on men's shoulders, to the oven.

Many of the vases, bottles, and pans of ordinary quality were
very similar to those made in Egypt at the present day, as we see
from the representations in the paintings, and from those found in
the tombs, or in the ruins of old towns ; and judging from the
number of Coptic words applied to the different kinds, their
names were as varied as their forms. Coptos and its vicinity were
always noted for this manufacture ; the clays found there were
peculiarly suited for porous vases to cool water ; and their
qualities are fully manifested, at the present day, in the *goolleh*
or *bardak* bottles, of the neighbourhood, made at the modern
towns of Kéneh and Ballás.

That the forms of the modern *goollehs* are borrowed from those
of an ancient time is evident, from the fragments found amidst
the mounds of ancient towns and villages, as well as from the
many preserved entire ; and a local tradition asserts that the
modern manufacture is borrowed from, and has succeeded without
interruption to, that of former days.

It is impossible to fix the period of the invention of the potter's
wheel, and the assertion of Pliny, who attributes it to Corœbus
the Athenian, is disproved by the evidence of the Egyptian

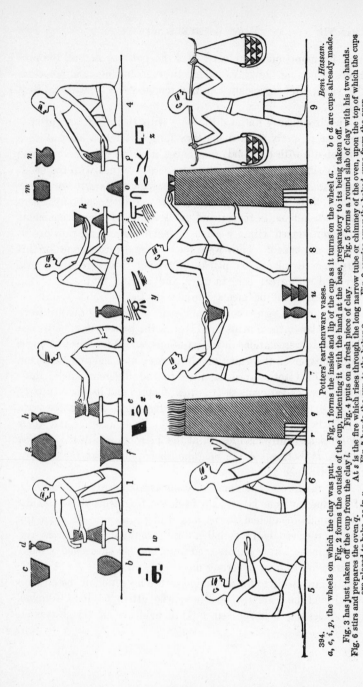

394.   *Potters' earthenware vases.*   *Beni Hassan.*

a, e, i, p, the wheels on which the clay was put.   Fig. 1 forms the inside and lip of the cup as it turns on the wheel a. $b c d$ are cups already made.
Fig. 2 forms the outside of the cup, indenting it with the hand at the base, preparatory to its being taken off.
Fig. 3 has just taken off the cup from the clay l.   Fig. 4 puts on a fresh piece of clay.   Fig. 5 forms a round slab of clay with his two hands.
Fig. 6 stirs and prepares the oven q.   At s is the fire which rises through the long narrow tube or chimney of the oven, upon the top of which the cups
are placed to bake, as in v.   Fig. 7 hands the cup to the baker 8.   Fig. 9 carries away the baked cups from the oven.

monuments, which prove it was known previous to the arrival of Joseph, and consequently long before the foundation of Athens.

But Pliny's chapter of inventions abounds with errors of this kind, and serves to show how commonly the Greeks adopted the discoveries of other nations, particularly of Egypt and Phœnicia, and claimed them as their own : even the art of cutting stones is attributed to Cadmus of Thebes ; and Thales of Miletus is said to have enlightened the Egyptians, under whom he had long been studying, by teaching them to measure the altitude of a pyramid, or other body, by its shadow, at the late period of 600 B.C.   But we cannot suppose that the Greeks taught their instructors a discovery, of which men so skilful in astronomy and mathematics could not have been ignorant ; and however superior they afterwards became in all branches of science, they were in their infancy long after the decline of Egypt.

The Egyptians displayed much taste in their gold, silver, porcelain, and glass vases, but when made of earthenware, for ordinary purposes, they were frequently devoid of elegance, and scarcely superior to those of England before the taste of Wedgewood substituted the graceful forms of Greek models, for some of the unseemly productions of our old potteries. Though the clay of Upper Egypt was particularly suited to porous bottles, it could not be obtained of a sufficiently fine quality for the manufacture of vases like those of Greece and Italy ; in Egypt, too, good taste did not extend to all classes, as in Greece ; and vases used for fetching water from a well, or from the Nile, were of a very ordinary kind, far inferior to those carried by the Athenian women to the fountain of Kallirhoë.

The Greeks, it is true, were indebted to Egypt for much useful knowledge, and for many early hints in art, but they speedily surpassed their instructors ; and in nothing, perhaps, is this more strikingly manifested than in the productions of the potter.

Carpenters and cabinet-makers were a very numerous class of workmen : and their occupations form one of the most important subjects in the paintings which represent the Egyptian trades.

Egypt produced little wood ; and with the exception of the date and *dôm* palms, the sycamore, tamarisk, and acacias, few trees of native growth afforded timber either for building, or for ornamental purposes.

The principal uses of the date and *dôm* trees have been already mentioned. *

For coffins, boxes, tables, doors, and other objects, which required large and thick planks, for idols and wooden statues, the sycamore was principally employed; and from the quantity discovered in the tombs alone, it is evident that the tree was cultivated to a great extent. It had the additional recommendation of bearing a fruit, to which the Egyptians were very partial; and a religious prejudice claimed for it, and the Persea, the name and rank of sacred fruit-trees. It is even now looked upon with favour; and when a foreigner is leaving the country, his Egyptian friends ask him if he has ever eaten any sycamore-figs, and on his answering in the affirmative, express their delight at the prospect of his return, saying, " whoever has eaten sycamore-figs is sure to come back to Egypt."

The tamarisk was preferred for the handles of tools, wooden hoes, and other things requiring a hard and compact wood; and of the acacia were made the planks and masts of boats, the handles of offensive weapons of war, and various articles of furniture. Large groves of this tree were cultivated in many parts of Egypt; especially in the vicinity of Memphis and Abydus; and besides its timber, the acacia was highly valued for the pods it produced, so useful for tanning, and for the gum, which exudes from the trunk and branches, now known under the name of gum Arabic. This tree is not less prized by the modern Egyptians, who have retained its name as well as its uses; *sont* being applied to this species of acacia, both in Arabic and the ancient Egyptian language.

Besides the *Sont*, or Acacia (Mimosa) Nilotica, the *Sellem*, *Sumr*, *Tulh*, *Fitneh*, *Lebbekh*, and other acacias, which grew in Egypt, were also adapted to various purposes; and some instances are met with of the wood of the *Egleeg* † or Balanites Ægyptiaca, and of different desert trees having been used by the Egyptian carpenters.

* Vol. i. p. 56.   † Or *Eqleeq*.

For ornamental purposes, and sometimes even for coffins, doors, and boxes, foreign woods were employed; deal and cedar were imported from Syria; and part of the contributions, exacted from the conquered tribes of Ethiopia, and Asia, consisted in ebony and other rare woods, which were annually brought by the chiefs, deputed to present their country's tribute to the Egyptian Pharaohs.

Boxes, chairs, tables, sofas, and other pieces of furniture were frequently made of ebony, inlaid with ivory; sycamore and acacia were veneered with thin layers, or ornamented with carved devices, of rare wood, applied, or let into them; and a fondness for this display suggested to the Egyptians the art of painting common boards, to imitate foreign varieties, so generally adopted in other countries at the present day.

The colours were usually applied on a thin coating of stucco, laid smoothly upon the previously prepared wood, and the various knots and grains, painted upon this ground, indicated the quality of the wood they intended to counterfeit.

The usual tools* of the carpenter were the axe, adze, hand-saw, chisels of various kinds (which were struck with a wooden mallet), the drill, and two sorts of planes (one resembling a chisel, the other apparently of stone, acting as a rasp on the surface of the wood, which was afterwards polished by a smooth body, probably also of stone†); and these with the ruler‡, plummet, and right angle§, a leather bag containing nails, the hone, and the horn of oil, constituted the principal, and perhaps the only, implements he used.

Some of the furniture of their rooms, the work of the cabinet-maker, I have already noticed‖, as well as the perfection to which they had arrived in the construction of the chairs and ottomans of their saloons; nor can I omit the mention of the art of dovetailing, already practised in the earliest Pharaonic ages, or the mode of applying two planks together in the same plane, by means of broad pins, or tongues, of hard wood. Of the former numerous

* Woodcut 395.   † Woodcuts 89, *fig.* 3, 392.   ‡ Woodcut 396, *e.*
§ Woodcut 390, *part* 2, *fig. v*; and 396, *f.*
‖ In vol. i., pp. 59 to 72, and 158 to 164.

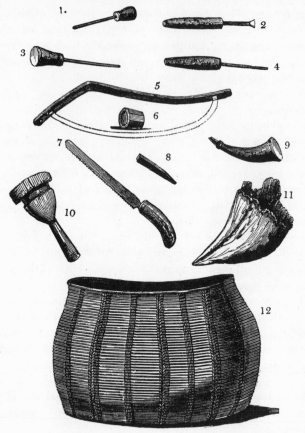

395.   *In the British Museum*
   Figs. 1, 2, 3, 4. Chisels and drills.   Fig. 9. Horn of oil.
        5. Part of drill.   10. Mallet.
        6. Nut of wood belonging to drill.   11. Bag for nails.
        7, 8. Saws.   12. Basket which held them.

instances occur, both in large and small objects, and no illustration of it is required; the latter is peculiar, and shows the great
care taken to make every thing durable, which characterizes all
the works of the Egyptians.

When two boards are joined together by our modern carpenters,
they fix small round pins horizontally, into corresponding parts of
the edges, which are then applied together, so as to form as it were

a single piece; but the cautious Egyptian carpenter was not content with this; and having used flat pins for the purpose about two inches in breadth, he secured these again, after the boards had been put together, by round pins or wooden nails, driven vertically through the boards, into each of the flat pins; and thus the possibility of the joint opening was effectually prevented, even should the glue, which was added as in our modern boxes, fail to hold them.

After the wood had been reduced to a proper size by the saw, the adze was the principal tool employed for fashioning it; and from the precision with which even the smallest objects are worked with it at the present day, by the unskilful carpenters of modern Egypt, we may form some idea of its use in the hands of their expert predecessors.

Many adzes, saws, and chisels, have been found at Thebes. The blades are all of bronze, the handles of the acacia or the tamarisk; and the general mode of fastening the blade to the handle appears to have been by thongs of hide. It is probable that some of those discovered in the tombs are only models, or unfinished specimens; and it may have been thought sufficient to show their external appearance, without the necessity of nailing them, beneath the thongs; for those they worked with were bound in the same manner, though I believe them to have been also secured with nails. Some, however, evidently belonged to the individuals in whose tombs they were buried, and appear to have been used; and the chisels often bear signs of having been beaten with the mallet.

The drill is frequently represented in the sculptures. Like all the other tools, it was of the earliest date, and precisely similar to that of modern Egypt, even to the nut of the *dóm** in which it turned, and the form of its bow with a leathern thong.

The chisel was employed for the same purposes, and in the same manner, as at the present day, and was struck with a wooden mallet, sometimes flat at the two ends, sometimes of circular or oval form; several of which last have been found at Thebes, and

* Woodcuts 390, *part* 2, *fig. s;* and 395; and vol. i. p. 56.

are in our European museums. The handles of the chisel were
of acacia, tamarisk, or other compact wood ; the blades of bronze ;
and the form of the points varied in breadth, according to the work for which they were intended.

The hatchet was principally used by boat-builders, and those who made large pieces of framework ; and trees were felled with the same instrument.*

The mode of sawing timber was primitive and imperfect, owing to their not having adopted the double saw ; and they were obliged to cut every piece of wood, however large, single-handed.   In order, therefore, to divide a beam into planks, they placed it, if not of very great length, upright between two posts, firmly fixed in the ground, and being lashed to them with cords, or secured with pins, it was held as in a vice.†

Among the many occupations of the carpenter, that of veneering is noticed in the sculptures of Thebes, as early as the time of the third Thothmes ; and the application of a piece of rare wood of a red colour, to a yellow plank of more ordinary kind, is clearly pointed out.   And in order to show that the yellow wood is of inferior quality, the workman is represented to have fixed his adze

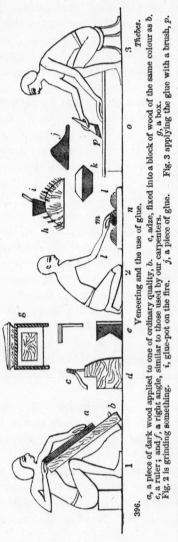

396.

Veneering and the use of glue.

Thebes.

a, a piece of dark wood applied to one of ordinary quality, *b.*   *c*, adze, fixed into a block of wood of the same colour as *b*,
e, a ruler ; and *f*, a right angle, similar to those used by our carpenters.   *g*, a box.
Fig. 2 is grinding something.   *i*, glue-pot on the fire.   *j*, a piece of glue.   Fig. 3 applying the glue with a brush, *p*.

* Woodcut 363, above in p. 18.   † Woodcut 398, *a*.

carelessly in a block of the same colour, while engaged in applying them together. Near him are some of his tools, with a box or small chest, made of inlaid and veneered wood, of various hues ; and in the same part of the shop are two other men, one employed in grinding something with a stone on a slab, and the other in spreading glue with a brush.

It might be conjectured that paint, or a varnish were here represented ; but the pot on the fire, the piece of glue with its concave fracture, and the workman before mentioned, applying the two pieces of wood together, decide the question, and attest the invention of glue nearly 3300 years ago. This is not, however, the only proof of its use at an early period, and several wooden boxes and coffins have been found, in which glue was employed to fasten the joints. It appears sometimes to be a fish glue.

Various boxes, shrines, articles of furniture, and other works of the cabinet-maker are frequently introduced in the paintings of Thebes, many of which present not inelegant forms, and are beautifully made. Several of the smaller objects, as boxes for trinkets and ointment, wooden spoons, and the like, have been mentioned among the furniture of their rooms ; where I have also described a curious substitute for a hinge, in some of those discovered at Thebes.*

Many boxes had lids resembling the curved summit of a royal canopy†, and were ornamented with the usual cornice‡ ; others had a simple flat cover ; and some few a pointed summit, resembling the shelving roof of a house.§ This last kind of lid was divided into two parts, one of which alone opened, turning on two small pins at the base, on the principle of the doors of their houses and temples ; and when necessary, the two knobs at the top|| could be tied together and sealed.¶

When not veneered, or inlaid with rare wood, the sides and lid were painted, and those intended for the tombs, to be deposited there in honour of the deceased, had usually funereal inscriptions,

* In chap. iii. p. 158 to 164.   † Woodcut 397, *figs.* 1, 2, 3, 6.
‡ *Fig.* 1.   § *Figs.* 4, 5, 8.
|| *Fig.* 4.   ¶ *See* vol. i. p. 163.

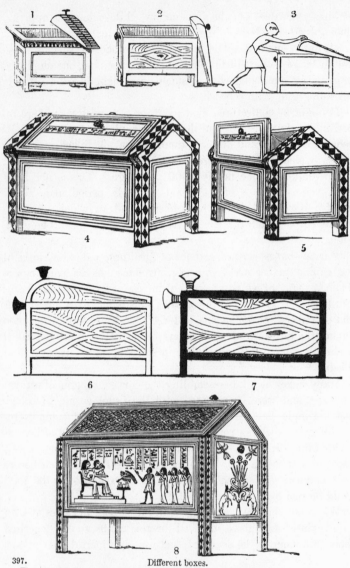

397.   Different boxes.
Figs. 1 and 2. Mode of placing the lid when the box was opened.
          3. Man opening a box, from a painting at Thebes.
     4 and 5. A painted box, showing how the lid opened.
     6 and 7. Boxes from the paintings of Thebes.
     8. Another painted box with a shelving lid, from Thebes, now at Alnwick Castle.

or religious subjects painted upon them, among which were offerings presented by members of their family.*

Several boxes have been found at Thebes; and in the British Museum is one remarkable for the brilliancy of the colours given to the ivory, with which it is inlaid.   The box is of ebony; the ivory, painted red and blue, is let into the sides and edges, and the lid is ornamented in the same manner.   There is in this a substitute for a hinge, similar to the one before mentioned, except that here the back of the cross bar, cut to a sharp edge along its whole extent, fits into a corresponding groove at the end of the box: and the two knobs are fixed in their usual place at the top and front.

The lids of many boxes were made to slide in a groove, like our small colour boxes; † others fitted into the body, being cut away at the edges for this purpose; and some turned on a pin at the back, as I have shown in the long-handled boxes before mentioned.‡

In opening a large box they frequently pushed back the lid, and then either turned it sideways § and left it standing across the breadth of the box, or suffered it to go to the ground; but in those of still larger dimensions, it was removed altogether and laid upon the floor.   Others with a pointed top had a projection under what may be called the end, or corbel of the gables, on the side that opened, in order that the lid might fall down and lie out of the way close to the side of the box, while the things were taken out of it.||

With the carpenters may be mentioned the wheelwrights, the makers of coffins, and the coopers; and this subdivision of one class of artisans shows that they had systematically adopted the partition of labour.

The makers of chariots and travelling carriages were of the same class; but both carpenters and workers in leather were employed in their manufacture; ¶ and chariots either passed through

* _Figs._ 4 and 8.   † Woodcut 184, p. 163, vol. i.
‡ Woodcuts 174, 175, and 178.   § Woodcut 397, _figs._ 1, 2, 3.
|| Woodcut 397, _figs._ 4, 5.   ¶ Vol. i. p. 377.

398.

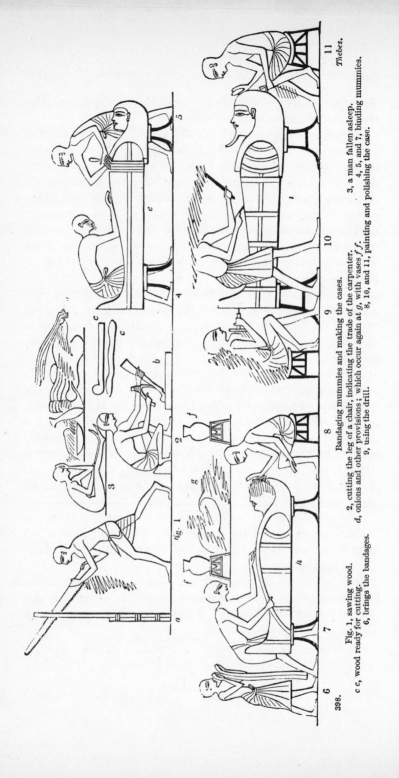

Bandaging mummies and making the cases.

Fig. 1, sawing wood. 2, cutting the leg of a chair, indicating the trade of the carpenter. 3, a man fallen asleep.

c c, wood ready for cutting. d, onions and other provisions; which occur again at g, with vases f f. 4, 5, and 7, binding mummies.

6, brings the bandages. 8, 10, and 11, painting and polishing the case.

9, using the drill.

Thebes.

the hands of both, or, which is more probable, chariot makers constituted a distinct trade.

Palanquins, canopies, and other wooden chests for travelling and religious purposes, were the work of cabinet makers or carpenters ; but the makers of coffins were distinct from both of these.   The undertakers, properly so called, were also a different class of people from these last, being attached to and even forming part of the sacerdotal order, though of an inferior grade.   Indeed the ceremonies of the dead were so numerous, and so many persons were engaged in performing the several duties connected with them, that no particular class of people can be said to have had the sole direction in these matters ; and we find that the highest orders of priests officiated in some, and in others those of a very subordinate station.   Thus the embalmers were held in the highest consideration, while those who cut open the body, when the intestines were removed, are said to have been treated with ignominy and contempt.   Those who swathed the body in bandages were called *Colchitæ* by the Greeks.

As in other trades, that of making coffins, or mummy cases, was a separate and distinct occupation, and it combined the work of the carpenter, the painter, and some others ; while at the same time the coffin-maker included in his labours the manufacture of boxes, wooden figures, and other objects connected with funerals.

The boat-builders may be divided into two separate and distinct trades, one of which formed a subdivision of the carpenters ; the other of the basket-makers, or the weavers of rushes and osiers, another very numerous branch.

The boats made by these last were a sort of canoe, or punt, used for fishing, and consisted merely of water plants or osiers, bound together with bands made of the stalks of the *common* papyrus.   They were very light, and some so small that they could easily be carried from one place to another ; and the Ethiopian boats, mentioned by Pliny, which were taken out of the water, and carried on men's shoulders past the rapids of the cataracts, were probably of a similar kind ; though Strabo describes the boats at the cataracts of Syene passing the falls in perfect security, and exciting the surprise of the beholders, before whom the boatmen delighted in displaying their skill.   These too are said by Celsius to have been made of the papyrus.

Papyrus boats are frequently noticed by ancient writers.   Plutarch describes Isis going in search of the body of Osiris " through the fenny country, in a bark made of the papyrus, whence it is supposed that persons using boats of this description are never attacked by crocodiles, out of fear and respect to the goddess; " and Moses is said to have been exposed in " an ark (or boat) of bulrushes, daubed with slime and with pitch." From this last we derive additional proof that the body of such boats was composed of rushes, which were bound together with the papyrus; and the mode of rendering them impervious to water is satisfactorily pointed out by the coating of pitch with which they were covered. Nor can there be any doubt that pitch was known in Egypt at that time, since we find it on objects which have been preserved of the same early date; and the Hebrew word *zift* is precisely the same as that used for " pitch " by the Arabs to the present day. It was also applied by the ancient Egyptians to " bitumen."

Pliny mentions boats " woven of the papyrus," the rind being made into sails, curtains, matting, ropes, and even into cloth; and observes elsewhere that the papyrus, the rush, and the reed, were all used for making boats in Egypt.

" Vessels of bulrushes " are again mentioned in Isaiah : Lucan alludes to the mode of binding or sewing them with bands of papyrus; and Theophrastus notices boats made of the papyrus,

399.   Making a papyrus boat.   *Tomb at the Pyramids*

and sails and ropes of the rind of the same plant. That small boats were made of these materials is certain ; and the sculptures of Thebes, Memphis, and other places, abundantly show that they were employed as punts, or canoes, for fishing in all parts of Egypt during the inundation of the Nile, particularly in the lakes and canals of the Delta. And the " Memphite bark bound together with the papyrus," that Lucan describes, is figured in the Memphite sculptures, as well as on the monuments of Upper Egypt.

There was another kind, in one of which Strabo crossed the Nile to the Island of Philæ, "made of thongs so as to resemble wicker-work ; " but it does not appear from his account whether it was formed of reeds bound together with thongs, or was like those made in Armenia, and used for going down the river to Babylon, which Herodotus describes, of osiers covered with hides (like British coracles), and which are represented on the Nimroud marbles. Strabo also mentions another, used on the canals during the inundation, of still more simple construction, in which, if we might substitute, what is probable, earthenware bottles or gourds for shells, we should recognise a modern Egyptian custom.

The Armenian boats were merely employed for transporting goods down the current of the Euphrates, and on reaching Babylon were broken up, the hides being put upon the asses which had been taken on board for this purpose, and the traders returning home by land. " They were round, in the form of a shield, without either head or stern, the hollow part of the centre being filled with straw." " Some were large, others small, and the largest were capable of bearing 5000 talents weight." They were, therefore, very different from the boats reported by the same historian to have been made in Egypt for transporting goods up the Nile, which he describes as being built in the form of ordinary boats, with a keel and a mast and sails.

" The Egyptian boats of burthen," he says, " are made of a thorn wood, very similar to the lotus of Cyrene, from which a tear exudes, called gum. Of this tree they cut planks measuring about two cubits, and having arranged them like bricks, they build the boat in the following manner :—They fasten the planks round firm long pegs, and, after this, stretch over the surface a series of girths, but without any ribs; and the whole is bound within by bands of papyrus. A single rudder is then put through the keel, and a mast of thorn-wood, and sails of the papyrus (rind), complete the rigging. These boats can only ascend the stream with a strong wind, unless they are towed by ropes from the shore; and, when coming down the river, they are provided with a hurdle made of tamarisk, sewed together with reeds, and a stone about two talents weight, with a hole in the centre. The hurdle is fastened to the head of the boat, and allowed to float on the water: the stone is attached to the stern, so that the former, carried down the river by the rapidity of the stream, draws after it the *baris* (for such is the name of these vessels), and the latter, dragged behind, and sinking into the water, serves to direct its course. They have many of these boats, some of which carry several thousand talents weight."

That boats of the peculiar construction he here describes were really used in Egypt is very probable; they may have been employed to carry goods from one town to another, and navigated in the manner he mentions; but we may be allowed to doubt their carrying several thousand talents, or many tons, weight; and we have the evidence of the paintings of Upper and Lower Egypt to show that the large boats of burthen were made of wooden planks, which men are seen cutting with saws and hatchets, and afterwards fastening together with nails and pins; and they were furnished with spacious cabins like those of modern Egypt. Those with planks, put together in the form of bricks, are also represented in the time of the 12th dynasty; but the use of the mallet and chisel, and the pins hammered into the holes to fasten the planks, show that they were not dependent on papyrus bands for their security; their construction was very like that of the modern Egyptian boats; and Herodotus has confounded the papyrus punt with the boat of burthen.

Pliny even goes farther than Herodotus, and speaks of papyrus vessels crossing the sea, and visiting the Isle of Taprobane* (Ceylon), which would throw the Chinese junk of modern days very far into the shade.

* Plin. vi. 22.

But though punts and canoes of osiers, papyrus, or reeds, may have been used on some occasions, as they still are, on the Nile and the lakes of Egypt, we know that the Egyptians had strong and well built vessels for the purposes of trade by sea, and for carrying merchandise, corn, and other heavy commodities on the Nile; and that, even if they had been very bold and skilful navigators, they would not have ventured to India, nor have defeated the fleets of Phœnicia, in their " paper vessels."

The sails, when made of the rind of the papyrus, were similar to those of the Chinese, which fold up like our Venetian blinds; but there is only one boat represented in the paintings, which appears to have sails of this kind, though so many are introduced there.   It is of very early date; and we cannot readily believe that a people, noted for their manufactures of linen and other cloths, would have preferred so imperfect a substitute as the rind of a plant, especially as they exported sail-cloth to Phœnicia for that very purpose.*

The construction of the various boats used on the Nile varied, according to the purposes for which they were intended.   The punts or canoes being either pushed with a pole, or propelled with a paddle,† had no mast, nor even rudder; and many of the small boats, intended merely for rowing, were unprovided with a mast or sails.   They were also without the raised cabin, common in large sailing boats, and the rowers appear to have been seated on the flat deck, which covered the interior from the head to the stern, pushing instead of pulling the oars, contrary to the usual custom in boats of larger dimensions.   The absence of a mast did not altogether depend on the size of the boat, since those belonging to fishermen, which were very small, were often furnished with a sail, besides three or four oars;‡ and some large boats, intended for carrying cattle and heavy goods, were sometimes without a mast.

In going up the Nile, they used the sail, whenever the wind

---

* Ezekiel xxvii. 7, In the lamentation of Tyre, "Fine linen, with broidered work from Egypt, was that which thou spreadest forth to be thy sail."

† *See* Contest of boatmen, woodcut 228, *fig.* 1.

‡ *See* Fishing scene, woodcut 420, part 1 *a*, in Chapter VIII.

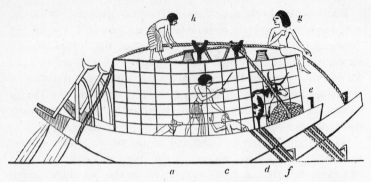

400.   Boats for carrying cattle and goods on the Nile.   *Thebes.*

a b, two boats, fastened to the bank by the ropes and pegs *f f*; in the cabin of one a man
inflicts the bastinado on a boatman. He is one of the stewards of the estate, and is accompanied by his dog. In the other boat is a cow, and a net of hay or chopped straw (*e*),
precisely the same as the *shenfeh* now used in Egypt.

was favourable; occasionally rowing, in those parts where the
windings of the river brought it too much upon the bows; for it
is probable that, like the modern Egyptians, they did not tack;
and when the wind was contrary, or during a calm, they generally
employed the tow-line, which was pulled by men on shore.

401. A boat with the mast and sail taken down, having a chariot and horses on board.
Eileithyias.

After they had reached the southernmost point of their journey
up the stream, the sail was no longer considered necessary; and
the mast and yards being taken down, were laid over the top of
the cabin, or on a short temporary mast, with a forked summit;
precisely in the same way as at the present day, on board the
cangias, and other masted rowing boats of Egypt. For as the

wind generally blows from the N.W., it seldom happens that the sail can be used in going down the Nile, and in a strong wind the mast and rigging are so great an incumbrance, that the boat is unable to make much way against it with oars.

The heavy boats of burden, which from their great size cannot be propelled by oars, are suffered to retain their masts and sails, and float down the river sideways at the rate of the stream, advantage being taken of the wind whenever the bends of the river permit; and the large *germs*, used for carrying corn during the inundation, are only employed when the water is very deep, and are laid up the rest of the year, and covered with matting from the sun. These, therefore, form exceptions to the ordinary boats of the Nile, and may be considered similar to some represented in the sculptures of Tel el Amarna; which are fastened to the shore by several large ropes, and are shown from the size of their cabins, the large awning in front for covering the goods they carried, and the absence of oars, to have been of unusual dimensions.

In the one given in the preceding wood-cut, from a tomb at Eileithyias, the size of the cabin, the horses taken on board with the chariot, and its height out of water, show that the common travelling boat was large and commodious; and we see that the cabin, as usual, was in the centre, with room enough on each side for the rowers to sit between it and the gunwale.

Large boats had generally one, small pleasure-boats two rudders, at the stern. The former traversed upon a beam, between two projecting heads, a short pillar or mast supporting it, and acting as the centre on which it moved; the latter were nearly the same in principle, except that they turned on a bar, or in a ring, by which they were suspended to the gunwale at either side : and in both instances the steersman directed them by means of a rope fastened to the upper extremity. The rudders consisted of a long broad blade and still longer handle; evidently made in imitation of the oars, by which they originally steered their boats, before they had so far improved them as to adopt a fixed rudder; and in order to facilitate its motion upon the mast or pillar, and to avoid the friction of the wood, a piece of bull's hide was introduced, as is the custom in the modern boats, between the mast and yard.

The oar was a long round wooden shaft, to which a flat board, either oval, circular, or of diamond shape, was fastened ; the same as still used on the Ganges, and in the Arabian Gulf. It turned either on a toll-pin, or in a ring, fastened to the gunwale of the boat ; and the rowers sat on the deck, on benches, or on low seats, or stood or knelt to the oar, sometimes pushing it forwards, sometimes, and indeed more generally, pulling it, as is the modern custom in Egypt, and most other countries.

At the head of the boat a man usually stood, with a long pole in his hand, to sound every now and then, and prevent its running upon any of the numerous sandbanks in the river (which, from their often changing at the time of the inundation, are not always known to the most skilful pilot) ; a precaution adopted not always in time by the modern boatmen of the Nile.

That the ancient Egyptian boats were built with ribs, like those of the present day, is sufficiently proved by the rude models discovered in the tombs of Thebes. It is probable that they had very little keel, in order to enable them to avoid the sand-banks, and to facilitate their removal from them when they struck ; and, indeed, if we may judge from the models, they appear to have been flat-bottomed. The boats now used on the Nile have a very small keel, particularly at the centre, where it is concave ; so that when the head strikes, they put to the helm, and the hollow part clears the bank : except in those cases where the impetus is too great, or the first warning is neglected.

The sails of the ancient boats appear to have been always square, with one yard above ; and none below in those of the oldest construction ; this last having been introduced when they abandoned the double mast of early times. The square sail is still retained in Ethiopia, where it is furled by forcibly rolling up the lower yard in the sail ; but in Egypt the only modern boats with square sails are a sort of lighter, employed for conveying stones from the quarries to Cairo and other places ; and these have only a yard at the top. All other boats have *latine* or triangular-shaped sails, which, in order to catch the wind when the Nile is low, are made of immense size : for unless they reach above its lofty banks, they are often prevented from benefiting by a side wind at that season of the year ; but the number of accidents which occur are a great objection to the use of such disproportionate sails.

The cabins of the Egyptian pleasure-boats were lofty and spacious ; but even in the smallest they did not extend over the whole breadth of the boat, as they do in the modern cangias, and merely occupied the centre ; the rowers sitting on either side, generally on a bench or stool. They were made of wood, with a door in front, or sometimes on one side, and they were painted within and without with numerous devices, in brilliant and lively colours. The same custom continued to the latest times, long after the conquest of the country by the Romans ; and when the Arabs invaded Egypt in 638, under Amer, the general of the Caliph Omer, one of the objects which struck them with surprise was the gay appearance of the painted boats of the Nile.

The lotus was one of their favourite devices, as on their furniture, the ceilings of rooms, and other places, and it was very common on the blade of the rudder, where it was frequently repeated at both ends, together with the eye of Osiris. But the place considered peculiarly suited to the latter emblem was the bow of the boat ; and the custom is still retained in some countries to the present day. In India and China it is very general ; and we even see the small barks that ply in the harbour of Malta bearing the eye on their bows, in the same manner as the boats of ancient Egypt. The Egyptians, however, appear to have confined it to boats used in the funeral ceremonies.

Streamers were occasionally attached to the pole of the rudder, and a standard was erected near the head of the vessel ; the latter generally a sacred animal, a sphinx, or some emblem connected with religion or royalty, like those belonging to the infantry ; and sometimes the top of the mast bore a shrine, or feathers, the symbol of the deity to whose protection they committed themselves during their voyage.

There is a striking resemblance, in some points, between the boats of the ancient Egyptians and those of India ; and the form of the stern, the principle and construction of the rudder, the cabins, the square sail, the copper eye on each side of the head, the line of small squares at the side, like false windows,* and the shape of the oars of boats used on the Ganges, forcibly call to mind those of the Nile, represented in the paintings of the Theban tombs.

The head and stern of the Egyptian pleasure-boats were usually ornamented with, or terminated in the shape of, a flower richly painted ; in the boats of burden they were destitute of ornament, and simply rounded off; and I have met with two only in which there was any resemblance to a beak. But this was in Nile boats, and is a mode of construction common in those of the present day. Nor are the ships of war, represented at Medeenet Haboo, furnished with beaks.

At the head, a forecastle frequently projected above the deck, in which the man who held the fathoming pole sometimes stood, and which answered as a small lock-up box, like the *hôn* of modern Nile boats; and occasionally there was at the

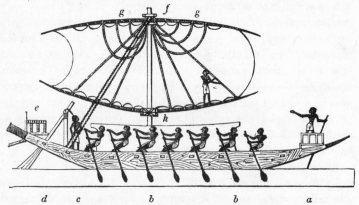

402. Boat of the Nile ; showing how the sail was fastened to the yards, and the nature of the rigging.   *Thebes.*

stern another of similar form, where the steersman sat.† They were both very generally adopted in the war galleys‡ ; where they were found of great service : the archers profiting by these

* Woodcut 402.   † Woodcut 402, *a* and *e*.
‡ Woodcut 351, vol. i. p. 412.

commanding positions to rake the enemy's decks, as they bore down upon a hostile galley.

There are no instances of boats with a rudder at both ends, said to have been used by some ancient nations; nor have any more than one mast and a single sail. Sometimes the rudder, instead of traversing in a groove, merely rested on the taffrel, and was suspended and secured by a rope, or band; but that imperfect method was confined to boats used in religious ceremonies on the Nile. The mallet and pegs for fastening the boat to the bank were kept in a particular place in the bows, as well as the landing plank, which were always in readiness, and under the surveillance of the man at the prow.

In some boats of burden, the cabin, or raised magazine, was very large, being used for carrying cattle, horses, and numerous stores; and it was sometimes made of open framework. As they often quitted these boats, to fetch other cattle, or to put them ashore, a boy was left on board to take charge of the stores; but this was not the only precaution: a dog was also kept tied up in the magazine; and its utility was often shown when the idle boy either wandered away during the absence of his masters, or fell asleep; for either of which delinquencies he was, if found out, liberally treated to the stick.* Both the sleeping underling and the bastinado are common representations in the paintings.

Unlike the modern Egyptians, they paid great attention to the cleanliness of their boats, the cabins and decks being frequently washed and swept; and this the Theban artists thought of sufficient importance to be indicated in the sculptures.

Herodotus states that the mast was made of the acanthus (Acacia, or Mimosa, Nilotica); but the trunk and limbs of this tree are not sufficiently long or straight; and for that purpose they doubtless preferred the fir, with which they were well acquainted, great quantity of the wood being annually imported into Egypt from Syria. The planks, the ribs, and the keel were of the acacia, which, from its resisting the effect of water for a length of time, was found well adapted for this purpose, as is fully proved by

* Woodcut 400.

modern experience. The foot of the mast was let into a strong beam, which crossed the whole breadth of the boat; it was supported by and lashed to a knee, rising to a considerable height before it ; and the many stout stays, fastened at the head, stern, and sides, sufficiently secured it, and compensated for the great pressure of the heavy yards and sail it carried. The sheets, halliards, and standing rigging, were all fastened "*within*" the gunwale, as at the present day, and the monuments confirm the statement of Herodotus respecting this peculiarity of the Egyptian boats.

In ships of war, the yard was allowed to remain aloft after the sail had been reefed ; but in the boats of the Nile, which had a yard at the top and bottom of the sail, as soon as it was furled, they lowered the upper yard, and in this position it remained until they again prepared for their departure. To loosen the sail from the lower yard must have been a tedious operation, if it was bound to it with the many lacings represented in some of the paintings ; but in these cases it may have been folded up between the two yards, as soon as the upper one was lowered ; the whole being lashed together by an outer rope.

It is uncertain whether they used blocks or pullies for raising and lowering the yards, or if the halliards merely passed through a smooth dead-sheave-hole near the top of the mast. The yards were evidently of very great size, and of two separate pieces, scarfed or joined together at the middle,* sometimes supported by five or six lifts, and so firmly secured that men could stand or sit upon them, while engaged in arranging the sail ; and from the upper yards were suspended several ropes, resembling the *horses* of our square-rigged ships,† and perhaps intended for the same purpose when they furled the sail. They had also braces and sheets to the upper and lower yards, for trimming the sails ; and each yard had its own halliards. Nor were the Egyptians ignorant of the pulley ; and one has actually been found in Egypt, which is now in the museum of Leyden. It was apparently intended for drawing water from a well. The sides

* Woodcut 402 *h*.   † Woodcut 402 *gg*.

are of tamarisk wood, the roller of fir; and the rope, of *leef* or fibres of the date-tree, which belonged to it, was found at the same time. But it is uncertain whether they introduced the pulley into the rigging of their boats.

Many of the sails were painted with rich colours, or embroidered with fanciful devices, representing the emblem of the soul of the king, flowers, and various patterns; some were adorned with cheques, and others were merely striped, like those of the present day. This kind of cloth, of embroidered linen, appears to have been made in Egypt expressly for sails, and was bought by the Tyrians for that purpose; but its use was confined to the pleasure-boats of the grandees, or of the king himself, ordinary sails being white; and the ship in which Antony and Cleopatra went to the battle of Actium was distinguished from the rest of the fleet by its purple sails, which were the peculiar privilege of the admiral's vessel. The sail of the large ship of Ptolemy Philopater, mentioned by Atticus, was, in like manner, of fine linen, ornamented with a purple border. Nor was this custom of late introduction; and the most highly decorated sails are those represented in the tomb of the third Remeses, at Thebes.*

The devices, painted or embroidered upon them, depended on fancy, and the same monarch had ships with sails of different patterns; but the boats used in sacred festivals upon the Nile were probably decorated with appropriate symbols, according to the nature of the ceremony, or the deity in whose service they were engaged. The edges of the sails were furnished with a strong hem or border, also neatly coloured, serving to strengthen it, and prevent an injury, and a light rope was generally sewed round it for the same purpose.

Some of the Egyptian vessels were of very great size. Diodorus mentions one of cedar wood, dedicated by Sesostris to the god of Thebes, 280 cubits, or 420 feet, long; another built in much later times by Caligula in Egypt, to transport one of the obelisks to Rome, carried 120,000 pecks of lentils as ballast; and Ptolemy Philopater built one of forty banks of oars, which was 280 cubits (about 420 feet) long, and 48 (about 72 feet) in

* " See woodcut at the end of this chapter."

height, or 53 (80 feet) from the keel to the top of the poop, with a crew of 400 sailors, besides 4000 rowers, and near 3000 soldiers. Philopater had another he used on the Nile, upwards of 300 feet in length, and 30 cubits (45 feet) in breadth, and nearly 40 (60 feet) high ; and Ptolemy Philadelphus had two of 30 banks, one of 20, four of 14, two of 12, fourteen of 11, thirty of 9, thirty-seven of 7, five of 6, seventeen of 5, and more than twice that number of 4 and 3 banks, with others of smaller size.

Of the origin of navigation no satisfactory conjecture can be offered, nor do we know to what nation to ascribe the merit of having conferred so important a benefit on mankind.

It is evident that the first steps were slow and gradual, and that the earliest attempts to construct vessels on the sea were rude and imperfect.

Ships of burden were originally mere rafts, made of the trunks of trees bound together, over which planks were fastened ; which Pliny states to have been first used on the Red Sea; but he is wrong in limiting the era of ship-building to the age of Danaus, and in supposing that rafts alone were employed until that period. Rafts were adopted, even to carry goods, long after the invention of ships, as they still are for some purposes on rivers and other inland waters ; but boats, made of hollow trees and various materials, covered with hides or pitch, were also of very early date, and to these may be ascribed the origin of planked vessels. Improvement followed improvement, and in proportion as civilisation advanced, the inventive genius of man was called forth to push on an invention, so essential to those communities, where the advantages of commerce were understood; and numerous causes contributed to the origin of navigation, and the construction of vessels for traversing the sea.

Whatever may have been the date of those expeditions which colonized various parts of Greece and other countries, the people to whom the art of navigation was most indebted, who excelled all others in nautical skill, and who carried the spirit of adventure far beyond any nation of antiquity, were the Phœnicians; and those bold navigators even visited the coast of Britain, in quest of tin.

The fleets of Sesostris, Amosis, and the Remeses, certainly date
at a very remote age, and some Phœnician sailors, sent by Neco
on a voyage of discovery, to ascertain the form of the African continent, actually doubled the Cape of Good Hope, about twenty-
one centuries before the time of Bartholomew Diaz, and Vasco
de Gama; but it was not till the discovery of the compass that
navigation became perfected, and the uncertain method of ascertaining the course by the stars gave place to the more accurate
calculations of modern times.

After the fall of Tyre, and the building of Alexandria, Egypt
became famous as a commercial country, and the emporium of
the East; the riches of India, brought to Berenice, Myos-Hormos,
and other ports on the Red Sea, passed through it, to be distributed over various parts of the Roman empire; and it continued to benefit by these advantages, until a new route was
opened to India by the Portuguese, round the Cape of Good Hope.

It is difficult to explain how, at that early period, so great a
value came to be attached to tin, that the Phœnicians should
have thought it worth while to undertake a voyage of such a
length, and attended with so much risk, in order to obtain it;
even allowing that a high price was paid for this commodity in
Egypt, and other countries, where, as at Sidon, the different
branches of metallurgy were carried to great perfection.   It was
mixed with other metals, particularly copper, which was hardened
by this alloy; it was employed, according to Homer, for the
raised work on the exterior of shields, as in that of Achilles;
for making greaves, and binding various parts of defensive
armour; as well as for household and ornamental purposes; and
it is remarkable, that the word *kassiteros*, used by the poet, is the
same as the Arabic name *kasdeer*, by which the metal is still
known in the East.   It is also called *kastira* in Sanscrit.

We have no means of ascertaining the exact period when the
Phœnicians first visited our coasts in search of tin; some have
supposed about the year 400 or 450 before our era: but that this
metal was employed many ages previously, is shown from the
bronze vessels and implements discovered at Thebes, and other
parts of Egypt.   It cannot, however, be inferred that the mines

of Britain were known at that remote period, since Spain and India may have furnished the Egyptians with tin; and the Phœnicians probably obtained it from these countries, long before they visited our distant coasts, and discovered the richness of their productive mines.   It is still produced in small quantities in Gallicia and another part of northern Spain.   Ezekiel says that the Tyrians received tin, as well as other metals, from Tarshish; and whether this was in India or not, there is sufficient evidence of the productions of that country having been known at the earliest times, as is proved by the gold of Ophir being mentioned in Job.   For if Phœnician ships did not actually sail to India, its productions arrived partly by land through Arabia, partly through more distant marts, established midway from India by the merchants of those (as of later) days; and we have evidence of their having already found their way to Egypt, at the early period of Joseph's arrival in that country, from the spices which the Ishmaelites were carrying to sell there.   And the amethyst, hæmatite, lapis lazzuli, and other objects discovered at Thebes, of the time of the third Thothmes, and succeeding Pharaohs, argue that the intercourse was constantly kept up.

The first mention of tin, though not the earliest proof of its use, is in connexion with the spoils taken by the Israelites from the people of Midian, in the year 1452 B.C., where they are commanded by Moses to purify " the gold and the silver, the brass, the *iron*, the *tin*, and the lead, by passing it through the fire; its combination with other metals is noticed by Isaiah, in the year 760 before our era, who alludes to it as an alloy mixed with a more valuable substance;* Ezekiel† shows that it was used for this purpose in connexion with silver; and bronze, a compound of tin and copper, is found in Egypt of the time of the 6th Dynasty, more than 2000 years B.C.

Strabo, Diodorus, Pliny, and other writers, mention certain islands discovered by the Phœnicians, which, from the quantity of tin they produced, obtained the name *Cassiterides*.   Though their locality is not given correctly by them, it is evident they

---

* Isaiah, i. 25.   † Ezek. xxii. 18, 20.

all allude to the cluster now known as the Scilly Isles; but these never produced tin, and the Phœnicians invented this story in order to conceal the fact of the mainland of Cornwall being the spot whence they obtained it. For, as Strabo says, the secret of their discovery was carefully concealed, and the Phœnician vessels continued to sail from Gades (Cadiz) in quest of this commodity, without its being known from whence they obtained it: though many endeavours were made by the Romans at a subsequent period to ascertain the secret, and to share the benefits of this lucrative trade.

So anxious, indeed, were the Phœnicians to retain their monopoly, that on one occasion, when a Roman vessel pursued a trader bound to the spot, the latter purposely steered his vessel on a shoal; preferring to suffer shipwreck, provided he involved his pursuers in the same fate, rather than disclose his country's secret; for which he was rewarded from the public treasury.

Pliny mentions a report of " white lead," or tin, being brought from certain islands of the Atlantic; yet he treats it as a " fable," and proceeds to state that it was found in Lusitania and Gallicia, and was the same metal known to the Greeks in the days of Homer by the name " *kassiteros.* " Diodorus and Strabo, after noticing the tin of Spain and the Cassiterides, affirm that it was also brought to Massillia (Marseilles) from the coast of Britain; but this was probably after it had been long known to the Phœnicians, who still kept their secret; and it was doubtless through their means that the natives of Britain prevented other foreigners going direct to the mines, supplying them, as they did, with pigs of tin, carried to Vectis, or the Isle of Wight; the established depôt where the traders from the Continent were accustomed to purchase the metal. And this having become the established line of commerce probably led to the choice of the neighbouring port of Southampton, as the place whence the Pilgrims in later times crossed over to the Seine.

Spain, in early times, was to the Phœnicians what America, at a later period, was to the Spaniards; and no one can read the accounts of the immense wealth derived from the mines of that country, in the writings of Diodorus and other authors, without being struck by the relative position of the Phœnicians towards the ancient Spaniards, and the followers of Cortez or Pizarro towards the inhabitants of Mexico or Peru.

" The whole of Spain," says Strabo, " abounds with mines . . . . and in no country are gold, silver, copper, and iron in such abundance or of such good quality : even the rivers and torrents bring down gold in their beds, and some is found in the sand ;" and the fanciful assertion of Posidonius, regarding the richness of the country in precious metals, surpassed the phantoms created in the minds of the conquerors of America.

The Phœnicians purchased gold, silver, tin, and other metals from the inhabitants of Spain and the Cassiterides, by giving in exchange earthenware vessels, oil, salt, bronze manufactures, and other objects of little value, like the Spaniards on their arrival at Hispaniola ; and such was the abundance of silver, that after loading their ships with full cargoes, they stripped the lead from their anchors, and substituted the same weight of silver.

Among those bronze implements were very probably the beautiful swords, daggers, and spear-heads found in this country, buried with the ancient Britons ; which are of such excellent workmanship and form, that they could only be the work of a highly civilized and skilful people ; and as they are neither of a Greek nor Roman type, it is difficult to attribute them to any other people than the Phœnicians.

A strong evidence of the skill of the Egyptians in working metals, and of the early advancement they made in this art, is derived from their success in the management of different alloys ; which, as M. Goguet observes, is further argued from the casting of the golden calf, and still more from Moses being able to burn the metal and reduce it to powder ; a secret which he could only have learnt in Egypt. It is said in Exodus, that " Moses took the calf which they had made, and burnt it in the fire, and ground it to powder, and strewed it upon the water, and made the children of Israel drink of it ;" an operation which, according to the French *savant,* " is known by all who work in metals to be very difficult."

" Commentators' heads," he adds, " have been much perplexed

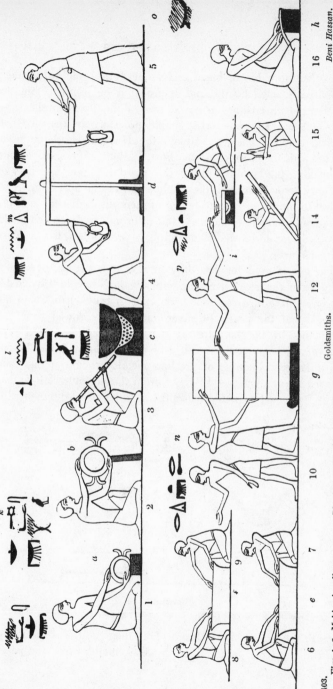

403. Figs. 1, 2. Making jewellery. 3. Blowing the fire for melting the gold. 4. Weighing the gold. 5. Clerk or scribe. 6, 7, 8, 9. Washing gold. 10. Superintendent. Goldsmiths. The remaining part relates to the preparation of the metal before it was worked.

Beni Hassan.

to explain how Moses burnt and reduced the gold to powder. Many have offered vain and improbable conjectures, but an experienced chemist has removed every difficulty upon the subject, and has suggested this simple process. In the place of tartaric acid, which we employ, the Hebrew legislator used natron, which is common in the East. What follows, respecting his making the Israelites drink this powder, proves that he was perfectly acquainted with the whole effect of the operation. He wished to increase the punishment of their disobedience, and nothing could have been more suitable ; for gold reduced and made into a draught, in the manner I have mentioned, has a most nauseous taste."

The use of gold for jewellery and various articles of luxury dates from the most remote ages. Pharaoh having "arrayed" Joseph "in vestures of fine linen, put a gold chain about his neck ; " and the jewels of silver and gold borrowed from the Egyptians by the Israelites at the time of their leaving Egypt (out of which the golden calf was afterwards made), suffice to prove the great quantity of precious metals wrought at that time into female ornaments. It is not from the Scriptures alone that the skill of the Egyptian goldsmiths may be inferred ; the sculp-

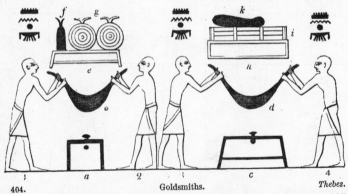

404.   Goldsmiths.   *Thebes.*

f g are articles of jewellery. The hieroglyphics read "goldsmith" or "worker in gold."

tures of Thebes and Beni Hassan afford their additional testimony, and the numerous gold and silver vases, inlaid work, and jewel-

lery, represented in common use, show the great advancement
they had made in this branch of art.

But gold was known in Egypt, and made into ornaments, long
before; and the same mode of washing and working it is figured
on the monuments of the 4th Dynasty.

The engraving of gold, the mode of casting it, and inlaying it
with stones, were evidently known at the same time; they are
mentioned in the Bible, and numerous specimens of this kind of
work have been found in Egypt.

The origin of the sign signifying gold has been happily explained by Champollion as the *bowl* in which the metal was
washed, the *cloth* through which it was strained, and the *dropping
of the water*, united into one character, at once indicative of the
process and the metal.

Much cannot, of course, be expected from the objects found in
the excavated tombs, to illustrate the means employed in smelting
the ore, or to disclose any of the secrets they possessed in metallurgy; and little is given in the paintings beyond the use of the
blow-pipe, the forceps, and the mode of concentrating heat by
raising cheeks of metal round three sides of the fire in which the
crucibles were placed.   Of the latter, indeed, there is no indication in these subjects, unless
it be in a preceding woodcut
(403, *fig. c.*) ; but their use
is readily suggested, and
some which have been found
in Egypt are preserved in
the museum of Berlin. They
are nearly five inches in
diameter at the mouth, and
about the same in depth, and
present the ordinary form

405.   Blowpipe, and small fireplace with cheeks to
confine and reflect the heat.   *Thebes.*

and appearance of those used at the present day.

At Beni Hassan, the process of washing the ore, smelting
or fusing the metal with the help of the blow-pipe, and fashioning

* Exod. xxxii. 4 ; xxviii. 9 and 11.

it for ornamental purposes, weighing it, and taking an account of
the quantity so made up, and other occupations of the goldsmith,
are represented; but, as might be supposed, these subjects merely
suffice, as they were intended, to give a general indication of the
goldsmith's trade, without attempting to describe the means employed.

From the mention * of earrings and bracelets, and jewels of
silver and gold, in the days of Abraham, it is evident that in
Asia, as well as in Egypt, the art of metallurgy was known at a
very remote period; and workmen of the same countries are noticed by Homer † as excelling in the manufacture of arms, rich
vases, and other objects inlaid or ornamented with metals. His
account of the shield of Achilles proves the art of working the
various substances of which it was made, copper, tin, gold, and
silver, to have been well understood at that time; and the skill
required to represent the infinity of subjects he mentions, was
such as no ordinary artisan could possess.

The ornaments in gold found in Egypt consist of rings, bracelets, armlets, necklaces, earrings, and numerous trinkets belonging
to the toilet, many of which are of the time of Osirtasen I. and
Thothmes III., about 3930, and 3290 years ago. Gold and silver
vases, statues, and other objects of gold and silver, of silver inlaid with gold, and of bronze inlaid with the precious metals,
were also common at the same time; and besides those manufactured in the country from the produce of their own mines, the
Egyptians exacted an annual tribute from the conquered provinces of Asia and Africa, in gold and silver, and in vases made
of those materials.

1   2   3

406.   Golden baskets, represented in the tomb of King Remeses III.   *Thebes.*

* Gen. xxiv. 47, 53.
† Hom. Iliad xxiii. 741. A silver cup, the work of the Sidonians, Od. iv. 618,
&c.; Iliad ii. 872, vi. 236; xvii. 474.

There was great elegance in the form of many of the oldest Egyptian vases, especially those of gold and silver. Much taste was also displayed in other objects as well as in the devices which ornamented them, among which may be mentioned the golden baskets in the tomb of Remeses III.

The gold mines of Egypt or of Ethiopia, though mentioned by Agatharcides and later writers, and worked even by the Arab Caliphs, long remained unknown, and their position has only been ascertained a few years since, by M. Linant and Mr. Bonomi. They lie in the Bisháree desert,—the land of Bigah (or of the " Bugaitæ" mentioned in the inscription at Axum)—about seventeen or eighteen days' journey to the south-eastward from Derow ; which is situated on the Nile, a little above Kom Ombo, the ancient Ombos.

Those two travellers met with some Cufic funereal inscriptions there, which from their dates show that the mines were worked in the years 339 A. H. (951 A. D.), and 378 A. H. (989 A. D.) ; the former being in the fifth year of the Caliph Mostukfee Billah, a short time before the arrival of the Fatemites in Egypt, the latter in the fourteenth of El Azeéz, the second of the Fatemite dynasty.

They continued to be worked till a much later period, and were afterwards abandoned, the value of the gold barely covering the expenses ; nor did Mohammed Ali, who sent to examine them and obtain specimens of the ore, find it worth while to re-open them.

The matrix is quartz : and so diligent a search did the Egyptians establish, throughout the whole of the deserts east of the Nile, for this precious metal, that I never remember to have seen a vein of quartz in any of the primitive ranges there, which had not been carefully examined by their miners ; certain portions having been invariably picked out from the fissures in which it lay, and broken into small fragments. The same was done in later times by the Romans ; and evidences of their searching for gold in quartz veins are even found in some parts of Britain.

The gold mines are said by Aboolfeda to be situated at El Allaga (or Ollagee) ; but Eshuranib (or Eshuanib), the principal place, is about three days' journey beyond Wadee Allaga according to Mr. Bonomi, to whom I am indebted for the following account of the mines. " The direction of the excavations depends on that of the strata in which the ore is found ; and the position of the various shafts differs accordingly. As to the manner of extracting the metal, some notion may be given by a description of the ruins at Eshuranib, the largest station, where sufficient remains to explain the process they adopted. The principal excavation, according to M. Linant's measurement, is about 180 feet deep : it is a narrow oblique chasm, reaching a considerable way down the rock. In the valley near the most accessible part of the excavation, are several huts, built of the unhewn fragments of the surrounding hills, their walls not more than breast high, perhaps the houses of the excavators or the guardians of the mine ; and separated from them by the ravine or course of the torrent is a group of houses, about three hundred in number, laid out very regularly in straight lines. In those nearest the mines lived the workmen who were employed to break the quartz into small fragments, the size of a bean, from whose hands the pounded stone passed to the persons who ground it in hand-mills, similar to those now used for corn in the valley of the Nile, made of a granitic stone ; one of which is to be found in almost every house at these mines, either entire or broken.

" The quartz thus reduced to powder was washed on inclined tables, furnished with two cisterns, all built of fragments of stone collected there ; and near these inclined planes are generally found little white mounds, the residue of the operation. Besides the numerous remains of houses in this station, are two large buildings, with towers at the angles, built of the hard blackish granitic, yet luminous, rock, that prevails in the district. The valley has many trees, and in a high part of the torrent bed is a sort of island, or isolated bank, on which we found many tombstones, some written in the ancient Cufic character, very similar to those at A'Souán."

Mr. Bonomi's account agrees very well with those given by Agatharcides and Diodorus ; who both mention the great labour of extracting the gold, and separating it from the pounded stone by frequent washings ; a process apparently represented in the tombs of the early time of the Osirtasens ; and the descriptions of the old " diggings" have acquired additional interest from those of modern days.

But in Australia and California they are carried on under more auspicious circumstances than those of old ; where the workers in the mines were principally captives taken in war, and men condemned to hard labour for crimes, or in consequence of offences against the government.   They were bound in fetters, and obliged to work night and day ; every chance of escape being carefully obviated by the watchfulness of the guards, who, in order that persuasion might not be used to induce them to relax in their duty, or feelings of compassion be excited for the sufferings of their fellow-countrymen, were foreign soldiers, ignorant of the Egyptian language.

Such was the system in the time of Diodorus ; but it is uncertain whether it was introduced under the Ptolemies, or had already existed under the later Pharaohs.   " The soil," says the historian, " naturally black, is traversed with veins of marble of excessive whiteness, surpassing in brilliancy the most shining substances ; out of which the overseers cause the gold to be dug, by the labour of a vast multitude of people ; for the kings of Egypt condemn to the mines notorious criminals, prisoners of war, persons convicted by false accusations, or the victims of resentment.   And not only the individuals themselves, but sometimes even their whole families are doomed to this labour ; with the view of punishing the guilty, and profiting by their toil.

" The vast numbers employed in these mines are bound in fetters, and compelled to work day and night without intermission, and without the least hope of escape ; for they set over them barbarian soldiers, who speak a foreign language, so that there is no possibility of conciliating them by persuasion, or the kind feelings which result from familiar converse.

" When the earth containing the gold is hard, they soften it by the application of fire, and when it has been reduced to such a state that it yields to moderate labour, several thousands (myriads) of these unfortunate people break it up with iron picks.   Over the whole work presides an engineer who views and selects the stone, and points it out to the labourers. The strongest of them, provided with iron chisels, cleave the marble-shining rock by mere force, without any attempt at skill; and in excavating the shaft below ground they follow the direction of the shining stratum, without keeping to a straight line.

" In order to see in these dark windings, they fasten lamps to their foreheads, having their bodies painted, sometimes of one and sometimes of another colour, according to the nature of the rock; and as they cut the stone it falls in masses on the floor, the overseers urging them to the work with commands and blows. They are followed by little boys, who take away the fragments as they fall and carry them out into the open air. Those who are above thirty years of age are employed to pound pieces of the stone, of certain dimensions, with iron pestles in stone mortars, until reduced to the size of a lentil. The whole is then trans-ferred to women and old men, who put it into mills arranged in a long row, two or three persons being employed at the same mill, and it is ground until reduced to a fine powder.

" No attention is paid to their persons; they have not even a piece of rag to cover themselves; and so wretched is their con-dition that every one who witnesses it deplores the excessive misery they endure. No rest, no intermission from toil, are given either to the sick or maimed : neither the weakness of age nor women's infirmities are regarded; all are driven to their work with the lash, till, at last, overcome with the intolerable weight of their afflictions, they die in the midst of their toil. So that these unhappy creatures always expect worse to come than what they endure at the present, and long for death as far preferable to life.

" At length the masters take the stone thus ground to powder, and carry it away to undergo the final process. They spread it upon a broad table a little inclined ; and, pouring water upon it, rub the pulverised stone until all the earthy matter is separated, which, flowing away with the water, leaves the heavier particles behind on the board. This operation is often repeated, the stone being rubbed lightly with the hand : they then draw up the useless and earthy substance with fine sponges, gently applied, until the gold comes out quite pure. Other workmen then take it away by weight and measure, and putting it with a fixed proportion of lead, salt, a little tin, and barley bran, into earthen crucibles well closed with clay, leave it in a furnace for five successive days and nights; after which it is suffered to cool. The crucibles are then opened, and nothing is found in them but the pure gold, a little diminished in quantity.

" Such is the method of extracting the gold on the confines of Egypt, the result of so many and such great toils. Nature, indeed, teaches that as gold is obtained with immense labour, so it is kept with difficulty, creating great anxiety, and attended in its use both with pleasure and grief."

In the early stages of society when gold first began to be used, idols, ornaments, or other objects, were made of the metal in its pure state, till being found too soft, and too easily worn away, an alloy was added to harden it, at the same time that it increased the bulk of the valuable material. As men advanced in experience, they found that the great ductility of gold enabled them to cover substances of all kinds with thin plates of the metal, giving all the effect of the richness and brilliancy they admired in solid gold ornaments; and the gilding of bronze, stone, silver, and wood, was speedily adopted.

The leaves so used were at first thick, but skill, resulting from experience, soon showed to what a degree of fineness they could be reduced; and we find that in Egypt substances of various kinds were overlaid with fine gold leaf at a very remote period, even in the time of the first Osirtasen. Some things still continued to be covered with thick leaf, but this was from choice, and not in consequence of any want of skill in the workmen; and in the early age of Thothmes III. they were already acquainted with the various methods of overlaying with gold leaf, gilding, inlaying, and beating gold into other metals, previously tooled with devices to receive it.

That the practice of applying it in leaf was common when the Israelites were in the country is evident from the direct mention of it in the Bible, the ark of shittim wood made by Moses being overlaid with pure gold; and the casting of the metal is noticed on the same occasion; nor can we doubt that the art was derived by the Jews from Egypt, or that the Egyptians had long before been acquainted with all those secrets of metallurgy, in which the specimens that remain prove them to have so eminently excelled.

The method devised by the Egyptians for beating out the leaf is unknown to us, but from the extreme fineness of some of that covering wooden and other ornaments found at Thebes, we may conclude it was done nearly in the same way as formerly in Europe, between parchment; and perhaps some membrane taken from the intestines of animals was also employed by them.

In Europe the skin of an unborn calf was at first substituted for the parchment previously used, but in the beginning of the 17th century, the German gold-beaters having obtained a fine pellicle from the entrails of cattle, found that they could beat gold much thinner than before, and this still continues to be used, and is known to us under the name of gold-beaters' skin. "About the year 1621," says Beckmann, "Merunne excited general astonishment, when he showed that the Parisian gold-beaters could beat an ounce of gold into sixteen hundred leaves, which together covered a surface of one hundred and five square feet. But in 1711, when the pellicles discovered by the Germans came to be used in Paris, Réaumur found that an ounce of gold in the form of a cube, five and a quarter lines at most in length, breadth, and thickness, and which covered only a surface of about 27 square lines, could be so extended by the gold-beaters as to cover a surface of more than $1466\frac{1}{2}$ square feet. This extension, therefore, is nearly one half more than was possible about a century before."

Many gilt bronze vases, implements of various kinds, trinkets, statues, toys, and other objects, in metal and wood, have been discovered in the tombs of Thebes: the faces of mummies are frequently found overlaid with thick gold-leaf; the painted cloth, the wooden coffin, were also profusely ornamented in this manner, and sometimes the whole body itself of the deceased, previous to its being enveloped in the bandages. Not only were small objects appertaining to the service of the gods, and connected with religion, or articles of luxury and show, in the temples, tombs, or private houses, so decorated; the sculptures on the lofty walls of an adytum, the ornaments of a colossus, the doorways of a temple, and parts of numerous large monuments were likewise covered with gilding, of which the wooden heifer which served as a sepulchre to the body of king Mycerinus's daughter, some of the mouldings in the temple of Kalabshi in Nubia, the statue of Minerva sent to Cyrene by Amasis, and portions of the Sphinx at the Pyramids may be cited as instances.

Gold is supposed to have been used for money some time before silver. In Egypt it was evidently known before silver, this being called " white *gold*; " and it was there the representative of money; while in Hebrew, *kussuf*, " silver," signified " money," like " argent " in French. In neither case was the money coined in early times. Gold was perhaps first stamped by the Lydians; but the oldest known Greek coins are the silver ones of Ægina, with a tortoise on one side.

Much gold was used for ornamental purposes. Its richness, durability, and freedom from tarnish, led the ancients to employ it very generally, and to a greater extent than in modern times, when South America has given us the abundance, and the name, of " plate." Silver was chiefly confined to money; and the demand for gold in houses (*Plin.* xxxiii. 17), and in jewellery, left silver free for the currency, and for a few other purposes. But though gold was preferred, it is still singular that so few pieces of silver plate seem to have been made by the Greeks and Romans.

The Egyptian sculptures represent silver as well as gold vases and ornaments, in the time of the third Thothmes, and silver rings and trinkets have been found of the same epoch; but gold was the favourite metal in Egypt, as afterwards in Greece and Rome; and the rich frequently had ornamental works, statues, and furniture of solid gold. Those who could not afford them were satisfied to have bronze overlaid with gold, at first with a thick, in after times with a thin coating, until in time gold-beating brought the external appearance of gold within the reach of less wealthy people; and gold leaf in modern days covers the wooden ornaments of the humblest house. Now that gold is in greater abundance, we may look to its coming again into more general use, instead of silver; which sinks into the appearance of pewter by the side of that rich metal; and to its taking the place of some of our paltry imitations.

If the use of gold preceded that of silver, the latter was not long in following it; and the earliest authority, the Bible, mentions both at a remote age. Abraham was said to have been " very rich in cattle, in *silver*, and in gold; " Abimelech gave him a thousand pieces of the former; and the use of silver as money is distinctly pointed out in the purchase of the field of Ephron, with its cave, which Abraham bought for " four hundred shekels of silver, current money with the merchant." On this occasion, as usual, the price paid was settled by *weight*, which was the origin and meaning of the name *shekel;* and the custom of weighing money was retained among the Egyptians, Hebrews, and other Eastern people, till a late period. Indeed, until a government stamp, or some fixed value, was given to money, this could be the only method of ascertaining the price paid, and of giving satisfaction to both parties. Thus Joseph's brethren,

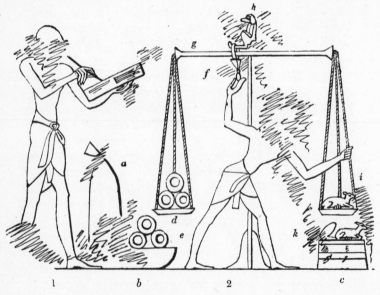

407.   *Kabbáneh* (Qabbáneh), or public weighers, and notaries.   *Thebes.*

when they discovered the money returned into their sacks, brought it back to Egypt, observing that it was "in full weight;" and the paintings of Thebes frequently represent persons in the act of weighing gold, on the purchase of articles in the market.

Egyptian money was in rings of gold and silver, a kind of currency that continues to this day in Sennaar and the neighbouring countries; but it is uncertain whether any of them had a government stamp to denote their purity or their value; and though so commonly represented, none have yet been found in the ruins or tombs of Thebes. They remind us of the "ring (*nuzm*) of gold" in Job (xlii. 11), given him with "a piece of money" by his friends.

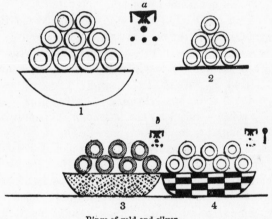

408.   Rings of gold and silver.   *Thebes.*

Gold when brought as tribute was often in bags, which were deposited in the royal treasury. These doubtless contained gold dust, which is mentioned by Job (xxviii. 6) as a well known form of that metal; and this is confirmed by " pure gold" being written over them. Though sealed, and warranted to contain a certain quantity, they were subjected to the usual ordeal of the scales by the cautious Egyptians. Money was sometimes kept ready weighed in known quantities for certain occasions, which, when intended as a present, or when the honesty of the person was beyond suspicion, did not require to be weighed; as when

Naaman gave "two talents of silver in two bags" to Gehazi (2 Kings v. 23; *see* Tobit ix. 5). The Egyptians had also unstamped copper money, called in the papyri "pieces of brass;" which, like the gold and silver, continued to be taken by weight even in the time of the Ptolemies; and it was only by degrees that the Greek coinage did away with the old imperfect system of weighing the price paid for every commodity.

But these princes were not the first who introduced coined money into Egypt: it had been current there during the Persian occupation of the country; and Aryandes, who was governor of Egypt, under Cambyses and Darius, struck silver coins, in imitation of the gold Darics of his sovereign, for which act of presumption he was condemned to death.

They are supposed to be those with an owl, and the Egyptian sceptres of Osiris, the crook and flail, on the obverse; and an archer on a hippocampus, with a dolphin, on the reverse.

The art of stamping money in Asia began in the dominions of Lydia. Herodotus says the Lydians were "the first people who coined gold and silver for their use;" and if Ægina also claims the earliest coinage, this does not contradict Herodotus, as it was only the earliest in relation to Greece. The oldest coins, that have been found, are the *staters* of Lydia, which date even a little before the very ancient ones of Cyzicus. They are not of pure gold, but of *Electrum,* or three parts gold and one of silver: probably owing to the two metals having been found together, and first stamped in that state. They were mere lumps, or dumps, of a certain weight; often cracked at the edge from being suddenly flattened by the blow. They were impressed with a lion's head, or other emblem, on one side only. Similarly rude were the old Æginetan coins, with a tortoise on one side, and on the other the mark of the block on which the lump of metal was fixed while struck. These last were all of silver, none of gold; and the oldest coins of real gold were those of Darius.

Phidon, king of Argos, is said to have invented weights and measures (that is in Greece), and to have established the silver coinage of Ægina B.C. 895: and though Pausanias thinks gold and silver money were unknown in the age of Polydorus, king of

Sparta (who died B.C. 724), the authority of the Parian Chronicle, and of Ælian, favour the earlier claims of Ægina. The coins of Syracuse and Magna Græcia date from 700 B.C.; having, like all others before 500 B.C., only a figure on one side; and the first silver coins of Athens were struck in 512 B.C. The gold Darics had only a figure on the obverse, representing an archer. They were coined about 500 B.C., and had not yet the round shape of later pieces, nor of the silver Darics, being 5-8ths of an inch long by 7-16ths. They were worth about 1*l.* 1*s.* 10*d.* each. These and other early coins therefore do not borrow their form from ring money; which may perhaps be traced in those of China.

Habit would naturally retain an original type for a long time; and sometimes even in Greece the archaic character of a coin was continued long after art had improved. Thus the old head of Minerva was repeated on the late Athenian drachm and tetra-drachm, because strangers were accustomed to it in commerce, and the Athenians were satisfied to use the well-known Corinthian didrachm for the same reason; as all people on the Mediterranean still welcome the pillar dollar of Spain.

The tradition of *pecunia* being called from *pecus*, and of the ox or sheep having been at first a substitute for money, as in Greece and Rome, accords with a custom still common among some people, of making them the standard of valuation; in Darfoor and Kordofan a piece of cotton cloth is reckoned equal to a sheep; and in Job (xlii. 11), the name *Kesíteh* (or "lamb") is employed to signify a "piece of money." Homer also reckons the value of certain things as equal to an ox; and in Solon's time a sheep was equivalent "to a bushel and a half of corn."

If stamped money was not used by the ancient Egyptians, we have evidence of weights and measures having been invented by them long before the Greeks existed as a nation: and it is probable that they were known even in Greece previous to the time of Phidon. (*See below*, p. 239, *on the use of the precious metals.*)

One kind of balance used for weighing gold differed slightly from those of ordinary construction, and was probably more delicately formed. It was made, as usual, with an upright pole, rising from a broad base or stand, and a cross beam turning on a pin at its summit; but instead of strings suspending the scales, was an arm on either side, terminating in a hook, to which the gold was attached in small bags. *

Large scales were generally a flat wooden board, with four ropes attached to a ring at the extremity of the beam; and those of smaller size were of bronze, one and a half inch in diameter, pierced near the edge in three places, for the strings.

The principle of the common balance was simple and ingenious; the beam passed through a ring suspended from a horizontal rod, immediately above and parallel to it, and when equally balanced, the ring, which was large enough to allow the beam to play freely, showed when the scales were equally poised, and had the additional effect of preventing the beam tilting, when the goods were taken out of one, and the weights suffered to remain in the other scale.† To the lower part of the ring a small plummet was fixed, and this being touched by the hand, and found to hang freely, indicated, without the necessity of looking at the beam, that the weight was just. The figure of a baboon was sometimes placed upon the top, as the emblem of the god Thoth, the regulator of measures, of time, and of writing, in his character of the moon; but there is no appearance of the goddess of Justice being connected with the balance, except in the judgment scenes of the dead.

The pair of scales was the ordinary and, apparently, only kind of balance used by the Egyptians; no instance of the steel-yard being met with in the paintings of Thebes, or of Beni Hassan: and the introduction of the latter is confined to a Roman era.

The Egyptians had another kind of balance, in which the equalisation of the opposite weights was ascertained by the plummet; and this last, whose invention has been ascribed by Pliny to Dædalus, is shown to have been known and applied in Egypt at least as early as the time of the Osirtasens.

For ordinary purposes copper was most commonly used; arms, vases, statues, instruments, and implements of every kind, articles of furniture, and numerous other objects, were made of this

* *See* woodcut 403, p. 136.　　　　† *See* woodcut 407, p. 148.

metal hardened by an alloy of tin, and even chisels for cutting stone, as well as carpenters' tools, and knives, were of bronze. It is generally allowed that copper or bronze was known long before iron, and though Tubal-Cain is said to have been "the instructor of every artificer in brass and *iron*," no direct mention is made of iron arms or tools till after the Exodus.

According to the Arundelian marbles, iron was known one hundred and eighty-eight years before the Trojan war, about 1370 years B.C., but Hesiod, Plutarch, and others limit its discovery to a much later period, after the capture of Troy. Homer, however, distinctly mentions its use:[*] and that there is little reason to doubt the *sideros* of the poet being iron, is shown by the simile, derived from the quenching of iron in water, which he applies to the hissing noise produced on piercing the eye of Polyphemus with the pointed stake, thus rendered by Pope:

> "And as when armourers temper in the ford
> The keen-edg'd poleaxe, or the shining sword,
> The red hot metal hisses in the lake,
> Thus in his eyeball hiss'd the plunging stake."

His "black *kyanus*" is also thought to be steel, as well as the *adamas* of Hesiod, who mentions the iron of the Idæi Dactyli in Crete; and the skill of the Chalybes in its manufacture dates from a very remote age. Among the earliest authorities for the use of iron, may be cited the bedstead of Og the king of Bashan, who is said to have lived about the year 1450 before our era; and Thrasyllus agrees with the Arundelian marbles in supposing iron to have been known before the Trojan war, or indeed one hundred and fourteen years previous to the foundation of Troy, 1537 before our era. On the other hand it has been argued, that offerings of iron in the temples of Greece distinctly showed the value attached to that metal, as well as its limited use for ordinary purposes, and rings of iron were worn by the ancients, some of which have been found in the tombs of Egypt. But these last are of very late date, long after iron was commonly used, and I possess one of them, engraved with the figure of Harpocrates, which is of a Ptolemaic, or rather of a Roman, era,

[*] Hom. Iliad, xxiii. 261, &c.

and which only claims some degree of interest, from its bearing a device noticed by Pliny as becoming fashionable at Rome in his time.

That iron, as early as the days of Lycurgus, was held in little estimation, is shown by that legislator forbidding the introduction of gold and silver in his republic, and restricting the Spartans to the use of iron; and some notion may be formed of its value at that time by the assertion of Plutarch, that it required a cart drawn by two oxen to carry the small sum of ten minæ.

The Jews appear to have been acquainted with two kinds of iron, previous to the Babylonish captivity; the *barzel*, which was in common use, and the northern iron, as well as steel: even as early as the days of Job iron was known; and Moses mentions an iron furnace.

One of the arguments against the early use of iron is the difficulty of smelting the ore, and of reducing it to a malleable state; and the various processes required to discover all its most useful properties render it less likely to be employed than a more ductile metal. Gold, silver, and copper were easily fused, and a single process sufficed to make them available for every purpose; the principal art required for fabricating implements of copper depending on the proper proportions and qualities of alloy introduced.

In the infancy of the arts and sciences, the difficulty of working iron might long withhold the secret of its superiority over copper and bronze; but it cannot reasonably be supposed that a nation so advanced, and so eminently skilled in the art of working metals as the Egyptians and Sidonians, should have remained ignorant of its use, even if we had no evidence of its having been known to the Greeks and other people; and the constant employment of bronze arms and implements is not a sufficient argument against their knowledge of iron, since we find the Greeks and Romans made the same things of bronze long after the period when iron was universally known.

Another argument, to show that bronze was used in Greece before iron, is derived from the word χαλκευς, " coppersmith," having in Greek the signification of "smith," whether applied to a worker of copper or iron. In Latin, on the contrary, *ferrum*, "an iron," is the word frequently applied to a sword; and some have hence argued the use of iron for those weapons, at the earliest period, among the Romans; which is confirmed by the treaty imposed upon them by Porsena, binding them not to use iron, except for agricultural implements. But long after iron was used by them, the Romans and Etruscans continued to make swords, daggers, spear-heads, and other offensive weapons of bronze, as well as their defensive armour; and the discovery of arms and tools of bronze ceases to argue an ignorance of iron.

To conclude, from the want of iron instruments, or arms, bearing the names of early monarchs of a Pharaonic age, that bronze was alone used, is neither just nor satisfactory; since the decomposition of that metal, especially when buried for ages in the nitrous soil of Egypt, is so speedy as to preclude the possibility of its preservation. Until we know in what manner the Egyptians employed bronze tools for cutting stone, the discovery of them affords no additional light, nor even argument; since the Greeks and Romans continued to make bronze instruments of various kinds so long after iron was known to them; and Herodotus mentions the iron tools used by the builders of the Pyramids.

Iron and copper mines are found in the Egyptian desert, which were worked in old times; and the monuments of Thebes, and even the tombs about Memphis, dating more than 4000 years ago, represent butchers sharpening their knives on a round bar of metal attached to their apron, which from its blue colour can only be steel; and the distinction between the bronze and iron weapons in the tomb of Remeses III., one painted red, the other blue, leaves no doubt of *both* having been used (as in Rome) at the same periods. In Ethiopia iron was much more abundant than in Egypt, and Herodotus states that copper was a rare metal there; though we may doubt his assertion of prisoners in that country having been bound with fetters of gold.

The speedy decomposition of iron would be sufficient to prevent our finding implements of that metal of an early period, and the greater opportunities of obtaining copper ore, added to the facility of working it, might be a reason for preferring the latter whenever it answered the purpose instead of iron. Bronze tools might also be made available for sculpturing and engraving stone ; though there is great difficulty in accounting for their use in mines and quarries, where the stone was frequently hewn with them ; as Agatharcides informs us in his account of the gold mines, and as was evidently done in cutting the limestone rock of the tombs at Thebes ; a bronze chisel having been found amidst the chippings of the stone, where it had been accidentally left by the workmen.

The hieroglyphics on obelisks and other granitic monuments are sculptured with a minuteness and finish which is surprising, even if they had used steel as highly tempered as our own.

Some are cut to the depth of more than two inches, the edges and all the most minute parts of the intaglio presenting the same sharpness and accuracy ; and I have seen the figure of a king in high relief, reposing on the lid of a granite coffin, which was raised to the height of nine inches above the level of the surface. What can be said, if we deny to men who executed such works as these the aid of steel, and confine them to bronze implements? Then, indeed, we exalt their skill in metallurgy far beyond our own, and indirectly confess that they had devised a method of sculpturing stone of which we are ignorant. In vain should we attempt to render copper, by the addition of certain alloys, sufficiently hard to sculpture granite, basalt, and stones of similar quality. No one who has tried to perforate or cut a block of Egyptian granite will scruple to acknowledge that our best steel tools are turned in a very short time, and require to be re-tempered : and the labour experienced by the French engineers, who removed the obelisk of Luxor from Thebes, in cutting a space less than two feet deep, along the face of its partially decomposed pedestal, suffices to show that, even with our excellent modern implements, we find considerable difficulty in doing what to the Egyptians would have been one of the least arduous tasks. The use of tools on granite is thus described by Sir R. Westmacott :—

"Granite, as most hard materials of that nature, being

generally worked with a pick of various strength, until reduced to a surface, the duration of the tool depends on its form; the more obtuse the longer it will work, remaining longer cold. In *jumping* (as it is termed) holes for the admission of bolts into fractured parts of granite, the tools are usually of strong tempered iron, about three-quarters of an inch in diameter, which resist the heat sometimes half an hour, seldom longer. One man holds, and turns, or moves the tool, whilst the other strikes it with a heavy hammer, the hole being supplied with water. Tools of less diameter are formed of steel, but these will not resist more than 300 strokes, when the points fly, and require to be fresh battered. Sculptors generally use tools formed of blistered steel, or of cast steel, the finer sort highly tempered by immersing them, when heated to a proper degree, into cold water."

Some have imagined that the granite, being somewhat softer at the time it is taken from the quarry, was more easily sculptured when the Egyptians put up the obelisks than at present, and thus satisfy themselves that the labour was considerably less; but this argument is entirely overthrown by the fact of other sculptures having been frequently added, one hundred, and one hundred and fifty, years after the erection of a monument, as in the lateral lines of hieroglyphics on obelisks; which are sometimes found more deeply cut and more beautifully executed than those previously sculptured. Others have suggested that the stone being stunned, as it is termed, in those places where it was to be sculptured, yielded more readily to the blow of the chisel; but neither is this sufficient to produce the effect proposed, nor an advantage exclusively enjoyed by the ancient Egyptians.

Thus, then, the facility they possessed of sculpturing granite is neither attributable to any process for bruising the crystals, nor to its softer state on coming from the quarry, and we have still to discover the means they employed with such wonderful success.

The hieroglyphics on the obelisks are rather engraved than sculptured; and, judging from the minute manner in which they are executed, we may suppose they adopted the same process as engravers, and even in some instances employed the wheel and drill. That they were acquainted with the use of emery powder is not at all improbable, since, being found in the islands of the Archipelago, it was within their reach; and if this be admitted, we can account for the admirable finish and sharpness of the hieroglyphics on granitic and basaltic monuments, and explain the reason of their preferring tools of bronze to those of harder and more compact steel: for it is evident the powder enters more readily into the former, and its action upon the stone is increased in proportion to the quantity retained by the point of the chisel; whence we now prefer tools of soft iron to hard steel for the same purpose.

As far as the sculpture or engraving of hieroglyphics, this explanation might suffice for their preference of bronze implements; but when we find tools used in *quarries* made of the same metal, we are unable to account for it, and readily express our surprise how they could render a bronze chisel capable of hewing stone. We know of no means of tempering copper, under any form or united with any alloys, for such a purpose. The addition of tin or other metals to harden it, if exceeding certain proportions, renders it too brittle for use; and that such is not the case is evident from the above-mentioned chisel I found at Thebes, which contains very little alloy, 100 parts being   94·0 copper,

$$5·9 \text{ tin,}$$
$$0·1 \text{ iron,}$$
$$\overline{100·0};$$

and its point is instantly turned by striking it against the very stone it was once used to cut. And yet when found the summit was turned over by the blows it had received from the mallet, while the point was intact, as if it had recently left the hands of the smith who made it.

It is difficult to say how it could have been used for cutting stone, and unless some medium was employed, as a sheath of steel or other protection to its point, the Egyptians must have possessed certain secrets in hardening or tempering copper, with which we are totally unacquainted. The size of this chisel is 9¼ inches in length; its diameter at the summit is 1 inch, and the point is 7-10ths of an inch in its greatest width: its weight 1 lb. 12 oz., and in general form it resembles those now used by the masons of modern Europe.

The skill of the Egyptians in compounding metals is abundantly proved by the vases, mirrors, arms, and implements of bronze, discovered at Thebes, and other parts of Egypt; and the numerous methods they adopted for varying the composition of bronze, by a judicious admixture of alloys, are shown in the many qualities of the metal. They had even the secret of giving to bronze, or brass, blades a certain degree of elasticity; as in the dagger of the Berlin Museum; which probably depended on the mode of hammering the metal, and the just proportions of peculiar alloys. (*See* vol. i. p. 148.)

Another remarkable feature in their bronze is the resistance it offers to the effect of the atmosphere; some continuing smooth and bright, though buried for ages, and since exposed to the damp of European climates. They had also the secret of covering the surface with a rich patina of dark or light green, or other colour, by applying acids to it; as was done by the Greeks and Romans, and as we do to the iron guns on board our men-of-war.

The colour of their bronze depended on the alloys. It generally had from twelve to twenty parts tin to eighty or eighty-five copper. When half tin it had a whitish appearance; and some Roman bronze was of a " liver colour," probably like our urns. Lackered brass has even been found, of Roman time. Yellow brass was a compound of zinc and copper; and a white and finer kind had a mixture of silver, which was used for mirrors, and is one quality of the so-called " Corinthian brass." Another, which was yellow, and very like gold in appearance, was partly made of that metal with copper; and its beauty has been proved by the discovery of a cup, still capable of receiving some portion of its original polish.

In Egypt, as in Greece, bronze ornaments were often gilt, but statues were preferred plain, or inlaid, or damaskened with gold or silver. Those of the Navarchai were, therefore, said by Plutarch to be blue from exposure to the air; and Pliny thinks the large colossus of Nero improved by the gilding having been scraped off, in spite of the scratches caused by the operation.

It is not known at what period they began to cast statues and other objects in bronze, or how long the use of beaten copper preceded the art of casting in that metal. No light is thrown on this point by the earlier paintings, nor is there any representation in later times, among the many subjects connected with the trades, arts, and occupations of the Egyptians, which relates to this process :—one of the many proofs that no argument against the existence of a custom ought to be derived from the circumstance of its not being indicated on the monuments.

Many bronzes have been found, evidently, from their style, of a very early period. A cylinder, with the name of Papi, of the 6th Dynasty, has every appearance of having been cast ; and other bronze implements of the same age bear still stronger evidence of having come from a mould ; all of which date more than two thousand years before our era.

Pausanias, in speaking of the art of casting metal, says the people of Pheneum in Arcadia pretended that Ulysses dedicated a statue of bronze to Neptune Hippius, in order that he might recover the horses he had lost, through the intervention of the Deity ; " indeed," he adds, " they showed me an inscription on the pedestal of the statue offering a reward to any person who should find and take care of the animals ; but I do not give credit to the whole of their statement, and no one can persuade me that Ulysses erected a *bronze* statue to Neptune. The art of fusing metal and casting it in a mould was not yet known; a statue was made in those times like a dress, successively, and in pieces, not at one time, or in a single mass, as I have already shown in speaking of the statue of Jupiter, surnamed the Most High.   In fact, the first who cast statues were Rhœcus the son of Philæus, and Theodorus the son of Telecles, both natives of Samos ; the latter the same who engraved the beautiful emerald in the ring of Polycrates."

The Samians were noted at an early period for their skill in this branch of art ; and before the foundation of Cyrene, or B.C. 630, they made a bronze vase, ornamented with griffins, supported on three colossal figures of the same metal, for the temple of Juno.   The art was also known at a very remote period in Italy.

Among the Etruscans, bronze statues were common, before the foundation of Rome ; and Romulus is said to have placed a statue of himself, crowned by Victory, in a four-horsed car of bronze, which had been captured at the taking of Camerium.

Pliny attributes the discovery of gold and the secret of smelting it to Cadmus, who is supposed to have gone to Greece 1493 years before our era; but this, like most of the inventions mentioned by him, was long before known to the Egyptians; and we may apply the same remark to the supposed discovery of Rhœcus and Theodorus.

It is uncertain whether the Egyptians possessed the art of damaskening or inlaying iron with gold, since, owing to the speedy decomposition of that metal, nothing made of iron has been preserved of a remote era ; but we may conclude, from their inlaying bronze in this manner, that it was not unknown to them.

Some have supposed that Glaucus of Chios was the inventor of this art, and that the stand of his silver vase presented to the temple of Delphi by Alyattes king of Lydia, which, according to Herodotus, was the most beautiful of all the offerings there, was made of iron inlaid with gold. But the description given of it by Pausanias will scarcely sanction this opinion, as he states " it consisted of several plates of iron, adjusted one over the other in the form of steps, the last, that is, those of the summit, curving a little outwards. It had the form of a tower, large at the base, and decreasing upwards, and the pieces of which it was composed were not fastened either with nails or pins, but simply soldered together."

The Greeks, however, were not ignorant of damaskening, and if the stand of Alyattes' vase was not so inlaid, it is certain they possessed the art, and ornamented goblets and other objects in that manner. The process was very simple: the iron was carved with various devices, and the narrow lines thus hollowed out were filled with gold, or with silver, which in some instances may have been soldered, but in others was simply beaten in with the hammer, the surface being afterwards filed and polished.

The term damaskening, though generally confined to iron or steel so inlaid (owing to its having been borrowed from the specimens of this work in the modern sword blades of Damascus), may with equal propriety be extended to any metal; and numerous instances of bronze inlaid with gold and silver occur in statues, scarabæi, and various ornamental objects discovered at Thebes and other places. Hard stones were also engraved in the same manner, and the intaglio filled with gold or silver beaten into it; a process commonly adopted at the present day by the Turks, and other Eastern people, in their *hookahs* or *nârgilehs*, and in the stone ornaments of their amber mouth-pieces.

The art of soldering metals had long been practised in Egypt before the time of Glaucus; and it is curious to find gold and bronze vases, made apparently in the same manner as the stand of that mentioned by Pausanias, represented at Thebes, in the tribute brought from Asia to the third Thothmes, and consequently dating many centuries previous to the Chian artist. They are shown to have been composed of plates of metal, imbricated, or overlapping each other, as Pausanias describes, and sometimes bound at intervals with bands of metal. Instances occur in the same sculptures of gold vases with stands formed of similar plates; which are interesting also from the elegance of their forms.

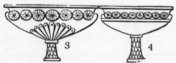

409.   Vases of the time of Thothmes III., imbricated, or ornamented with plates of metal.   *Thebes.*

In coarser work, or in those parts which were out of sight, the Egyptians soldered with lead, but we are ignorant of the time when it was first used for that purpose, though it could only have been after the discovery of tin; for, as Pliny justly observes, "lead can only be united by the addition of tin, nor is this last efficient without the application of oil." The oldest specimen of metal soldered with lead with which I am acquainted is the sistrum of Mr. Burton: its date, however, is uncertain; and though, from the style of the figures engraved upon it, we may venture to ascribe to it a Pharaonic age, the exact period when it was made cannot be fixed.

In early ages, before men had acquired the art of smelting ore, and of making arms and implements of metal, stones of various kinds were used, and the chasseur was contented with the pointed flint with which nature had provided him. The only effort of his ingenuity was to fix it in some kind of handle, or at the extremity of a reed, in order to make the knife, or the arrow; and we still witness the skill which some savage people of the present day display in constructing those rude weapons.

The Egyptians, at a remote period, before civilization dawned upon them, adopted the same; and we find that stone-tipped arrows continued to be occasionally used for hunting long after the metal head had been commonly adopted, and after the arts had arrived at the state of perfection in which they appear subsequently to the accession of the 18th dynasty. Long habit had reconciled them to the original reed shaft with its head of flint, and even to arrows made with a point of hard wood inserted into them, which were also the remnant of a primæval custom. Those, however, who preferred them of a stronger kind, adopted arrows of wood tipped with bronze heads; and these were considered more serviceable, and were almost invariably used in war.

The same prejudice in favour of an ancient and primitive custom retained the use of stone knives for certain purposes connected with religion among the Egyptians; and Herodotus tells us it was usual to make an incision in the body of the deceased, when brought to be embalmed, with an Ethiopic stone. This name, in all instances where the stone is said to be used for cutting, evidently signifies flint, which is shown by its frequent employment for that purpose among many people, and by our finding several flint knives in the tombs of Thebes. In other cases, the Ethiopic stone, mentioned by Herodotus, is evidently granite, so called from being common in Ethiopia; and it is possible that the flint received that name from its *black* colour.

The stone knives found in the excavations and tombs, many of which are preserved in our European museums, are generally of two kinds; one broad and flat like the blade of a knife, the other

narrow and pointed at the summit, several of which are preserved in the Berlin Museum (*fig.* 1).   These last are supposed
to have been used for making the incision in the side of the body,
for the purpose of removing the intestines, preparatory to the
embalming process already mentioned ; and, considering how
strongly men's minds are prepossessed in favour of early habits
connected with religion, and how scrupulous the Egyptians were,
above all people, in permitting the introduction of new customs
in matters relating to the gods, we are not surprised that they
should have retained the use of these primitive instruments in a
ceremony of so sacred a nature as the embalming of the dead.

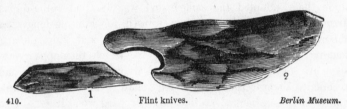

410.   Flint knives.   *Berlin Museum.*

The difference in the type of the metal implements of the Egyptians and early European people is very marked.   The former
continued always to use flat blades of metal for adzes and hatchets ;
those of Italy, Greece, the Tyrol, Gaul, Britain, Ireland, and other
parts of Europe, gradually changed the form of the flat blade
(which had succeeded to the stone hammer and hatchet), and
gave it projecting sides, then a transverse ridge in the centre to
prevent the shifting of the wooden handle fitted *upon* it, and to
withstand the shock of a blow ; and at length they made it into
a metal socket, with which the wood was shod.   The mode of
fastening the metal to the handle was the same in Europe as in
Egypt ; which was with thongs of hide (as is still done in the
South Sea Islands and other places) ; but our various forms of
celtes, or "hatchets," were unknown to, and are readily distinguished from the tools of, the Egyptians.

Besides the various trades already noticed, were public weighers
and common notaries, answering to the *kabbáneh* of modern
Egypt.   The business of the former was to ascertain the exact
weight of everything they were called upon to measure, in the

public street or market, where they temporarily erected their scales, and where the law compelled them to adjust the sale of each commodity with the strictest regard to justice, without favouring either the buyer or seller. All things sold by weight were submitted to this test, and the value of the money paid for them was settled by the same unquestionable criterion.

A scribe or notary marked down the amount of the weight, whatever the commodity might be; and this document, being given or shown to the parties, completely sanctioned the bargain, and served as a pledge that justice had been done them.

The same custom is still retained by the modern Egyptians, the scales of the public *kabbáneh* in the large towns being a criterion to which no one can object; and the weight of meat, vegetables, honey, butter, cheese, wood, charcoal, and other objects, having been ascertained, is returned in writing on the application of the parties.

The notaries were merely public writers, like the modern *katebs* of Egypt, or the *scrivani* of Italy, who for a small trifle compose and pen a petition to government, settle accounts, and write letters, or other documents not requiring the priest or the lawyer, for those who are untaught, or too idle to do so for themselves. These persons, however, must not be confounded with the "royal" or "priestly scribes"—men of high rank, of the military or sacerdotal class; and they were only on a par with the shopkeepers and master tradesmen, most of whom learnt to write; while the working men were contented to occupy their time in acquiring a knowledge of the art to which they were brought up.

Certain persons were also employed in the towns of Egypt, as at the present day in Cairo and other places, to pound various substances in large stone mortars; and salt, seeds, and other things were taken in the same manner by a servant to these shops, whenever it was inconvenient to have it done in the house. The pestles they used, as well as the mortars themselves, were precisely similar to those of the modern Egyptians; and their mode of pounding was the same; two men alternately raising ponderous metal pestles with both hands, and directing their falling

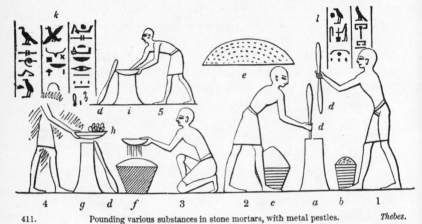

411.   Pounding various substances in stone mortars, with metal pestles.   *Thebes.*

a g i, mortars.   *d d,* pestles.   Figs. 1 and 2, alternately raising and letting fall the pestles into the mortar.   Figs. 3 and 4, sifting the substance after it is pounded; the coarser parts, *h,* being returned into the mortar to be again pounded.

point to the centre of the mortar, which is now generally made of a large piece of granite, or other hard stone, scooped out into a long narrow tube, to little more than half its depth. When the substance was well pounded, it was taken out, and passed through a sieve, and the larger particles were again returned to the mortar, until it was sufficiently and equally levigated; and this, and the whole process here represented, so strongly resemble the occupation of the public pounders at Cairo, that no one, who has been in the habit of walking in the streets of that town, can fail to recognise the custom, or doubt of its having been handed down from the early Egyptians, and retained without alteration to the present day.

The occupation of the cooper was comparatively limited in Egypt, where water and other liquids were carried, or kept, in skins and earthenware jars; and wooden barrels were little suited to its arid climate. Barrels were not, therefore, in common use there; and the skill of the cooper was only required to make wooden measures for grain, which were bound with hoops either of wood or metal, and resembled in principle those used by the modern Egyptians for the same purpose; though in form some approached nearer to the small barrels, or kegs, of modern Europe.

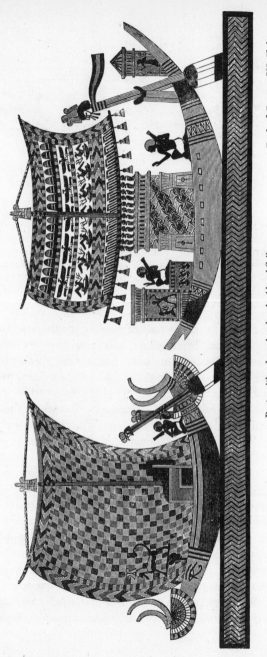

Boats with coloured and embroidered Sails.

Tomb of Remeses III. Thebes.

Cattle during the Inundation in the Delta.

CHAPTER VIII.

THE FIFTH CLASS — PASTORS, POULTERERS, SHOPS, FOWLERS, FISHERMEN, LABOURERS, BRICKMAKERS, AND COMMON PEOPLE — JEWS — PEOPLE GIVING AN ACCOUNT OF THEIR MODE OF LIVING — LAWS — JUDGES — CRIMES AND PUNISHMENTS — THIEVES — DEBTORS — SALES AND DEEDS — MARRIAGES — PARENTS — LAWGIVERS — PROVINCES AND GOVERNORS — REVENUES —GOLD — MENSURATION — THREE SEASONS — INTERCALATION — SOTHIC YEAR — LAND MEASURES — CUBIT — WEIGHTS AND MEASURES.

THE fifth class was composed of pastors, poulterers, fowlers, fishermen, labourers, brickmakers, and common people. The pastors were divided into oxherds, shepherds, goatherds, and swineherds; but even among them a gradation of rank was observed; and those who tended the herds and flocks while grazing were inferior in position to the managers of stock in the farmyard, who prepared provender for them when the Nile covered the lands. Those too who understood the veterinary art and took care of the sick cattle were men of skill and intelligence, who held a higher post among the pastors. But they were all looked upon by the Egyptian aristocracy as people who followed a disgraceful employment; and it is therefore not surprising that Pharaoh should have treated the Israelites with that contempt which it was usual for the Egyptians to feel towards " shepherds ;" or that Joseph should have warned his brethren on their arrival, of this aversion of the Egyptians, and of their considering every shepherd an abomination. And from his recommending them to request they might dwell in the land of Goshen, we may conclude it was with a view to avoid as much as possible those who were not shepherds like themselves, or to obtain a settlement in the land peculiarly adapted for pasture.   It is also probable that much of Pharaoh's cattle was kept there, since the monarch gave orders that if any of those strangers were remarkable for skill in the management of herds, they should be selected to overlook his own cattle, after they were settled in the land of Goshen. This part of the country received at a later time the name of *Bucolia;* and the northern part of the Delta, with the lands lying to the east of the Damietta branch of the Nile, are still preferred for grazing cattle.

The hatred borne against shepherds by the Egyptians was not owing solely to their contempt for that occupation ; this feeling originated in another and a far more powerful cause—the occupation of their country by a pastor race, who had committed great cruelties during their possession of the country.   And as if to prove how much they despised every order of pastors, the artists, both of Upper and Lower Egypt, delighted on all occasions in caricaturing their appearance.

The swineherds were the most ignoble, and of all the Egyptians the only persons who are said not to have been permitted to enter a temple ; and even if this statement is exaggerated, it tends to show with what contempt they were looked upon by the individuals from whom Herodotus received his information, and how far they ranked beneath any others of the whole order of pastors.   Indeed (as I have before stated) the same is still the case in India, where the swineherds are the very lowest class, and are so despised that no others will associate with them.

The skill of these people in rearing animals of different kinds was the result, says Diodorus, of the experience they had inherited from their parents, and subsequently increased by their own observation ; and the spirit of emulation, which is natural to all men, constantly adding to their stock of knowledge, they introduced many improvements unknown to other people.   Their sheep were twice shorn, and twice brought forth lambs in the course of one year ; and though the climate was the chief cause of these phenomena, the skill and attention of the shepherd were also necessary ; nor, if the animals were neglected, would unaided nature alone suffice for their continuance.

But of all the discoveries to which any class of Egyptians attained, the one that the historian considered most worthy of admiration was their artificial process of hatching the eggs of fowls and geese ; which has been continued to the present day by their Copt successors. The modern process, like that of ancient times, is this : they have ovens expressly built for the purpose ; and persons are sent round to the villages to collect the eggs from the peasants, which, being given to the rearers, are all placed on

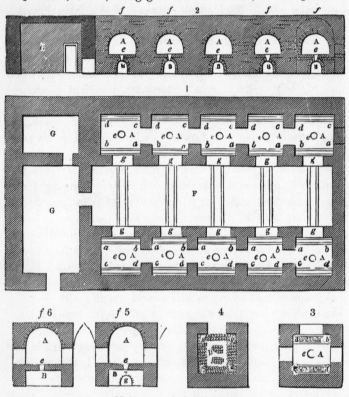

412.   Modern ovens for hatching eggs.

Fig. 1. Plan of the building, showing the form of the upper rooms A A, the entrance-room G G, and the passage F. At *a a* are the fires ; *e e* the aperture communicating with the oven.
 2. Section of the same, showing the upper rooms A and B.
 3. Plan of upper room, in which the fires are placed at *a b* and *c d*.
 4. Lower room in which the eggs are placed.
 5, 6. Sections from the back and front of the upper and lower rooms A and B.

mats, strewed with bran, in a room about eleven feet square, with a flat roof, and about four feet high, over which is another chamber of the same size, with a vaulted roof and about nine feet high ; a small aperture in the centre of the vault (at f), admitting light during the warm weather, and another (e) of larger diameter, immediately below, communicating with the oven through its ceiling. By this also the man descends to observe the eggs ; but in the cold season both are closed, and a lamp is kept burning within ; another entrance at the front part of the oven, or lower room, being then used for the same purpose, and shut immediately on his quitting it. By way of distinction, I call the vaulted (A) the upper room, and the lower one (B) the oven. In the former are two fires in the troughs $a \, b$, and $c \, d$, which, based with earthen slabs, three quarters of an inch thick, reach from one side to the other against the front and back walls. These fires are lighted twice a day : the first dies away about midday ; and the second, lighted at 3 p.m., lasts until 8 o'clock. In the oven, the eggs are placed on mats strewed with bran, in two lines corresponding to, and immediately below, the fires $a \, b$ and $c \, d$, where they remain half a day. They are then removed to $a \, c$ and $b \, d$; and others (from two heaps in the centre) are arranged at $a \, b$ and $c \, d$ in their stead ; and so on, till all have taken their equal share of the warmest positions ; to which each set returns again and again, in regular succession, till the expiration of six days.

They are then held up, one by one, towards a strong light ; and if the eggs appear clear, and of an uniform colour, it is evident they have not succeeded ; but if they show an opaque substance within, or the appearance of different shades, the chickens are already formed ; and they are returned to the oven for four more days, their positions being changed as before. At the expiration of the four days they are removed to another oven, over which, however, are no fires. Here they lie for five days in one heap, the apertures (e, f) and the door (g) being closed with tow to exclude the air ; after which they are placed separately about one or two inches apart, over the whole surface of the mats, which are sprinkled with a little bran. They are at this time continually turned, and shifted from one part of the mats to another, during six or seven days, all air being carefully excluded; and are constantly examined by one of the rearers, who applies each singly to his upper eyelid. Those which are cold prove the chickens to be dead, but warmth greater than the human skin is the favourable sign of their success.

At length the chicken, breaking its egg, gradually comes forth : and it is not a little curious to see some half exposed and half covered by the shell; while they chirp in their confinement, which they show the greatest eagerness to quit.

The total number of days is generally twenty-one, but some eggs with a thin shell remain only eighteen. The average of those that succeed is two-thirds, which are returned by the rearers to the proprietors, who restore to the peasants one-half of the chickens; the other being kept as payment for their expenses.

The size of the building depends, of course, on the means or speculation of the proprietors; but the general plan is usually the same, being a series of eight or ten ovens and upper rooms, on either side of a passage about 100 feet by 15, and 12 in height. The thermometer in any part is not less than 86° or 88° Fahr.; but the average heat in the ovens does not reach the temperature of fowls, which is 104°.

Excessive heat or cold are equally prejudicial to this process; and the only season of the year at which they succeed is from the 15th of Imsheer (23rd of February) to the 15th of Baramoodeh (24th of April), beyond which time they can scarcely reckon upon more than two or three in a hundred.

The great care bestowed by the shepherds on the breed of sheep, was attended with no less important results; and the selection of proper food for them at particular seasons, and the mode of treating them when ill, were their constant study. Indeed their skill in curing animals was carried to the greatest perfection; and Cuvier's discovery of the left *humerus* of a mummied ibis fractured and reunited, evidently through the intervention of human art, fully confirms the fact.

Those who exercised the veterinary art were of the class of

1   2   3   4   5   6   7

Beni Hassan.

413.

Herdsmen and poulterers treating sick animals and geese.

Fig. 1. Feeding a sick goose.
2. In the original, this figure shows more skill in the drawing than is usual in Egyptian sculpture.
3. Feeding an oryx.
4, 5. Treatment of goats.   The foreleg is tied up to prevent the animal rising while the medicine is administered to it.
7. Forces a ball of medicated food taken from the vase before him into the ox's mouth.

shepherds.   They took the utmost care of the animals, providing
them with proper food, which they gave them with the hand,
and preparing for them whatever medicine they required, which
they forced into their mouths.   Their medical aid was not confined to oxen and sheep ; it extended also to the oryx, and other
animals of the desert they tamed or bred in the farmyard ; and
the poulterers bestowed the same care on the geese and fowls

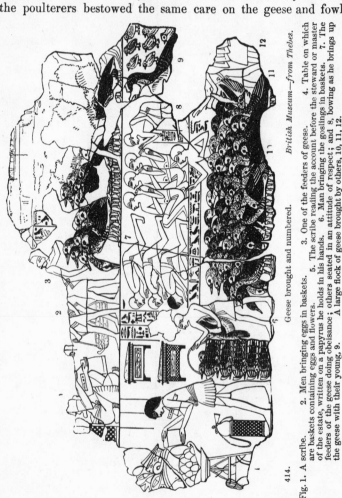

British Museum—from Thebes.

Geese brought and numbered.

414.   Fig. 1. A scribe.   2. Men bringing eggs in baskets.   3. One of the feeders of geese.   4. Table on which
are baskets containing eggs and flowers.   5. The scribe reading the account before the steward or master
of the estate, written on a papyrus he holds in his hands.   6. Man bringing the goslings in baskets.   7. The
feeders of the geese doing obeisance ; others seated in an attitude of respect ; and 8, bowing as he brings up
the geese with their young, 9.   A large flock of geese brought by others, 10, 11, 12.

And such was their attention to the habits of different animals, and the patient treatment of them, that the wildest and most timid were rendered so tame as to be driven, like the sheep and goats; and the wild geese and other birds were brought to the stewards, whenever an inventory was made of the live stock on the estate.

The pastors were a class apart from the agriculturists, and were held in disrepute, partly from the nature of their occupation, partly from the prejudices of the Egyptians against all herdsmen. But this did not extend to the farmers who bred cattle or sheep; it was confined to the poor people who kept them; and as if to show how degraded a class they were, they are represented, as at Beni Hassan and the tombs near the Pyramids, lame, or deformed, dirty, unshaven, and even of a ludicrous appearance; and often clad in dresses made of matting, similar in quality to the covering thrown over the backs of the oxen they are tending.

415.   A deformed oxherd.   *Tombs near the Pyramids.*

They generally lived in sheds made of reeds; deriving a scanty nourishment from the humblest and coarsest food; but they were overlooked by other persons of a superior condition among the pastoral class. There were also overseers of the shepherds, who regulated everything respecting the stock;—which were to graze in the field, which to be stall-fed;—and their duty was also to give reports at certain periods to the scribes attached to the stewards' office, who examined them preparatory to their being presented to the owner of the estate. In these nothing

was omitted; and every egg was noted in the account, and
entered with the chickens and goslings.   And in order to prevent

416.   Giving an account to two scribes of the stock on the estate.   *Thebes.*
Before fig. 1 is the sachel, and above fig. 2 the box for holding writing implements and
papyri.   They are writing on boards: in their left hands are the inkstands with black and
red ink.

any connivance, or a question respecting the accuracy of a report, two scribes received it from the superintendents at the same
moment.   Everything was done in writing.   Bureaucratie was
as consequential in Egypt as in modern Austria, or France;
scribes were required on every occasion, to settle public or
private questions; no bargain of consequence was made without
the vouchure of a written document; and the sale of a small
piece of land required sixteen witnesses.   Either the Egyptians
were great cheats, or a very cautious people—probably both; and
they would have been in an agony of mind to see us so careless,
and so duped in many of our railway and other speculations.

The shepherds on the estate were chosen by the steward, who
ascertained their character and skill, before they were appointed
to their various duties; and Pharaoh in like manner commanded
Joseph, who was superintendent " over all the land of Egypt,"
to select from among his brethren such as were skilful in the
management of the flocks or herds, and " make them rulers over
his cattle."

There was also the honorary office of " superintendent of the

herds;" but this was very different from the duty of any one in
the class of shepherds: it was a high and distinguished post,
being held by persons of rank belonging to the priestly and
military classes, who were called "superintendents of the cattle

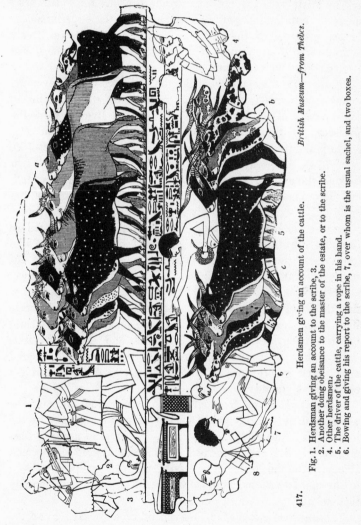

British Museum—from Thebes.

Herdsmen giving an account of the cattle.

Fig. 1. Herdsman giving an account to the scribe, 3,
2. Another doing obeisance to the master of the estate, or to the scribe.
4. Other herdsmen;
5. The driver of the cattle, carrying a rope in his hand.
6. Bowing and giving his report to the scribe, 7, over whom is the usual sachel, and two boxes.

417.

of the king," or " of some god ;" and one of the former, named Honofr, whose wife was one of the sacred women of Amun, is mentioned in a very beautiful papyrus in the British Museum.

The cattle were brought into a court attached to the steward's house, or into the farmyard, and counted by the superintendent in the presence of the scribes; and the bastinado was freely administered if any fraud was detected, or if any shepherd had neglected the flocks committed to his care.

In the accompanying woodcut the numbers written over the animals correspond to the report made to the steward, who, in the presence of the master of the estate, receives it from the overseer, or the head shepherd. First come the oxen, over which is the number 834, then cows 220, goats 3234, asses 760, rams 974; followed by a man carrying the young lambs in baskets slung upon a pole. The steward leaning on his staff, and accompanied by what was then a fashionable dog, "with a curly tail," stands on the left of the picture; and in another place the scribes are making out the statements presented to them by the different persons employed on the farm. The tomb where this subject occurs is at the Pyramids, dating upwards of 4000 years ago, when the Egyptians had already the same customs as at a much later period. How long before this they had reached this state of civilization; had laid aside their arms; had decimal as well as duodecimal calculation, and the reckoning by units, tens, hundreds, and thousands, it is impossible to determine; but these, as well as the use of squared stone, even granite, and many other arts, were known to them before the Pyramids were built.

Many birds which frequented the interior and skirts of the desert, and were highly prized for the table, were caught by the fowlers, as the partridge, *gutta* (*pterocles*, or sand-grouse), bustard, and quail; and waterfowl of different descriptions, which abounded in the Valley of the Nile, afforded endless diversion to the sportsman, and profit to those who gained a livelihood by their sale.

Fowling was a favourite amusement of all classes; and the

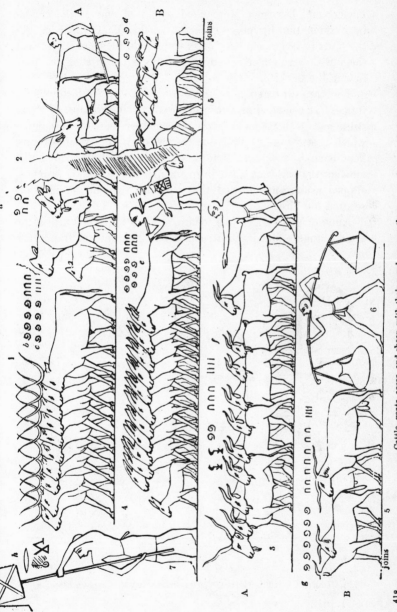

Cattle, goats, asses, and sheep, with their numbers over them.
Fig. 1. The number 834 over long-horned oxen. Fig. 2. 220 cows with calves. Fig. 3. 3234 goats.   Fig. 4. 760 asses.   Fig. 5. 974 sheep.
Fig. 7 gives in the account to the steward of the estate.   In the original, the two upper lines join the two lower ones at A and B.

In a Tomb near the Pyramids.

418.

fowlers and fishermen were subdivisions of one of the classes into which the Egyptians were divided. They either caught the birds in large clap-nets, or in traps; and they sometimes shot them with arrows, or felled them with a throw-stick, as they flew in the thickets. (*See* vol. i. p. 234 to 236.)

The trap was generally made of network, strained over a frame. It consisted of two semicircular sides or flaps, of equal sizes, one or both moving on the common bar, or axis, upon which they rested. When the trap was set, the two flaps were kept open by means of strings, probably of catgut, which, the moment the bait that stood in the centre of the bar was touched, slipped aside, and allowed the two flaps to collapse, and thus secured the bird.

Anotner kind, which was square, appears to have closed in the same manner; but its construction was different, the framework

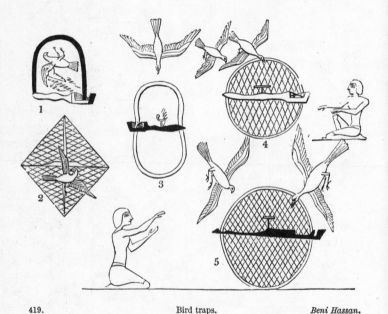

419.   Bird traps.   *Beni Hassan.*

Fig. 1. Trap closed, and the bird caught in it; the net-work of it has been effaced, as also in fig. 3. The other traps are open.

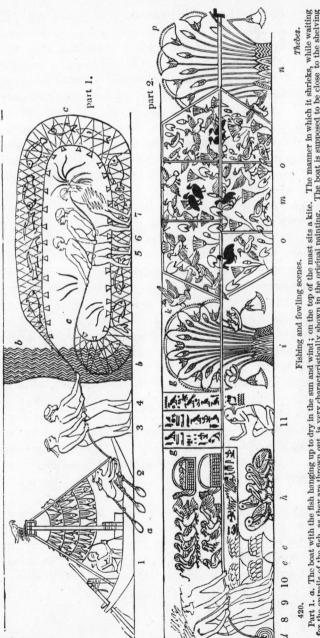

part 1.

part 2.

Thebes.

Fishing and fowling scenes.

420. Part 1. *a.* The boat with the fish hanging up to dry in the sun and wind; on the top of the mast sits a kite. The manner in which it shrieks, while waiting for the entrails of the fish, as they are thrown out, is very characteristically shown in the original painting. The boat is supposed to be close to the shelving bank to which they are dragging the net. The water is represented by zigzag lines at *b*, which, to prevent confusion, I have not continued over the net.

Part 2. Figs. 8, 9, 10, 11, pull the rope that the net may collapse; 11 makes a sign with his hand to keep silence and pull; at *p* the rope is fixed; at *f, g, e,* are geese and baskets of their young and eggs; *h,* are pelicans; *i* and *n,* papyrus plants.

running across the centre, and not, as in the others, round the edges of the trap.

And so skilful were they in making traps, that they were strong enough to hold the hyæna; and in the one which caught the robber in the treasury of Rhampsinitus, the power of the spring, or the mechanism of the catch, was so perfect that his brother was unable to open it, or release him.

Similar in ingenuity, though not in strength, were the nets made by the convicts banished to Rhinocolura by Actisanes, which, though made of split straws, were yet capable of catching many of the numerous quails that frequented that desert region at a particular period of the year.

The clap-net was of different forms, though on the same general principle as the traps. It consisted of two sides or frames, over which the network was strained; at one end was a short rope, which they fastened to a bush, or a cluster of reeds, and at the other was one of considerable length, which, as soon as the birds were seen feeding in the area within the net, was pulled by the fowlers, causing the two sides to collapse.*

As soon as they had selected a convenient spot for laying down the net, in a field or on the surface of a pond, the known resort of numerous wild fowl, they spread open the two sides or flaps. and secured them in such a manner that they remained flat upon the ground, until pulled by the rope. A man, crouched behind some reeds, growing at a convenient distance from the spot, from which he could observe the birds as they came down, watched the net, and enjoining silence by placing his hand over his mouth, beckoned to those holding the rope to keep themselves in readiness, till he saw them assembled in sufficient numbers; when a wave of his hand gave the signal for closing the net.

The Egyptian mode of indicating silence is evidently shown, from these scenes, to have been by placing "the hand on their mouth," (as in Job xxix. 9), not as generally supposed, by approaching the forefinger to the lips; and the Greeks erroneously concluded that the youthful Harpocrates was the deity of silence,

* Woodcut 420, part 2.

from his appearing in this attitude ; which, however humiliating
to the character of a deity, was only illustrative of his extreme

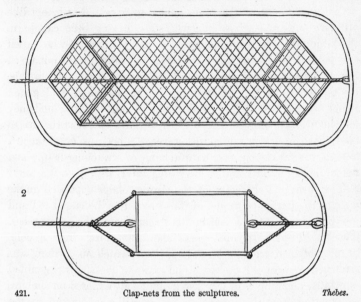

421.   Clap-nets from the sculptures.   *Thebes.*

youth, and of a habit common to children in every country,
whether of ancient or modern times.

The poulterers may be divided into two grades,—the rearers,
and those who sold poultry in the market; the former living in
the country and villages, the latter in the towns.   They fed them
for the table ; and besides the number required for private consumption, a great many were exclusively fattened for the service
of the temple, as well as for the sacred animals, and for the
daily rations of the priests and soldiers, or others who lived at
the government expense.   The birds were principally geese,
ducks, teal, quails, and some small birds, which they were in the
habit of salting, especially in Lower Egypt, where they ate "all
sorts of birds and fish, not reckoned sacred, either roasted or
boiled."   For besides geese and pigeons, which abounded in
Egypt, many of the wading tribe—the ardea and several others—
were esteemed for the table, and even introduced among the

choice offerings to the gods.   But the favourite was the *Vul-panser* of the Nile, known to us as " the Egyptian goose," which, with some others of the same genus, were tamed and kept like ordinary poultry.   Those in a wild state, having been caught in the large clap-nets, were brought to the poulterers, who salted and potted them in earthenware jars ; and others were put up in the shops for immediate sale.   Like other rearers of animals, the poulterers paid great attention to the habits of wild geese, which were tamed to feed in flocks, like our turkies ; and they had doubtless perceived that, besides warmth, chickens require to have their food constantly within reach ; perhaps even buried, that they may exercise their natural habit of scratching it up ; and not to have a great quantity after long intervals.

The form and character of the various shops depended on the will, or the particular trade, of the person they belonged to ; and many no doubt sat and sold in the streets, as at the present day. The poulterers suspended geese and other birds from a pole, or on nails, in front of the shop, over which an awning was stretched to keep off the sun ; and many of the shops resembled our stalls, being open in front, with the goods exposed on shelves, or hanging from the inner wall, as is still the custom in the *bazárs* of eastern towns.

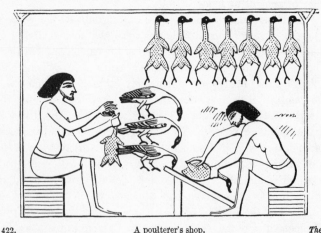

422.   A poulterer's shop.   *Thebes.*

The distribution of labour seems to have been as well understood by the Egyptians as in modern times; one plucked, another opened and trussed, and a third potted, or hung up the birds; and the same variety of offices was allotted to different individuals in other trades.   Part of the occupation

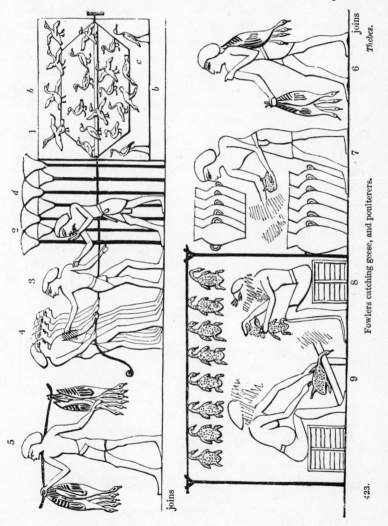

Fowlers catching geese, and poulterers.

423.

of poulterers was to collect eggs of wild birds; and whenever
these could be procured they were carefully collected and submitted to the management of the rearers, like those of tame
fowl.   The same care was taken to obtain the young of gazelles,
and other wild animals of the desert, whose meat was reckoned
among the dainties of the table; and by paying proper attention to their habits, they were enabled to collect many
head of antelopes, which formed part of the herds of the
Egyptian nobles.   And in order to give an idea of the pains
they took in rearing these timid animals, and to show the great
value of the possessions of the deceased, they are introduced with
the cattle, in the sculptures of the tombs.

Those who were fishermen by trade, and gained a livelihood
by it, generally used the net in preference to the line; though
on some occasions they employed the latter, seated or standing
on the bank.   But these last were poor people who could not
afford the expense of nets; and the use of their very simple line
was mostly confined, as at the present day, to those who depended on skill or good luck for a precarious subsistence.   If
we may believe Ælian—that most unsophisticated fish, the
Thrissa of the Lake Mareotis, "was caught by singing to it,

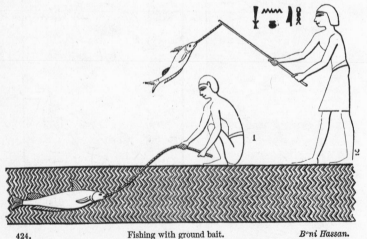

424.   Fishing with ground bait.   *Bᵉni Hassan.*
                 These fish are the *Shilbeh*, or rather the *Arábrab.*

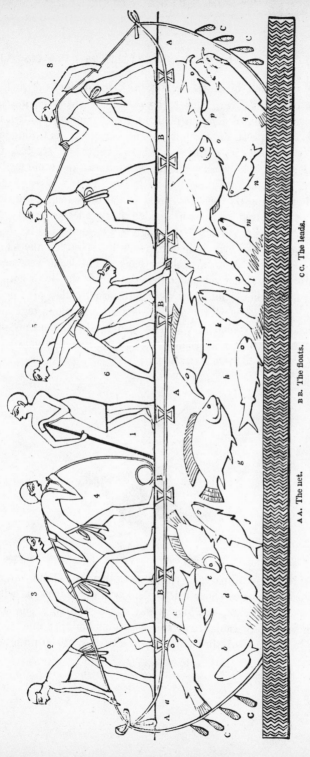

425.

A A. The net.   B B. The floats.   C C. The leads.

Fishing with a drag-net.

Tomb near the Pyramids

and by the sound of *crotala* (clappers) made of shells;" and so musically inclined was this species, and so sharp in hearing sounds even out of its own element, that " dancing up, it leapt into the nets spread for the purpose, giving great and abundant sport." Indeed, if Plato and others are to be trusted, the Egyptians not only caught, but tamed fish, with the same facility as land animals.

Fishermen mostly used the net. It was of a long form, like the common drag net, with wooden floats on the upper, and leads on the lower side ; * but though it was sometimes let down from a boat, those who pulled it generally stood on the shore, and landed the fish on a shelving bank. The leads were occasionally of an elongated shape, hanging from the outer cord or border of the net ; but they were most usually flat, and, being folded round the cord, the opposite sides were beaten together ; a satisfactory instance of which is seen in the ancient net preserved in the Berlin Museum ; and this method continues to be adopted by the modern Egyptians.

426.   Leads, with part of a net.   *Berlin Museum.*

Besides the ordinary Egyptian net, they sometimes used a smaller kind, for catching fish in shallow water, furnished with a pole on either side, to which it was attached, exactly similar to one now used in India ; and the fisherman holding one of the poles in either hand, thrust it below the surface of the water, and

* *See* woodcut 425.

awaited the moment when a shoal of small fry passed over it. And this, or a smaller landing-net, secured the large fish, which had been wounded with the spear, or entangled with the hook.

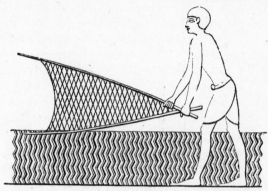

427.　　　　　　　　A sort of landing-net.　　　　　　*Thebes.*

When they employed the drag-net, and even when they pulled it to the shore, a boat sometimes attended, in which the fish were deposited as soon as caught; those intended for immediate use, to be eaten fresh, being sent off to market when the day's sport was finished; and the others being opened, salted, and hung up to dry in the sun.*

Some were cut in half, and suspended on ropes were left to dry in the sun and the open air; sometimes the body was simply laid open with a knife from the head to the tail, the two sides being divided as far as the back bone; and many were contented with taking out the intestines, and removing the head and tip of the tail, and exposing them, when salted, to the sun.

When caught, the small fish were generally put into baskets, but those of a larger kind were suspended to a pole, borne by two or more men over their shoulders, or were carried singly in the hand, slung at their back, or under the arm; all which methods are adopted by the modern fishermen at the Cataracts of A'Souán, and in other parts of the country.

Great was the consumption of fish in Egypt, as we know from

* Woodcuts 420, 428.

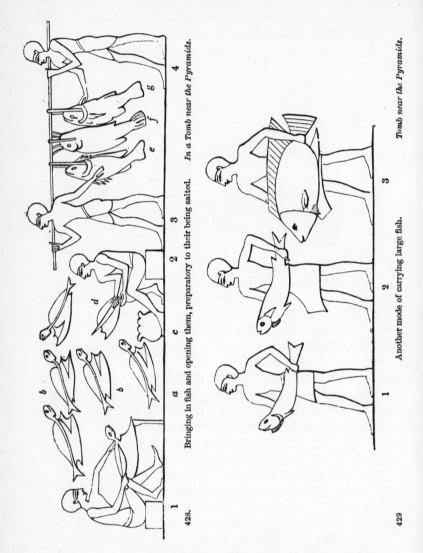

Bringing in fish and opening them, preparatory to their being salted.   In a Tomb near the Pyramids.

428.

Another mode of carrying large fish.   Tomb near the Pyramids.

429

the sculptures and other good authority; the "fishers" of the
Nile, and "they that cast angle into the brooks," "they that
spread nets," and they "that make sluices and ponds for fish,"

are mentioned in the Bible;* and the Israelites remembered with regret "the fish which (they) did eat in Egypt freely." † They were eaten either fresh or salted; and at a particular month of the year, on the 9th day of the first month (Thoth), every person was obliged, by a religious ordinance, to eat a fried fish before the door of his house, with the exception of the priests, who were contented to burn it on that occasion.‡

Some fish were particularly prized for the table, and preferred as being more wholesome, as well as superior in flavour to others; among which we may mention the *búlti*§, the *ḳishr*,‖ the *benni*,¶ the *shall*,** the *shilbeh*,†† and *arábrab*, the *byad*,‡‡ the *ḳarmoot*,§§ and a few others; but it was unlawful to touch those which were sacred, as the oxyrhinchus, the phagrus, and the lepidotus: and the inhabitants of the city of Oxyrhinchus objected even to eat any fish caught by a hook, lest it should have been defiled by the blood of one they held so sacred.

The oxyrhinchus was probably the *mizdeh*, a mormyrus remarkable among the fish of the Nile for its pointed nose, as the word *oxyrhinchus* implies; and a prejudice is still felt

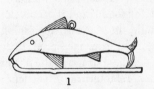 or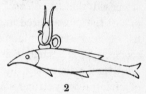

1   2

430.   The Oxyrhinchus fish, in bronze.

against it in some parts of Upper Egypt. Indeed, *mizdeh* is not very unlike the Coptic name of the city of (Oxyrhinchus) Mge. It is often represented in the sculptures, and in bronze; and in the temple of the Great Oasis this fish is accompanied by the name of Athor, or Venus, showing it to have been one of her emblems.

431. At the Oasis.

* Isaiah xix. 8, 10.
‡ Plut. de Is. s. 7.
‖ Perca Nilotica.
** Silurus Shall.
‡‡ Silurus Bajad.

† Numb. xi. 5.
§ Or *booltee*, Labrus Niloticus.
¶ Cyprinus Benni, or C. Lepidotus.
†† The Silurus Schilbe Niloticus.
§§ Silurus Carmuth.

The phagrus was the eel; and the reason of its sanctity, like that of the former, was owing to its being unwholesome; and the best way of preventing its being eaten was to assign it a place among the sacred animals of the country.

The lepidotus is still uncertain; from its name it was a scaly fish; and representations of it in bronze are not uncommon, which

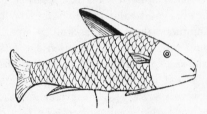

432.   Bronze Lepidotus (in my possession).

show it to be the Cyprinus Lepidotus or Benni; though the *Kishr*, the *bulti*, and the *Kelb el Bahr* or *Salmo Dentex* (all wholesome, and the best of the insipid fish of the Nile) have each been invited to accept the name. It might reasonably be supposed that the *Raad*, or Electric fish of the Nile, would be one of the most sacred and forbidden for food; and it seems not to be represented among those caught in the ancient fishing scenes. It is a small fish; and the one I saw measured little more than a foot long, by 4 inches in depth. But it had the power of giving a very strong shock. It is the Melapterurus Electricus; and may have been the ancient *Latus*.

The name *Raad*, "thunder," is very remarkable, since the modern Egyptians are quite ignorant of the cause of its peculiar powers; and if it was borrowed by them from their predecessors, the question naturally arises, were they acquainted with electricity?

Like the sacred quadrupeds, they were not all regarded with the same reverence in different parts of the country; and the people of Cynopolis were in the habit of eating the oxyrhinchus, which " was the origin of a civil war between the two cities, till both sides, after doing each other great mischief, were severely punished by the Romans."

Besides the fish cured, or sent to market for the table, a very great quantity was set apart expressly for feeding the sacred animals and birds,—as the cats, crocodiles, ibises, and others ; and some of the large reservoirs, attached to the temples, were used as well for keeping fish as for the necessary ablutions of the devout, and for various purposes connected with religion.

The quantity of fish in Egypt was a very great boon to the poor classes, and when the Nile overflowed the country the inhabitants of the inland villages benefited by this annual gift of the river, as the land did by the fertilizing mud deposited upon it.   The canals, ponds, and pools, on the low lands, continued to abound in fish, even after the inundation had ceased ; and it was then that their return to the Nile was intercepted by closing the mouths of the canals.   The same happens at the present day, *and so numerous are they, that the tax upon the profits now paid annually by the poor peasants to the Turkish government on the fish of a small canal amounts to 21*l*.

The revenue from the fisheries was much larger in old times ; though we may not believe that " while the water retired from the Lake Mœris (which Ælian quaintly calls the ' fish harvest ') the royal treasury received daily a talent of silver (supposed to be 193*l*. 15*s*. English), and during the other six months, when the water flowed from the Nile into the lake, 20 *minæ*" (about 64*l*. 12*s*.).   The sum said to have been derived from this source was given as a dowry to the queen, for the purchase of jewels, ointments, and other things connected with her toilet—a very liberal provision, being upwards of 94,000*l*. a-year ; and when this formed only a portion of the pin-money of the Egyptian queens, who also received the revenues of the town of Anthylla, famous for its wines, they had no reason to complain of the allowance they enjoyed.

Though the fish of the Nile were a great benefit, their quality was not such as would satisfy modern taste, being insipid, and often muddy in flavour ; but the Egyptians, like many others who live on rivers, were not connoisseurs in fish ; and those of the sea were scarcely known to them, though the waters of the Mediterranean and the Arabian Gulf might have afforded them many excellent kinds.   The sea was looked upon by them with abhorrence; political reasons had led the government in old times to increase that aversion ; and prejudice prevented their appreciating the good things it contained, which might have raised their taste above the carp-and-tench-level of their inexperience.

Of the various kinds of labourers few are worthy of notice, except the brickmakers ; and their employment derives considerable interest from the detailed notice of it in the Bible, according as it does so remarkably with the Egyptian paintings. Brickmaking, a mere manual occupation, with nothing to stimulate the clever workman to improvement, was only followed by the meanest of the community, who had not even the satisfaction of working for themselves ; for bricks were a government monopoly, and the pay for a tale of them was a small remuneration for this laborious drudgery in mud.

The use of crude bricks baked in the sun was universal throughout the country, for private and for many public buildings, and the dry climate of Egypt was peculiarly suited to those simple materials. They had the recommendation of cheapness, and even of durability ; and those made 3000 years ago, whether with or " without straw," are even now as firm and fit for use as when first put up in the reigns of the Amunophs and Thothmes, whose names they bear. When made of the Nile mud, or alluvial deposit, they required straw to prevent their cracking ; but those formed of clay (now called *Háybeh*), taken from the torrent beds on the edge of the desert, held together without straw ; and crude brick walls frequently had the additional security of a layer of reeds or sticks placed at intervals to act as binders. The courses of bricks were also disposed occasionally in horizontal curves, or a succession of concave and convex lines, throughout the length of the wall ; and this undulating arrangement was even adopted in stone, especially in quays by the river side.

Burnt bricks were not used in Egypt, and when found they are known to be of Roman time. Enclosures of gardens, or granaries, sacred circuits surrounding the courts of temples, walls of fortresses and towns, dwelling-houses and tombs, and even some few of the temples themselves were of crude brick, with stone columns and gateways ; and so great was the demand, that the government foreseeing the profit to be obtained from a monopoly of them, undertook to supply the public at a moderate price, thus preventing all unauthorised persons from engaging in their manufacture.   And, in order more effectually to obtain their end, the seal of the king, or of some privileged person, was stamped upon the bricks at the time they were made ; and bricks so marked are found both in public and private buildings ; some having the ovals of a king, and some the name and titles of a priest, or other influential person.   Those which bear no characters either formed part of a tale, of which the first only were stamped, or were from the brick-fields of individuals, who had obtained a licence from government to make them for their own consumption.

The employment of numerous captives, who worked as slaves, would in any case have enabled the government to sell the bricks at a lower price than those persons who had recourse solely to free labour ; so that, without the necessity of a prohibition, they must soon have become an exclusive manufacture ; and we find that, independent of native labourers, a great many foreigners were constantly engaged in the brick-fields at Thebes, and other parts of Egypt.   The Jews, of course, were not excluded from this drudgery ; and, like the captives detained in the Thebaïd, they were condemned to the same labour in Lower Egypt.   They not only erected granaries, treasure cities, and many public monuments for the Egyptian monarch ; but the materials used in building them were the work of their hands ; and the number of persons constantly employed in making bricks may be readily accounted for by the extensive supply required, and kept by the government for sale.

To meet with Hebrews in the sculptures cannot reasonably be expected, since the remains in that part of Egypt where they lived have not been preserved ; but it is curious to discover other foreign captives occupied in the same manner, overlooked by similar " taskmasters,"* and performing the very same labours as the Israelites described in the Bible ; and no one can look at

* *Figs.* 3 and 6 in woodcut 433.

o 2

Thebes.

433.   Foreign captives employed in making bricks at Thebes.

Fig. 1. Man returning after carrying the bricks.   Figs. 4, 5. Men carrying bricks.

Figs. 7, 9, 12, 13. Digging and mixing the clay or mud.   Figs. 3, 6. Taskmasters.

Figs. 8, 14. Making bricks with a wooden mould, *d, h.*

the paintings of Thebes, representing brick-makers, without a feeling of the highest interest. That the scene in the accompanying wood-cut is at the capital of Upper Egypt is shown by the hieroglyphics, which state, that the " bricks" (*tôbi*) are made for a building at " Thebes " (*fig.* 9, *e*) ; and this occurrence of the word implying bricks, similar both in modern Arabic * and ancient Coptic, gives an additional value to the picture.

It is not very consistent, nor logical, to argue, that because the Jews made bricks, and the persons here introduced are so engaged, these must necessarily be Jews : since the Egyptians and their captives were constantly required to perform the same task ; and the great quantity made at all times is proved by the number of buildings, which still remain, constructed of those materials. And a sufficient contradiction is given to that conclusion, by their being said to be working at Thebes, where the Jews never were, and by the names of various Asiatic captives of the time being recorded in the same tomb, among which no mention is made of Jews.

With regard to the features of foreigners resembling the Jews, it is only necessary to observe that the Egyptians adopted the same character for all the inhabitants of Syria ; as may be seen in the sculptures of Karnak and other places, where those people occur, as well as in one of the sets of figures in Belzoni's tomb ; and the brick-makers, far from having what is considered the very Jewish expression found in many of those figures, have not even the long beard, so marked in the people of Syria and the prisoners of Shesonk (Shishak). They are represented as a white people, like others from Asia introduced into the paintings, and some have blue eyes and red hair, which are also given to the people of Rot-ñ-n in this same tomb. Indeed if I were disposed to think them Jews, I should rather argue it from many of these figures *not* having the large nose and dark eyes and hair we consider as Jewish types ; for some of these brickmakers are painted yellow, with blue eyes and small beards. Others are red with a *rétroussé* nose. (*Woodcut* 434, *fig.* 2.)

These last may be Egyptians, or people of Pount who are re-

* " Tob " or "toob," in Arabic " a brick :" in Coptic " tôbi."

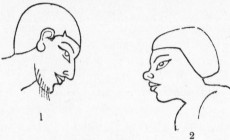

1   2

434.   Two of the Brickmakers.   *Thebes.*

presented bringing tribute in the same tomb.   The fact of some
having small beards, others merely the " stubble-field " of an
unshaven chin, might accord with Jews as well as with the Rot-n̄-n,
or other northern races ; but their making bricks at Thebes, and
the name of Jews not being mentioned in the whole tomb, are
insuperable objections.

   And here I may mention a remarkable circumstance, that the
Jews of the East to this day often have red hair and blue eyes,
with a nose of delicate form and nearly straight, and are quite
unlike their brethren of Europe ; and the children in modern
Jerusalem have the pink and white complexions of Europeans.
The Oriental Jews are at the same time unlike the other Syrians
in features ; and it is the Syrians who have the large nose that
strikes us as the peculiarity of the western Israelites.   This
prominent feature was always a characteristic of the Syrians ;
but not of the ancient, nor of the modern, Jews of Judæa ; and
the Saviour's head, though not really a portrait, is evidently a
traditional representation of the Jewish face, which is still traceable at Jerusalem.   No real portrait of Him was ever handed
down ; and Eusebius, of Cæsarea, pronounced the impossibility of
obtaining one for the sister of Constantine ; but the character of
the Jewish face would necessarily be known in those early days,
(in the 4th century), when the first representations of Him were
attempted ; and we should be surprised to find any artist abandon
the style of features thus agreed upon for ages, and represent the
Saviour with those of our western Jews.   Yet this would be
perfectly correct if the Jews of His day had those features ; and
such would have been, in that case, His traditional portrait.

I had often remarked the colour and features of the Jews in the East, so unlike those known in Europe, and my wish to ascertain if they were the same in Judæa was at length gratified by a visit to Jerusalem ; where I found the same type in all those really of eastern origin ; and the large nose is there an invariable proof of mixture with a western family. It may be difficult to explain this great difference in the eastern and western face (and the former is said to be also found in Hungary) ; but the subject is worthy of investigation, as is the origin of those Jews now living in Europe, and the early migrations that took place from Judæa long before the Christian era. These would be more satisfactory than mere speculations on the Lost Tribes.

The occupations of the common people in Egypt were carefully watched by the magistrate, and no one was allowed to live an idle life, useless to himself, and to the community. It was thought right that the industrious citizen should be encouraged, and distinguished from the lazy or the profligate ; and in order to protect the good and detect the wicked, it was enacted that every one should at certain times present himself before the magistrates, or provincial governors, and give in his name, his place of abode, his profession or employment, and the mode in which he gained his livelihood ; the particulars being duly registered in the official report. The time of attendance was fixed, and those from the same parish proceeded in bodies to the appointed office, accompanied by their respective banners, and each individual being introduced singly to the registering clerks, gave in his statement and answered the necessary questions. In approaching these functionaries, they adopted the usual forms of respect before a superior ; making a profound bow, one hand falling down to the knee, the other placed over the mouth to keep the breath from his face. The same mark of deference was expected from every one, as a token of respect to the court, on all occasions ; when accused before a magistrate, and when attending at the police office to prefer a complaint, or to vindicate his character from an unjust imputation ; and when a culprit sought to deprecate punishment, or to show great deference before a superior, he frequently placed one hand across his breast to the opposite shoulder.

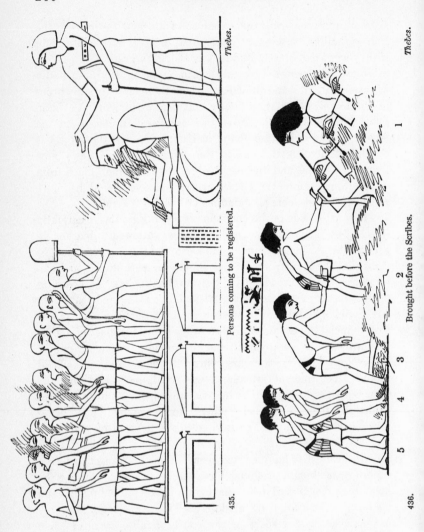

Thebes.

Persons coming to be registered.

435.

Thebes.

1

2

3

4

5

Brought before the Scribes.

436.

The custom of giving an account of their occupations was not
of late introduction; it was adopted in old times; and the above
representations are of the time of the 18th dynasty. It appears
that they not only enrolled their names and gave in the various
particulars required of them, but were obliged to have a passport

from the magistrates ; and this may possibly be the paper presented in the preceding woodcut to the scribe ; for a document of that kind was required for every ship quitting a port, and all the precautions respecting a man's mode of life would have been useless if he could leave his town for another part of the country without some notice being required on his departure, and some vouchure being shown by him on his arrival at a new place of abode. The tiresome system of passports is exactly what the scrutiny of the cautious " paternal government " of Egypt would have invented ; their formula may be recognised in the description of persons, who were parties to the sale of estates, and other private or public contracts ; and in a deed of the time of Cleopatra Cocce, and Ptolemy Alexander I., written in Greek, and relating to the sale of a piece of land at Thebes, five individuals are thus described :—" Pamonthes, aged about forty-five, of middle size, dark complexion and handsome figure, bald, round faced, and straight nosed ; Snachomneus, aged about twenty, of middle size, sallow complexion, round faced, and straight nosed ; Semnuthis Persineï, aged about twenty-two, of middle size, sallow complexion, round faced, flat nosed, and of quiet demeanour ; and Tathlyt Persineï, aged about thirty, of middle size, and sallow complexion, round faced, and straight nosed—the four being children of Petepsais, of the leather-cutters of the Memnonia ; and the Nechutes the less, the son of Asos, aged about forty, of middle size, sallow complexion, cheerful countenance, long face, and straight nose, with a scar upon the middle of his forehead."

During this examination before the magistrates, if excesses were found to have been committed by any one, in an irregular course of life, he was sentenced to the bastinado ; but a false statement, or the proof of being engaged in unlawful pursuits, entailed upon him the punishment of a capital crime.

Another, and a fuller account of his conduct was required in the Confession, which the soul of every Egyptian was doomed to make at his death, before he could receive his last passport to eternal happiness.

The laws of the Egyptians were partly a compilation from decisions of learned judges in noted cases; as in some modern countries, and as with the Bedouins, who are guided by pre-

cedents and the opinions of their *ḳádis*, handed down from past
times, rather than by the fixed law of the Ḳoran.   They had
also a grand code of laws and jurisprudence, known as the
celebrated " Eight Books of Hermes," which it was incumbent
on those high-priests called " prophets" to be thoroughly versed
in, and which the king, who held that office, was also required and
entitled to know.   It was not only in Egypt that the kings were
judges ; it was usual in many eastern countries to entrust the
laws and their administration to them ; and Xenophon, who
ascribes the origin of the custom in Asia to Cyrus, says that
those who wished to present petitions to the king attended at the
gate of the palace.*   It was probably from a similar custom that
the Turkish title " the Sublime Porte " (or " lofty gate ") was
derived ; and the same idea is contained in the common Oriental
expression *Ana fee bab Allah*, " I am waiting at God's gate"
(for help), in cases of complete distress.

We are acquainted with few of the laws of the ancient Egyptians ; but the superiority of their legislature has always been
acknowledged as the cause of the duration of an empire, which
lasted with the same form of government for a much longer
period than the generality of ancient states.   Indeed the wisdom
of that people was proverbial, and was held in such consideration
by other nations, that we find it taken by the Jews as the standard
to which superior learning† in their own country was willingly
compared ; and Moses had prepared himself for the duties of a
legislator, by becoming versed "in all the wisdom of the Egyptians."

Besides their right of enacting laws, and of superintending all
affairs of religion, and the state, the kings administered justice
to their subjects on those questions which came under their immediate cognisance, and they were assisted in the management
of state affairs by the advice of the most able and distinguished
members of the priestly order.   With them the monarch consulted upon all questions of importance relating to the internal
administration of the country ; and previous to the admission of

* *Comp.* 2 Sam. xix. 8, and Esther, and other parts of the Bible.
† Of Solomon ; 1 Kings, iv. 30.

Joseph to the confidence of Pharaoh, the opinion of his ministers was asked as to the expediency of the measure.*

His edicts appear to have been issued in the form of a *firmán*, or written order, like the Hot e' Sheréef, " handwriting of the Descendant of the Prophet," (or the Turkish Sultan,) and like the royal commands in all Oriental countries ; and from the expression used by Pharaoh in granting power to Joseph, we may infer that the people who received his order adopted the same Eastern mode of acknowledging their obedience and respect for the sovereign, now shown to a *firmán ;* the expression in the Hebrew † being, " according to thy word shall all people *kiss* " (be ruled), and evidently alluding to the custom of *kissing* the signature attached to those documents.   They were also expected to " bow the knee ‡ " in the presence of the monarch and chiefs of the country, and even to prostrate themselves to the ground, as Joseph's brethren did before him.

Causes of ordinary occurrence were decided by those who held the office of judges ; and the care with which persons were elected to this office is a proof of their regard for the welfare of the community, and of their earnest endeavours to promote the ends of justice.   None were admitted to it but the most upright and learned individuals ; and, in order to make the office more select, and more readily to obtain persons of known character, ten only were chosen from each of the three cities—Thebes, Memphis, and Heliopolis ; a body of men, says Diodorus, by no means inferior either to the Areopagites of Athens, or to the senate of Lacedæmon.

These thirty individuals constituted the bench of judges ; and at their first meeting they elected the most distinguished among them to be president, with the title of Arch-judge.   His salary was much greater than that of the other judges, as his office was

* Gen. xli. 38, " And Pharaoh said unto his servants (ministers), Can we find such a one as this is ?"   Gen. l. 7, " The elders of his (Pharaoh's) house."   And Isaiah xix. 11, " The wise counsellors of Pharaoh."

† Gen. xli. 40.

‡ Gen. xli. 43.   The word *abrek* אברך is very remarkable, as it is used to the present day by the Arabs, when requiring a camel to *kneel* and receive its load, and is derived from *rûkbeh* the " knee."   Hence too *báraka* a " blessing," from " kneeling " in prayer.

more important, and the city to which he belonged enjoyed the privilege of returning another judge, to complete the number of the thirty from whom he had been chosen. They all received ample allowances from the king, in order that, possessing a sufficiency for their maintenance and other necessary expenses, they might be above the reach of temptation, and be inaccessible to bribes; for it was considered of primary importance that all judicial proceedings should be regulated with the most scrupulous exactitude; sentences pronounced by authorised tribunals always having a decided influence, either salutary or prejudicial, on the affairs of common life. They felt that precedents were thereby established, and that numerous abuses frequently resulted from an early error, which had been sanctioned by the decision of some influential person; and for this reason they weighed the talents, as well as the character, of the judge.

The first principle was, that offenders should be discovered and punished, and that those who had been wronged should be benefited by the interposition of the laws; since the least compensation which can be made to the oppressed, and the most effectual preventive of crime, are the speedy discovery and exposure of the offender. On the other hand, if the terror which hangs over the guilty in the hour of trial could be averted by bribery or favour, nothing short of distrust and confusion would pervade all ranks of society; and the spirit of the Egyptian laws (as Diodorus shows) was not merely to hold out the distant prospect of rewards and punishments, nor simply threaten the future vengeance of the gods, but to apply the more persuasive stimulus of present retribution.

Besides the care taken by them that justice should be administered according to the real merits of the case, and that before their tribunals no favour or respect of persons should be permitted, another very important regulation was adopted, that justice should be gratuitously administered; and it was consequently accessible to the poor as well as to the rich. The very spirit of their laws was to give protection and assistance to the oppressed, and everything that tended to promote an unbiassed judgment was peculiarly commended by the Egyptian sages.

When a case was brought for trial, it was customary for the arch-judge to put a golden chain round his neck, to which was suspended a small figure of Truth, ornamented with precious

437.   The goddess of Truth and Justice.   *Thebes.*

stones.   This was, in fact, a representation of the goddess who was worshipped under the double character of Truth and Justice, and whose name, Thmei, appears to have been the origin of the Hebrew Thummim — a word, according to the Septuagint translation, implying "truth," and bearing a further analogy in its plural termination.   And what makes it more remarkable, is that the chief priest of the Jews, who, before the election of a king, was also the judge of the nation, was alone entitled to wear this honorary badge ; and the Thummim, like the Egyptian figure, was studded with precious stones of various colours.   The goddess was represented " having her eyes closed,"

438.   The goddess of Truth, "with her eyes closed." *Thebes.*

purporting that the duty of a judge was to weigh the question according to the evidence he had heard, and to trust rather to his mind than to what he saw, and was intended to warn him of that virtue which the Deity peculiarly enjoined : an emblematic idea, very similar to " those statues at Thebes of judges without hands, with their chief or president at their head having his eyes turned downwards," signifying, as Plutarch says, " that Justice ought neither to be accessible to bribes, nor guided by favour and affection."

It is not to be supposed that the president and the thirty judges above mentioned were the only house of judicature in the country ; each city, or capital of a nome, had no doubt its own " County court," for the trial of minor and local offences ; and it is probable that the assembly returned by the three chief cities resided wherever the royal court was held, and performed many of the same duties as the senates of ancient times. And that this was really the case appears from Diodorus mentioning the thirty judges and their president, represented at Thebes in the sculptures of the tomb of Osymandyas.

The president, or arch-judge, having put on the emblem of Truth, the trial commenced ; and the eight volumes which contained the laws of the Egyptians were placed close to him, in order to guide his decision, or to enable him to solve a difficult question, by reference to that code, to former precedents, or to the opinion of some learned predecessor. The complainant stated his case. This was done in writing ; and every particular that bore upon the subject, the mode in which the alleged offence was committed, and an estimate of the damage, or the extent of the injury sustained, were inserted.

The defendant then, taking up the deposition of the opposite party, wrote his answer to each of the plaintiff's statements, either denying the charge, or endeavouring to prove that the offence was not of a serious nature ; or, if obliged to admit his guilt, suggesting that the damages were too high, and incompatible with the nature of the crime. The complainant replied in writing ; and the accused having brought forward all he had to say in his defence, the papers were given to the judges ; and if no witnesses could be produced on either side, they decided upon the question according to the deposition of the parties. Their opinion only required to be ratified by the president, who then proceeded, in virtue of his office, to pronounce judgment on the case; and this was done by touching the party who had gained the cause with the figure of Truth. They considered that this mode of proceeding was more likely to forward the ends of justice, than when the judges listened to the statements of pleaders; eloquence having frequently the effect of fascinating the mind, and tending to throw a veil over guilt, and to pervert truth. The persuasive arguments of oratory, or those artifices which move the passions and excite the sympathy of the judges, were avoided; and thus neither did an appeal to their feelings, nor the tears and dissimulation of an offender, soften the just rigour of the laws. And while ample time was afforded to each party to proffer or to disprove an accusation, no opportunity was given to the offender to take advantage of his opponent, but poor and rich, ignorant and learned, honest and dishonest, were placed on an equal footing; and it was the case, rather than the persons, upon which the judgment was passed.

The laws of the Egyptians were handed down from the earliest times, and looked upon with the greatest reverence. They had the credit of having been dictated by the gods themselves, and Thoth (Hermes, Mercury, or the Divine Intellect) was said to have framed them for the benefit of mankind.

The names of many of the earliest monarchs and sages, who had contributed to the completion of their code, were recorded and venerated by them; and whoever, at successive periods, made additions to it was mentioned with gratitude as a benefactor of his country.

Truth or justice was thought to be the main cardinal virtue among the Egyptians, inasmuch as it relates more particularly to others; prudence, temperance, and fortitude being relative qualities, and tending chiefly to the immediate benefit of the individual who possesses them. It was, therefore, with great earnestness that they inculcated the necessity of fully appreciating it; and falsehood was not only considered disgraceful, but when it entailed an injury on any other person was punishable by law. A calumniator of the dead was condemned to a severe punishment ; and a false accuser was doomed to the same sentence which would have been awarded to the accused, if the offence had been proved against him ; but to maintain a falsehood by an oath was deemed the blackest crime, and one which, from its complicated nature, could be punished by nothing short of death. For they considered that it involved two distinct crimes—a contempt for the gods, and a violation of faith towards man ; the former the direct promoter of every sin, the latter destructive of all those ties which are most essential for the welfare of society.

The wilful murder of a freeman, or even of a *slave*, was punished with death, from the conviction that men ought to be restrained from the commission of sin, not on account of any distinction of station in life, but from the light in which they viewed the crime itself ; while at the same time it had the effect of showing, that if the murder of a slave was deemed an offence deserving of so severe a punishment, they ought still more to shrink from the murder of one who was a compatriot and a free-born citizen.

In this law we observe a scrupulous regard to justice and humanity, and have an unquestionable proof of the great advancement made by the Egyptians in the most essential points of civilisation. Indeed, the Egyptians considered it so heinous a crime to deprive a man of life, that to be the accidental witness of an attempt to murder, without endeavouring to prevent it, was a capital offence, which could only be palliated by bringing proofs of inability to act. With the same spirit they decided, that to be present when any one inflicted a personal injury on another, without interfering, was tantamount to being a party, and was punishable according to the extent of the assault ; and every one who witnessed a robbery was bound either to arrest, or, if that was out of his power, to lay an information, and to prosecute the offenders : and any neglect on this score being proved against him, the delinquent was condemned to receive a stated number of stripes, and to be kept without food for three whole days.

Although, in the case of murder, the Egyptian law was inexorable and severe, the royal prerogative might be exerted in favour of a culprit, and the punishment was sometimes commuted by a mandate from the king.   Sabaco, indeed, during the fifty years of his reign, "made it a rule not to punish his subjects with death," whether guilty of murder or any other capital offence, but, "according to the magnitude of their crimes, he condemned the culprits to raise the ground about the town to which they belonged.   By these means the situation of the different cities became greatly elevated above the reach of the inundation, even more than in the time of Sesostris ;" and either on account of a greater proportion of criminals, or from some other cause, the mounds of Bubastis were raised considerably higher than those of any other city.

The same laws that forbade a master to punish a slave with death took from a father every right over the life of his offspring ; and the Egyptians deemed the murder of a child an odious crime, that called for the direct interposition of justice. They did not, however, punish it as a capital offence, since it appeared inconsistent to take away life from one who had given it to the child, but preferred inflicting such a punishment as would induce grief and repentance.   With this view they ordained that the corpse of the deceased should be fastened to the neck of its parent, and that he should be obliged to pass three whole days and nights in its embrace, under the surveillance of a public guard.

But parricide was visited with the most cruel of chastisements ; and conceiving, as they did, that the murder of a parent was the most unnatural of crimes, they endeavoured to prevent its occurrence by the marked severity with which it was avenged.   The criminal was therefore sentenced to be lacerated with sharpened reeds, and after being thrown on thorns he was burnt to death.

When a woman was guilty of a capital offence, and judgment had been passed upon her, they were particularly careful to ascertain if the condemned was in a state of pregnancy ; in which case her punishment was deferred till after the birth of the child, in order that the innocent might not suffer with the guilty, and thus the father be deprived of that child to which he had at least an equal right.

But some of their laws regarding the female sex were cruel and unjustifiable ; and even if, which is highly improbable, they succeeded by their severity in enforcing chastity, and in putting an effectual stop to crime, yet the punishment rather reminds us of the laws of a barbarous people than of a wise and civilized state. A woman who had committed adultery was sentenced to lose her nose, upon the principle that, being the most conspicuous feature, and the chief, or, at least, an indispensable, ornament of the face, its loss would be most severely felt, and be the greatest detriment to her personal charms ; and the man was condemned to receive a bastinado of one thousand blows. But if it was proved that force had been used against a free woman, he was doomed to a cruel mutilation.

The object of the Egyptian laws was to preserve life, and to reclaim an offender. Death took away every chance of repentance, it deprived the country of his services, and he was hurried out of the world when least prepared to meet the ordeal of a future state. They, therefore, preferred severe punishments, and, except in the case of murder, and some crimes which appeared highly injurious to the community, it was deemed unnecessary to sacrifice the life of an offender.

In military as well as civil cases, minor offences were generally punished with the stick ; a mode of chastisement still greatly in vogue among the modern inhabitants of the valley of the Nile, and held in such esteem by them, that convinced of (or perhaps by) its efficacy, they relate "its descent from heaven as a blessing to mankind."

If an Egyptian of the present day has a government debt or tax to pay, he stoutly persists in his inability to obtain the money, till he has withstood a certain number of blows, and considers himself compelled to produce it ; and the ancient inhabitants, if not under the rule of their native princes, at least in the time of the Roman emperors, gloried equally in the obstinacy they evinced, and the difficulty the governors of the country experienced in extorting from them what they were bound to pay ;

whence Ammianus Marcellinus tells us, " an Egyptian blushes if
he cannot show numerous marks on his body that evince his endeavours to evade the duties."

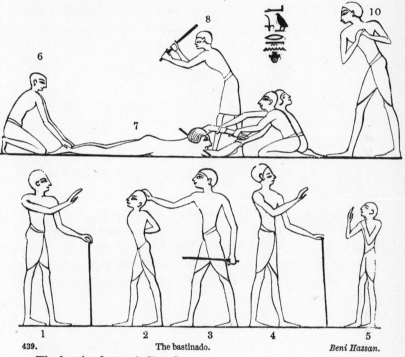

439.   The bastinado.   Beni Hassan.

The bastinado was inflicted
on both sexes, as with the
Jews. Men and boys were
laid prostrate on the ground,
and frequently held by the
hands and feet while the
chastisement was adminis-
tered ; but women, as they
sat, received the stripes on
their back, which was also
inflicted by the hand of a
man. Nor was it unusual

440.   Women bastinadoed.   Beni Hassan.

for the superintendents to stimulate labourers to their work by the persuasive powers of the stick, whether engaged in the field or in handicraft employments ; and boys were sometimes

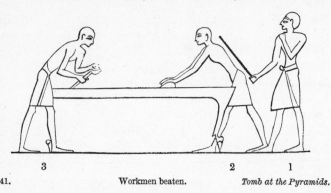

3   2   1
441.   Workmen beaten.   *Tomb at the Pyramids.*

beaten without the ceremony of prostration, the hands being tied behind their back, while the punishment was applied.

It does not, however, appear to have been from any respect to the person, that this less usual method was adopted ; nor is it probable that any class of the community enjoyed a peculiar privilege on these occasions, as among the modern Moslems, who, extending their respect for the Prophet to his distant descendants of the thirty-sixth and ensuing generations, scruple to administer the stick to a *Sheréef* until he has been politely furnished with a mat, on which to prostrate his guilty person. Among other amusing privileges in modern Egypt, is that conceded to the grandees, or officers of high rank. Ordinary culprits are punished by the hand of persons usually employed on such occasions ; but a Bey, or the governor of a district, can only receive his chastisement from the hand of a Pasha, and the aristocratic *daboss* (mace) is substituted for the vulgar stick. This is no trifling privilege : it becomes fully *impressed* upon the sufferer, and renders him, long after, sensible of the peculiar honour he has enjoyed ; nor can any one doubt that an iron mace, in form not very unlike a chocolate-mill, is a *distingué* mode of punishing men who are proud of their rank.

Having noticed the pertinacity of the modern Egyptians in

resisting the payment of their taxes, I shall introduce the following story as remarkably illustrative of this fact. In the year 1822, a Copt Christian, residing at Cairo, was arrested by the Turkish authorities for the non-payment of his taxes, and taken before the Kehia, or deputy of the Pasha. " Why," inquired the angry Turk, "have you not paid your taxes? "—" Because," replied the Copt, with a pitiable expression, perfectly according with his tattered appearance, " I have not the means." He was instantly ordered to be thrown upon the floor, and bastinadoed. He prayed to be released, but in vain : the stick continued without intermission, and he was scarcely able to bear the increasing pain. Again and again he pleaded his inability to pay, and prayed for mercy : the Turk was inexorable ; and the torments he felt at length overcame his resolution : they were no longer to be borne. " Release me," he cried, " and I will pay directly."—" Ah, you Giower! go." He was released, and taken home, accompanied by a soldier, and the money being paid, he imparted to his wife the sad tidings. " You coward! you fool! " she exclaimed ; " what, give them the money on the very first demand! I suppose after five or six blows, you cried, ' I will pay, only release me ;' next year our taxes will be doubled through your weakness ; shame! "—" No, my dear," interrupted the suffering man, " I assure you I resisted as long as it was possible ; look at the state I am in, before you upbraid me. I paid the money, but they had trouble enough for it ; for I obliged them to give me at least a hundred blows before they could get it." She was pacified ; and the pity and commendation of his wife, added to his own satisfaction in having shown so much obstinacy and courage, consoled him for the pain, and, perhaps, in some measure, for the money thus forced from him.

Hanging was the customary mode of punishment, in ancient Egypt, for many capital crimes ; and the criminals were kept " bound " in prison till their fate was decided ; whether it depended on the will of the sovereign, or the decision of the judges. These places of confinement were under the immediate superintendence, and within the house, of the chief of the police, or " captain of the guard," " an officer of Pharaoh," who was probably the captain of the watch, like the *Zábut* of the modern Egyptian police.*

The character of some of the Egyptian laws was quite consonant with the notions of a primitive age. The punishment was directed more particularly against the offending member : and adulterators of money, falsifiers of weights and measures, forgers of seals or signatures, and scribes who altered any signed document by erasures or additions, without the authority of the parties, were condemned to lose both their hands.

But their laws do not seem to have sanctioned the gibbet, or the exposure of the body of an offender; for the conduct of Rhampsinitus, in the case of the robbery of his treasure, is mentioned by Herodotus as a singular mode of discovering an accomplice, and not as an ordinary punishment; if indeed the whole story is not the invention of a Greek *cicerone*.

Thefts, breach of trust, and petty frauds were punished with the bastinado; but robbery and housebreaking were sometimes considered capital crimes, and deserving of death; as is evident from the conduct of the thief, when caught by the trap in the treasury of Rhampsinitus, and from what Diodorus states respecting Actisanes. This monarch, instead of putting robbers to death, instituted a novel mode of punishing them, by cutting off their noses, and banishing them to the confines of the desert, where a town was built, called Rhinocolura, from the peculiar nature of their punishment; and thus, by removing the bad, and preventing their corrupting the good, he benefited society, without depriving the criminals of life; at the same time that he punished them severely for their crimes, by obliging them to live by their labours, and derive a precarious sustenance from quails, or whatever they could catch, in that barren region. Commutation of punishment was the foundation of this part of the convict system of Egypt, and Rhinocolura was their Norfolk Island, where a sea of sand separated the worst felons from those guilty of smaller crimes; who were transported to the mines in the desert, and condemned to work for various terms, according to their offence.

* Gen. xxxix. 1, 20; xl. 3, 22.

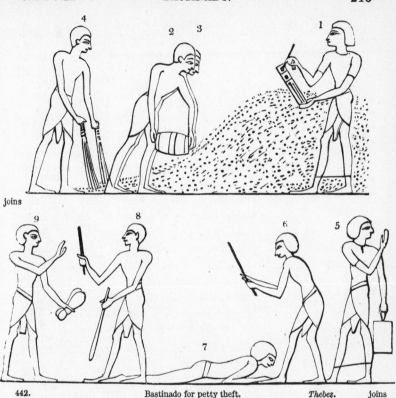

joins

442.   Bastinado for petty theft.   *Thebes.*   joins

Blindly following the old-fashioned notion of merely *punishing*
for offences committed, the Egyptian Government had never
thought of *preventing* crime by educating the youth of the poor,
and checking the supply of future criminals by thwarting vice in
embryo ; they did, however, attempt it in some degree by preventing idleness, and requiring each to account for his mode of life ;
and they could scarcely be expected in those early days to have
arrived at a system we have only just adopted ; and which has
been so ably carried out in Scotland.   Our next problem, on the
return of criminals to society, when transportation shall have
ceased, has yet to be solved ; and we shall be fortunate if we
excel the Egyptians as far in this, as in the case of juvenile
offenders.

The Egyptians had a singular custom respecting theft and burglary. Those who followed the *profession* of thief gave in their names to the chief of the robbers; and agreed that he should be informed of every thing they might thenceforward steal, the moment it was in their possession. In consequence of this the owner of the lost goods always applied by letter to the chief for their recovery: and having stated their quality and quantity, the day and hour when they were stolen, and other requisite particulars, the goods were identified, and, on payment of one quarter of their value, they were restored to the applicant, in the same state as when taken from his house.

For being fully persuaded of the impracticability of putting an entire check to robbery, either by the dread of punishment, or by any method that could be adopted by the most vigilant police, they considered it more for the advantage of the community, that a certain sacrifice should be made in order to secure the restitution of the remainder, than that the law, by taking on itself to protect the citizen, and discover the offender, should be the indirect cause of greater loss. And that the Egyptians, like the Indians, and I may say the modern inhabitants of the Nile, were very expert in the art of stealing, we have abundant testimony from ancient authors.

It may be asked, what redress could be obtained, if goods were stolen by thieves who failed to enter their names on the books of the chief; but, it is evident that there could be few of those private speculators, since by their interfering with the interests of all the *profession*, the detection of such egotistical persons would have been certain; and thus all others were effectually prevented from robbing, save those of the privileged class.

The salary of the chief was not merely derived from his own demands upon the goods stolen, or from any voluntary contribution of the robbers themselves, but was probably a fixed remuneration granted by the government, as one of the chiefs of the police; nor is it to be supposed that he was any other than a respectable citizen, and a man of integrity and honour. The same may be said of the modern "*shekh* of the thieves" at Cairo, where this very ancient office is still retained.

The great confidence reposed in the public weighers rendered it necessary to enact suitable laws in order to bind them to their duty ; and considering how much public property was at their mercy, and how easily bribes might be taken from a dishonest tradesman, the Egyptians inflicted a severe punishment as well on the weighers as on the shopkeepers, who were found to have false weights and measures, or to have defrauded the purchaser in any other way ; and these, as well as the scribes who kept false accounts, were punished (as before stated) with the loss of both their hands ; on the principle, says Diodorus, that the offending member should suffer ; while the culprit was severely punished, that others might be deterred from the commission of a similar offence.

As in other countries, their laws respecting debt and usury underwent some changes, according as society advanced, and as pecuniary transactions became more complicated.

Bocchoris (who reigned in Egypt about the year 800 B. C., and who, from his learning, obtained the surname of Wise), finding that in cases of debt many causes of dispute had arisen, and instances of great oppression were of frequent occurrence, enacted, that no agreement should be binding unless it was acknowledged by a written contract ; and if any one took oath that the money had not been lent him, that no debt should be recognised, and the claims of the suing party should immediately cease.   This was done, that great regard might always be had for the name and nature of an oath, at the same time that, by substituting the unquestionable proof of a written document, the necessity of having frequent recourse to an oath was avoided, and its sanctity was not diminished by constant repetition.

Usury was in all cases condemned by the Egyptian legislature; and when money was borrowed, even with a written agreement, it was forbidden to allow the interest to increase to more than double the original sum.   Nor could the creditors seize the debtor's person : their claims and right were confined to the goods in his possession, and such as were really his own ; which were comprehended under the produce of his labour, or what he had received from another individual to whom they lawfully belonged. For the person of every citizen was looked upon as the property of the state, and might be required for some public service, connected either with war or peace; and, independent of the injustice of subjecting any one to the momentary caprice of his creditor, the safety of the country might be endangered through the avarice of a few interested individuals.

This law, which was borrowed by Solon from the Egyptian code, existed also at Athens; and was, as Diodorus observes, much more consistent with justice and common sense than that which allowed the creditor to seize the person, while it forbade him to take the ploughs and other implements of husbandry. For if, continues the historian, it is unjust thus to deprive men of the means of obtaining subsistence, and of providing for their families, how much more unreasonable must it be to imprison those by whom the implements were used!

To prevent the accumulation of debt, and to protect the interests of the creditor, another remarkable law was enacted by Asychis, which, while it shows how greatly they endeavoured to check the increasing evil, proves the high respect paid by the Egyptians to the memory of their parents, and to the sanctity of their religious ceremonies. By this it was pronounced illegal for any one to borrow money without giving in pledge the body of his father, or the tomb of his ancestors; and, if he failed to redeem so sacred a deposit, he was considered infamous; and, at his death, the celebration of the accustomed funeral obsequies was denied him, and he could not enjoy the right of burial either in that tomb or in any other place of sepulture; nor could he inter his children, or any of his family, as long as the debt was unpaid, the creditor being put in actual possession of the family tomb.

In the large cities of Egypt, a fondness for display, and the usual allurements of luxury, were rapidly introduced; and considerable sums were expended in furnishing houses, and in many artificial caprices. Rich jewels and costly works of art were in great request, as well among the inhabitants of the provincial capitals, as at Thebes and Memphis: they delighted in splendid equipages, elegant and commodious boats, numerous attendants, horses, dogs, and other requisites for the chase; and, besides, their houses, their villas, and their gardens, were laid out with no ordinary expense. But while the funds arising from extensive farms, and the abundant produce of a fertile soil, enabled the rich to indulge extravagant habits, many of the less wealthy envied the enjoyment of those luxuries which fortune had denied to them; and, prompted by vanity, and a silly desire of imitation, so common in civilised communities, they pursued a career which speedily led to an accumulation of debt, and demanded the interference of the legislature; and it is probable that a law, so severe as this must have appeared to the Egyptians, was only adopted as a measure of absolute necessity, in order to put a check to the increasing evil.

The necessary expenses of the Egyptians were remarkably small, less, indeed, than of any people; and the food of the poorer classes was of the cheapest and most simple kind. Owing to the warmth of the climate, they required few clothes, and young children were in the habit of going without shoes, and with little or no covering to their bodies; and so trifling was the expense of bringing up a child, that, as Diodorus affirms, it never need cost a parent more than 20 drachms (13 shillings English), until arrived at man's estate. It was, therefore, luxury, and the increasing wants of an artificial kind, which corrupted the manners of the Egyptians, and rendered such a law necessary for their restraint; and we may conclude, that it was mainly directed against those who contracted debts for the gratification of pleasure, or with the premeditated intent of defrauding an unsuspecting creditor.

In the mode of executing deeds, conveyances, and other civil contracts, the Egyptians were peculiarly circumstantial and minute; and the great number of witnesses is a singular feature in those documents. In the time of the Ptolemies, sales of property commenced with a preamble, containing the date of the king in whose reign they were executed; the name of the president of the court, and of the clerk by whom they were written, being also specified. The body of the contract then followed. It stated the name of the individual who sold the land, the description of his person, an account of his parentage, profession, and place of abode, the extent and nature of the land, its situation and boundaries, and concluded with the name of the purchaser, whose parentage and description were also added, and the sum for which it was bought.   The seller then vouched for his undisturbed possession of it ; and, becoming security against any attempt to dispute his title, the name of the other party was inserted as having accepted it, and acknowledged the purchase. The names of witnesses were then affixed ; and, the president of the court having added his signature, the deed was valid.   Sometimes the seller formally recognised the sale in the following manner :—" All these things have I sold thee : they are thine, I have received their price from thee, and will make no demand upon thee for them from this day ; and if any person disturb thee in the possession of them, I will withstand the attempt ; and, if I do not otherwise repel it, I will use compulsory means," or, " I will indemnify thee."

But, in order to give a more accurate notion of the form of these contracts, I shall introduce a copy of the whole of one of them, as given by Dr. Young, and refer the reader to others occurring in the same work.   " Translation of the enchorial papyrus of Paris, containing the original deed relating to the mummies :—' This writing dated in the year 36, Athyr 20, in the reign of our sovereigns Ptolemy and Cleopatra his sister, the children of Ptolemy and Cleopatra the divine, the gods Illustrious : and the priest of Alexander, and of the Saviour gods, of the Brother gods, of the (Beneficent gods), of the Father-loving gods, of the Illustrious gods, of the Paternal god, and of the Mother-loving gods, being (as by law appointed) : and the prize-bearer of Berenice the Beneficent, and the basket-bearer of Arsinoë the Brother-loving, and the priestess of Arsinoë the Father-loving, being as appointed in the metropolis (of Alexandria) ; and in (Ptolemaïs) the royal city of the Thebaïd ? the guardian priest for the year ? of Ptolemy Soter, and the priest of king Ptolemy the Father-loving, and the priest of Ptolemy the Brother-loving, and the priest of Ptolemy the Beneficent, and the priest of Ptolemy the Mother-loving; and the priestess of queen Cleopatra, and the priestess of the princess Cleopatra, and the priestess of Cleopatra, the (queen) mother, deceased, the Illustrious; and the basket-bearer of Arsinoë the Brother-loving (being as appointed): declares: The Dresser? in the temple of the Goddess, Onnophris, the son of Horus, and of Senpoëris, daughter of Spotus? ("aged about forty, lively,") tall (" of a sallow complexion, hollow-eyed, and bald"); in the temple of the goddess to (Horus) his brother? the son of Horus and of Senpoëris, has sold, for a price in money, half of one third of the collections for the dead " priests of Osiris?" lying in Thynabunum . . . in the Libyan suburb of Thebes, in the Memnonia . . . likewise half of one third of the liturgies: their names being, Muthes, the son of Spotus, with his children and his household; Chapocrates, the son of Nechthmonthes, with his children and his household; Arsiesis, the son of Nechthmonthes, with his children and his household; Petemestus, the son of Nechthmonthes; Arsiesis, the son of Zminis, with his children and his household; Osoroëris, the son of Horus, with his children and his household; Spotus, the son of Chapochonsis, surnamed? Zoglyphus (the sculptor), with his children and his household: while there belonged also to Asos, the son of Horus and of Senpoëris, daughter of Spotus? in the same manner one half of a third of the collections for the dead, and of the fruits and so forth . . . he sold it on the 20th of Athyr, in the reign of the King ever-living, to (complete) the third part: likewise the half of one third of the collections relating to Peteutemis, with his household, and . . . likewise the half of one third? of the collections and fruits for Petechonsis, the bearer of milk, and of the . . . place on the Asian side, called Phrecages, and . . . the dead bodies in it: there having belonged to Asos the son of Horus one half of the same: he has sold to him in the month of . . . the half of one third of the collections for the priests of Osiris? lying in Thynabunum, with their children and their households: likewise the half of one third of the collections for Peteutemis, and also for Petechonsis, the bearer of milk, in the place Phrecages on the Asian side : I have received for them their price in silver . . . and gold; and I make no further demand on thee for them from the present day . . . before the authorities . . . (and if any one shall disturb thee in the possession of them, I will resist him, and, if I do not succeed, I will indemnify thee?) . . . Executed and confirmed. Written by Horus, the son of Phabis, clerk to the chief priests of Amonrasonther, and of the contemplar? Gods, of the Beneficent gods, of the Father-loving gods, of the Paternal god, and of the Mother-loving gods.   Amen.

" ' Names of the witnesses present :—

ERIEUS, the son of Phanres Erieus.
PETEARTRES, the son of Peteutemis.
PETEARPOCRATES, the son of Horus.
SNACHOMNEUS, the son of Peteuris.
SNACHOMES, the son of Psenchonsis.
TOTOES, the son of Phibis.
PORTIS, the son of Appollonius.
ZMINIS, the son of Petemestus.
PETEUTEMIS, the son of Arsiesis.
AMONORYTIUS, the son of Pacemis.
HORUS, the son of Chimnaraus.
ARMENIS (rather Arbais), the son of Zthenaetis.
MAESIS, the son of Mirsis.
ANTIMACHUS, the son of Antigenes.
PETOPHOIS, the son of Phibis.
PANAS, the son of Petosiris.' "

In this, as in many other documents, the testimony required is very remarkable, sixteen witnesses being thought necessary for the sale of a moiety of the sums collected on account of a few tombs, and for services performed to the dead, the total value of which was only 400 pieces of brass; and the name of each person is introduced, in the true Oriental style, with that of his father. Nor is it unreasonable to suppose that the same precautions and minute formulas were observed in similar transactions during the reigns of the Pharaonic kings, however great may have been the change introduced by the Ptolemies and Romans into the laws and local government of Egypt.

Of the marriage contracts of the Egyptians we are entirely ignorant, nor do we even find the ceremony represented in the paintings of their tombs. We may, however, conclude that they were regulated by the customs usual among civilised nations; and, if the authority of Diodorus can be credited, women were indulged with greater privileges in Egypt than in any other country. He even affirms that part of the agreement entered into at the time of marriage was, that the wife should have control over her husband, and that no objection should be made to her *commands*, whatever they might be; but, though we have sufficient to convince us of the superior treatment of women among the Egyptians, as well from ancient authors as from the sculptures that remain, it may fairly be doubted if those indulgences were carried to the extent mentioned by the historian, or that command extended beyond the management of the house, and the regulation of domestic affairs.

It is, however, remarkable that the royal authority and supreme direction of affairs were entrusted without reserve to women, as in those states of modern Europe where the Salic law has not been introduced; and we not only find examples in Egyptian history of queens succeeding to the throne, but Manetho informs us that the law, according this important privilege to the other sex, dated as early as the reign of Binothris, the third monarch of the second dynasty.

In primitive ages the duties of women were very different from those of later and more civilized periods, and varied of course according to the habits of each people. Among pastoral tribes they drew water, kept the sheep, and superintended the herds as well as flocks. As with the Arabs of the present day, they prepared both the furniture and the woollen stuffs of which the tents themselves were made, ground the corn, and performed other menial offices. They were also engaged, as in ancient Greece, in weaving, spinning, needlework, embroidery, and other sedentary occupations within doors. The Egyptian ladies in like manner employed much of their time with the needle; and the sculptures represent many females weaving and using the spindle. But they were not kept in the same secluded manner as those of ancient

Greece, who, besides being confined to certain apartments in the house, most remote from the hall of entrance, and generally in the uppermost part of the building, were not even allowed to go out of doors without a veil, as in many Oriental countries at the present day. The Egyptians treated their women very differently, as the accounts of ancient authors and the sculptures sufficiently prove. At some of the public festivals women were expected to attend—not alone, like the Moslem women at a mosque, but in company with their husbands or relations; and Josephus states that on an occasion of this kind, " when it was the custom for women to go to the public solemnity, the wife of Potiphar, having pleaded ill health in order to be allowed to stay at home, was excused from attending," and availed herself of the absence of her husband to talk with Joseph. (*See* vol. i. pp. 4, 144.)

That it was the custom of the Egyptians to have only one wife, is shown by Herodotus and the monuments, which present so many scenes illustrative of their domestic life ; and Diodorus is wrong in supposing that the laity were allowed to marry any number, while the priests were limited to one. (*See* vol. i. p. 5.)

But a very objectionable custom, which is not only noticed by Diodorus, but is fully authenticated by the sculptures both of Upper and Lower Egypt, existed among them from the earliest times, the origin and policy of which it is not easy to explain— the marriage of brother and sister—which Diodorus supposes to have been owing to, and sanctioned by, that of Isis and Osiris ; but as this was purely an allegorical fable, and these ideal personages never lived on earth, his conjecture is of little weight ; nor does any ancient writer offer a satisfactory explanation of so strange a custom.

In the time of the Patriarchs, as in the case of Abraham and Sarah, and among the Athenians, it was lawful to marry a sister by the father's side, not, however, if born of the same mother ; but that this restriction was not observed in Egypt, we have sufficient evidence from the marriages of several of the Ptolemies.

Though the Egyptians confined themselves to one wife, they, like the Jews and other Eastern nations, both of ancient and modern times, scrupled not to admit other inmates to their *hareem*, most of whom appear to have been foreigners, either taken in war, or brought to Egypt to be sold as slaves. They became members of the family, like those in Moslem countries at the present day, and not only ranked next to the wives and children of their lord, but probably enjoyed a share of the property at his death. These women were white or black slaves, according to the countries from which they were brought; but, generally speaking, the latter were employed merely as domestics, who were required to wait upon their mistress and her female friends. The former, likewise, officiated as servants, though they of course held a rank above the black slaves.

The same custom prevailed among the Egyptians regarding children, as with the Moslems and other Eastern people; no distinction being made between their offspring by a wife or any other woman, and all equally enjoying the rights of inheritance; for, since they considered a child indebted to the father for its existence, it seemed unjust to deny equal rights to all his progeny.

In speaking of the duties of children in Egypt, Herodotus declares, that if a son was unwilling to maintain his parents he was at liberty to refuse, but that a daughter, on the contrary, was compelled to assist them, and, on refusal, was amenable to law. But we may question the truth of this statement; and, drawing an inference from the marked severity of filial duties among the Egyptians, some of which we find distinctly alluded to in the sculptures of Thebes, we may conclude that in Egypt much more was expected from a son than in any civilised nation of the present day; and this was not confined to the lower orders, but extended to those of the highest ranks of society. And if the office of fan-bearer was an honourable post, and the sons of the monarch were preferred to fulfil it, no ordinary show of humility was required on their part; and they walked on foot behind his chariot, bearing certain insignia over their father during the triumphal processions which took place in commemoration of his victories, and in the religious ceremonies over which he presided.

It was equally a custom in the early times of European history, that a son should pay a marked deference to his parent; and no prince was allowed to sit at table with his father, unless through his valour, having been invested with arms by a foreign sovereign, he had obtained that privilege ; as was the case with Alboin, before he succeeded his father on the throne of the Lombards. The European nations were not long in altering their early habits, and this custom soon became disregarded ; but a respect for ancient institutions, and those ideas, so prevalent in the East, which reject all love of change, prevented the Egyptians from discarding the usages of their ancestors ; and we find this and many other primitive customs retained, even at the period when they were most highly civilised.

In the education of youth they were particularly strict ; and " they knew," says Plato, " that children ought to be early accustomed to such gestures, looks, and motions as are decent and proper, and not to be suffered either to hear or learn any verses and songs, than those which are calculated to inspire them with virtue ; and they consequently took care that every dance and ode introduced at their feasts or sacrifices should be subject to certain regulations." They particularly inculcated respect for old age ; and the fact of this being required even towards strangers, argues a great regard for the person of a parent ; for we are informed that, like the Israelites and the Lacedæmonians, they required every young man to give place to his superiors in years, and even, if seated, to rise on their approach.

Nor were these honours limited to their lifetime : the memory of parents and ancestors was revered through succeeding generations : their tombs were maintained with the greatest respect ; liturgies were performed by their children, or by priests at their expense ; and we have previously seen what advantage was taken of this feeling, in the laws concerning debt.

Guided by the same principle, the Egyptians paid the most marked respect to their monarch, as the father of his people. He was obeyed with courteous submission, his will was tantamount to a law, and such implicit confidence did they place in his judgment that he was thought incapable of error. He was the representative of the Divinity on earth : the Gods were supposed to communicate through him their choicest benefits to man ; and they believed that the sovereign power had been delegated to him by the will of the Deities themselves.   They entertained a strong feeling of gratitude for the services done by him to the state ; and the memory of a monarch who had benefited his subjects was celebrated after death with the most unbounded honours.   " For of all people," says Diodorus, " the Egyptians retain the highest sense of a favour conferred upon them, deeming it the greatest charm of life to make a suitable return for benefits they have received ;" and from the high estimation in which the feeling of gratitude was held among them, even strangers felt a reverence for the character of the Egyptians.   Through this impulse, they were induced to solemnise the funeral obsequies of their kings with the enthusiasm described by the historian ; and to this he partly attributes the unexampled duration of the Egyptian monarchy.   (*See* vol. i. p. 314.)

It is only doing justice to the modern Egyptians to say that gratitude is still a distinguishing trait of their character ; and this is one of the many qualities inherited by them, for which their predecessors were remarkable ; confirming what I have before stated, that the general peculiarities of a people are retained, though a country may be conquered, and nominally peopled by a foreign race.   (*See* vol. i. p. 2, 3.)

Another remarkable feature of the Egyptian laws was the sanctity with which old edicts were upheld.   They were closely interwoven with the religion of the country, and said to be derived from the Gods themselves ; whence it was considered both useless and impious to alter such sacred institutions.   Those innovations only were introduced by their monarchs, which were loudly called for by circumstances ; and we neither read of any attempts on the part of the people to alter or resist the laws, nor on that of their rulers to introduce a more arbitrary mode of government.

The Egyptians were particularly remarkable for their great love for their country ; which is also inherited by their successors. They considered it to be under the immediate protection of the Gods, and the centre of the world ; they even called it the " world " itself ; and it was thought to be the favoured spot where all created beings were first generated, while the rest of the earth was barren and uninhabited.

But as society advanced, it necessarily happened that some alterations were required, either in the reformation of an existing code, or in the introduction of additional laws; and among the different legislators of the Egyptians are particularly noticed the names of Mnevis, Sasyches, Sesostris, Bocchoris, Asychis, Amasis, and even the Persian Darius. The great merit of the first of these seems to have consisted in inducing the people to conform to those institutions which he pretended to have received from Hermes, the Egyptian Mercury; " an idea," says Diodorus, " which has been adopted with success by many other ancient lawgivers, who have inculcated a respect for their institutions, through the awe that is naturally felt for the majesty of the Gods." The additions made by Sasyches chiefly related to matters of religious worship; and Sesostris, in addition to numerous regulations of a military nature, is said to have introduced some changes into the agricultural system. He divided all the land of Egypt, with the exception of that which belonged to the priests and soldiers, into squares of equal areas, assigning to each peasant his peculiar portion, or a certain number of these *arouras*, for which he annually paid a fixed rent; and having instituted a yearly survey of the lands, any deficiency, resulting from a fall of the bank during the inundation, or other accidental causes, was stated in the returns, and deducted for in the government demands. Of the laws of Bocchoris and Asychis respecting debt, I have already spoken; and the former is said to have introduced many others relating to the kings, as well as to civil contracts and commerce, and to have established several important precedents in Egyptian jurisprudence. (*See above*, pp. 217, 218.)

Amasis was particularly eminent for his wisdom, and for the many salutary additions he made to the laws of his country. He remodelled the system of provincial government, defining the duties of the nomarchs with peculiar precision; and his conduct in the management of affairs was so highly approved by the people, that their respect for him was scarcely inferior to that

shown to his most glorious predecessors. Nor was Darius, though
a Persian, and of a nation justly abhorred by the Egyptians,*
denied those eulogiums which the mildness of his government,
and the introduction of laws tending to benefit the country,
claimed for him; and they even granted him the title of Divus,
making him partaker of the same honours which were bestowed
on their native princes.   But the Ptolemies in after times
abrogated some of the favourite laws of the country ; and though
much was done by them, in repairing the temples, and in executing
very grand and useful works, and though several of those sovereigns courted the good will of the Egyptians, yet their name
became odious, and Macrobius has stigmatised their sway with
the title of " tyranny."

After the king and council, the judges or magistrates of the
capital held the most distinguished post ; and next to them may
be considered the nomarchs, or governors, of districts.

The whole of Egypt was divided into nomes, or districts, the
total of which, in the time of Sesostris, amounted to thirty-six ;—
afterwards increased to fifty-three.

The limits of Egypt were the Mediterranean to the north, and
Syene, or the Cataracts, to the south ; and the cultivated land
east and west of the Nile, contained within this space, or between
the latitude 31° 37′ and 24° 3′, was all that constituted the
original territory of the Pharaohs : though the Mareotis, the
Oases, the Nitriotis, and even part of Libya were attached to their
dominions, and were considered part of the country.

The main divisions of Egypt were " the Upper and Lower
regions ;" and this distinction, which had been maintained from
the earliest times, was also indicated by a difference in the dia-
lects of the language.   Thebes and Memphis enjoyed equal rank
as capitals of Egypt ; and every monarch at his coronation
assumed the title of " lord of the two regions," or " the two
worlds."   But a change afterwards took place in the division of

---

* Though Cambyses was so execrated, his conduct was at first conciliatory;
and a monument in the Louvre proves that he confirmed the leading men in their
offices, and did not interfere with their customs until the Egyptians became
turbulent.

the country, and the northern portion was subdivided into the two provinces of Heptanomis and Lower Egypt. The latter extended from the sea to the head of the Delta, and advancing to the natural boundary of the low lands, which is so strongly marked by the abrupt ridge of the modern Mokuttum, it included the city of Heliopolis within its limits.

Heptanomis, or Middle Egypt, extended thence to the Theban castle, which marked the frontier a few miles above Tanis, and which appears to have occupied the site of the present town of Dahroot; and its name, Heptanomis, was derived from the seven nomes, or districts, it contained, which were those of Memphis, Aphroditopolis, Crocodilopolis, or Arsinoë, Heracleopolis, Oxyrhinchus, Cynopolis, and Hermopolis.

The limits of the Thebaïd remained the same, and extended to the cataracts of Syene; but it appears that the Oases were all attached to the province of Heptanomis. The chief towns of the three provinces were Thebes, Memphis, and Heliopolis; the same from which the bench of judges was elected.

According to Diodorus, the celebrated Sesostris was the first who divided the country into nomes; but it is more reasonable to suppose that long before his time, or at least before that of Remeses the Great, or even of Osirtasen, all necessary arrangements for the organization of the provinces had already been made, and that this was one of the first plans suggested for the government of the country.

The office of nomarch was at all times of the highest importance, and to his charge were committed the management of the lands, and all matters relating to the internal administration of the district. He regulated the assessment and levying of the taxes, the survey of the lands, the opening of the canals, and all other agricultural interests of the country, which were under the immediate superintendence of certain members of the priestly order; and, as his residence was in the chief town of the nome, all causes respecting landed property, and other accidental disputes, were referred to him, and adjusted before his tribunal. The division of the country into thirty-six parts, or nomes, continued to be maintained till a late period, since in Strabo's time the number was still the same; ten, says the geographer, being assigned to the Thebaïd, ten to the Delta, and sixteen to the intermediate province; though some changes were afterwards introduced both in the nomes and provinces of Egypt. The nomes, he adds, were subdivided into local governments, and these again into minor jurisdictions; and we may conclude that the three offices of nomarchs, toparchs, and the third or lowest grade, answered to those of bey, kashef, and ḳýmaḳám of the present day. The distinctive appellation of each nome, in later times at least, was derived from the chief town, where the governor resided, and the rank of each nomarch depended on the extent of his jurisdiction. But of the condition of Egypt in the early period of its history little is known; owing to the scanty information obtained by those Greeks who visited it, or to the loss of their writings, as well as to the jealousy of the Egyptians towards foreigners, to whom little or nothing was imparted respecting the institutions and state of the country.

They prevented all strangers from penetrating into the interior; and if any Greek was desirous of becoming acquainted with the philosophy of their schools, he was tolerated, rather than welcomed, in Egypt; and those who traded there were confined to the town of Naucratis, in the same manner that Europeans are now obliged to live in the Frank quarter of a Turkish, or a Chinese, city. And when, after the time of Amasis and the Persian conquest, foreigners became better acquainted with the country, its ancient institutions had begun to lose their interest, and the Egyptians mourned under a victorious and cruel despot. Herodotus, it is true, had ample opportunity of examining the state of Egypt during his visit to the country; but he has failed to give us much insight into its laws and institutions.

Strabo mentions some of the offices which existed in Egypt in his time; but, though he asserts that many of them were the same as under the Ptolemies, we are by no means certain that they answer to those of an earlier period. "Under the eparch," says the geographer, "who holds the rank of a king, is the dicæodotes, that is, the lawgiver or chancellor, and another officer, who is called the privy-purse, or private accountant, whose business it is to take charge of everything that is left without an owner, and which falls of right to the emperor. These two are also attended by freedmen and stewards of Cæsar, who are entrusted with affairs of greater or less magnitude. . . . . But of the natives who are employed in the government of the different cities, the principal is the exégétés, or expounder, who is dressed in purple, and is honoured according to the usages of the country, and takes care of what is necessary for the welfare of the city: the register, or writer of commentaries: the archidicastes, or chief judge: and, fourthly, the captain of the night."

From all that can be collected on this subject, we may conclude, that in early times, after the king, the senate, and others connected with the court, the principal persons employed in the management of affairs were the judges of different grades, the rulers of provinces and districts, the government accountants, the chief of the police, and those officers immediately connected with the administration of justice, the levying of taxes, and other similar employments; and that the principal part of them were chosen either from the sacerdotal or the military class.

During the reigns of the latter Ptolemies, considerable abuses crept into the administrative system: intrigues, arising out of party spirit and conflicting interests, corrupted men's minds: integrity ceased to be esteemed: every patriotic feeling became extinguished: the interests of the community were sacrificed to the ambition of a successful candidate for a disputed throne: and the hope of present advantage blinded men to future consequences. New regulations were adopted to suppress the turbulent spirit of the times: the government, no longer content with the mild office of protector, assumed the character of chastiser of the people: and Egypt was ruled by a military force, rendered doubly odious, from being, in a great measure, composed of foreign mercenaries. The military class had lost its consequence, its privileges were abolished, and the harmony once existing between it and the people was entirely destroyed. Respect for the wisdom of the sacerdotal order, and the ancient institutions of Egypt, began to decline: and the influence once possessed by the priests over the public mind could only be traced in the superstitious reverence shown by fanatics to the rites of a religion, now much corrupted and degraded by fanciful doctrines; and if they retained a portion of their former privileges, by having the education of youth entrusted to them, as well as the care of the national records, the superintendence of weights and measures, the surveying of the lands, and the equal distribution of the annual payments, they lost their most important offices— the tutelage and direction of the councils of government, and the right of presiding at the courts of justice.

The provincial divisions of Egypt varied at different times, particularly after the Roman conquest. The country, as already stated, consisted originally of two parts, Upper and Lower Egypt; afterwards of three, the Thebaïd: Heptanomis, or Middle Egypt: and the Delta, or Lower Egypt: but Heptanomis, in the time of Arcadius, the son of Theodosius the Great, received the name of Arcadia; and the eastern portion of the Delta, about the end of the fourth century, was formed into a separate province called Augustamnica, itself divided into two parts. The Thebaïd was also made to consist of Upper and Lower, the line of separation passing between Panopolis and Ptolemaïs Hermii.

Under the Romans, Egypt was governed by a præfect, or eparch, aided by three officers, who superintended the departments of justice, revenue, and police, throughout the country, the inferior charges being chiefly filled by natives; and over each of the provinces a military governor was appointed, who was subordinate to the præfect in all civil affairs, though frequently intruding on his jurisdiction, when it was necessary to use military coercion in the collection of the taxes. But as the condition of Egypt under the Ptolemies and Romans is not directly connected with the manners and customs of the ancient Egyptians, it is unnecessary to describe the changes that took place during their rule.

Judging from the sculptures of Thebes, the tribute annually received in early times by the Egyptians, from nations they had subdued in Asia and Northern Ethiopia, was of immense value, and tended greatly to enrich the coffers of the state; and the quantity of gold in dust, rings, and bars, and silver in rings and ingots, copper, iron, lead, and tin (?), the various objects of luxury, vases of glass, porcelain, gold, silver, and other metals, ivory, ebony, and different woods, precious stones, horses, dogs, oxen, wild animals, trees, seeds, fruits, bitumen, incense, gums, perfumes, spices, and other foreign productions there described, perfectly accord with the statements of ancient authors. And though they are presented to the king, as chief of the nation, we may conclude they formed part of the public revenue, and were not solely intended for his use; especially in a country where royalty was under the restraint and guidance of salutary laws, and where the welfare of the community was not sacrificed to the caprice of a monarch.

According to Strabo, the taxes, even under Ptolemy Auletes, the father of Cleopatra, the most negligent of monarchs, amounted to 12,500 talents, or between three and four millions sterling; and the constant influx of specie resulting from commercial intercourse with foreign nations, who purchased the corn and manufactures of Egypt, during the very careful administration of its native sovereigns, necessarily increased the riches of the country, and greatly augmented the revenue at that period.

Among the exports were yarn, fine linen cloth, and embroidered work, purchased by the Tyrians and Jews; chariots and horses, bought by the merchants of Judæa in the time of Solomon at 600 and 150 shekels of silver; and other commodities, produced or manufactured in the country.*

The Egyptians also derived important advantages from their intercourse with India and Arabia; and the port of Philoteras, which, there is reason to believe, was constructed at a very remote period, long before the Exodus of the Israelites, was probably the emporium of that trade. It was situated on the western coast of the Red Sea, in latitude 26° 9'; and though small, the number of ships its basin would contain sufficed for a constant traffic between Egypt and Arabia, no periodical winds there interfering with the navigation, at any season of the year.

* 2 Chron. i. 16, 17; 1 Kings, x.; and Ezek. xxvii. 7.

It is not probable that they had a direct communication with India at the same early epoch; but they were supplied through Arabia with the merchandise of that country; and even an indirect trade was capable of opening to them a source of immense wealth. And that the productions of India did actually reach Egypt we have positive testimony from the tombs of Thebes.

The Scripture history shows the traffic established by Solomon with India, through the Red Sea, to have been of very great consequence, producing, in one voyage, no less than 450 talents of gold*; and to the same branch of commerce may be ascribed the main cause of the flourishing condition of Tyre itself. And if the Egyptian trade was not so direct as that of Solomon and the Tyrians, it must still be admitted that *any* intercourse with India at so remote a period would have been highly beneficial to the country, since it was enjoyed with little competition, and consequently afforded increased advantages.

The other harbours in this part of the Arabian Gulf,—Myos Hormos, Berenice, Arsinoë, Nechesia, and Leucos Portus,— were built in later times; and the lucrative trade they enjoyed was greatly increased after the conquest of Egypt by the Romans; 120 vessels annually leaving the coast of Egypt for India, at midsummer, about the rising of the dog-star, and returning in the month of December or January. " The principal objects of oriental traffic," says Gibbon, " were splendid and trifling : silk (a pound of which was esteemed not inferior in value to a pound of gold), precious stones, and a variety of aromatics." When Strabo visited Egypt the Myos Hormos seems to have superseded Berenice, and all the other maritime stations on the coast; and indeed it possessed greater advantages than any other, except Philoteras and Arsinoë, in its overland communication with the Nile. Yet Berenice, in the later age of Pliny, was again preferred to its rival. From both ports the goods were taken on camels by an almost level road across the desert to Coptos, and thence distributed over different parts of Egypt; and, in the time of the Ptolemies and Cæsars, those particularly suited for

---

* 2 Chron. viii. 18; 1 Kings, ix. 26.

exportation to Europe went down the river to Alexandria, where they were sold to merchants who resorted to that city at a stated season.

At a subsequent period, during the reigns of the Arab Caliphs, Apollinopolis, Parva, or Koos, succeeded Coptos, as the rendezvous of caravans from the Red Sea; and this town flourished so rapidly, in consequence of the preference it enjoyed, that in Aboolfeda's time it was second only to Fostat, the capital of Egypt; until it ceded its place to Keneh, as Myos Hormos was destined to do in favour of Kossayr. Philoteras, however, continued to be resorted to after the Arab conquest; and it was during the reigns of the Egyptian caliphs that the modern Kossayr took the place of that ancient port.

The Myos Hormos, called also Aphrodité, stood in latitude 27° 22', upon a flat coast, backed by low mountains, distant from it about three miles; where a well, the Fons Tadnos, supplied the town and ships with water. The port was more capacious than those of Berenice and Philoteras; and though exposed to the winds, it was secure against the force of a boisterous sea. Several roads united at the gates of the town, from Berenice and Philoteras on the south, from Arsinoë on the north, and from Coptos on the west; and stations supplied those who passed to and from the Nile with water and other necessaries.

Berenice owed its foundation to Ptolemy Philadelphus, who called it after the name of his mother, the wife of Lagus or Soter. The town was extensive, and was ornamented with a small but elegant temple of Sarapis; and though the harbour was neither deep nor spacious, its position in a receding gulf tended greatly to the safety of the vessels lying within it, or anchored in the bay. A road led thence direct to Coptos, furnished with the usual stations, or *hydreumas;* and another, which also went to the emerald mines, joined, or rather crossed it, from Apollinopolis Magna.

Arsinoë, which stood at the northern extremity of the Red Sea, near the modern town of Sooez, was founded by the second Ptolemy, and so named after his sister. Though vessels anchored there rode secure from the violence of the sea, its exposed situation, and the dangers they encountered in working up the narrow extremity of the gulf, rendered its position less eligible for the Indian trade than either Myos Hormos or Berenice; and had it not been for the convenience of establishing a communication with the Nile by a canal, and the shortness of the journey across the desert in that part, it is probable it would not have been chosen for a sea-port.

The small towns of Nechesia and the Leucos Portus were probably of Roman date, though the natural harbours they possess may have been used at a much earlier period. Their positions are still marked by the ruins on the shore, in latitude 24° 54′ and 25° 37′, where I discovered them in 1826, while making a survey of this part of the coast from Sooez to Berenice. The former stands in, and perhaps gave the name to, the Wadee Nukkaree; the latter is called E'Shoona, or "the Magazine," and, from being built of very *white* limestone, was readily indicated by the Arabs when I inquired of them the site of the White Harbour.

Many other ports, the "Portus multi" of Pliny, occur along the coast, particularly between Berenice and Kossayr; but though they all have landmarks to guide boats in approaching their rocky entrances, which are openings in the coral reefs, none of them have any remains of a town, or the vestiges of habitations.

The principal objects introduced in early times into Egypt, from Arabia and India, were spices and various oriental productions, required either for the service of religion, or the purposes of luxury; and a number of precious stones, lapis lazzuli, and other things brought from those countries, are frequently discovered in the tombs of Thebes, bearing the names of Pharaohs of the 18th dynasty. The mines of their own desert did, indeed, supply the emeralds they used; and these were worked as early, at least, as the reign of Amunoph III., at the beginning of the 15th century B.C., but many other stones must have come from India; and some plants, as the Nymphæa Nelumbo, seem to have been introduced from that country.

Though we cannot ascertain the amount or exact quality of the various imports, of the goods re-exported from Egypt, or the proportion which these last bore to the internal consumption, it is reasonable to conclude that every article of luxury was a source of revenue to the government; and that both native and foreign productions coming under this denomination, whether exported, or sold in Egypt, tended to enrich the state, to which they belonged, or paid a duty.

That the riches of the country were immense is proved by the appearance of the furniture and domestic utensils, and by the great quantity of jewels of gold, and silver, precious stones, and other objects of luxury in use among them in the earliest times; their treasures became proverbial throughout the neighbouring states,* and a love of pomp and splendour continued to be the ruling passion of the Egyptians till the latest period of their existence as an independent state.

The wealth of Egypt was principally derived from taxes, foreign tribute, monopolies, commerce, mines, and above all from the productions of a fruitful soil. The wants of the poorer classes were easily satisfied; the abundance of grain, herbs, and esculent plants, afforded an ample supply to the inhabitants of the valley of the Nile, at a trifling expense, and with little labour; and so much corn was produced in this fertile country, that after sufficing for the consumption of a very extensive population, it offered a great surplus for the foreign market; and afforded considerable profit to the government, being exported to other countries, or sold to the traders who visited Egypt for commercial purposes.

The gold mines of the Bisharee desert were in those times very productive; and, though we have no positive notice of their first discovery, there is reason to believe they were worked at the earliest periods of the Egyptian monarchy. The total of the annual produce of the gold and silver mines (which Diodorus, on the authority of Hecatæus, says, was recorded in the tomb of Osymandyas at Thebes, apparently a king of the 19th dynasty) is stated to have been 3200 myriads, or 32 millions of *minæ*,

---

* " Greater riches than the treasures in Egypt." Ep. Heb. xi. 26. "The pomp of Egypt." Ezek. xxxii. 12. *Comp.* also the jewels of silver and gold which the Jews borrowed from the Egyptians. Exod. xii. 35.

—a weight of that country, called by the Egyptians *mn* or *mna*, 60 of which were equal to one talent. The whole sum amounted to 133 millions of our money; but it was evidently exaggerated.

The position of the silver mines is unknown; but the gold mines of Allaga (already mentioned)*, and other quartz "diggings," have been discovered, as well as those of copper, lead, iron, and emeralds, all of which are in the desert near the Red Sea; and the sulphur, which abounds in the same districts, was not neglected by the ancient Egyptians.

The abundance of gold and silver in Egypt and other ancient countries, and the sums reported to have been spent, accord well with the reputed productiveness of the mines in those days; and, as the subject has become one of peculiar interest, it may be well to enquire respecting the quantity and the use of the precious metals in ancient times. They were then mostly confined to the treasuries of princes, and of some rich individuals; the proportion employed for commercial purposes was small, copper sufficing for most purchases in the home market; and nearly all the gold and silver money (as yet uncoined) was in the hands of the wealthy few. The manufacture of jewellery and other ornamental objects took up a small portion of the great mass; but it required the wealth and privilege of royalty to indulge in a grand display of gold and silver vases, or similar objects of size and value.

The mines of those days, from which was derived the wealth of Egypt, Lydia, Persia, and other countries, afforded a large supply of the precious metals; and if most of them are now exhausted, or barely retain evidences of the treasures they once gave forth, there can be no doubt of their former productiveness; and it is reasonable to suppose that gold and silver abounded in early times in those parts of the world which were first inhabited, as they did in countries more recently peopled. They may never have afforded at any period the immense riches of a California or an Australia, yet there is evidence of their having been sufficiently distributed over various parts of the old world.

* In chap. vii. p. 141.

For though Herodotus (iii., 106) says that the extremities of the earth possess the greatest treasures; those extremities may approach or become the centre, i. e., of civilisation, when they arrive at that eminence which all great countries in their turn seem to have a chance of reaching; and Britain, the country of the greatly coveted tin, once looked upon as separated from the rest of mankind, is now one of the commercial centres of the world. The day, too, may come when Australia and California will be rivals for a similar distinction; and England, the rendezvous of America in her contests with Europe, will yield its turn to younger competitors.

The greatest quantity of gold and silver in early times was derived from the East; and Asia and Egypt possessed abundance of those metals. The trade of Colchis, and the treasures of the Arimaspês and Massagetæ, coming from the Ural (or from the Altai) mountains, supplied much gold at a very early period, and Indian commerce sent a large supply to western Asia. Spain, the Isle of Thasos, and other places, were resorted to by the Phœnicians, particularly for silver; and Spain, for its mines, became the "El Dorado" of those adventurous traders.

The mines of the Eastern desert, the tributes from Ethiopia and Central Africa, as well as from Asia, enriched Egypt with gold and silver; but it was long before Greece (where in heroic times the precious metals were scarcely known) obtained a moderate supply of silver from her own mines; and gold only became abundant there after the Persian war.

Thrace and Macedonia produced gold, as well as other countries, but confined it to their own use, as Ireland employed the produce of its mines; and as early Italy did, when its various small states were still free from the Roman yoke; and though the localities from which silver was obtained in more ancient times are less known, it is certain that it was used at a very remote period; and (as before stated) it was commonly employed in Abraham's time for mercantile transactions.

Gold is mentioned on the Egyptian monuments of the 4th dynasty, and silver was probably of the same early time; but gold was evidently known in Egypt before silver, which is consistent with reason, gold being more easily obtained than silver, and frequently near the surface or in streams. (*See above*, p. 147.)

The relative value and quantity of the precious metals in the earliest times, in Egypt and Western Asia, are not known ; and even if a greater amount of gold were found mentioned in a tribute, this could be no proof of the silver being more rare, as it might merely be intended to show the richness of the gifts. In the tribute brought to Thothmes III. by the southern Ethiopians and three Asiatic people, the former present scarcely any silver, but great quantities of gold in rings, ingots, and dust. The Asiatic people of Pount bring two baskets of gold rings, and one of gold dust in bags, a much smaller amount of gold than the Ethiopians, and no silver; those of Kufa, or Kaf, more silver than gold, and a considerable quantity of both made into vases of handsome and varied shapes; and the Rot-ñ-n (apparently living on the Euphrates) present rather more gold than silver, a large basket of gold and a smaller one of silver rings, two small silver and several large gold vases, which are of most elegant shape, as well as coloured glass or porcelain cups, and much incense and bitumen. The great Asiatic tribute to the same king at Karnak, speaks in one place of 100 ingots (or pounds weight?) of gold and silver, and afterwards of 401 of silver ; but the imperfect preservation of that record prevents our ascertaining how much gold was brought, or the relative proportions of the two metals.

M. Léon Faucher, indeed, suggests that " the value of silver in some countries originally equalled, if it did not exceed, that of gold . . . and the laws of Menes state that gold was worth two and a half times more than silver. . . . Everywhere, except in India, between the fifth and sixth centuries B.C., the relative value of gold and silver was 6 or 8 to 1, as it was in China and Japan at the end of last century." In Greece it was, according to Herodotus, as 13 to 1 ; afterwards, in Plato's and Xenophon's time, and more than 100 years after the death of Alexander, as 10 to 1, owing to the quantity of gold brought in through the Persian war ; when the value of both fell so much, that in the time of Demosthenes it was five times less than at the death of Solon.

The relative price of gold and silver continued for a long time at 10 to 1 (Liv. xxxviii. 11), except when occasional events altered the equilibrium by an increase of one of those metals; as when the taking of Syracuse, and the plunder of the treasury by Julius Cæsar, reduced the proportions to 7 and 9 to 1. But these sudden changes, as Humboldt says, were owing to the less general commercial relations of the world, and they could not have happened with the rapidity of communication in the present day.

Under the Empire, the produce of the silver mines of Asia, Thrace, and Spain, again raised the value of gold, and the proportions were 18 to 1 in the time of Theodosius II.; but the skill required for working silver was so deficient during the middle ages and in the sixteenth century, that they were brought to 11 and 12 to 1. Before the discovery of America, they were 11 and 10 to 1 in England ; and, after great fluctuations, they were in Newton's time 16 to 1, becoming at length about 14¼ to 1 ; which may again be altered by the modern discoveries of California and Australia, unless another Potosi affords fresh supplies of silver. But owing to the constant export of gold, the extent of trading operations, the rapidity of communication throughout the world, and the quantity required to keep up the equilibrium after restoring the deficiency in many countries, a long time must elapse before the effects of these new gold supplies on the general circulation will be felt, or the value of gold be sensibly altered beyond its relative proportion to silver.

Though it may not be possible to arrive at any satisfactory conclusion, respecting the quantity of gold and silver taken from the mines ; employed in objects of art and luxury ; or in circulation as money in Egypt and other countries; I shall introduce a few facts derived from the accounts of ancient authors, relating to the amount of wealth amassed, and the purposes to which those precious metals were applied. I shall also show some of the fluctuations that have taken place in the supply of them at various periods ; and shall endeavour to establish a comparison between the quantity said to have been in use in ancient and modern times.

When we read of the enormous wealth amassed by the Egyptian and Asiatic kings, or the plunder by Alexander and the Romans, we wonder how so much could have been obtained ; for, even allowing for considerable exaggeration in the accounts of early times, there is no reason to disbelieve the private fortunes of individuals at Rome, and the sums squandered by them, or even the amount of some of the tributes levied in the East.   Of ancient cities, Babylon is particularly cited by Herodotus and others, for its immense wealth.   Diodorus (ii. 9) mentions a golden statue of Jupiter at Babylon 40 feet high, weighing 1000 Babylonian talents ; another of Rhea, of equal weight, having two lions on its knees, and near it silver serpents of 300 talents each ; a standing statue of Juno weighing 800 talents, holding a snake, and a sceptre set with gems ; as well as a golden table of 500 talents weight, on which were two cups weighing 300 talents, and two censers each of 300 talents weight, with three golden bowls, one of which, belonging to Jupiter, weighed 1200 talents, the others each 600 ; making a total of at least 6900 talents, reckoned equal to 11,000,000 sterling.   And the golden image of Nebuchadnezzar, 60 cubits, or 90 feet, high, at the same ratio would weigh 2250 talents.

David, who had not the Indian and Arabian trade afterwards obtained by Solomon, left for the building of the temple 100,000 talents of gold and 1,000,000 of silver ;* and the sum given by him of his " own proper good," " over and above all prepared for the holy house," was " 3000 talents of gold " and " 7000 of refined silver ;" besides the chief men's contributions † of 500 talents and 10,000 drachms of gold, 10,000 talents of silver, and an abundance of brass, iron, and precious stones.

The annual tribute of Solomon ‡ was 666 talents of gold, besides that brought by the merchants, and the present from the Queen of Sheba of 120 talents ; and the quantity of gold and silver used in the temple and his house was extraordinary.   Mr. Jacob, in his valuable work on the precious metals, has noticed many of these immense sums, collected in old times.   Among them are the tribute of Darius, amounting to 9880 talents of silver and 4680 of gold, making a total of 14,560, estimated at

---

* 1 Chron. xxii. 14.   † 1 Chron. xxix. 3, 4, 7.
‡ 2 Chron. ix. 13 ; 1 Kings, x. 14.

about 3¼ millions sterling; the sums taken by Xerxes to
Greece; the wealth of Crœsus; the riches of Pytheus, king of
a small territory in Phrygia, possessing gold and silver mines,
who entertained the army of Xerxes, and gave him 2000 talents
of silver and 4,093,000 staters of gold (equal to 4,770,000
pounds of our money, or according to Larcher 3,600,000); the
treasures acquired by Alexander, in Susa and Persia, exclusive
of that found in the Persian camp and in Babylon, said to have
amounted to 40,000 or 50,000 talents; the treasure of Persepolis rated at 120,000 talents; that of Pasagarda at 6000; and
the 180,000 talents collected at the capture of Ecbatana; besides
6000 which Darius had with him, and were taken by his mur-
derers. "Ptolemy Philadelphus is stated by Appian to have
possessed treasure to the enormous amount of 740,000 talents;"
either "178 millions, or at least a quarter of that sum;" and
fortunes of private individuals at Rome show the enormous
wealth they possessed. "Crassus had in lands 1,614,583*l*., besides as much more in money, furniture, and slaves; Seneca,
2,421,875*l*.; Pallas, the freedman of Claudius, an equal sum;
Lentulus, the augur, 3,229,166*l*.; Cæc. Cl. Isidorus, though he
had lost a great part of his fortune in the civil war, left by his
will 4116 slaves, 3600 yoke of oxen, 257,000 other cattle, and
in ready money 484,375*l*. Augustus received by the testaments
of his friends 32,291,666*l*. Tiberius left at his death 21,796,875*l*.,
which Caligula lavished away in less than one year; and Vespasian, at his succession, said that to support the state he required
quadrigenties millies, or 322,916,666*l*. The debts of Milo
amounted to 565,104*l*. J. Cæsar, before he held any office,
owed 1300 talents, 251,875*l*.; and when he set out for Spain
after his prætorship, he is reported to have said, that ' Bis
millies et quingenties sibi deesse, ut nihil haberet,' or ' that he
was 2,018,229*l*. worse than nothing.' When he first entered
Rome, in the beginning of the civil war, he took out of the
treasury 1,095,979*l*., and brought into it at the end of it
4,843,750*l*.; he purchased the friendship of Curio, at the commencement of the civil war, by a bribe of 484,373*l*., and that of
the consul L. Paulus by 1500 talents, about 279,500*l*.; Apicius

wasted on luxurious living 484,375*l.*; Caligula laid out on a supper 80,729*l.*; and the ordinary expense of Lucullus for a supper in the Hall of Apollo was 50,000 drachms, or 1614*l.* The house of Marius, bought of Cornelia for 2421*l.*, was sold to Lucullus for 16,152*l.*; the burning of his villa was a loss to M. Scaurus of 807,291*l.*; and Nero's golden house must have cost an immense sum, since Otho laid out in furnishing a part of it 403,645*l.*" * But though Rome was greatly enriched by conquest, she never obtained possession of the chief wealth of Asia; and the largest quantity of the precious metals was always excluded from the calculations of ancient writers.

The whole revenue of the Roman Empire under Augustus is " supposed to have been equal to 40 millions of our money ;" and at the time of his death (A.D. 14) the gold and silver in circulation throughout the empire is supposed to have amounted to 358,000,000*l.*; which at a reduction of 1 grain in 360 every year for wear, would have been reduced by the year A.D. 482 to 87,033,099*l*; and when the mines of Hungary and Germany began to be worked, during the seventh and ninth centuries, the entire amount of coined money was not more than about 42 at the former, and 33 or 34 millions sterling at the latter, period ; so that if no other supply had been obtained, the quantity then circulating would long since have been exhausted.

" The loss by wear on silver" is shown by Mr. Jacob " to be four times that of gold ;" that on our shillings is estimated at more than one part in a hundred annually ; and " the smaller the pieces, the greater loss do they suffer by abrasion." " The maximum of durability of gold coins seems to be fixed at 22 parts, in 24, of pure gold with the appropriate alloys. When the fineness ascends or descends from that point, the consumption by abrasion is increased." It is from its ductility that gold wears so much less than silver ; and many ancient gold coins (as those of Alexander and others), though evidently worn by use, nearly retain their true weight, from the surface being partly transferred into the adjacent hollows, and not entirely rubbed off as in silver.

The quantity of the precious metals, formerly used for the

* Adams' Roman Antiquities, p. 438-440.

purposes of luxury, greatly diminished after the decline of the Roman empire, and in the middle ages they were sparingly employed except for coinage ; ornamental work in gold and silver, mostly executed by first-rate artists, being confined to men of rank, till the opening of new mines added to the supply ; which was afterwards increased by the abundant treasures of America ; and the quantity applied to ornamental purposes then began to vie with that of olden times. M. Léon Faucher even calculates the annual abstraction of the precious metals from circulation by use for luxury, disasters at sea, and export, at 5 millions sterling, in Europe and the United States.

The silver from the American mines exported to Europe in 100 years, to 1630, gave an addition to the currency of 1 million sterling annually, besides that used for other purposes, or re-exported ; and from 1630 to 1830 from $1\frac{1}{2}$ to 2 millions annually ; an increase in the quantity used for currency having taken place, as well as in that exported to India, and employed for purposes of luxury. Humboldt states the whole quantity of gold from the American mines, up to 1803, to be 162 millions of pounds in weight, and of silver 7178 millions, or 44 of silver to 1 of gold.

Again, the total value of gold produced during three centuries to 1848, including that from Russia, has been estimated at 565 millions ; and the total annual quantity of gold, before the discovery of the Californian fields, has been reckoned at about 10,000,000*l.* That from California and Australia already amounts yearly to 34,000,000*l.* (or 3 2-5ths times as much as previously obtained), and is still increasing ; but though far beyond the supply afforded by the discovery of America, the demand made upon it by the modern industry of man, together with the effect of rapid communication, and of the extension of trade, as well as by the great deficiency of gold in the world, will prevent its action being felt in the same way as when the American supply was first obtained ; and still less will be the effect now, than it would have been in ancient times, if so large and sudden a discovery had then been made. For, as Chevalier says, " Vast as is the whole amount of gold in the world, it sinks into insignificance when contrasted with the aggregate product of other branches of human industry. If they increase as fast as the gold, little or no alteration will take place in its value ; which depends on the relation between it and the annual production of other wealth."

According to another calculation, all the gold now in the world is supposed to be equal to about 682 millions ; but the whole amount of either of the two precious metals in old times is not easily ascertained, nor can any definite comparison be established between their former and present value. And still less in Egypt, than in Greece and Rome ; no standard of calculation being obtainable from the prices of commodities there, or from any other means of determining the value of gold and silver.

In the infancy of her existence as a nation, Egypt was contented with the pursuits of agriculture ; but in process of time, the advancement of civilisation and refinement led to numerous inventions, and to improvements in the ordinary necessaries of life, and she became at length a great manufacturing country, famed amongst foreigners for the excellence of her fine linen, her cotton and woollen stuffs, cabinet work, porcelain, glass, and numerous branches of industry. That the Egyptians should be more known abroad for their manufactures, than for those occupations which related solely to themselves, might be reasonably expected, in consequence of the exportation of the commodities in which she excelled, and the ignorance of foreigners respecting the internal condition of a country from which they were excluded by the jealousy of the natives ; though, judging from the scanty information imparted to us by the Greeks, who in later times had opportunities of examining the valley of the Nile, it appears that we have as much reason to blame the indifference of strangers who visited the country, as the exclusiveness of the Egyptians.

There are fortunately other sources of information, which give an insight into many of their pursuits ; and, independent of what may be gleaned from Herodotus and Diodorus, the paintings, in the tombs of Thebes and Lower Egypt, show the experience they had acquired in the management of their lands and herds, and the different duties connected with husbandry ; as well as their progress in various arts, and even in scientific knowledge.

In considering the state of agriculture in Egypt, we ought not to confine its importance to the direct and tangible benefits it annually conferred upon the people, by the productiveness of the soil ; the influence it had on the manners, and scientific acquirements, of the people is no less obvious ; and to the peculiar nature of the Nile, and the effects of its inundation, has been reasonably attributed the early advancement of the Egyptians in geometry and mensuration. Herodotus, Plato, Diodorus, Strabo, Clemens of Alexandria, Iamblichus, and others, ascribe the origin of geometry to changes which annually took place from the inundation, and to the consequent necessity of adjusting the claims of each person respecting the limits of the lands ; and, though Herodotus may be wrong in limiting the commencement of those observations to the reign of Sesostris, his remark tends to the same point, and confirms the general opinion that this science had its origin in Egypt.

It is reasonable to suppose, that as the inundation subsided, litigation often occurred between neighbours respecting the limits of their unenclosed fields ; and the fall of a portion of the bank, carried away by the stream during the rise of the Nile, frequently made great alterations in the extent of land near the river side ; a mode of determining the quantity which belonged to each individual was therefore very necessary, both for settling disputes with a neighbour, and for ascertaining the tax due to government. But it is difficult to fix the period when the science of mensuration commenced ; if we have ample proofs of its being known in the time of Joseph, this does not carry us far back into the ancient history of Egypt ; and there is evidence of geometry and mathematics having already made nearly the same progress at the earliest period of which any monuments remain, as in the later era of the Great Remeses.

Besides the mere measurement of superficial areas, it was of the highest importance to agriculture, and to the interests of the peasant, to distribute the benefits of the inundation in due proportion to each individual, that the lands which were low might not enjoy the exclusive advantages of the fertilising water, by constantly draining it from those of a higher level. For this purpose they were obliged to ascertain the various elevations of the country, and to construct accurately levelled canals and dykes ; and, if it be true that Menes, their first king, turned the course of the Nile into a new channel he had made for it, we have a proof of their having, long before his time, arrived at considerable knowledge in this branch of science ; since so great an undertaking could only have been the result of long experience.

These dykes were succeeded or accompanied by the invention of sluices, and all the mechanism appertaining to them ; the regulation of the supply of water admitted into plains of various levels, the report of the exact quantity of land irrigated, the depth of the water, and the time it continued upon the surface, which determined the proportionate payment of the taxes, required much scientific skill ; and the prices of provisions for the ensuing year were already ascertained by the unerring prognostics of the existing inundation. Hence they were led to make minute observations respecting the increase of the Nile during that season : Nilometers, for measuring its gradual rise or fall, were constructed in various parts of Egypt, and particular persons were appointed to observe each daily change, and to proclaim the favourable or unfavourable state of this important phenomenon. On these reports depended the time chosen for opening the canals, whose mouths were closed until the river rose to a fixed height; upon which occasion grand festivities were proclaimed throughout the country, in order that every person might show his sense of the great benefit vouchsafed by the Gods to the land of Egypt. The introduction of the waters of the Nile into the interior, by means of these canals, was allegorically construed into the union of Osiris and Isis; the instant of cutting away the dam of earth which separated the bed of the canal from the Nile was looked forward to with the utmost anxiety; and many omens were consulted in order to ascertain the auspicious moment for this important ceremony.

Superstition added greatly to the zeal of a credulous people. The Deity, or presiding Genius, of the river was propitiated by suitable oblations, both during the inundation, and about the period when it was expected; and Seneca tells us, that on a particular fête the priests threw presents and offerings of gold into the river near Philæ, at a place called the Veins of the Nile, where they first perceived the rise of the inundation. It was reasonable that the grand and wonderful spectacle of the inundation should excite in them feelings of the deepest awe for the divine power, to which they were indebted for so great a blessing : and a plentiful supply of water was supposed to be the result of the favour of the Gods, as a deficiency was attributed to their displeasure, punishing the sins of an offending people.

On the inundation depended all the hopes of the peasant ; it affected the revenue of the government, both by its influence on the scale of taxation, and by the greater or less profits on the exportation of grain and other produce; and it involved the comforts of all classes. For in Upper Egypt no rain fell to irrigate the land ; it was a country which did not look for showers to advance its crops ; and if " these fell in Lower Egypt, they were confined to that district, and heavy rain was a prodigy in the Thebaïd." But though, speaking generally, it may be said not to rain there, heavy storms did occasionally fall in the vicinity of Thebes, as is proved by the appearance of the deep ravines worn by water in the hills, about the tombs of the Kings, probably, as now, after intervals of fifteen or twenty years ; and modern experience shows that slight showers fall at Thebes, about five or six times a year ; in Lower Egypt much more frequently ; and at Alexandria almost as often as in the South of Europe.

The result of a favourable inundation was not confined to tangible benefits ; it had the greatest effect on the mind of every Egyptian by long anticipation ; the happiness arising from it, as the regrets on the appearance of a scanty supply of water, being far more sensibly felt than in countries which depend on rain for their harvest, where future prospects are not so soon foreseen. The Egyptian, on the other hand, was able to form a just estimate of his crops even before sowing the seed, or preparing the land for its reception.

Other remarkable effects may likewise be partially attributed to the interest excited by the expectation of the rising Nile; and the accurate observations required for fixing the seasons, and the period of the annual return of the inundation, contributed greatly to the early study of astronomy in the valley of the Nile. The precise time when these and other calculations were first made by the Egyptians, it is impossible now to determine; but from the height of the inundation being already recorded in the reign of the kings of the 12th dynasty, we may infer that constant observations had been made, and Nilometers constructed, even before that early period; and astronomy, geometry, and other sciences are said to have been known in Egypt in the time of the hierarchy which preceded the accession of their first king, Menes.

We cannot, however, from the authority of Diodorus and Clemens of Alexandria, venture to assert that the books of Hermes which contained the science and philosophy of Egypt, all date before the reign of Menes; the original work, by whomsoever it was composed, was probably very limited and imperfect; and the famous books of Hermes were not all written at the same period; like the Jewish collection of poems received under the name of David's Psalms, some of which date after the Babylonish captivity. Nor was Thoth, Hermes, or Mercury, a real personage, but (as I have before stated) a deified form of the divine intellect, which being imparted to man had enabled him to produce this effort of genius; and the only argument in favour of the high antiquity of any portion of this work is the tradition of the people, supported by the positive proof of the great mathematical skill of the Egyptians in the time of Menes, by the change he made in the course of the Nile. It may also be inferred from their advancement in the arts and sciences at this early period, that many ages of civilization had preceded the accession of their first monarch.

At all events, we may conclude that to agriculture and the peculiar nature of the river, the accurate method adopted by the Egyptians in the regulation of their year is to be attributed; that by the return of the seasons, so decidedly marked in Egypt, they were taught to correct those inaccuracies, to which an approximate calculation was at first subject; and that thus the calendar, which could not long be suffered to depend on the vague length of a solar revolution, was necessarily brought round to a fixed period.

It is highly probable that the Egyptians, in their infancy as a nation, divided their year into twelve lunar months; the twenty-eight years of Osiris's reign being derived, as Plutarch says, from the number of days the moon takes to perform her course round the earth; and it is worthy of remark that the hieroglyphic signifying "month" was represented by the crescent of the moon, as is abundantly proved from the sculptures and the authority of Horapollo. From this we also derive another very important conclusion; that the use of hieroglyphics was of a far more remote date than is generally supposed, since they existed previous to the adoption of solar months.

The substitution of solar for lunar months was the earliest change in the Egyptian year. It was then made to consist of twelve months of thirty days each, making a total of 360 days: but as it was soon discovered that the seasons were disturbed, and no longer corresponded to the same months, five additional days were introduced at the end of the last month, Mesoré, in order to remedy the previous defect in the calendar, and to insure the returns of the seasons to fixed periods.

The twelve months were Thoth, Paopi, Athor, Choeak, Tobi, Mechir, Phamenoth, Pharmuthi, Pachons, Paoni, Epep, Mesoré: and the year being divided into three seasons, each period comprised four of these months. That containing the first four was styled the season of the "plants;" the next *perhaps* of the "manifestation," or "appearance, of the inundation;" and the last season of the "tanks of water," which had been laid up when the Nile subsided. The 1st of Thoth, in the time of Julius Cæsar, fell on the 29th of August; and Mesoré, the last month, began on the 25th of July; as may be seen in the accompanying woodcut, where I have introduced the modern names given them by the Copts, who still use them in preference to the lunar months of the Arabs; and, indeed, the Arabs themselves are frequently guided by the Coptic months in matters relating to agriculture, particularly in Upper Egypt.

1st Season.

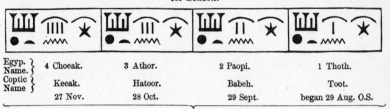

Egyp. Name.	4 Choeak.	3 Athor.	2 Paopi.	1 Thoth.
Coptic Name	Keeak.	Hatoor.	Babeh.	Toot.
	27 Nov.	28 Oct.	29 Sept.	began 29 Aug. O.S.

2nd Season.

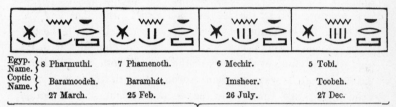

Egyp. Name.	8 Pharmuthi.	7 Phamenoth.	6 Mechir.	5 Tobi.
Coptic Name.	Baramoodeh.	Baramhát.	Imsheer.	Toobeh.
	27 March.	25 Feb.	26 July.	27 Dec.

3rd Season.

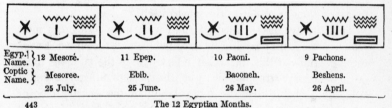

Egyp. Name.	12 Mesoré.	11 Epep.	10 Paoni.	9 Pachons.
Coptic Name.	Mesoree.	Ebib.	Baooneh.	Beshens.
	25 July.	25 June.	26 May.	26 April.

443   The 12 Egyptian Months.

A people who gave any attention to subjects so important to their agricultural pursuits, could not long remain ignorant of the deficiency which even the intercalation of the five days left in the adjustment of the calendar; and though it required a period of 1461 years for the seasons to recede through all the twelve months, and to prove by the deficiency of a whole year the imperfection of this system, yet it would be obvious to them, in the lapse of a very few years, that a perceptible alteration had taken place in the relative position of the seasons; and the most careless observation would show, that in 120 years, having lost a whole month, or thirty days, the rise of the Nile, the time of sowing and reaping, and all the periodical occupations of the

peasant, no longer coincided with the same month. They therefore added a quarter day to remedy the defect, making every
fourth year to consist of 366 days; which, though still subject
to a slight error, was a sufficiently accurate approximation; and
the length of each year was computed from one heliacal rising of
the Dog-star to another. It was therefore called the "Sothic
year;" and Censorinus says "it was termed by the Greeks
'κυνικον,' by the Latins 'canicularem,' because its commencement is taken from the rising of the Dog-star on the first day of
the month, called by the Egyptians Thoth." But that day was
not made the beginning of the year *because* Sothis rose heliacally
upon it; the Sothic period was fixed *when* it coincided with it;
and the beginning of the year, or the first of Thoth, was, perhaps,
originally at a very different season; though they even pretended in later times that the commencement of the Sothic
period corresponded with the beginning of the world. Some
have supposed that the name Thoth was formerly applied to the
first day alone, and not to the month itself.

That the five days, called of the Epact, were added at a most
remote period, may readily be credited; and so convinced were
the Egyptians of this, that they referred it to the fabulous times
of their history, wrapping it up in the guise of allegory; and it
is highly probable that the intercalation of the quarter day, or
one day in four years, was also of very early date. The first
direct notice of the five days is on a box at Turin of the time of
Amunoph III.; but M. de Rougé has shown they were used in
the 12th dynasty, and that the fête of Sothis was celebrated at
the same period.

The Sothic period, as is well known, was fixed in the year
1322 before our era, when the Egyptians had ascertained
by observation that 1460 Sothic were equal to 1461 solar
years, the seasons having in that time passed through every part
of the year, and returned again to the same point. They thus
established a standard for adjusting their calendar, under the
name of the Sothic period; and though for ordinary purposes,
as the dates of their kings and other events, they continued to

use the vague year of 365 days, every calculation could thus be corrected, by comparing the time of this last with that of the Sothic or sidereal year. When the idea first occurred to them is unknown; but the oath imposed on the Egyptian Kings "that they would not intercalate any month or day, but that the sacred year of 365 days should remain as instituted in ancient times," evidently had for its object the employment of both the years for a counter-reckoning in present and past records; and as the Sothic period was fixed in 1322 B.C. from observations, it is evident that these must have been continued during the time that elapsed up to that year, which would throw back the beginning of their observations to a very remote age. The king in whose reign the Sothic period was fixed is said to be Menophres; but the name he is known by on the monuments has not yet been ascertained, though he seems to have lived about the beginning of the 19th dynasty.

The astronomical subjects and various data to be derived from the monuments, will doubtless some day clear up most essential points relating to Egyptian Chronology; and though we must sometimes depend upon conjecture, it is satisfactory, considering the general uncertainty of history, to have arrived at a fair approximation in Egyptian dates. Those I have ventured to assign to the Pharaohs only pretend to a similar approximation; but the rising of Sothis in the reign of Thothmes III., now calculated by the learned M. Biot to correspond to between 1464 and 1424 B.C., shows that my placing his reign from 1495 to 1456 B.C. only differed from his real date by about 30 years.

The pursuits of agriculture did not prevent the Egyptians from arriving at a remarkable pre-eminence as a manufacturing nation; and that they should successfully unite the advantages of an agricultural and a manufacturing country is not surprising, when we consider that in those early times the competition of other manufacturing countries did not interfere with their market; and though Tyre and Sidon excelled in various manufactures, many branches of industry brought exclusive advantages to the Egyptian workman. Even in the flourishing days of the Phœnicians, Egypt exported linen to other countries, and she probably enjoyed at all times an entire monopoly in this, and every article she manufactured, with the caravans of the interior of Africa.

The Egyptian land measure was the aroura (or arura), a square of 100 cubits, covering an area of 10,000 cubits, and like our acre solely employed for measuring land. It contained 29,184 square feet English, (the cubit being full 20½ inches,) and was little more than ¾ of an English acre. The other measures of Egypt were the schœne, equal to 60 stades in length, which served like the stade of Greece, the parasang of Persia, and the more modern mile, for measuring distance; the cubit, which Herodotus says was equal to that of Samos; and the palm and digit, which were parts of the cubit. Though the stade is often used by Greek writers in giving measurements in Egypt, it was not an Egyptian measure; and generally speaking it was equal to 600 Greek feet. They also mention the plethrum in giving the length of some buildings, as the Pyramids; but this was properly a Greek square measure, containing 10,000 square feet. When used as a measure of length it was estimated at 100 feet; though, if Herodotus's measurement of the Great Pyramid be correct, it could not complete 100 of our feet, as he gives the length of each face 8 plethra. But little reliance can be placed on his measurements, since in this he exceeds the true length; and to the face of the third Pyramid he only allows 3 plethra, which, calculating the plethrum at 100 feet, is more than half a plethrum short of the real length,—each face, according to the measurement of Colonel Howard Vyse, being 354 feet.

The total length of each face of the Great Pyramid when entire I believe to have been 754 or 755 feet, which would be exactly 440 cubits; but neither this, nor the courts of the temples, the statues, and other monuments can be depended upon for the exact length of that Egyptian measure.

Happily other data of a less questionable nature are left us for this purpose, and the graduated cubit in the Nilometer of Elephantine, and the wooden cubits discovered in Egypt, suffice o establish its length, without the necessity of conjecture.

Some have supposed that the Egyptian cubit varied at different periods, and that it consisted at one time of 24, at another of 32 digits ; or that there were two cubits of different lengths,—one of 24 digits or 6 palms, the other of 32 digits or 8 palms, employed for different purposes. Some have maintained, with M. Girard, that the cubit used in the Nilometer of Elephantine consisted of 24 digits, others that it contained 32; and numerous calculations have been deduced from these conflicting opinions, respecting the real length of the cubit. But a few words will suffice to show the manner in which that cubit was divided, the number of its digits, and its real length; and respecting the supposed change in the cubit used in the Nilometers of Egypt, I shall only observe, that people far more prone to innovation than the Egyptians would not readily tolerate a similar deviation from long-established custom; and it is obvious that the greatest confusion would have been caused throughout the country, and that agriculture would have suffered incalculable injuries, if the customary announcement of a certain number of cubits for the rise of the Nile had been changed, through the introduction of a cubit of a different length.

The Nilometer in the island of Elephantine is a staircase between two walls descending to the Nile, on one of which is a succession of graduated scales containing one or two cubits, accompanied by inscriptions recording the rise of the river at various periods, during the rule of the Cæsars. Every cubit is divided into fourteen parts, each of 2 digits, giving 28 digits to the cubit ; and the length of the cubit is 1 ft. 8⅝ in., or 165 eighths, which is 1 ft. 8.625 in. to each cubit, and 0·736 in. to each digit.

The wooden cubit, published by M. Jomard, is also divided into 28 parts or digits, and therefore accords, both in its division, and, as I shall show, very nearly in length, with the cubit of Elephantine. In this last we learn, from the inscriptions accompanying the scales, that the principal divisions were palms and digits; the cubit being 7 palms or 28 digits : and the former in like manner consisted of 7 palms or 28 digits. The ordinary division, therefore, of the cubit was as follows :

The Cubit in the Nilometer of Elephantine.			Feet.	Inches.
1 digit			0	0·736
4	1 palm		0	2·946
28	7	1 cubit	1	8·625

The full division of the wooden Egyptian cubits, which have been found, appears to be :—

Parts of the Cubit.							Cubit of the Nilometer.	Cubit of Memphis according to Jomard.
							Inches English.	Inches English.
$\frac{1}{16}$ of a digit							0·04603	0·04569
16	1 digit						0·7366	0·73115
	2	1 condyle					1·4732	1·4623
	4	2	1 palm				2·9464	2·9247
	5	..	..	1 hand			3·6830	3·6557
	6	..	..	..	1 kubdeh, or fist with thumb erect			4·4196	4·3869
	8	..	2	..	..	1 dichas, or 2 palms . .		5·8928	5·8494
	11	..	..	..	..	..	1 fitr or forefinger span	8·1026	8·0428
	13	..	..	..	..	..	1 shibr, spithamé, or full span.	9·5758	9·5051
	28	..	7	..	..	..	1 cubit . . .	20·6250	20·47291

There is no indication of a foot, and the 15 last digits are solely occupied with fractional parts, beginning with a 16th, and ending in $\frac{1}{2}$ a digit, from which we may conclude that the smallest measurement in the Egyptian scale of length was the 16th of a digit, or the 26th of an inch.

The lengths of different Egyptian cubits are :—

	Millimètres.	English Inches.
Cubit in the Turin Museum, according to my measurement	$522\frac{4}{10}$ or	20·5730
The same, according to M. Jomard	$522\frac{7}{10}$,,	20·5786
Another, he gives	523 ,,	20·6180
Another	524 ,,	20·6584
M. Jomard's cubit of Memphis	520 ,,	20·4729
Cubit of Elephantine according to M. Jomard . .	527 ,,	20·7484
The same, according to my measurement . .	.. ,,	20·6250
Part of a cubit found by me at A'Souán . .	apparently about	21·0000
The cubit at the Pyramids according to Mr. Perring .	. . . .	20·6280
Mr. Harris's cubit from Thebes	. . . .	20·6500

The careless manner in which the graduation of the scales of the Nilometer at Elephantine has been made by the Egyptians, renders the precise length of its cubit difficult to determine; but as I have carefully measured all of them, and have been guided by their general length as well as by the averages of the whole, I am disposed to think my measurement as near the truth as possible; and judging from the close approximation of different wooden cubits, whose average M. Jomard estimates at 523·506 millimètres, we may conclude that they were all intended to represent the same measures, strongly arguing against the supposition of different cubits having been in use, one of 24 and others of 28 and 32 digits; and indeed, if at any time the Egyptians employed a cubit of a different length, consisting of 24 digits, it is not probable that it was used in their Nilometers, for architectural purposes, or for measuring land.

And if, when cited from ancient authors, I have calculated the cubit at 1½ foot, this is only because custom has reconciled us to that approximate measurement.

The principal Egyptian measures of weight were the talent, and the mina; the former called in Coptic *ginshôr*, the latter *emna* or *amna*, and in the hieroglyphics *men*, or *mna*.

The talent is supposed to have contained 60 minæ, and the mina 100 drachms, as in Greece; but the uncertainty about their real value is so great, that the talent has been reckoned at 114 or 113, at 91, 86¾, or even 65 lbs. Troy; and the mina in the same proportion. It seems really to have been about 40 lbs. Troy and the mina 16¼ ounces.

The mina, *mna*, or *men*, is often mentioned on the monuments, and from their reckoning upwards of 2000 minæ, (as of " *sift*," *zift*, or bitumen,) it was evidently used for large quantities, where we should rather have expected the talent, and was, like our pound, the standard weight. The name is quite Egyptian, and of a more common form than any other in the language; and it is found applied to weights at least as early as the 18th dynasty, followed by a square, indicative of a " weight." It seems also to be related to the Arabic word *mana* " to count," (and the "*mna*, " mene," of Daniel,) from which Al-manach is supposed to be derived.

s 2

The weights represented, when they are engaged in weighing gold and silver and other commodities, are in the form of a whole ox, a bull's head, and a conical mass, as well as the square representing the mina; and the three first seem to be the whole, the half, and another subdivision of the talent, or 60, 30, and 20 or 10 minæ. The adoption of the bull for the talent may have originated in the original mode of bartering, and accords with Homer's reckoning the bull as a standard of value. Indeed it is said to have represented a talent. Thus the *pecunia* of the Romans was taken from *pecus*.

The Egyptians had also a measure, or weight, apparently of the same name, *mn* or *mna*, used for gold and silver, and followed by a similar square sign; which Mr. Birch supposes to have been divided like our pound into 16 parts or ounces, no higher number having been found than 15. These have also a square sign after them, determinative of weight, and are called *kit* or *kiti*, the Coptic name of the drachma and didrachma.

The idea of the mina being equivalent to our pound seems to be confirmed by the weights, in the form of lions and ducks, brought by Mr. Layard from Nimroud,* (now in the British Museum); as the most perfect of the large ducks, which was ½ a talent, or 30 minæ, weighs little more than 484 ounces, or 40 lbs. troy and 4 ozs. Each mina is therefore 16⅓ ounces; and the close approximation in the weight of the lions and ducks shows they represented the same quantity.

Of the Egyptian measures of capacity one was small, answering to the modern *mid*, or nearly 2½ pecks English; another larger, also used for measuring grain, distinguished by the king's crook that surmounts it, which, as M. de Rougé suggests, may point to its value fixed by royal authority; or be a royal, *i. e.* a large measure. It may perhaps be the origin of the modern Egyptian *ardéb* (the *ertôb* of the Copts, and the Medish artaba), equal nearly to 5 English bushels; and the smaller one is shown to be the one employed for measuring grain when taken to, or from, the

---

* See Layard's Nineveh and Babylon, p. 601. In the woodcut he gives, p. 602, the supposed ring on the back of the crouched lion is only the same conical weight seen in the scales.

granary; being the standard like the modern *mid*, which in size and shape it so much resembled. This name is very like the Latin *modius*.

The modern ardéb contains 8 *mid*; and the latter 4 *roftów*, or 3 *roob*; and according to another calculation the ardéb is made to consist of 6 *waybeh*, a name answering to the *ouôpi* of the Copts, which was equal to 4 *roob*. The half ardéb, or mid, was called also *koros* in Coptic.

There was another measure used both for liquids, as wine; and for dry substances, as incense and bitumen; which had likewise a name very like *mn* or *mina*.

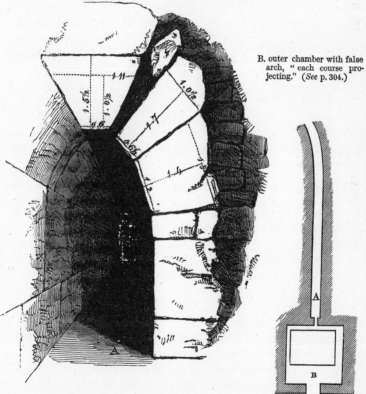

B. outer chamber with false arch, " each course projecting." (*See* p. 304.)

N.   Arch at Tusculum, in Italy (built while the Kings ruled at Rome?).

o. View of the modern town of Manfaloót, showing the height of the banks of the Nile in summer. In the mountain range, opposite Manfaloót, are the large crocodile mummy caves of Maábdeh.

CHAPTER IX.

EGYPTIAN ART — REMAINS OF NINEVEH — HUMAN FIGURE — DRAWING AND PAINTING — ARCHITECTURE — ORDERS OF ARCHITECTURE — SOME DEVICES COPIED FROM NATURE — TOO GREAT SYMMETRY AVOIDED — USE OF LARGE STONES — ANTIQUITY OF THE ARCH — BRICKS — PROGRESS OF ARCHITECTURE — USE OF LIMESTONE — COLOSSI — MONOLITHS — MACHINERY — MASONS — EARLY EGYPTIAN INVENTIONS — DRESSES — WIGS — DRESSES OF WOMEN — ORNAMENTS — OINTMENTS — MIRRORS — DOCTORS — MAGIC.

THE interest that attaches to Egyptian art is from its great antiquity. We see in it the first attempts to represent what in after times, and in some other countries, gradually arrived, under better auspices, at the greatest perfection; and we even trace in it the germ of much that was improved upon by those, who had a higher appreciation of, and feeling for, the beautiful. For, both in ornamental art, as well as in architecture, Egypt exercised in early times considerable influence over other people less advanced than itself, or only just emerging from barbarism: and the various conventional devices, the lotus flowers, the sphinxes, and other fabulous animals, as well as the early Medusa's head, with a protruding tongue, of the oldest Greek pottery and sculptures, and the ibex, leopard, and above all the (Nile) "goose and sun," on the vases, show them to be connected with, and frequently directly borrowed from, Egyptian fancy.   It was, as it still is, the custom of people to borrow from those who have attained to a greater degree of refinement and civilization than themselves; the nation most advanced in art led the taste; and though some had sufficient invention to alter what they adopted, and to render it their own, the original idea may still be traced whenever it has been derived from a foreign source.   Egypt was long the dominant nation, and the intercourse established at a very remote period with other countries, through commerce or war, carried abroad the taste of this the most advanced people of the time; and so general seems to have been the fashion of their ornaments, that even the Nineveh marbles present the winged globe, and other well-known Egyptian emblems, as established elements of Assyrian decorative art.   This fact would suffice to disprove the early date of the marbles hitherto discovered, which are in fact of a period comparatively modern in the history of Egypt; and recent discoveries have fully justified the opinion I ventured to express, when they were first brought to this country : 1°, that they are not of archaic style, and that original Assyrian art is still to be looked for; 2°, that they give evidences of the decadence, not the rise, of art ; and 3°, that they have borrowed much from Egypt, long the dominant country in power and art, and will be found to date within 1000 B.C.   This, however, is far from lessening their importance; for the periods they chiefly illustrate—those of Shalmaneser and Sennacherib, so closely connected with Hebrew history—give an interest to them, which the oldest monuments of Assyria would fail to possess.

While Greece was still in its infancy, Egypt had long been the leading nation of the world ; she was noted for her magnificence, her wealth, and power, and all acknowledged her pre-eminence in wisdom and civilization.   It is not, therefore, surprising that the Greeks should have admitted into their early art some of the forms then most in vogue ; and though the won-

derful taste of that gifted people speedily raised them to a point
of excellence, never attained by the Egyptians or any others, the
rise and first germs of art and architecture must be sought in the
valley of the Nile.   In the oldest monuments of Greece, the
sloping or pyramidal line constantly predominates ; the columns
in the oldest Greek order are almost purely Egyptian, in the proportions of the shaft, and in the form of its shallow flutes without
fillets ; and it is a remarkable fact that the oldest Egyptian
columns are those which bear the closest resemblance to the
Greek Doric.

Though great variety was permitted in objects of luxury, as
furniture, vases, and other things depending on caprice, the
Egyptians were forbidden to introduce any material innovations
into the human figure, such as would alter its general character ;
and all subjects connected with religion retained to the last the same
conventional type.   A god in the latest temple was of the same
form, as when represented on monuments of the earliest date ;
and King Menes would have recognised Amun, or Osiris, in a
Ptolemaic or a Roman sanctuary.   In sacred subjects the law
was inflexible ; and religion, which has frequently done so much
for the development and direction of taste in sculpture, had the
effect of fettering the genius of Egyptian artists.   No improvements, resulting from experience and observation, were admitted
in the mode of drawing the human figure ; to copy nature was
not allowed ; it was therefore useless to study it, and no attempt
was made to give the proper action to the limbs.   Certain rules,
certain models had been established by the priesthood ; and the
faulty conceptions of ignorant times were copied and perpetuated
by every successive artist.   For, as Plato and Synesius say, the
Egyptian sculptors were not suffered to attempt anything contrary to the regulations laid down regarding the figures of the
gods ; they were forbidden to introduce any change, or to invent
new subjects and habits ; and thus the art, and the rules which
bound it, always remained the same.

Egyptian bas-relief appears to have been, in its origin, a mere
copy of painting, its predecessor.   The first attempt to represent
the figures of gods, sacred emblems, and other subjects consisted

in drawing, or painting, simple outlines of them on a flat surface, the details being afterwards put in with colour ; but in process of time these forms were traced on stone with a tool, and the intermediate space between the various figures being afterwards cut away, the once level surface assumed the appearance of a basrelief.   It was, in fact, a pictorial representation on stone, which is evidently the character of all the bas-reliefs on Egyptian monuments ; and which readily accounts for the imperfect arrangement of their figures.

Deficient in conception, and above all in a proper knowledge of grouping, they were unable to form those combinations which give true expression ; every picture was made up of isolated parts, put together according to some general notions, but without harmony, or preconceived effect. The human face, the whole body, and everything they introduced, were composed in the same manner, of separate members placed together one by one according to their relative situations : the eye, the nose, and other features composed a face ; but the expression of feelings and passions was entirely wanting ; and the countenance of the king, whether charging an enemy's phalanx in the heat of battle, or peaceably offering incense in a sombre temple, presented the same outline and the same inanimate look.   The peculiarity of the front view of an eye, introduced in a profile, is thus accounted for : it was the ordinary representation of that feature added to a profile, and no allowance was made for any change in the position of the head.

It was the same with drapery : the figure was first drawn, and the drapery then added, not as part of the whole, but as an accessory ; they had no general conception, no previous idea of the effect required to distinguish the warrior or the priest, beyond the impressions received from costume, or from the subject of which they formed a part ; and the same figure was dressed according to the character it was intended to perform. Every portion of a picture was conceived by itself, and inserted as it was wanted to complete the scene ; and when the walls of the building, where a subject was to be drawn, had been accurately ruled with squares, the figures were introduced, and fitted to this mechanical arrangement. The members were appended to the body, and these squares regulated their form and distribution, in whatever posture they might be placed.

As long as this conventional system continued, no great change could take place, beyond a slight variation in the proportions, which at one period became more elongated, particularly in the reign of the second Remeses; but still the general form and character of the figures continued the same, which led to the remark of Plato, " that the pictures and statues made ten thousand years ago, are in no one particular better or worse than what they now make." And taken in this limited sense—that no nearer approach to the beau ideal of the human figure, or its real character, was made at one period than another—his remark is true, since they were always bound by the same regulations, which prohibited any change in these matters, even to the latest times; as is evident from the sculptures of the monuments erected after Egypt had long been a Roman province. All was still Egyptian, though of bad style; and if they then attempted to finish the details with more precision, it was only substituting ornament for simplicity; and the endeavour to bring the proportions of the human figure nearer to nature, with the retention of its conventional type, only made its deformity greater, and showed how incompatible the Egyptian was with any other style.

The proportions of the human figure did not, as I have just said, continue always the same. During the 4th and other early dynasties it differed from that of the Augustan age of the 18th and 19th; and another change took place under the Ptolemies. The chief alteration was in the height of the knee from the ground, which was higher during the 18th and 19th than in the ancient and later periods. The whole height of the figure in bas-reliefs and paintings was then divided into nineteen parts; and the wall having been ruled in squares, according to its intended size, all the parts of it were put in according to their established positions; the knee, for instance, falling on the sixth line. But the length of the foot was not, as in Greece, the standard from which they reckoned; for being equal to 3 spaces, it could not be taken as the base of 19; though the height of the foot being 1 might

444.   Mode of drawing the human figure on a wall, previous to its being sculptured or painted ; showing the proportions during the 18th and 19th dynasties.   *Thebes.*

answer for the unit. (*See* Müller's Ancient Art, p. 392, on Greek forms.)

In the composition of modern paintings three objects are required : one main action ; one point of view ; and one instant of time : and the proportions and harmony of the parts are regulated by perspective ; but in Egyptian sculpture these essentials were disregarded : every thing was sacrificed to the principal figure ; its colossal dimensions pointed it out as a centre to which all the rest was a mere accessory ; and, if any other was made equally conspicuous, or of equal size, it was still in a subordinate station, and only intended to illustrate the scene connected with the hero of the piece.

In the paintings of the tombs greater licence was allowed in the representation of subjects relating to private life, the trades, or the manners and occupations of the people ; and some indication of perspective in the position of the figures may occasionally be observed : but the attempt was imperfect, and, probably, to an Egyptian eye, unpleasing ; for such is the force of habit, that even where nature is copied, a conventional style is sometimes preferred to a more accurate representation.

In the battle scenes on the temples of Thebes, some of the figures representing the monarch pursuing the flying enemy, despatching a hostile chief with his sword, and drawing his bow, as his horses carry his car over the prostrate bodies of the slain, are drawn with much spirit ; and the position of the arms gives a perfect idea of the action which the artist intended to portray ; still, the same imperfections of style, and want of truth, are observed ; there is action, but no sentiment, expression of the passions, nor life in the features ; it is a figure ready formed, and mechanically *varied* into movement ; and whatever position it is made to assume, the point of view is the same : the identical profile of the human body with the anomaly of the shoulders seen in front. It is a description, rather than a representation.

But in their mode of portraying a large crowd of persons they often show great cleverness ; and, as their habit was to avoid uniformity, the varied positions of the heads give a truth to the subject without fatiguing the eye. Nor have they any symmetrical arrangement of figures, on opposite sides of a picture, such as we find in some of the very early paintings in Europe.

In the representation of animals, they appear not to have been restricted to the same rigid style ; but genius once cramped can scarcely be expected to make any great effort to rise, or to succeed in the attempt ; and the same union of parts into a whole, the same preference for profile, and the same stiff action, are observable in these as in the human figure. Seldom did they attempt to draw the face in front, either of men or animals ; and when this was done, it fell far short of the profile, and was composed of the same juxtaposition of parts. It must, however, be allowed, that in general the character and form of animals were admirably portrayed ; the parts were put together with greater truth ; and the same conventionality was not maintained, as in the shoulders and other portions of the human body. Nor will I deny that great life and animation are given to the antelope, and many wild beasts, in the hunting scenes of the Theban tombs.

The mode of representing men and animals in profile is primitive, and characteristic of the commencement of art : the first attempts made by an uncivilised people are confined to it ; and until the genius of artists bursts forth, this style continues to hold its ground. From its simplicity it is readily understood ; the most inexperienced perceive the object intended to be represented, and no effort is required to comprehend it. Hence it is that, though few combinations can be made under such restrictions, those few are perfectly intelligible, the eye being aware of the resemblance to the simple exterior ; and the modern uninstructed peasant of Egypt, who is immediately struck with and understands the paintings of the Theban tombs, if shown an European drawing, is seldom able to distinguish men from animals ; and no argument will induce him to tolerate foreshortening, the omission of those parts of the body concealed from his view by the perspective of the picture, or the introduction of shadows, particularly on the human flesh.

Bas-relief may be considered the earliest style of sculpture. It originated in those pictorial representations which were the primæval records of a people anxious to commemorate their victories, the accession or the virtues of a king, and other events connected with their history. These were the first purposes to which the imitative powers of the mind were applied; but the progress was slow, and the infant art (if it may be so called) passed through several stages ere it had the power of portraying real occurrences, and imitating living scenes. The rude outlines of a man holding a spear, a sword, or other weapon, or killing a wild animal, were first drawn, or scratched, upon a rock, as a sort of hieroglyphic; but in process of time the warrior and a prostrate foe were attempted, and the valour of the prince who had led them to victory was recorded by this simple group.

As their skill increased, the mere figurative representation was extended to that of a descriptive kind, and some resemblance of the hero's person was attempted; his car, the army he commanded, and the flying enemies, were introduced; and what was at first scarcely more than a symbol, aspired to the more exalted form and character of a picture. Of a similar nature were all their historical records; and these pictorial illustrations were a substitute for written documents. Rude drawing and sculpture, indeed, long preceded letters, and we find that even in Greece, to describe, draw, engrave, and write, were expressed by the same word, γραφειν.

The want of letters, and the inability to describe an individual, his occupations, or his glorious actions, led them in early ages to bury with the body some object which might indicate the character of the deceased. Thus, warriors were interred with their arms; artisans with the implements they had used; the oar was placed over the sailor; and *paterœ*, and other utensils connected with his office, or the emblems of the deity in whose service he had been employed, were deposited in the sepulchre of a priest. In those times a simple mound was raised over chieftains, sometimes with a rough stone pillar placed upon it, but no inscription; and even, at a later period, when they intended to show the occupations of the deceased, an allegorical emblem was often engraved on the levelled surface of the stone, and the implements continued to be buried with them, after writing was invented.

Poetry and songs also supplied the want of writing to record the details of events ; and tradition handed down the glorious achievements of a conqueror, and the history of past years, with the precision and enthusiasm of national pride. The poetry was recited to the sound of music ; whence the same expression often implied the " ode " and the " song ;" and as laws were recorded in a similar manner, the word νομος signified, as Aristotle observes, both a " law " and a " song."

Man *attempted* sculpture long before he *studied* architecture : a simple hut, or a rude house, answered every purpose as a place of abode, and a long time elapsed before he sought to invent what was not demanded by necessity.

Architecture is a creation of the mind ; it has no model in nature, and it requires great imaginative powers to conceive its ideal beauties, to make a proper combination of parts, and to judge of the harmony of forms altogether new and beyond the reach of experience. But the desire in man to imitate and to record what has passed before his eyes, in short, to transfer the impression from his own mind to another, is natural in every stage of society ; and however imperfectly he may succeed in representing the objects themselves, his attempts to indicate their relative position, and to embody the expression of his own ideas, are a source of the highest satisfaction.

As the wish to record events gave the first, religion gave the second impulse to sculpture. The simple pillar of wood or stone, which was originally chosen to represent the deity, afterwards assumed the human form, the noblest image of the power that created it ; though the *Hermæ* of Greece were not, as some have thought, the origin of statues, but were borrowed from the mummy-shaped gods of Egypt.

Pausanias thinks that " all statues were in ancient times of wood, particularly those made in Egypt ; " but this must have been at a period so remote as to be far beyond the known history of that country ; though it is probable that when the arts were in their infancy the Egyptians were confined to statues of that kind ; and they occasionally erected wooden figures in their temples, even till the times of the latter Pharaohs.

Long after men had attempted to make out the parts of the

figure, statues continued to be very rude ; the arms were placed directly down the side to the thighs, and the legs were united together ; nor did they pass beyond this imperfect state in Greece, until the age of Dædalus. Fortunately for themselves and for the world, the Greeks were allowed to free themselves from old habits; while the Egyptians, at the latest periods, continued to follow the imperfect models of their early artists, and were for ever prevented from arriving at excellence in sculpture : and though they made great progress in other branches of art, though they evinced considerable taste in the forms of their vases, their furniture, and even in some architectural details, they were for ever deficient in ideal beauty, and in the mode of representing the natural positions of the human figure.

In Egypt, the prescribed automaton character of the figures effectually prevented all advancement in the statuary's art ; the limbs being straight, without any attempt at action, or, indeed, any indication of life : they were really *statues* of the person they represented, not the person " living in marble ;" in which they differed entirely from those of Greece. No statue of a warrior was sculptured in the varied attitudes of attack and defence; no wrestler, no *discobolus*, no pugilist exhibited the grace, the vigour, or the muscular action of a man ; nor were the beauties, the feeling, and the elegance of female forms displayed in stone : all was made to conform to the same invariable model, which confined the human figure to a few conventional postures.

A sitting statue, whether of a man or woman, was represented with the hands placed upon the knees, or held across the breast ; a kneeling figure sometimes supported a small shrine or sacred emblem ; and when standing, the arms were placed directly down the sides of the thighs, one foot (and that always the left) being advanced beyond the other, as if in the attitude of walking, but without any attempt to separate the legs.

The oldest Egyptian sculptures on all large monuments were in low relief, and, as usual at every period, painted (obelisks and everything carved in hard stone, some funereal tablets, and other small objects, being in intaglio) ; and this style continued in vogue until the time of Remeses II., who introduced intaglio very generally on large monuments; and even his battle scenes at

Karnak and the Memnonium are executed in this manner.   The reliefs were little raised above the level of the wall ; they had generally a flat surface with the edges softly rounded off, far surpassing the intaglio in effect ; and it is to be regretted that the best epoch of art, when design and execution were in their zenith, should have abandoned a style so superior ; which, too, would have improved in proportion to the advancement of that period.

Intaglio continued to be generally employed, until the accession of the 26th dynasty, when the low relief was again introduced ; and in the monuments of Psammitichus and Amasis are numerous instances of the revival of the ancient style.   This was afterwards universally adopted, and a return to intaglio on large monuments was only occasionally attempted, in the Ptolemaic and Roman periods.

The intaglio introduced by Remeses may, perhaps, be denominated *intaglio rilievato*, or relieved intaglio.   The sides of the *incavo*, which are perpendicular, are cut to a considerable depth, and from that part to the centre of the figure (or whatever is represented) is a gradual swell, the centre being frequently on a level with the surface of the wall.   On this all the parts of dress, features, or devices, are delineated and painted, and even the perpendicular sides are ornamented in a corresponding manner, by continuing upon them the adjoining details.

In the reign of Remeses III. a change was made in the mode of sculpturing the intaglios, which consisted in carving the lower side to a great depth, while the upper face inclined gradually from the surface of the wall till it reached the innermost part of .the intaglio ; its principal use was for the hieroglyphics, in order to enable a person standing immediately beneath, and close to the wall on which they were sculptured, to distinguish and read them ; and the details upon the perpendicular sides, above mentioned, had the same effect.

It was a peculiarity of style not generally imitated by the successors of Remeses III., and hieroglyphics bearing this character may serve to fix the date of monuments, wherever they are found, to the age of that monarch.   After his reign no great encouragement appears to have been given to the arts; the subjects represented on the few monuments of the epoch intervening between his death, and the accession of the 26th dynasty, are principally confined to sacred subjects, in which no display of talent is shown; and the records of Sheshonk's victories at Karnak are far from partaking of the vigour of former times, either in style, or in the mode of treating the subject.

After the accession of the 26th dynasty some attempt was made to revive the arts, which had been long neglected; and independent of the patronage of government, the wealth of private individuals was liberally employed in their encouragement. Public buildings were erected in many parts of Egypt, and beautified with rich sculpture; the city of Saïs, the royal residence of the Pharaohs of that dynasty, was adorned with the utmost magnificence; and extensive additions were made to the temples of Memphis, and even to those of the distant Thebes.

The fresh impulse thus given to art was not without effect; the sculptures of that period exhibit an elegance and beauty which might even induce some to consider them equal to the productions of an earlier age; and in the tombs of the Assaseef, at Thebes, are many admirable specimens of Egyptian art. To those, however, who understand the true feeling of this peculiar school, it is evident, that though in minuteness and finish they are deserving of the highest commendation, yet in grandeur of conception and in boldness of execution, they fall far short of the sculptures of Sethos, and the second Remeses.

The skill of the Egyptian artists in drawing bold and clear outlines is, perhaps, more worthy of admiration than anything connected with this branch of art; and in no place is the freedom of their drawing more conspicuous than in the figures in the unfinished part of Belzoni's tomb at Thebes. It was in the drawing alone that they excelled, being totally ignorant of the correct mode of colouring a figure; and their painting was not an imitation of nature, but merely the harmonious combination of certain hues, which they well understood. Indeed, to this day the harmony of positive colours is thoroughly felt in Egypt and the East; and it is strange to find the little perception of it in Northern Europe, where theories take upon themselves to explain to the mind what the eye has not yet learnt, as if a grammar could be written before the language is understood.

Drawing was always a principal point in ancient art. The Greeks made it their great study, knowing how it improved the accuracy of the eye and the management of the hand, as well as the perception of the beautiful; and the most extraordinary correctness must have been acquired to enable Apelles to draw the line within that of Protogenes.

The neglect that drawing has experienced in England is now, we may hope, in a fair way of being remedied; for to many a real *line* has been almost unknown; and while the French have persevered so successfully in drawing, we have seldom been alive to its importance; occasionally excusing ourselves from the trouble by some such subterfuge as, " there is no outline in nature." How often indeed is a line made up of a few dotted strokes; and many a youth, as yet unacquainted with the proper use of a pencil, thinks that the brush will at once enable him to acquire excellence in art!

Of the quality of the pencils used by the Egyptians for drawing and painting, it is difficult to form any opinion. Those generally employed for writing were a reed or rush, many of which have been found with the tablets or inkstands belonging to the scribes; and with these, too, they probably sketched the figures in red and black upon the stone or stucco of the walls. To put in the colour, we may suppose that brushes of some kind were used; but the minute scale on which the painters are represented in the sculptures prevents our deciding the question.

Habits among men of similar occupations are frequently alike, even in the most distant countries; and we find it was not unusual for an Egyptian artist, or scribe, to put his reed pencil behind his ear, when engaged in examining the effect of his painting, or listening to a person on business, like a clerk in the counting-house of an European town.

Painters and scribes deposited their writing implements in a box with a pendent leather top, which was tied up with a loop or thong; and a handle or strap was fastened to the side, to enable

them to carry it more conveniently. Their ordinary wooden
inkstand was furnished with two or more cavities for holding
the colours, and a tube in the centre for the pens or reeds ; and

445. A scribe writing on a tablet. *c* and *d* are two cases for carrying writing materials.
Thebes.

446. Scribe with his inkstand upon the table. One pen is put behind his ear, and he is
writing with another. *Thebes.*

certain memoranda were frequently written at the back of it,
when a large piece of papyrus, or the wooden slab, was not
at hand. An idle moment was often occupied in making rough
sketches on a piece of stone or on some other common material ;
and subjects of greater size were drawn in a happy mood of fancy,
upon a papyrus : for the Egyptians (as I have already said)
were addicted to caricature, and some papyri in the British and
other museums show that even religious subjects were not exempt
from it ; and one in the Turin collection presents a severe libel
on the taste and conduct of women.

Of painting, apart from sculpture, and of the excellence to

which it attained in Egypt, we can form no accurate opinion,
nothing having come down to us of a Pharaonic period, or of
that epoch when the arts were at their zenith in Egypt; but that,
already, in the time of Osirtasen, they painted on panel, is shown
by one of the subjects at Beni Hassan, where two artists are
engaged in a picture representing a calf, and an antelope overtaken by a dog.   The painter holds his brush in one hand, and

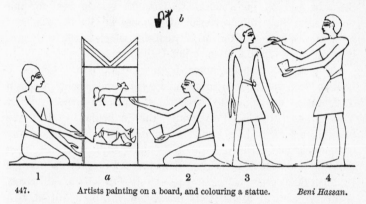

447.   Artists painting on a board, and colouring a statue.   *Beni Hassan.*

his palette or saucer of colour in the other; but, though the
boards stand upright, there is no indication of a contrivance to
steady or support the hand.   The Greeks drew and painted in
the same manner without that help.

   Mention is made of an Egyptian painting by Herodotus, who
tells us that Amasis sent a portrait of himself to Cyrene, probably on wood, and in profile; for the full face is rarely represented either in their paintings, or bas-reliefs.   The faces of the
kings in the tombs and temples of Egypt are unquestionably
portraits; but they are always in profile; and the only ones in
full face are on wood, and of late time.   Two of these are preserved in the British Museum, but they are evidently Greek, and
date, perhaps, even after the conquest of Egypt by the Romans.
It is therefore vain to speculate on the nature of their painting, or
their skill in this branch of art; and, though some of the portraits
taken from the mummies may prove that encaustic painting with
wax and naphtha was adopted in Egypt, the time when it was

first known there is uncertain, nor can we conclude from a specimen of Greek time, that the same was practised in a Pharaonic age.

Fresco painting was entirely unknown in Egypt; and the figures on walls were always drawn and painted after the stucco was quite dry. But they sometimes coated the colours with a transparent varnish, which was also done by the Greeks; and the wax said by the younger Pliny to have been used for this purpose, on the painted exterior of a house at Stabia, may have been a substitute for the usual varnish; which last would have been far more durable under a hot Italian sun.

Pliny states, in his chapter on inventions, that " Gyges, a Lydian, was the earliest painter in Egypt; and Euchir, a cousin of Dædalus according to Aristotle, the first in Greece; or, as Theophrastus thinks, Polygnotus the Athenian." But the painting represented in Beni Hassan evidently dates before any of those artists. Pliny, in another place, says, " the origin of painting is uncertain : the Egyptians pretend that it was invented by them 6000 years before it passed into Greece; a vain boast, as every one will allow." It must, however, be admitted, that all the arts (however imperfect) were cultivated in Egypt long before Greece existed as a nation ; and the remark he afterwards makes, that painting was unknown at the period of the Trojan war, can only be applied to the Greeks ; as is shown by the same unquestionable authority at Beni Hassan, dating about 900 years before the time usually assigned to the taking of Troy.

It is probable that the artists, in Egypt, who painted on wood, were in higher estimation than mere decorators ; as was the case in Greece, where "no artists were in repute but those who executed pictures on wood, for neither Ludius nor any other wall painter was of any renown." The Greeks preferred moveable pictures, which could be taken away in case of fire, or sold if necessary ; and as Pliny says, " there was no painting on the walls of Apelles' house " (or " no painting by Apelles on the walls of a house "). The painting and decoration of buildings was another and an inferior branch of art. The pictures were put up in temples, as the works of great masters in later times in churches ; but they were not dedications, nor solely connected with sacred subjects ; and the temple was selected as the place of security, as it often was as a repository of treasure. They had also picture galleries in some secure place ; as in the Acropolis of Athens.

Outline figures on walls were in all countries the earliest style of painting ; they were in the oldest temples of Latium ; and in Egypt they preceded the more elaborate style, that was after-wards followed by bas-relief and intaglio. In Greece, during the middle period, which was that of the best art, pictures were painted on wood, by the first artists ; and Raoul-Rochette thinks that if any of them painted on walls, this was accidental ; and the finest pictures being on wood were in after times carried off to Rome. This removal was lamented by the Greeks " as a spo-liation " ; which having left the walls bare accounts for Pausanias saying so little about pictures in Greece. Historical compositions were of course the highest branch of art ; though many of the greatest Greek artists, who seem to have excelled in all styles, often treated inferior subjects ; and some (as in later times) com-bined the two highest arts of sculpture and painting.

In the infancy of art figures were represented in profile ; but afterwards they were rare in Greece ; and art could not reach any degree of excellence until figures in a composition had ceased to be in profile ; and it was only in order to conceal the loss of an eye that Apelles gave one side of the face, in his portrait of Antigonus.

The oldest paintings were also, as Pliny admits, *monochrome*, or painted of one uniform colour ; like those of Egypt ; and indeed statues in Greece were at first of one colour, doubtless red like those of the Egyptians, Romans, and Etruscans. For not only bas-reliefs were painted, which as parts of a coloured building was a necessity, but statues also ; and as art advanced they were made to resemble real life. For that statue by Scopas, of a Bacchante, with a disembowelled fawn, whose cadaverous hue contrasted with the rest, at once shows that it was *painted*, and not of a *monochrome* colour ; and the statues of Praxiteles, painted for him by Nicias, would not have been preferred by that sculptor to his other works, if they had merely been stained red.

The blue eyes of Minerva's statue; the inside of her shield painted by Pannæus, and the outside by Phidias, (originally a painter himself), could only have been parts of the whole coloured figure; Pannæus assisted in painting the statue of Olympian Jupiter; and ivory statues were said to have been prevented turning yellow by the application of colour.

If the artists of Greece did not paint on walls, it was not from any mistaken pride, since even the greatest of them would paint statues not of their own work; and those in modern days who study decorative art will do well to remember that to employ superior taste in ornamental composition is no degradation, and that the finest specimens of decorative work in the middle ages were executed by the most celebrated artists.

Egyptian architecture evidently derived much from the imitation of different natural productions, as palm trees, and various plants of the country; but Egyptian columns were not borrowed from the wooden supports of the earliest buildings. Columns were not introduced into the interior of their houses until architecture had made very great progress; the small original temple, and the primitive dwelling, consisted merely of four walls; and neither the column nor its architrave were borrowed from wooden constructions, nor from the house. And though the architrave was derived in Egypt as elsewhere, from constructed buildings, that member originated in the *stone* beam, reaching from pillar to pillar, in the temples. And if the square stone pillar was used in the quarry, the stone architrave was unknown to the Egyptians, until they found reason to increase the size of, and add a portico to, their temples. And that the portico was neither a necessary, nor an original, part of their temples is plainly shown by the smaller sanctuaries being built, even at the latest times, without it. Some members of Egyptian architecture, it is true, were derived from the woodwork of the primitive house or temple; as the overhanging cornice, and the torus that runs up the ends of the walls, which it separates from the cornice; the former being the projecting roof of palm branches, and the other the framework of reeds bound together, which secured the mud (or bricks) composing the walls.

The early houses of Egypt were of mud; and the *masses* of that material, used in making their walls, afterwards led to the simple invention of *large* sun-baked bricks. The flat roof was of palm-beams, covered with branches of the same tree, and a thick coating of mud laid upon them completed the whole. But it was not till luxury had been introduced that the column performed a part in an Egyptian mansion; and the temple of early Egypt was a simple quadrangular chamber. (*See a complete Temple in Frontispiece, Vol. I.*)

Square pillars were the first used; and their presence in the old temples is consistent with the fact of their having been the first kind adopted there. They are found in some of the earliest constructed porticoes, and in the peristyles of the old peripteral temples. This square pillar originated in the stone quarry, where too it appears without any architrave; a mere mass, often rather irregular, left to support the roof; and when in after times large tombs and temples were excavated in the rock, they in their turn borrowed from constructed monuments; and the pillar was no longer permitted to support the roof, without the intervening architrave.

Thus then, constructed buildings were indebted to the quarry for the pillar; and rock-hewn monuments derived from the former the architrave and plinth. The same spirit of imitation also led to the introduction of square dentils over an architrave, as in the façade of a tomb at Beni Hassan; and the ceiling of one of the rock tombs at the Pyramids imitating the palm beams of a house, is another proof that the two borrowed from each other. In these, the rock monuments imitated timber roofs; but this was long after columns and architraves had been used in temples, and architecture was then only dependent for new features on caprice or taste.

As painted decoration preceded sculpture, the ornaments (in later times carved in stone) were at first represented in colour; and the mouldings of Egyptian monuments were then merely painted on the flat surfaces of the walls and pillars. The next step was to chisel them in relief. The lotus blossom, the papyrus head, water-plants, the palm-tree, and the head of a goddess, were among the usual ornaments of a cornice, or a pillar; and these favourite devices of ancient days continued in after times to be repeated in relief, when an improved style of art had substituted sculpture for the mere painted representation. But when the square pillar had been gradually converted into a polygonal shape, the ornamental devices not having room enough upon its narrow *facettes*, led to the want and invention of another form of column; and from that time a round shaft was surmounted by the palm-tree capital, or by the blossom, or the bud of the papyrus; which had hitherto only been painted, or represented in relief, upon the flat surfaces of a square pillar. Hence the origin of new orders differing so widely from the polygonal column.

It is a curious fact that both the Egyptians and the Greeks began with the same simple polygonal column; the severe grandeur of which we admire in both styles of architecture. Those at Beni Hassan are 3 feet 4 inches in diameter, and 16 feet 8½ inches high.* They have sixteen faces or grooves, each about eight inches wide, and so slight and elegant that their depth does not exceed half an inch; and one of the faces, which is not hollowed into a groove, is left for the introduction of a column of hieroglyphics. The old and new orders continued, for some time, to divide the taste of the early Egyptian architects; until at length when the size and height of Egyptian buildings had increased beyond the scale adapted to the old polygonal shaft, the more elongated style of the new columns superseded the use of their rival; and in the later periods of the native dynasties these, with the varieties that grew out of them, were employed to the entire exclusion of the old order.

It is uncertain when the new columns were invented; but the water-plant capital with the blossom and bud of the lotus and the papyrus, and probably also the palm-tree column, were used at least as early as the 6th dynasty; and the most elegant of the water-plant columns are those in the tombs of Beni Hassan, where they were used contemporaneously with the polygonal and fluted order. A capital, resembling a bunch of flax, or other flowers, is also represented in early paintings supporting wooden canopies.

* *See* Woodcut 449.

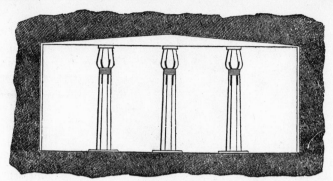

448.   Section of one of the *southern* grottoes of Beni Hassan.

The palm-tree, and water-plant, columns were not therefore in imitation of the wooden support of the early roof; they owed their origin to the devices painted, and afterwards sculptured, on the face of the square pillar, which was carved into a round shaft and capital to imitate the shape of the plant itself; and the binding together of a number of water-plants, to form a column, was evidently not taken from a similar frail support, but was a fanciful caprice, borrowed from the *ornaments* of the old pillar.

The formation of the polygonal and circular fluted column was evidently owing to the four corners of the square pillar having been first cut off for convenience. This converted it into an octagonal shaft; and in course of time, the eight sides having been again subdivided, the number was increased to 12, 16, 20, and 32 ; and these flat *facettes* being hollowed into grooves presented the actual form of the fluted column. It was doubtless from this, the oldest Egyptian order, that the Greeks borrowed their Doric shaft; and it is not impossible that the Doric capital may even have been taken from that of the water-plant column ; since by removing the upper part, and bringing down the abacus, it gives the very shape of the Doric capital.* The annuli also round the neck of that early Greek column seem also to be taken from the bands tied round the cluster of water-plants ; which are an anomaly in a single shaft where there is *nothing to bind.*

The Egyptian column, like that of Greece, was constructed of

* Woodcut 449, *figs.* 5 and 6.

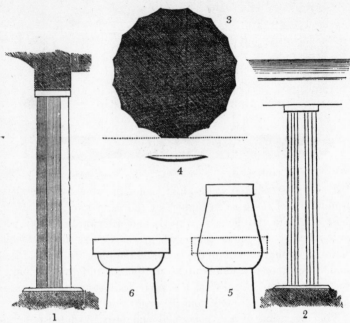

449.   Fig. 1. Columns in the portico of the northern grottoes of Beni Hassan.
     2. Columns of the interior.
     3. Horizontal section of fig. 2, showing the grooves.
     4. One of the grooves on a larger scale.
     5. An Egyptian capital, which seems to have been the origin of the Doric, fig. 6.

several pieces; but it consisted of half (not of whole) drums, with
the joint placed alternately one way and the other; each two at
right angles with those next below and above them, sometimes secured by dovetailed cramps.   Whole drums were never used,
except in a few small granite shafts; and the only columns of a
single piece were of that stone; which were also of moderate
dimensions, and nearly confined to temples in the Delta.

Nor were the Egyptian drums secured or adjusted with the precision of those in the Parthenon, and other Greek buildings, by
means of a cramp and socket in the centre, round which the upper
drums were turned, till the two moistened surfaces had been ground
together, and their edges made to fit with the greatest nicety;
leaving a slightly concave space around the cramp.

Egyptian columns may be classed in eight *orders*, as in the accompanying wood-cut, where, being drawn to the same scale,
their respective dimensions are shown.   For though columns of
the same order vary very much in different buildings, an average
proportion may be assigned to them; which indeed is all that can
be done in those of Greece, though they varied less than in
Egyptian architecture.   In point of antiquity the first was certainly the square pillar; then the polygonal and round fluted
column of the second order; and soon afterwards the third and
fourth came into use.   But the fourth and fifth, though used long
before, were not common till the 18th dynasty, and the fourth
assumed a larger size than any other, as at Karnak and Luxor.
The sixth, though mostly in Ptolemaic and Roman temples, dates
at least as early as the 18th dynasty; as does the eighth, which

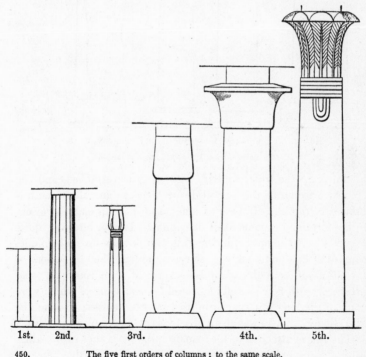

1st.   2nd.   3rd.   4th.   5th.

450.   The five first orders of columns; to the same scale.

6th.   7th, or Composite.   8th, or Osiride.

450 a. The remaining three orders of columns, and the *scale.*

is, in fact, the square pillar, with a figure attached, and the evident original of the Caryatide of Greece; but the seventh is limited to the age of the Ptolemies, and has an endless variety in the form and ornaments of its capital. It was, however, quite Egyptian, and in no way indebted to Greek taste for its introduction. Of the same kind were the columns described by Athenæus (v. 103), with circular capitals, set round with rose-like ornaments, or with flowers and interlaced leaves; some of which were made of the long tapering form used in their houses; to which he also alludes. There was also a pilaster surmounted by a cow's head.

The figure attached to the square pillar was that of the king, in the form of Osiris, whence I have given it the name of

" Osiride pillar." But it did not support any member of the building; the sacred person of a king could not be subjected to such a degradation, and it was merely ornamental. Not so the figures, and heads, of captives made to support thrones, tables, or various parts of architecture ; and vanquished chiefs performed the duties of consoles, over the window-sills in the palace of the third Remeses in Thebes ;

451. Heads of enemies once supporting something now removed. *Thebes*.

as they decorated the sandals, and thrones, of other Pharaohs.

The oldest existing monuments in the world are the Pyramids and the tombs about them, which date as far back as the 4th, and perhaps 3rd, dynasty, and show at what a remote period sculpture and the use of squared stone in horizontal courses were practised in Egypt. The employment of squared granite blocks, and the beauty of the masonry in the interior of the Pyramids (which has not been surpassed, if even equalled, at any subsequent age), also prove the degree of skill the Egyptians had reached at a time long anterior to the building of the walls of Tiryns, and, consequently, to the rudest attempts in masonry in Italy or Greece. How long they took to arrive at that perfection it is difficult to determine ; but the period between the builders of the Pyramids and the reign of Tosorthrus, the second king of the 3rd dynasty, said by Manetho to have first used squared stone, is evidently much too short ; and we may conclude that it was known to them, as well as the engineering skill required for changing the course of the Nile, even before the reign of Menes.

Another very remarkable invention of those early times was the glazed tiles used for lining the walls of a chamber in the pyramid of Sakkára, and bearing the name of a king of the 3rd or 4th dynasty, the employment of which in wainscoting Egyptian rooms is mentioned by Athenæus (v. 104). He describes them of a white and black colour, here and there intermixed with slabs of alabaster; but they made them of various hues; and those at Sakkára are blue and white.

For their devices the Egyptians frequently selected objects which were favourites with them, as the lotus and other flowers, and these, as well as various animals or their heads, were adopted, to form a cornice, particularly in their houses and tombs, or to ornament fancy articles of furniture and of dress. In this they committed an error, which the Greeks, with a finer perception of taste and adaptability, rightly avoided. These refined people knew that in architecture conventional devices had a much more pleasing effect than objects merely copied from nature; for, besides the incongruity of an actual representation of flowers to compose mouldings and other decorative parts of architecture, the *imperfect* imitation in an *unsuitable* material has a bad effect. To represent figures on buildings in their proper and dignified places belongs to sculpture, which then exercises its talent in the way eminently suited to it, and it is the province of art to imitate nature both in sculpture and painting. But neither the works of the sculptor should be degraded by being made merely decorative, nor should decorative design attempt to pass beyond its own sphere. The latter remark applies equally to embroidery and household furniture: even tapestry goes out of its own province when it invades that of painting; and our worsted work mistakes its capabilities, when it represents men and other natural objects in staircase outlines, and transfers them from their proper place, a picture, to its conventional squares.

The Greeks preferred taking the sentiment of natural objects to making a direct copy of them when intended for ornament, and it is evident that their elegant honeysuckle moulding would lose all its beauty, if it were converted into a close representation of the real flower and its leaf-bud. There is a pleasure in the variety arising from harmonious combination applied to ornament, which could never be obtained to the same extent by the mere imitation of natural objects; and the custom of depending solely on the latter is the result of poverty of invention, and the refuge of a mind deficient in talent and taste. Such was their perception of beauty that the Greeks at once saw it wherever it was to be found ; and they presented the *sentiment* of it to the eye ; thus relieving the spectator from the common-place inquiry about the exact representation of an object,—generally, too, in a position where it would have no right to be found.   They did the same in copying from " the Barbarian ;" and, when they perceived in any of his devices the germ of the beautiful, they adopted, or adapted, it ; making it, with a small modification, what it was capable of being ; and when, thus remodelled, it became their own.

And well might we in modern times imitate their example, instead of striving to make what is merely *new*, and thinking more of originality than excellence.   It would be no discredit if we knew how to borrow and improve, like the Greeks ; and when we can do this we may hope to have an object of taste recommended to us, not because it is the "*newest*," but because it is the "*best*," and to cease to be guided by fashion in our selection.

We have abundant proofs of the length of time that the same devices, and the same subjects, for decorative purposes, continued to be used by the Greeks.   They remained favourites because they were elegant; and many of the fancy ornaments, in trinkets and furniture, continued the same also among the Egyptians for ages, who at the same time did not reject any novelty if worthy of adoption ; and they even admitted many alterations, unknown to their ancestors, in the architecture of the temple and the tomb.   But neither they nor the Greeks committed the error of preferring any work of taste because it was new, or not of native growth ; and we who in England too often refuse due honour to "a prophet in his own country," would do ourselves more credit by showing a full appreciation of the exquisite designs of a Flaxman, than by seeking some far inferior production of a foreign hand.   To combine, like the Greeks, excellence in sculpture with decorative taste is the highest merit, and those who possess them both will know how to combine them for architectural purposes ; but many people, and above all the Arabs, have shown how decorative art may be fully effective, even without the assistance of its more exalted companion.   Who indeed can look at the endless variety and exquisite beauty of

Saracenic ornaments without appreciating them? and the harmony produced by those combinations affords the same gratification to the eye, that music does to the ear.

It must, however, be allowed that the Egyptians did not
always confine themselves to the mere imitation of natural objects
for ornament, and their ceilings and cornices offer numerous
graceful fancy devices ; among which are the *guilloche*, miscalled
Tuscan border, the *chevron*, and the scroll pattern. These are
even met with in a tomb of the time of the 6th dynasty ; they were
therefore known in Egypt many ages before they were adopted
by the Greeks ; and the most complicated form of the guilloche
covered a whole Egyptian ceiling, upwards of a thousand years
before it was represented on those comparatively late objects
found at Nineveh.

Not only the tomb and house, but all parts of the temple
were coloured, both within and without ; and this variety served
as a relief to the otherwise sombre appearance of the massive
straight walls of the exterior. Colour was an essential part of
Egyptian architecture, and some of the mouldings and other
details were made out solely by it, without any sculptured indication of them ; as was often done on the monuments of Greece. The
ceilings of Egyptian temples were painted blue and studded with
stars, to represent the firmament (as in early European churches) ;
and on the part over the central passage, through which the king
and the religious processions passed, were vultures and other
emblems ; the winged globe always having its place over the
doorways. The whole building, as well as its sphinxes and other
accessories, were richly painted ; and though a person unaccustomed to see the walls of a large building so decorated, might
suppose the effect to be far from pleasing, no one who understands the harmony of colours will fail to admit that they perfectly understood their distribution and proper combinations, and
that an Egyptian temple was greatly improved by the addition
of painted sculptures.

The introduction of colour in architecture was not peculiar
to the Egyptians ; it was common to the Etruscans, and even to
the Greeks ; and the mention made of it by ancient authors is

confirmed by its having been found on the monuments of Sicily and Greece.

In the temple of Theseus at Athens, vestiges of colours are seen on the ground of the frieze, on the figures themselves, and on the ornamental details. The Parthenon presents remains of painting on some members of the cornice; many coloured devices remain on the upper part of the walls in the interior; and the ground of the frieze, containing the reliefs of the Panathenaic procession, was blue. The Propylæa of the Acropolis and the Choragic monument of Lysicrates also offer traces of colour; as did the Ionic temple on the Ilissus; and vestiges of red, blue, and green, have been discovered on the metopes of a temple at Selinus in Sicily. In one of these, the figure of Minerva has the eyes and eyebrows painted; her drapery and the girdle of Perseus are also ornamented with coloured devices; and the whole ground of this, and of two other metopes, is red.

Red and blue seem to have been generally used for the ground; and these two, with green and yellow, were the principal colours introduced in Greek architecture, many members of which were also gilt, as the shields, guttæ, and other prominent details; but many suppose that the shafts of columns were always white, and that the coloured parts were confined to the entablature and pediment.

In Egyptian buildings, indeed, it sometimes happened, that the shafts of columns were merely covered with white stucco, without any ornament, and even without the usual line of hieroglyphics; and the same custom of coating certain kinds of stone with stucco was common in Greece. The Egyptians put this layer of stucco, or paint, over stone, whatever its quality might be; and we are surprised to find the beautiful granite of obelisks, and other monuments, concealed in a similar manner; but it was occasionally allowed to retain its own red hue, the sculptures being painted green, or sometimes blue, red, and other colours.

Whenever they employed sandstone, it was absolutely necessary to cover it with a surface of a smoother and less absorbent nature, to prevent the colour being too readily imbibed by so porous a stone; and a coat of calcareous composition was laid on before the paint was applied.   When the subject was sculptured, either in relief or intaglio, the stone was coated, after the figures were cut, with the same substance, to receive the final colouring; and it had the additional advantage of enabling the artist to finish the figures and other objects, with a precision and delicacy in vain to be expected on the rough and absorbent surface of sandstone.

They sometimes coated the inside walls of a sanctuary, a tomb, or a house, with granite, or some other kind of stone, or stained them to imitate it; and the adytum of the temple of Osiris at Abydus was lined with oriental alabaster.   They also used, for interiors of houses and tombs, the black and white tiles already mentioned (which were similar to those afterwards made by the Arabs and the Dutch); and cased the exterior of a limestone or sandstone building with granite; and a great portion of the third pyramid was covered with this " Ethiopian stone of various hues," which still remains.

Their colours were principally blue, red, green, black, yellow, and white.   The red was an earthy bole; the yellow an iron ochre; the green was a mixture of a little ochre with a pulverulent glass, made by vitrifying the oxides of copper and iron with sand and soda; the blue was a glass of like composition without the ochreous addition; the black was bone or ivory black; and the white a very pure chalk.   They were mixed with water; and apparently a little gum to render them tenacious and adhesive.   With the Egyptians the favourite combination of colour was red, blue, and green; when black was introduced, yellow was added to harmonise with it: and in like manner they sought for every hue its congenial companion.   They also guarded against the false effect of two colours in juxtaposition, as of red and blue, by placing between them a narrow line of white or yellow.   They had few mixed colours; though purple, pink, orange, and brown, are met with; and frequently on papyri.   The blue, which is very brilliant, consists of fine particles of blue glass, and may be considered equivalent to our smalt; it seems to be the same that Vitruvius describes, which he supposes to have been first made at Alexandria; and it also agrees with the artificial *kyanus* of Theophrastus, invented in Egypt, which he says was laid on thicker than the native (or lapis lazzuli).   The thickness of the blue on the ceilings in Belzoni's tomb confirms his remark.   The green is also a glass in powder, mixed with particles of colourless glass, to which it owes its brightness.

Gilding was employed in the decoration of some of the ornamental details of the building; and was laid on a purple ground, to give it greater richness; an instance of which may be seen in the larger temple at Kalabshee, in Nubia.   It was sparingly employed, and not allowed to interfere, by an undue quantity, with the effect of the other colours; which they knew well how to introduce in their proper proportions; and such discords as light green and strawberry-and-cream were carefully avoided.

The Egyptians showed considerable taste in the judicious arrangement of colours for decorative purposes; they occasionally succeeded in *form*, as in the shapes of many of their vases, their furniture, and their ornaments; and they had still greater knowledge of *proportion*, so necessary for their gigantic monuments; but though they knew well how to give to their buildings the effect of grandeur, vastness, and durability, they had little idea of the beautiful; and were far behind the Greeks in the appreciation of form.   It is, however, rare to find any people who combine colour, form, and proportion; and even the Greeks occasionally failed to attain perfection in their beautiful vases, some of which are faulty in the handles and the foot.

For knowledge of proportion no people in later times have equalled the Italians.   It is most remarkable in their public buildings; where, though perfection of form may be sometimes wanting, the first impressions arising from harmony of proportion conceal the faults that afterwards become apparent to the eye; and show the importance of a thorough knowledge of it.

We are now making a laudable effort to disseminate taste among the whole community; the Great Exhibition of 1851 has, among other good effects, made people think a little more for themselves; and a revival of architecture, as well as of mediæval ornament, has directed the eye to better models than those of Georgian times. And as we have no prescribed rules like those of the Egyptians, and no Louis XIV. and XV. splendid monstrosities, to give us preconceived notions in favour of the utter decomposition of an outline, there is no reason and no excuse for taste not flourishing, and not pervading even those least alive to it.

But it is not by mere patronage of the great that art and taste are to be made to flourish in a country; all must be made sensible of the charm and the effect they produce; and the feeling for them must become general. Encouragement may be advantageously given, and their progress may be greatly advanced by such praiseworthy assistance; but for a people to attain to excellence in them, the masses, and particularly the middle classes, must learn how to appreciate what is good, and how to discountenance the bad. It was the general taste in Greece that made the arts flourish—they were intelligible to all; and many a column, or other portion of a public edifice, was raised at the combined expense of several poor subscribers. It is an error to suppose that the religion of Greece had peculiarly the tendency to encourage the fine arts. Christian story abounds in noble subjects, with many feelings of a far more exalted kind than those portrayed by the Greeks; and historical compositions are not confined to any one people, nor to any age. To make art and taste flourish and endure, they must be generally encouraged; and it is not to the grandees of any country, who condescendingly permit their names to appear at the head of a list of patrons, that these must trust; and to obtain any good result, the judgment of the public must be cultivated. It is vain for any artists or artisans to excel in painting, sculpture, or ornamental art, if the taste of the country is deficient, and if busts or portraits are more prized than fine statues or good historical compositions; and how often, when good works are produced in decorative art, is the talented inventor obliged to discontinue them, because he finds no encouragement! He "must live;" and he is, therefore, compelled to satisfy the demand of the purchasers, by making something more consonant with their bad taste.

It is, therefore, with great satisfaction that we now look forward to the effect of the schools of design, and the well-directed energies of those who have such important objects in view; and when taste becomes general, we shall cease to have committees sanctioning what is bad. Indeed, it might always be better to submit the selection of works of art to a single individual of sound judgment, who should be, and feel that he was, *responsible*, than to leave it to the doubtful decision of a number—some indifferent, some who never attend, some put there for their name alone, none individually responsible, and many glad to shift the blame or the trouble upon some very active member, who, often being the most busy, and tiresome in the inverse ratio of his talents, gets his own way in opposition to less assuming and more capable men.

Another great impediment to the extension of taste is the notion that beauty of design is only to be sought in expensive ornamental objects, and those connected with the arts; but so long as it is confined to them, and not introduced into all the ordinary utensils of common life, it will be possessed by few, and will be a sort of exotic plant. Beauty of form, and proportion, exquisite detail, and high finish, are found in the vases and commonest objects among the Greeks; they were afterwards prized by the Romans, and looked upon as rarities by them as by modern collectors; but among those who originated them they were appreciated by all. "Arts of production" must not be independent of the arts of design—they must go together; and as the commonest lamp, strainer, or other things used for ordinary purposes, were beautiful in Greece, so must they be with those who strive to arrive at similar refinement. It is not by making what is elegant dear to the purchaser that art and taste will flourish; this is an impediment, not an encouragement to them; and until the beautiful is within the reach of all, and appreciated by all, it is vain to hope for excellence in any country.

The sculptures of an Egyptian temple mostly represented the king making offerings to the Triad of the city, and to the principal deities worshipped there ; the king's name, who erected or enlarged the building, was frequently repeated in the dedications upon the architraves, as well as on the ornamental cornices, and other places ; and as it was his right to make the offerings in the temple, he alone was represented pouring out libations, and making sacrifices before the gods.   On the outer walls similar subjects were repeated ; but in the large temples, especially of the çapital, the chief places both of the outer and inner walls were occupied by battle scenes, representing the victories obtained by the monarch over the enemies of Egypt ; and upon the great towers of the façade he was portrayed routing them in battle, or in the act of smiting the captive " Heads," or " chiefs, of the Gentiles," in the presence of the great deity of the place.

Among the peculiarities of Egyptian architecture, one of the most important is the studied avoidance of uniformity, in the arrangement of the columns, and many of the details.   Of these some are evident to the eye, others are only intended to have an influence on the general effect, and are not perceptible without careful examination.   Thus the capitals of the columns in the great hall at Karnak are at different heights, some extending lower down the shaft than others ; evidently with a view to correct the sameness of symmetrical repetition, and to avoid fatiguing the sight with too much regularity.   This is not to be perceived until the eye is brought on a level with the lower part of the capitals ; and its object was only effect, like that of many curved lines introduced in a Greek temple, as at the Parthenon.

But the Egyptians often carried their dislike of uniformity to an extreme, beyond even what is justified by the study of variety. Where they avoided that extreme their motive was legitimate ; and it is remarkable that they were the first people whose monuments offer instances of that diversity, which forms so essential a characteristic of Saracenic and Gothic architecture.

This feeling increased, rather than diminished, after the accession of the Ptolemies ; and intercourse with the Greeks had not the effect of inducing the Egyptians to adopt any of the notions of symmetry, which prevailed in their monuments.   Those therefore who imagine that the great variety then in vogue, from the juxtaposition of columns of different orders, was introduced by the Ptolemies, attribute it to a very improbable cause; for if any change had been introduced by the Greeks, it would have been that of greater uniformity; and the arrangement of columns, each with a different capital in the same portico, is evidently the result of Egyptian taste. It shows the same progress which our decorated made from the more simple, but still varied, character of our early pointed style. The decorated and flamboyant each grew out of its predecessor; but no one looks for their origin in a *different* style of architecture; and in like manner the more ornamented column and the more *varied* arrangements of the details, in later Egyptian buildings, arose out of the old Egyptian style, and did not certainly proceed from the *uniformity* of Greek taste.

Our perpendicular style, though really derived from its varied predecessors, did undergo a change, and one that at last deprived it of the principal characteristic of the pointed style; it even admitted by degrees an incipient taste for greater uniformity (which about a century later Europe unequivocally welcomed back, by a return to classic architecture); and though it did not positively fraternise with the renaissance, it lost that great feature—variety, which peculiarly distinguished its Gothic parent. In one part overloaded with fretwork, in another with an endless repetition of monotonous lines, it strove to make rich what it ceased to make beautiful; and at last departed so far from the Gothic type, that one portion of a perpendicular edifice cast in metal might almost serve to construct the rest.

Egyptian architecture was at first simple, as was the Greek, and both had the severe fluted column, which as I have shown originated in the still more simple square pillar of an Egyptian quarry. The Greeks varied their style by the introduction of the Ionic, and a basket capital with leaves which by degrees took the form of the Corinthian; borrowing from the Ionic, and from the basket capital of Egypt, and varying the ornaments, as they had before modified the volutes; for these were also derived from the Egyptian columns attached to the canopies of the kings. But here the variety ended; or at least they did not go the length of the

Egyptians in placing columns of different orders one by the other in the same portico. This was confined to the taste of Egyptian (and of the later Gothic) architects. And though the original Egyptian column was so simple, no foreign influence introduced the change : it was of native growth ; and the water-plant and other columns, as I have already shown, date from the time of the earliest periods before the invasion of the Shepherds. Their formation too was consistent with the style of their decoration.

But while the architecture of the Egyptians and that of the Greeks had some points of resemblance in certain details, their general character was essentially distinct ; and the Egyptian flat roof had a totally different effect from the pediment, or gable, of a Greek temple. The plans of their sacred buildings were also quite dissimilar, and the circular form of the early Greek tomb was unknown in Egypt. The Egyptians, too, a cautious people, made durability their chief object, and they never sought for that beauty, to which the Greeks were so successful in attaining. If certain nations, like individuals, are gifted with peculiar talents, none have been favoured with the same variety as the Greeks ; and all their habits and feelings were eminently suited to the development of taste. Not so those of the Egyptians, who, independently of the restrictions imposed upon them, were deficient in the requisites for that purpose. They wanted the imaginative faculty of the Greeks ; they thought chiefly of carrying out a particular object ; and their speculative powers led to abstruse theories, not to the ideal conceptions required for excellence in art.

With regard to the pyramidal or sloping line in Egyptian buildings, it is scarcely necessary to say that its object was greater solidity ; and its use is one of many arguments against the opinion that Egyptian temples had their origin in excavated monuments ; for it is evident that the pyramidal line can neither be required, nor be consistently introduced, in the walls of a rock temple, and wherever the sloping line does occur there, it is merely in the ornamental mouldings, and is one more evidence of the imitation of a constructed monument. Another misconception, respecting Egyptian architecture, is that they *began* with

large buildings *because* the mountains gave them the power of
excavating to any depth, and extending the front to any length :
which is disproved by the fact that the oldest sanctuaries were of
very *small* dimensions ; *large* monuments were erected *before*
large rock temples were made ; and the mere irregular quarry
(opened solely to supply materials) did not bear any resemblance
to the plan or general character of a temple.   The attempt, too,
to account for the use of large blocks, from the " facility of transport " in a level country, and the preference given by the Greeks
to smaller or shorter architraves, from the difficulty of conveying
them from the quarries in a hilly country, is equally unsatis-
factory, and is far from being consistent with the positions of
many early Greek temples, and with what may be observed in
other countries, since we find that in the mountainous districts
of Syria heavier blocks were used than in the temples of
Egypt.

If the employment of large blocks were thus to be accounted
for, it would be difficult to explain how the Syrians acquired the
habit, or obtained the experience, which enabled them to move the
enormous stones at Baalbek, far heavier than any in Egypt, being
upwards of 60 feet long by 9 broad and 12 feet thick.   Some
stones in the walls of Jerusalem are more than 20 feet in length ;
and massive columns, of a single piece, were raised in temples
on the mountain summits of Syria.   It was therefore as common
a practice to use large blocks in the mountainous Syria, as in the
level Egypt ; so that neither the great breadth of the Egyptian, nor
the narrowness of Greek, or any other intercolumniations, can
be accounted for by the facility, or difficulty, of transporting long
blocks of stone to serve as architraves.   Nor was size originally
a condition in the edifices of the Egyptians.   They began, as did
the Greeks, with small monuments, which increased in scale with
the increase of wealth and the advancement of art ; and though
as their taste was developed, the Egyptians preferred monuments
of large size, the origin of this preference must not too hastily be
attributed to the facility of transporting the blocks, nor even to
the convenience of obtaining materials near at hand ; since the
granite quarries of Syene were upwards of 130 miles from

Thebes, or five times as much from Memphis; and the monoliths of that material erected in the Delta were conveyed more than 800 miles. The same hasty conclusion has been made about the largest colossi being peculiar to Egypt. But that of Olympian Jove was 60 feet high; that of Apollo, mentioned by Pausanias. was 30 cubits, or 45 feet; and the colossus of Rhodes, measuring 105 feet, far exceeded any in Egypt.

The arch was employed in Egypt at a very early period; and crude brick arches were in common use in roofing tombs at least as early as Amunoph I., in the 16th century before our era. And since I first discovered one at Thebes bearing his name, others have been found of the age of Thothmes III. (his fourth successor) and of Remeses V. It even seems to have been known in the time of the 12th dynasty, judging from the representation of what appear to be vaulted granaries at Beni Hassan.

That it should have originated in a country where wood was rare is consistent with probability; and it has been conjectured that the chambers in the large brick pyramids near Memphis were arched. Those at Thebes, of a rather later period, were so roofed; nor is it unreasonable to suppose that in the other large ones they had the same construction; and the superiority over the stone pyramids, boasted in the inscription upon that of Asychis, has been supposed to consist in its vaulted chambers. It is also evident that in the time of Osirtasen the vaulted ceilings of rock-tombs were made in imitation of arches; and the arch seems to have been particularly used in sepulchral monuments.

The earliest stone arches are of the time of a Psammitichus, in the 7th century before our era. One of these is at Sakkára, but from the thin slabs of stone forming its roof, it is a far less satisfactory instance of the arch than some of those near the pyramids of Geezeh of the same date; though an arch being of stone is no stronger proof of its existence, than are those of brick at Thebes; which are on the same principle, the bricks (like the stones) radiating to a common centre. For it is not necessary that an arch should be of any particular material; nor does the principle of the arch depend on its having a keystone; and arches, both round and pointed, are found at all ages without it. The same is the case in Egypt, and the small chapels before the pyramids of Ethiopia have instances of round and pointed arches, with and without the keystone.

Numerous crude brick arches, of different dates, exist in Thebes, besides the small pyramids * already alluded to, some of which are of very beautiful construction. The most remarkable are the doorways of the enclosures surrounding the tombs in the Assaseéf, which are composed of two or more concentric semicircles of brick, as well constructed as any of the present day. They are of the time of Psammitichus and other princes of the 26th dynasty, immediately before the invasion of Cambyses. All the bricks radiate to a common centre : they are occasionally pared off at the lower part, to allow for the curve of the arch, and sometimes the builders were contented to put in a piece of stone to fill up the increased space between the upper edges of the bricks. In those roofs of houses or tombs, which were made with less care, and required less solidity, the bricks were placed longitudinally, in the direction of the curve of the vault, and the lower ends were then cut away considerably, to allow for the greater opening between them ; and many were grooved at the sides, in order to retain a greater quantity of mortar between their united surfaces.

Though the oldest stone arch, whose age has been positively ascertained, dates only in the time of the second Psammitichus,† we cannot suppose that the use of stone was not adopted by the Egyptians, for that species of construction, previous to his reign ; even if none of the arches of the pyramids in Ethiopia should prove to be anterior to his era. Nor does the absence of the arch in temples, and other large buildings, excite our surprise, when we consider the style of Egyptian monuments ; and no one who understands the character of their architecture could wish for its introduction. In some of the small temples of the Oasis, the Romans attempted this innovation, but the appearance of the chambers so constructed fails to please ; and the introduction of an imitation of the arch into a building at Abydus, bearing the name of Sethi, or Osirei, was owing to its being a sepulchral monument. Here the roof is formed of single blocks of stone

* One is introduced into woodcut 452, *fig.* 1.   † Vignette P., Chap. x.

reaching from one architrave to the other, which, instead of being placed in the usual manner, stand upon their edges, in order to allow room for hollowing out an arch in their thickness ; but its effect is by no means good.   (*Woodcut* 452, *fig.* 3.)

Like the Egyptians, the Greeks abstained from introducing the arch into their monuments, being unsuited to a style already formed ;—an objection not felt by the Romans, who modified what they borrowed, so far as to adopt the arch, and break through the horizontal line of Greek architecture ; thus establishing the first elements of the vertical of later times ; and the great benefits conferred by the arch in covering large spaces, where crowded assemblies were to meet, are well demonstrated by a comparison of our churches, and the Great Hall of Karnak, with its forest of columns to support the roof.   But the Greeks were not ignorant of the arch ; instances of it still remain ; and Posidonius claims its invention for Democritus, who was born B.C. 460.   The arched tunnel of brick under the Euphrates at Babylon, mentioned by Diodorus, also shows that it was known at a remote age in other countries, as well as in Egypt.   (*See also Vignette N., end of Chap. VIII.*)

Another imitation of the arch occurs in a building at Thebes. Here, however, a reason may perhaps be given for its introduction, in addition to its being a tomb, and not bound to accord with the ordinary rules of architecture laid down for Egyptian temples.   The chambers lie under a friable rock, and are cased with masonry, to prevent the fall of its crumbling stone ; but instead of being roofed on the principle of the arch, they are covered with a number of large blocks, placed horizontally, one projecting beyond that immediately below it, till the uppermost two meet in the centre, the interior angles being afterwards ounded off to form the appearance of a vault.

This building dates in the 15th century B.C., consequently many years after the Egyptians had been acquainted with the art of vaulting ; and the reason of their preferring such a mode of construction probably arose from their calculating the great difficulty of repairing an injured arch in this position, and the consequences attending the decay of a single block ; nor can any one suppose, from the great superincumbent weight applied to

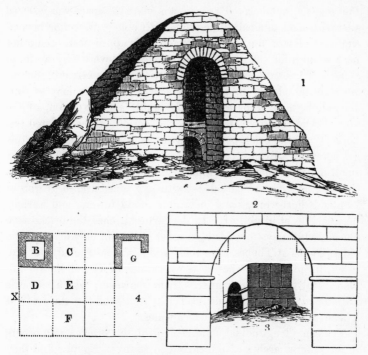

452.   Fig. 1. Vaulted rooms and doorway of a crude brick pyramid at Thebes.
          2. An imitation of an arch at Thebes.
          3. Another at Abydus.
          4. Mode of commencing a quarry.

the *haunches*, that this style of building is devoid of strength, and of the usual durability of an Egyptian fabric, or pronounce it ill suited to the purpose for which it was erected.

This was either an imitation of an arch, or a method of older times used before its invention ; and we have other instances, in Italy, of false and true arches being employed contemporaneously, by people well acquainted with the principle of forming *voussoirs* with stones radiating to a common centre.

The first deviation from the mode of roofing with flat stones was what is called the pent-shaped roof ; formed by the application of two sets of stones, inclined towards each other, at an angle of about 100°, as over the entrance to the Great Pyramid and the roof of the Queen's chamber.   The next was when the space was covered over with slabs of small dimensions, each course projecting beyond the one below it, until the uppermost ones approached each other near enough for the remaining space to be covered by a single stone.   These two, used at the same time in the Great Pyramid, were also employed by the early Greeks; and they may be considered the first steps towards the want, and invention, of the arch.   And this seems to confirm the notion of the boasted superiority of the brick pyramid having consisted in supplying this desideratum.   Bricks certainly led to its invention; and thus small materials have contributed to the greatest variety in construction at different periods :—witness groined arches, as well as long-and-short-work, opus incertum, round towers, and various peculiarities of brickwork.   In the earliest arches, the bricks were placed lengthways towards each other; and not only many of the oldest tombs at Thebes have their roofs so constructed, but the stones forming the arches at the pyramids of Gebel Berkel are placed in the same manner.   This, however, was afterwards abandoned; and the beautiful brick arches of the Assaseéf at Thebes resemble those of modern times.

The same longitudinal arrangement of the bricks again occurs in the pointed arches of the early Christians in Egypt; and they give evidence of being a first essay of a new principle.   Doubtful as to the power of an arch of this form, they only used it at first to cover passages, and other small spaces; and many consisted only of 1, 2, or 3 very long bricks in height, with a portion of one placed between the two uppermost ones as a key.   They are, however, remarkable from their antiquity, being about the 7th century of our era; and though a much older pointed arch is found at Gebel Berkel, as well as in Italy, and the pointed arch seems to be *imitated* in the time of the 18th dynasty, that style of building does not appear to have come into common use in the East much before the 9th century.   But it was then very general, and though some dream of pointed arches having been invented in Europe, from the intersection of two round arches, we may be sure that the East gave us the first notion of the new principle; and that we derived it from the Saracens; as they composed their architecture from the Byzantine and Persian styles, and the earliest pointed *architecture*, if not the first pointed arches, should be looked for in Asia Minor, and about Constantinople. As the Greeks instructed the Romans, the Byzantine Christians worked for the Saracens, and gave them the first notions of a style, which they afterwards modified according to their views.   The cupola introduced a new feature into the mosk, whose original simple courts, and small round arches, were humble imitations of Roman buildings; the golden mosaics of Byzantium, themselves descended from the "golden vaults" of Imperial Rome, decorated the walls and arched ceilings of Damascus houses, as they enriched the apses of Italian basilicas ; and the Byzantine or Romanesque style spread its influence over Europe and the East.   But the stream of taste was diversified according to the ground over which it flowed.   As yet one general system was not acknowledged, as in later times when Gothic architecture was the same, with slight variations, throughout Europe ; each people at first made their own selection, in the principles or the mouldings they imitated ; in England the rude Saxon, with its long-and-short-work,—the common house construction even before the age of Justinian ; the more decorated Norman ; and the Italian Lombard style, were all indebted to the Roman and the Byzantine ; and from the arrival of a fresh element from the East, itself of cognate origin, arose the pointed style of Western Europe.   Such was the progress of architecture from the earliest times ; each system borrowing, adopting, or recasting the component parts of its predecessor, according to the wants, climate, materials, or taste of the new country of its growth.

The most ancient buildings in Egypt were constructed of limestone, hewn from the mountains bordering the valley of the Nile to the East and West, extensive quarries of which may be seen at El Māsara, Nesleh Shekh Hassan, El Maabdeh, and other places ; and that it was used long before sandstone is proved by the tombs of the pyramids, as well as those monuments themselves, and by the vestiges of old substructions and ruins in Upper Egypt. Limestone continued to be occasionally employed for building even after the accession of the 12th dynasty ; but so soon as the durability of sandstone was ascertained, the quarries of Silsilis were opened, and those materials were universally adopted, and preferred for their even texture, and the ease with which they were wrought.

The extent of the quarries at Silsilis is very great; and it is not by the size and scale of the monuments of Upper Egypt alone that we are enabled to judge of the stupendous works executed by the ancient Egyptians; these would suffice to prove the character they bore, were the gigantic ruins of Thebes and other cities no longer in existence; and safely may we apply the expression, used by Pliny in speaking of the porphyry quarries, to those of Silsilis, " they are of such extent, that masses of any dimensions might be hewn from them."

In opening a new quarry, when the stone could not be taken from the surface of the rock, and it was necessary to cut into the lower part of its perpendicular face, they pierced it with a horizontal shaft; beginning with a square trench, and then breaking away the stone left in the centre (as indicated in woodcut 452, *fig.* 4, by the space B), its height and breadth depending of course on the size of the stones required. They then cut the same around C, and so on to any extent in a horizontal direction, after which they extended the work downwards, in steps, taking away E, and leaving D for the present, and thus descending as far as they found convenient, or the stone continued good. They then returned, and cut away the steps D, F, and all the others, reducing each time one step in depth, till at last there remained at X a perpendicular wall; and when the quarries were of very great horizontal extent, pillars were left at intervals to support the roof.

453.   Removing a stone from the quarries of El Māsara.

In one of the quarries at El Māsara, the mode of transporting the stone is represented. It is placed on a sledge, drawn by oxen, and is supposed to be on its way to the inclined plane that led to the river; vestiges of which may still be seen a little to the south of the modern village.

Sometimes, and particularly when the blocks were large and ponderous, men were employed to drag them, and those condemned to hard labour in the quarries, as a punishment, were required to assist in moving a certain number of stones, according to the extent of their offence, ere they were liberated; which seems to be proved by this expression, " I have dragged 110 stones for the building of Isis at Philæ," in an inscription at the quarries of Gertassy in Nubia. In order to keep an account of their progress, they frequently cut the initials of their name, or some private mark, with the number, on the rock whence the stone was taken, as soon as it was removed : thus, c. xxxii., pd. xxxiii. ; pd. xxxiiii., and numerous other signs occur at the quarries of Fateereh.

All large blocks were taken from the quarry on sledges ; and in a grotto behind E'Dayr, a Christian village between Antinoë and El Bersheh, is the representation of a colossus, which a number of men are employed in dragging with ropes—a subject doubly interesting from being of the early age of Osirtasen II., and one of the very few paintings which throw any light on the method employed by the Egyptians for moving weights.

It is not necessary that the colossus should have been hewn in the hill of El Bersheh ; and this picture, though it refers to what *really happened*, may also represent one of the occupations of the Egyptians, like the trades, gardening-scenes, and other subjects. At all events the statue could not have been placed in the tomb, as some suppose, being too large for the doorway ; and traces of it must have remained.

One hundred and seventy-two men, in four rows, of forty-three each, pull the ropes attached to the front of the sledge ; and grease is poured from a vase by a person standing on the pedestal of the statue, in order to facilitate its progress as it slides over the ground, which was probably covered with a bed of planks, though they are not indicated in the painting. (*See Frontispiece.*)

Some of the persons employed in this laborious duty appear to be Egyptians, the others are foreign slaves, who are clad in the costume of their country ; and behind are four rows of men, who, though only twelve in number, may be intended to represent the " superintendents," and the set which relieved the others when fatigued.

Below are persons carrying vases of the liquid, or perhaps water, for the use of the workmen, and some implements connected with the transport of the statue, followed by taskmasters with their wands of office. On the knee of the figure stands a man who claps his hands to the measured cadence of a song, to mark the time and insure their simultaneous draught ; for it is evident that, in order that the whole power might be applied at the same instant, a sign of this kind was necessary ; and the custom of singing at their work was usual in every occupation of the Egyptians, as it now is in that country, in India, and many other places. Nor is it found a disadvantage among the modern sailors of Europe, when engaged in pulling a rope, or in any labour which requires a simultaneous effort. Above are seven companies of soldiers, *unarmed*, holding green twigs in their hands.

The height of the statue was 13 cubits, 19½ ft., or really 22 ft. 2½ in. ; and of lime, or freestone ; as the colour and the hieroglyphics inform us. It was bound to the sledge by double ropes, which were tightened by means of long pegs inserted between them, and twisted round until completely braced ; and, to prevent injury from the friction of the ropes, a compress of leather, lead, or other substance, was introduced at the part where they touched the statue.

It is singular that the position of the ring to which all the ropes were attached for moving the mass was confined to one place at the front of the statue, and did not extend to the back part of the sledge ; but this was owing to the shortness of the body ; and, when of great length, it is probable that ropes were fixed at intervals along the sides, in order to give an opportunity of applying a greater moving power. For this purpose, in blocks of very great length (as the columns at Fateereh, which are about 60 ft. long, and 8½ ft. in diameter), certain pieces of stone were left projecting from the sides, like the trunnions of a gun, to which several ropes were attached, each pulled by its own set of men.

Small blocks of stone were sent from the quarries by water to their different places of destination in boats, or rafts ; and if any land-carriage was required, they were placed on sledges and rollers; but those of very large dimensions were dragged the whole way by men, overland, in the manner here represented. The immense weight of some shows that the Egyptians were well acquainted with mechanical powers, and the mode of applying a locomotive force with the most wonderful success; and the use of grease for large weights in preference to rollers is consistent with modern experience.

The obelisks transported from the quarries of Syene, at the first cataracts, in latitude 24° 5′ 23″, to Thebes and Heliopolis, vary in size from seventy to ninety-three feet in length. They are of one single stone; and the largest in Egypt, which is that of the great temple at Karnak, I calculate to weigh about 297 tons. This was brought about 138 miles from the quarry to where it now stands, and those taken to Heliopolis passed over a space of more than 800 miles. The power, however, to move the mass was the same, whatever might be the distance, and the mechanical skill which transported it five, or even one, would suffice for any number of miles.

In examining the ruins of western Thebes, and reading the statements of ancient writers regarding the stupendous masses of granite conveyed by this people for several hundred miles, our surprise is greatly increased. We find in the plain of Koorneh two colossi of Amunoph III., of a single block each, forty-seven feet in height, which contain about 11,500 cubic feet, and are made of a stone not known within several days' journey of the place; and at the Memnonium, is another of Remeses II., which when entire weighed upwards of 887 tons, and was brought from A'Sooán to Thebes, a distance, as before stated, of more than 130 miles. This is certainly a surprising weight, and we cannot readily suggest the means adopted for its transport, or its passage of the river; but the monolithic temple, said by Herodotus to have been taken from Elephantine to Buto, in the Delta, was still larger, and far surpassed in weight the pedestal of Peter the Great's statue at St. Petersburgh, which last is calculated at about 1200 tons.

He also mentions a monolith at Saïs, of which he gives the

following account :—" What I admire still more, is a monument
of a single block of stone, which Amasis transported from the
city of Elephantine.   Two thousand men, of the class of boatmen, were employed to bring it, and were occupied three years
in this arduous task.   The exterior length is twenty-one cubits
(31½ ft.) ; the breadth fourteen (21 ft.) ; and the height eight (12
ft.) ; and, within, it measures eighteen cubits twenty digits (28 ft.
3 in.) in length ; twelve (18 ft.) in breadth ; and five (7½ ft.) in
height.   It *lies* near the entrance of the temple, not having been
admitted into the building, in consequence, as they say, of the
engineer, while superintending the operation of dragging it
forward, having sighed aloud, as if exhausted with fatigue, and
impatient of the time it had occupied ; which being looked upon
by Amasis as a bad omen, he forbade its being taken any further.   Some, however, state that it was in consequence of a man
having been crushed beneath it, while moving it with levers."

Herodotus's measurement is given as it lay on the ground ;
his length is properly its height, and his height the depth, from
the front to the back ; for, judging from the usual form of these
monolithic monuments, it was doubtless like that of the same
king at Tel-et-Mai, the dimensions of which are 21 ft. 9 in.
high, 13 ft. broad, and 11 ft. 7 in. deep ; and internally 19 ft.
3 in., 8 ft., and 8 ft. 3 in.

The weight of the Saïte monolith cannot certainly be compared
to that of the colossus of Remeses ; but when we calculate the
solid contents of the temple of Latona at Buto, our astonishment
is unbounded ; and we are perplexed to account for the means
employed to move a mass which, supposing the walls to have
been only 6 ft. thick (for Herodotus merely gives the external
measurement of forty cubits, or 60 ft. in height, breadth, and
thickness), must have weighed upwards of 6000, or at the lowest
computation of 5000 tons.

The skill of the Egyptians was not confined to the mere moving of immense weights ; their wonderful knowledge of mechanism
is shown in the erection of obelisks, and in the position of large
stones, raised to a considerable height, and adjusted with the
utmost precision ; sometimes, too, in situations where the space

will not admit the introduction of the inclined plane. Some of the most remarkable are the lintels and roofing stones of the large temples ; and the lofty doorway leading into the grand hall of assembly, at Karnak, is covered with sandstone blocks, 40 ft. 10 in. long., and 5 ft. 2 in. square.

In one of the quarries at A'Sooán (Syene) is a granite obelisk, which, never having been finished or separated from the rock, remains in its original place. The depth of the quarry is so small, and the entrance to it so narrow, that it would have been impossible for them to turn the stone, in order to remove it by that opening ; they had therefore to lift it out of the hollow in which it had been cut ; and this was the case with all the other shafts previously hewn in the same quarry. Such instances as these suffice to prove the wonderful mechanical knowledge of the Egyptians ; and we may question whether our engineers could raise weights with the same facility, without using some of those modern appliances, which were quite unknown to that ancient people.

Pliny mentions several obelisks of very large dimensions, some of which were removed to Rome, where they now stand.

The Egyptians naturally looked on those monuments with feelings of veneration, being connected with their religion, and the glorious memory of their monarchs ; and at the same time perceived that, in buildings constructed as their temples were, the monotony of numerous horizontal lines required a relief of this kind ; but the same feelings cannot influence others, and few' motives can be assigned for their removal to Europe, beyond the desire of possessing what requires great difficulty to obtain.

I will not pretend to say that the ancient Romans committed the same strange outrage to taste as their modern successors, who have destroyed the effect of the most graceful part of these monuments, by crowning the apex, which should of course termi-nate in a point, with stars, rays, or other whimsical additions ; and, however habit may have reconciled the eye to such a monstrosity, every one who understands the beauty of form, and the harmony of lines, must observe and regret the incongruity of balls and weather-cocks on our own spires.

Pliny says, that the first Egyptian king who erected an obelisk was Mitres, who held his court at Heliopolis, the city of the Sun, to whom they were there dedicated; as to Amun at Thebes. Many others were raised by different monarchs, and "Ramises" made one 99 feet in height, "on which he employed 20,000 workmen." "And, fearing lest the engineer should not take sufficient care to proportion the power of the machinery to the weight he had to raise, he ordered his own son to be bound to the apex, more effectually to guarantee the safety of the monument."

The same writer describes a method of transporting obelisks from the quarries down the river, by lashing two flat-bottomed boats together, side by side, which were admitted into a trench, cut from the Nile to the place where the stone lay, laden with a quantity of ballast exactly equal to the weight of the obelisk; which, so soon as they had been introduced beneath the transverse block, was all taken out; and the boats rising, as they were lightened, bore away the obelisk in lieu of their previous burden. But we are uncertain if this method was adopted by the Egyptians; and though he mentions it as the invention of one Phœnix, he fails to inform us at what period he lived.

No insight is given into the secrets of their mechanical knowledge, from the sculptures, or paintings of the tombs, though so many subjects are there introduced. Our information, connected with this point, is confined to the use of levers, and a sort of crane; which last is mentioned by Herodotus, in describing the mode of raising the stones from one tier to another, when they built the Pyramids. He says it was made of short pieces of wood;—an indefinite expression, conveying no notion either of its form or principle;—and every stone was raised to the succeeding tier by a different machine.

Diodorus tells us, that machines were not invented at that early period, and that the stone was raised by mounds or inclined planes; but we may be excused for doubting his assertion, and thus be relieved from the effort of imagining an inclined plane five hundred feet in perpendicular height, with a proportionate base.

Whatever may have been the means employed, they evidently had acquired great facility in moving large blocks; and this was

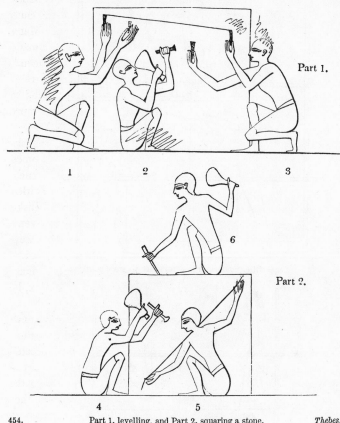

454.   Part 1. levelling, and Part 2. squaring a stone.   *Thebes.*
                Figs. 2, 4, 6, are using the chisel and mallet.

often a temptation to a later king to appropriate the monuments
of a predecessor in embellishing a temple. Thus Tirhakah took
the two lions of Amunoph III. from Soleb (the *name* of which
place they bear) to Gebel Birkel; which was an easy task, when
obelisks were transplanted from Memphis and Heliopolis to
Alexandria, and afterwards to Rome; and Amunoph's lions have
at last found a place in the British Museum.

It is true, that the occupations of the mason and the statuary
are sometimes alluded to in the paintings; the former, however,

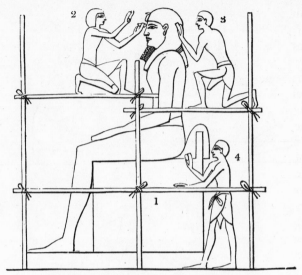

455.   Large sitting colossus of granite, which they are polishing.

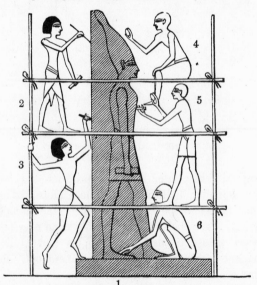

456.   Standing figure of a king, and, like the former, painted to represent granite.
Figs. 4, 6, are polishing it; and figs. 2 and 3 painting and sculpturing the hieroglyphics at the back.   *Thebes.*

are almost confined to the levelling or squaring a stone, and the use of the chisel.　Some are represented polishing and painting statues of men, sphinxes, and small figures; and two instances occur of large granite colossi, surrounded with scaffolding, on which men are engaged in chiselling and polishing the stone; the painter following the sculptor to colour the hieroglyphics he had engraved at the back of the statue.　(Woodcut 455, *fig.* 2.)

The usual mode of cutting large blocks from the quarries was by a number of metal wedges, which were struck at the same instant along its whole length; sometimes, however, they seem to have been of highly dried wood, which, being driven into holes previously cut for them by a chisel, and then saturated with water, split the stone by their expansion; and the troughs frequently found along the whole line of the holes, where the wedges were inserted, argue strongly in favour of this opinion.

Such a method could only be adopted when the wedges were in an horizontal position, upon the upper surface of the stone; but those put into the sides were impelled by the hammer only.

To separate the lower part of a ponderous mass from the rock, we may suppose they cut under it, leaving long pieces here and there to support it, like beams, which traversed its whole depth from the front to the back; and then having introduced wooden rafters into the open spaces which were cleared away, they removed the remainder of the stone, and the block rested on the wood.　This was also the process in the quarry at Baalbek.

Some have imagined that they used the same means now practised in India, of lighting a fire along the whole length of the mass, in the direction where they intended it should split; and then pouring water upon it, cracked the stone in that part by its sudden action: but this is very doubtful, and the presence of the holes for the wedges sufficiently proves the method they usually employed.

Among the remarkable inventions of a remote era among the Egyptians, may be mentioned bellows and siphons.　The former were used at least as early as the reign of Thothmes III., being represented in a tomb bearing the name of that Pharaoh.　They consisted of a leather bag, secured and fitted into a frame, from

which a long pipe extended for carrying the wind to the fire.
They were worked by the feet, the operator standing upon them,
with one under each foot, and pressing them alternately, while
he pulled up each exhausted skin with a string, he held in his
hand.   In one instance we observe from the painting, that when
the man left the bellows, they were raised, as if full of air ; and
this would imply a knowledge of the valve. (*Woodcut* 457, *k, o.*)

457.   Bellows.   *Thebes.*

a, b, k, o, the leather case.   *c, e, l, n,* the pipes conveying the wind to the fire. *d, m,* the fire.
          h, q, charcoal.   *k* and *o* are raised as if full of air.

It is uncertain when bellows were first invented ; the earliest
contrivance of this kind was probably a mere reed or pipe, which
we find used by goldsmiths in the age of Osirtasen, and also at a
late period, after the invention of bellows ; and the tubes of these
last appear even in the time of Thothmes III. to have been
simply of reed, tipped with a metal point, to resist the action of
the fire.

The first step was to add the sack containing the air ; and

various improvements succeeded each other in the form and principle of the bellows : there are, however, no means of ascertaining
the period when they assumed their present form ; and the merit
of the late invention of *wooden* bellows is still disputed.   Strabo
ascribes the bellows to Anacharsis, but with the evident conviction that these (the double anchor), and the potter's wheel, were of
an age far anterior to the Scythian philosopher, which is fully
proved by the paintings of Thebes.

The ordinary hand-bellows now used for small fires in Egypt
are a sort of bag made of the skin of a kid, with an opening at
one end (like the mouth of a common carpet bag), where the
skin is sewed upon two pieces of wood ; and these being pulled
apart by the hands, and closed again, the bag is pressed down,
and the air thus forced through the pipe at the other end.   It is,
perhaps, an ancient invention, but I find no indication of it in
the paintings.

The bellows with sides of wood, made at the present day, are
a more perfect construction than these last, or the foot-bellows of
the time of Thothmes.   They are supposed to have been known
to the Greeks, though I confess, the

> "———— taurinis follibus auras
> Accipiunt redduntque"

of Virgil is rather calculated to convey the idea of bellows made
of ox leather without wooden sides.

Siphons are shown to have been invented in Egypt, at least as
early as the reign of Amunoph II. in the 15th century before
our era ; and they again occur in the paintings of the third Remeses.   In a tomb at Thebes, bearing the name of Amunoph,
their use is unequivocally pointed out, by one priest pouring a
liquid into some vases, and the other drawing it off, by applying
the siphon to his mouth, and thence to a large vase ; and it is
not improbable that they owed their invention to the necessity of
allowing the Nile water to deposit its thick sediment in vases,
which could not be moved without again rendering it turbid,
whether by inclining the vessel, or dipping a cup into it with the
hand.   They seem to be of a pliant material, from their bending
(at *f* and perhaps at *g*, in Woodcut 458).

458.   Siphons used about the year 1430 B.C.   *Thebes.*
1 Pours a liquid into vases from the cup *b* ; and 2 draws it off by the siphons *a*.

Julius Pollux says they were used for tasting wine; and
Heron of Alexandria, the first writer of consequence who mentions them, and who lived under Ptolemy Euergetes II., shows
them to have been employed as hydraulic machines on a grand
scale, for draining lands, or conveying water over a hill from one
valley to another. Their name, siphon, is evidently oriental,
and derived from the word *siph* or *sif*, to "imbibe," or "draw
up with the breath," analogous to, and perhaps the origin of, our
own expression "to sip." They had also invented the syringe,
used for injecting liquids into the head and body of mummies
during the embalming process; and an instrument is often represented in the sculptures of early times, which has the appearance
of a portable pump.

Respecting the numerous inventions of the Egyptians little information is to be obtained; but I have mentioned their skill in
cutting hard stones, and various branches of art; and we may
conclude they tested gold by a stone. And if they applied the
name *Bashan*, or *Basan* (whence *basanos*), to a basaltic stone
on which gold makes no mark (nor does it on that of the "Basanite
mountain"), this was probably because it included all basalts;

some of which test gold as well as our basanite,—a slate to which the name has since been transferred, and confined.

I have also shown that Herodotus, and others, ascribe the origin of geometry to the Egyptians; but the period when it commenced is uncertain. Anticlides pretends that Mœris was the first to lay down the elements of that science, which he says was perfected by Pythagoras; but the latter observation is merely the result of the vanity of the Greeks, which claimed for their countrymen (as in the case of Thales, and other instances) the credit of enlightening a people on the very subjects which they had visited Egypt for the purpose of studying.

The discovery of the pole, the sundial, and the division of the day into twelve hours, are said by Herodotus to have been derived by the Greeks from the Babylonians. Of the two former we have no indication in the sculptures to prove the epoch when they were known in Egypt; but there is reason to believe that the day and night were divided, each into twelve hours, by the Egyptians, some centuries before that idea could have been imparted to the Greeks from Babylon.

Sufficient data cannot, of course, be expected from the sculptures of the tombs, and the accidental introduction of their occupations, to enable us to form an accurate opinion respecting the extent of their knowledge, the variety of their inventions, or the skill of their workmen in different branches of art. The objects buried with the dead were frequently mere models of those they used; and the pains taken in making them depended on the sums expended by the friends of the deceased after his death. It was left to their good intentions or their superstitious feelings to decide of what quality they should be, or what labour should be bestowed upon them; and if the kind regards of a friend frequently induced some to incur considerable expense in providing such objects, many, on the other hand, were less scrupulous in the last duties to their departed relative. The former purchased ornaments of the most costly materials, as agate, basalt, granite, alabaster, onyx, jasper, gold, and precious stones; the latter were contented with common porcelain, wax, limestone, or wood. But even the best which have been found in the tombs, are evidently of inferior quality; and, like their vases and chairs, none have been discovered equal in beauty to those represented in the paintings, with the exception of a few rings and some female ornaments, which had been actually worn by the deceased.

The paintings, again, indicate a very small portion of their inventions: many, with which we know they were acquainted, are omitted; and the same remark applies to some of their most common occupations, to the animals they kept, and to the ordinary productions of their country. No exact notion can even be formed of their costume and the dresses of various grades, either among men or women, though so frequently represented, partly owing to their conventional style of drawing figures, partly to their want of skill in depicting drapery; it is, therefore, only the most simple portion of their dress which can be understood.

Ordinary workmen, and indeed all the lower orders, were clad in a sort of apron, or kelt, sometimes simply bound round the loins, and lapping over in front *; and others had short drawers, extending half way to the knee.† The same kind of apron was worn by the higher orders, under an ample dress of fine linen reaching to the ankles,‡ and provided with large sleeves.§ The apron was generally fastened by a girdle, or by a sort of sash, tied in front in a bow or knot ‖: it was sometimes folded over, with a centre-piece falling down in front, beneath the part where it overlapped; and some of the poor classes, while engaged in laborious occupations, were contented with a roll of linen passed between the legs from the back to the front of the girdle ¶. This last is frequently used at the present day by the peasants, when drawing water by the *shadoof;* some of whom are satisfied with a few leaves, in Adam-like, or in River-God, simplicity.

Herodotus mentions some Egyptian dresses, which he describes of linen, with a fringe on the border around the legs, called *calasiris;* over which they wore a cloak of white wool, similar, no doubt, to the *bornous* of the present day, so common in Egypt and the coast of Barbary. (*See above*, p. 91, and vol. i., p. 333.)

* Woodcut 459.   † Woodcut 384, *fig.* 1, and *fig.* 2 *j*.
‡ Woodcut 156, *figs.* 6, 8.   § Woodcuts 251 and 30, *fig.* 5.
  Woodcut 407.   ¶ Woodcut 459, *fig.* 7.

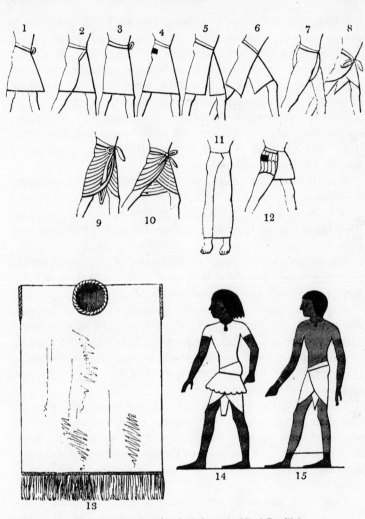

459.   Men's dresses.   13 a shirt from the work of Prof. Rosellini.

The same custom of edging their dresses with fringes was common to the Israelites, who were ordered to make them "in the borders of their garments;" "a blue riband" being "put upon the fringe;" and, as already observed, they were only

the ends of the threads composing the woof, left in order to
prevent the cloth unravelling; the blue riband added by the
Israelites being intended to strengthen it, and prevent its tearing.
These fringed dresses are occasionally represented in the paintings; and pieces of cloth have been found with the same kind
of border; which in some instances has been sewed on.

Some people wore a sort of shirt with loose or light sleeves,
open at the neck, where it was tied with strings; and except that
it was linen, instead of wool, it was not unlike the *bisht* of the
modern inhabitants of Upper Egypt.

The dresses of the priests, which excepting those of ceremony
were much the same as of other persons of rank, have been
already mentioned; as well as the goeffreying process, by which
the folds or waving lines were impressed upon the fine linen they
wore.*

The princes wore a dress very like that of the sacred scribe,
the apron wound round the body, and divided into three different
folds, over which was a garment with large sleeves; but their
distinguishing mark was a peculiar badge at the side of the head,
descending to the shoulder, and frequently adorned and terminated
with a gold fringe. This, I suppose to have contained the lock
of hair, indicative of youth, which is seen in the statues of
Harpocrates, and frequently represented on the heads of children;
as I have already shown.†

The robes of the sovereign varied, of course, according to his
immediate occupation. When engaged as high-priest, they much
resembled those worn by the principal functionaries of the sacerdotal order, with the exception of the apron and head-dress, which
were of peculiar form, and belonged exclusively to his rank as
king.

This apron was richly ornamented in front with lions' heads,
and other devices, probably of coloured leather; and the border
was frequently formed of a row of asps, the emblems of royalty.
Sometimes the royal name, with an asp on each side, as *supporters*,
was embroidered upon it, the upper part being divided into square

* In vol. i. p. 334; and vol. ii. p. 92.
† *See* vol. i. p. 311, and woodcuts 279, 105, *fig.* 2.

compartments of different colours; but it is not improbable, that this formed an appendage to the girdle, rather than to the apron; and several straps falling down at the side of the centre-piece show that it was tied in front, and came over the folds of the apron, and even of the upper robes.

460.　　　　　　　　　　Dress of the king.

2, 3, the king's apron.　3, is from a statue of Amunoph III. in the museum at Alnwick Castle.　4, wreath of the crown of Sabaco's statue at the Isle of Argo.

The head-dress of the king, on state occasions, was the crown of the Upper or of the Lower country, or the *pshent*, the union of the two. Every king, after the sovereignty of the Thebaïd and Lower Egypt had become once more vested in the same person, put on this double crown at his coronation; and we find in the grand representation given of this ceremony at Medeenet Haboo, that the principal feature of the proclamation, on his ascension to the throne, was the announcement to the four sides of the world, that " Remeses had put on the crown of the Upper and Lower country." (*See crowns and head-dresses in Woodcut* 461.)

He even wore his crown during the heat of battle; sometimes merely a wig; but a helmet made apparently of woollen stuff with a thick nap, not very unlike the modern Persian cap, was generally preferred; and, in religious ceremonies, he put on a striped head-dress, probably of linen, which descended in front over the breast, and terminated behind in a sort of *queue* bound with riband. This last is the one generally worn by sphinxes; which were emblems of the king.

When crowned, the king invariably put on the two crowns at the same time, though on other occasions he was permitted to wear each separately, whether in the temple, the city, or the field of battle : and he even appeared in his helmet during the ceremonies in honour of the gods. On some occasions he wore a short wig, on which a band was fastened, ornamented with an asp, the emblem of royalty.

It may appear singular that so warm a covering to the head should have been adopted in the climate of Egypt; but when we recollect that they always shaved the head, and that the reticulated texture of the groundwork, on which the hair was fastened, allowed the heat of the head to escape, while the hair effectually protected it from the sun, it is evident that no better covering could have been devised, and that it far surpassed in comfort and coolness the modern turban; which is always found by those who are in the habit of wearing it to be very agreeable in hot weather, provided all the particulars are attended to, which the Turks find so essential, but which those Europeans who merely put it on for effect, too often neglect.

The upper portion of the wig was frequently made with curled, and not with plaited hair, this last being confined to the sides and lower part, as is the case in the wigs preserved in the British and Berlin museums; but the whole was sometimes composed of a succession of plaits, commencing from the centre of the crown, extending downwards, and increasing in length towards the bottom. Some smaller wigs, worn by persons of rank, consisted of short locks of equal length, arranged in uniform

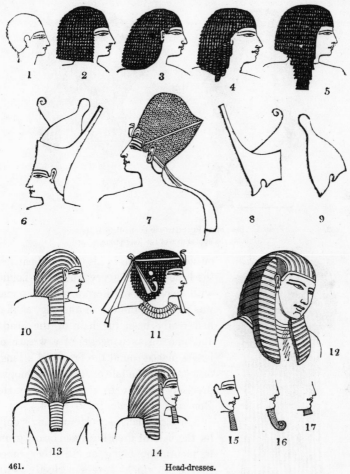

461.   Head-dresses.

1, a close cap.   2, 3, 4, 5, wigs.   6, the crown *Pshent* of the Upper and Lower country, or
9 and 8 united. 10 to 14, royal head-dresses. 15, beard of a god. 17, of a king. 16, of
a private individual of rank.

lines; imitations of which appear to have been made in woollen
or other stuffs, under the denomination of false wigs, for the use of
those who could not afford the more expensive quality of real hair.

Wigs were worn both within the house and out of doors, like
the turban of the present day; and a priest might even officiate

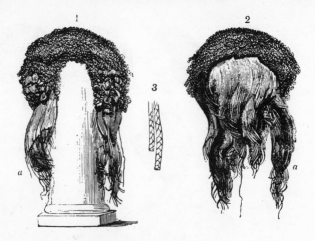

462.   Front and back of an Egyptian wig in the British Museum.
              3, shows the appearance of the long plaits, *a, a.*

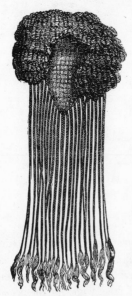

463. Wig about 2¼ feet in length,
seen in front. *Berlin Museum.*

on some occasions in his wig. At parties, the head-dress of every guest was bound with a chaplet of flowers, and ointment was put upon the top of the wig, as if it had really been the hair of the head; and one instance occurs of a wreath of leaves placed round the crown of a king, on a statue in the Isle of Argo, in Ethiopia, precisely similar to those worn by the Romans. (*Woodcut* 460, *fig.* 4.)

The Egyptians, says Herodotus, "only let the hair of their head and beard grow in mourning, being at all other times shaved;" which agrees perfectly with the authority of the sculptures, and of the Bible, where Joseph is said to have "shaved himself," when sent for from prison by Pharaoh. So particular, indeed, were they on this point, that to have neglected it was a subject of reproach and ridicule; and whenever they intended to convey the idea of a man of low condition, or a slovenly person, the artists represented him with a beard. It is amusing to find that their love of caricature was not confined to the lower orders, but extended even to the king: and the negligent habits of Remeses VII. are indicated in his tomb at Thebes, by the appearance of his chin, blackened by an unshorn beard of two or three days' growth. But it was likewise given as the test of hardships undergone in a severe campaign; and the warlike character of Remeses the Great is pointed out in the same manner.

The Egyptians did not confine the privilege of shaving to freeborn citizens, like the Romans, who obliged slaves to wear their beards and hair long, and only permitted them the use of a cap after they had been enfranchised: and though foreigners, who were brought to Egypt as slaves, had beards on their arrival in the country, we find that so soon as they were employed in the service of this civilised people, they were obliged to conform to the cleanly habits of their masters; their beard and heads were shaved; and they adopted a close cap.

The priests were remarkable for their love of cleanliness, which was carried so far, that they shaved the whole body every three days, and performed frequent daily ablutions, bathing twice a day and twice during the night. It was not confined to their order; every Egyptian prided himself on the encouragement of habits, which it was considered a disgrace to neglect: we can, therefore, readily account for the disgust they felt on seeing the squalid appearance and unrefined habits of their Asiatic neighbours, whose long beards were often the subject of ridicule to the Egyptian soldier; and for their abhorrence of the bearded and long-haired Greeks; which was so great, that, according to Herodotus, " no Egyptian of either sex would on any account kiss the lips of a Greek, make use of his knife, his spit and cauldron, or taste the meat of an animal which had been slaughtered by his hand." The same habits of cleanliness are also indicated by the " changes of raiment" given by Joseph to his brethren, when they set out to fetch their father to Egypt.

Barbers may be considered the offspring of civilisation; and as a Roman youth, when arrived at the age of manhood, cut off his beard, and consecrated it to some deity, as a token of his having emerged from a state of childhood, so a people, until they have adopted the custom of shaving, may be supposed to retain a remnant of their early barbarism.

With the Egyptians it was customary to shave the heads even of young children, leaving only certain locks at the front, sides, and back; and those of the lower classes were allowed to go out in the sun with the head exposed, without the protection of a cap; which is the reason assigned by Herodotus for the hardness of the Egyptian skulls, compared with those of other people. " I became acquainted," says the historian, " with a remarkable fact, which was pointed out to me by the people living in the neighbourhood of the field of battle, where the Egyptians and the army of Cambyses fought; the bones of the killed being still scattered about, those of the Persians on one side, and of the Egyptians on the other. I observed that the skulls of the former were so soft, that you could perforate them with a small pebble; while those of the latter were so strong, that with difficulty you could break them with a large stone. The reason of which, as they told me, and I can readily believe it, is that, the Egyptians being in the habit of shaving their heads from early youth, the bone becomes thickened: and hence, too, they are never bald; for, certainly, of all countries, nowhere do you see fewer bald people than in Egypt. The Persians, on the contrary, have soft skulls, in consequence of their keeping the head covered from the sun, and enveloped in soft caps. I also observed the same of those who were killed in the battle between Achæmenes and Inarus the Libyan."

It was usual for the lower orders to work in the sun without any covering to the head, as the modern peasants of Egypt, who appear (*fortunately*) to inherit from their predecessors skulls of uncommon hardness; and we see the same class of persons repre-sented in the paintings with and without a cap, whether in the house or in the open field.

Persons of all classes occasionally wore caps, some of which were large, others fitting tight to the head; but these last were considered far less becoming than the wig, and suited rather to the lower orders than to persons of rank. Women always wore their own hair, and they were not shaved even in mourning, or after death.

The use of wigs was not confined to the Egyptians of all people of antiquity; the Romans, under the emperors, also adopted a sort of peruke, called *capillamentum* or *galerus*, though it seems rather to have been worn by women than men; and Juvenal describes Messalina putting on a wig of flaxen hair to conceal her own black locks, when she left the palace in disguise.

The most singular custom of the Egyptians was that of tying a false beard upon the chin, which was made of plaited hair, and of a peculiar form, according to the person by whom it was worn. Private individuals had a small beard, scarcely two inches long; that of a king was of considerable length, square at the bottom; and the figures of gods were distinguished by its turning up at the end. No man ventured to assume, or affix to his image, the beard of a deity; but after their death, it was permitted to substitute this divine emblem on the statues of kings, and all other persons who were judged worthy of admittance to the Elysium of futurity; in consequence of their having assumed the character of Osiris, to whom the souls of the pure returned, on quitting their earthly abode. The form of the beard, therefore, readily distinguishes the figures of gods and kings, in the sacred subjects of the temples; and the allegorical connexion between the sphinx and the monarch is pointed out by its having the kingly beard, as well as the crown, and other symbols of royalty.

This title of "Osiris" seems, in the oldest times, to have been confined to the deceased kings (as Mr. Birch has observed); and it was only on, or a little before, the accession of the 18th dynasty, that it was given to "goodmen" of all ranks, at their death.

The dresses of children of the lower classes were very simple; and as Diodorus informs us, the expenses incurred in feeding and clothing them amounted to a mere trifle. "They feed them," he says, "very lightly, and at an incredibly small cost; . . . . . and since most of them are brought up, on account of the mildness of the climate, without shoes, and, indeed, without any other clothing, the whole expense incurred by the parents does not exceed 20 drachmæ (13 shillings) each; and this frugality is the true reason of the populousness of Egypt." But the children of the higher orders were often dressed like grown persons, with a loose robe, reaching to the ankles, and sandals.

Infants do not appear to have been swaddled, as among the Jews, Greeks, and Romans. When too young to walk, if taken out by a mother or nurse, they were carried in a shawl, suspended at her back, or before her; a custom still retained by the women

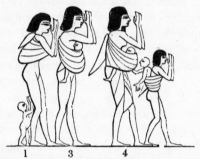

464.   Women carrying their children in a funeral procession.   *Thebes.*

1   3   4

of the Moghrebin Arabs; and in Ethiopia they were carried in baskets, supported at the mother's back by a band passing over her forehead.*

Sometimes, though nearly or entirely naked, the neck of an Egyptian child was decorated with a string of beads; and occasionally a *bulla*, or charm, was suspended in the centre, representing the symbol of truth and justice, which has been supposed also to indicate the heart, and is usually found in the balance of the judgment scenes, as a representative of the good works of the deceased. A *bulla* of this kind was worn by the youthful deity Harpocrates.

It was probably of gold, or hard stone, like those of the Romans; and others worn by the poorer classes, as at Rome, and in modern Egypt, were of leather. They were supposed to prompt the wearer to virtue and wisdom, to keep off the evil eye, or to

* Woodcut 354.

avert misfortune ; and superstition induced many to appeal to
them in danger, and derive from them omens of forthcoming
events. Sometimes a charm consisted of a written piece of
papyrus tightly rolled up, and sewed into a covering of linen, or
other substance, several of which have been found at Thebes ;
and emblems of various deities were appended to necklaces for
the same purpose.

Ladies and men of rank paid great attention to the beauty of
their sandals : but on some occasions those of the middle classes
who were in the habit of wearing them, preferred walking bare-
footed ; and in religious ceremonies, the priests frequently took
them off, while performing their duties in the temple.

The sandals varied slightly in form ; those worn by the upper
classes, and by women, were usually pointed and turned up at
the end, like our skaits, and many Eastern slippers of the present
day. Some had a sharp flat point, others were nearly round.

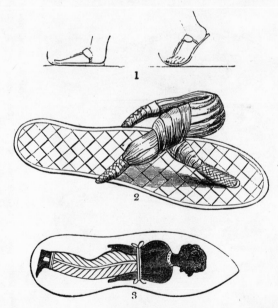

465.　　　　　　　　　　　Sandals.　　　　　　*Berlin Museum.*
1, From the sculptures.　　　2, In the Berlin Museum ; made of the papyrus.
　　　　　　　3, Figure of a captive on the sole.

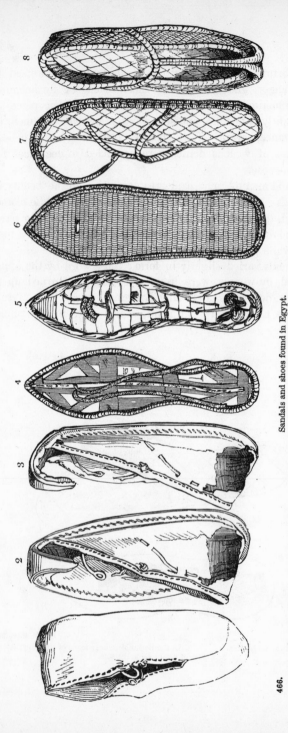

466.

Sandals and shoes found in Egypt.

1, 2, 3. Shoes of green leather, probably of Greek time. Mr. Salt's Collection. 4, 5. Upper and lower side of a pair of sandals, made of palm leaves and the papyrus, 11 inches long and 3 broad. In the Museum of Alnwick Castle. 6. Sole of a sandal, 1 foot long and 3¼ inches broad. Alnwick Castle. 7. A sandal; and 8. A sandal with sides like a shoe. Both in the Berlin Collection.

They were made of a sort of woven, or interlaced work, of palm leaves and papyrus stalks, or other similar materials; sometimes of leather; and were frequently lined within with cloth, on which the figure of a captive was painted *; that humiliating position being considered suited to the enemies of their country, whom they hated and despised—an idea agreeing perfectly with the expression which so often occurs in the hieroglyphic legends, accompanying a king's name, when his valour and victories are recorded on the sculptures: " You have trodden the impure Gentiles under your powerful feet."

Shoes, or low boots, were also common in Egypt, many having been found at Thebes†; but these I believe to have been of late date, and to have belonged to Greeks; for, since no persons are represented in the paintings wearing them, except foreigners, we may conclude they were not adopted by the Egyptians, at least in a Pharaonic age. They were of leather, generally of a green colour; laced in front with thongs, which passed through small loops on either side; and were principally used, as in Greece and Etruria, by women.

The dresses of women consisted sometimes of a loose robe or shirt, reaching to the ankles, with tight, or full sleeves, and fastened at the neck like those of the men, with a string ‡; over which they often wore a sort of petticoat, secured at the waist by a girdle; and this last, in mourning, while bewailing the death of a relative, was frequently their only dress.§

Such was the costume of the lower classes of women; and, sometimes indeed, as at the present day, it consisted merely of the loose shirt or robe, without shoes or sandals.

The higher orders wore a petticoat, or gown, secured at the waist by a coloured sash, or by straps over the shoulders; and above this was a large loose robe, made of the finest linen, with full sleeves,‖ and tied in front below the breast: and during some religious ceremonies¶ the right arm was taken out of the sleeve, and left exposed as in the funeral processions. The petticoat or

* Woodcut 465, *fig.* 3.
‡ Woodcut 125, *fig.* 2.
‖ Woodcut 282, *fig.* 5.
† Woodcut 466, *figs.* 1, 2, 3.
§ Woodcut 280.
¶ Woodcut 282, *figs.* 1, 2, and 3.

467.   Dresses of women.

The sash in figs. 1 and 2, though represented at the side, is to be understood as tied in front. In fig. 3 the side hair appears to be fixed by a comb; and before it, on the cheek, the short hair is arranged in separate plaits. 4 shows the shirt tied at the neck: it is a terra cotta statue.

gown was of richly coloured stuff, presenting a great variety of patterns, not unlike our modern chintzes, the most elegant of which were selected for the robes of deities and the dresses of queens.

Slaves or servants were not allowed to wear the same costume as ladies, and their mode of dressing the hair was different. They generally bound it at the back part of the head, into a sort of loop, or ranged it in one or more long plaits at the back, and eight or nine similar ones were suffered to hang down at either side of the neck and face.* They wore a long tight gown, tied at the neck, with short close sleeves, reaching nearly to the elbow: and sometimes a long loose robe was thrown over it, when employed to dance, or to present themselves on festive occasions.

* Woodcuts 151 and 158.

Ladies wore their hair long, and plaited. The back part was made to consist of a number of strings of hair, reaching to the bottom of the shoulder blades, and on each side other strings of the same length descended over the breast. The hair was plaited

in the triple plait, the ends being left loose ; or, more usually, two or three plaits were fastened together at the extremity by a woollen string of corresponding colour. Around the head was bound an ornamental fillet, with a lotus bud, by way of *feronière*, falling over the forehead ; and the strings of hair, at the sides, were separated and secured with a comb, or a band, ornamented in various ways according to the fancy of the wearer : and occasionally a round stud, or pin, was thrust into them at the front.

468.   Head-dress of a lady, from a mummy case.

The short hair at the side of the face, which the ingenuity of ancient Roman, and modern European ladies, has, by the aid of gum, compelled to lie in an immovable curve upon the cheek, was interwoven with several of its longer neighbours ; and these being bound together at the end with string, fell down before the, earring which they partially concealed ; or in a simple corkscrew curl. Many of the mummies of women have been found with the hair perfectly preserved, plaited in the manner I have mentioned ; the only alteration in its appearance being the change of its black hue, which became reddened by exposure to great heat, during the process of embalming.

The ancient mode of plaiting the hair seems to have been very similar to that of the women in modern Ethiopia, where, too, young girls wear a girdle, or rope, of twisted hair, leather, or other materials, decorated with shells, round the hips.*

The earrings, most usually worn by Egyptian ladies, were large, round, single hoops† of gold, from one inch and a half, to two inches and one-third, in diameter, and frequently of a still greater size ; or

* *See* woodcuts 98, 125, 151.   † Woodcuts 474, *fig.* 5, and 159.

made of six rings soldered together*; sometimes an asp, whose body was of gold set with precious stones, was worn by persons of rank, as a fashionable caprice; but it is probable that this emblem of majesty was usually confined to members of the royal family.

Earrings of other forms have also been found at Thebes, but their date is uncertain; and it is difficult to say if they are of an ancient Egyptian age, or of Greek introduction. Of these the most remarkable are a dragon,† and another of fancy shape, which is not inelegant.‡ Some few were of silver, and plain hoops, like those made of gold already noticed, but less massive, being of the thickness of an ordinary ring. At one end was a small opening, into which the curved extremity of the other caught after it had been passed through the ear; § and others were in the form of simple studs.

Though gloves do not appear to have been worn by Egyptian women, they were known as early as the 18th dynasty, and brought as part of a tribute to Thothmes III. by the Rot-n̄-n, an Asiatic people; and long linen gloves, ornamented with a blue stripe, have been found in Egypt.

They wore many rings, sometimes two and three on the same

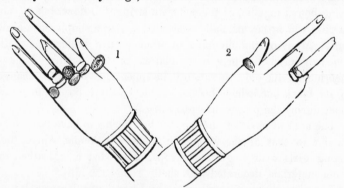

469.   Hands of a wooden figure of a woman.   On the lid of a mummy case in Mr. Salt's Collection, now in the British Museum.   1. The left; 2. the right hand.

* Woodcut 474, *figs.* 6 and 7.
† Woodcut 470, *fig.* 10, not unlike one of the Chinese dragons.
‡ Woodcut 470, *fig.* 21.   § Woodcut 474, *fig.* 5.

finger: the left was considered the hand peculiarly privileged to bear those ornaments, and it is remarkable that its third finger was decorated with a greater number than any other, and was considered by them, as by us, *par excellence* the ring finger, though there is no evidence of its having been so honoured at the marriage ceremony. They even wore a ring on the thumb; and I have seen, upon the right hand of a wooden figure, a ring on the thumb, and two on the third finger; and upon the left, one upon the thumb and little finger, two on the fore and second finger, and three on the third. One on the third finger is in the form of a *trochus* shell, very common in the Red Sea.

Some rings were simple; others were made with a scarabæus, or an engraved stone; and they were occasionally in the form of a shell, a knot, a snake, or some fancy device. They were mostly of gold; and this metal seems to have been always preferred to silver, for rings and other articles of jewellery. Silver rings, however, are occasionally met with; and two in my possession, which were accidentally found in a temple at Thebes, are engraved with hieroglyphics, containing the name of the royal city.

Bronze was seldom used for rings, though frequently for signets. Some have been discovered of brass and iron (the latter of a Roman time); but ivory and blue porcelain were the materials of which those worn by the lower classes were usually made. The scarabæus was the favourite form both for rings and the ordinary ornaments of necklaces; in some the stone, flat on both faces, turned on pins, like many of our seals at the present day, and the ring itself was bound round at each end, where it was inserted into the stone, with gold wire. This was common not only to rings but to signets, and was intended for ornament as well as security.

One of the largest signets I have seen, contained twenty pounds worth of gold. (*Woodcut* 470, *figs.* 4, 5, 6, 7.)

It consisted of a massive ring, half an inch in its largest diameter, bearing an oblong plinth, on which the devices were engraved one inch long, $\frac{6}{10}$ths in its greatest, and $\frac{4}{10}$ths in its smallest, breadth. On one face was the name of King Horus,

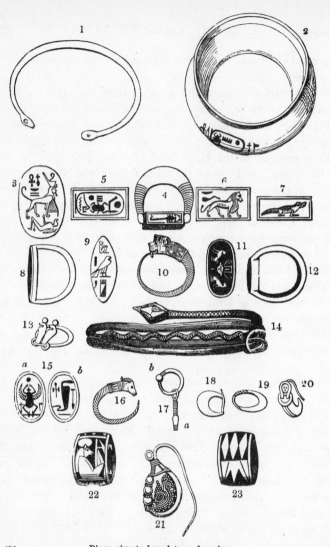

470.   Rings, signets, bracelets, and earrings.

Fig. 1. Bronze bracelet, or bangle, in the Museum of Alnwick Castle.   2. Gold bracelet in the Leyden Museum, bearing the name of Thothmes III., 1¼ inch high, and 3 inches in diameter.   3. Scarabæus of amethyst, with a sphinx, emblematic of the king trampling on a prostrate enemy ; over it is the expression "Good God, Lord of the world."   4. A gold signet, mentioned in the last page.   5, 6, 7. The three other sides of the plinth.   8. A gold ring.   9. The engraved face of it.   10. A gold earring, about 1¼ inch in diameter. 11. The face of it, of the real size.   12. A gold ring, in my possession, four-fifths of an inch in diameter.   13. Gold ring with two asps.   14. A snake bracelet of gold.   15. A stone scarabæus.   16. Gold earring.   17. Gold earring with two pearls, a and b.   18, 19. 20. Other gold earrings.   21. Gold earring, 1 inch high and six-tenths broad.   22, 23 Ring of porcelain, or blue glazed pottery. Museum of Alnwick Castle.

of the 18th dynasty; on the other a lion, with the legend "lord of strength," referring to the monarch; on one side a scorpion, and on the other a crocodile.

Two cats sitting back to back, and looking round towards each other, with an emblem of the goddess Athor between them, seem to have been a favourite device on gold rings; and I have seen three or four of this pattern. (*fig.* 11.)

They also had large gold anklets or bangles, armlets, and bracelets, frequently inlaid with precious stones or enamel, and worn by men as well as women. Some were simple bands, or rings of metal; others in the shape of snakes—the last a favourite device among women in all ages, who still continue to be ignorant of the connexion between their taste and Eve's temptation by the serpent, so gravely set forth by Clemens in condemnation of this graceful ornament. Kings are often represented with armlets and bracelets; and in the Leyden Museum is a gold bracelet bearing the name of the third Thothmes, which was doubtless once worn by that monarch. (*fig.* 2.)

Handsome and richly ornamented necklaces were a principal part of the dress, both of men and women; and some idea may be formed of the number of jewels they wore, from those borrowed by the Israelites at the time of the Exodus, and by the paintings of Thebes. They consisted of gold, or of beads of various qualities and shapes, disposed according to fancy, generally with a large drop or figure in the centre. Scarabæi, gold, and cornelian bottles, or the emblems of Goodness and Stability, lotus flowers in enamel, amethysts, pearls, false stones, imitations of fish, frogs, lions, and various quadrupeds, birds, reptiles, flies, and other insects, shells and leaves, with numerous figures and devices, were strung in all the variety which their taste could suggest; and the sole museum of Leyden possesses an infinite assortment of those objects, which were once the pride of the ladies of Thebes.

Some wore simple gold chains in imitation of string, to which a stone scarabæus, set in the same precious metal, was appended; but these probably belonged to men, like the *torques* of the

z 2

471. Various necklaces. *From the Leyden Museum.* B. is composed of small covered cups, of bronze gilt. I b is the other end of I a. These leaves are of gold, inlaid with lapis lazuli and green and red stones. M a, a sort of gold *torques* or chain, of which a stone scarabæus found in gold forms the centre ornament. U in the possession of the late Mr. Madox. V W X Y Z, gold catches of necklaces, one sliding into the other.

Romans.* A set of small cups, or covered saucers, of bronze gilt, hanging from a chain of the same materials, were sometimes worn by women, a necklace of which has been found, belonging to a Theban lady — offering a striking contrast in their simplicity to the gold leaves inlaid with lapis lazzuli,† red and green stones, of another she wore; which served, with many more in her possession, to excite the admiration of her friends.

The devices engraved on scarabæi, rings, and other objects of ornamental *luxe*, varied according to the caprice of individuals. Rings frequently bore the name of the wearer; others of the monarch in whose reign he lived; others, again, the emblems of certain deities; and many were mere fanciful combinations. The greater number consisted of scarabæi, mounted upon a gold ring passing through them: the scarabæus itself was of green stone, cornelian, hæmatite, granite, serpentine, agate, lapis lazzuli, root of emerald, amethyst, and other materials; and a cheaper kind was made of limestone, stained to imitate a harder and dearer quality; or of the ordinary blue pottery. Cylinders of stone or blue pottery, bearing devices or hieroglyphics, were also common in necklaces and as signets; one of which, bearing the name of Osirtasen I. (in the Alnwick Museum), proves them to have been of the earliest date in Egypt, and the origin of, rather than derived from, the Cylinders of Assyria. From the number of scarabæi discovered, some have hastily supposed they served as money; but they were either ornamental, funereal, or historical: and some of these last of great size, bearing the name of Amunoph III. and his queen Taia, relate to his conquests, his lion hunts, her parentage, or to public works executed during their reign.

Of the various objects of the toilet, found at Thebes, and other places, the principal are bottles, or vases, for holding ointment, and *kohl* or collyrium for the eyes, mirrors, combs, and the small boxes, spoons, and saucers already mentioned. The ointment was scented in various ways; some preserved in the

* Pharaoh "put a gold chain about (Joseph's) neck," Gen. xli. 42; and "a ring upon Joseph's hand." *See* woodcut 471, *fig.* M.

† Woodcut 471, *figs.* B, I. *a.*

museum at Alnwick Castle has retained its odour for several centuries ; and the great use of ointment by the Egyptians is sufficiently indicated in the paintings representing the reception of guests.

With the exception of the little found in the tombs, we have nothing to guide us respecting the nature of Egyptian ointments. Some appear to be made with a nut oil, but it is probable that animal, as well as vegetable, grease was employed for this purpose ; the other ingredients depending on the taste of the maker, or the purchaser. Julius Pollux mentions a black kind made in Egypt, and speaks of the *sagdas* (*psagdæ*) as an ointment of that country. Theophrastus, on the contrary, states that Egyptian ointments were colourless; but we can readily account for this variance of opinion, by supposing that they had in view two different qualities : which is further proved, by the fact of our finding them both preserved at Thebes. (*See pp.* 23, 27, 32, *and vol.* i. p. 259.)

Ointment was frequently kept in *alabaster* bottles, or vases (whence the Greeks applied the name of *alabastron*, even to one made of other materials) : sometimes in those of the onyx, or other stone, glass, ivory, bone, or shells ; specimens of all of which have been discovered in the tombs.

Strabo says that the common people, both men and women, used the oil of the *kikki*, or castor-berry, for anointing themselves ; the general purpose to which it was applied being for lamps : and many oils, as from the *simsim*, olive, almond, flax, *selgam* (cole-seed), *seemga*, lettuce, and other vegetable productions, were extracted in Egypt. (*See above, p.* 23 *to* 32.)

The Egyptian combs were usually of wood, and double ; one side having large, the other small teeth ; the centre part was frequently ornamented with carved work, and, perhaps, inlaid. They were about four inches long, and six deep ; and those with a single row of teeth were sometimes surmounted with the figure of an ibex, or other animal.

The custom of staining the eyelids and brows, with a moistened powder of a black colour, was common in Egypt from the earliest times ; it was also introduced among the Jews and

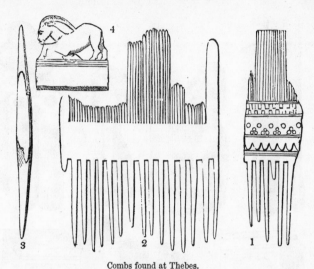

472.   Combs found at Thebes.
1. Comb with the centre part ornamented.   3. Side view of fig. 2.
      4. An ibex, supposed to have formed the top of a comb.

Romans; and is retained in the East to the present day. It is thought to increase the beauty of the eye; which is made to appear larger by this external addition of a black ring; and many even suppose the stimulus its application gives to be beneficial to the sight. It is made in various ways. Some use antimony, black oxide of manganese, preparations of lead, and other mineral substances: others the black powder of burnt almonds, or frankincense; and many prefer a mixture of different ingredients for making the *Kohl*.

Mr. Lane is perfectly correct in stating that the expression "painted her face," which Jezebel is said to have done, when Jehu came to Jezreel, is in the Hebrew, "painted her eyes;" the same is again mentioned in Jeremiah and Ezekiel; and the lengthened form of the ancient Egyptian eye, represented in the paintings, was probably produced, as Mr. Lane supposes, by this means.

Many of the *Kohl* bottles have been found in the tombs, together with the bodkin used for applying the moistened powder. They are of various materials, usually stone, wood, or pottery, sometimes composed of two, sometimes of four and five separate

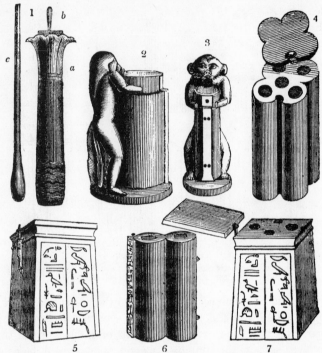

473.   Boxes or bottles, holding the *Kohl* for staining the eyelids.
1. In the British Museum.   *c* is the bodkin for applying the *Kohl*. The others are in the
Museum of Alnwick Castle.

cells, apparently containing each a mixture, differing slightly in its
quality and hue, from the other three.   Many were simple round
tubes, vases, or small boxes : some were ornamented with the figure
of an ape, or monster, supposed to assist in holding the bottle
between his arms, while the lady dipped into it the pin, with which
she painted her eyes ; and others were in imitation of a column
made of stone, or rich porcelain of the choicest manufacture.

Pins and needles were also among the articles of the toilet,
which have been occasionally found in the tombs.   The former
are frequently of considerable length, with large gold heads ;
and some, of a different form, tapering gradually to a point,
merely bound with gold at the upper end, without any projecting
head (seven or eight inches in length), appear to have been in-

tended for arranging the plaits or curls of hair; like those used in England, in the days of Elizabeth, for nearly the same purpose.

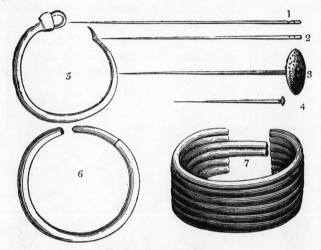

474.   Needles, pins, and earrings.

1, 2. Bronze needles, in the Museum of Alnwick Castle, 3 and 3¼ inches long. 3. Large gold-headed pin, in the Berlin Collection. 4. Another of smaller size. 5. Silver earring in my possession, one and four-tenths of an inch in diameter. 6. Gold earring in the Berlin Museum, one and one-third of an inch in diameter. 7. Another, seen from above.

Some needles were of bronze, from three to three and a half inches in length; but as few have been found, we are not able to form any opinion respecting their general size and quality, particularly of those used for fine work, which must have been of a very minute kind.

The custom of staining the fingers red with *henneh* (the pounded leaves of the Lawsonia) was probably of very ancient date in Egypt and the East; and some have attributed the Greek metaphor of "rosy-fingered Aurora" to its use in the East.

One of the principal objects of the toilet was the mirror. It was of mixed metal, chiefly copper, most carefully wrought and highly polished; and so admirably did the skill of the Egyptians succeed in the composition of metals, that this substitute for our modern looking-glass was susceptible of a lustre, which has even been partially revived at the present day, in some of those discovered at Thebes, though buried in the earth for many centuries.

The mirror itself was nearly round, inserted into a handle of wood, stone, or metal, whose form varied according to the taste of the owner. Some presented the figure of a female, a flower, a column, or a rod ornamented with the head of Athor, a bird, or a fancy device; and sometimes the face of a typhonian monster was introduced to support the mirror, serving as a contrast to the

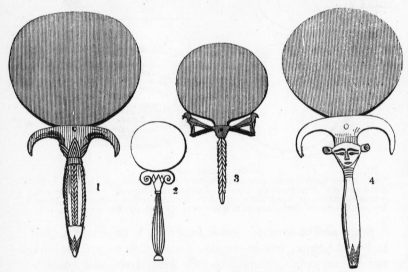

475. Metal mirrors. (*See* Woodcut 476, *fig.* 1.)
1, 3, 4, From Mr. Salt's Collection. 2, from a painting at Thebes. 4 is about 11 inches high.

features whose beauty was displayed within it. The same kind of metal mirror was used by the Israelites, who doubtless brought them from Egypt; and the brazen laver made by Moses for the tabernacle was composed " of the *looking-glasses* of the women, which assembled at the door of the tabernacle of the congregation." A similar one is also used to this day in China and Japan.

When walking from home, Egyptian gentlemen frequently carried sticks, varying from three or four to about six feet in length, occasionally surmounted with a knob imitating a flower, or with the more usual peg projecting from one side, some of which have

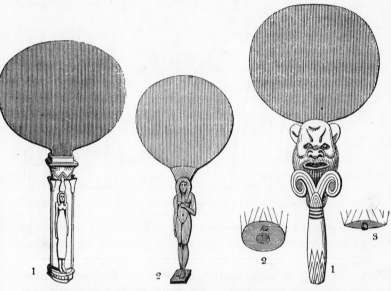

Other metal mirrors.

476.   Fig. 1. From Mr. Salt's Collection; with a wooden handle.   Fig. 2. In the Museum of Alnwick Castle.

475 a. Was in the possession of Dr. Hogg. 2 and 3 show the bottom of the handle, to which something has been fastened.

been found at Thebes. Many were of *cherry*-wood, only three feet three inches long; and those I have seen with the lotus head

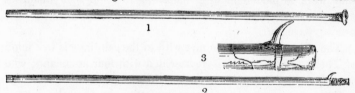

477.   Walking sticks found at Thebes.   2 is of cherry-wood, in Mr. Salt's Collection. 3 shows the peg at the side.

were generally about the same length. Others appear to have been much longer; the sculptures represent them at least six feet; and one brought to England by Mr. Madox was about five feet in length. Some were ornamented with colour and gilding.

On entering a house they left their stick in the hall, or at the door; and poor men were sometimes employed to hold the sticks

478.   Priests and other persons of rank walking with sticks.   *Thebes.*

of the guests who had come to a party on foot, being rewarded by
the master of the house for their trouble with a trifling compensation in money, with their dinner, or a piece of meat to carry to
their family.   The name of each person was frequently written
on his stick, in hieroglyphics, for which reason a hard wood was
preferred, as the acacia, which seems to have been more generally
used than any other; and on one found at Athribis, the owner
had written—" O my stick! the support of my legs," &c.

We have little knowledge of the nature of their baths; but as
they were forbidden in deep mourning to indulge in them, we
may conclude they were considered as a luxury, as well as a
necessary comfort.

The only instance I have met with in the paintings is in a tomb
at Thebes, where a lady is represented with four attendants, who
wait upon her, and perform various duties.

One removes the jewellery and clothes she has taken off, or
suspends them to a stand in the apartment; another pours water
from a vase over her head, as the third rubs her arms and body
with her open hands; and a fourth seated near her holds a sweet-
scented flower to her nose, and supports her as she sits.   A
similar subject is treated nearly in the same manner on some of
the Greek vases, the water being poured over the bather, who
kneels, or is seated on the ground.

Warm as well as cold baths were used by the Egyptians, though for ordinary ablutions cold water was preferred; and both were probably recommended medicinally when occasion required.

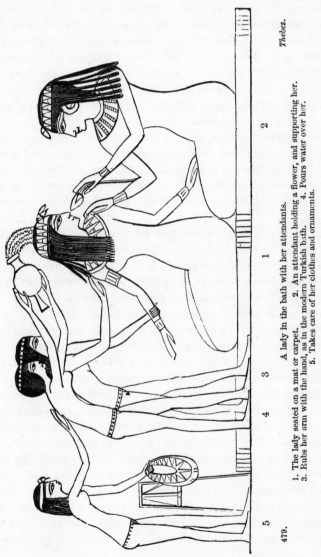

Thebes.

479.

A lady in the bath with her attendants.

1. The lady seated on a mat or carpet.   2. An attendant holding a flower, and supporting her.
3. Rubs her arm with the hand, as in the modern Turkish bath.   4. Pours water over her.
5. Takes care of her clothes and ornaments.

The Egyptians paid great attention to health, and " so wisely," says Herodotus, " was medicine managed by them, that no doctor was permitted to practise any but his own peculiar branch. Some were oculists, who only studied diseases of the eye; others attended solely to complaints of the head; others to those of the teeth; some again confined themselves to complaints of the intestines; and others to secret and internal maladies; accoucheurs being usually, if not always, women." And it is a singular fact, that their dentists adopted a method, not very long practised in Europe, of stopping teeth with gold, proofs of which have been obtained from some mummies of Thebes.

They received certain salaries from the public treasury; and after they had studied those precepts which had been laid down from the experience of their predecessors, they were permitted to practise; and, in order to prevent dangerous experiments being made upon patients, they might be punished if their treatment was contrary to the established system: and the death of a person entrusted to their care, under such circumstances, was adjudged to them as a capital offence. If, however, every remedy had been administered according to the sanatory law, they were absolved from blame; and if the patient was not better, the physician was allowed to alter the treatment after the third day, or even before, if he took upon himself the responsibility.

Though paid by Government as a body, it was not illegal to receive fees for their advice and attendance; and demands could be made in every instance except on a foreign journey, and on military service; when patients were visited free of expense.

The principal mode adopted by the Egyptians for preventing illness was attention to regimen and diet; " being persuaded that the majority of diseases proceed from indigestion and excess of eating;" and they had frequent recourse to abstinence, emetics, slight doses of medicine, and other simple means of relieving the system, which some persons were in the habit of repeating every two or three days. " Those who live in the corn country," as Herodotus terms it, were particular for their attention to health. " During three successive days, every month, they submitted to a regular course of treatment; from the conviction that illness was wont to proceed from some irregularity in diet;" and if preventives were ineffectual, they had recourse to suitable remedies, adopting a mode of treatment very similar to that mentioned by Diodorus.

The employment of numerous drugs in Egypt has been mentioned by sacred and profane writers; and the medicinal properties of many herbs which grow in the deserts, particularly between the Nile and Red Sea, are still known to the Arabs; though their application has been but imperfectly recorded and preserved.

" O virgin, daughter of Egypt," says Jeremiah, " in vain shalt thou use many medicines, for thou shalt not be cured;" and Homer, in the Odyssey, describes the many valuable medicines given by Polydamna, the wife of Thonis, to Helen while in Egypt, " a country whose fertile soil produces an infinity of drugs, some salutary and some pernicious; where each physician possesses knowledge above all other men." Pliny makes frequent mention of the productions of that country, and their use in medicine; he also notices the physicians of Egypt; and as if their number was indicative of the many maladies to which the inhabitants were subject, he observes, that it was a country productive of numerous diseases. In this, however, he does not agree with Herodotus, who affirms that, " after the Libyans, there are no people so healthy as the Egyptians, which may be attributed to the invariable nature of the seasons in their country."

Pliny even says, that the Egyptians examined the bodies after death, to ascertain the nature of the diseases of which they had died; and we can readily believe that a people, so far advanced in civilisation and the principles of medicine, as to assign to each physician his peculiar branch, would have resorted to this effectual method of acquiring knowledge and experience.

It is evident that the medical science of the Egyptians was sought and appreciated even in foreign countries; and we learn from Herodotus, that Cyrus and Darius both sent to Egypt for medical men. In later times too, they continued to be celebrated for their skill: Ammianus says it was enough for a doctor to say he had studied in Egypt to recommend him; and Pliny

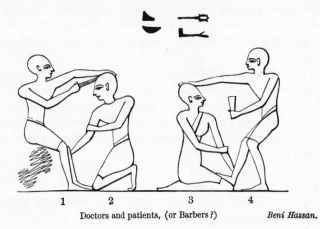

1   2   3   4

480.   Doctors and patients, (or Barbers ?)   *Beni Hassan.*

mentions medical men going from Egypt to Rome.   But though
their physicians are often noticed by ancient writers, the only
indication of medical attendance appears to be in the paintings of
Beni Hassan ; and even there it is uncertain whether a doctor, or
a barber, be represented.

Their doctors probably felt the pulse ; as Plutarch shows they
did at Rome, from this saying of Tiberius, "a man after he has
passed his thirtieth year, who *puts forth his hand* to a physician,
is ridiculous ; " whence our proverb of " a fool or a physician
after forty."

Diodorus tells us, that dreams were regarded in Egypt with
religious reverence, and the prayers of the devout were often
rewarded by the gods, with an indication of the remedy their
sufferings required ; and magic, charms, and various supernatural
agencies, were often resorted to by the credulous ; who " sought
to the idols, and to the charmers, and to them that had familiar
spirits, and to the wizards."   (*Isaiah*, xix. 3.)

Origen also says, that when any part of the body was afflicted
with disease, they invoked the demon to whom it was supposed to
belong, in order to obtain a cure.

In cases of great moment oracles were consulted ; and a Greek
papyrus found in Egypt mentions divination " through a boy with
a lamp, a bowl, and a pit ;" which resembles the pretended power

of the modern magicians of Egypt. The same also notices the mode of discovering theft, and obtaining any wish; and though it is supposed to be of the 2nd century, the practices it alludes to are doubtless from an old Egyptian source; and other similar papyri contain recipes for obtaining good fortune and various benefits, or for causing misfortunes to an enemy. Some suppose the Egyptians had even recourse to animal magnetism, and that dreams indicating cures were the result of this influence; and (though the subjects erroneously supposed to represent it apply to a very different act) it is not impossible that they may have discovered the mode of exercising this art, and that it may have been connected with the strange scenes recorded at the initiation into the mysteries. If really known, such a power would scarcely have been neglected; and it would have been easy to obtain thereby an ascendency over the minds of a superstitious people.

Indeed the readiness of man at all times to astonish on the one hand, and to court the marvellous on the other, is abundantly proved by present and past experience. That the nervous system may be worked upon by it to such a degree, that a state either of extreme irritability, or of sleep and coma, may be induced, in the latter case paralysing the senses so as to become deadened to pain, is certain; and a highly sensitive temperament may exhibit phenomena beyond the reach of explanation; but it requires very little experience to know that we are wonderfully affected by far more ordinary causes; for the nerves may be acted upon to such an extent, by having as we commonly term it " our teeth set on edge," that the mere filing a saw would suffice to drive any one mad, if unable to escape from its unceasing discord. What is this but an effect upon the nerves? and what more could be desired to prove the power of any agency? And the world would owe a debt of gratitude to the professors of animal magnetism, if instead of making it, as some do, a mere exhibition to display a power, and astonish the beholders, they would continue the efforts already begun, for discovering all the beneficial uses to which it is capable of being applied. We might then rejoice that, as astrology led to the more useful knowledge of astronomy, this influence enabled us to comprehend our nervous system, on which so many conditions of health depend, and with which we are so imperfectly acquainted.

The cure of diseases was also attributed by the Egyptians to *Exvotos* offered in the temples. They consisted of various kinds. Some persons promised a certain sum for the maintenance of the sacred animals ; or whatever might propitiate the deity ; and after the cure had been effected, they frequently suspended a model of the restored part, in the temple ; and ears, eyes, distorted arms, and other members, were dedicated as memorials of their gratitude and superstition.

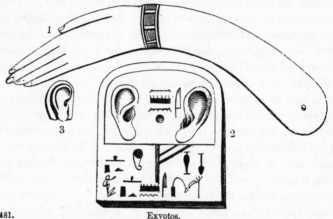

481.   Exvotos.
1. Ivory hand, in Mr. Salt's Collection.   2. Stone tablet, dedicated to Amunre, for the recovery of a complaint in the ear; found at Thebes.   3. An ear of terra cotta in my possession, from Thebes.

Sometimes travellers, who happened to pass by a temple, inscribed a votive sentence on the walls, to indicate their respect for the deity, and solicit his protection during their journey ; the complete formula of which contained the adoration (*proskunéma*) of the writer, with the assurance that he had been mindful of his wife, his family, and friends ; and the reader of the inscription was sometimes included in a share of the blessings it solicited. The date of the king's reign and the day of the month were also added, with the profession and parentage of the writer. The complete formula of one *proskunéma* was as follows : " The adoration of Caius Capitolinus, son of Flavius Julius, of the fifth troop of Theban horse, to the goddess Isis, with ten thousand names.　And I have been mindful of (or have made an adoration for) all those who love me, and my consort, and children, and all my household, and for him who reads this.　In the year 12 of the emperor Tiberius Cæsar, the 15 of Paüni."

The Egyptians, according to Pliny, claimed the honour of having invented the art of curing diseases.　Indeed, the study of medicine and surgery appears to have commenced at a very early period in Egypt, since Athothes, the second king of the country, is stated to have written upon the subject of anatomy ; and the schools of Alexandria continued till a late period to enjoy the reputation, and display the skill, they had inherited from their predecessors.　Hermes was said to have written six books on medicine, the first of which related to anatomy ; and the various recipes, known to have been beneficial, were recorded, with their peculiar cases, in the memoirs of physic, inscribed among the laws deposited in the principal temples.

The embalmers were probably members of the medical profession, and the Bible states that "the physicians embalmed" Jacob.

482.　　　　　　　　　Funeral Boat, or Baris.　　　　　　　*Thebes.*

P. Tomb at Saḳḳara, arched with stone, of the time of Psammitichus, or Psamatik, II., whose name occurs on the roof to the left, and in other places.

CHAPTER X.

FUNERAL RITES — OFFERINGS TO THE DEAD — TOMBS — FUNERAL PRO-CESSIONS — TRIALS OF THE DEAD — SACRED LAKE — BURIAL — EMBALMING — SARCOPHAGI — PAPYRI, &c.

THE great care of the Egyptians was directed to their condition after death ; that last state towards which their present life was only the pilgrimage ; and they were taught to consider their abode here merely as an "inn" upon the road. They looked forward to being received into the company of that Being, who represented the Divine Goodness, if pronounced worthy at the great judgment

day; and the privilege of being called by his name was the ful-
filment of all their wishes. Every one was then the same; all
were " equally noble ;" there was no distinction of rank beyond
the tomb ; and though their actions might be remembered on
earth with gratitude and esteem, no king or conqueror was
greater than the humblest man after death ; nor were any honours
given to them as heroes. And if ceremonies were performed
to the deceased, they were not in honour of a man translated to
the order of the gods, but of that particular portion of the
divine essence which constituted the soul of each individual,
and returned to the Deity after death. Every one, therefore,
whose virtuous life entitled him to admission into the regions
of the blessed, was supposed to be again united to the Deity, of
whom he was an emanation ; and, with the emblem of Thmei,
purporting that he was judged or justified, he received the holy
name of Osiris. His body was so bound up as to resemble the
mysterious ruler of Amenti or *Hades;* it bore some of the emblems peculiar to him ; and the beard, of a form which belonged
exclusively to the gods, was given to the deceased in token of his
having assumed the character of that deity. (*See above,* p. 329.)

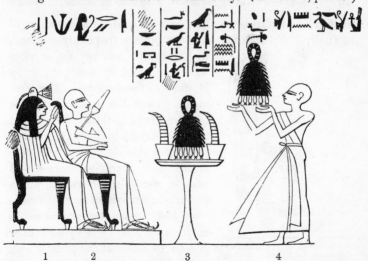

1   2   3   4

483. Services performed to the dead by one of the family. Here it is a son. The principal
         part of the offering consists of onions. (*See* Vol. i., p. 324.)   *Thebes.*

Offerings were also made to the god Osiris himself, after the burial, in the name of the deceased ; and certain services or liturgies were performed for him by the priests, at the expense of the family ; their number depending upon their means, or the respect they were inclined to pay to the memory of their parent. If the sons or relations were of the priestly order, they had the

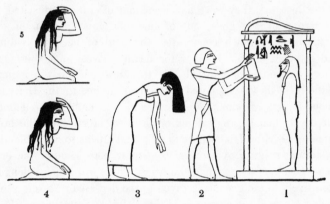

484.   The members of the family present when the services were performed.   *Thebes.*

privilege of officiating on these occasions ; and the members of the family had permission, and were perhaps frequently expected,

485.   A woman embracing, and weep-
ing before, her husband's mummy.
Thebes.

to be present, whether the services were performed by strangers, or by relations of the deceased. The cere-monies consisted of a sacrifice, similar to those offered in the temples, vowed for the deceased to one or more gods (as Osiris, Anubis, and others con-nected with *Amenti*) : incense and libation were also presented ; and a prayer was sometimes read, the rela-tions and friends being present as mourners. They even joined their prayers to those of the priest ; and, embracing the mummied body, and

bathing its feet with their tears, they uttered those expressions of

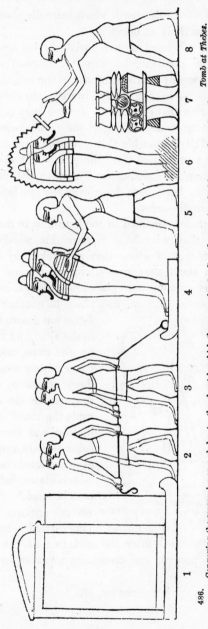

Tomb at Thebes.

486.   Conveying the mummies on a sledge to the closet in which they were kept, after the services had been performed to them. The priest (fig. 8) is pouring oil (?) over them. On the altar are three vases of oil, cakes, a basket of grapes, and some other things (which were indistinct from being much defaced). Below are two glass bottles of wine. Even in this serious subject the Egyptian artists could not refrain from their love of caricature; and one of the mummies (fig. 4) is falling down upon the priest, who supports it with his hands.

grief, and praises of the deceased, which were dictated by their feelings on so melancholy an occasion.

The priest who officiated at the burial service was selected from the grade of Pontiffs who wore the leopard skin; but various other rites were performed by one of the minor priests to the mummies previous to their being lowered into the pit of the tomb, as well as after that ceremony. Indeed they continued to be administered at intervals, as long as the family paid for their performance; and it is possible that upon the cessation of this payment, or after a stipulated time, the priests had the right of transferring the tomb to another family, which the inscriptions within them show to have been done, even though belonging to members of the priestly order.

When the mummies remained in the house, or in the chamber of the sepulchre, they were kept in moveable wooden closets, with folding doors, out of which they were taken by the minor functionaries to a small altar, before which the priest officiated. The closet and the mummy were placed on a sledge, in order to facilitate their movement from one place to another; and the

1   2   3

487.   Pouring oil (?) over a mummy.—The priest (fig. 1) has a napkin on his shoulder. Fig. 2 holds a papyrus. The mode of placing the napkin is remarkable, being the same as now adopted in the East by servants while guests are washing their hands before meals.   *Tomb at Thebes*.

latter was drawn with ropes to the altar, and taken back by the same means when the ceremony was over. On these occasions, as in the prayers for the dead, they made the usual offerings of incense and libation, with cakes, flowers, and fruit; and even anointed the mummy, oil or ointment being poured over its head.* Sometimes several priests attended. One carried a napkin over his shoulder, to be used after the anointing of the mummy; another brought a papyrus roll containing a prayer, or the usual

* Woodcuts 486, 487.

ritual deposited in the tombs with the dead; and others had
different occupations according to their respective offices.

These funeral oblations answer exactly to the *inferiæ* or *pa-
rentalia* of the Romans, consisting of victims, flowers, and libations; when the tomb was decked with garlands and wreaths of
flowers, and an altar was erected before it for presenting the
offerings. And that this last was done also by the Egyptians, is
proved by the many small altars discovered outside the doors of
the catacombs at Thebes.

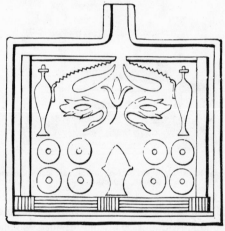

488. An altar, in the British Museum, showing that the trench is for carrying off the
libation. The lower device is the ordinary hieroglyphic signifying " *chosen*," as applied to
offerings.

It was not unusual to keep the mummies in the house, after they
had been returned by the embalmers to the relations of the
deceased, in order to gratify the feelings which made them desirous of having those they had loved in life as near them as
possible after death; or to give time to the family to prepare a
tomb for their reception. Many months often elapsed between
the ceremony of embalming and the actual burial; and it was
during this period that the liturgies were performed before the
mummy, which were afterwards continued at the tomb. One
inscription upon the coffin of a woman shows that the burial
took place a whole year after her death, and some were doubtless
kept, for various reasons, much longer. It was during this

interval that feasts were held in honour of the dead, to which the friends and relations were invited; as was customary among the Greeks and other people of antiquity.

Small tables made of reeds or sticks bound together, and interlaced with palm leaves, were sometimes placed in the tombs, bearing offerings of cakes, ducks, or other things, according to the wealth or inclination of the donors; one of which, found at Thebes, is now in the British Museum. On the lower compart-

489.   A table found in a tomb by Mr. Burton, on which are a duck trussed, and another
                cut open, with cakes.   *British Museum.*

ment, or shelf, are cakes; the central shelf has a duck, cut open at the breast and spread out, "but not divided asunder;" and at the top is a similar bird, trussed in the usual mode when brought to an Egyptian table. Similar offerings "for the dead" were strictly forbidden by the law of Moses; and it was doubtless the Egyptian custom that the Hebrew legislator had in view when he introduced this wise prohibition.

Though the privilege of keeping a mummy in the house was sanctioned by law and custom, care was always taken to assign some plausible reason for it, since they deemed it a great privilege to be admitted to the repositories of the dead, as their final resting-place. To be debarred from the rites of burial reflected a severe disgrace upon the whole family; and the most influential individual could not be admitted to the very tomb he had built for himself, until acquitted before that tribunal which sat to judge his conduct during life.

The tombs of the rich consisted of one or more chambers, ornamented with paintings and sculpture, the plans and size of which depended on the expense incurred by the family of the deceased, or on the wishes of the individuals who purchased them during their lifetime. They were the property of the priests; and a sufficient number being always kept ready, the purchase was made at the "shortest notice;" nothing being requisite to complete even the sculptures, or inscriptions, but the insertion of the deceased's name, and a few statements respecting his family and profession. The numerous subjects representing agricultural scenes, the trades of the people, in short the various occupations of the Egyptians, were already introduced. These were common to all tombs, varying only in their details and the mode of their execution; and were intended as a short epitome of human life, which suited equally every future occupant.

In some instances all the paintings of the tomb were finished, and even the small figures representing the future occupant were introduced; those only being left unsculptured which being of a large size required more accuracy in the features in order to give his real portrait; and sometimes even the large figures were completed before the tomb was sold, the only parts left unfinished being the hieroglyphic legends containing his name and that of his wife. Indeed the fact of their selling old mummy cases, and tombs belonging to other persons, shows that they were not always over scrupulous about the likeness of an individual, provided the hieroglyphics were altered and contained his real name: at least when a motive of economy reconciled the mind of a purchaser to a *second-hand* tenement for the body of his friend. Those who could afford it bought a family tomb; but this was generally confined to the owner and his wife, and their children.

Besides the upper rooms of the tomb, which were ornamented with the paintings already mentioned, were one or more pits, varying from 20 to 70 feet in depth; at the bottom or "sides" of which were recesses, like small chambers, for depositing the coffins; recalling the expression, "whose tombs are in the side of the pit," and the metaphor, "going down to the pit," applied to death. And well might the verse of the Psalmist, "our bones are scattered at the grave's mouth, as when one cutteth and cleaveth wood upon the earth," accord with the state of many an Egyptian pit a few years ago; when, to the disgrace of Christian excavators, the Moslems were obliged to interfere, and bury the bones recklessly scattered by them over the ground.

The pit was closed with masonry after the burial had been performed, and sometimes re-opened to receive other members of the family. The upper apartments were richly ornamented with painted sculptures, being rather a monument in honour of the deceased than the actual sepulchre; and they served for the reception of his friends, who frequently met there, and accompanied the priests when performing the services for the dead. Each tomb, and sometimes each apartment, had a wooden door, either of a single or double valve, turning on pins, and secured by bolts or bars, with a lock; which last was protected by a seal of clay, upon which the impress of a signet was stamped when the party retired. Remains of the clay have even been found adhering to some of the stone jambs of the doorways, in the tombs of Thebes; and the numerous stamps buried near them were probably used on those occasions.

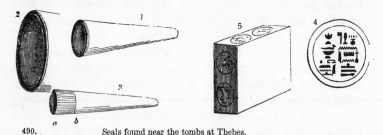

490.   Seals found near the tombs at Thebes.

1, 2. An instance of one with a raised edge round the stamped part.
3. Another stained with red ochre from *a* to *b*.
4. Style of the inscription on some of them.
5. A brick stamped in a similar manner.

Similar seals were used for securing the doors of temples, houses, and granaries.

Tombs were built of brick and stone, or hewn in the rock, according to the position of the Necropolis. Whenever the mountains were sufficiently near, the latter was preferred; and these were generally the most elegant in their design, and in the variety of their sculptures, not only at Thebes, but in other

parts of Egypt.   Few, indeed, belonging to wealthy individuals
were built of masonry, except those at the pyramids in the vicinity
of Memphis.   But Egyptian tombs were never circular, as many
in Asia Minor, Etruria, and Greece.

The sepulchres of the poorer classes had no upper chamber.
The coffins were deposited in pits in the plain, or in recesses
excavated at the side of a rock, which were closed with masonry,
like the pits within the large tombs.   Mummies of the lower
orders were buried together in a common repository; and the
bodies of those whose relations had not the means of paying for
their funeral, after being "merely cleansed by some vegetable
decoctions, and kept in an alkaline solution for seventy days,"
were wrapped up in coarse cloth, in mats, or in a bundle of palm
sticks, and deposited in the earth.

Some tombs were of great extent; and when a wealthy individual bought the ground, and had an opportunity during a long
life of making his family sepulchre according to his wishes, it was
frequently decorated in the most sumptuous manner.   And so
much consequence did the Egyptians attach to them, that people
in humble circumstances made every effort to save sufficient to
procure a handsome tomb, and defray the expenses of a suitable
funeral.   This species of pomp increased as refinement and
luxury advanced; and in the time of Amasis and other monarchs
of the 26th dynasty, the funeral expenses so far exceeded what it
had been customary to incur during the reigns of the early
Pharaohs, that the tombs of some individuals far surpassed in
extent, if not in splendour of decoration, those of the kings
themselves.

Many adorned their entrances with gardens, in which flowers
were reared by the hand of an attached friend, whose daily care
was to fetch water from the river, or from the wells on the edge
of the cultivated land; and the remains of alluvial soil brought
for this purpose, may still be traced before some of the sepulchres
at Thebes.   Those tombs at Memphis and the Pyramids, which
are of masonry, differ in their plan, and in many instances in the
style of their sculptures; the subjects, however, generally relate
to the manners and customs of the Egyptians; and parties, boat

scenes, fishing, fowling, and other ordinary occupations of the people, are portrayed there, as in the sepulchres of Thebes.

"When any one died, all the females of his family, covering their heads and faces with mud, and leaving the body in the house, ran through the streets, with their bosoms exposed, striking themselves, and uttering loud lamentations." Their friends and relations joined them as they went, uniting in the same demonstrations of grief; and when the deceased was a person of consideration, many strangers accompanied them, out of respect to his memory. Hired mourners were also employed to add, by their feigned demonstrations of grief, to the real lamentations of the family, and to heighten the show of respect paid to the deceased. "The men, in like manner, girding their dress below their waist, went through the town smiting their breast," and throwing dust upon their heads; but the mourners consisted chiefly of women, as is usual in Egypt at the present day; and we may suggest "dust," rather than "mud," on a dry Egyptian road.

Of the magnificent pomp of a royal funeral in the time of the Pharaohs no adequate idea can be formed from the processions represented in the tombs of ordinary individuals; and from the marked distinction always maintained between the sovereign and the highest subjects in the kingdom, we may readily believe how greatly the funeral processions of the wealthiest individuals fell short of those of the kings. From the pomp of ordinary funerals, therefore, may be inferred the grand state in which the body of a sovereign was conveyed to the tomb.

In the funeral processions of the Egyptian grandees the order was frequently as follows :—

First came several servants carrying tables laden with fruit, cakes, flowers, vases of ointment, wine and other liquids, with three young geese and a calf for sacrifice, chairs and wooden tablets, napkins, and other things. Then others bringing the small closets in which the mummy of the deceased and of his ancestors had been

491. Closets containing figures of gods.

kept, while receiving the funeral liturgies previous to burial, and which sometimes contained the images of the Gods. They also carried daggers, bows, sandals, and fans; each man having a kerchief or napkin on his shoulder. Next came a table of offerings, fauteuils, couches, boxes, and a chariot; and then the charioteer with a pair of horses yoked in another car, which he drove as he followed on foot, in token of respect to his late master. After these were men carrying gold vases on a table, with other offerings, boxes, and a large case upon a sledge borne on poles by four men, superintended by two functionaries of the priestly order; then others bearing small images of his ancestors, arms, fans, the sceptres, signets, collars, necklaces, and other things appertaining to the king, in whose service he had held an important office. To these succeeded the bearers of a sacred boat, and that mysterious eye of Osiris, as God of Stability, so common on funeral monuments,—the same which was placed over the incision in the side of the body when embalmed; as well as on the prow and rudder of the funeral boat; was the emblem of Egypt; and was frequently used as a sort of amulet, and deposited in the tombs. Others carried the well-known small images of blue pottery representing the deceased under the form of Osiris, and the bird emblematic of the soul. Following these were seven or more men, bearing upon staves, or wooden yokes, cases filled with flowers and bottles for libation; and then seven or eight women, having their heads bound with fillets, beating their breasts, throwing dust upon their heads, and uttering doleful lamentations for the deceased, intermixed with praises of his virtues.

One woman is seen in the picture turning round, in the act of adoration, towards a sacred case containing a sitting Cynocephalus, the emblem of the God of Letters, placed on a sledge drawn by four men; the officiating high priest or pontiff, clad in a leopard skin, following, having in his hand the censer and vase of libation, and accompanied by his attendants bearing the various things required for the occasion.

Next came the hearse, placed in the consecrated boat upon a sledge, drawn by four oxen and by seven men, under the direction of a superintendent, who regulated the march of the pro-

cession. A high functionary of the priestly order walked close
to the boat, in which the chief mourners, the nearest female rela-
tives of the deceased, stood or sat at either end of the sarcophagus ; and sometimes his widow, holding a child in her arms,
united her lamentations with prayers for her tender offspring,
who added its tribute of sorrow to that of its afflicted mother.

The sarcophagus was decked with flowers ; and on the sides
were painted alternately the emblems of Stability and Security (?)
two by two (as on the sacred arks or shrines) upon separate
panels, one of which was sometimes taken out to expose to view
the head of the mummy within.

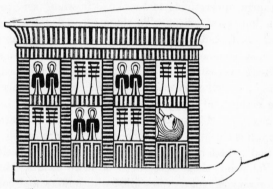

492.   The mummy's head, seen at an open panel of the coffin.   *Thebes.*

Behind the hearse followed the male relations and friends of
the deceased ; some beating their breasts; others, if not giving
the same tokens of grief, at least showing their sorrow by their
silence and solemn step, as they walked, leaning on their long
sticks.   These closed the procession.

Arrived at the sacred lake, the coffin was placed in the *baris*,
or consecrated boat of the dead, towed by a larger one furnished
with sails and oars, and having frequently a spacious cabin ;
which, in company with other sailing boats carrying the mourners
and all those things above mentioned appertaining to the funeral,
crossed to the other side.   Arrived there, the procession went in
the same order to the tomb; at which the priest offered a
sacrifice, with incense and libation; the women still continuing

their lamentations, united with prayers and praises of the deceased.

It frequently happened that the deceased, with his wife, if dead at the time of his funeral, was represented seated under a canopy, in lieu of the coffin.   Before him stood an altar laden with offerings; and a priest, opening a long roll of papyrus, read aloud the funeral ritual, and an account of his good deeds, " in order to show to Osiris and the Assessors the extent of his piety and justice during his life." (*Woodcut* 482.) When the boats reached the other side of the lake, the yards were lowered to the top of the cabin; and all those engaged in the ceremony left them and proceeded to the tomb; from which they appear to have returned by land, without recrossing the lake.

Such was the funeral procession of a *basilico-grammat,* or royal scribe, a member of the priestly order.   He lived during the four successive reigns of Thothmes III., Amunoph II., Thothmes IV., and Amunoph III., and held the office of tutor to one of the young princesses, as the sculptures inform us, which represent him nursing her on his knee, while entertaining a party of friends.

The funerals of other persons differed in the order of the procession, as well as in the pomp displayed on the occasion; and the mode of celebrating them appears to have depended on the arrangements made by the family, except in those particulars which were prescribed by law. The funeral of *Nofr-Othph,* a priest of Amun at Thebes, is thus described on the walls of his tomb; the scene of which lies partly on the lake, and partly on the way thence to the sepulchre itself :—

First came a large boat, conveying the bearers of flowers, cakes, and numerous things appertaining to the offerings,—tables, fauteuils, and other pieces of furniture; as well as the friends of the deceased, whose consequence is shown by their dresses and long walking-sticks,—the peculiar mark of Egyptian gentlemen. This was followed by a small skiff holding baskets of cakes and fruit, with a quantity of green palm-branches, which it was customary to strew in the way as the body proceeded to the tomb; the smooth nature of their leaves and stalks being particularly well adapted to enable the sledge to glide over them.

In this part of the picture the love of caricature common to the Egyptians is shown to have been indulged in, even in the serious subject of a funeral; and the retrograde movement of the large boat, which has grounded and is pushed off the bank, striking the smaller one with its rudder, has overturned a large table loaded with cakes and other things upon the rowers seated below, in spite of all the efforts of the *prowman*, and the earnest vociferations of the alarmed steersman.

In another boat men carried bouquets, and boxes supported on the usual yoke over their shoulders; and this was followed by two others, one containing the male, the other the female mourners, standing on the roof of the cabin, beating themselves, uttering cries, and making other demonstrations of excessive grief. Last came the consecrated boat, bearing the hearse, which was surrounded by the chief mourners, and the female relations of the deceased. A high priest burnt incense over the altar, which was placed before it; and behind it stood the images of Isis and Nepthys. They were the emblems of the Beginning and the End, and were thought to be always present at the head and feet of the dead who had led a virtuous life, and who were deemed worthy of admission into the regions of the blessed.

Arrived at the opposite shore of the lake, the procession advanced to the catacombs, crossing the sandy plain which intervened between them and the lake; and on the way several women of the vicinity, carrying their children in shawls suspended at their side or at their back, joined in the lamentation. The mummy being taken out of the sarcophagus, was placed erect in the chamber of the tomb; and the sister or nearest relation, embracing it, commenced a funeral dirge, calling on her relative with every expression of tenderness, extolling his virtues, and bewailing her own loss. In the mean time the high priest presented a sacrifice of incense and libation, with offerings of cakes and other customary gifts, for the deceased; and the men and women without continued the ululation, throwing dust upon their heads, and making other manifestations of grief.

Many funerals were conducted in a more simple manner; the procession consisting merely of the mourners and priests, with the hearse conveyed, as usual, on a sledge drawn by two or three oxen, and by several men, who aided in pulling the rope.   The priest who wore the leopard skin dress and who performed the sacrifice was in attendance, burning incense and pouring out a libation as he went; and behind him walked a functionary of an inferior grade, clad in a simple robe, extending a little below the knees and standing out from the body.   In form it was not altogether unlike a modern Abbaíeh, and was made of some stiff substance,

with two holes in front, through which the arms passed, in order to enable him to hold a long taper.   At the head and foot of the hearse was a female, who generally clasped one arm with her hand in token of grief, her head being bound with a fillet, her bosom exposed, and her dress supported, like that of mourning women, by a strap over the shoulder.   She some-times wore a scarf tied across her hips; much in the same manner as Egyptian women now put on their shawls both in the house and when going out of doors. She may be a type of mourning, the "chief mourner," or one who had some peculiar office on these occasions.

493.   A peculiar attendant at a funeral. (*See* p. 373.)

A procession of this kind was all that attended the funeral of a person who held the office of " scribe, of weights and measures;" but the pomp displayed in these ceremonies depended on the sums expended by the family, and other circumstances.   In another funeral the order of the procession was as follows:—

First came eight men throwing dust upon their heads, and giving other demonstrations of grief; then six females, in the usual attire of mourners, preceding the hearse, which was drawn by two oxen—in this instance unassisted by men, two only being near them ; one uttering lamentations, and the other driving them with a goad or a whip.   Immediately before the sledge bearing the coffin was the *sprinkler*, who, with a brush dipped in a vase, or with a small bottle, threw water upon the ground, and perhaps also on those who passed.   The same is done in the funeral ceremonies of the East at the present day, being supposed to keep off the evil eye.   Next came the high priest, who, turning round to the hearse, offered incense and libation in honour of the deceased, the chief mourner being seated in the boat before it : other men followed ; and the procession closed with eight or more women, beating themselves, throwing dust on their heads, and singing the funeral dirge.   Arrived at the tomb, which stood beneath the western mountain of Thebes, the mummy was taken from the hearse ; and being placed upright, incense was burnt, and a libation was poured out before it by the high priest as he stood at the altar, while other functionaries performed various ceremonies in honour of the deceased.   The hierogrammat or sacred scribe then read aloud from a tablet, or a roll of papyrus, his eulogy, and a prayer to the Gods in his behalf ; and the same was sometimes read from the boat, immediately after the deceased had passed that ordeal which gave him the right to cross the sacred lake.

The order of the procession which accompanied the body from the sacred lake to the catacombs was the same as before they had passed it : the time occupied by the whole march depending, of course, on the position of the tomb, and the distance from which the body had been brought ; some coming from remote towns or villages, and others from the city itself, or the immediate vicinity.

The tomb, in the subject above described, is represented at the base of the western mountain of Thebes, which agrees perfectly with its actual position ; and from this, as from several other similar paintings, we learn that, besides the excavated chambers hewn in the rock, a small building crowned by a roof of conical or pyramidical form stood before the entrance.   It is probable that many, if not all the pits in the plain below the hills, were once covered with buildings of this kind, which, from their perishable materials, crude brick, have been destroyed after a lapse of so many ages.   Indeed we find the remains of some of them, and occasionally even of their vaulted chambers, with the painted stucco on the walls.

Many other funerals occur on the tombs, which vary only in some details from those already mentioned.   I cannot however omit to notice another instance of palm branches strewed in the way, and the introduction of two tables or altars for the deceased and his wife,—one bearing a profusion of cakes, meat, fruit, vegetables, and other customary gifts; and the other numerous utensils and insignia, as flabella, censers, ostrich feathers, asps, and emblems, together with the leg of a victim, placed upon a napkin spread over the table.   Another is curious, from its showing that

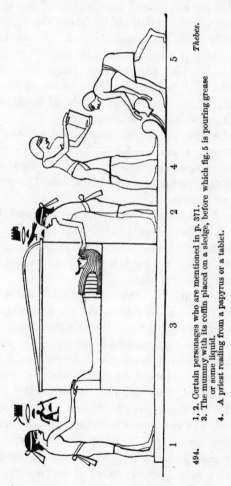

Thebes.

494.   1, 2. Certain personages who are mentioned in p. 371.
        3. The mummy with its coffin placed on a sledge, before which fig. 5 is pouring grease
           or some liquid.
        4. A priest reading from a papyrus or a tablet.

grease was sometimes poured upon the ground or platform on which the sledge of the hearse passed, as was done in moving a colossus or any great weight by the same process.

The hearse containing the mummy was generally closed on all sides ; but it was sometimes open, partially or entirely ; and the body was seen placed upon a bier, ornamented, like some of the couches in their houses, with the head and feet of a lion. Sometimes the mummy was placed on the top of the sarcophagus, within an open hearse ; and three friends of the deceased, or the functionaries destined for this office, took it thence to convey it to the tomb, where it received the accustomed services previous to interment in the pit ; an affectionate hand often crowning it with a garland of " *immortelles*," bay leaves, or fresh flowers ; and depositing, as the last duty of a beloved friend, some object to which while alive he had been attached.

Such are the principal funeral processions represented in the tombs of Thebes. It remains for me to describe the preparatory rites, and the remarkable ceremony that took place on arriving at the lake, before permission could be obtained to transport the body to the opposite shore.

The body having been conveyed to the embalmers, the afflicted family during seventy (or seventy-two) days continued their lamentations at home, singing the funeral dirge, and fulfilling all the duties required both by custom and their own feelings on the mournful occasion.

During this period they abstained from all amusements ; the indulgence in every kind of luxury, as " the bath, wine, delicacies of the table, or rich clothing ;" " they suffered their beard and hair to grow ;" and endeavoured to prove, by this marked neglect of their personal comfort and appearance, how entirely their thoughts were absorbed by the melancholy event that had befallen them. But they did not cut themselves in token of grief ; and the command given to the Israelites, " Ye shall not cut yourselves, nor make any baldness between your eyes for the dead," does not refer to a custom of the Egyptians, but of those people among whom they were about to establish themselves in Syria ; as is distinctly stated of the votaries of Baal.

The body, when embalmed, was restored to the family, and having been deposited in its case, which was generally enclosed in two or three others, all richly painted, " it was placed in a room of the house, upright against the wall," until the tomb was ready, and all the necessary preparations had been made for the funeral.   The *coffin* or mummy case was then " carried forth," and deposited in the *hearse*, drawn upon a sledge, as already described, to the sacred lake of the nome ; notice having been previously given to the judges, and a public announcement made of the appointed day.   Forty-two judges having been summoned, and placed in a semicircle, near the banks of the lake, a boat was brought up, provided expressly for the occasion, under the direction of a boatman called, in the Egyptian language, *Charon ;* " and it is from hence," says Diodorus, " that the fable of Hades is said to be derived, which Orpheus introduced into Greece."

" When the boat was ready for the reception of the coffin, it was lawful for any person who thought proper to bring forward an accusation against the deceased.   If it could be proved that he had led an evil life, the judges declared accordingly, and the body was deprived of the accustomed sepulture ; but if the accuser failed to establish what he had advanced, he was subject to the heaviest penalties.   When there was no accuser, or when the accusation had been disproved, the relations ceased from their lamentations, and pronounced encomiums on the deceased. They did not enlarge upon his descent, as is usual among the Greeks, for they hold that all the Egyptians are equally noble ; but they related his early education and the course of his studies ; and then praising his piety and justice, his temperance, and the other virtues he possessed, they supplicated the gods below to receive him as a companion of the pious.   This announcement was received by the assembled multitude with acclamations ; and they joined in extolling the glory of the deceased, who was about to remain for ever with the virtuous in the regions of Hades.   The body was then taken by those who had family catacombs already prepared, and placed in the repository allotted to it."

" Some," continues the historian, " who were not possessed of catacombs constructed a new apartment for the purpose in their own house, and set the coffin upright against the firmest of the walls : and the same was done with the bodies of those who had been debarred the rites of burial on account of the accusation brought against them, or in consequence of debts they or their sons had contracted. These last, however, if their children's children happened to be prosperous, were released from the impediments of their creditors, and at length received the ceremony of a magnificent burial. It was, indeed, most solemnly established in Egypt that parents and ancestors should have a more marked token of respect paid them by their family, after they had been transferred to their everlasting habitations. Hence originated the custom of depositing the bodies of their deceased parents as pledges for the payment of borrowed money ; those who failed to redeem those pledges being subject to the heaviest disgrace, and deprived of burial after their own death."

The grief and shame felt by the family, when the rites of burial had been refused, were excessive.

It is true that the duration of this punishment was limited according to the extent of the crimes of which the accused had been guilty ; and when the devotion of friends, aided by liberal donations in the service of religion, and the influential prayers of the priests, had sufficiently softened the otherwise inexorable nature of the gods, the period of this state of purgatory was doubtless shortened ; and Diodorus shows that grandchildren, who had the means and inclination, might avail themselves of the same method of satisfying their creditors and the gods.

The form of the ritual read by the priest in pronouncing the acquittal of the dead is preserved in the tombs, usually at the entrance passage ; in which the deceased is made to enumerate all the sins forbidden by the Egyptian law, and to assert his innocence of each. They are supposed by Champollion to amount to forty-two, being equal in number to the assessors, who were destined to examine the deceased, at his final judgment, respecting the peculiar crime which it was his province to punish.

Every large city, as Thebes, Memphis, and some others, had

its lake, at which the same ceremonies were practised ; and it is probable, from what Diodorus says of the " lake of the *nome*," that the capital of each province had one in its immediate vicinity, to which the funeral procession of all who died within the jurisdiction of the *nomarch* was obliged to repair. Even when the priests granted a dispensation for the removal of a body to another town, as was sometimes done in favour of those who desired to be buried at Abydus and other places, the previous ceremony of passing through this ordeal was doubtless required at the lake of their own province.

Those persons who, from their extreme poverty, had no place prepared for receiving their body when denied the privilege of passing the sacred lake, appear to have been interred on the shores they were forbidden to leave ; and I have found the bones of many buried near the site of the lake of Thebes, which appeared to be of bodies imperfectly preserved, as of persons who could not afford the more expensive processes of embalming. This was like remaining on the wrong side of the Styx ; and Diodorus has shown that the fables of the Acherusian lake, of Hecate, of Cerberus, of Charon and the Styx, owed their origin to these Egyptian ceremonies.

Of Charon it may be observed that both his name and character are taken from Horus, who had the peculiar office of steersman in the sacred boats of Egypt ; and the piece of money given him for ferrying the dead across the Styx appears to have been borrowed from the gold or silver plate put into the mouth of the dead by the Egyptians. For though they did not intend it as a reward to the boatman, but rather as a passport to show the virtuous character of the deceased, it was of equal importance in obtaining for him admittance into the regions of the blessed.

The Egyptian custom of depositing cakes in the tombs probably led to the Greek notion of sending a cake for Cerberus, which was placed in the mouth of the deceased ; and it was by means of a similar one, drugged with soporiferous herbs, and given to the monster at a hungry hour, that Æneas and the Sibyl obtained an entrance into the lower regions.

The judge of the dead is recognised in Osiris ; the office of

Mercury, the conductor of souls, is the same as that of Anubis; the figure of Justice without a head, and the scales of Truth or Justice at the gate of Amenti, occur in the funereal subjects of the Egyptian tombs; and the hideous animal who guards the approach to the mansion of Osiris, and is called " the devourer of the wicked," is a worthy prototype of the Greek Cerberus.

It was not ordinary individuals alone who were subjected to a public ordeal at their death—the character of the king himself was doomed to undergo the same test; and if any one could establish proofs of his impiety or injustice, he was denied the usual funereal obsequies when, in the presence of the assembled multitude, his body was brought to the sacred lake, or, as Diodorus states, to the vestibule of the tomb. " The customary trial having commenced, any one was permitted to present himself as an accuser. The pontiffs first passed an encomium upon his character, enumerating all his noble actions, and pointing out the merit of each, to which the people, who were assembled to the number of several thousands, if they felt those praises to be just, responded with favourable acclamations. If, on the contrary, his life had been stained with vice or injustice, they showed their dissent by loud murmurs: and several instances are recorded of Egyptian monarchs having been deprived of the honour of the customary public funeral by the opposing voice of the people." " The effect of this," adds the historian, " was that succeeding kings, fearing so disgraceful a censure after death, and the eternal stigma attached to it, studied by their virtuous conduct to deserve the good opinion of their subjects; and it could not fail to be a great incentive to virtue, independent of the feelings arising from a wish to deserve the gratitude of men, and the fear of forfeiting the favour of the gods."

The custom of refusing funeral rites to a king was not confined to Egypt; it was common also to the Jews*, who forbade a wicked monarch to repose in the sepulchres of his fathers. Thus Joash, though " buried in the city of David," was not interred " in the sepulchres of the kings †;" Manasseh ‡ " was buried in

---

* 1 Kings, xiv. 13; 2 Kings, ix. 10.   † 2 Chron. xxiv. 25.
‡ 2 Kings, xxi. 18 and 26.

the garden of his own house," and several other kings of Judah and Israel were denied that important privilege. And the speech of Samuel, on giving up his post of judge, " Whom have I defrauded ? " and the answer of the people, prove that the custom was adopted by the Jews before they had the kingly form of government.* That the same continued to the time of the Asmodeans, is shown by the conduct of Alexander Janneus, who, feeling the approach of death, charged his wife, " on her return to Jerusalem, to send for the leading men among the Pharisees, and show them his body, giving them leave, with great appearance of sincerity, to use it as they might please,—whether they would dishonour the dead body by refusing it burial, as having suffered severely through him, or whether in their anger they would offer any other injury to it. By this means, and by a promise that nothing should be done without them in the affairs of the kingdom, it was hoped that a more honourable funeral might be obtained than any she could give him, and that his body might be saved from abuse by this appeal to their generosity." They had also the custom of instituting a general mourning for a deceased monarch whose memory they wished to honour.

But the Egyptians allowed not the same extremes of degradation to be offered to the dead as the Jews sometimes did to those who had incurred their hatred ; and the body of a malefactor, though excluded from the precincts of the necropolis, was not refused to his friends that they might perform the last duties to their unfortunate relative.

" The Egyptians," according to Herodotus, " were the first to maintain that the soul of man is immortal ; that after the death of the body it always enters into that of some other animal which is born ; and when it has passed through all those of the earth, water, and air, it again enters that of a man, which circuit it accomplishes in 3000 years." The doctrine of transmigration is mentioned by Plutarch, Plato, and other ancient writers as the general belief among the Egyptians, and it was adopted by Pythagoras and his preceptor Pherecydes, as well as other philosophers of Greece.

* 1 Sam. xii. 4, 5.

Opinions varied respecting it; and some maintained that the soul passed through different bodies till it returned again to the human shape, and that all events which had happened were destined to occur again after a certain period, in the identical order and manner as before. The same men were said to be born again, and to fulfil the same career; and the same causes were thought to produce the same effects, as stated by Virgil. This was termed κυκλος αναγκης, "the circle (or orbit) of necessity."

It is even supposed that the Egyptians preserved the body, in order to keep it in a fit state to receive the soul which once inhabited it; and that their tombs were decorated so richly in order to be ready for their owners on a future occasion. But this is contradicted by the fact of the tombs being sold to later occupants; and by animals being also embalmed, the preservation of whose bodies was not ascribable to any idea connected with the soul; and the custom arose rather from a sanitary regulation for the benefit of the living, and from that feeling of respect for the dead which is common to all men.

And since it is distinctly shown that all virtuous men became " Osiris," and returned again to the Good Being whence their souls emanated, their coming to earth again at any period is improbable; and the bad alone were condemned to that degradation, going through a state of purgatory, by passing into the bodies of animals. This, which accords with the belief of the Hindoos, is more consistent with what we know of the notions of the Egyptians; and there is reason to believe from the monuments, that the souls which underwent transmigration were those of men whose sins were of a sufficiently moderate kind to admit of that purification; the unpardonable sinner being condemned to eternal fire. The Buddhists have the same notion of the soul of man passing into the bodies of animals; and even the Druids believed in the migration of the soul, though they confined it to human bodies.

The judgment scenes, found in the tombs and on the papyri, sometimes represent the deceased conducted by Horus alone, or accompanied by his wife, to the region of Amenti. Cerberus is present as the guardian of the gates, near which the scales of

Justice are erected; and Anubis, " the director of the weight," having placed a vase representing the good actions, or the heart, of the deceased in one scale, and the figure or emblem of Truth in the other, proceeds to ascertain his claims for admission. If on being "weighed" he is "found wanting," he is rejected; and Osiris, the judge of the dead, inclining his sceptre in token of condemnation, pronounces judgment upon him, and condemns his soul to return to earth under the form of a pig, or some other unclean animal. Placed in a boat, it is removed, under the charge of two monkeys, from the precincts of Amenti, all communication with which is figuratively cut.off by a man who hews away the earth with an axe after its passage; and the commencement of a new term of life is indicated by those monkeys, the emblems of Thoth, as Time. But if, when the sum of his deeds have been recorded, his virtues so far predominate as to entitle him to admission to the mansions of the blessed, Horus, taking in his hand the tablet of Thoth, introduces him to the presence of Osiris; who, in his palace, attended by Isis and Nepthys, sits on his throne in the midst of the waters, from which rises the lotus, bearing upon its expanded flower the four Genii of Amenti.

Other representations of this subject differ in some of the details; and in the judgment scene of the royal scribe, whose funeral procession has been described, the deceased advances alone in an attitude of prayer to receive judgment. On one side of the scales stands Thoth, holding a tablet in his hand; on the other the Goddess of Justice; and Horus, in lieu of Anubis, performs the office of director of the balance, on the top of which sits a Cynocephalus, the emblem of Thoth. Osiris, seated as usual on his throne, holding his crook and flagellum, awaits the report from the hands of his son Horus. Before the door of his palace are the four Genii of Amenti, and near them three deities, who either represent the assessors, or may be the three assistant judges, who gave rise to the Minos, Æacus, and Rhadamanthus of Greek fable. In these the *Min* and *Amenti* are very Egyptian.

Another, figured in the side adytum of the Ptolemaic temple of Dayr el Medeeneh, at Thebes, represents the deceased approaching in a similarly submissive attitude, between two figures of Truth or Justice; whose emblem, the ostrich feather, he holds in his hand. The two figures show the double capacity of that goddess, corresponding to the Thummim, or "two Truths," and according well with the statement of Diodorus respecting her position "at the gates of Truth." Horus and Anubis superintend the balance, and weigh the actions of the judged; whilst Thoth inscribes them on his tablet, which he prepares for presentation to Osiris, who, seated on his throne, pronounces the final judgment, permitting the virtuous soul to enjoy the blessings of eternal felicity. Before him four Genii of Amenti stand upon a lotus flower; and a figure of Harpocrates, seated on the crook of Osiris between the scales and the entrance of the divine abode, which is guarded by Cerberus, is intended to show that the deceased on admission to that pure state must be born again, and commence a new life, cleansed from all the impurities of his earthly career. It also represents the idea common to the Egyptians and other philosophers, that to die was only to assume a new form—that nothing was annihilated—and that dissolution was merely the forerunner of reproduction. Above, in two lines, sit the forty-two assessors, the complete number mentioned by Diodorus; whose office was to assist in judging the dead.

Many similar subjects occur on funeral monuments, few of which present any new features. One, however, is singular, from the Goddess of Justice being herself engaged in weighing the deceased, in the presence of Thoth, who is represented under the form of a Cynocephalus, having the horns and globe of the Moon upon its head, and a tablet in its hand. Instead of the usual vase, the figure of the deceased himself is placed in one of the scales, opposed to that of the Goddess; and close to the balance sits Cerberus with open mouth, ready to perform his office of " devourer of the wicked."

Another may also be noticed, from the singular fact of the Goddess of Justice, who here introduces the deceased, being without a head, as described by Diodorus; from the deceased holding in each hand an ostrich feather, the emblem of Truth; and from Cerberus being represented standing upon the steps of the divine abode of Osiris, as if in the act of announcing the arrival of Thoth with the person of the tomb.

Sometimes the deceased wore round his neck the same vase, which in the scales typified his good actions; or bore on his head the ostrich feather of Truth. They were both intended to show that he had been deemed worthy of admission to the mansions of the just; and in the same idea originated the custom of placing the name of the Goddess after that of virtuous individuals who were dead, implying that they were " judged," or " justified."

The Goddesses Athor and Netpe, in their respective trees, the Persea and Sycamore-fig, frequently presented the virtuous after death with the fruit and drink of heaven; which call to mind the ambrosia and nectar of Greek fable.

The process of embalming is thus described by ancient writers: —" In Egypt," says Herodotus, " certain persons are appointed by law to exercise this art as their peculiar business; and when a dead body is brought them they produce patterns of mummies in wood, imitated in painting; the most elaborate of which are said to be of him (Osiris), whose name I do not think it right to mention on this occasion. The second which they show is simpler and less costly; and the third is the cheapest. Having exhibited them all, they inquire of the persons who have applied to them which mode they wish to be adopted; and this being settled, and the price agreed upon, the parties retire, leaving the body with the embalmers.

" In preparing it according to the first method, they commence by extracting the brain from the nostrils by a curved iron probe, partly cleansing the head by these means, and partly by pouring in certain drugs; then making an incision in the side with a sharp Ethiopian stone, they draw out the intestines through the aperture. Having cleansed and washed them with palm wine, they cover them with pounded aromatics; and afterwards filling the cavity with powder of pure myrrh, cassia, and other fragrant substances, frankincense excepted, they sew it up again. This being done, they salt the body, keeping it in natron during seventy days; to which period they are strictly confined. When the seventy days are over, they wash the body, and wrap it up entirely in bands of fine linen smeared on their inner side with gum, which the Egyptians generally use instead of glue. The relations then take away the body, and have a wooden case made in the form of a man, in which they deposit it; and when fastened up, they keep it in a room in their house, placing it upright against the wall. This is the most costly mode of embalming.

" For those who choose the middle kind, on account of the expense, they prepare the body as follows. They fill syringes with oil of cedar, and inject this into the abdomen, without making any incision or removing the bowels; and taking care that the liquid shall not escape, they keep it in salt during the specified number of days. The cedar oil is then taken out; and such is its strength that it brings with it the bowels, and all the inside, in a state of dissolution. The natron also dissolves the flesh; so that nothing remains but the skin and bones. This process being over, they restore the body without any further operation.

" The third kind of embalming is only adopted for the poor. In this they merely cleanse the body by an injection of *syrmæa*, and salt it during seventy days; after which it is returned to the friends who brought it.

" The bodies of women of quality are not embalmed directly after their death, and it is customary for the family to keep them three or four days before they are subjected to that process."

The account given by Diodorus is similar to that of the historian of Halicarnassus. " The funerals of the Egyptians are conducted upon three different scales,—the most expensive, the more moderate, and the humblest. The first is said to cost a talent of silver (about 250*l*. sterling); the second 22 minæ (or 60*l*.); and the third is extremely cheap. The persons who embalm the bodies are artists who have learnt this secret from their ancestors. They present to the friends of the deceased who apply to them an estimate of the funeral expenses, and ask them in what manner they wish it to be performed; which being agreed upon, they deliver the body to the proper persons appointed to that office. First, one, who is denominated the scribe, marks upon the left side of the body, as it lies on the ground, the extent of the incision which is to be made; then another, who is called *paraschistes* (the *dissector*), cuts open as much of the flesh as the law permits with an Ethiopian (flint) stone, and immediately runs away, pursued by those who are present, throwing stones at him amidst bitter execrations, as if to cast upon him all the odium of this necessary act. For they look upon every one who has offered violence to, or inflicted a wound or any other injury upon a human body, to be hateful ; but the embalmers, on the contrary, are held in the greatest consideration and respect, being the associates of the priests, and permitted free access to the temples as sacred persons.

" As soon as they have met together to embalm the body thus prepared for them, one introduces his hand through the aperture into the abdomen, and takes every thing out, except the kidneys and heart. Another cleanses each of the viscera with palm wine and aromatic substances. Lastly, after having applied oil of cedar and other things to the whole body for upwards of *thirty* days, they add myrrh, cinnamon, and those drugs which have not only the power of preserving the body for a length of time, but of imparting to it a fragrant odour. It is then restored to the friends of the deceased. And so perfectly are all the members preserved, that even the hairs of the eyelids and eyebrows remain undisturbed, and the whole appearance of the person is so unaltered that every feature may be recognised. The Egyptians, therefore, who sometimes keep the bodies of their ancestors in magnificent apartments set apart for the purpose, have an opportunity of contemplating the faces of those who died many generations before them ; and the height and figure of their bodies being distinguishable, as well as the character of the countenance, they enjoy a wonderful gratification, as if they lived in the society of those they see before them."

On the foregoing statements of the two historians, I may be permitted some observations.

First. The wooden figures kept as patterns are similar (except in size) to those small ones of glazed pottery, representing the deceased in the form of Osiris, so common in our collections.

Secondly. It is evident from the mummies which have been found in such abundance at Thebes and other places, that in the three different modes of embalming several gradations existed ;

some of which differ so much in many essential points as almost to justify our extending the number mentioned by the historians.

Thirdly. The extraction of the brain by the nostrils is proved by the appearance of the mummies found in the tombs ; and some of the crooked instruments (always of bronze) supposed to have been used for this purpose have been discovered at Thebes.

Fourthly. The incision in the side is, as Diodorus says, on the left. Over it the sacred eye of Osiris was placed, and through it the viscera were returned when not deposited in the four vases.

Fifthly. The second class of mummies without any incision in the side are often found in the tombs ; but it is also shown from the bodies at Thebes that the incision was not always confined to those of the first class, and that some of an inferior kind were submitted to this simple and effectual process.

Sixthly. The sum stated by Diodorus of a talent of silver can only be a general estimate of the expense of the first kind of embalming ; since the various gradations in the style of preparing them prove that some mummies must have cost far more than others : and the sumptuous manner in which many persons performed the funerals of their friends kept pace with the splendour of the tombs they made, or purchased for their reception.

Seventhly. The execrations with which the *paraschistes* was pursued could only have been a religious form, from which he was doubtless in little apprehension ; an anomaly not altogether without a parallel in other civilised countries.

Eighthly. Diodorus is in error when he supposes the actual face of the body was seen after it was restored to the family ; for even before it was deposited in the case, which Herodotus says the friends made for it, the features, as well as the whole body, were concealed by the bandages which enveloped them. The resemblance he mentions was only in the mummy case, or the cartonage which came next to the bandages ; and, indeed, whatever number of cases covered a mummy, the face of each was intended as a representation of the person within, as the lower part was in imitation of the swathed body.

Diodorus mentions three different classes of persons who assisted in preparing the body for the funeral,—the scribe, who regulated the incision in the side; the *paraschistes*, or cutter; and the embalmers. To these may be added the undertakers, who wrapped the body in bandages, and who had workmen in their employ to make the cases in which it was deposited.* Many different trades and branches of art were constantly called upon to supply the undertakers with those things required for funereal purposes: as the painters of mummy cases; those who made images of stone, porcelain, wood, and other materials; the manufacturers of alabaster, earthenware, and bronze vases; those who worked in ivory; the leather-cutters, and many others. And it is not improbable that to the undertakers, who were a class of priests, belonged a very large proportion of the tombs kept for sale in the cemeteries of the large towns.

The number of days, seventy or seventy-two, mentioned by the two historians, is confirmed by the Scripture account of Jacob's funeral; and this arbitrary period cannot fail to call to mind the frequent occurrence of the numbers 7 and 70, which are observed in so many instances both among the Egyptians and Jews. But there is reason to believe that it comprehended the whole period of the mourning, and that the embalming process only occupied a portion of it; forty being the number of days expressly stated by the Bible to have been assigned to the latter, and "three score and ten" to the entire mourning.

The custom of embalming bodies was not confined to the Egyptians: the Jews adopted this process to a certain extent, "the manner of the Jews" being to bury the body "wound in linen clothes with spices;" as Lazarus was swathed with bandages.

The embalmers were probably members of the medical profession, as well as of the class of priests. Joseph is said to have "commanded the physicians to embalm his father;" and Pliny states that during this process certain examinations took place, which enabled them to study the disease of which the deceased had died. They appear to have been made in compliance with an order from the government, as he says, the kings of Egypt had the bodies opened after death to ascertain the nature of their

* *See* above, pp. 117, 118, 119.

diseases, by which means alone the remedy for phthisical complaints was discovered.

Certain regulations respecting the bodies of persons found dead were wisely established in Egypt, which, by rendering the district or town in the immediate vicinity responsible in some degree for the accident, by fining it to the full cost of the most expensive funeral, necessarily induced those in authority to exercise a proper degree of vigilance, and to exert their utmost efforts to save any one who had fallen into the river, or was otherwise exposed to the danger of his life. From these too we may judge of the great responsibility they were under, for the body. of a person found murdered within their jurisdiction.

" If a dead body," says Herodotus, " was accidentally found, whether of an Egyptian or a stranger, who had been taken by a crocodile, or drowned in the river, the town upon the territory of which it was discovered was obliged to embalm it according to the most costly process, and to bury it in a consecrated tomb. None of the friends or relations were permitted to touch it; this privilege was accorded to the priests of the Nile alone, who interred it with their own hands, as if it had been something more than the corpse of a human being."

Herodotus fails to inform us what became of the intestines, after they had been removed from the body of those embalmed according to the first process; but the discoveries made in the tombs clear up this important point, and enable us to correct the improbable account given by Porphyry.. The latter writer says, " When the bodies of persons of distinction were embalmed, they took out the intestines and put them into a vessel, over which (after some other rites had been performed for the dead) one of the embalmers pronounced an invocation to the Sun in behalf of the deceased. The formula, according to Euphantus, who translated it from the original into Greek, was as follows:—' O thou Sun, our sovereign lord! and all ye Deities who have given life to man! receive me, and grant me an abode with the eternal Gods. During the whole course of my life I have scrupulously worshipped the Gods my fathers taught me to adore; I have ever honoured my parents, who begat this body; I have killed no one; I have not defrauded any, nor have I done an injury to any man; and if I have committed any other fault during my life, either in eating or drinking, it has not been done for myself, but for these things.' So saying, the embalmer pointed to the vessel containing the intestines, which was thrown into the river ; the rest of the body, when properly cleansed, being embalmed."

Plutarch gives a similar account of their " throwing the intestines into the river," as the cause of all the faults committed by man, "the rest of the body when cleansed being embalmed ;" which is evidently borrowed from the same authority as that of Porphyry, and given in the same words. But the positive evidence of the tombs, as well as our acquaintance with the religious feelings of the Egyptians, sufficiently prove this to be one of the many idle tales by which the Greeks have shown their ignorance of that people ; and no one who considers the respect with which they looked upon the Nile, the care they took to remove all impurities which might affect their health, and the superstitious prejudice they felt towards every thing appertaining to the human body, could for an instant suppose that they would on any consideration be induced to pollute the stream, or insult the dead, by a similar custom.

But the inaccurate statements of the Greeks respecting Egypt and the Egyptians are numerous ; and not only have we to censure them for failing to give much interesting information, which they might have acquired after their intercourse with the country became unrestrained, but to regret that what they tell us can seldom be relied on, unless confirmed by the monuments.

It might appear incredible that errors could have been made on the most common subjects, on things relating to positive customs which daily occurred before the eyes of those who sought to inquire into them, and are described by Greek writers who visited the country. But when we observe the ignorance of Europeans respecting the customs of modern Egypt,—of Europeans, who are a people much less averse to inquire into the manners of other countries, much more exposed to the criticism of their compatriots in giving false information than the ancient Greeks, and to whom the modern inhabitants do not oppose the same impediments in examining their habits as did the ancient Egyptians;—when we recollect the great facilities they enjoy of becoming acquainted with the language and manners, and still find many Italians, French, and others, who have resided ten, twenty, or more years in Egypt, with a perfect knowledge of Arabic, and enjoying opportunities for constant intercourse with the people, ignorant of their most ordinary customs, we can readily account for the misconceptions of the Greeks respecting the habits or opinions of the ancient Egyptians.

As far as the invocation of the Sun, and the confession pronounced by the priest (rather than the embalmer) on the part of the deceased, the account of Porphyry partakes of the character of truth; though the time when this was done should rather be referred to the ceremony on the sacred lake, or to that of depositing the body in the tomb. The confession, indeed, is an imperfect portion of that recorded in the sculptures, which has been already mentioned. (p. 376.)

As soon as the intestines had been removed from the body, they were properly cleansed, and embalmed in spices and various substances, and deposited in four vases. These were afterwards placed in the tomb with the coffin, and were supposed to belong to the four Genii of Amenti, whose heads and names they bore. Each contained a separate portion. The vase with a cover representing the human head of Amset held the stomach and large intestines; that with the cynocephalus head of Hapi* contained the small intestines; in that belonging to the jackal-headed Smautf were the lungs and heart; and for the vase of the hawk-headed Kebhnsnof were reserved the gall-bladder and the liver. They differed in size and the materials of which they were made. The most costly were of oriental alabaster, from 10 to 20 inches high, and about one-third of that in diameter, each having its inscription, with the name of the particular deity whose head it bore. Others were of common limestone, and even of wood; but these last were generally solid, or contained nothing, being merely emblematic, and intended only for those whose intestines were returned into the body. They were generally surmounted by the heads above mentioned, but they sometimes had human heads;

* See List of Woodcuts, in vol. i., note on 278.

and it is to these last more particularly that the name of Canopi has been applied, from their resemblance to certain vases made by the Romans to imitate the Egyptian taste. I need scarcely add that this is a misnomer, and that the application of the word Canopus to any Egyptian vase is equally inadmissible.

Such was the mode of preserving the internal parts of the mummies embalmed according to the most expensive process. And so careful were the Egyptians to show proper respect to all that belonged to the human body, that even the sawdust of the floor where they cleansed it was taken and tied up in small linen bags, which, to the number of twenty or thirty, were deposited in vases and buried near the tomb.

In those instances where the intestines, after being properly cleansed and embalmed, were returned into the body by the aperture in the side, images of the four Genii of Amenti, made of wax, were put in with them, as the guardians of the portions particularly subject to their influence; and sometimes, in lieu of them, a plate of lead, or other material bearing upon it a representation of these four figures. Over the incision the mysterious eye of Osiris was placed, whether the intestines were returned or deposited in the vases.

For the classification of "Egyptian Mummies," and the different modes of Embalming, I refer to Mr. Pettigrew's work; where they are arranged under these general heads:—

    I. Those with the ventral incision.

    II. Those without any incision.

  I. Of the mummies with the incision are,

    1. Those preserved by balsamic matter.

    2. Those preserved by natron.

  1. Those dried by balsamic and astringent substances are either filled with a mixture of resin and aromatics, or with asphaltum and pure bitumen.

When filled with resinous matter they are of an olive colour; the skin dry, flexible, and as if tanned; retracted and adherent to the bones. The features are preserved, and appear as during life. The belly and chest are filled with resins, partly soluble in spirits of wine. These substances have no particular odour by which they can be recognised; but when thrown upon hot coals a thick smoke is produced, giving out a strong aromatic smell. Mummies of this kind are dry, light, and easily broken ; with the teeth, hair of the head, and eyebrows well preserved. Some of them are gilt on the surface of the body ; others only on the face, or the sexual parts, or on the head and feet.

The mummies filled with bitumen are black ; the skin hard and shining, and as if coloured with varnish ; the features perfect ; the belly, chest, and head filled with resin, black and hard, and having a little odour. Upon being examined they are found to yield the same results as the Jews' pitch met with in commerce. These mummies are dry and heavy. They have no smell, and are difficult to develop or break. They have been prepared with great care, and are very little susceptible of decomposition from exposure to the air.

2. The mummies with ventral incisions, prepared by natron, are likewise filled with resinous substances, and also asphaltum. The skin is hard and elastic : it resembles parchment, and does not adhere to the bones. The resins and bitumen injected into these mummies are little friable, and give out no odour. The countenance of the body is little altered, but the hair is badly preserved : what remains usually falls off upon being touched. These mummies are very numerous, and if exposed to the air they become covered with an efflorescence of sulphate of soda. They readily absorb humidity from the atmosphere.

Such are the characteristic marks of the first quality of mummies, according to the mode of embalming the body. They may also be distinguished by other peculiarities ; as,

1. Mummies of which the intestines were deposited in vases.

2. Those of which the intestines were returned into the body.

The former included all mummies embalmed according to the most expensive process (for though some of an inferior quality are found with the incision in the side, none of the first quality were embalmed without the removal of the intestines) ; and the body, having been prepared with the proper spices and drugs, was enveloped in linen bandages, sometimes measuring 1000 yards in length. It was then enclosed in a cartonage fitting closely to the mummied body, which was richly painted, and covered in front with a network of beads and bugles arranged in a tasteful form, the face being laid over with thick gold-leaf, and the eyes made of enamel. The three or four cases, which successively covered the cartonage, were ornamented in like manner with painting and gilding ; and the whole was enclosed in a sarcophagus of wood or stone, profusely charged with painting or sculpture. These cases, as well as the cartonage, varied in style and richness, according to the expense incurred by the friends of the deceased. The bodies thus embalmed were generally of priests of various grades. Sometimes the skin itself was covered with gold-leaf ; sometimes the whole body, the face, or the eyelids ; sometimes the nails alone. In many instances the body or the cartonage was beautified in an expensive manner, and the outer cases were little ornamented ; but some preferred the external show of rich cases or sarcophagi.

Those of which the intestines were returned into the body, with the wax figures of the four Genii, were placed in cases less richly ornamented ; and some of these were, as already stated, of the second class of mummies.

II. Those without the ventral incision were also of two kinds :

1. Salted, and filled with bituminous matter less pure than the others.

2. Simply salted.

(1.) The former mummies are not recognisable ; all the cavities are filled, and the surface of the body is covered with thin mineral pitch. It penetrates the body, and forms with it one undistinguishable mass. These mummies, M. Rouger conceives, were submerged in vessels containing the pitch in a liquid state. They are the most numerous of all kinds : they are black, dry, heavy, and of disagreeable odour, and very difficult to break. Neither the eyebrows nor hair are preserved, and there is no gilding upon them. The bituminous matter is fatty to the touch, less black and brittle than the asphaltum, and yields a very strong odour. It dissolves imperfectly in alcohol, and when thrown upon hot coals emits a thick smoke and disagreeable smell. When distilled, it gives an abundant oil ; fat, and of a brown colour and fœtid odour. Exposed to the air, these mummies soon change, attract humidity, and become covered with an efflorescence of saline substances.

(2.) The mummies simply salted and dried are generally worse preserved than those filled with resins and bitumen. Their skin is dry, white, elastic, light, yielding no odour, and easily broken ; and masses of adipocere are frequently found in them. The features are destroyed ; the hair is entirely removed ; the bones are detached from their connexions with the slightest effort, and they are white like those of a skeleton. The cloth enveloping them falls to pieces upon being touched. These mummies are generally found in particular caves which contain great quantities of saline matters, principally the sulphate of soda.

Of the latter also several subdivisions may be made, according to the manner in which the bodies were deposited in the tombs ; and some are so loosely put up in bad cloths and rags, as barely to be separated from the earth or stones in which they have been buried. Some are more carefully enveloped in bandages, and arranged one over the other without cases in the same common tomb, often to the number of several hundred ; a visit to one of which has been well described by Belzoni.

Some have certain peculiarities in the mode of their preservation. In many the skulls are filled with earthy matter in lieu of bitumen ; and some mummies have been prepared with wax and tanning, a remarkable instance of which occurs in that opened by Dr. Granville,—for a full account of which I refer the reader to his work, descriptive of the body and its mode of preservation. I cannot, however, omit to mention a wonderful proof of the skill of the embalmers in this as in so many other instances, who, by means of a corrosive liquid, had removed the internal tegument of the skull, and still contrived to preserve the thin membrane below, though the heat of the embalming matter afterwards poured into the cavity had perforated the suture and scorched the scalp.

It has been a general and a just remark that few mummies of children have been discovered,—a singular fact, not easily accounted for, since the custom of embalming those even of the earliest age was practised in Egypt.

Greek mummies usually differed from those of the Egyptians in the manner of disposing the bandages of the arms and legs. The former had the arms placed at the sides, and bound separately ;

but the arms as well as the legs, and even the fingers of the Egyptians, were generally enclosed in one common envelope, without any separation in the bandages. In these last the arms were extended along the side, the palms inwards and resting on the thighs, or brought forwards over the groin; sometimes even across the breast; and occasionally one arm in the former, the other in the latter position. The legs were close together, and the head erect. These different modes of arranging the limbs were common to both sexes, and to all ages; though we occasionally meet with some slight deviations from this mode of placing the hands. But no Egyptian is found with the limbs bandaged separately, as those of Greek mummies; though instances may occur of the latter having the arms enveloped with the body.

Sometimes the nails and the whole hands and feet were stained with the red dye of the *henneh;* and some mummies have been found with the face covered by a mask of cloth fitting closely to it, and overlaid with a coating of composition, so painted as to resemble the deceased, and to have the appearance of flesh. But these are of rare occurrence, and I am unable to state if they are of an Egyptian or Greek epoch. This last is most probable; especially as we find that the mummies which present the portrait of the deceased painted on wood, and placed over the face, are always of Greek time. Some remarkable instances of these are preserved in the collections of Europe; and one upon a coffin sent to England by Mr. Salt, which has been figured by Mr. Pettigrew, is now in the British Museum.

On the breast was frequently placed a scarabæus, in immediate contact with the flesh. These scarabæi, when of stone, had their

495.   A stone scarabæus; covered with wings, and the sun and asps, of silver.
In my possession.

extended wings made of lead or silver; and when of blue pottery, the wings were of the same material. On the cartonage and case, in a corresponding situation above, the same emblem was also placed, to indicate the protecting influence of the Deity; and in this last position it sometimes stood in the centre of a boat, with the Goddesses Isis and Nepthys on either side in an attitude of prayer. On the outer cases the same place was occupied by a similar winged scarabæus, or the winged globe, or a hawk, or a ram-headed vulture or hawk, or both these last, or the same bird with the head of a woman, or by the Goddess Netpe; and sometimes a disk was supported by the beetle, having within it a hawk and the name of Re.

The mode of painting the mummy cases differed according to the rank of the persons, the expense incurred in their decoration, and other circumstances; and such was their variety, that few resembled each other in every particular. There was also a very great difference at different periods; which extended even to the shape of the mummy case. I shall, therefore, in describing them, confine my remarks to their general character, and to the most common representations figured upon them, from the 18th to the 26th dynasty.

In the first quality of mummies, the innermost covering of the body, after it had been swathed in the necessary quantity of bandages, was the *cartonage*. This was a pasteboard case fitting exactly to its shape; the precise measure having been carefully taken, so that it might correspond to the body it was intended to cover, and to which it was probably adjusted by proper manipulation while still damp. It was then taken off again, and made to retain that shape till dry, when it was again applied to the bandaged body, and sewed up at the back. After this it was painted and ornamented with figures and numerous subjects: the face was made to imitate that of the deceased, and frequently gilded; the eyes were inlaid; and the hair of females was made to represent the natural plaits, as worn by Egyptian women.

The subjects painted upon the cartonage were the four Genii of Amenti, and various emblems belonging to Deities connected with the dead. On the breast was placed the figure of Netpe, with expanded wings, protecting the deceased; sacred arks, boats, and other things were arranged in different compartments; and Osiris, Isis, Nepthys, Anubis, Sokari, and other Deities, were frequently introduced. In some instances, Isis was represented throwing her arms round the feet of the mummy, with this appropriate legend, " I embrace thy feet;" at once explanatory of, and explained by, the action of the Goddess. A long line of hieroglyphics, extending down the front, usually contained the name and quality of the deceased, and the offerings presented for him to the Gods ; and transverse bands frequently repeated the former, with similar donations to other Deities. But as the arrangement and character of these sacred ornaments vary in nearly all the specimens of mummies, it would be tedious to introduce more than a general notion of their character. Even the cartonage and different cases of the same mummy differ, in all except the name and description of the deceased ; and the figure of Netpe is sometimes replaced by a winged Sun, or a scarabæus. This Goddess, however, always occurs in some part of the coffin, and often with outspread arms at the bottom of the inner case, where she appears to receive the body into her embrace, as the protectress of the dead.

The face of the cartonage was often covered with thick gold leaf, and richly adorned ; the eyes inlaid with brilliant enamel ; the hair imitated with great care, and adorned with gold : and the same care was extended to the three cases which successively covered it, though each differed from the next ; the innermost being the most ornamented. Rich necklaces were placed or represented on the neck of each, for all were made in the form of the deceased ; and a net-work of coloured beads was frequently spread over the breast, and even the whole body, worked in rich and elegant devices.

The outer case was either of wood or stone. When of wood, it had a flat or a circular summit, sometimes with a short square pillar rising at each angle. The whole was richly painted, and some of an older age frequently had a door represented near one of the corners. At one end was the figure of Isis, at the other Nephthys ; and the top was painted with bands or fancy devices. In others the lid represented the curving top of the ordinary Egyptian canopy (*figs*. 9, 1, 2).

The stone coffins, usually called sarcophagi, were of oblong shape, having flat straight sides, like a box, with a curved or pointed lid. Sometimes the figure of the deceased was represented upon the latter in relief, like that of the queen of Amasis in the British Museum; and some were in the form of a king's name, or royal oval. Others were made in the shape of the

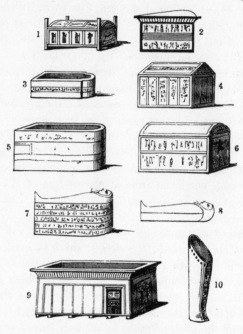

496.   Different forms of mummy cases.

1, 2, 4. Of wood.   3, 5, 6, 7, 8. Of stone.
9. Of wood, and of early time—before the 18th dynasty.
10. Of burnt earthenware.

mummied body, whether of basalt, granite, slate, or limestone, specimens of which are met with in the British Museum and other collections. I have even seen one of this form, found during my stay at Thebes, of a red earthenware, very similar to our tiles, made in two pieces sewed together, small holes having been made in the clay before it was burnt for this purpose. The upper part was broken off, but it was evidently a continuation of the human figure in the form of the mummy it contained.

With regard to the question when the custom of embalming the body ceased in Egypt, it may be observed that some are of opinion that it ceased at an early time, when Egypt became a Roman province. But this has been fully disproved by modern discoveries; and it not only appears that the early Christians embalmed their dead, but according to " St. Augustine, mummies were made in his time, at the beginning of the fifth century." The custom may not have been universal at that period; and it is more probable that it gradually fell into disuse, than that it was suddenly abandoned from any accidental cause connected with change of custom, or from religious scruple.

The disposition of various objects placed with the dead varied in different tombs according to the rank of the person, the choice of the friends of the deceased, or other circumstances, as their number and quality depended on the expense incurred in the funeral. For, besides the richly decorated coffins, many vases, images of the dead, papyri, jewels, and other ornaments were deposited in the tomb; and tablets of stone or wood were placed near the sarcophagus, engraved or painted with funeral subjects and legends relating to the deceased. These last resembled in form the ordinary Egyptian shield, being squared at the base, and rounded at the summit; and it is probable, as already observed, that their form originated in the military custom of making the shield a monument in honour of a deceased soldier.

Many of the objects buried in the tomb depended on the profession or occupation of the individual. A priest had the insignia of his office; as the scribe his inkstand or palette; the high priest the censer; the hieraphoros a small model of a sacred shrine, or a figure bearing an image or emblem of a deity; and others according to their grade. In the soldier's tomb were deposited his arms; in the mariner's a boat; and the peculiar occupation of each artisan was pointed out by some implement employed in his trade.

Besides the four vases with the heads of the Genii of Amenti, were many of smaller size; of alabaster, hard stone, glass, porcelain, bronze, and other materials, many of which were of exquisite workmanship; but these were confined to the sepulchres of the rich, as were jewellery and other expensive ornaments.

Papyri were likewise confined to persons of a certain degree of wealth; but small figures of the deceased, of wood or vitrified earthenware, were common to all classes, except the poorest of the community. These figures are too well known to need a

detailed description.   They usually present a hieroglyphic
inscription, either in a vertical line down the centre, or in
horizontal bands round the body, containing the name and quality
of the deceased, with the customary presentation of offerings for
his soul to Osiris, a chapter from the ritual, or some funereal
formula.   In the hands of these figures are a hoe and a bag of
seed.   Their arms are crossed in imitation of certain representations of Osiris, whose name and form the dead assumed; and
their beard indicates the return of the human soul, which once
animated that body, to the Deity from whom it emanated.

I do not enter into a minute description of all the modes of
arranging the objects in the tombs, the endless variety of Egyptian mummies, or the subjects of their painted cases.   I have
confined myself to a general view of this, as of other subjects
connected with the manners and customs of this ancient and
remarkable people; and now, having accompanied the Egyptians
to the tomb, I take my leave of them with this wish,

" Sedibus ut saltem placidis in morte quiescant."

Q.   Mummy-pit.   A woman searching for ornaments.   *Thebes.*

INDEX.

Flute, Minerva's aversion for the, i. 127.

Fly-fishing. *See* Fishing.

Food, i. 166–168.

—— of the peasants, i. 167; ii. 3.

—— of the poor people and shepherds, ii. 175.

—— of poor people simple and cheap, i. 179; ii. 219, 330.

"Fool or a physician at forty," origin of, ii. 352.

Foot, watering with the, i. 34.

——, standard, or unit for the human figure, ii. 266.

Foot-machine, i. 34.

Footmen, running, i. 76.

Footstools, i. 68.

Foreleg and shoulder, called "the chosen part," i. 264.

Forks not used at dinner, i. 181.

—— known to the Jews and Etruscans, but not used at table, i. 182.

—— used in an Egyptian kitchen, i. 174, 175.

—— of wood used by the peasants, ii. 42, 45.

Fortification, regular system of, i. 407.

Fowling, a great amusement, i. 234.

Fox, i. 227, 245.

—— dog, i. 231.

Fringes on dresses (sometimes sewed on). ii. 91, 322. *See* Dresses with fringes.

Fruit in wicker baskets, i. 43.

—— gathering, i. 40, 41, 43, 44.

Fruit trees, i. 36, 55, 57.

Fruits on the altar, i. 259.

Fullers, ii. 106.

Funerals, mourners at, ii. 366.

Funerals of kings, ii. 366.

——, some grand, ii. 366–373.

Furniture of Egyptian rooms, i. 58–72.

Fyoom, or Arsinoïte nome, i. 49, 229, 244, 304.

——, extremity of the, artificially irrigated, i. 307.

——, remains of vineyards on the western borders of, i. 49; ii. 20.

——, wild boars found in the, i. 244.

Game, preserves for, i. 37.

——, parks and covers for, i. 215.

Game-cart, substitute for the, i. 218.

Games in honour of the gods, i. 282.

—— most usual, i. 188, 189.

—— of ball, i. 198–200.

Games, various, i. 192–207.

—— of single-stick, i. 206, 207.

——, board of, found by Dr. Abbott, i. 194, 195. See *Mora* and Draughts.

Gardens, i. 25, 32, 35–37.

Garlands or chaplets, i. 57, 79–81.

Garments worn at feasts, i. 81.

Gazelle, i. 214–216, 219, 220, 223–225, 227, 247.

Geese, boxes in the form of, i. 161.

—— fed, i. 215. *See* Goose.

—— potted, ii. 185.

Geography, in the books of Hermes, i. 274.

Geometry, i. 321.

——, arithmetic, and astronomy, ii. 319.

—— invented in Egypt, ii. 248, 251.

Gilding, ii. 145–147.

Giraffe, i. 231, 247.

Gladiators not employed in Egypt, i. 210.

Glass, early use of—blowers, bottles and blowpipe, and glazed pottery, ii. 58.

—— bottles, ii. 58, 67.

—— bottles of various colours, ii. 60.

—— beads with name of Amun-m̄-het, ii. 59.

—— beads, ii. 64, 65. *See* Beads.

—— beads rarely found with a name, ii. 60.

——, discovery or invention of, ii. 60.

——, Egyptians famed for particular kinds of, ii. 60.

——, counterfeits of precious stones, ii. 60, 63. *See* Precious Stones.

—— shows advance of luxury, ii. 65.

—— of many colours attempted at Venice, ii. 61.

—— mosaics of pictures in Venice, ii. 61, 63.

——, false emeralds of, ii. 63, 64.

——, coloured, 60, 63–65, 67, 71.

——, coloured imitations of murrhine vases, ii. 71.

—— applied to various uses, ii. 65.

—— coloured porcelain, ii. 66, 71. *See* Vitrified.

——, cut, ground, and cast, ii. 67.

—— cut by the diamond, emery powder, and wheel, ii. 67.

—— bottles inclosed in wicker casing, ii. 67, 68.

—— lamps, ii. 71, 72.

Glazed tiles in Egypt, ii. 287, 292.

Gloves, i. 283; ii. 336.

—— brought by the Rot-n̄-n, i. 397.

Tabret, or timbrel (the *Taph* of the Jews), i. 129, 130, 140.
Talent, ii. 259, 260.
Tamarisk, ii. 37.
—— wood, use of, ii. 110.
—— tree, sacred to Osiris, i. 256.
Tambourine, i. 98, 129.
—— of various kinds, i. 129.
—— used in sacred music, i. 129.
—— played by goddesses, i. 129.
Tanning skins; pods of the acacia (*sont*), bark of *séaleh* and rhus, for, ii. 106.
Tapestry (*tapeta*) carpets, ii. 92.
Taste, ii. 288, 289. *See* Inapplicableness.
——, encouragement of, ii. 293-295.
Taxes, very great in Egypt, ii. 234.
Temenos. See Grove.
Temperance, exhortations to, i. 53, 187.
Temple, dedication of a, i. 271, 272.
——, a complete. *See* Frontispiece, vol. i.
Temples, subjects represented in the, i. 264.
——, coloured, ii. 290.
——, sculptures of, ii. 295.
—— not derived from excavated monuments, ii. 298.
——, or sanctuaries, at first small, ii. 299.
Tentyris (now Dendera), i. 242, 307.
Tentyrites overcame the crocodile, i. 242.
Testudo and battering ram, i. 387-389.
Thales, improbable story of, teaching his instructors, ii. 109, 319.
Thanksgivings, i. 260. *See* Grace.
—— after victory, i. 278, 416.
Theban dynasty, i. 307.
Thebes, pavilion of Remeses III.; two colossi of the plain before the temple of Amunoph III.; vignettes C, E, i. 73, 141, 306.
——, i. 306, 331, 407.
——, capital of Upper Egypt, ii. 229, 230.
—— and Memphis had no walls round them, i. 409.
——, tombs of the kings at, i. 394.
——, plain of, formerly of less breadth, i. 306.
Theft, ii. 216.
——, mode of discovering, by divination, ii. 353.
Thieves had a chief, to whom they reported what they stole, and to whom the person robbed applied, ii. 216.
Thimble-rig, i. 203.
This, the Thinite dynasty, i. 307.
Thomson, Mr., on linen and mummy cloths, ii. 73-77, 79, 80.
Thoth, the Mercury or Hermes of Egypt, i. 274, 275.
——, books of Hermes, or, i. 274.
——, fête of, i. 299.
——, the intellect, i. 123.
—— month of, i. 299.
——, the Moon and God of letters, with an Ibis head, i. 328.
——, answered to Time, ii. 381.
Thothmes, the kings, i. 308.
—— III., i. 153, 308, 395, 397, 399, 418.
——, rising of Sothis in reign of, and date of, ii. 255.
Threshers, song of the, ii. 43.
Threshing. *See* Wheat; *see* Ornan.
Throwstick, i. 235, 237.
—— not on the principle of the *boomerang* of Australia, i. 235.
Thummim. *See* Truth.
Thyrsus carried by the priests, i. 291.
—— suggested by the staff or ivy-bound flower, i. 285.
Tiles, glazed, ii. 288, 292.
Tin, early use of, ii. 133, 134.
—— taken to the Isle of Wight as a depôt, ii. 135.
—— called *Kassiteros* in Greek, and *Kastira* in Sanscrit, ii. 133.
—— sought in Britain by the Phœnicians, ii. 134, 135.
——, some found in Spain even now, ii. 134.
Tirhaka, i. 308.
——, captives of, i. 393, 395-398.
Tnephachthus' curse of Menes, i. 173.
Toersha, a people of Asia, i. 398.
Toes, a strap held between the, ii. 104.
Tokkari, an Asiatic people, i. 392.
——, carts of the, i. 392.
Tomb of Remeses III., i. 77, 108.
——, some not allowed to be buried in their own, i. 314, 325; ii. 376, 379.
Tombs and funeral rites, ii. 356-400.
——, visit of women to the (as at present), i. 93; ii. 364.
—— of the kings, i. 394.
—— of poor people, ii. 365.
—— all finished except the name of the owner, and ready for sale, ii. 363.
——, seals of the, ii. 364.